MW01620811

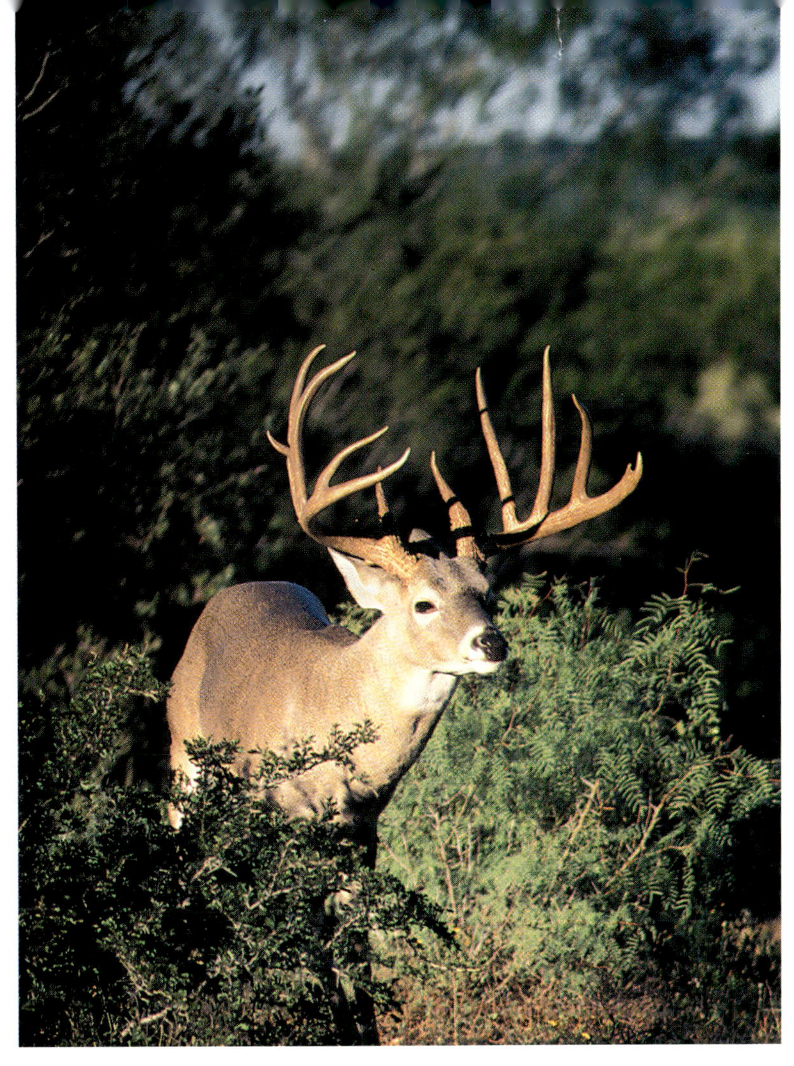

OBSERVING & EVALUATING WHITETAILS

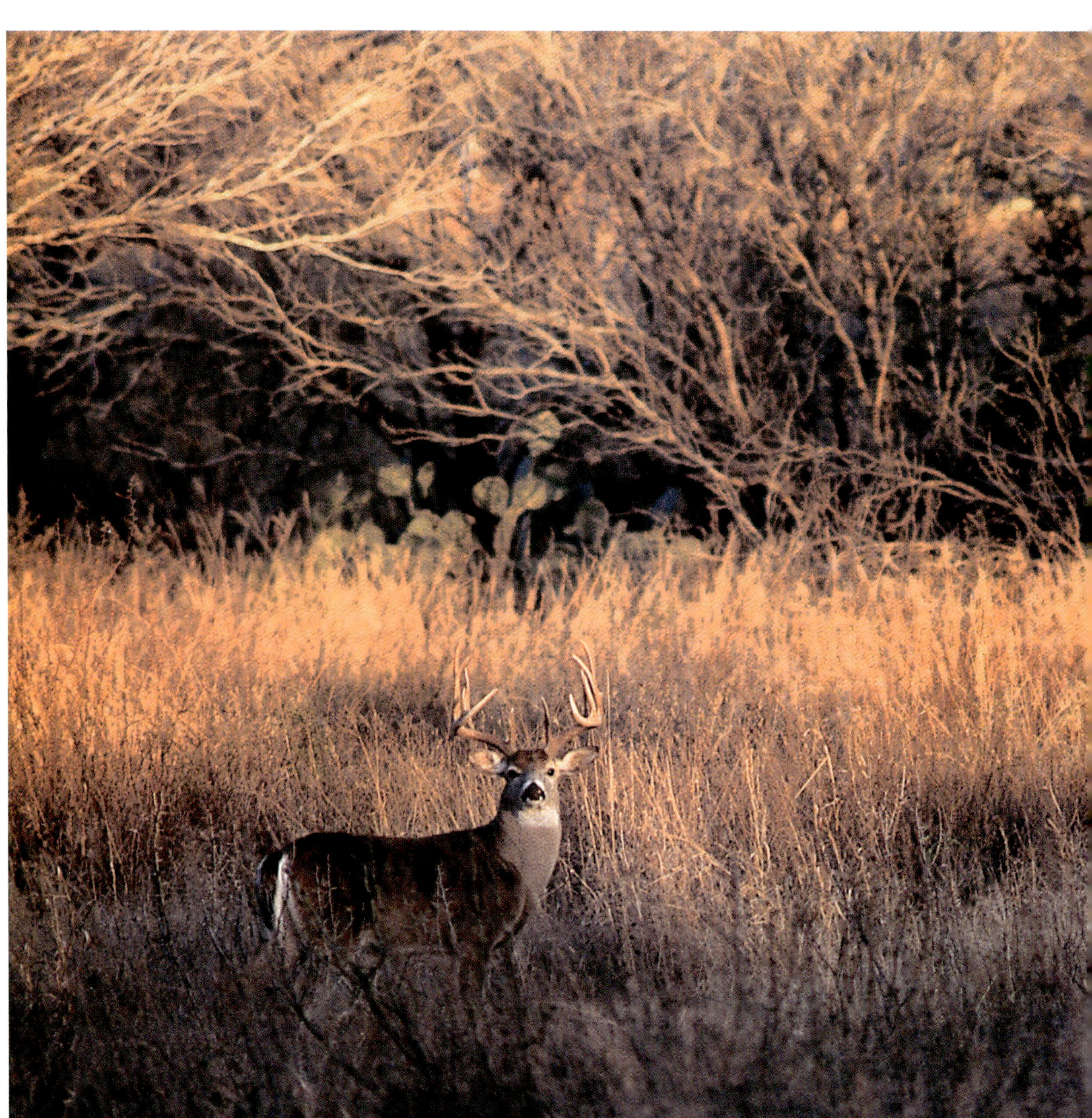

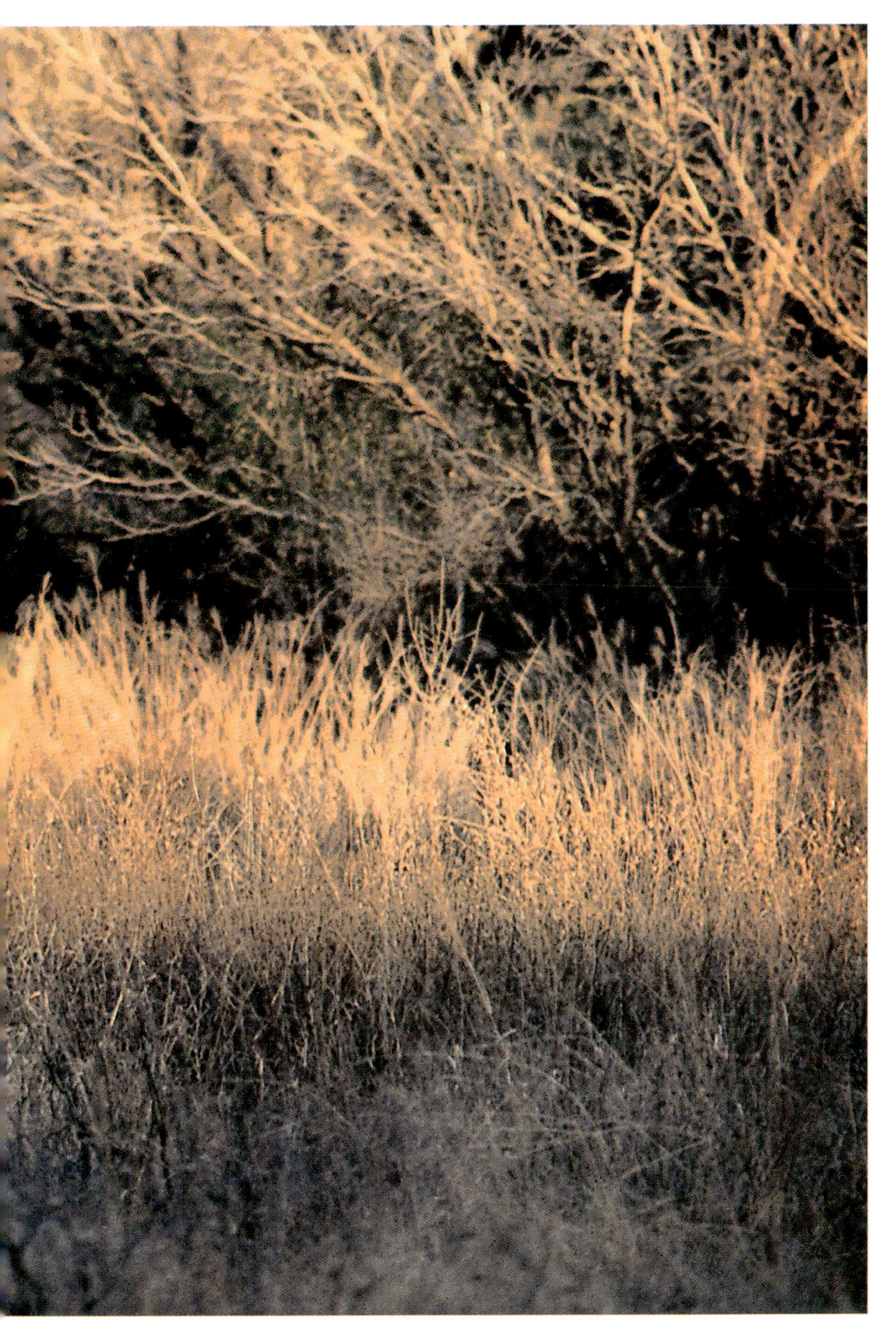

Text by Dave Richards & Al Brothers

Photography by Dave Richards

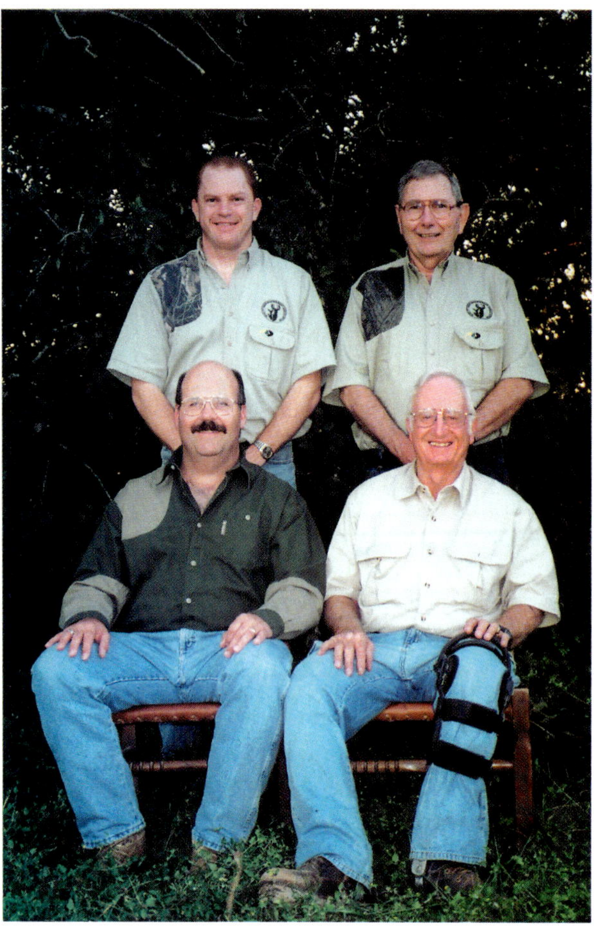

Front (left to right): Dave Richards and Al Brothers
Back: Brian Murphy and Dr. R. Larry Marchinton

Dave Richards became interested in photographing wildlife over 25 years ago, fueled by his desire to capture on film the array of wildlife he encountered in the woods and swamps on hunting and fishing trips as a boy. He has traveled much of the West including Alaska photographing a variety of species from waterfowl to grizzly bears. However, his primary love is photographing big south Texas whitetails. Over the years hundreds of his photos have graced the covers and pages of numerous publications, books, and ad campaigns. He is also a manufacturers rep for several leading companies in the hunting and fishing industry. Dave and his wife Beth live with their two sons near Boerne in the Texas hill country.

Al Brothers is a wildlife biologist and private whitetail consultant on more than 200,000 acres in South Texas. He is co-author of the landmark book, "Producing Quality Whitetails," which sparked the nationwide quality deer management movement. Al's previous employment includes wildlife manager for the Zachry Land and Cattle Company and wildlife biologist for the Texas Parks and Wildlife Service. He has received numerous awards including Excellence in Wildlife Management from the Southeastern Section of The Wildlife Society.

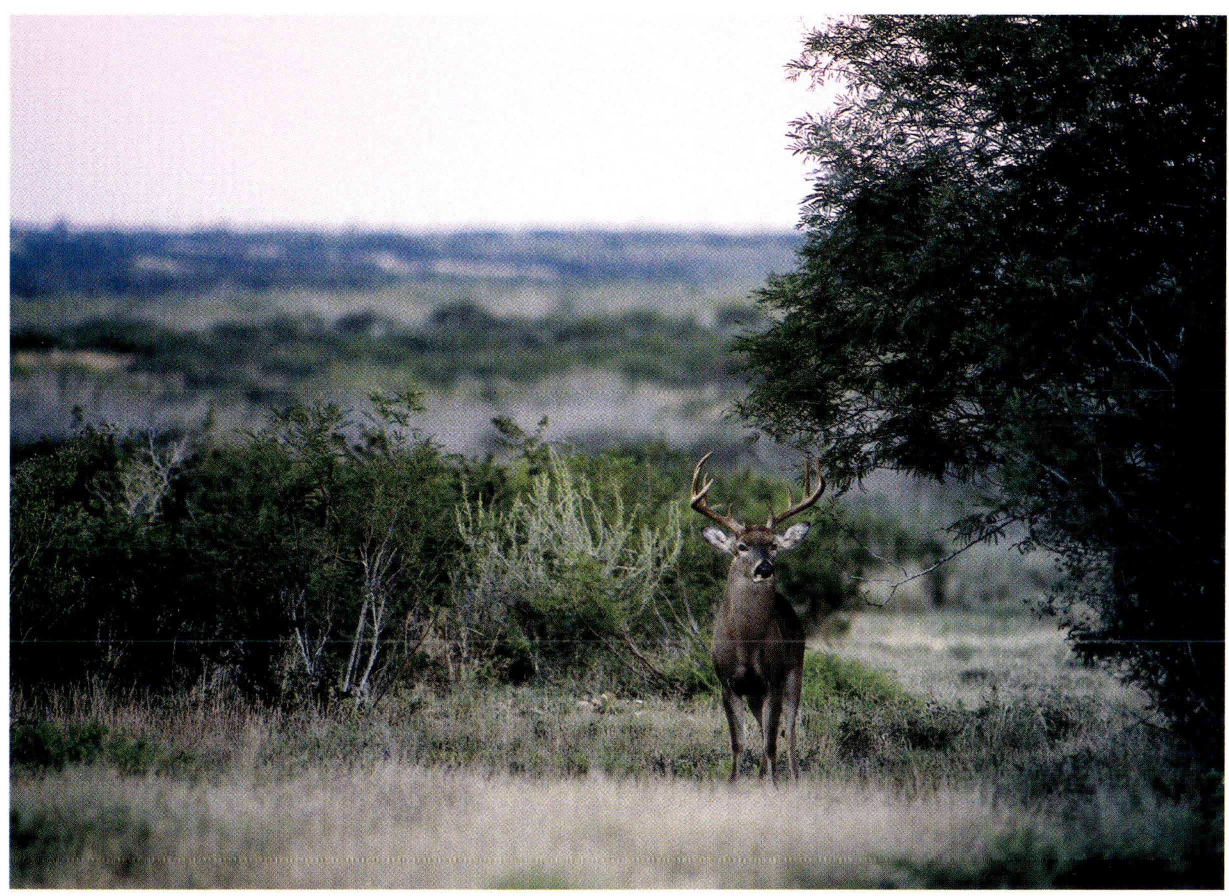

Dr. R. Larry Marchinton is a professor emeritus at The University of Georgia where he taught wildlife biology and management for 30 years. He has authored or co-authored more than 200 technical and popular articles on white-tailed deer and has contributed to numerous books and videos. He is recognized internationally as a pioneer in deer behavior and quality deer management. He was awarded the 1997 Deer Management Career Achievement Award by The Wildlife Society and the 2002 Joe Hamilton Lifetime Achievement Award from the Quality Deer Management Association.

Brian Murphy is a wildlife biologist and the executive director of the Quality Deer Management Association. Brian worked previously as a deer research coordinator for The University of Georgia (UGA) and as a deer biologist for the Australian government. He has authored more than 100 popular and scientific articles on deer biology and management and is the recipient of the E.L. Cheatum Wildlife Excellence Award from UGA and the National Conservation Award from the Australian Deer Association.

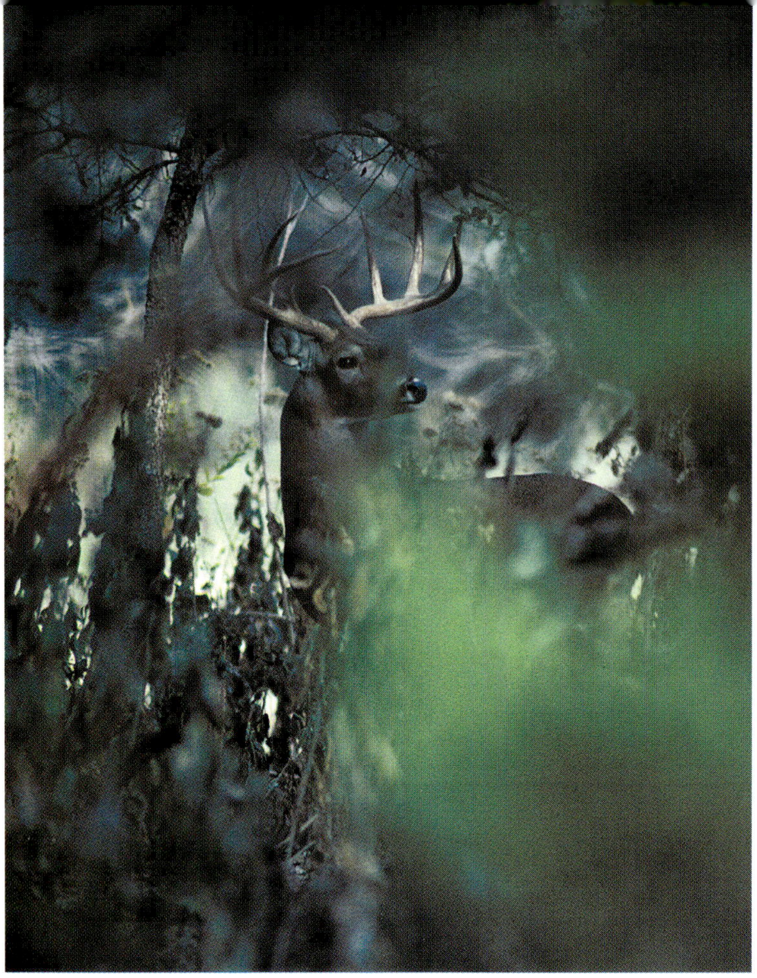

Published by Dave Richards Wilds of Texas Photography, LLC
Boerne, TX

To purchase additional copies of this book, contact the Quality Deer Management Association at (800) 209-3337 or online at www.QDMA.com.

Library of Congress Control Number 2003098736
ISBN No. 0-9747780-0-1 hardcover
ISBN No. 0-9747780-1-X softcover
ISBN No. 0-9747780-2-8 leather bound

Printed in USA

Editors: Betty Marchinton, Dr. R. Larry Marchinton,
Brian Murphy, and Lindsay Thomas Jr.
Graphic Design: Gini Knight, Lindsay Thomas Jr.

Our sincere thanks

go to the following sponsors who helped make this project possible.

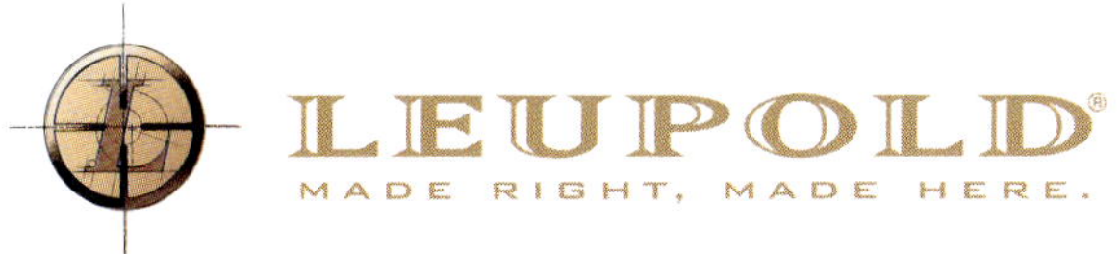

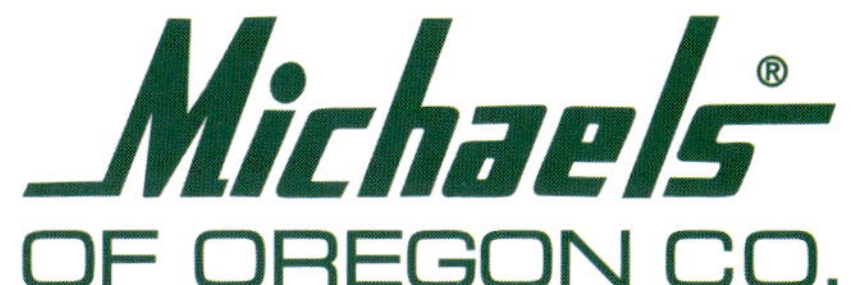

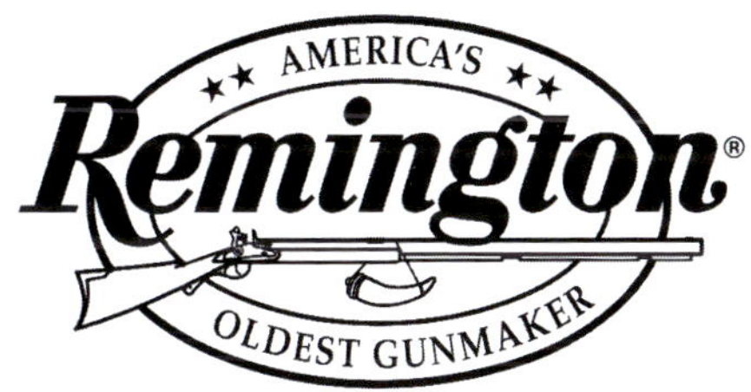

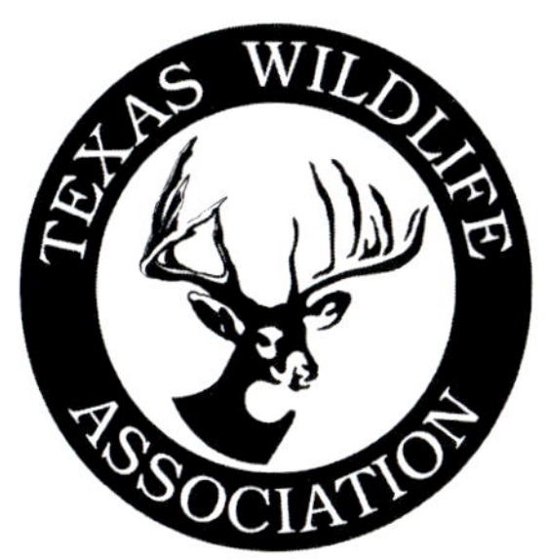

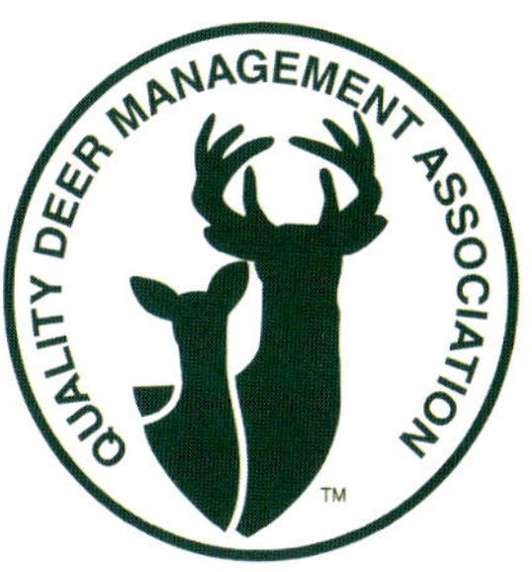

Please refer to the end of the book for more information regarding these sponsors.

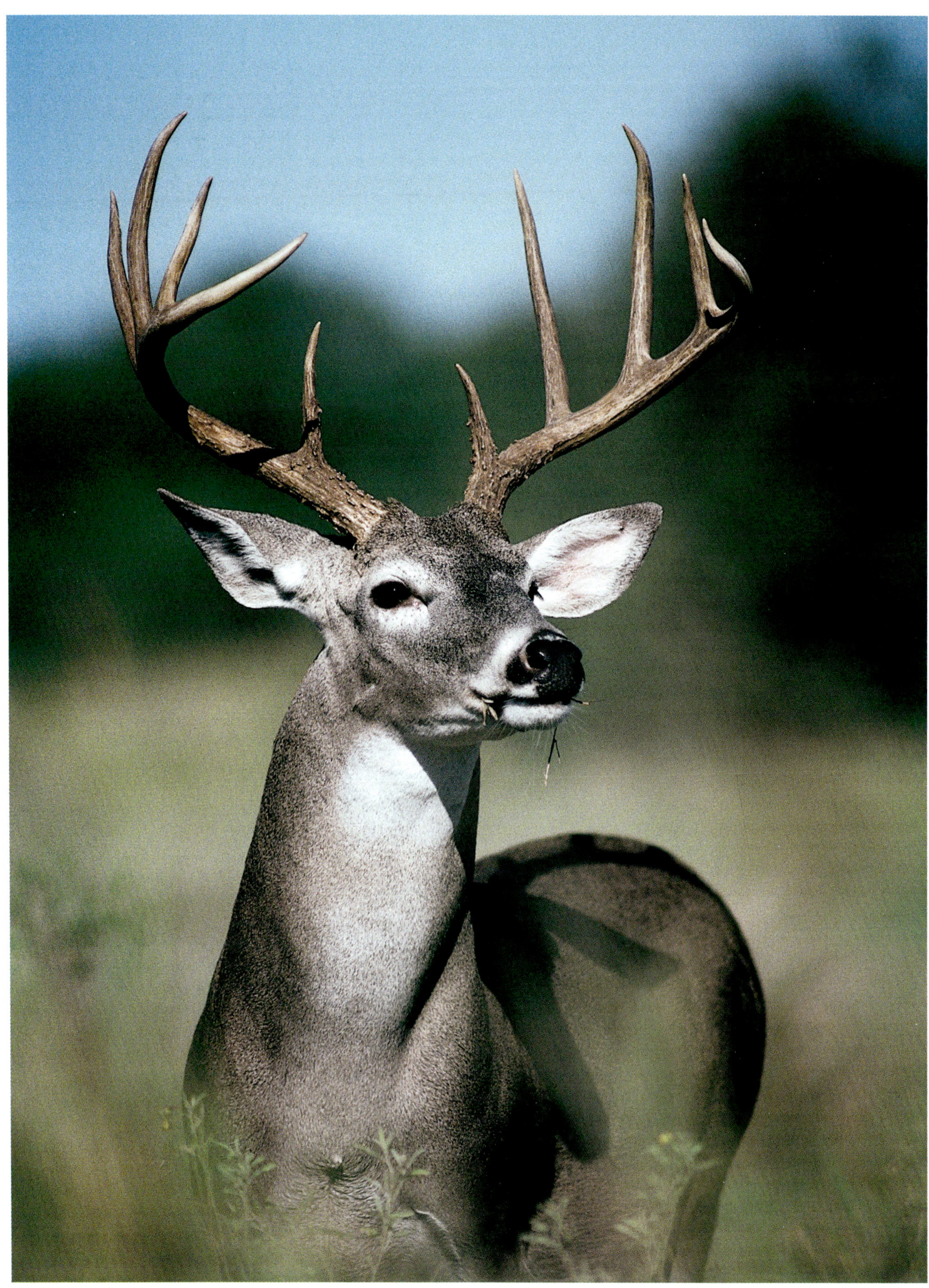

Contents

CHAPTER 1 -------- 22 Whitetail Communication and Sensory Capabilities

CHAPTER 2 -------- 36 Whitetail Antler Development

CHAPTER 3 -------- 44 Aging Whitetails on the Hoof

CHAPTER 4 -------- 76 Buck Aging Sequences

CHAPTER 5 -------- 124 Aging Whitetails by Behavior

CHAPTER 6 -------- 146 Aging Whitetails After Harvest

CHAPTER 7 -------- 154 Estimating Boone & Crockett Score on the Hoof

CHAPTER 8 -------- 166 Examples of Live Bucks with Known Boone & Crockett Scores

CHAPTER 9 -------- 206 Whitetail Antler Anomalies

CHAPTER 10 ------- 214 Whitetail Parasites, Diseases, and Anomalies

CHAPTER 11 ------- 222 Conclusion

CHAPTER 12 ------- 226 Additional Information

Dedication

Raised in a cow camp, sleeping on the earth many nights a year is how Roy Hindes Jr. and his brother Bob grew up in south Texas. Roy spent much of his time hunting for camp meat with the cook, Enrique Gonzales. It was from these hunts for their daily sustenance that Roy gained a wealth of knowledge from Enrique about hunting and the outdoors. It was a tough but adventuresome lifestyle that could have only been from an earlier era and could not be duplicated in today's modern world.

As Roy got older, Graves Peeler, a close friend of the family, took a shining to Roy. There is no doubt their mutual love of hunting was a big part of their friendship. Roy became a "crack shot" with his left eye after a roping accident permanently blinded his dominant right eye. This feat showed that the young man of only 18 years had the courage to be a cut above, which added to the admiration Graves held for his young friend.

Graves was a bachelor who worked for the Texas Southwestern Cattle Raisers Association, a job which gained him many friendships and access to hunt just about anywhere he wanted. Together Graves and Roy made 14 hunting trips to Arizona and New Mexico during the late '40s and '50s. Roy always shot an open-sighted 30-30 and used to tell everyone, "You can kill anything with a 30-30." However, on Roy's first trip out West, he learned from Graves how to shoot a scoped rifle and continued to do so from then on.

As the years passed, the hunting out West began to decline, and Roy began noticing what was happening to the wildlife on public lands. He believed that his home state of Texas would become the big-game hunting destination of the future because it was almost entirely owned by private landowners who could do what was necessary to manage their wildlife. It was from those early experiences that "Big Roy," as he is called by all who knew him, gained the insight and grasped the vision that has established the Hindes Ranch as one of the finest whitetail herds in the country. It did not happen overnight, and it did not come easy. However, because Big Roy stood tall from his fence lines fighting poachers and fighting for better management laws, both Texas whitetails and Texas whitetail managers have benefited greatly.

In the beginning the Hindes' deer hunting was poor at best. They had heavy hunting pressure from neighboring properties. A good buck was lucky to have a spread greater than his ears, and 10-pointers were rare. Big Roy knew he had to stop the overharvest of young bucks on his property and, in 1973, began constructing a high fence encompassing almost 20 square miles of the brush country.

At the time Roy Hindes III ("Little Roy") was attending college in Uvalde, Texas, and heard about Al Brothers' work on whitetails at H.B. Zachry's ranch. Little Roy came home and talked to his dad, and they began realizing that many of the same principles that related to cattle management also related to deer management. In the weeks and months that followed, the Hindes developed friendships with Al and Murphy Ray, Jr. and began implementing the principles that Al had used successfully on the Zachry Ranch. The results of their determined efforts can be seen throughout these pages, as many of these tremendous bucks are the result of

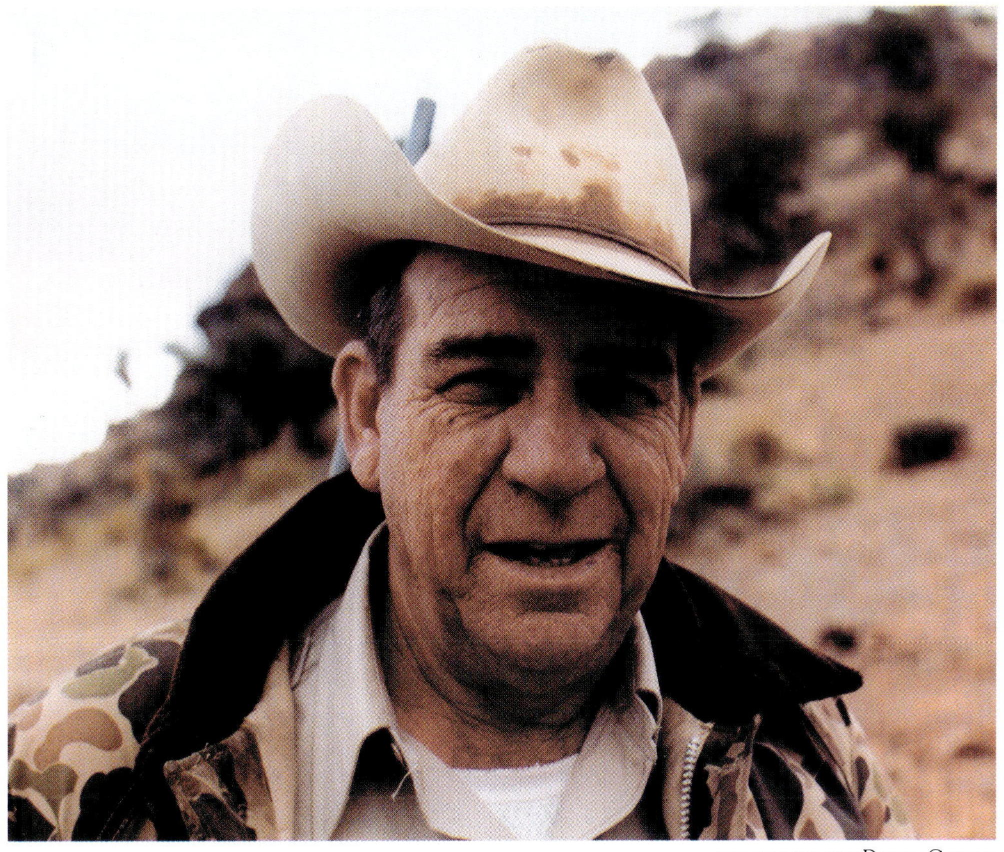

PHOTO COURTESY DUANE CORLEY

30 years of intensive management.

Big Roy loved spending hours observing their white-tailed deer through his spotting scope, and as the seasons passed, he began to notice physical changes in his bucks. It was four to five years into their management program before he began seeing mature bucks. Al Brothers recalls that Big Roy was the first person ever to suggest to him that deer could be aged on the hoof by their physical attributes, and Al was skeptical at the time. However, after getting together, Al knew Big Roy was right. Not only was Big Roy pioneering the techniques for aging live whitetails, he was creating a whitetail herd that would one day draw hunters from all parts of the nation in pursuit of one of its record bucks.

Big Roy Hindes was a true pioneer of whitetail management, and through his many successes and failures he blazed a clearer path for others to follow. I became friends with Big Roy in the latter years of his life, and our last conversation was much like our first — visiting about the good Lord, our families, their hunting dogs, and the Hindes' whitetails. He has gone home to be with the Lord leaving behind his lovely wife of 50 years, Fannie Grace, and his loving family who are determined to carry on his legacy.

Big Roy's vision, character, courage, determination, and sweat poured out during his lifelong love of white-tailed deer. His passion and dedication led to improved management practices for whitetails and their habitat and to a wider trail for whitetail managers and enthusiasts to follow. This is why I am proud to dedicate this book to him as a friend, mentor, and legend in white-tailed deer management.

Acknowledgements

James 1:16-17 tells us "Do not be deceived, my beloved brethren. Every good thing bestowed and every perfect gift is from above, coming down from the Father of lights, with whom there is no variation, or shifting shadow." The book you hold is evidence of one of the many very good things Jesus Christ has blessed my life with. I am forever grateful to the good Lord for creating and growing such a magnificent animal as the white-tailed deer to marvel at and enjoy and for enabling me to have the tremendous opportunity to observe and photograph them in so many extraordinary places over the years. As I've worked on this project I have realized the greatest blessings have been the time spent with God in His awesome creation and the many wonderful friendships my family and I have been blessed with by those who share the same admiration for these wonderful mammals.

Behind every photograph and concept written in these pages there are many individuals who helped me in innumerable ways that I wish to thank. A married man can only be as good as the life mate he has joined with, and I am forever grateful to my best friend and wife, Beth. She has been a tremendous gift to me through her constant love, wisdom, Godly character, and support, and without her typing abilities this book would have never made it to the publisher in time. I wish to thank my sons James and Joseph for their young, eager eyes, hungry minds, and willing spirits to learn about all the outdoor world holds for them, which rekindles my own spirit. I wish to thank my mom and dad for your love and understanding when you looked at your young son's pictures of blurred images of snakes, squirrels, bird nests, and coyote dens and paid the store clerk for them anyway. Thank you for all of your encouraging words that helped me believe they were good, giving me the hope and courage to chase my dreams. Thank you most of all for always sharing your time in God's great outdoors, giving me a love for it and a desire to share that love with others. I want to thank my brothers Steve, Jim, Don, and Larry for all the great memories we have had in the deer woods and on the water over the years and for your desire to pass it on to our children.

I want to thank Little Roy Hindes, a great friend and brother in Christ, whose knowledge, gracious help, and friendship have been a tremendous blessing to me over the years. Through your mom and dad's vision and your entire family's dedication you have demonstrated what being a good steward of the land and its wildlife is, as few ever will. I can never express my gratitude enough for you and your family's help and willingness to share your years of knowledge and experience about white-tailed deer. Everyone in your family has contributed in many ways to help this book become a reality. So I wish to extend my heartfelt thanks to Roy Jr.(late) and Fannie Grace Hindes, Roy III and Pam Hindes, Roy IV (Cuatro) and Kelli Hindes, and John and Kristi Schulte.

Working on this project with Al Brothers has truly been a dream come true. Al, I cannot thank you enough for your help in co-authoring and editing this book, enabling it to be more than a photographer's observations, but also biologically sound through your years of experience and knowledge. Thank you also for enlarging my circle of friends by opening yours. You have become a great friend, and it has been an honor and a privilege to work with you. I want to thank Dr. Larry Marchinton for the privilege of including his chapter on white-tailed deer's sensory and communication capabilities. Sharing his years of research in this book enables us all to continue to learn and become more knowledgeable about white-tailed deer, and to your wife Betty for her editorial skills. To Brian Murphy, Lindsay Thomas Jr., Gini Knight, James Guthrie, and all the folks at Quality Deer Management Association who helped in editing, layout, and publishing this book I want to say thanks for all your vision, creativity, professionalism, and hard work. Your standard of excellence is visible on every page.

I also want to thank Leupold, Michaels of Oregon, Remington Arms, Quality Deer Management Association, and Texas Wildlife Association for their sponsorship and belief in supporting this project so whitetail managers and hunters will become more knowledgeable about managing white-tailed deer in hopes that future generations will be able to enjoy the best whitetail herds ever known. I wish to thank a few individuals from each sponsor that were instrumental to this project. Mike Slack and Cyndi Flannigan of Leupold. Todd Seyfert of Michaels of Oregon. Ray Murski for Remington Arms. Brian Murphy of Quality Deer Management Association and Kirby Brown, David Langford, and David Brimager of the Texas Wildlife Association.

A special thanks to Klint Graf, Bill Reaves, Kim and Robyn Hicks, Wyman Meinzer, Mike Biggs, and Mark McDonald for your friendships, advice, and help with this project and my photography over the years.

I wish to thank Gary Grant for the numerous doors and opportunities you have opened for me and for the privilege to do what I do as a manufacturers representative and as a photographer.

Cy Angelloz, Clay Applewhite, Steve Ashenfelter, Darwin Avant, David Baxter, Jimmy Biella, Larry Blomquist, Mark Bower, Larry Bozka, Gordon Buescher, John Burdett, Charles Butcher, Charlie Cantwell, Jeff Copeland, Lance Cote, Joe and Jane Craigo, Robbie Curtis, Jimmy Dieringer, Amos DeWitt, David Drinkard, Ronnie Eckel, Terry Erwin, Doug Ferrer, (late)Adrian Fitzmorris, Dave Fulson, George Garza, Ken Graf, Kyle Green, Bob Glick, Horace Gore, David Groce, Steve Hall, Denny and Susan Hallmark, Joe Hamilton, Rod Haydel, Tom Hicks, Roque Hines, Rick Hodges, Richard Hurt, Robbie Hurt, Luther James, Tim Jeanes, John Jefferson, Greg Jenkins, Charlie Jones, Jerry Johnston, Dr. James Kroll, Joe Klutsch, Mike Leggett, Jim Lowe, Richard Magee, Abel Martinez, Boyd McMullen, Dr. Karl Miller, Jim Miller, Gene Naquin, Bobby Nolan, Bobby Parker Jr., Billy Patterson, John Pierce, Dale Priour, Murphy Ray, Keith Ray, Matt Richards, Marcus Richards, Scott Rupp, Jimmy Rutledge, Ray Sasser, (late)Louis Schriener, Greg Simons, Tom Snyder, Jerry Smith, Wayne Spahn, Marvin Spivey, John Stein, Kenny Stephens, Rick Stovall, Brad Swanson, Larry Teague, Greg Tinsley, Mike Vanatter, Tom Vining, Pat Walters, Keith Warren, Larry Weishuhn, Ronnie Wells, Pat West, Gordon Whittington, Sid Williams, Mike Winkler, Red and Mary Wood, John Wooters, David Wright, and many friends at Texas Parks & Wildlife Department. You have all made an impact and a difference in my photography, hunting experiences, and life, and I am forever grateful.

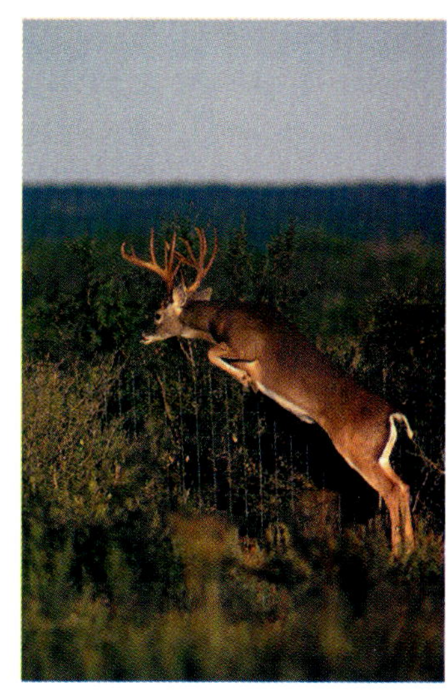

Dave Richards

My thanks go to all Dave mentioned plus a very special thanks to Larry and Betty Marchinton and Brian Murphy and James Guthrie of the Quality Deer Management Association. I know that we left many individuals out who have helped our efforts through the years, and our thoughts and sincere gratitude are extended to you.

Al Brothers

Foreword

By Al Brothers

It has been both an honor and a pleasure to assist Dave Richards in compiling his "labor of love" legacy. The countless hours, days, and nights Dave has devoted to this effort will be of benefit whether you are a landowner, hunter, deer manager, or just someone who enjoys wildlife. It is our wish that this book will help maintain and enhance white-tailed deer and their habitat for future generations to enjoy. My sincere hope is that everyone who reads and studies this book will be inspired to become a better hunter, manager, and conservationist.

The first chapter on whitetail communication was written by renowned whitetail expert Dr. R. Larry Marchinton. To Larry, a close and dear friend, we extend our thanks for your contribution to this book. Chapter 6 on aging whitetails by tooth eruption and wear was compiled by our good friend Brian Murphy, executive director of the Quality Deer Management Association (QDMA) who helped create a comprehensive aging poster on this subject for the QDMA. We are very grateful to Brian and QDMA for this valuable addition.

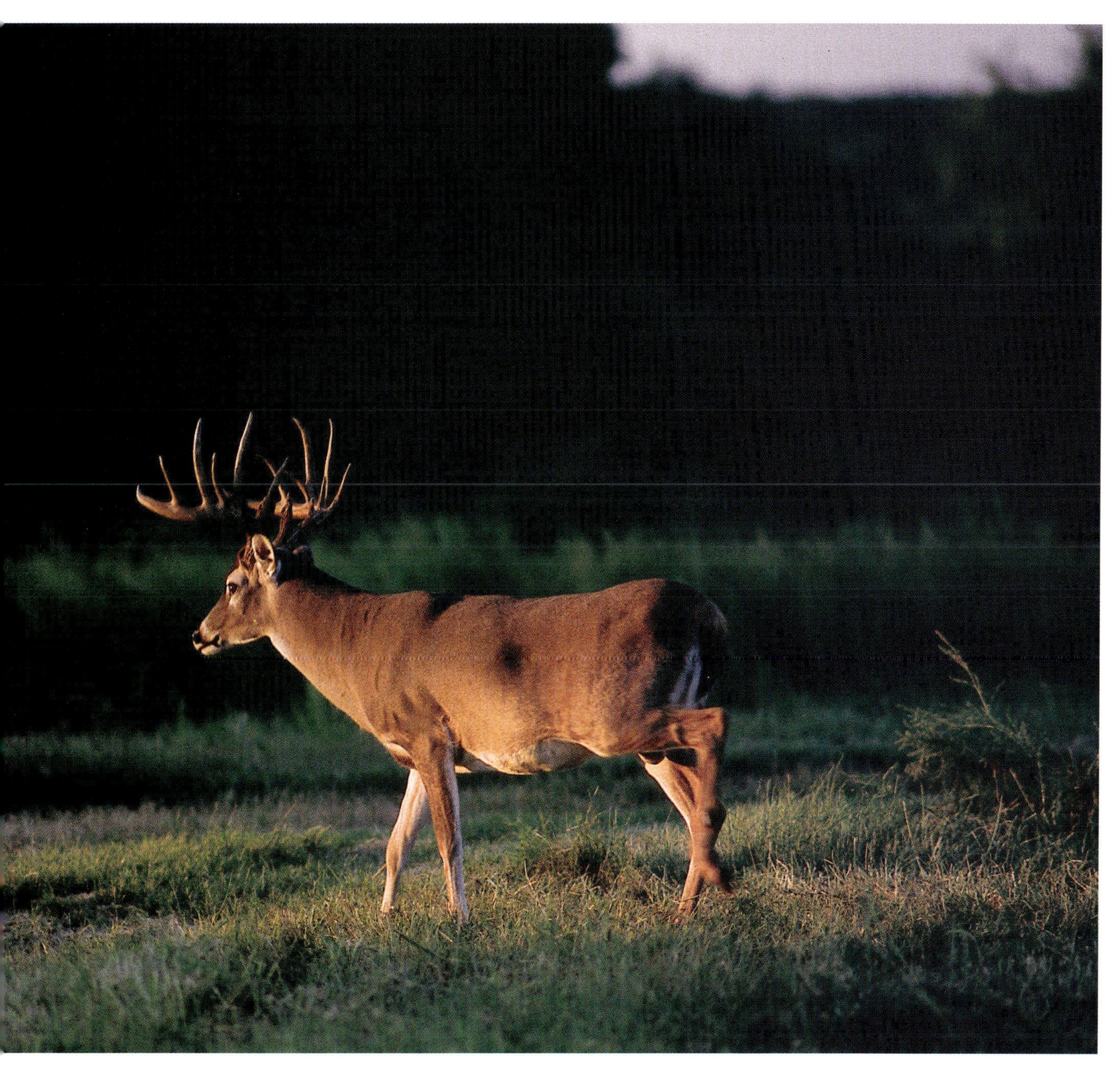

Introduction

By Dave Richards

From the time I was old enough to see out a car window in whitetail country, I was always peering out hoping to glimpse one. My wife Beth will tell you I'm still that way today. Beth has been involved in quite a few U-turns over the years as I groped for my camera after seeing a good buck. While my early desires were simply to obtain glimpses of deer, those desires led to a lifelong pursuit of those fascinating mammals.

As I hunted, observed, and learned more about whitetails, I realized I was only peeling back thin layers of a very extensive subject matter. The more layers I peeled back, the more I discovered there was to learn. After 30 years of hunting and photographing white-tailed deer, I am convinced this is an inexhaustible study. I wish this book contained all the answers to questions about whitetails, but I am still peeling back layers and exposing more to ponder and study. However, what will be evident through these pages are numerous insights that will enable the deer hunter/manager to become more proficient at aging, judging, and analyzing white-tailed deer.

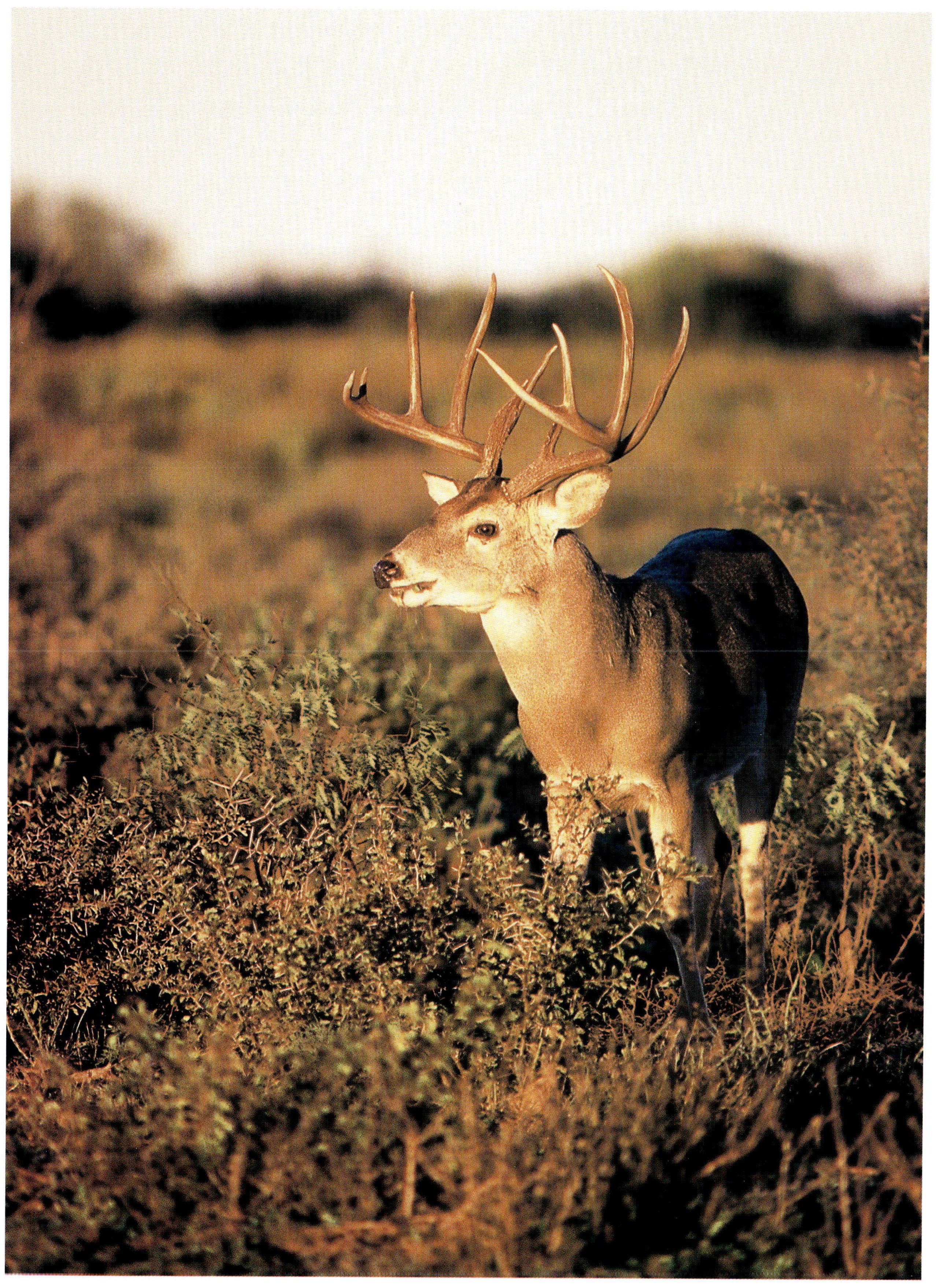

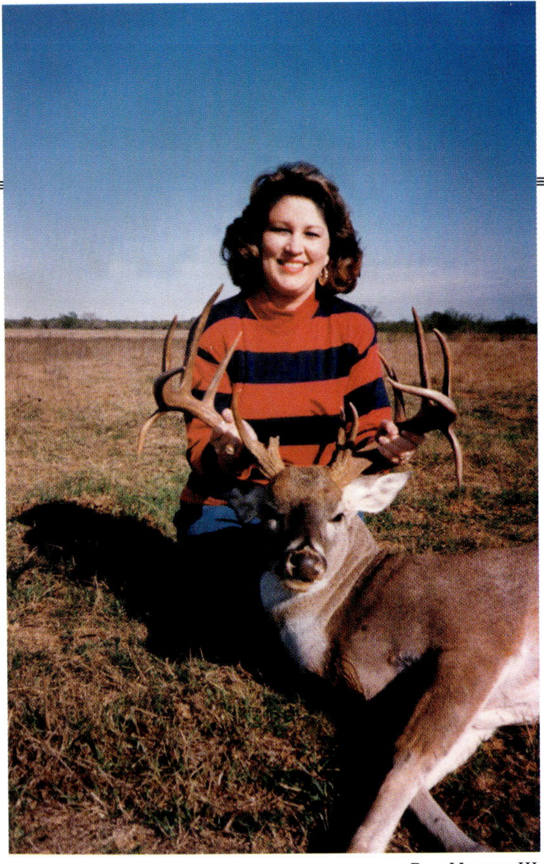

PHOTO COURTESY ROY HINDES III

The thrill of harvesting a buck like this that you worked hard to produce on your property is clearly evident in Pam Hindes' expression as she holds a beautiful double drop-tine buck she harvested from their ranch.

Aging and judging is by no means an exact science. Every deer is an individual, which results in exceptions to generally accepted standards or averages. Many factors can influence a whitetail's appearance including age, nutrition, habitat quality, health, weather extremes, rainfall, injury, breeding activity, and genetics. Most bucks in this book are at the top of the management scale and the result of 30 years of intensive management. While these deer may not be the same size as those in your area, the principles and methods for aging and judging them will be the same. For example, while bucks in central Texas are smaller than those in south Texas, the body and behavioral characteristics used to observe and analyze them are the same.

Initially, it is important to develop the skills to classify bucks into yearlings (1 1/2 years old), immature (2 1/2 to 4 1/2 years old), mature (5 1/2 to 7 1/2 years old), and post-mature (8 1/2+ years). However, many hunters and managers desire a higher level of competence. By raising the standard from broad age groups to specific years, a smaller margin of error will result. Many times, when classifying bucks by groups and pulling the trigger on a buck judged as mature, you could be short-changing yourself and the deer herd. The buck could have been a 4 1/2-year-old with the potential to grow 20 or 30 additional inches of antler in one or two more years. This situation can usually be avoided by becoming more proficient at aging and judging.

Through these pages, you will see many bucks just realizing their antler potential at 4 1/2 years but not fulfilling their full potential until later in life. By letting them "walk," you increase your chances of harvesting a larger buck — maybe the largest of your life — in a couple of years. Little Roy Hindes once told me that his dad always said, "You will never lose by allowing a big buck to walk, because he will be spreading his genes in your herd." Another reason you would not lose is that some bucks will continue to grow great antlers up to 8 1/2 and sometimes 9 1/2 years of age. Therefore, do not rush a decision on a buck you are unfamiliar with. With many bucks you will have more opportunities. It must be remembered that every buck is an individual, every hunt is unique, and that quick decisions are often required. However, quick decisions should be the exception rather than the rule. The more you observe mature bucks and the characteristics that distinguish them from younger bucks, the more likely you will be correct when a quick decision must be made. Finally, for optimum herd management it is necessary to identify mature and dominant females by physical and behavioral characteristics. The ability to identify fawns (6 to 10 months) and to discern whether they are male or female also is very important.

Like many whitetail hunters I thought I could age deer fairly well after several years of hunting and photographing them. My terminology was like many hunters — he is young or he is a shooter — and that pretty well covered the bases. Young was a clearly recognizable, 1 1/2 to 3 1/2-year-old with a thin neck, long legs, tight stomach, and a young face. A "shooter" was a buck whose brisket and neck had no discernible difference where they met, a full stomach area, sagging back, and sometimes wrinkles under the chin.

For most landowners interested in managing deer at that time, that was more than sufficient. They were simply pleased that a hunter was making a concerted effort to help and not simply shooting the first 10-point that passed by. However, my deer aging got upgraded, overhauled, and improved several years ago the first time Big Roy and Little Roy Hindes picked me up after I had been sitting in one of their deer stands and I started describing the different bucks I had seen that morning. The magic question was thrown out by Big Roy after I described each buck I had seen: "Well, how old was he?" I've heard that question a thousand times in my conversations with all three generations of Hindes over the years about almost every buck seen since that morning years ago. This question caused me to quickly realize their knowledge of aging deer was at the collegiate level while mine was still in elementary school. That realization caused me to start asking a lot of questions, like, "What made you think that buck was 4 1/2 and not 5 1/2?" Sometimes it was his physical characteristics, sometimes it was his reaction to other deer, and others it was because the Hindes had observed him the previous year and estimated his age at 3 1/2. Often it was a combination of multiple criteria.

It was in the late 1970s the first time Little Roy remembers his dad taking him out on the ranch to show him that deer could be aged on the hoof. At the time Little Roy remembers being very skeptical. Big Roy told him to grab the spotting scope, and they headed out to observe deer that afternoon. Big Roy said, "Now look at that buck on the left, do you see how small he is? He is an 18-month-old buck. Now look at the buck to the right approaching him. Do you see he has a lot bigger body? He is an older buck. Now look, there is a third buck approaching. He is a little bigger than the first buck but not near the size of the big buck. I think he is a 2 1/2-year-old. Get your gun up and shoot him, and we'll go see what he is." Little Roy explained to me that they were quite proficient at aging deer by their teeth at that time. So he raised his rifle and dropped the buck. And, when they toothed him, he was 2 1/2 years old. Little Roy knew immediately his dad was on to something.

As Little Roy reflects, he believes it was through his dad's many hours of observing bucks through his spotting scope that he began to notice the differences in body characteristics as bucks matured and realized they could effectively age deer. It is also why Big Roy believed the spotting scope was one of the most important tools for aging and judging deer.

Some two decades later, lessons learned that afternoon between father and son have paid off season after season with many high-scoring bucks for hunters fortunate enough to hunt on the Hindes Ranch. The Hindes had raised the bar on judging deer, much like a sharpshooter fine tunes his shooting skills until he can hit the same hole with each bullet. The Hindes had mastered the art of judging age because it was necessary to achieve the level of management they desired.

A buck's body matures at 4 1/2 years of age, but usually his antlers will add several inches of growth each year until he is 7 1/2 and sometimes even 8 1/2 years old. If the Hindes had just shot mature bucks, they would still have killed some very good bucks but would not be consistently harvesting 180 to 200+ Boone & Crockett class deer.

I realized through observation, record keeping, photography, and studying their whitetails at every opportunity, the Hindes were selectively managing their harvest by age class with remarkable results. I also realized how fortunate I was to have the opportunity to benefit from their extensive knowledge and to share my photography and insights with other ranchers and hunters.

This book has been a work in progress for several years, and there were numerous times I would obtain a unique photo of a particular buck and Big Roy or Little Roy would comment, "That needs to go in your book." Over the years I have been fortunate to photograph and discuss many magnificent whitetails with the Hindes family and have learned a great deal from them. From the first conversations about compiling this information, the Hindes family felt they had been blessed by the Lord and were willing to share what they knew for the benefit of others. I also have been blessed to know them as friends and be in a position to observe and photograph many of their monstrous bucks.

My photographs and data grew over the years, and I was overjoyed when Al Brothers agreed to coauthor this book. The addition of his knowledge, years of experience, and understanding as a whitetail manager/biologist to my observations and photographs will ensure more can be learned from our combined experiences. Our hope is that as you thumb through these pages your knowledge and appreciation for North America's premier big-game animal, the white-tailed deer, will be taken to new heights and you will enjoy it as much as we have enjoyed putting it together.

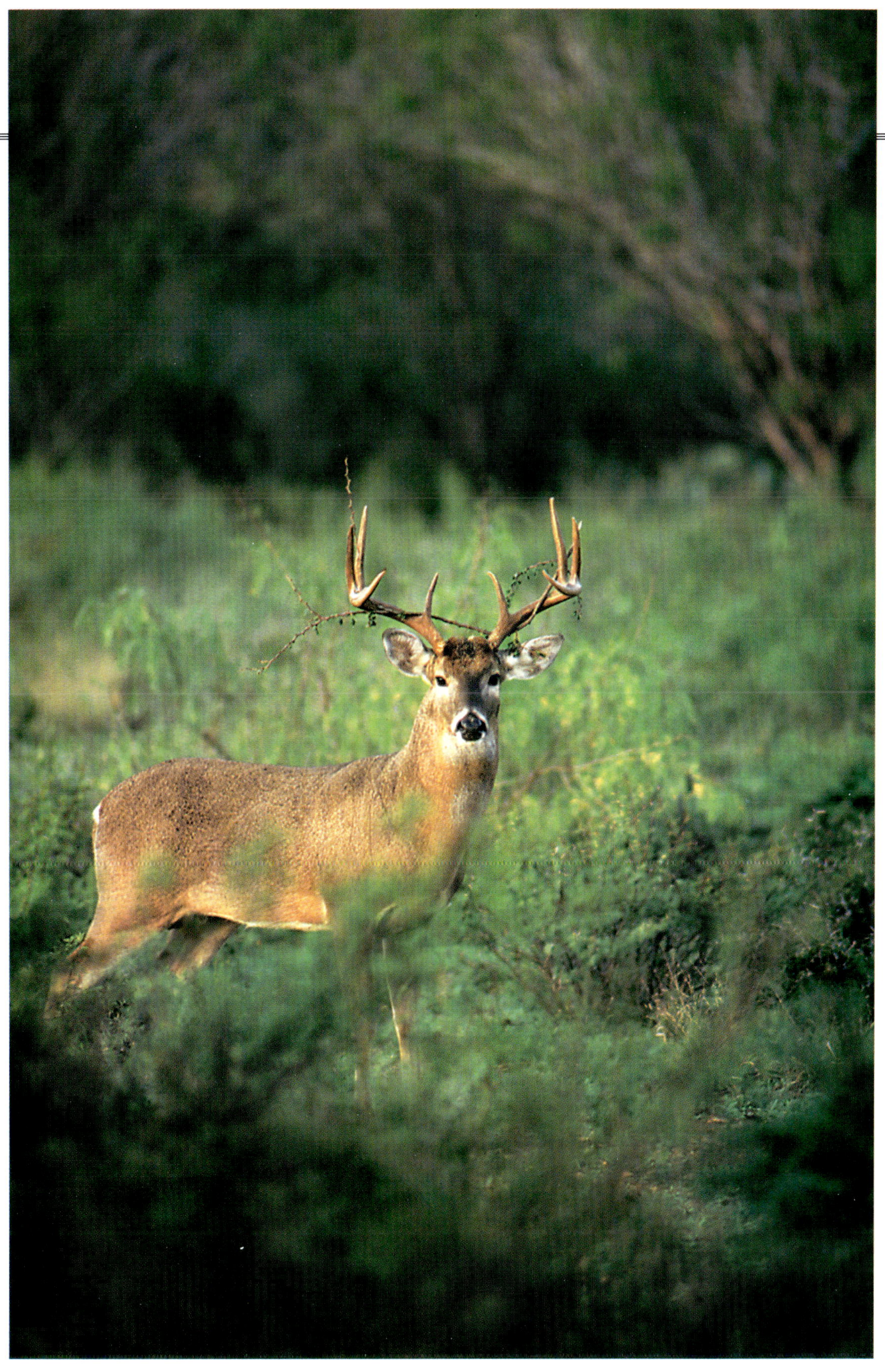

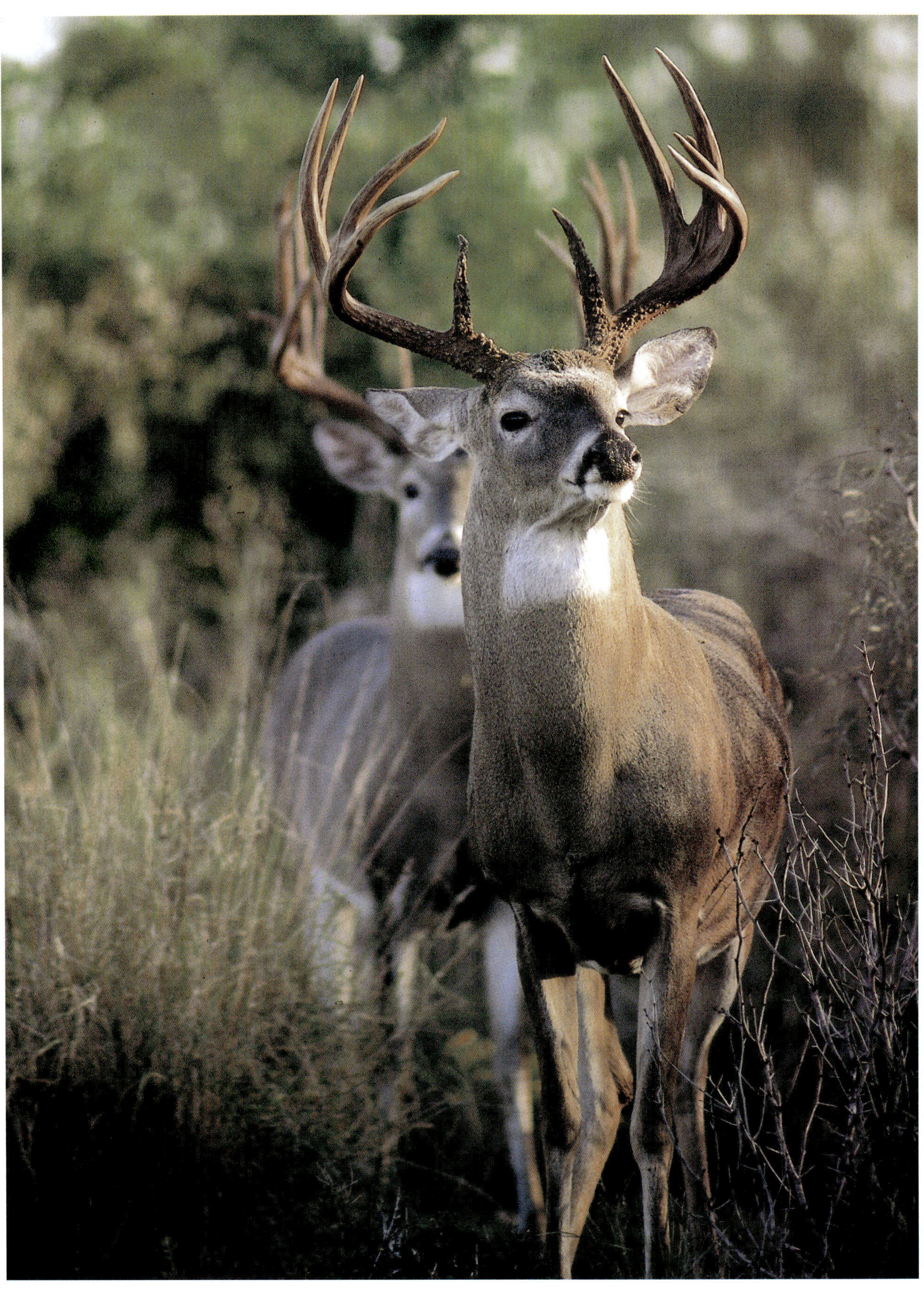

1 Whitetail Communication and Sensory Capabilities

By Dr. R. Larry Marchinton

Like humans, white-tailed deer have five senses they use to learn about their environment and communicate with each other. These include the ears for hearing, eyes for seeing, tongue for tasting, skin and hair for touch, and last but not least the nose for smelling. Some of these sensory organs function much better than ours, some not as well or differently, and others we don't really know about. We will briefly discuss each of a deer's sensory capabilities and how they use them. Also, we will review the various scent glands, vocalizations, and behaviors used to communicate. The astute deer hunter or observer can learn to decode much of this "deer language."

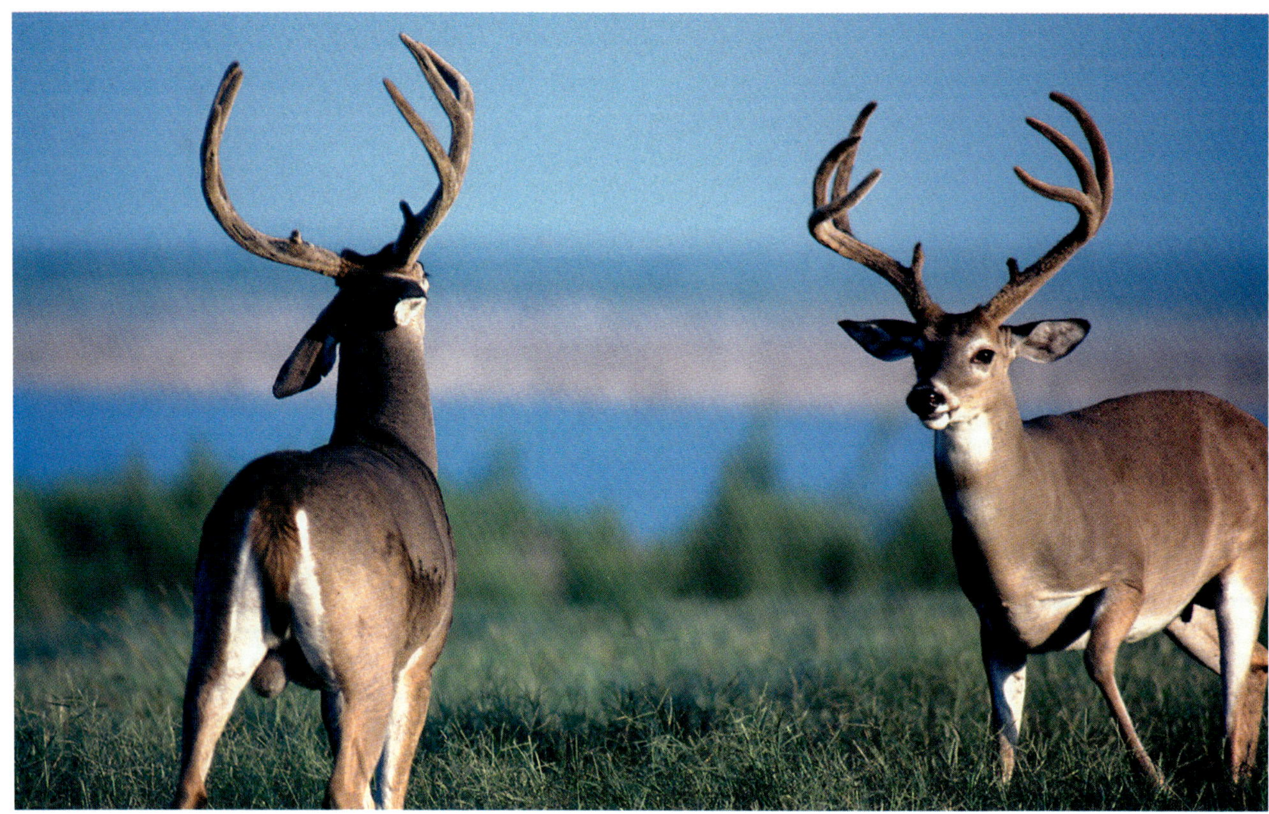

Body language represents a large portion of whitetail communication. The buck on the left is using the position of his ears, head, and antlers to send a clear message to the approaching buck.

What do Deer Feel?

As far as we know, no research has been done on this subject. We assume they have a sense of "touch" similar to ours, but they also have an excellent system of tactile hairs we don't have. These are "deer whiskers," also called vibrissae. They are specialized hairs located in complex patterns around a whitetail's mouth, nose, and eyes. Most hunters have rarely given them a second look or thought — if they have noticed them at all. Vibrissae are thought to provide "tactile" function (that is, a sense of touch) to help animals feel the presence of objects close to the mouth, nose, or eyes. They seem especially common in mammals that are at least partly active at night. Mammals, such as humans, that have lost or never had much of a sense of smell rarely have true vibrissae. This fact suggests that vibrissae are linked with smell as well as touch. Although we have no proof, vibrissae's greatest importance to animals with an acute sense of smell may be to determine wind direction. Perhaps they are used to "feel" air movement and the direction from which a scent is coming. Whether the scent is that of a dangerous predator (e.g., a hunter) or valuable food source, "whiskers" may be as important to deer as the nose itself.

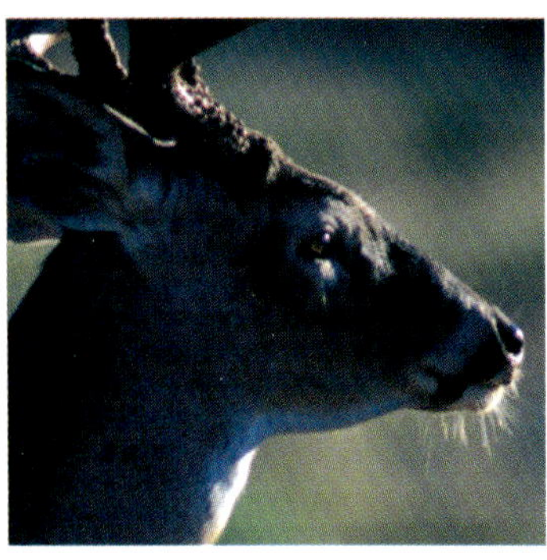

The "whiskers," or vibrissae, around the muzzle of a whitetail play an important role in sensory capabilites. One use may be sensing wind direction.

What do Deer Taste?

Little is known about a deer's ability to taste. We know they can distinguish subtle differences in plants, such as the difference between fertilized and unfertilized plants or the difference between white oak and red oak acorns based on tannin levels. However, it remains unclear if this is actually taste or smell or both.

What do Deer See?

There has been much debate on whether a deer sees in black and white, if they can only see an object when it moves, and how well they see in the dark. Let's first look at some of the physical differences between a deer's eye and ours.

1. Deer have a wider-opening pupil (light gathering ability increases by the square of the pupil's diameter). We have not directly measured this, but if a deer's pupil diameter is three times ours, it will gather nine times the light.

2. Deer, and many other mammals, have a reflective layer in the back of the retina called the tapetum. This is what causes their eyes to shine in the dark. This allows the light not absorbed by receptor cells to be recycled, increasing vision under low light conditions. Humans have a poorly-developed tapetum and, therefore, see poorly under low light conditions.

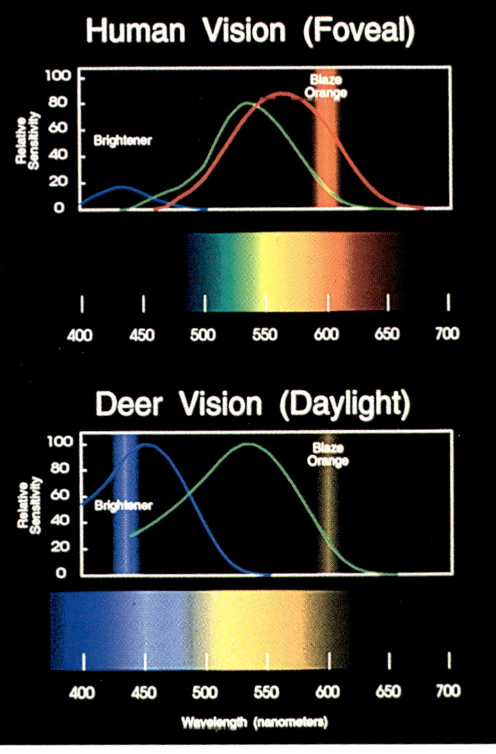

3. The human lens contains a yellowish filter that blocks ultraviolet light (UV). This filter protects our eyes from damaging UV light, which is important for long-lived species like humans. It also enhances our acuity (ability to see sharp details) much like yellow shooting glasses. Deer do not appear to have this filter, so we would expect them to have somewhat less acuity in daylight and to depend more on movement to identify objects. The lack of a filter allows deer more sensitivity in the shorter wavelengths, especially in dim light; perhaps even allowing some vision into the UV range.

4. Vision is accomplished when light strikes the rods and cones located in the retina. Deer have more rods but fewer cones than humans. Rods are about 1,000 times as sensitive as cones and responsible for vision in dim light. Photopigments on the cones are responsible for color vision. Humans have three types of cone photopigments: ones with peak sensitivity in the blue (short) wavelength, ones in the green (medium) wavelength, and ones in the red (long) wavelength. This is why we see in three basic colors, or trichromatically.

In an effort to better understand the whitetail's visual capabilities, a cooperative study was conducted in 1992 between The University of Georgia, University of California at Santa Barbara, and the Medical College of Wisconsin. In this study, a series of highly sophisticated trials were conducted to determine the structure of a deer's eye and the types of photoreceptors they have on their rods and cones. From this, we concluded that:

1. Deer have two cone pigments, which likely allow dichromatic color vision. As previously mentioned, humans have three cone photopigments allowing trichromatic color vision.

2. One of their cone photopigments is very similar in sensitivity to our photopigment that peaks in the short (blue) wavelengths suggesting little UV filtering. However, we found no evidence of a specialized cone

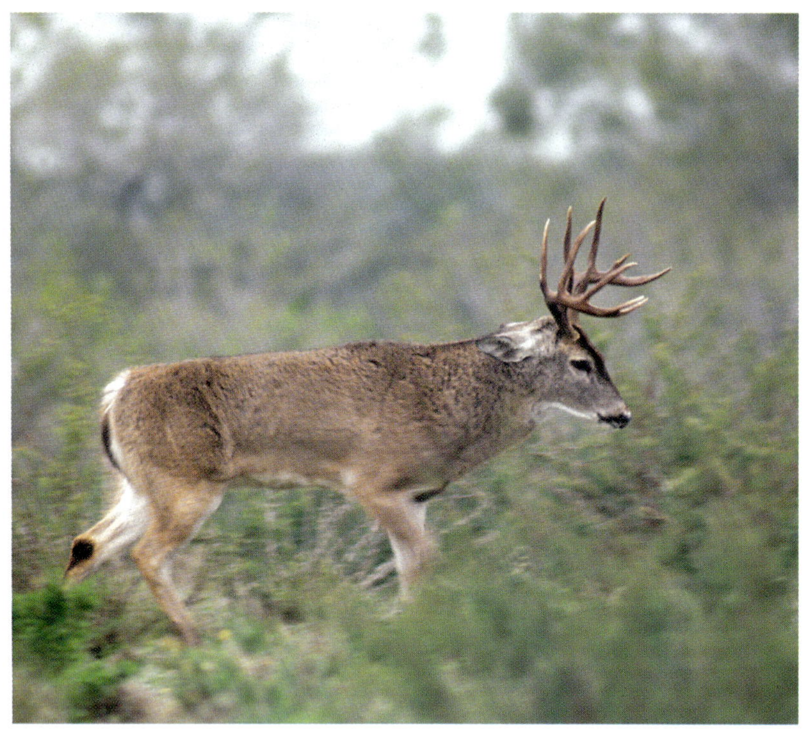

This is classic behavior during the peak of the rut on well-managed properties. Note the body language displayed by this mature buck as it approaches another mature buck — hair raised, ears down and back. Even its posture communicates attitude. Note also the dark tarsal gland.

photopigment sensitive to UV light like some animals.

3. Their second cone photopigment is sensitive to wavelenths that are intermediate between a human's medium (green) and long (red) cone photopigments. In other words, it has a peak sensitivity to wavelengths we perceive as yellow. Consequently, deer are relatively insensitive to long wavelengths of light and therefore likely cannot discriminate a red tomato on a green vine or a hunter in blaze orange against a brown forest background. They may see somewhat like a human with red/green color blindness.

The bottom line is that nobody can say for sure, but deer probably see something like what we call blue and yellow. They may see in the blues or violets better than we do (I do not wear blue jeans while deer hunting anymore). Due to the larger number of rods, larger pupils, tapetum, and lack of UV filter, they can definitely see much better at night than we do. Depending so heavily on rods reduces visual acuity and makes movement more important to their vision.

Body Language

Whitetails communicate information by their postures. For example, tail erection indicates alarm. The position of the ears is another powerful communicator. It may suggest the direction of potential danger if pointed forward or a warning if laid back against the neck. The hair on the body can be erected to indicate a general "bad mood" threat. The way a deer walks can communicate volumes about its feelings or "attitude." All of these body signals communicate to other deer, but they can be "read" equally well by the knowledgeable human observer.

What Can Deer Smell?

Deer live in a world of odors. It is hard for us to fathom the importance deer place on their ability to smell. It is safe to say the nose is their most important sense organ. We must rely on sophisticated equipment to attempt to decipher the information a whitetail receives through its nose. Hunting magazines are full of advertisements for buck lures of every description — many with grand claims and guarantees. On the other side of the coin are agriculturists and houndsmen. Deer present a huge problem to those wishing to grow ornamental or agricultural plants preferred by deer or to train their dogs to run raccoon, fox, or rabbits — but not deer. Hound magazines are full of scents guaranteed to make your dog regret he ever thought of running a deer. So fortunes are spent by some people trying to lure deer and others trying to repel deer or train hounds not to chase them. All of this relates to scent communication, and one thing is certain — deer make much use of scents. Unfortunately, most popular speculation is based on uncritical observation. My students, colleagues, and I at The University of Georgia have studied deer scent communication for more than 30 years but still do not claim to have all the answers. In fact, sometimes I believe we have only examined the "tip of the iceberg." Let's look at some of what we do know.

The Scent Glands of the White-tailed Deer

Interdigital Glands

Members of the deer family have interdigital glands on all four feet. These are small, sparsely-haired sacs about the size of our thumbnail, that open between the hooves by a short, wide duct. They usually contain a yellowish, cheesy material with a strong, pungent smell similar to rancid butter. This secretion accumulates from sloughed skin and the product of oil glands and leaves a scent trail wherever a deer walks. Our studies have identified at least 46 different compounds associated with interdigital secretions, some of which occur in greater concentrations in dominant bucks than in younger bucks. The trails deer leave are undoubtedly important in providing them with a sense of home range familiarity, and there have been observations of deer back-trailing themselves to return home from strange locations. An interesting note is that the components of this scent have different volatility, which cause the scent to change with time. This gradual change in a smell could be what tells a deer how old the track is and which is the front and which is the back trail. On the negative side for the deer, this scent trail can also be followed by predators.

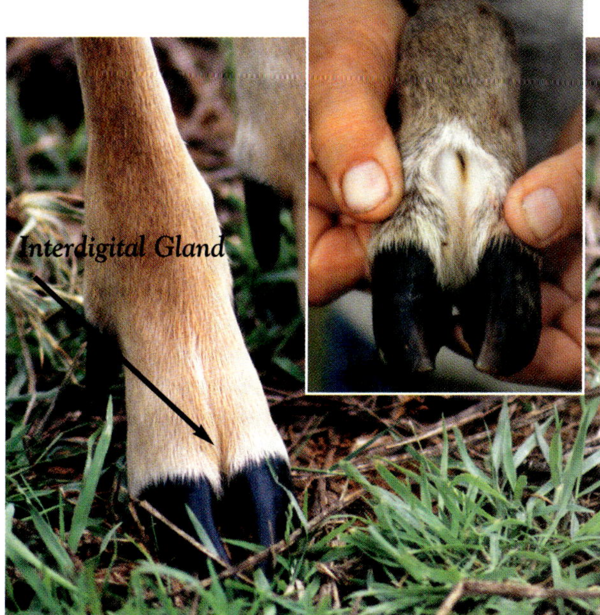

The interdigital glands, located between the hooves on all four feet on whitetails, leave a scent trail wherever the deer walks.

Metatarsal Glands

The metatarsal glands are found on the outside

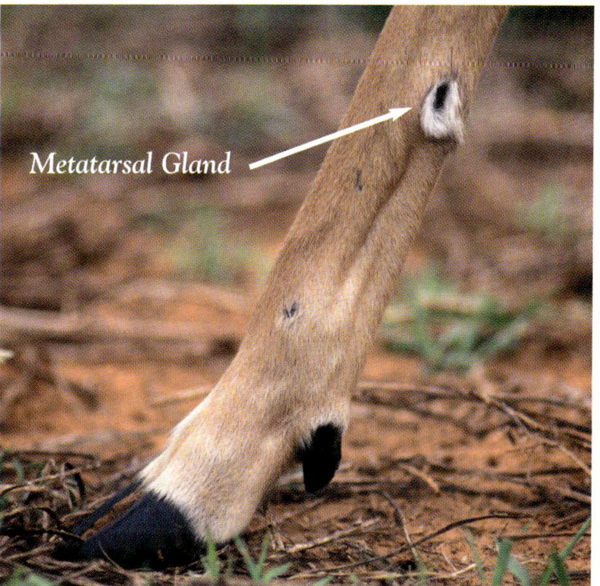

The metatarsal gland is located on the outside of the hind leg. The function of this gland remains unclear.

of a deer's hind legs. These glands have a curious structure — an oval ring of white hairs surrounding a black callous. There is some evidence they are the source of an alarm scent in black-tailed deer. However, our work at The University of Georgia has been unable to show this gland has any function in white-tailed deer. It is interesting to note that white-tailed deer in Central and South America do not even have this gland.

Tarsal Glands

Tarsal glands are tufts of hair on the inside of the deer's hind legs. We believe they may be the most important scent glands in whitetails. They seem to communicate identity and social status. A behavior pattern, which we refer to as rub urination, is often associated with tarsal glands. It involves an animal urinating on the tarsal glands while rubbing them together and results in a scent trail being left during the animal's subsequent movements. This urination posture differs from that during normal urination, as in the latter the hind legs are well apart. After urinating on the tarsal glands, a deer usually licks the inside of his hind legs, including the glands. Interestingly, during the rut, dominant bucks generally do not lick the urine off their tarsal glands. This, and possibly a change in the composition of the urine itself, results in long, dark stains down the inside of the hind legs in the most dominant bucks. One could argue that a buck with extremely prominent staining down the leg at least "thinks" he is the biggest and baddest buck in his neck of the woods.

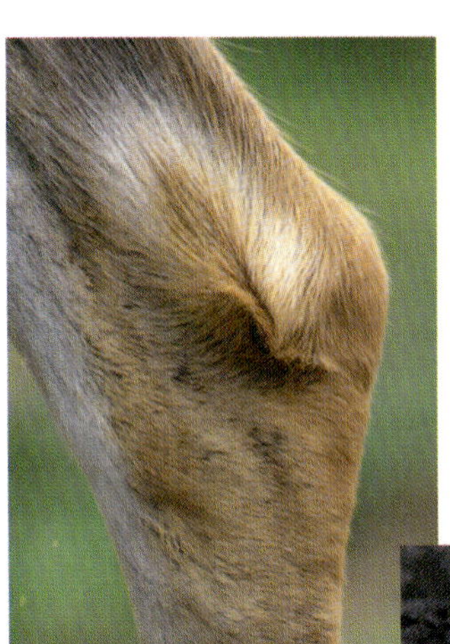

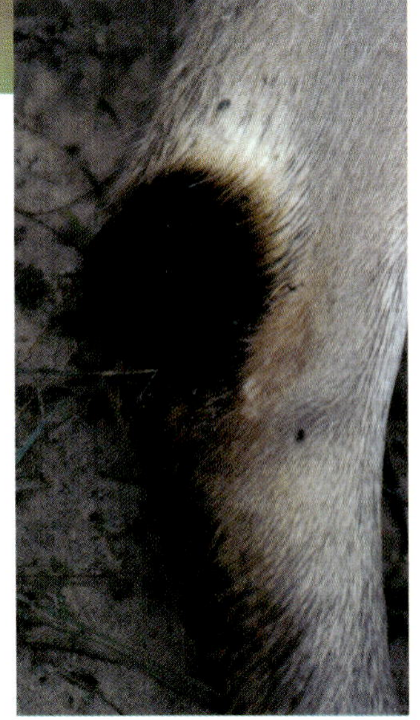

Tarsal glands, located on the inside of a deer's hind legs, may be the most important scent glands in whitetails, communicating identity and social status. During the rut, the tarsal glands of bucks become stained and dark (right), with the stain running down the leg from the gland on the most dominant bucks.

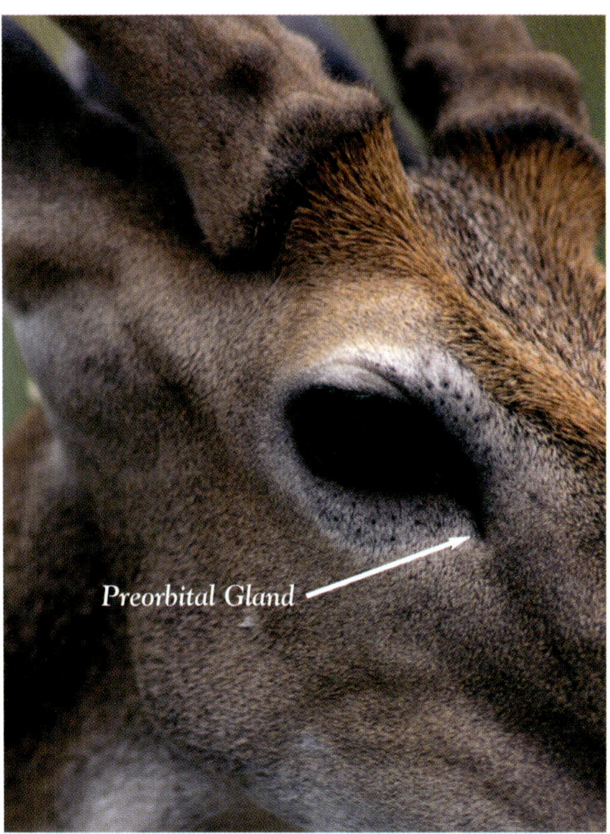

A whitetail's preorbital glands are located just in front of each eye and may play a role in scent communication at scrape sites.

Preorbital Glands

These are found just in front of the eye. They contain few scent-producing cells and are poorly developed in whitetails as compared to some other

The forehead gland is a patch of specialized sweat cells located in the skin from the eyes to the antlers. A buck's forehead gland becomes particularly active during the rut, causing a darkening of the hair of the forehead on most bucks. Bucks deposit scent from this gland on rubs and on the limbs overhanging scrapes.

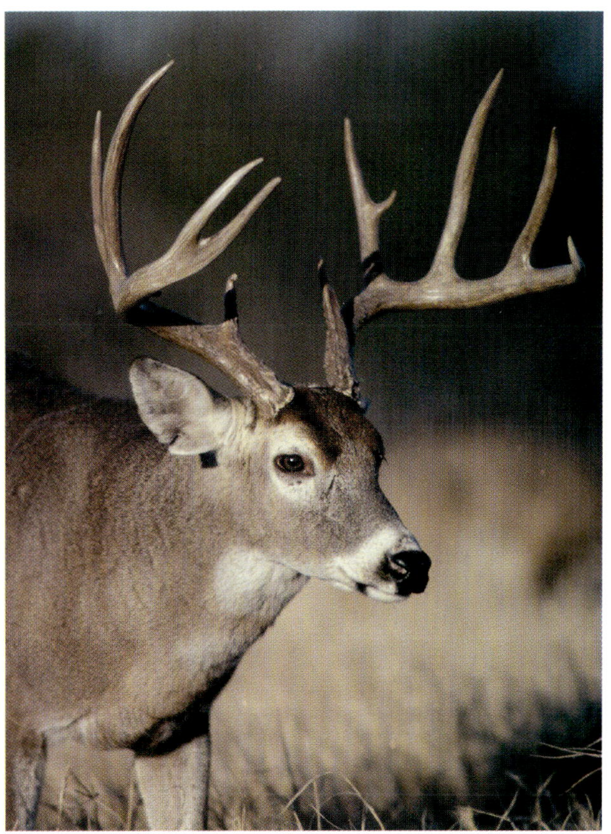

ungulates like elk or sambar deer. They can be flared open and in does may function in visual communication with fawns. Sometimes they seem to be used in marking the branches overhanging scrapes. If they have a function resulting from this apparent marking behavior it would have to involve scent.

Nasal, Forehead, and Preputial Glands

There are other glands on whitetails discovered by University of Georgia researchers. The first is the nasal gland. They are within each nostril and are about the size of an almond. This is a strange place for a scent gland, because the constant presence of an odor would inhibit the ability to smell it. They might be just for lubrication, but we have speculated they could produce an alarm scent expelled during the snort. If such an alarm scent is produced, it would remain in the air warning other deer of possible danger. No experimental evidence for this has been demonstrated.

Another gland is the forehead gland. It is composed of specialized sweat cells in the patch of skin from the eyes to antlers. This gland was discovered by taking biopsy samples from the forehead of several deer in our pens. Samples were also collected from hunter-killed deer. We found that the glands of adults of both sexes were inactive during the summer. During the rut, the glands of does were moderately active while those of bucks were highly active. Because the gland is much more active and prominent in bucks, experienced observers can use this to separate the sexes, even if the antlers are obscured. We also found that dominant bucks, irrespective of age, had more active cells than their subordinates. It is obvious that bucks are leaving scent on rubs and possibly branches over scrapes that relays information to other deer.

The preputial gland is comprised of glandular cells in the penile prepuce of bucks. They could provide smells that communicate sexual status but are not thought to be a primary source for such odors. This gland is thought to play an important role in sexual communication in many gregarious deer species such as red deer, elk, and fallow deer.

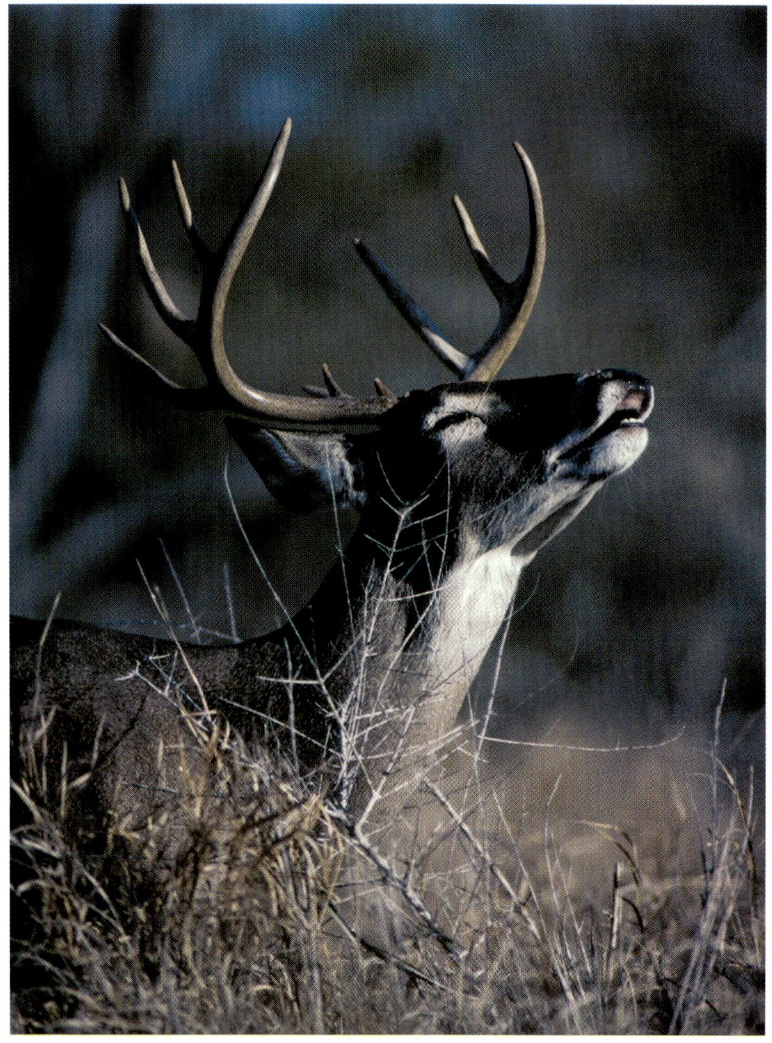

This buck is performing a lip-curl or flehmen behavior, which draws the scent from doe urine into the sensory pit of the vomeronasal organ, located in the roof of the mouth.

Vomeronasal Organ

Although not a gland, the vomeronasal organ is very important to chemical communication in deer. This organ is located on the roof of the mouth and used as an additional chemical sensory organ. It is a "sixth" sense, but not the supernatural kind. You may have seen a deer perform lip curl or flehmen behavior. The buck will sniff and lick the spot where a doe has urinated. The buck then curls up his nose and inhales. By doing so, he draws chemicals from the urine into his mouth and then into the sensory pit of the vomeronasal organ. Interestingly, the nerve connections of this organ do not access the portion of the brain that controls behavior but rather that which controls sexual physiology. Therefore, we believe this organ is involved in a "priming effect," which ensures the buck is ready for mating, but not for determining the immediate reproductive status of a doe. In other words, the vomeronasal organ takes in chemical messengers called "primer" pheromones, which affect the buck subconsciously and maintain his sexual drive. On the other hand, the main olfactory system (nose) receives information in the form of "releaser" pheromones, which the buck is consciously aware of and which can affect his immediate behavior such as identifying a doe in heat or fleeing from danger.

Urine

We have studied both buck and doe urine. In the case of doe urine, it is evident the components which indicate a doe is in heat (i.e., estrus) are derived from the reproductive tract and not from the urine itself. However, urine that is passed from a doe during normal urination may pick up important primer and/or releaser pheromones from her reproductive tract via glands in her external genitalia.

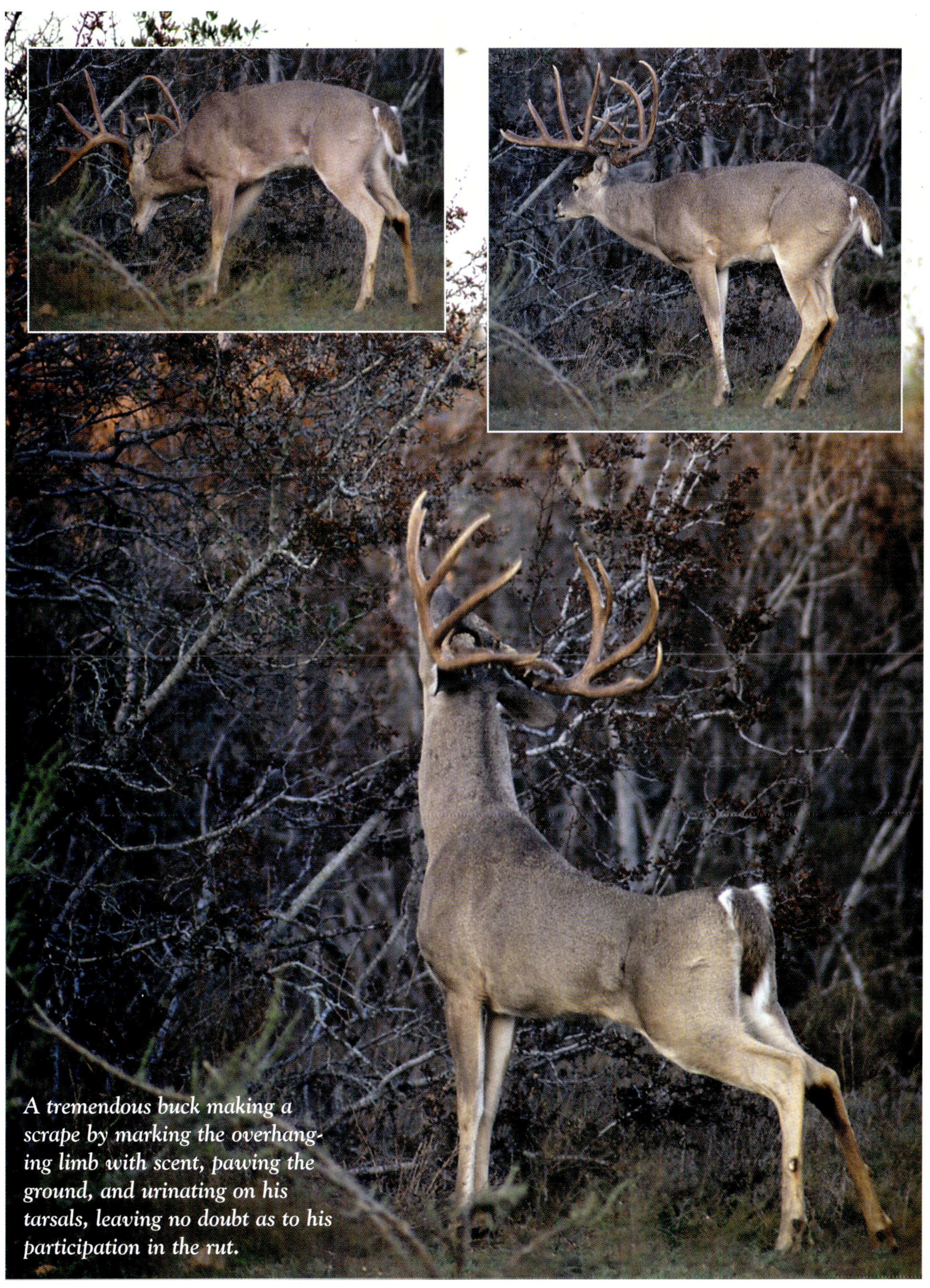

A tremendous buck making a scrape by marking the overhanging limb with scent, pawing the ground, and urinating on his tarsals, leaving no doubt as to his participation in the rut.

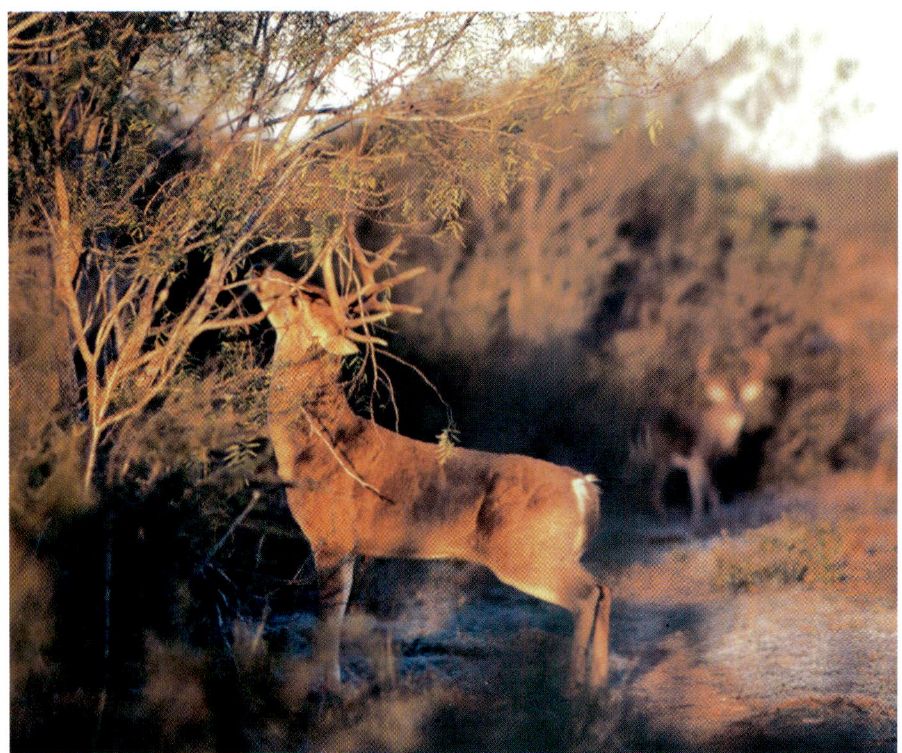

Both visual and scent information play key roles in the communication network of whitetails.

Signposts

White-tailed deer rubs and scrapes were first identified as signposts through research at The University of Georgia (UGA). Signposts are places where visual and olfactory information, primarily from the urine and the various scent glands, are presented for other deer to receive. They are a major part of the whitetail's communication network and one from which the astute human observer can learn much.

What do Deer Hear?

Little research has been done on what and how well white-tailed deer hear. One study many years ago at UGA indicated their hearing range closely approximated that of humans (i.e., they hear best between about 100 and 10,000 Hz). A few other small studies have basically substantiated this. It seems clear that, unlike dogs and cats, they do not hear in the very high frequencies. Interestingly, if this is true, the widely advertised ultrasonic "deer whistles" for preventing deer-car collisions would not be effective.

How do Deer Talk?

Whitetails send olfactory and visual "notes" to each other with signposts and body language. They also have a vocal language of sorts. In a study at UGA (similar work was done at Mississippi State University), approximately 400 deer vocalizations were recorded of which 90 were selected for sonagraphic analysis. We identified 12 different calls in five categories.

Alarm and Distress Calls

Snort — The snort is probably the most widely recognized of the whitetail's calls. Some snorts sound like sharp blasts of "white noise," while oth-

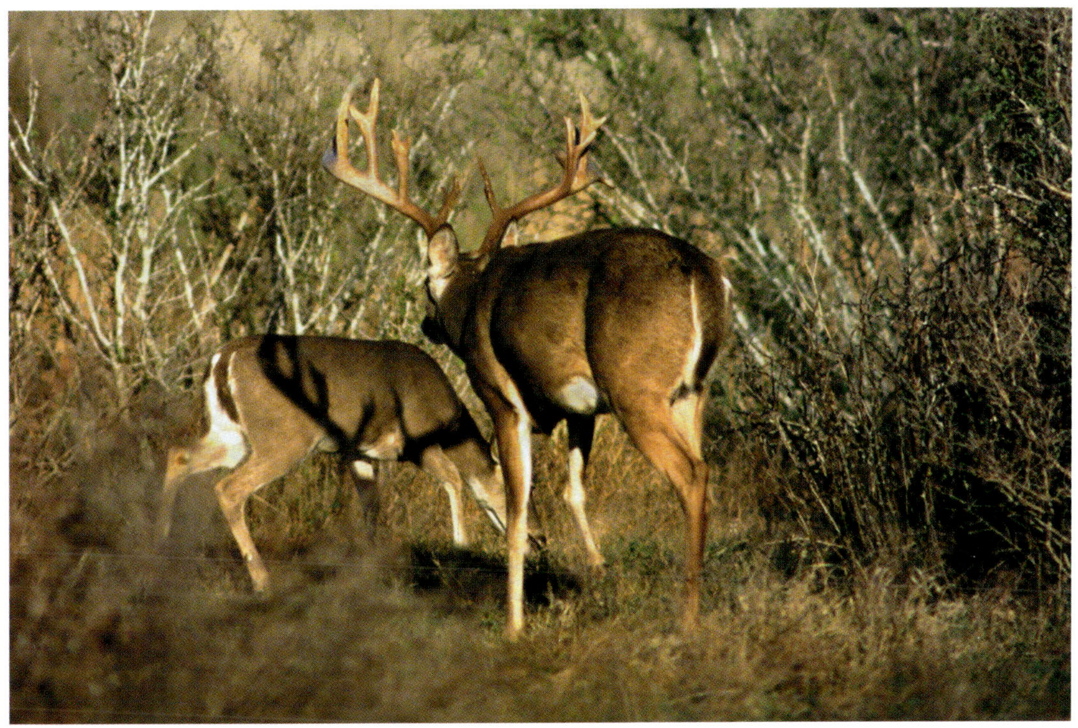

Most hunters are familiar with the tending grunt, given by bucks during courtship. When imitated by hunters, this call can be an effective lure for non-tending bucks.

ers have a moderate whistling quality. The snort is often used to express alarm and is given singly or in a series. It is made occasionally by both sexes, but primarily by members of doe groups.

Bawl — The bawl is a very intense vocalization given when deer are being traumatized. It is a voiced sound of high tonality given with the mouth open. Its pitch generally decreases with age. Large males, especially, have deeper, heavier bawls. Bawls are given by deer of all ages in situations of extreme distress and may function as another alarm call. Badly frightened deer have been heard to make this sound, but we hear it most often when deer are injured or restrained. Deer, other than nursing does, generally respond to a bawl by fleeing. The fawn bawl is an effective way of calling does in the summer and, to a lesser extent, in early fall.

Aggressive Calls

We identified three aggressive vocalizations. They consist of a basic call with successive elements added as the intensity of the encounter escalates.

Low grunt — The low grunt is used by both sexes throughout the year and occurs during the least aggressive interactions. It consists of a low guttural grunt coupled with intention postures and is used frequently by dominant animals of either sex to displace subordinates. Usually given singly, it is a voiced sound of low pitch, tonality, and intensity and of brief duration given with the mouth open or closed. Often, if the deer it is directed to hesitates, the encounter escalates into a rush and foreleg kick by the dominant animal.

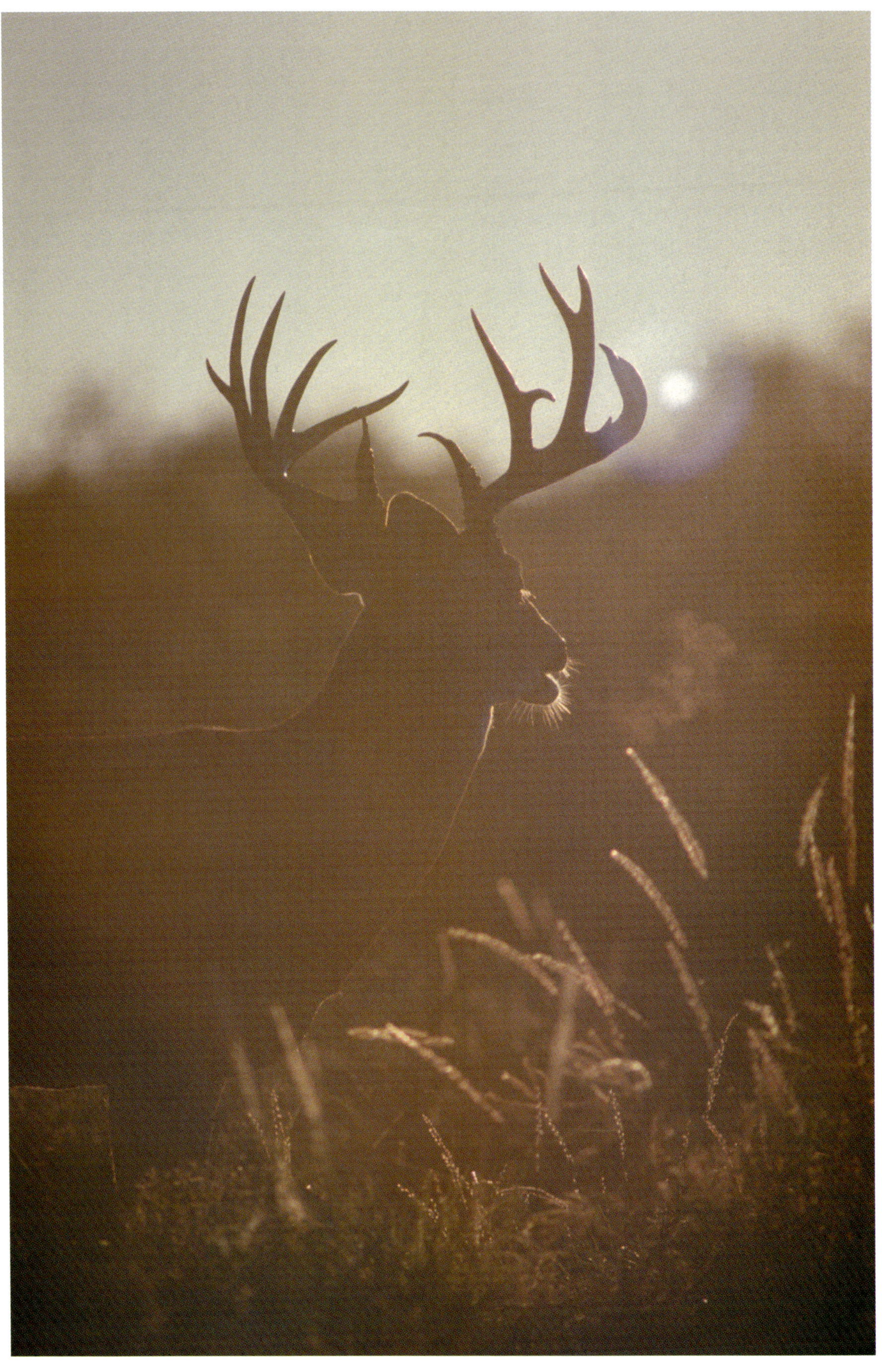

Grunt-snort — In more intense encounters by either sex, one to four rapid snorts are added to the basic grunt. Occasionally given by does, this call is generally emitted by bucks during the breeding season.

Grunt-snort-wheeze — This is a buck's most intense aggressive vocalization. It consists of the grunt-snort followed by a drawn-out wheezing sound made through pinched nostrils. Although difficult to imitate, it can be a powerful hunting tool when properly used, but is likely to call in only the largest, most dominant bucks.

Maternal-Neonatal Calls

Maternal grunt — This call is a voiced sound of moderate pitch, low tonality, and short duration given at intervals of a few seconds as a means of the doe communicating with her fawn. The call is of low intensity, often audible to humans for only a few yards. If a fawn fails to respond, the doe calls more loudly and can be heard further.

Mew — The primary sound of the newborn fawn is the mew, a voiced sound of high pitch and tonality and low intensity.

Bleat — The bleat is a higher-level, care-soliciting vocalization of the fawn. The intensity and duration of this call are proportional to the degree of deprivation of the fawn. Whereas the mew is inaudible at distances of a few yards, bleats can carry 100 yards or more. Bleats are also heard when fawns are disturbed and usually result in investigations by nursing does.

Nursing whine — It usually is made as the fawn is actively suckling or searching for a nipple.

Mating Calls

Tending grunt — The tending grunt is given by males during courtship of a doe in estrus. Although highly variable, this call is a voiced sound of moderate intensity, low tonality, moderate pitch, and often is longer in duration than the other grunts described. When used by hunters, this can be an effective call for luring non-tending bucks.

Bellow — We have heard this call on only a few occasions. Usually it was made during periods of intense sexual frustration or aggression.

Contact Call

It is heard when a member of a group becomes separated and serves to maintain vocal contact with one another when visual contact is lost. This call is a voiced grunt of moderate pitch, intensity, and tonality. It is similar to the maternal grunt, but often much louder. Hunters listening carefully may hear it from 50 to 100 yards away. Grunt calls or mouth imitations of does grunting can be effective at luring bucks, particularly young ones.

It usually requires experience for the hunter or field observer to recognize "deer talk." Deer vocalizations often are mistaken for insects or other background noises. With much practice and a good ear, students of white-tailed deer can find themselves in or even a part of a whole new world of deer "conversation." Knowledge of deer communications allows the observer to establish a relationship with this fascinating animal that most humans never dreamed possible.

I would like to express my appreciation to Dr. Karl V. Miller and the many UGA graduate students who have helped in the research presented in this chapter.

Hunters may not realize the wide range of vocalizations whitetails use for communication. Researchers have identified a dozen different calls.

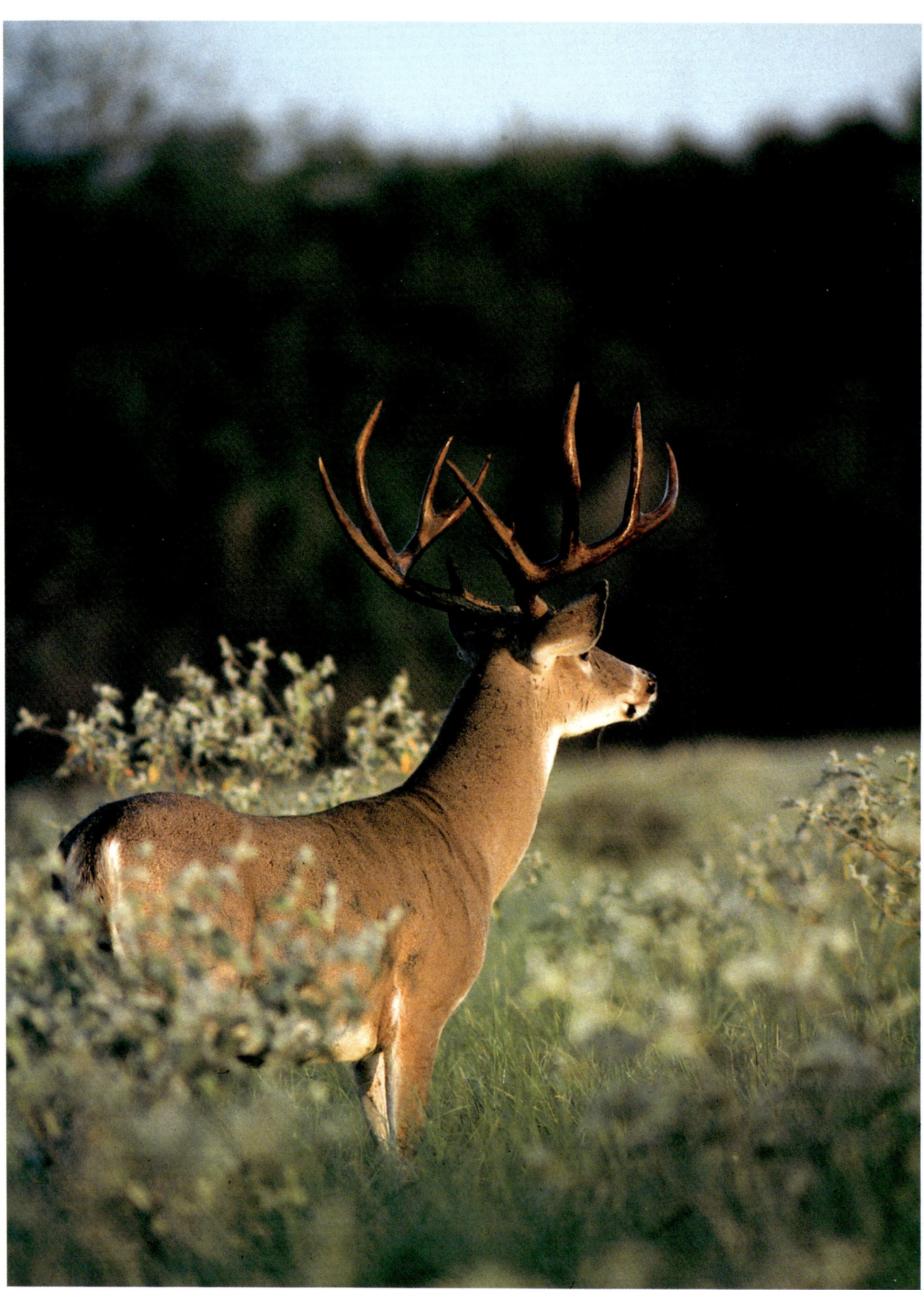

2

Whitetail Antler Development

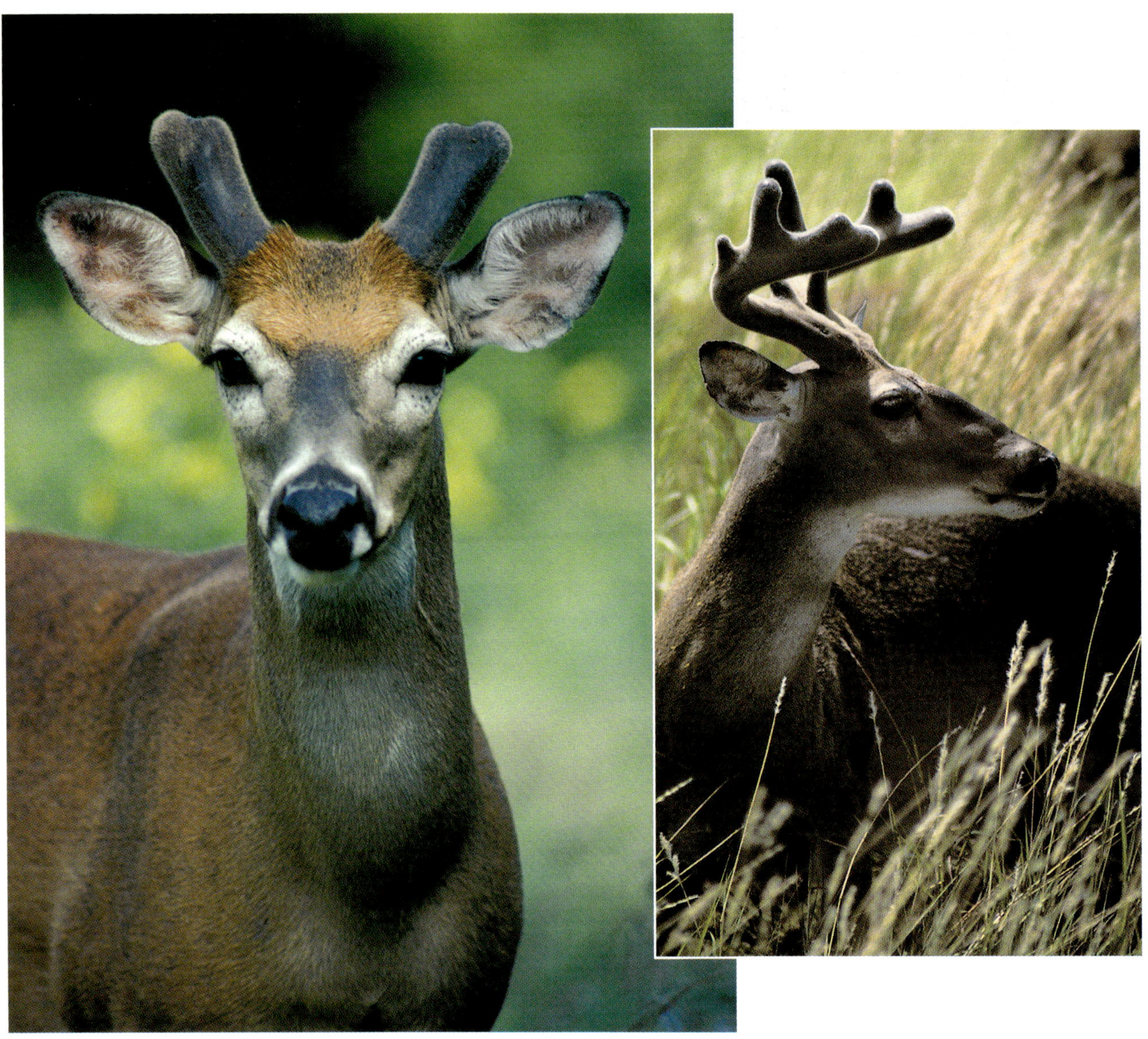

When holding a deer antler, whether it is a shed or still connected to a buck, you are holding a magnificently created piece of nature. For many, antlers are sought for their natural beauty, which is clearly understandable, as no two are exactly alike. Antlers are grown in every shape and configuration imaginable, which is one reason why they have enamored hunters for thousands of years. As a hunter matures and learns the processes antlers go through from growth and maturation to utilization and casting, antlers attain an entirely new value.

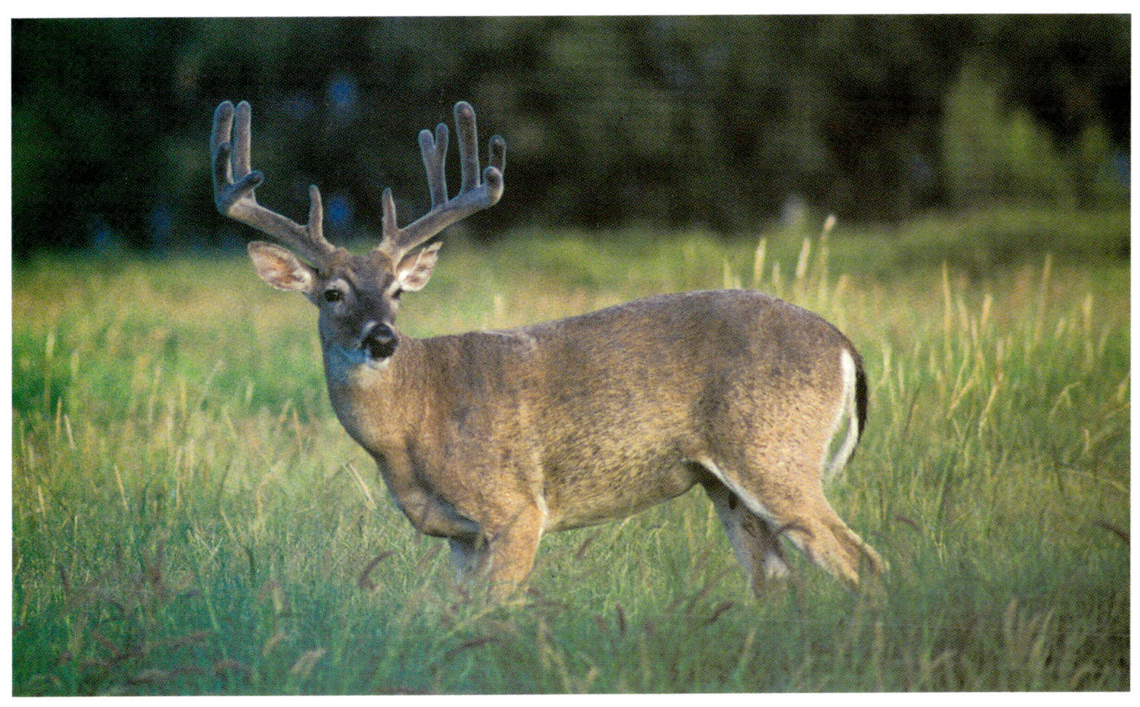

Growing antlers draw enormous amounts of nutrients from reserves in the blood and skeletal system, and growth can approach a half-inch or more per day.

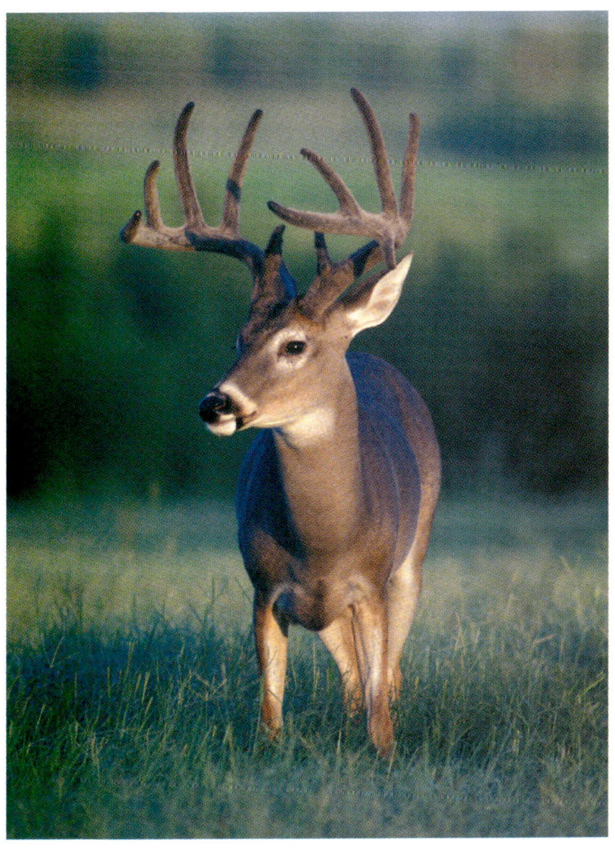

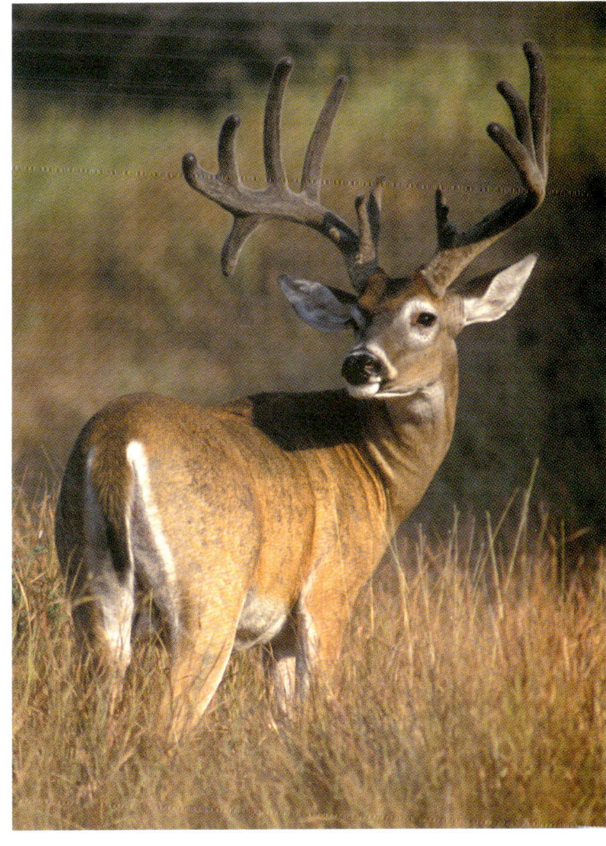

As fall approaches, decreasing daylight triggers hormonal changes, which restrict blood supply to the growing antler resulting in antler hardening and velvet shedding.

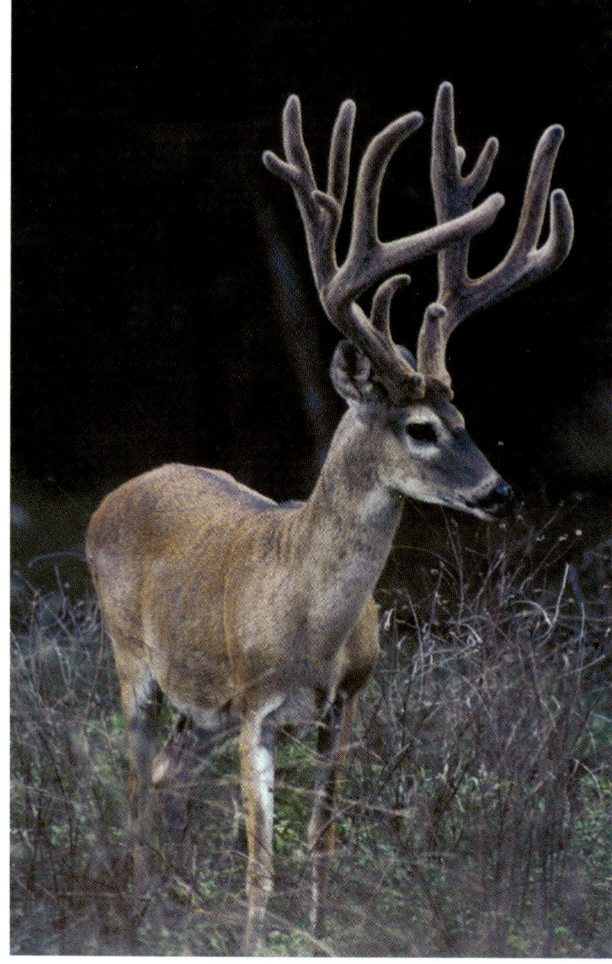

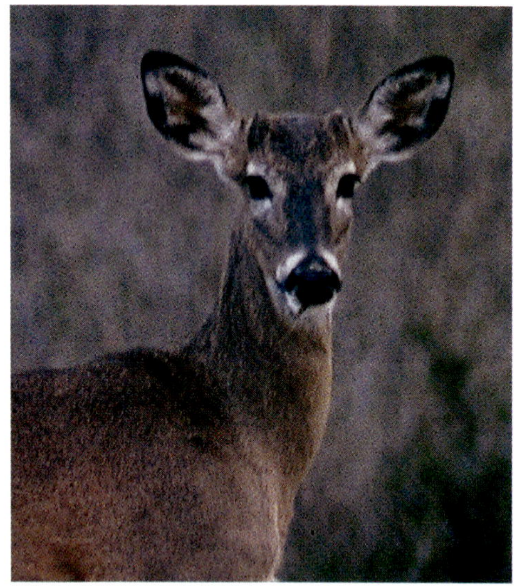

In the first few months of a buck fawn's life, pedicles form on the skull plate of his forehead. It is from these pedicles that future antlers will grow. The following spring, at approximately 10 to 12 months of age, increasing daylight triggers hormonal changes which cause the antlers to begin growing. They start as protrusions covered by a specialized skin called velvet, which contains numerous blood vessels. The large amount of nutrients transported in the blood supply to the developing antler can result in a half-inch or more of growth per day. In fact, antlers grown by members of the Cervidae (deer) family are likely the fastest growing tissue found in any mammal. As fall approaches, decreasing daylight triggers hormonal changes, which restrict blood supply to the growing antler resulting in antler hardening and velvet shedding. A buck will rub off the velvet, and the new antlers will be worn for several months depending on climate, nutrition, age, and health.

Finally, hormonal changes in late winter result in casting of the antlers. When cast, the buck's pedicles are typically bloody but quickly heal and soon support the beginning of the next year's antler growth. The reason some bucks cast their antlers earlier than others is not clearly understood. Most researchers cite physical condition, nutrition, and age as the primary causes. The poorer the physical

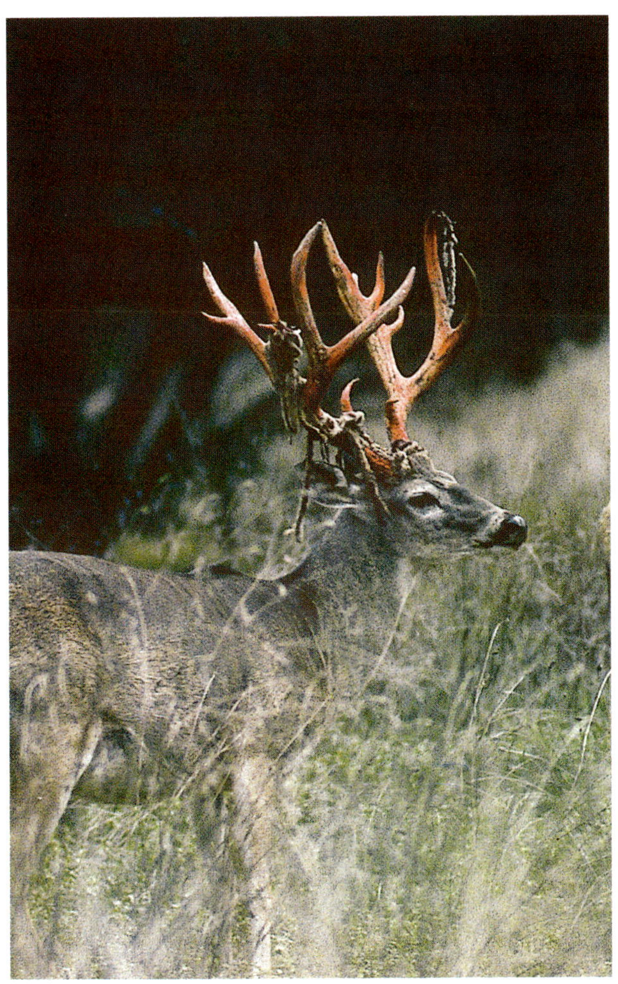

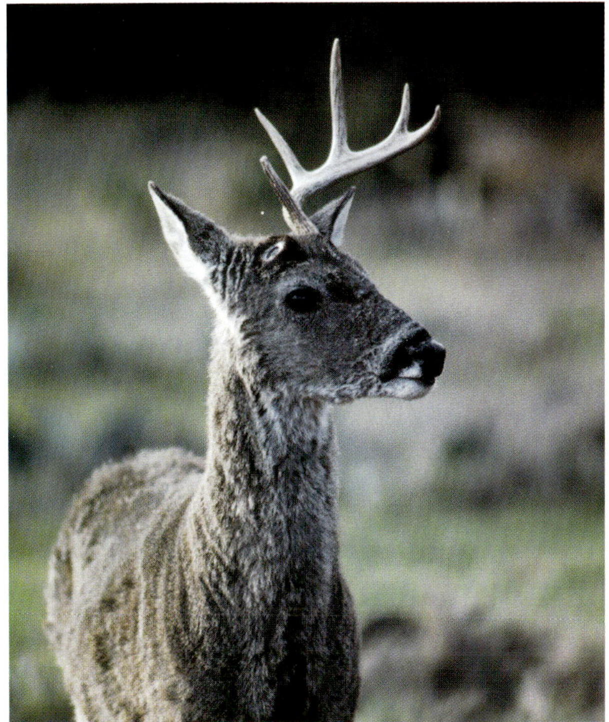

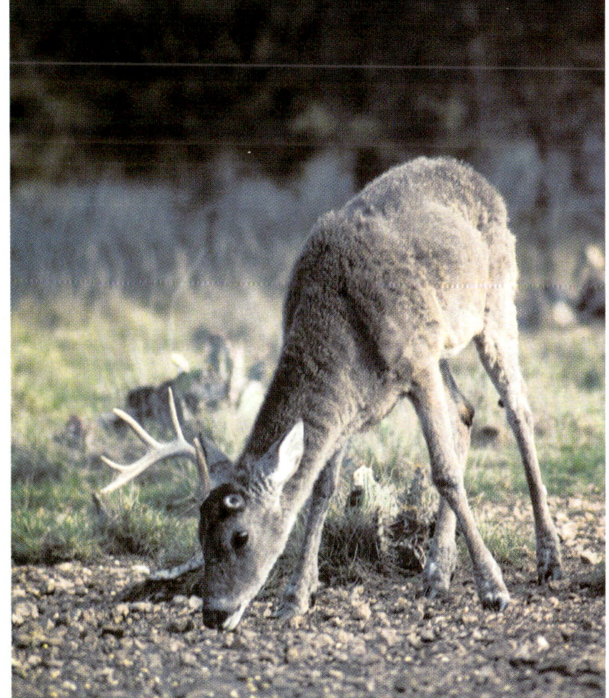

condition, especially when a buck is past his prime, the earlier the casting. Another theory is that a buck spending the post-rut period with does instead of being by himself or with a buck bachelor group may cause delayed antler casting. This is thought to be due to elevated testosterone levels caused by extended breeding activities.

While most hunters realize that age and genetics affect antler growth, nutrition is equally if not more important. Dietary levels of energy, calcium, phosphorus, protein, and vitamins are directly correlated to antler size. As such, insufficiencies in any of these components can adversely affect antler growth. Protein and energy are important not only

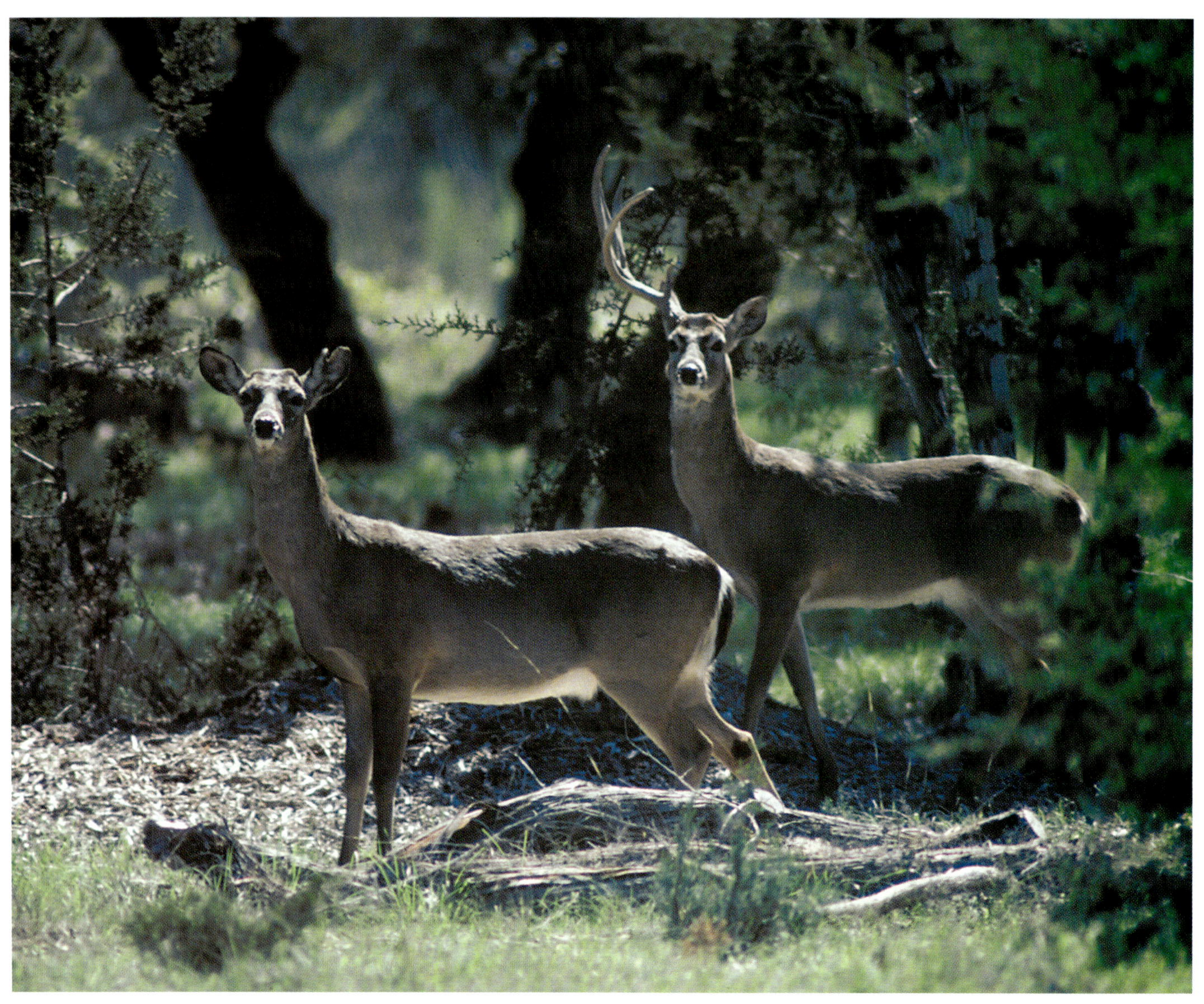

Most researchers believe that physical condition, age, and available nutrition are the main factors that cause some bucks to cast their antlers earlier than others.

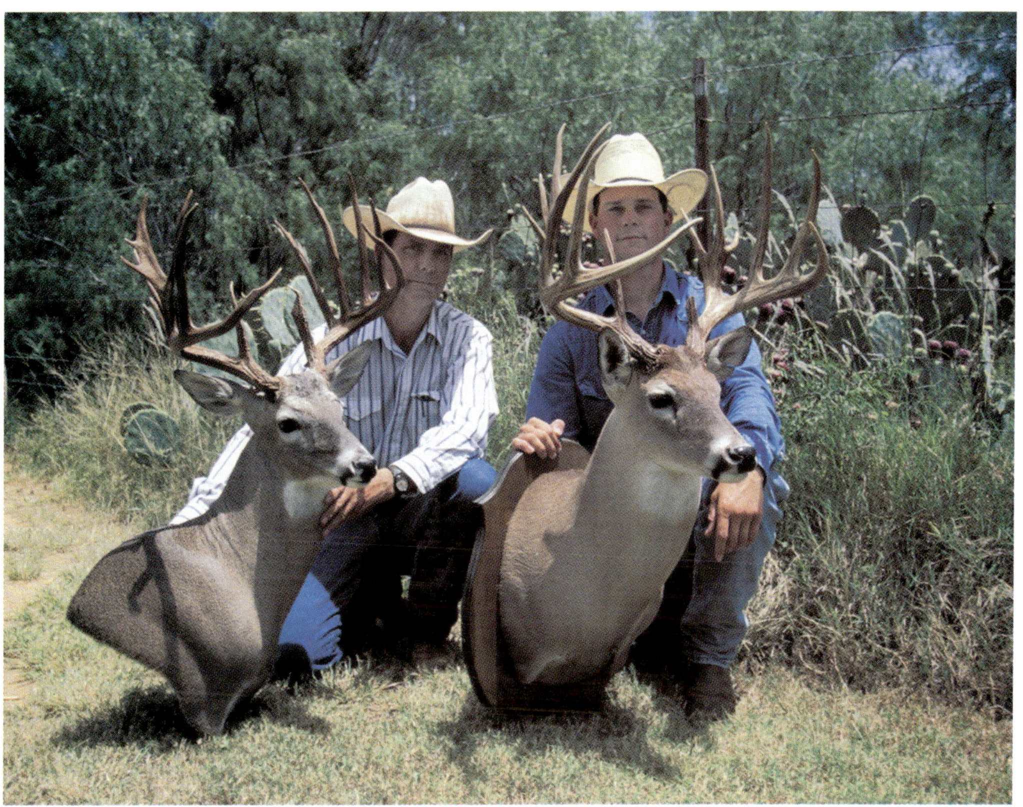

Little Roy (left) and Cuatro Hindes (right) hold mounted heads of two 6 1/2-year-old bucks that lived several miles from one another at the same time on their ranch. Both bucks display several of the same antler characteristics making one wonder about the possibility of a shared genetic background.

during antler growth but also one to two months prior to the start of growth. Poor nutrition during late winter and early spring can adversely affect antler growth, even when nutritional levels may be optimal the last 60 to 80 days of growth. Sixteen percent protein is considered by most researchers to be the minimum for optimum antler and body development. Since body size and antler quality are directly correlated to nutrition, it must be remembered that the genetic potential for antler growth cannot be realized if nutritional intake is chronically deficient, even for mature bucks.

It has long been known that a buck's antlers will increase in overall size and mass from 1 1/2 to 5 1/2 years of age. For years, most deer managers have assumed that a buck will produce his largest antlers in his fifth or sixth year. However, recent research suggests that many bucks produce their largest antlers between 6 1/2 and 8 1/2 years of age.

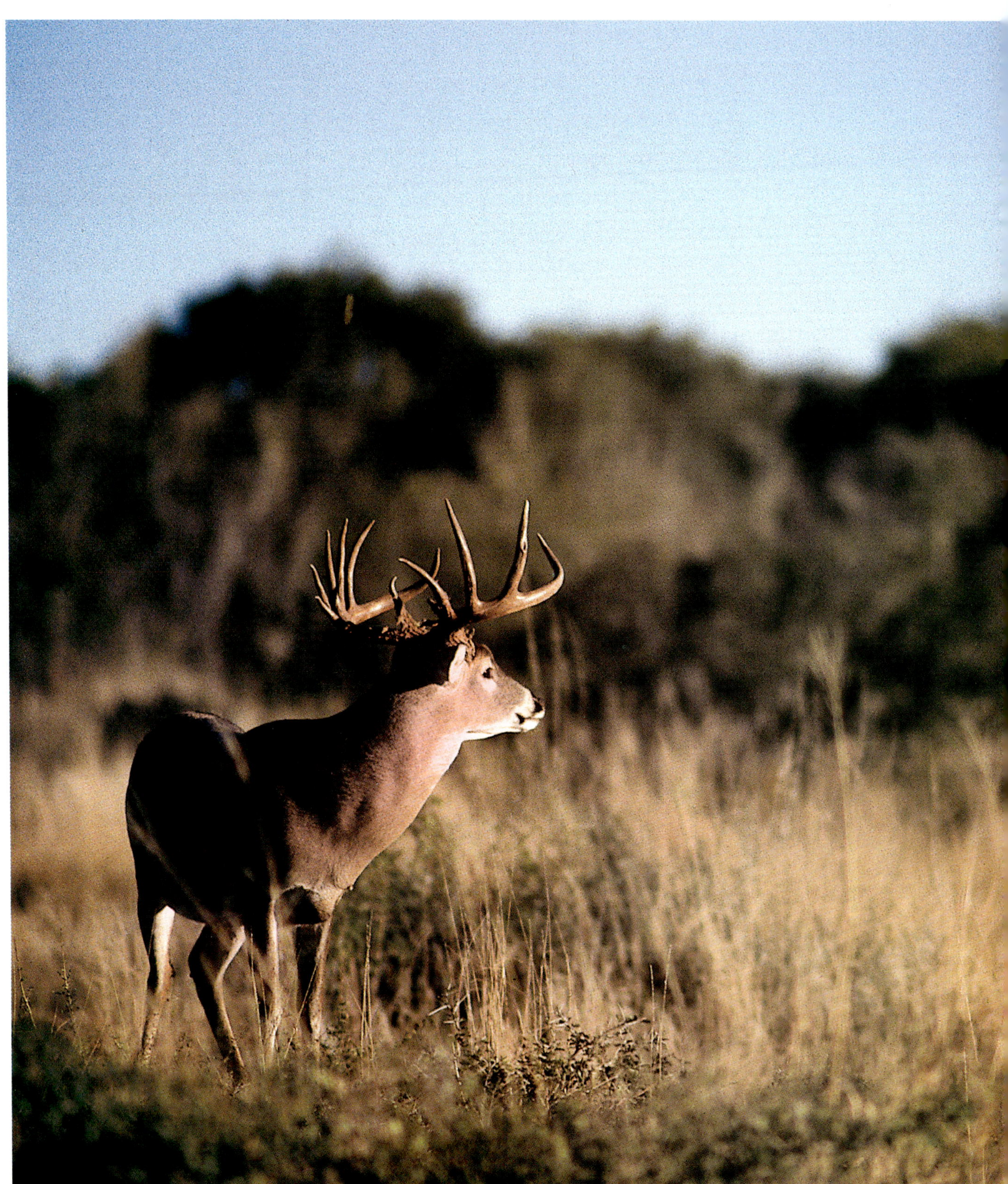

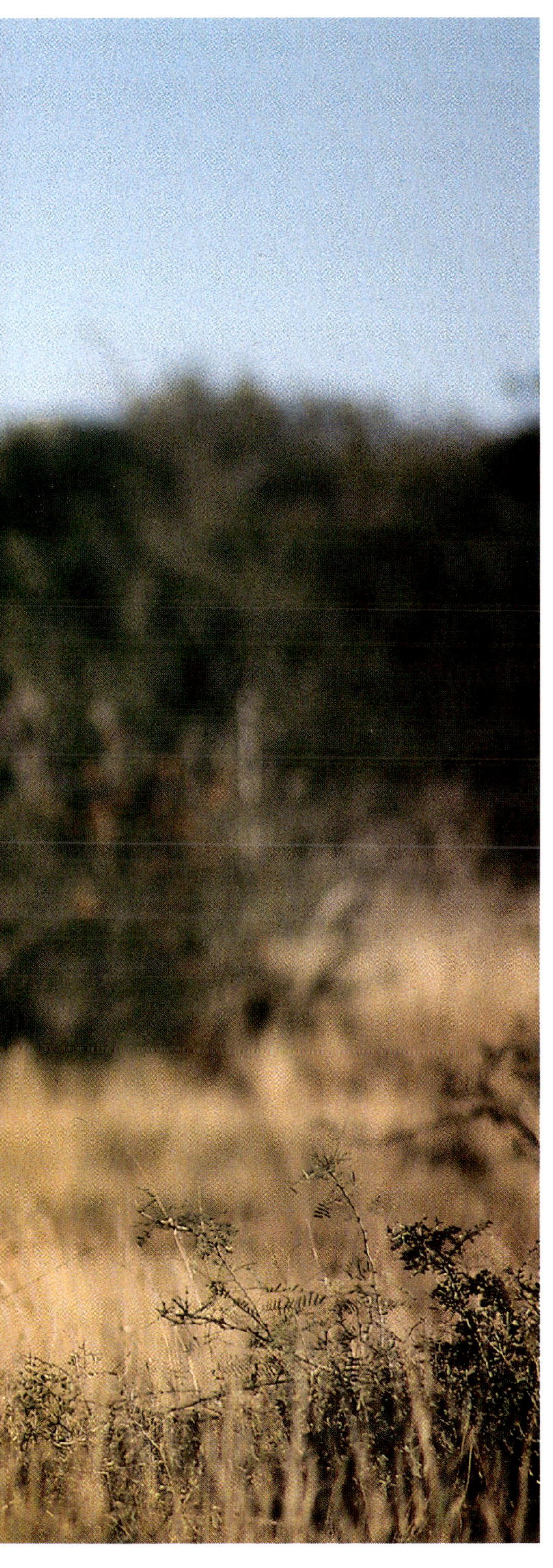

3 Aging Whitetails on the Hoof

Under the best of circumstances, aging white-tailed deer on the hoof is a calculated guess. Even when all proper methods have been utilized and all available information analyzed, you will still make mistakes. It is also important to understand that every deer herd is unique and that numerous variables must be considered before you can consistently age deer on a particular property.

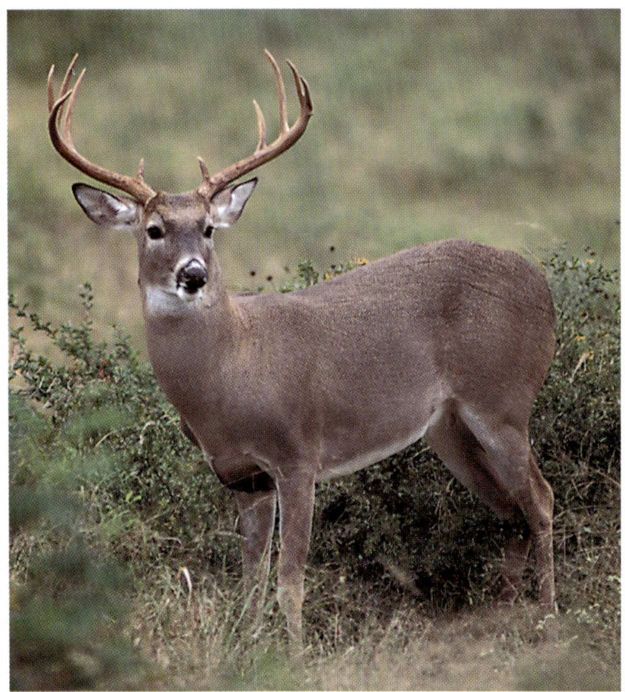
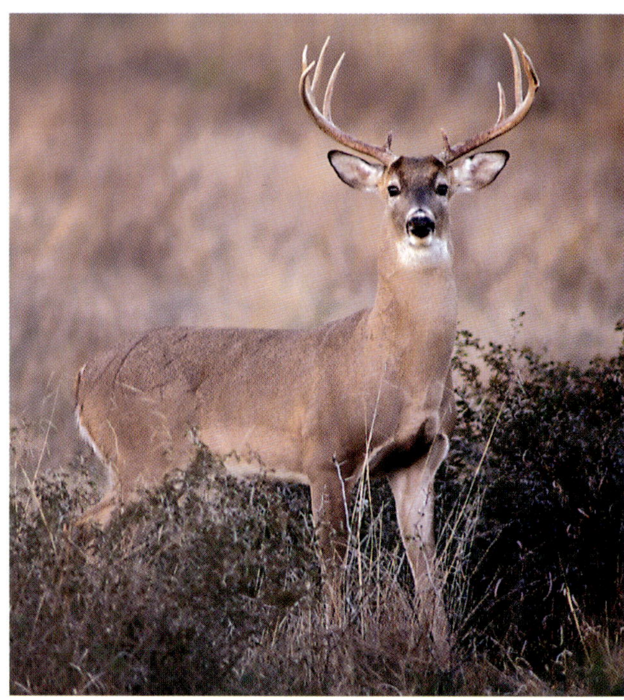

Note the weight loss on this 3 1/2-year-old buck from October until January. Also, notice there is relatively little difference in neck size. The observer must always consider the time of year and rutting activity when aging bucks.

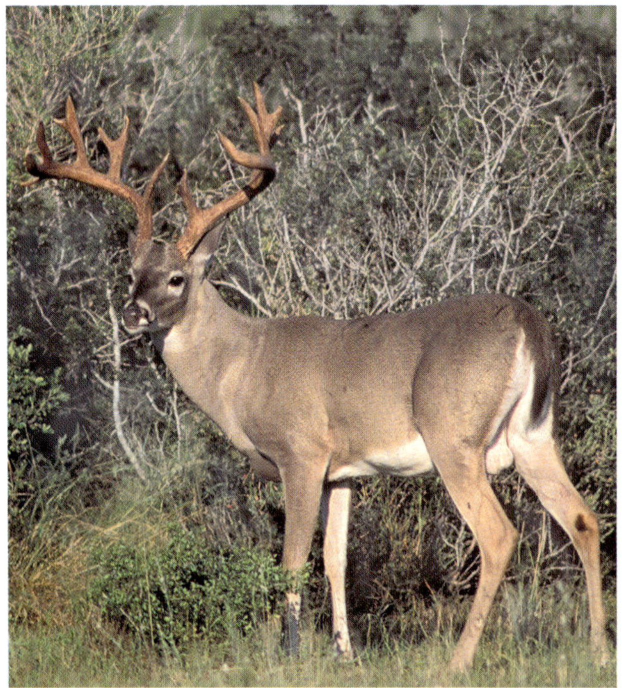
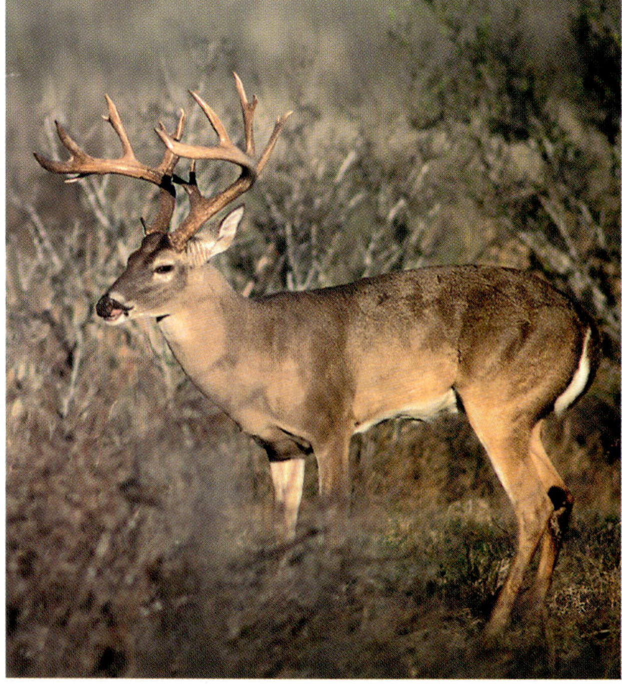

Along with weight loss on this 4 1/2-year-old buck from October (left) until January (right), note the staining of the tarsal area. By January, the stain extended to the hoof along with loss of hair from urine scalding. Bucks can lose considerable weight during the rut and resemble a younger buck during the post-rut.

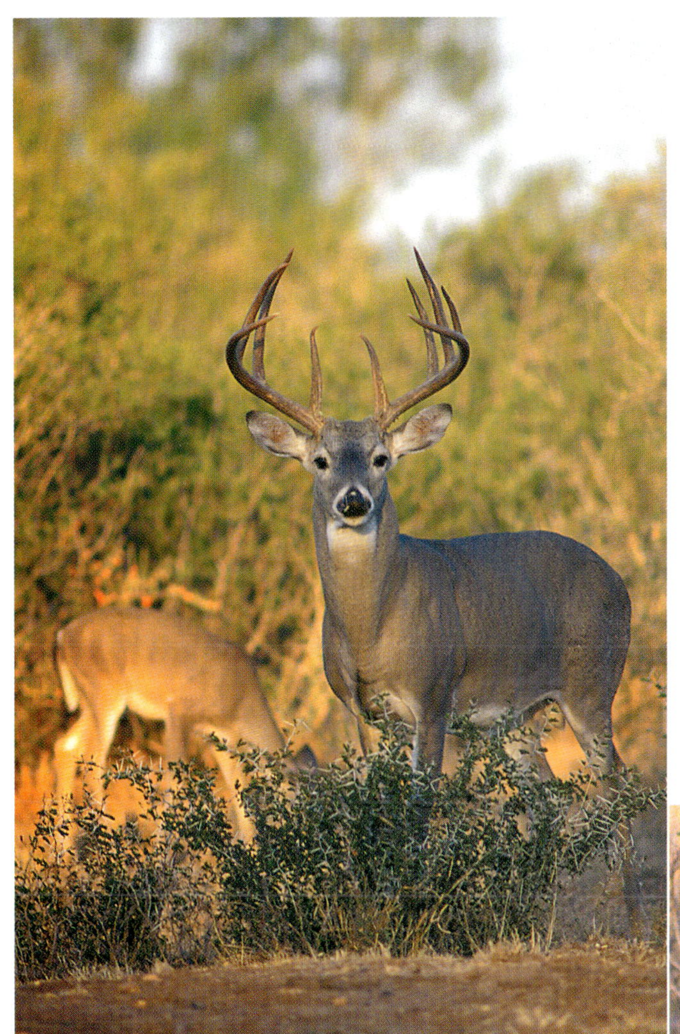

One factor to consider is how nutrition, or lack thereof, has affected the deer you are trying to age. Has there been an extended drought or periods of above-average rainfall that could have affected body and antler development? Other potential considerations include: How many years has the property been under management? Is the property high fenced or low fenced? Does the ranch feed high protein, and, if so, how long has the feeding program been in place? Does the ranch plant food plots and what do those plots contain? Any situations you can think of that could affect deer nutrition are pertinent. Different nutritional levels affect deer body growth and development and can cause variations among deer from different properties.

This 7 1/2-year-old exhibits weight loss, increased neck size, antler breakage from fighting, and extreme tarsal scalding from September (above) to December (right). During the rut a buck's increased neck size can make him appear entirely different than he did in late summer and early fall, as this buck clearly demonstrates.

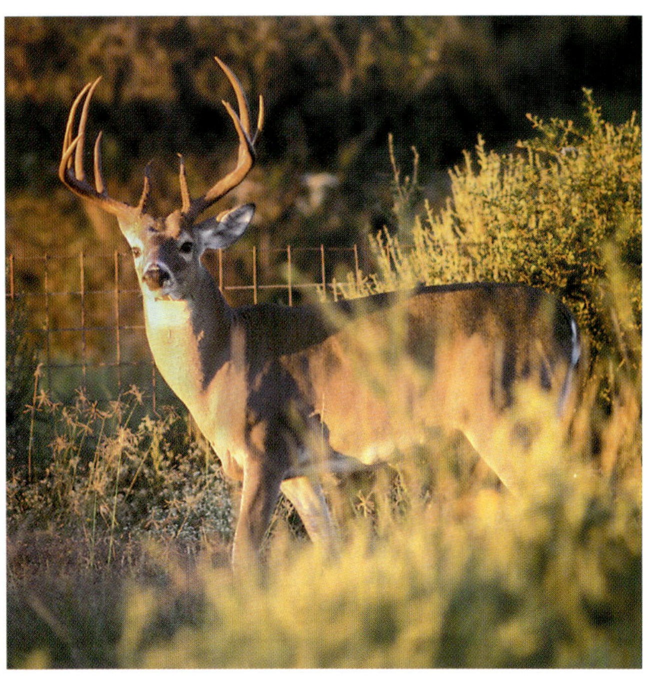

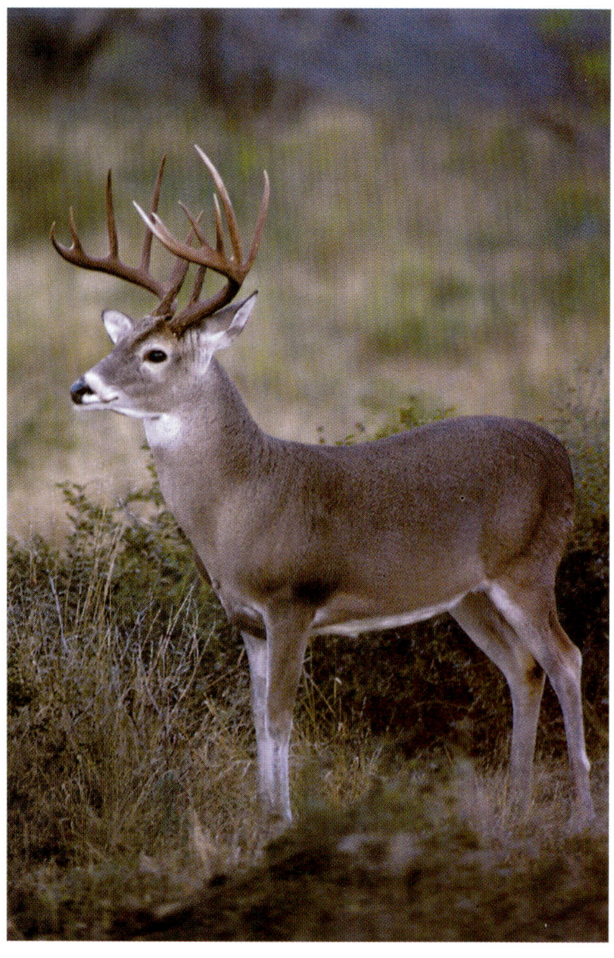

This 6 1/2-year-old demonstrates sequential neck swelling, tarsal staining, and weight loss throughout this October (above), early November (right), and post-rut January (below) photo series. Many factors can influence the degree to which a buck's body changes during this time frame such as nutrition, weather, buck-to-doe ratios, and level of activity during the rut.

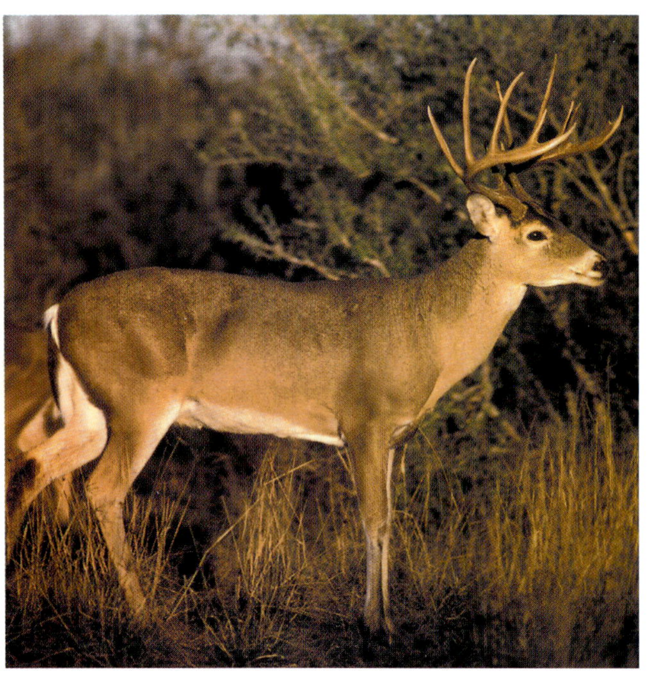

In most situations, deer herds provided high-quality, supplemental feeds have heavier body weights and larger antlers at younger ages than those relying solely on natural habitat. This is an important consideration when estimating age. Another major consideration is time of year. The characteristics we have focused on are best recognized during the rut. This focus is intentional, as hunting season typically occurs during the rut. A buck's body is on a physical roller coaster throughout the year, which greatly affects how old he appears. During the summer months, much of a mature buck's nutritional intake is directed to antler development and body growth, though his neck remains quite thin. In the fall, about the time he rubs the

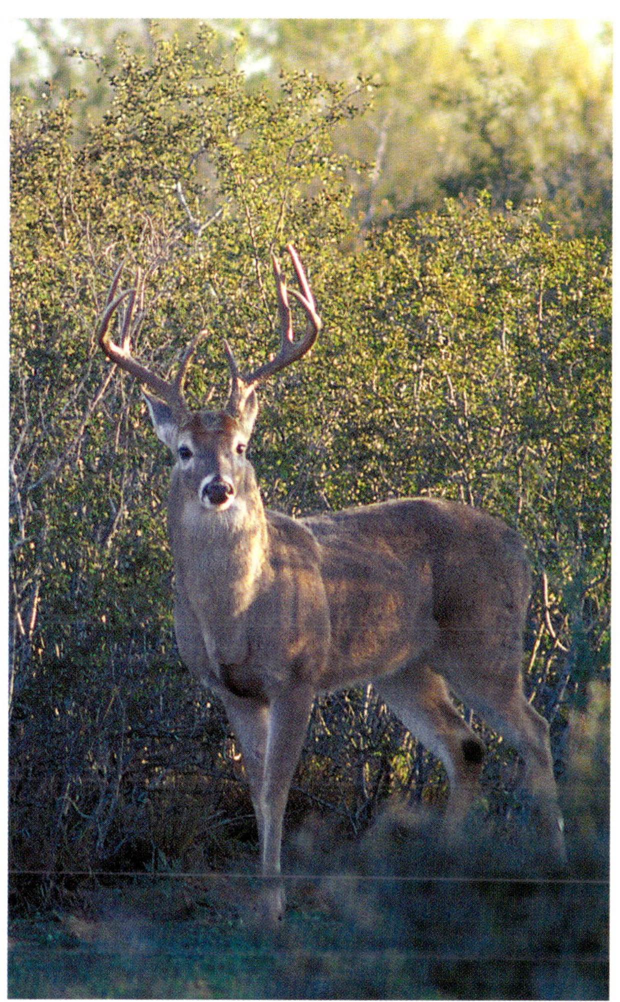

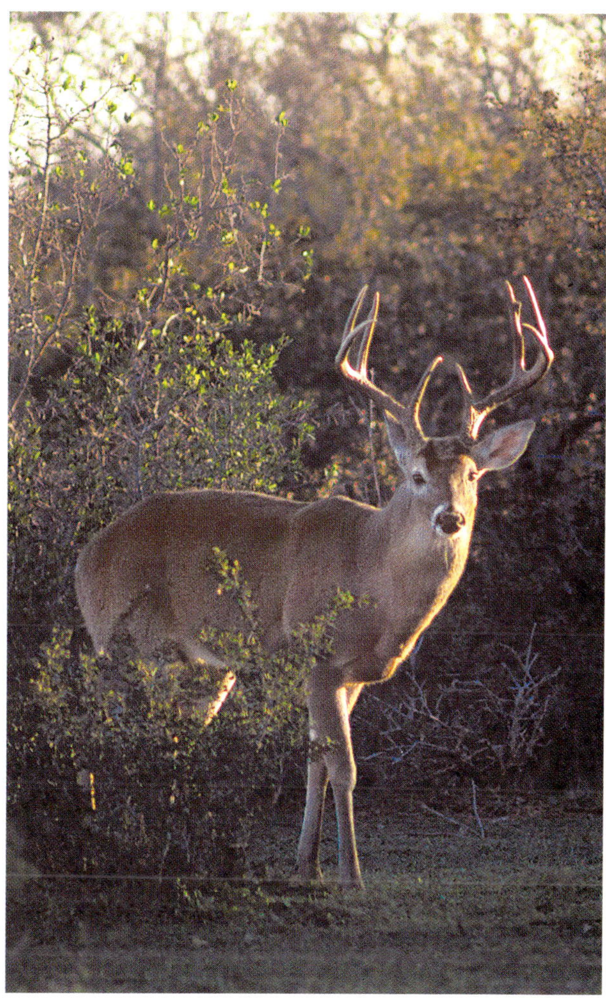

This photo series, taken over less than two minutes, demonstrates the visual differences of a buck as he approaches with other bucks present. Initially, he approaches with hair erect (above) attempting to appear as mature as possible to help establish his place in the hierarchy of the bucks present. However, after a short time his hair flattens (upper and lower right), and it is evident he is only 3 1/2. When the hair is erected, bucks will appear larger, falsely indicating older age. If possible when other bucks are present, observe for a longer period of time for better clarification. This is one reason so many hunters experience ground shrinkage after shooting a buck when he first appears.

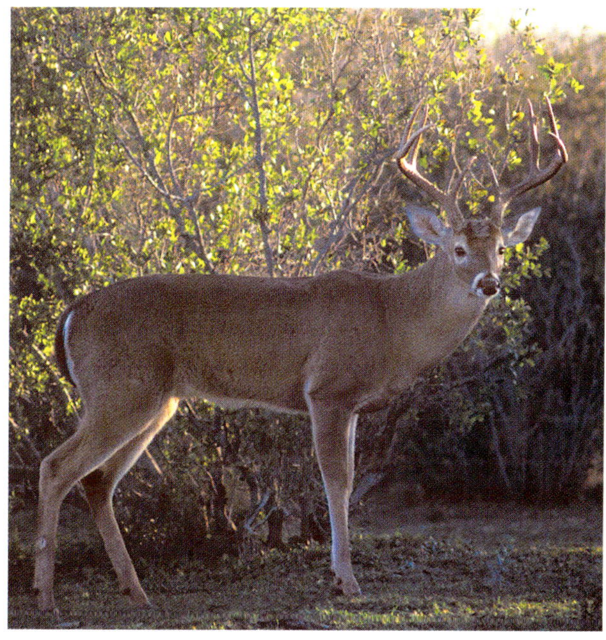

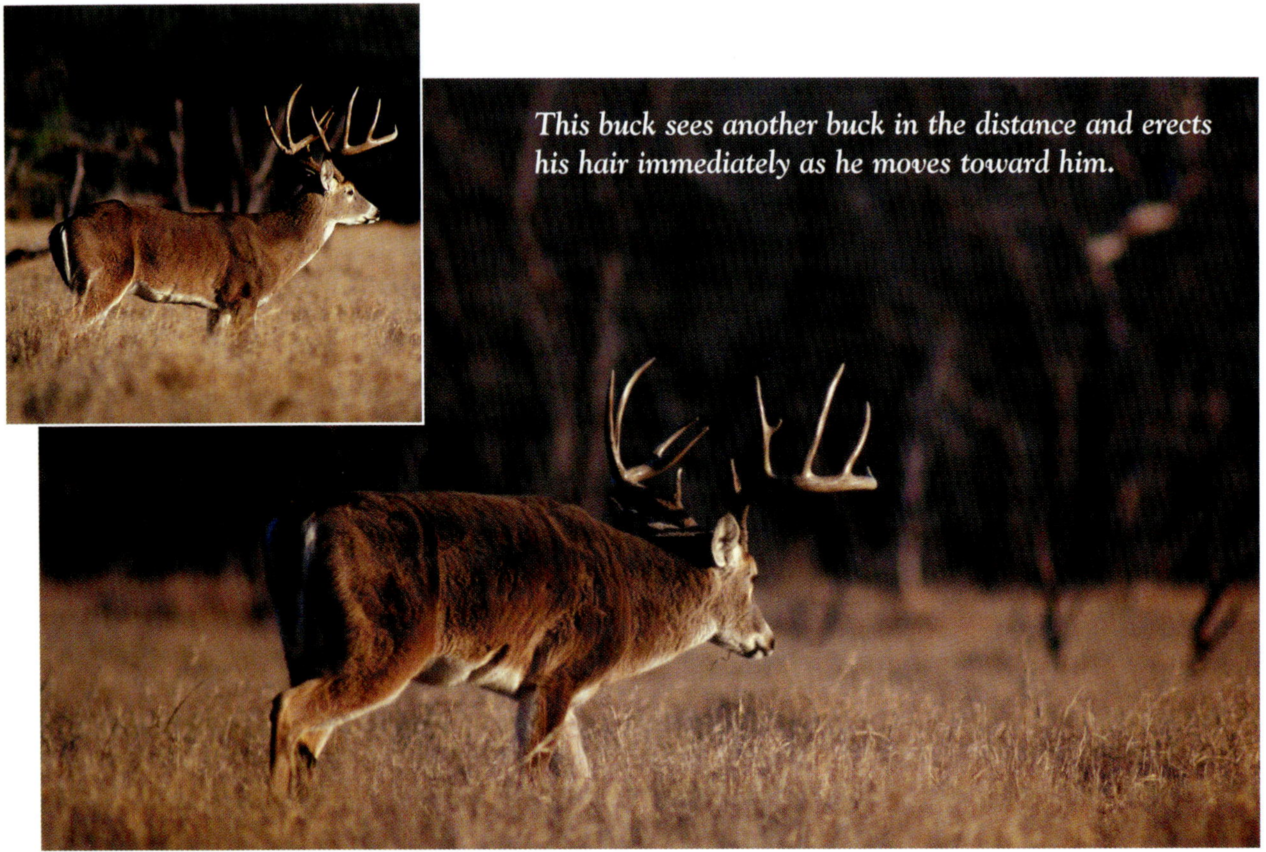
This buck sees another buck in the distance and erects his hair immediately as he moves toward him.

velvet from his antlers, his nutritional intake is directed to increasing muscle mass, particularly in his neck and chest as he prepares for the rut. This weight and muscle mass gain takes place in just eight to 10 weeks and can drastically alter how a buck appears. Later, as a buck participates in the rut by chasing does and fighting other bucks, he will lose the recently gained weight. By mid-January he will appear thin and often gaunt. Thus, the buck you got a glimpse of in mid-December that looked like a muscle-bound 5 1/2-year-old super buck may look like a typical 4 1/2-year-old by mid-January.

With the numerous variables involved, it is clear that trying to age a buck in a few critical seconds during a hunt is not a simple matter, and sometimes mistakes will occur. There are definitely bucks that are mature shooters and some that are immature nonshooters. However, there are a lot of 3 1/2- to 5 1/2-year-old-bucks that, depending on season, lighting, distance, behavior, and body angle, can appear older than they really are. I have taken photographs of the same buck only seconds apart. Sometimes these photographs are only a few steps apart, and because of the lighting and the buck's hair being raised in response to another buck's presence, you would say he is a shooter. Then a few steps later he is a nonshooter. First impressions are why many bucks are taken before their time. Light, angle, and behavior affect how a buck appears. Often minute-by-minute changes in perception occur, especially if other bucks are present. This is when observation time can be your best friend or worst enemy. If you are in a rush while hunting, time will be your enemy, because you may rush the shot before making a fair judgment. However, if possible, allow time for the buck to approach closer and your adrenaline to slow. Then, start analyzing him, comparing him to other deer by body, antler characteristics, and behavior toward them. By doing so, the odds of making a correct decision turn rapidly in your favor.

When a buck approaches and other bucks are present, always be slower in your judgment of age. Many times a buck will come in with hair erect and appear much older. Let him relax and flatten his hair before judging. Often I have seen a buck appear 200 to 300 yards away and immediately think he is a big mature buck. He will appear dark and huge against the light-colored grass, and his slow swagger just adds to the false information my eyes are telling my brain. A few moments later another buck will be seen crossing the same sendero (a long clearing in thick brush) in close proximity to the first buck. The new buck doesn't seem to have the time to notice the first buck and moves on quickly. Then with the same speed of flipping an electrical switch the big, mature buck deflates. He lays his hair back down and immediately appears two years younger than first thought. This scenario describes how one buck's behavior toward another buck can fool you. Little Roy has told me on more than one occasion that they almost never shoot a deer the first time they see it unless it is a spike or unless they have someone with them who also knows deer and agrees it is a shooter.

Then there are early mornings in predawn light. As I watch through my Leupold binoculars

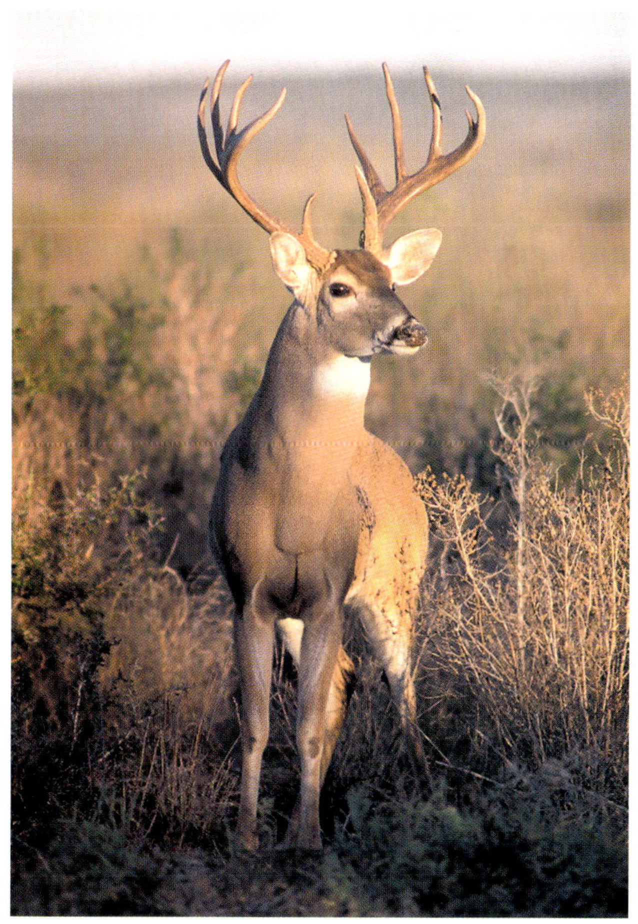

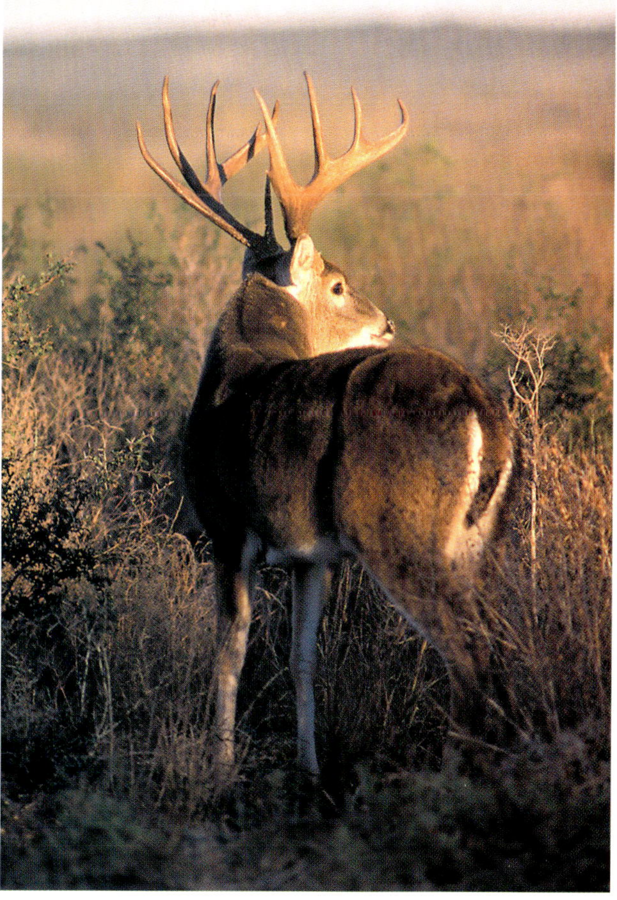

This buck is watching something in the distance. It is immediately evident the object of his attention is another buck of similar age and status when he erects his hair and angles his body. The approaching buck was a long distance away but clearly had this buck's attention.

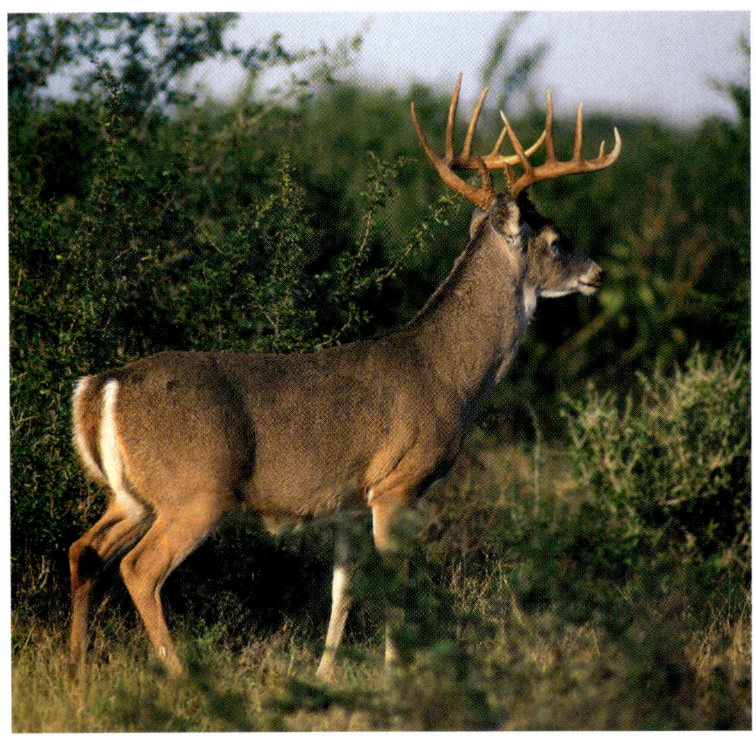

Another example of a mature buck demonstrating the long stare (above) and then erecting his hair within seconds as the approaching buck draws closer (below).

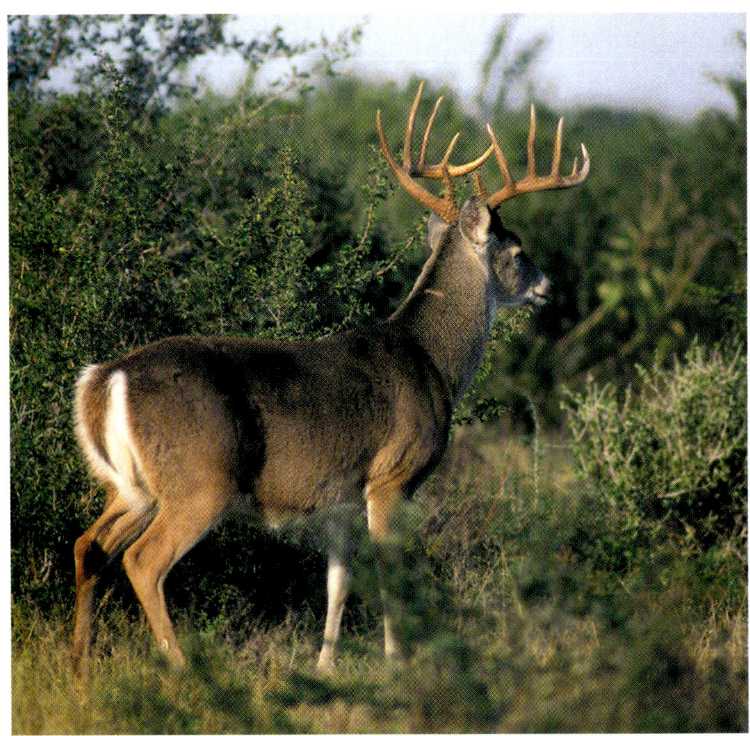

there is a dark shape that materializes like a ghost into the sendero. It is a huge-bodied whitetail with a lot of headgear that is feeding closer and closer. After several long minutes, the dark night begins to change to shades of gray, and the buck, which had appeared heavy horned and mature in the dark, loses two years and 20 inches of antler in a matter of 10 minutes. That is another of the many scenarios that can cause you to misjudge a buck's age.

The angle from which you are viewing a particular buck also can lead to an aging mistake. Most hunters are familiar with the statement, "You never age or judge a buck as he is going away from you." This angle makes a buck appear much bigger than he really is. However, going away is not the only angle that can deceive you. The angle that occurs when a buck's head is down and feeding often exaggerates the fullness of his stomach. Often how a buck postures with his head held high from straight-on can make him appear heavier and older. I have seen some big 4 1/2-year-olds from the frontal view that could trigger a wrong decision if a split second was all the time available. The frontal view can be useful to judge facial characteristics relative to age, but the best angle is from the side. The side angle is best for observing how the neck and brisket join, how full the stomach area is, and if the back is straight or sagging. However, it is always best to view the buck from multiple angles. The more time you can watch a buck from different angles, analyze and put each piece of the puzzle together, the better your aging decision will be.

Distance is a variable that has a

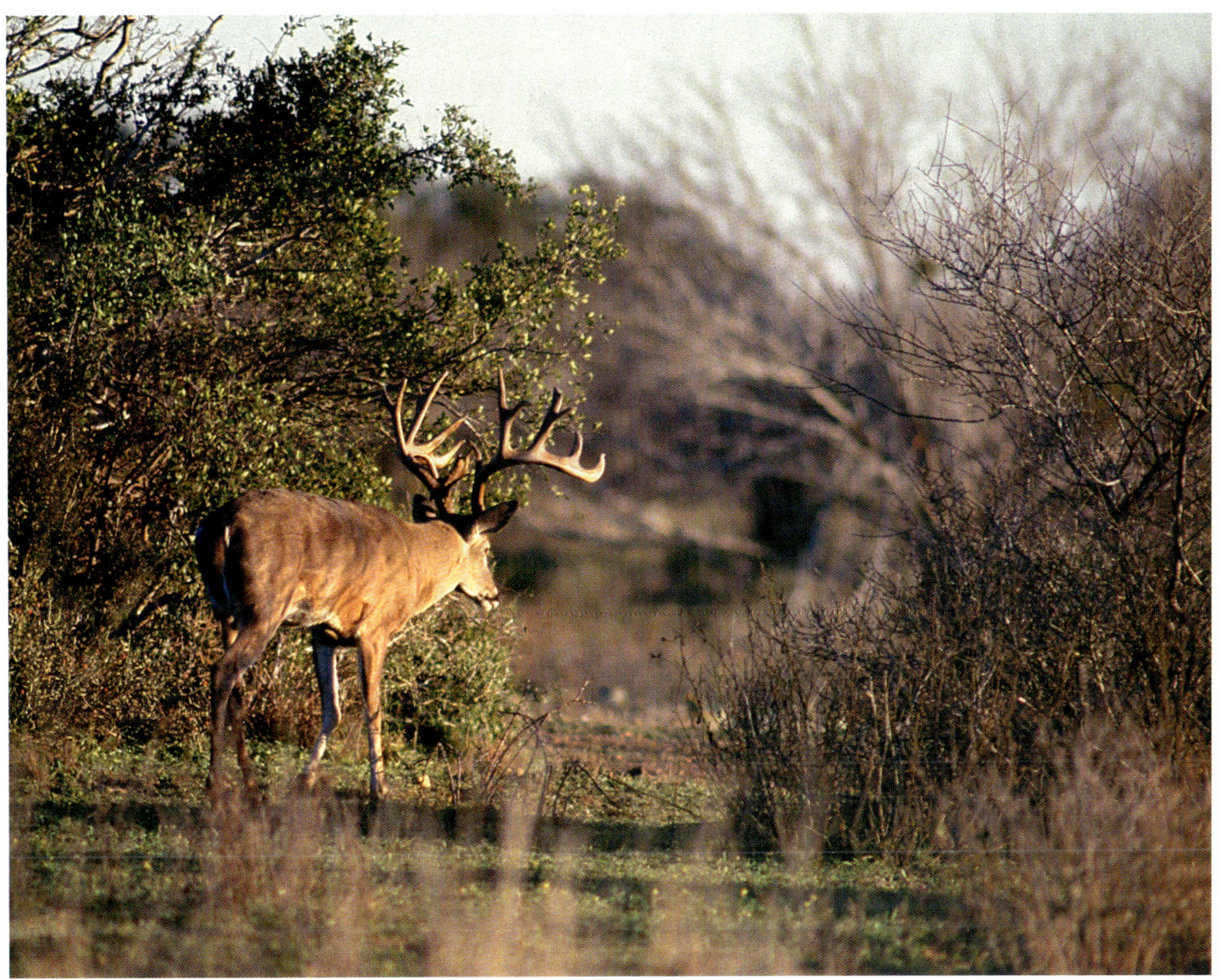

Try to judge a buck from as many angles as possible, keeping in mind the worst angle is going directly away or angling away. However, there are always exceptions to every rule, as this buck is clearly a keeper from any angle.

way of creating ground shrinkage once the trigger has been pulled. The closer you can observe deer the better. A good spotting scope and the best pair of binoculars you can afford are extremely important if you desire to minimize mistakes. High-quality optics will enable you to see the subtle details such as wrinkles under the chin, age in the face, thickening and graying of hair on the forehead, dimples in the neck and body, and the condition of the hocks. In recent times, there has been an increasing emphasis on shooting deer at longer distances. Attempting to judge deer at 200 yards or more without extremely good optics is poor judgment and preparation. In the past few years, binoculars and spotting scopes have been continually improved. A very good pair of binoculars can be purchased for $250 to $500, and a good spotting scope can be purchased for $200 to $900. The bottom line is that good optics are essential for anyone seriously interested in aging deer.

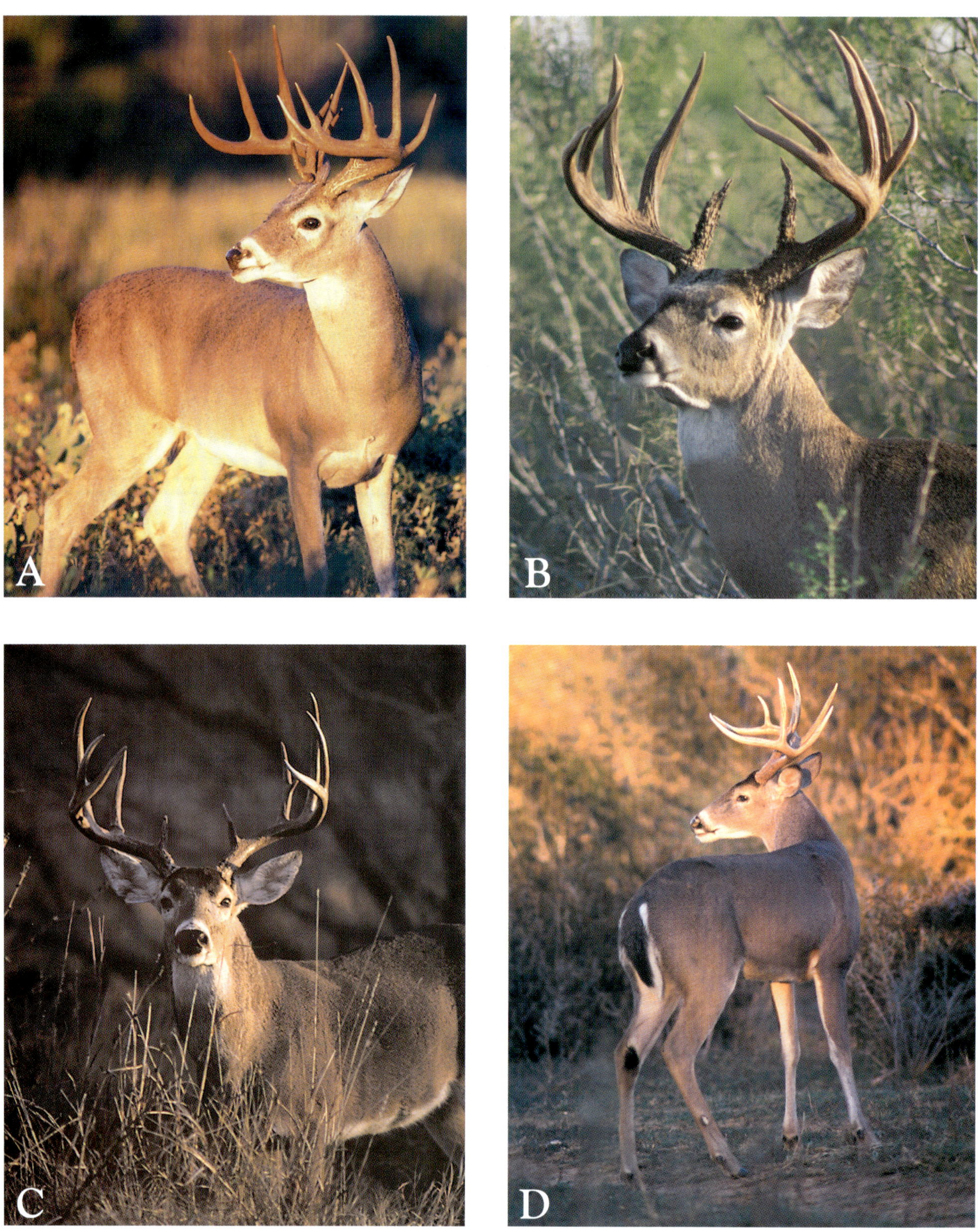

When aging a buck in the field, look for how the neck joins the brisket (A), loose skin under the chin (B), how the hair on the forehead gland appears (C — noticeably thicker and darker), and the degree of staining in the tarsal area (D). These are some of the key sources of information needed to age a buck correctly.

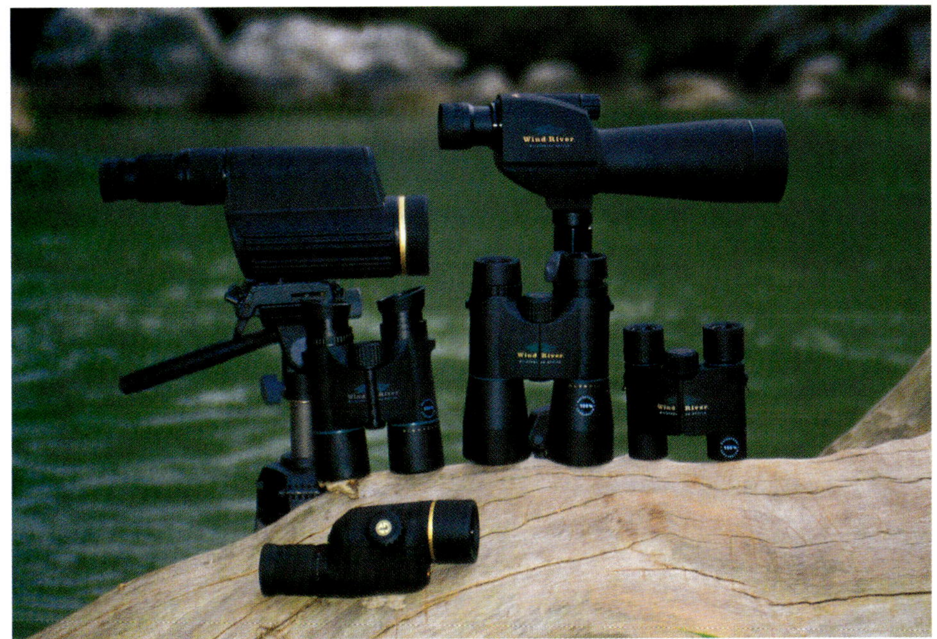

Using high quality optics like these Leupold spotting scopes and WindRiver binoculars is extremely important for anyone who is serious about aging and judging whitetails. The resolution, clarity, and light transmitting qualities of these products will prove invaluable when observing deer in the wide array of conditions encountered in the field.

If the first time you observe a deer he is 5 1/2 or older, you will have a very difficult time trying to determine an exact age. You will run into difficulties many times during the hunting season, but the more bucks you can identify on sight and become familiar with the sooner more of your bucks will start living to 6 1/2 and 7 1/2 years old. In fact, the earlier you can recognize a particular buck and correctly age him, the more accurate you will be, and the more successful your management program will be.

People often look incredulous when I talk about a specific buck I have observed over a period of years. Yet if I ask them whether they have any trouble identifying their friends on a regular basis the answer is always a resounding no. The shortcoming is that most landowners and hunters have not spent enough time looking closely at deer to pick out individual characteristics to help identify them later.

The key to identifying individual bucks is to carefully scrutinize each one you see, regardless of age or size. While antler shape and size can be helpful, facial and body characteristics are more reliable, especially after age three. Look for any unique markings or features. Are the ears black-tipped or brown? Are there big white eye patches or almost no eye patches at all? Is a white throat patch present, and what shape is it? Is the throat patch round or rectangular? Is the throat patch distinct or faded? Is there a double throat patch? Are there any unusual body colorations? Is there a dark stripe of hair down the neck or back? Are extremely white forelegs present making it appear as if he is wearing socks? What color is the top of the tail? Is it solid brown or solid black? Is part of the tail missing? Some bucks' tails appear as if they have been partially dipped in black while others have more white surrounding the entire tail.

Next, focus on the face. What color are the eyes? Are they extremely dark, appearing black, or are they very light, causing the eyes to take on an amber appearance? Do the eyes appear close or far apart? Are the eyes slanted, making it appear as if

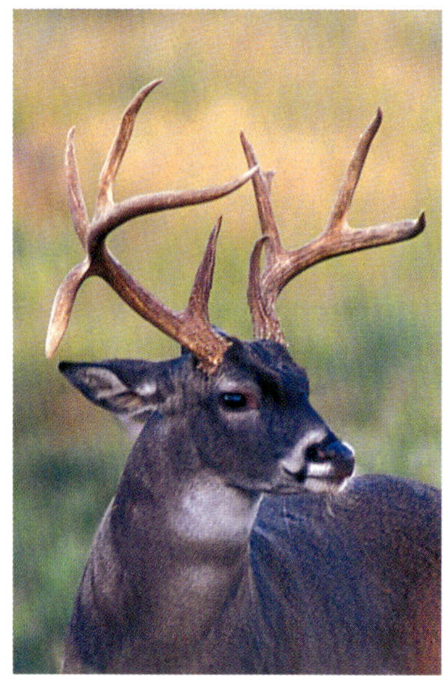

Though next year this buck may or may not have a drop tine, his dark face with a very small white eye patch, small white spot beneath the throat patch, and small white spot near the base of the right ear are all good features by which he can be identified throughout life.

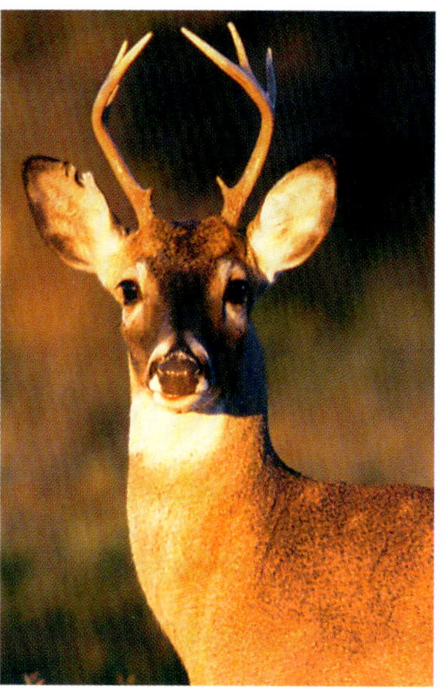

The notch in the upper margin of the right ear will mark this 1 1/2-year-old buck for life. Without this type of lifelong mark, most 1 1/2-year-olds are extremely hard do identify the next year.

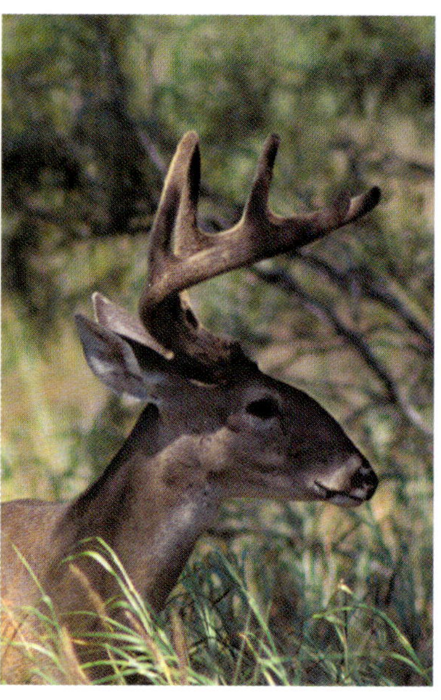

The prominent Roman (humped) nose is a give away on identifying this buck.

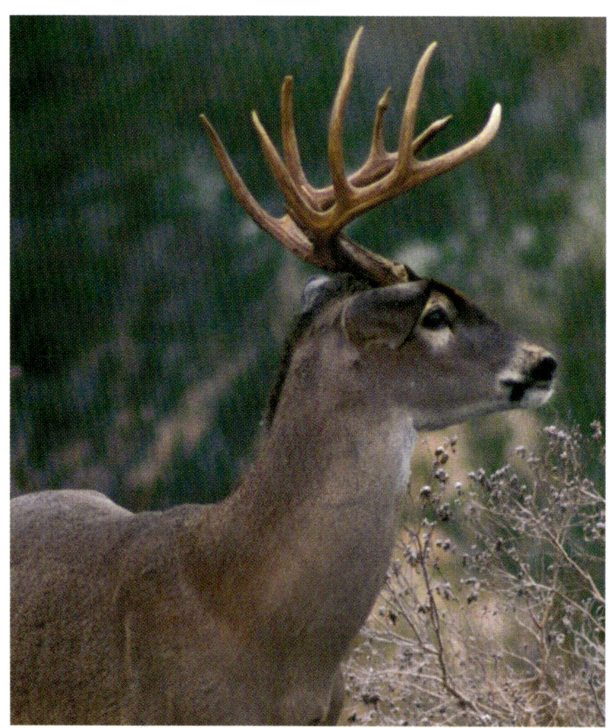

A band of long, dark hair down the back of the neck identifies this buck.

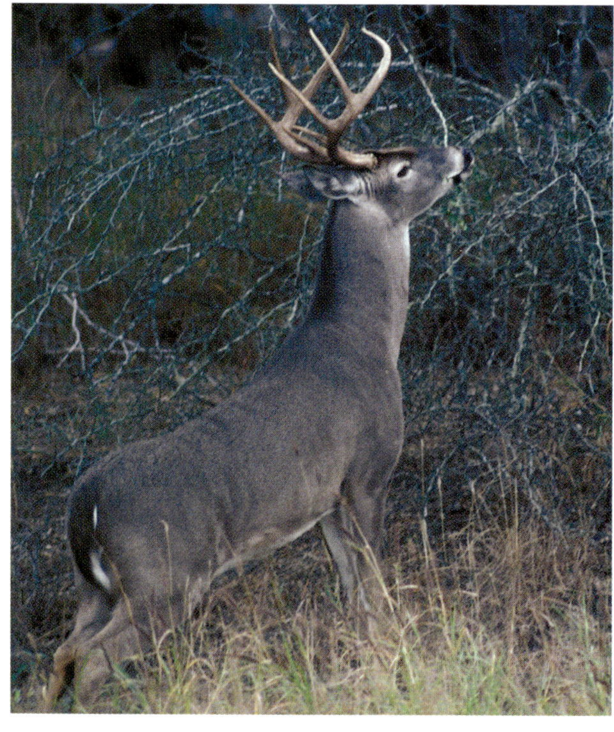

A band of dark hair down the neck and a dark tail will aid in identifying this buck in the future.

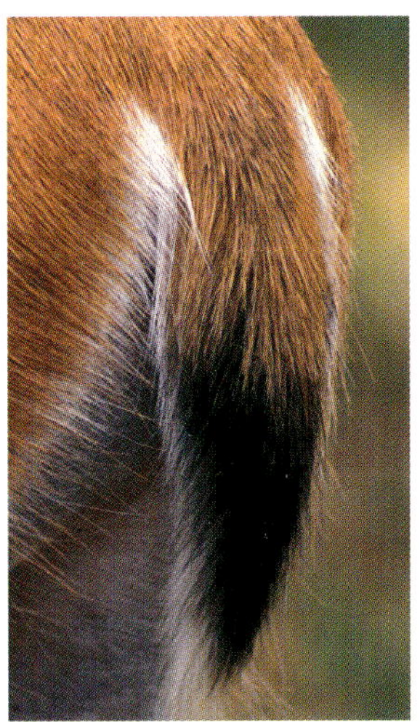

he is squinting, or is he wide-eyed, giving the appearance the eyes are bulging out? Are the ears held up or laid flat? Does one ear droop? Is there a tear, hole, or gap in the ear? Does the face appear long or short and stubby? Is there a pointed, dainty nose, a Roman nose, or a wide, flat nose? How is the head held when standing? Is it held high as if surveying the country? Some bucks have this trait. What about the gait? Some bucks can be identified by their peculiar walking gait even from a distance. Most bucks will have one or more identifiable markings or characteristics that will enable positive identification.

Throughout this book are several bucks I have photographed over the years that have easily-identifiable features. Look them over and see how well you pick up their unique features that distinguish them from other bucks. This will be good practice for recognizing individual bucks on your own property or lease in the future.

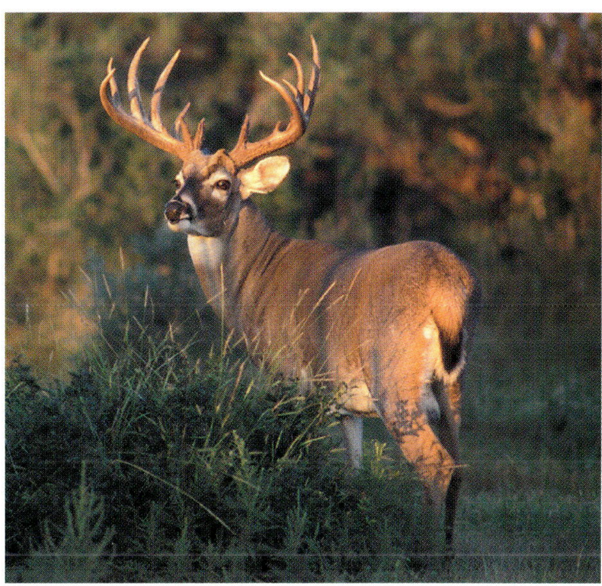

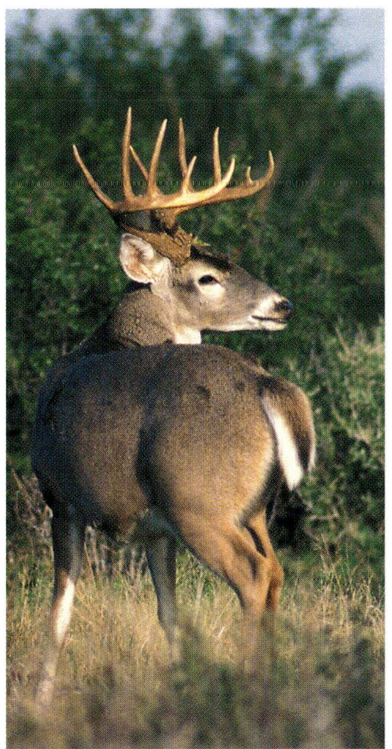

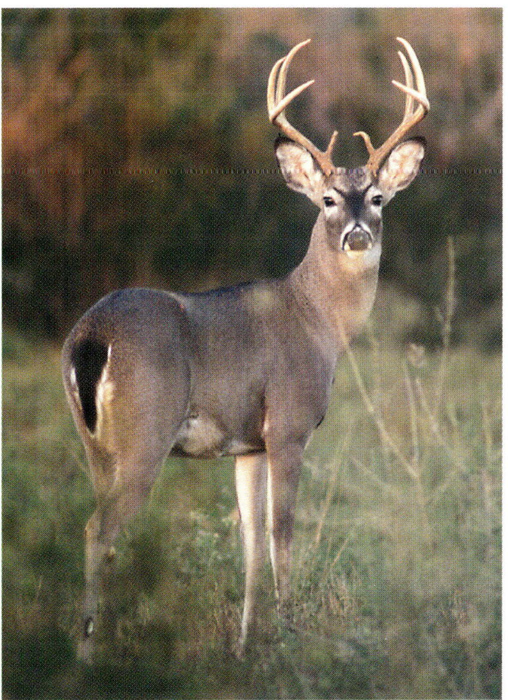

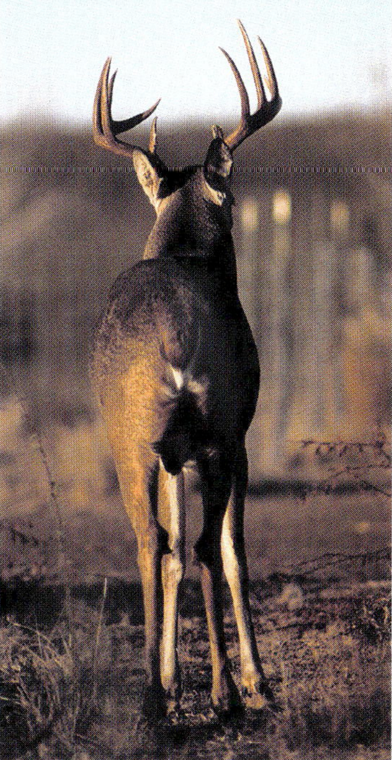

A careful observer will notice the various color patterns on these deer's tails which will help identify them throughout their lives. Notice the last buck is missing the lower half of his tail altogether.

Age Classes -

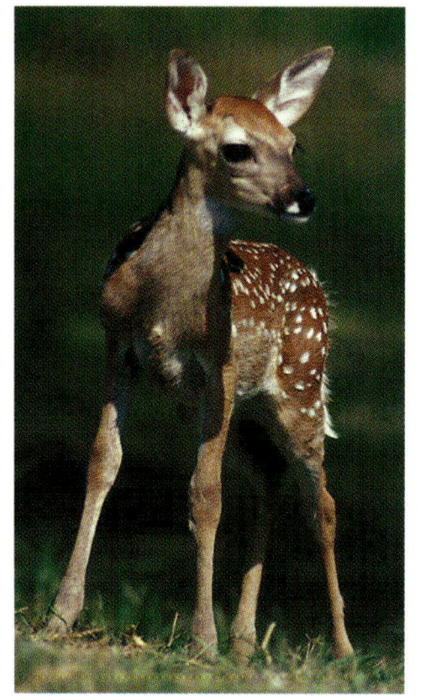

Buck Fawns

It is important not to mistake buck fawns for mature does. They are this year's fawns and usually still with their mothers early in the season. Note the small nubs

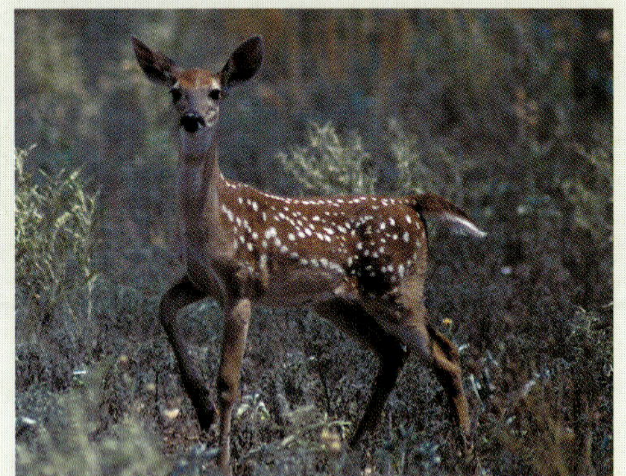

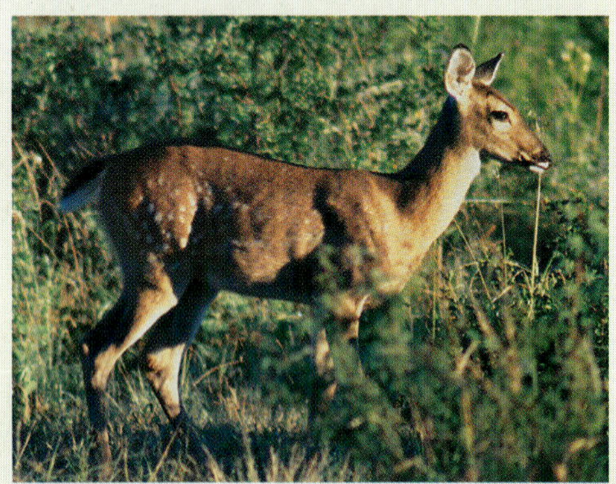

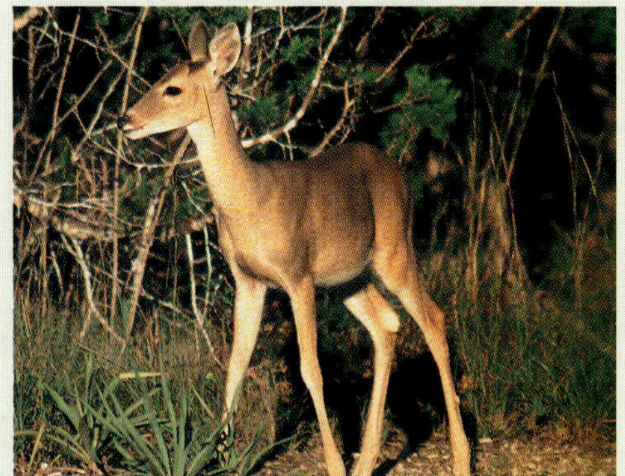

Above (top to bottom):
Fawn development showing the transition from spots to normal pelage and pedicle development from summer to late fall.

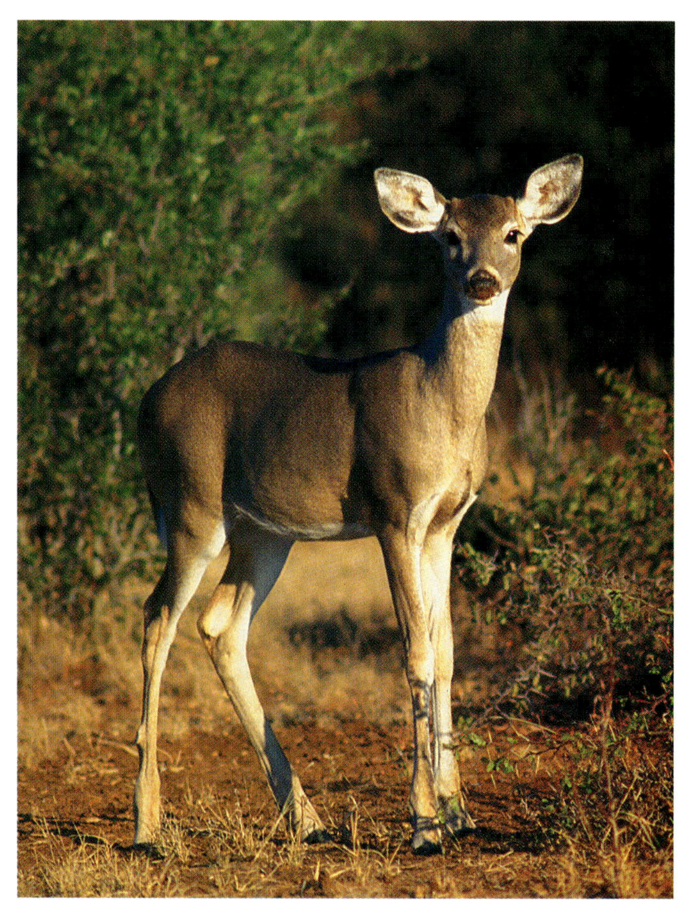

barely visible on their heads. A good spotting scope or pair of binoculars is a must to identify these young bucks. Look at the length of the head — it will be shorter and more compact than older deer. Also, look at the shape of the forehead. Buck fawns have flat foreheads while does have rounded foreheads. This feature becomes more pronounced later in the season. Buck fawns often are separated from their mothers during the breeding season and commonly observed traveling and feeding alone. These young bucks are often the first deer to appear at a feeding area or food plot. Thus, it is wise to never shoot a lone antlerless deer, especially at long distances. Always ensure other antlerless deer are present to allow a size comparison.

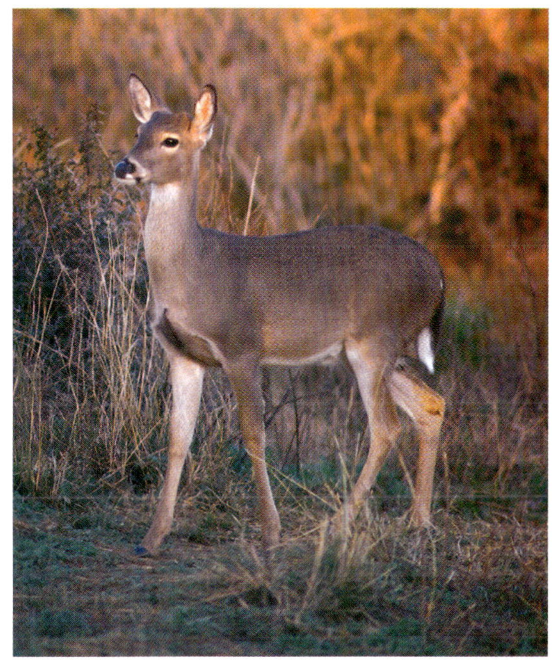

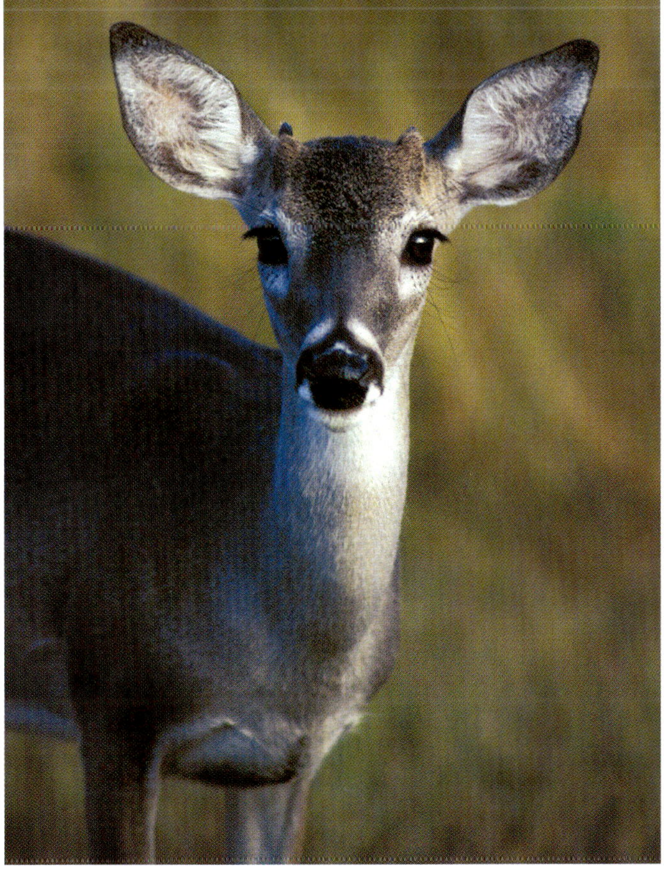

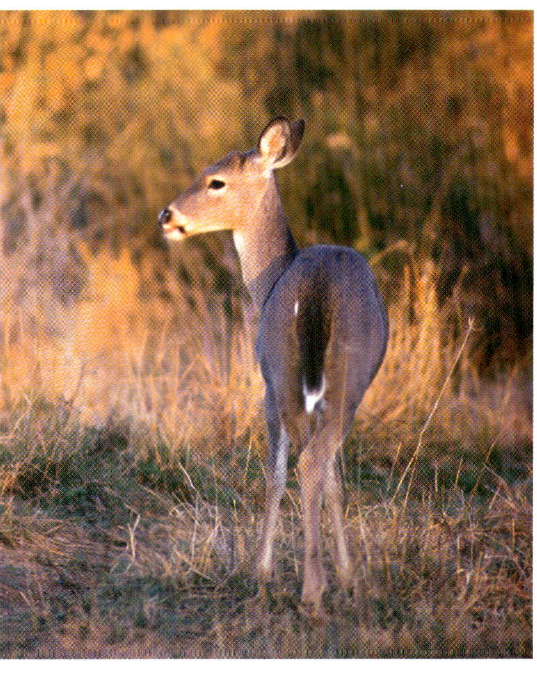

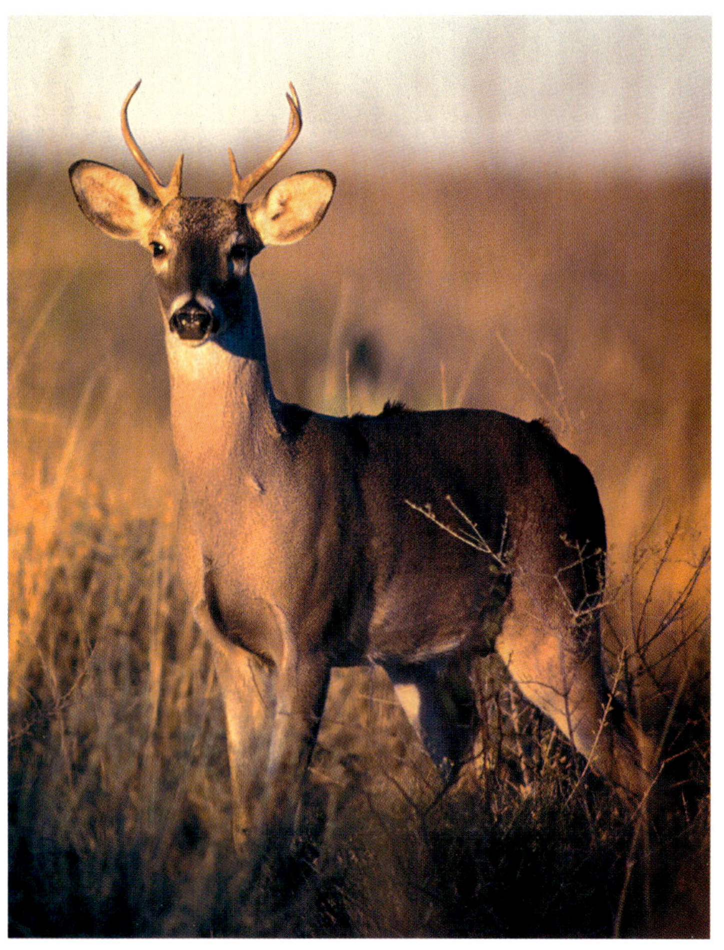

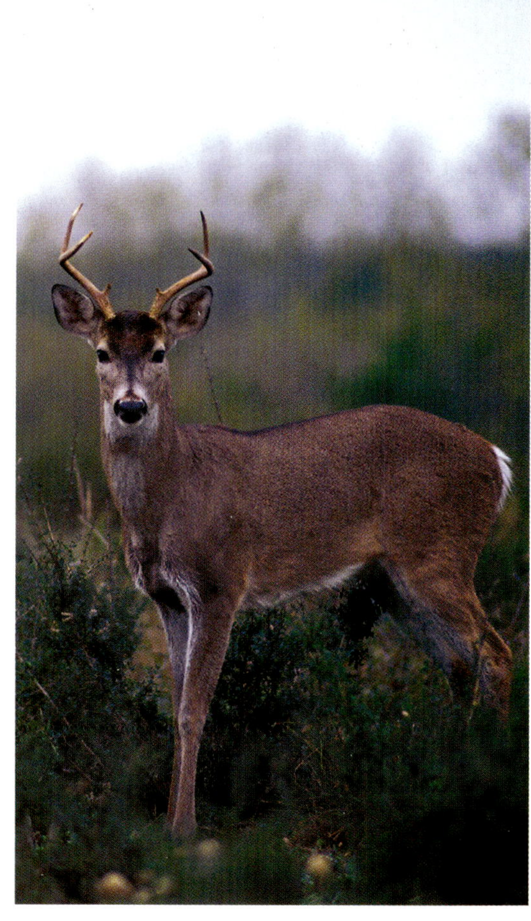

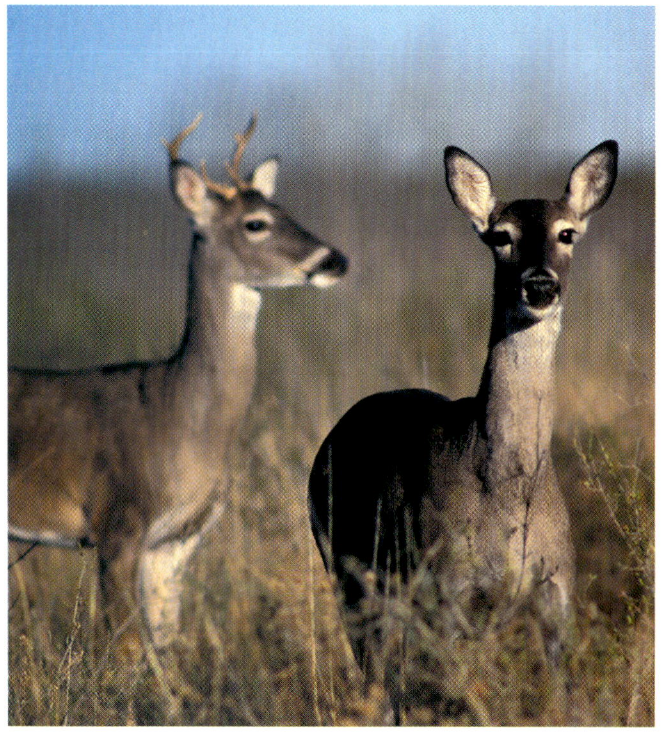

1 1/2-Year-Olds

As you can see, 1 1/2-year-old bucks appear dainty with baby faces and thin necks. Their legs appear long and slender, and their torso is slim like a doe's. In a photo of a 1 1/2-year-old buck, cover the antlers with your thumb and you will see that the body resembles a doe. Yearling buck antler development is highly variable, ranging from tiny spikes to 10 or more points. But, even super 1 1/2-year-old bucks

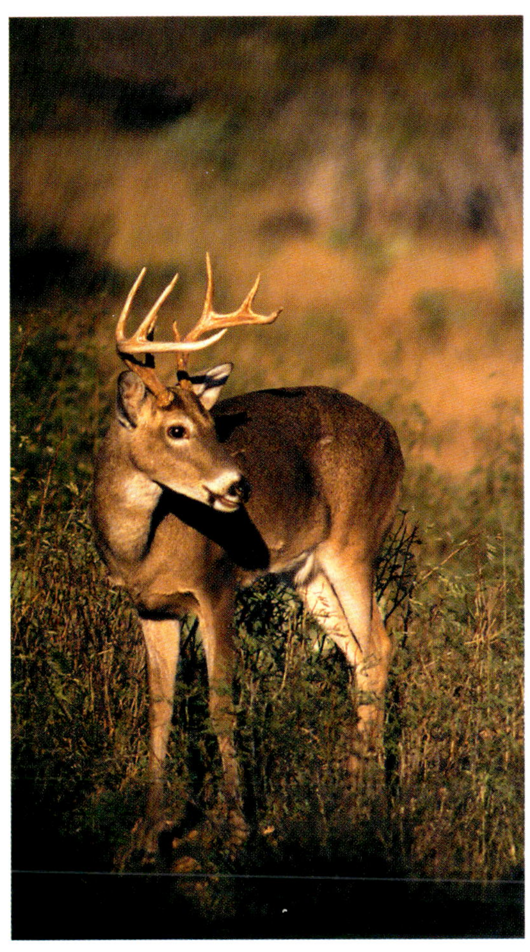

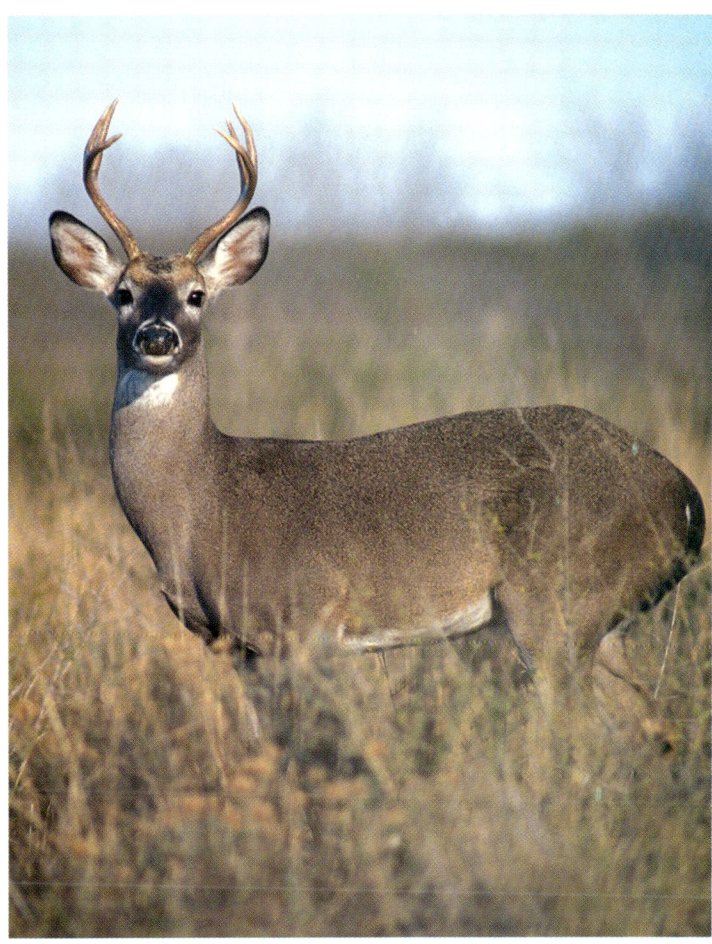

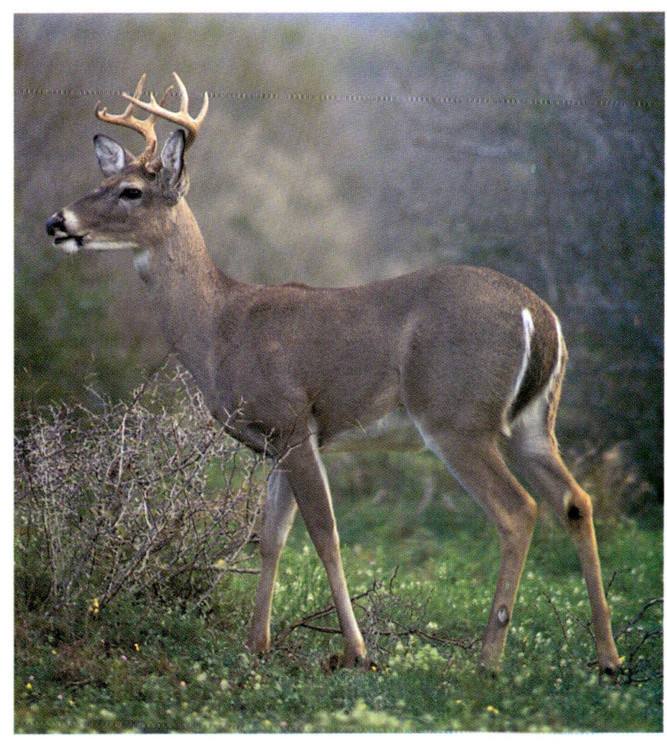

with multiple points will have small, thin antlers. Likewise, regardless of the number of points, the length of their main beams will be short compared to older bucks. Their tarsal area will be small and lightly colored. Some 1 1/2-year-old bucks will still be traveling with their mothers into the rut, but most will have dispersed. It is at this age that many relocate and establish separate home ranges from their mothers.

2 1/2-Year-Olds

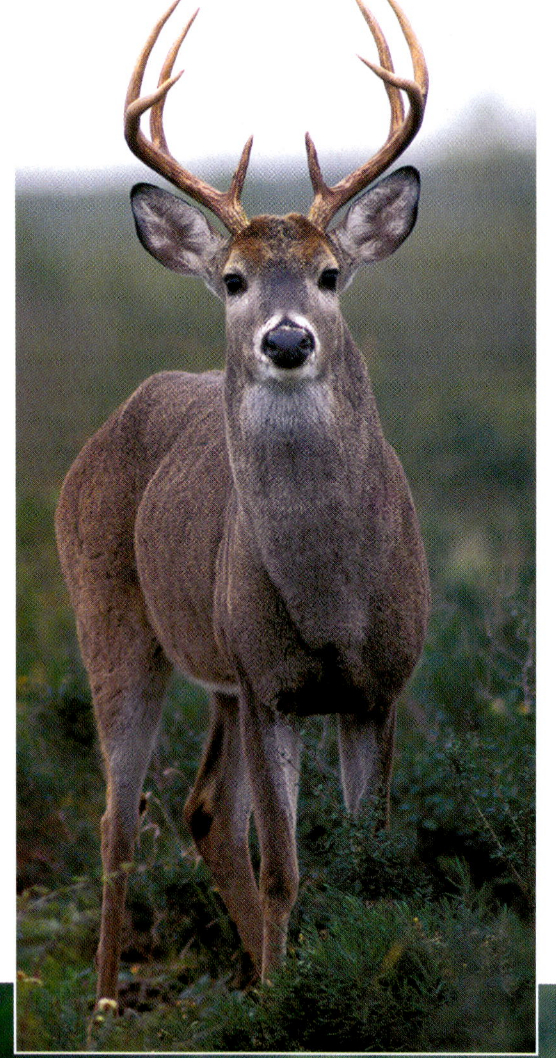

The best way to describe the bodies of 2 1/2-year-old bucks is gangly and awkward. Their legs appear to be growing too fast for their body. Their bodies, while thicker than those of 1 1/2-year-olds, still have legs and necks that appear stretched in proportion. Their back and stomach area will appear very taut, and their face appears larger than their thin neck from a frontal view. The head will appear long from the side. For the first time, their antlers will begin to catch your eye, which is probably why 2 1/2 is the average age of whitetail bucks harvested in many areas. The truth is their antlers are just starting to grow. Most 2 1/2-year-olds are big travelers during the rut, because they typically are not active breeders in herds with balanced adult sex ratios and good buck age structure. Lack of breeding is not from lack of desire but due to competition and dominance from older bucks. During the rut their tarsal glands may be dark, but the very darkest area is usually very small and round in appearance.

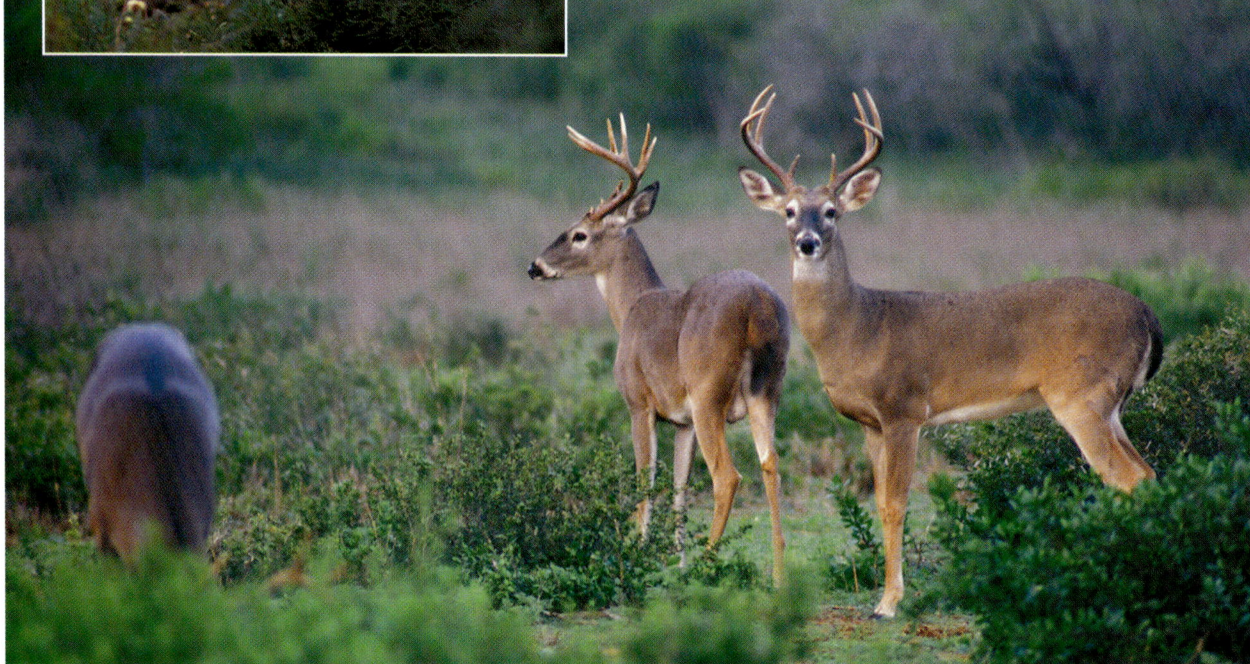

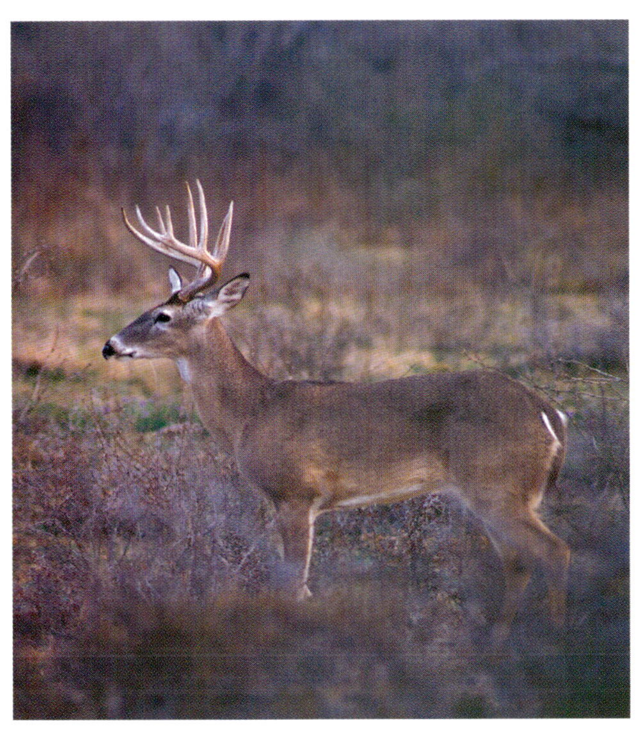
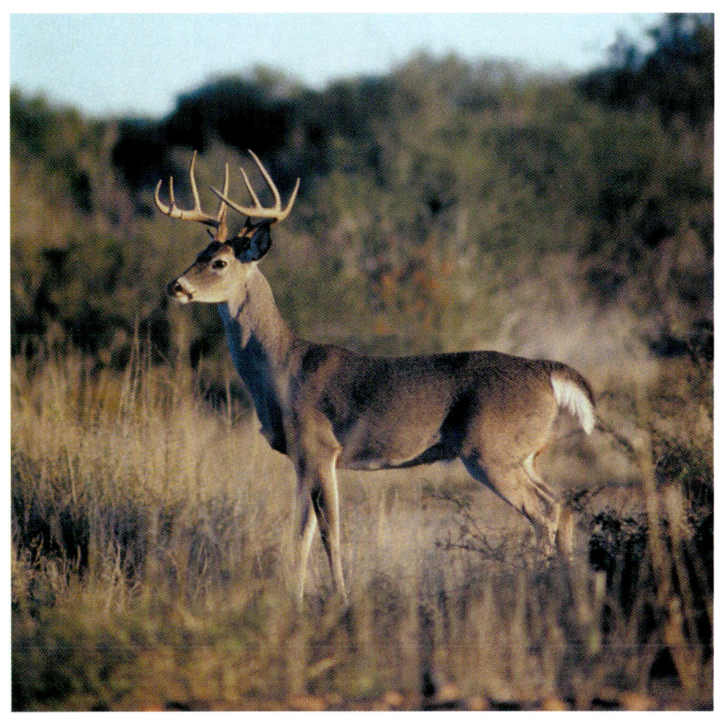
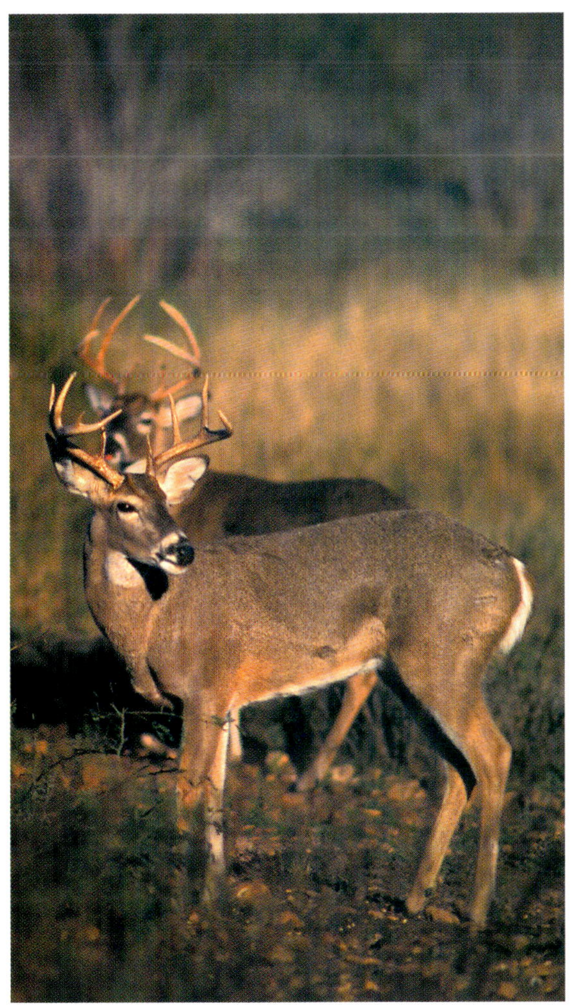
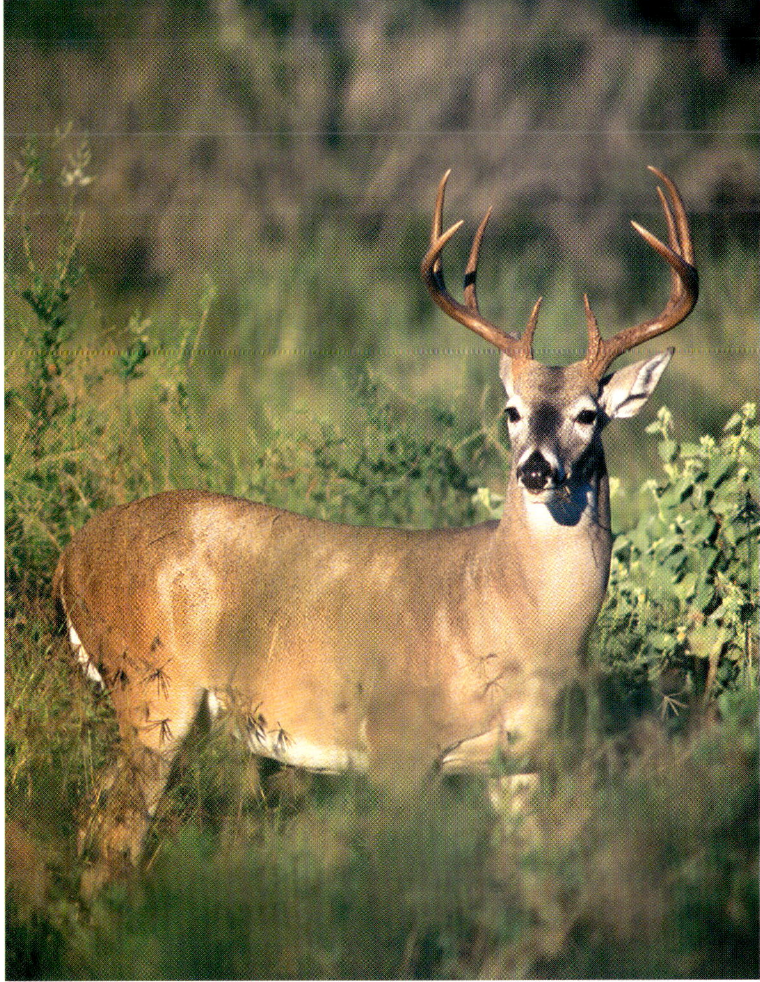

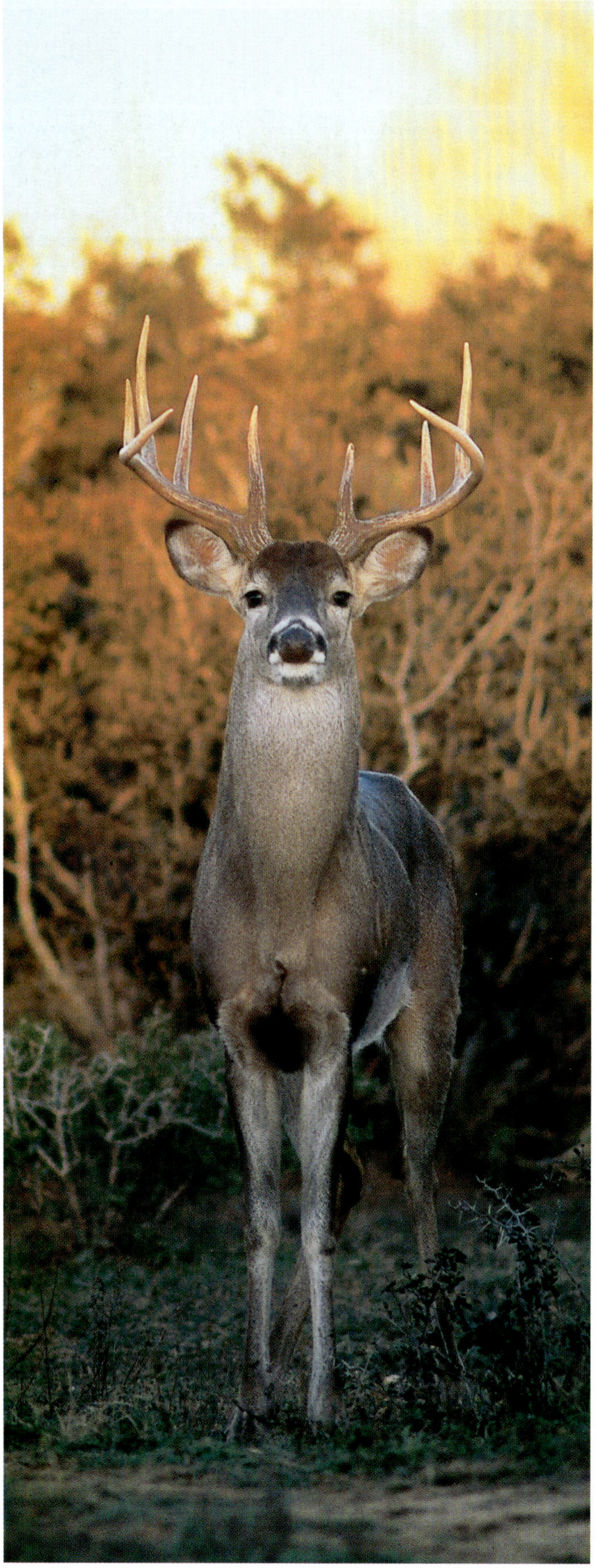

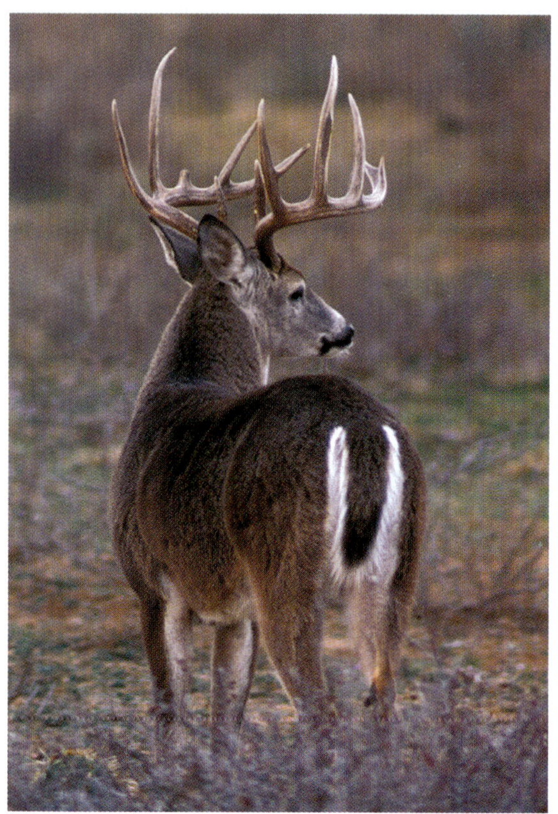

3 1/2-Year-Olds

A fuller neck and deeper chest are characteristics of a 3 1/2-year-old. As the bucks pictured demonstrate, their neck muscles are expanding from increased hormones and use during the rut but are still not as large or thick as a fully-mature buck. Their chest is beginning to appear larger than their rump, but their back and stomach are still straight and taut. Also, their neck is still distinct by four or five inches from their brisket. Their tarsals will be dark during the rut but usually will appear small, and the dark staining from urine usually does not extend down the leg to the hoof.

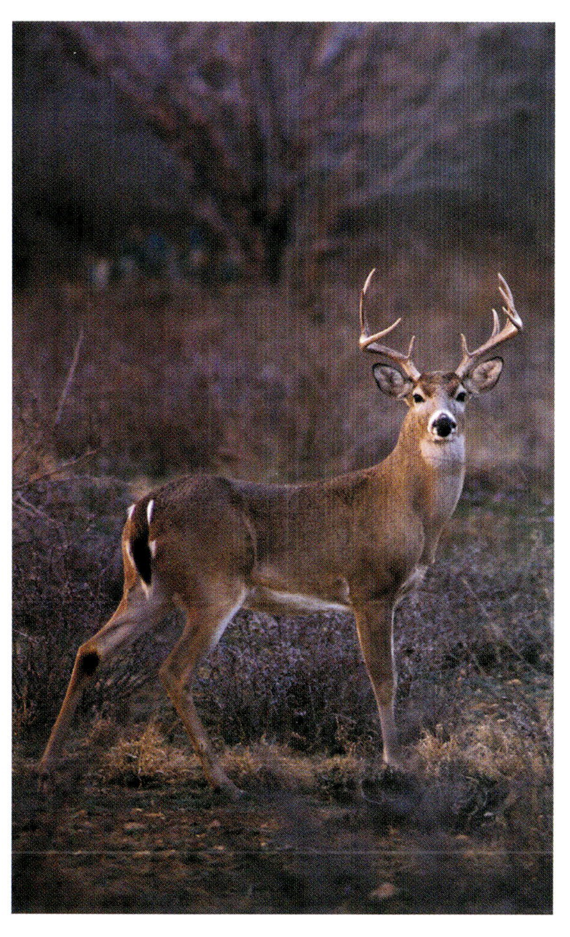

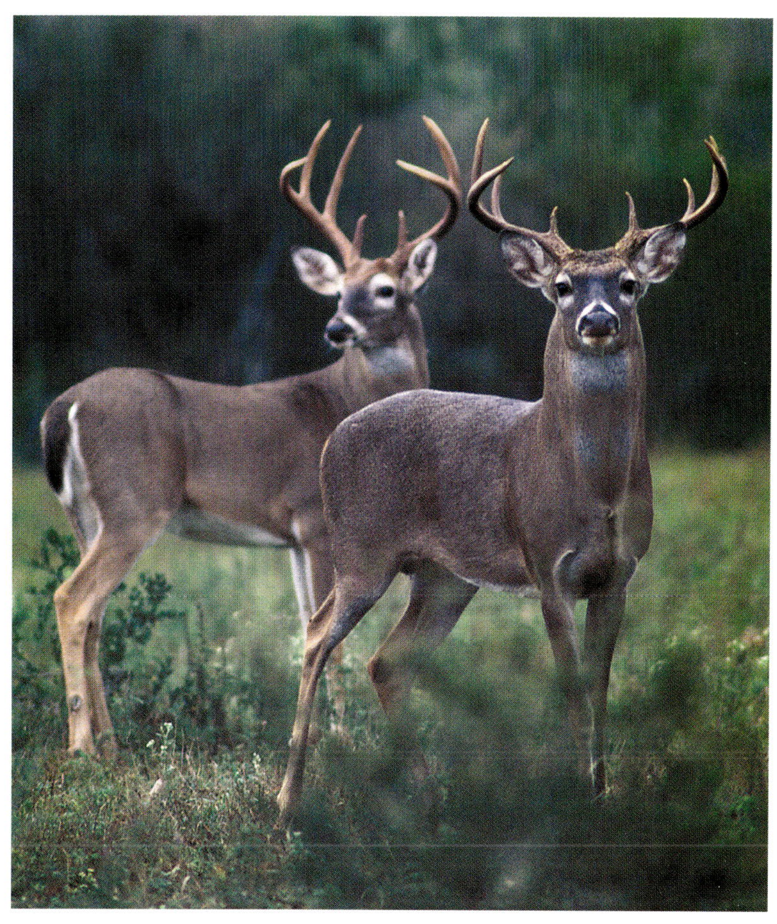

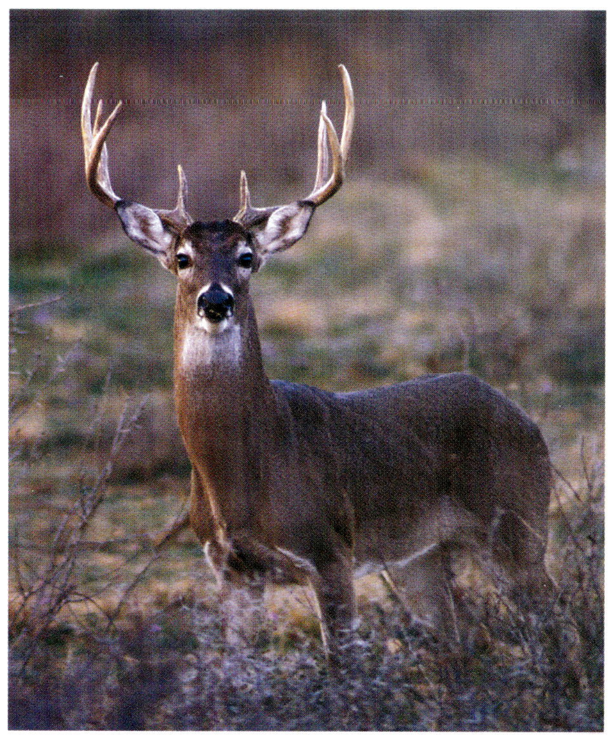

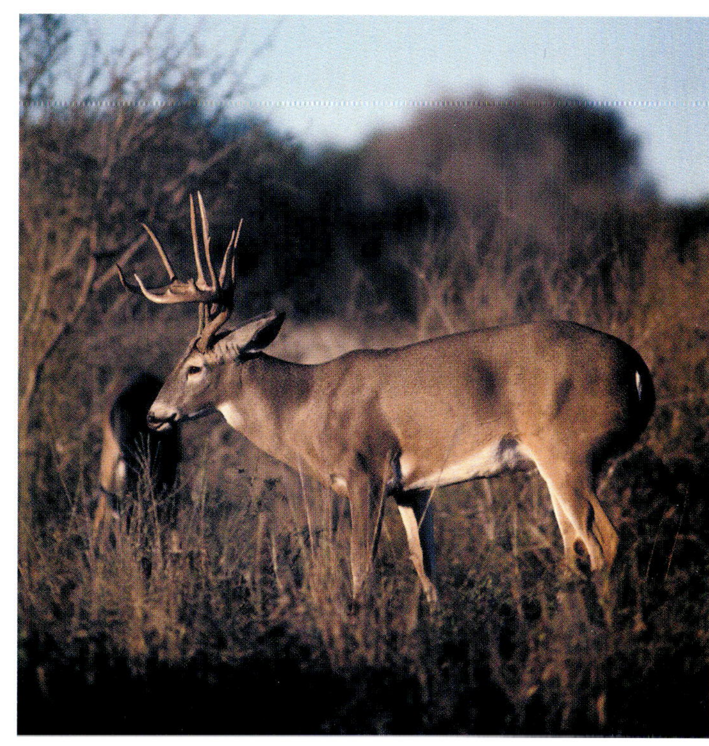

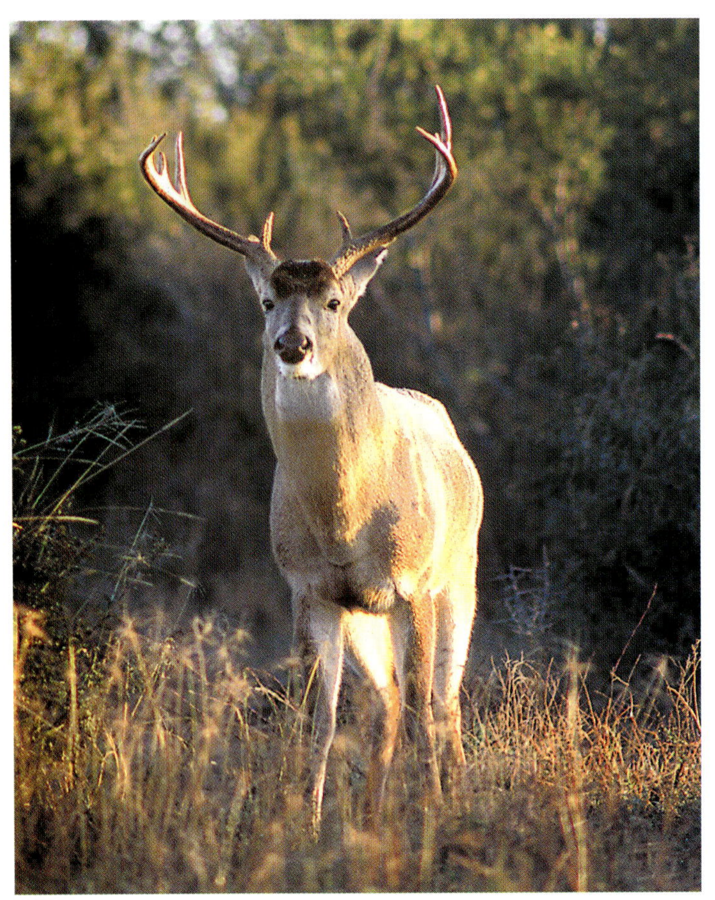

4 1/2-Year-Olds

When bucks reach 4 1/2 they attain skeletal maturity and begin exhibiting many characteristics of full maturity. Their rump will appear full and rounded. Their neck will be more muscular and their body thicker and fuller but still trim. Their stomach and back will not appear to sag, and their jaw skin will be tight. This is the first time their legs do not appear longer than they should for their body. Their legs may even appear slightly short for the thickened body. During the rut, their tarsals will be noticeably large and dark due to repeated urinating and rubbing. In many respects, 4 1/2-year-old bucks are similar to young athletes in their early 20s. Their bodies have reached full size but are muscular and lean. The majority of 4 1/2-year-old bucks will have a significant increase in antler growth over the previous year. For the first time, much of the nutritional intake is directed to antler growth instead of muscle and skeletal growth. Bucks at this age can grow very respectable antlers making them difficult for hunters to pass. Focus your attention on the body and face when aging, especially if the buck has very good antlers. Typically, 4 1/2-year-olds breed more does than any other age class. This is because they are in prime physical condition and quite competitive in the dominance hierarchy.

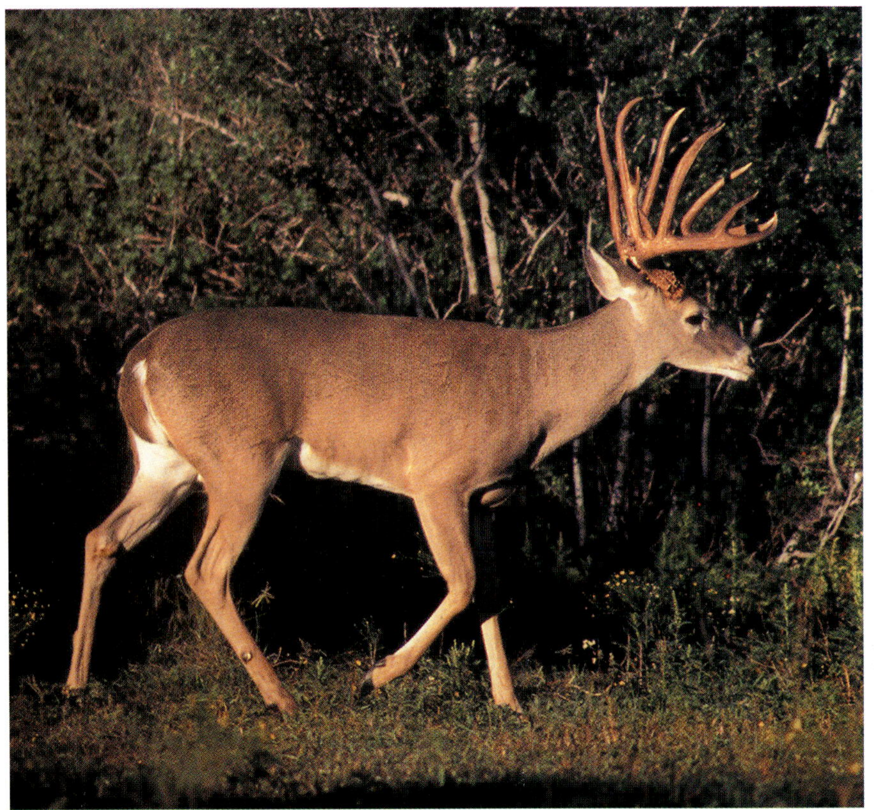

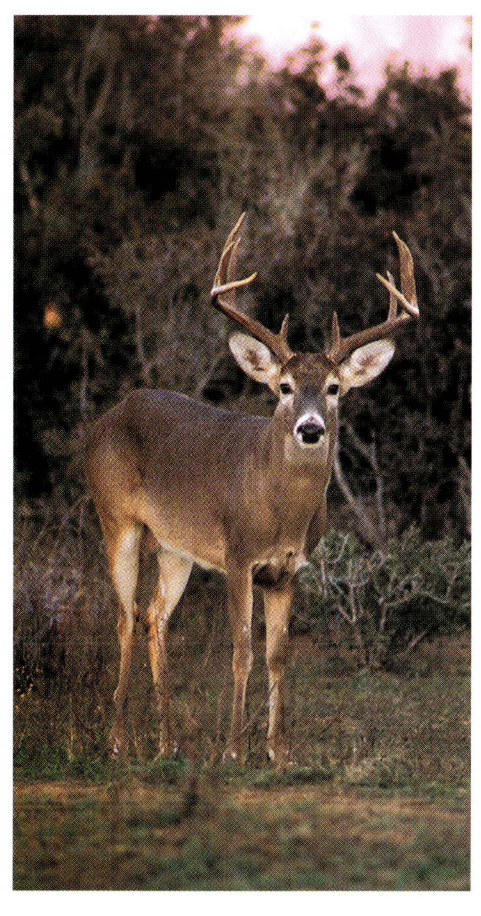
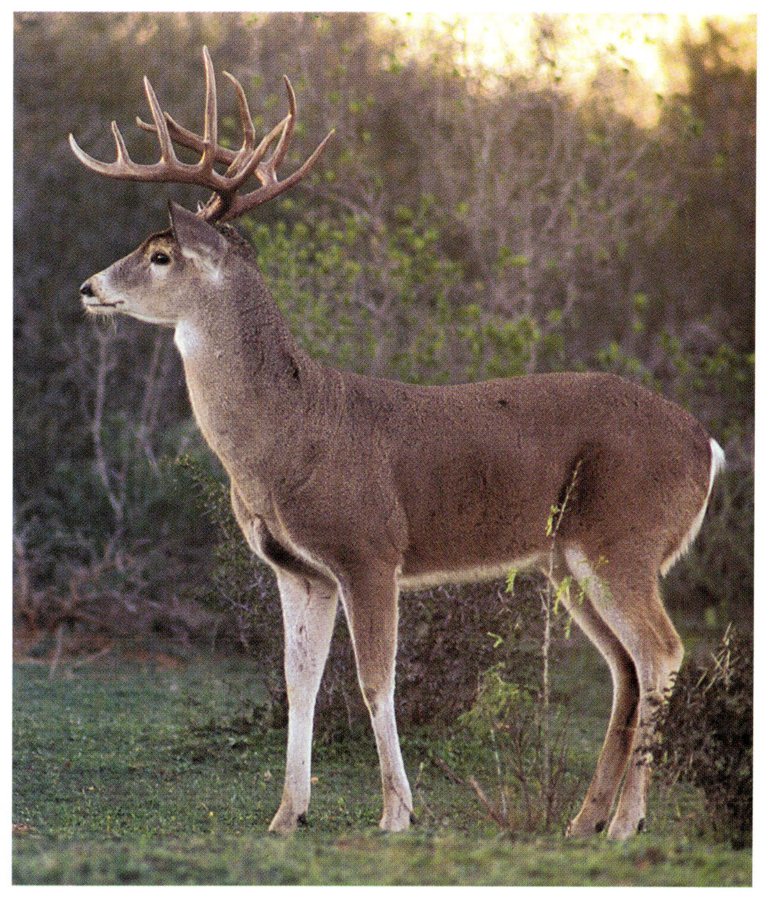
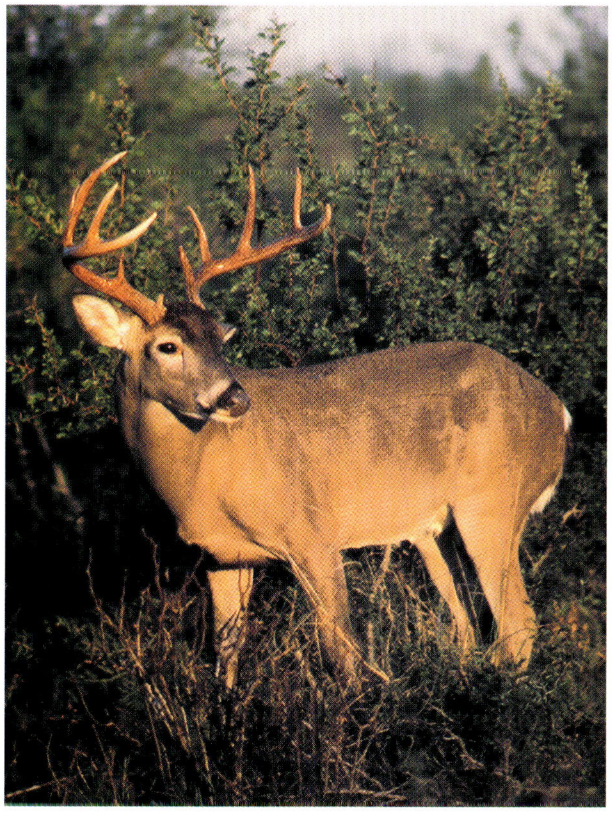
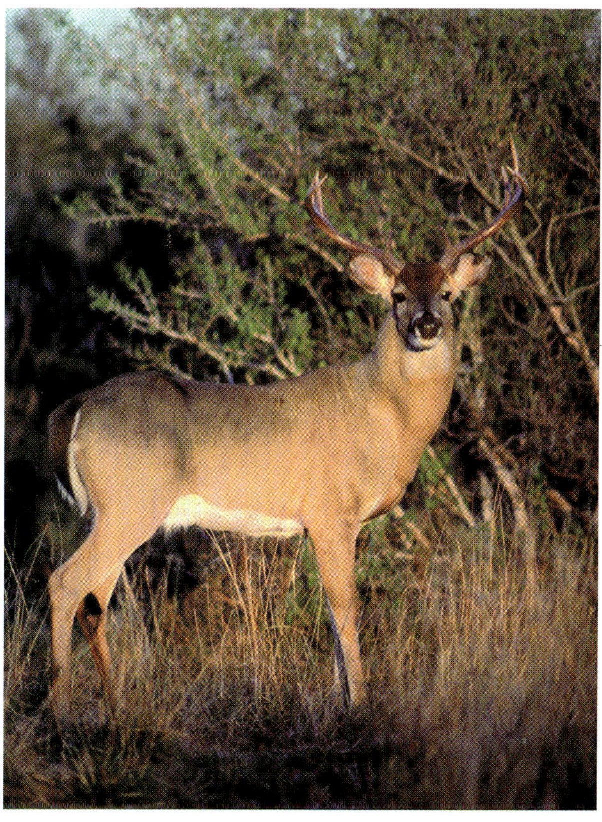

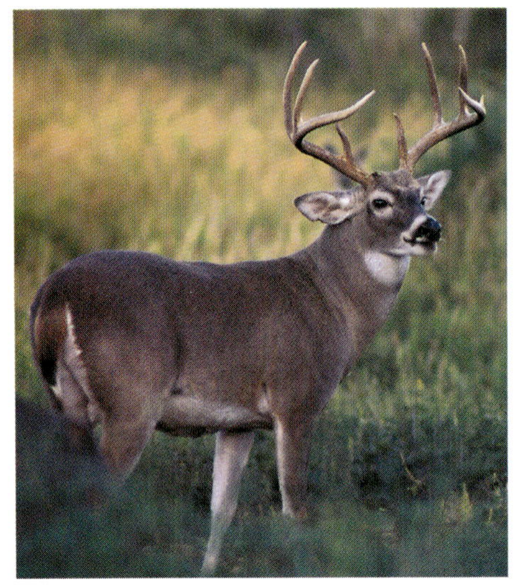

5 1/2-Year-Olds

At 5 1/2 years old, most bucks will be carrying the largest set of antlers they have ever grown. Their bodies also exhibit some noticeable changes. Typically, their stomach and back have a noticeable sag. Their neck will swell considerably during the rut, making the neck and brisket appear to be one continuous muscle. Also, their neck, while being very big, will appear muscular and firm and not flabby. The tarsals will be noticeably large and very dark with many bucks having staining down the inside of the leg to the hoof. Late in the rut their legs may even appear slightly white under the tarsals where the urine has scalded their hide. Also at 5 1/2, the forehead gland appears noticeably thicker and darker because of increased secretions from the specialized sweat glands underneath. Finally, 5 1/2-year-old bucks' legs will appear short almost to an exaggerated extent, due to the fuller and fatter bodies.

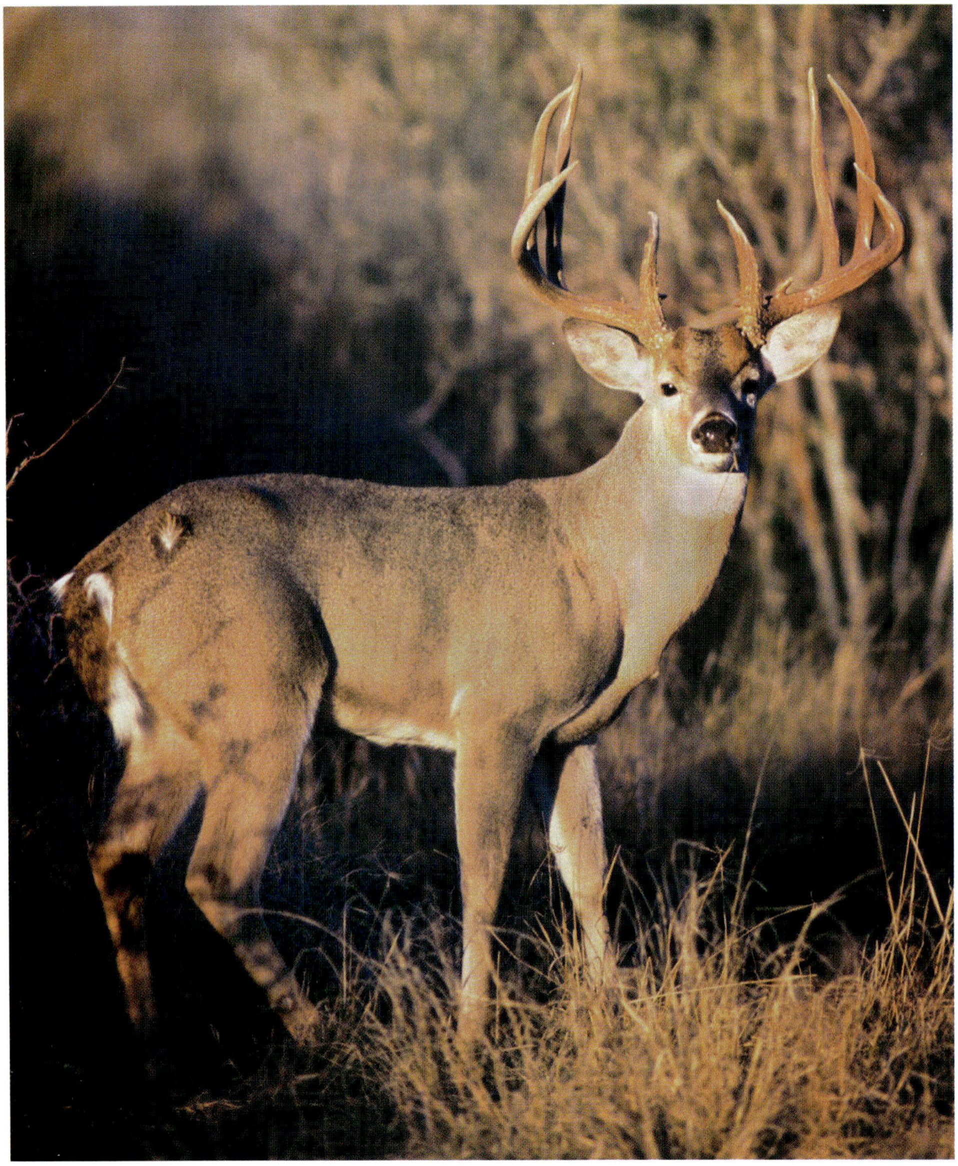

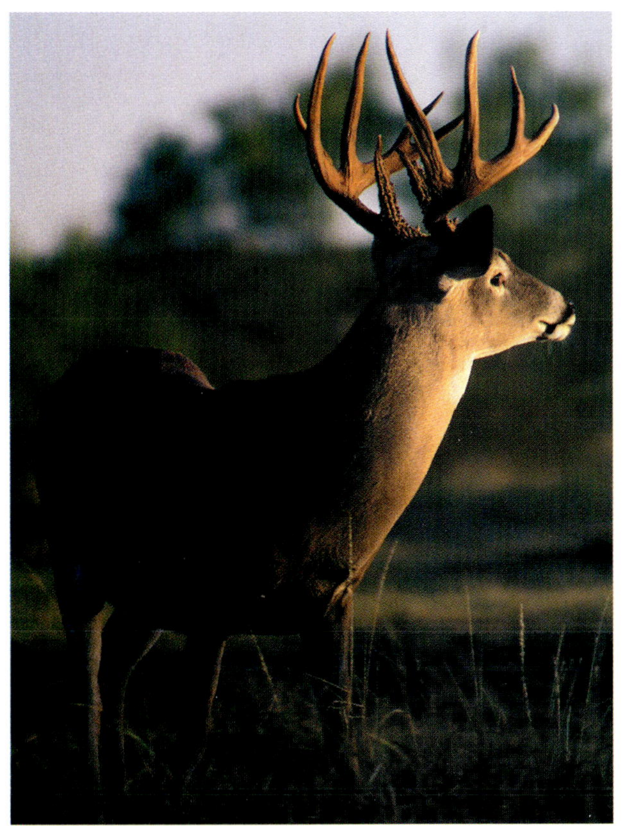

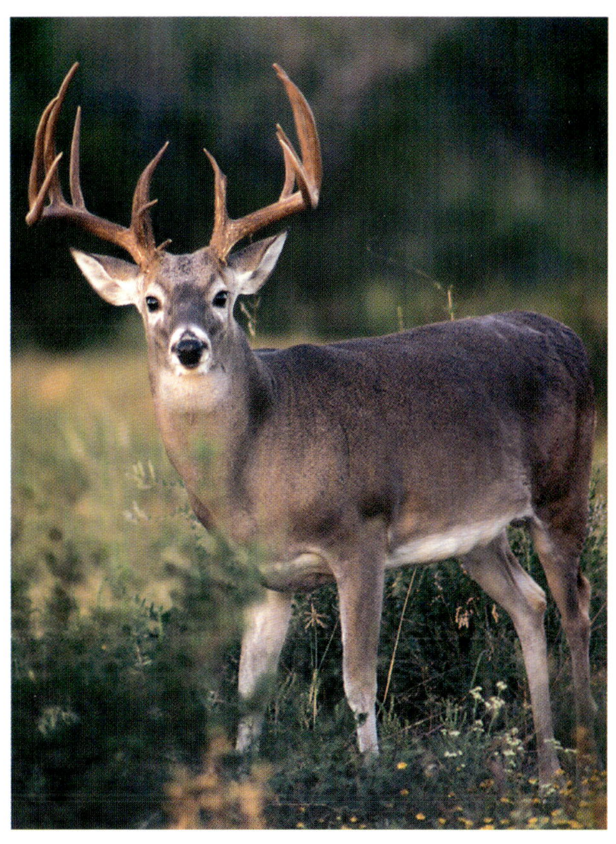

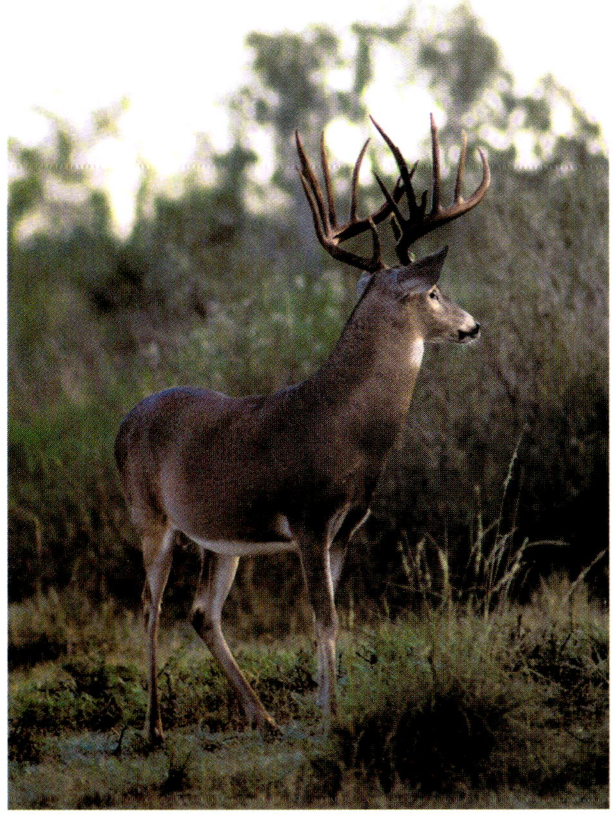

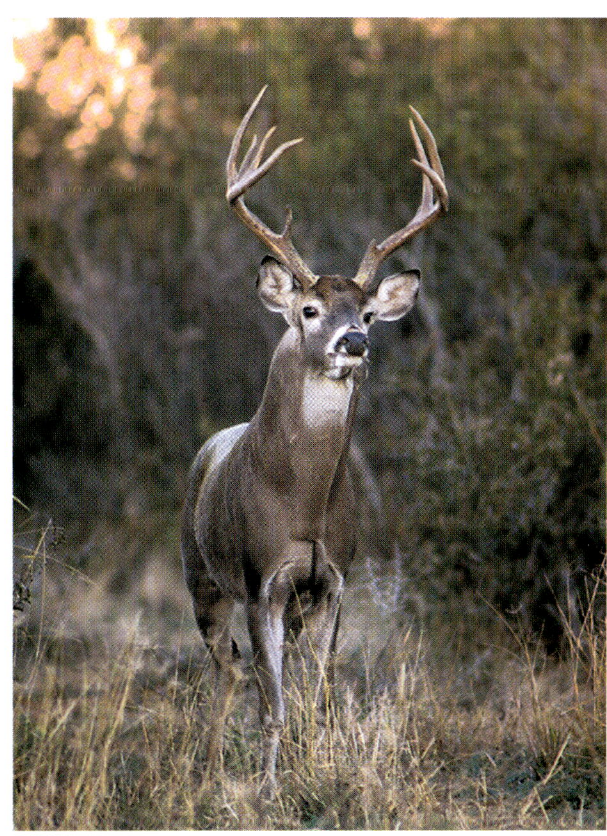

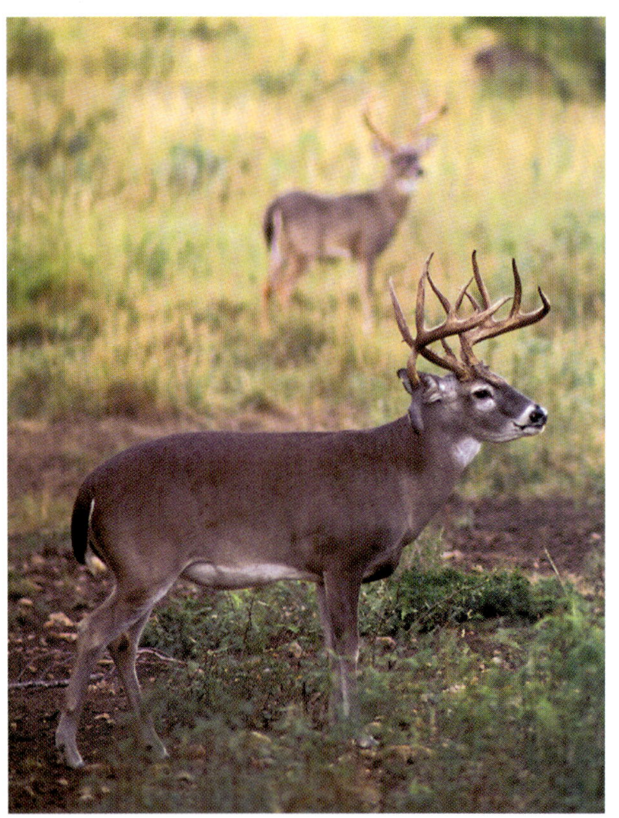

6 1/2-Year-Olds

At 6 1/2 years old, there is no doubt a buck is mature. During the rut, their neck will often be almost as thick as their body and will connect to their brisket as if one, continuous muscle. Their face will appear small in proportion to the thickness of their neck from a frontal view. Their body will be heavy and appear rippled, especially in the chest and neck areas. Throughout most of the year they will have a sagging stomach, except during the post-rut due to weight loss. Their back will also sag, making their front shoulders appear taller. The hair patch on their forehead is noticeably thicker and darker, and the chin will show ripples and may sag. Their tarsals and lower inside legs will be darkly stained down to the hoof. Late in the rut, they may have a large, grayish-white area under the tarsal where it has been scalded from urine. Finally, many bucks this age will have testicles that appear larger and descended lower than normal.

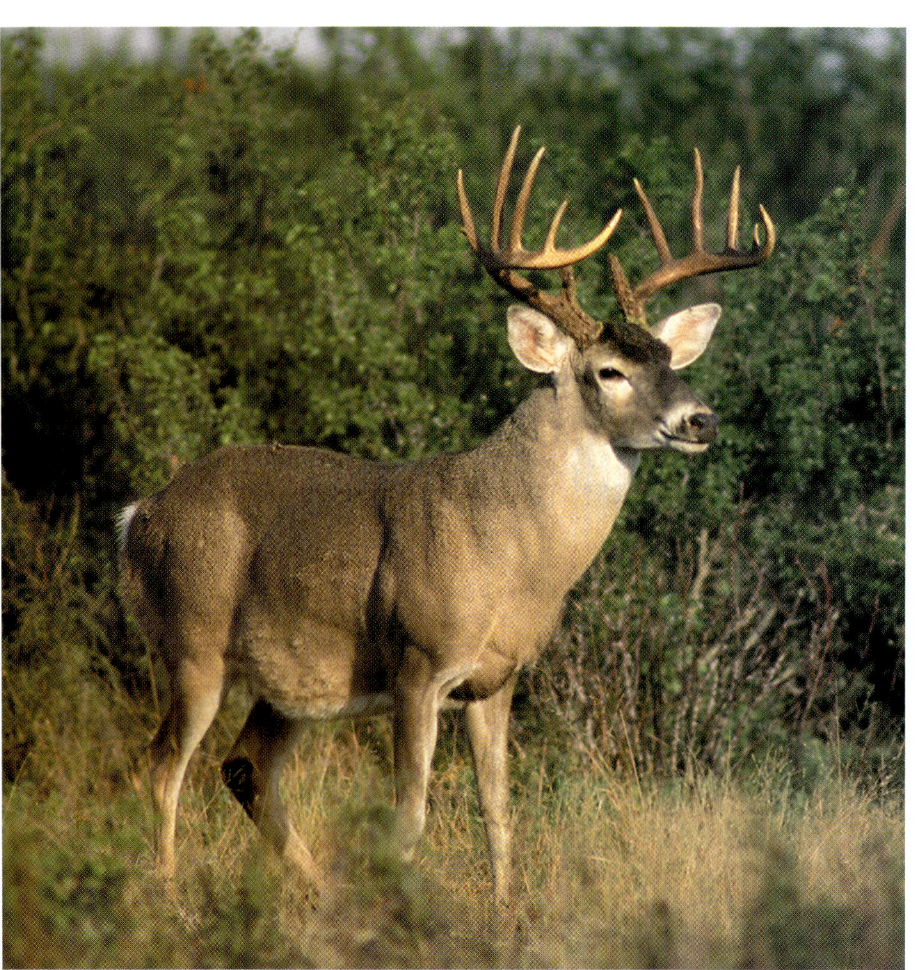

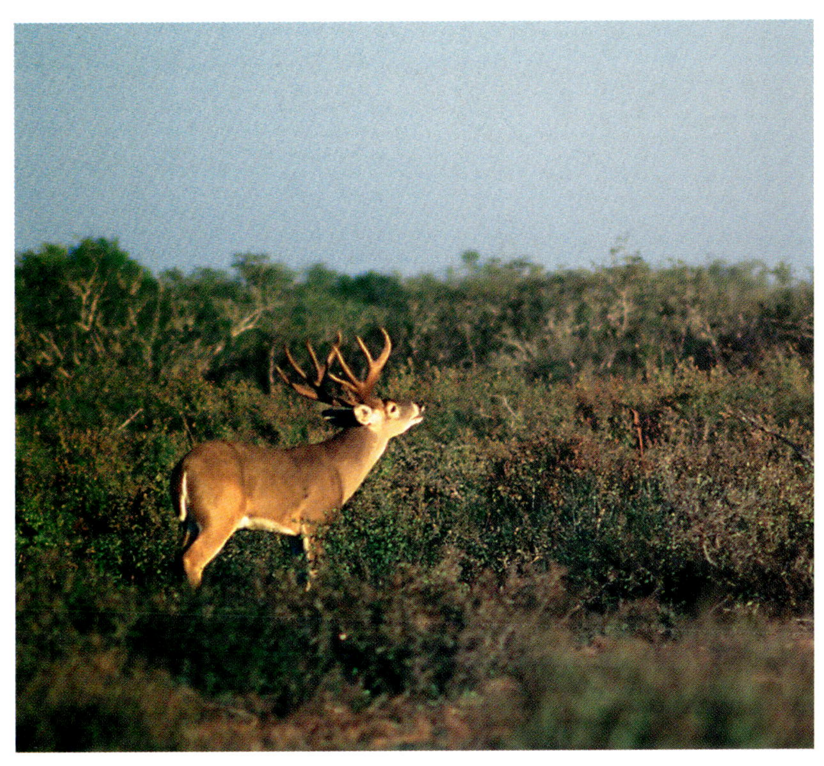

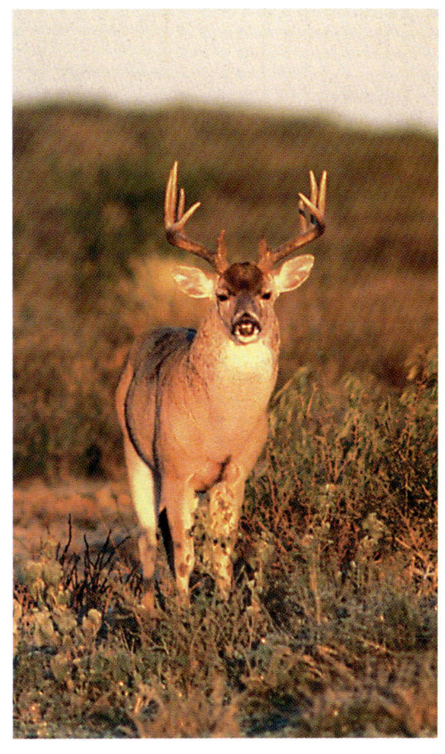

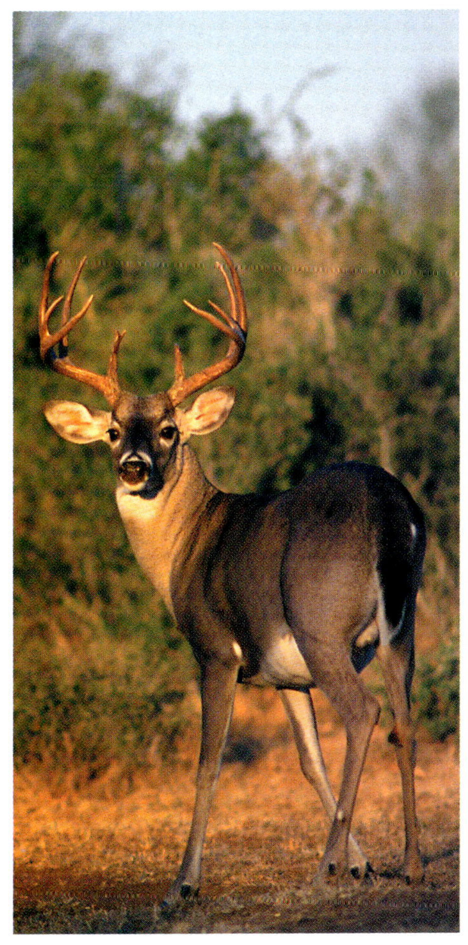

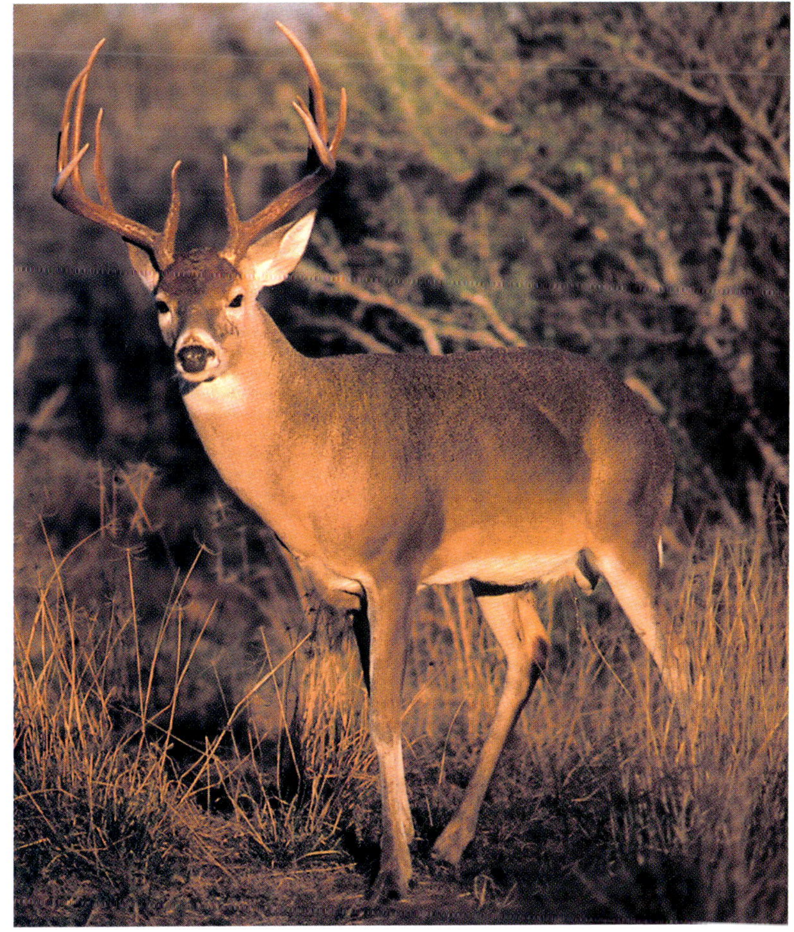

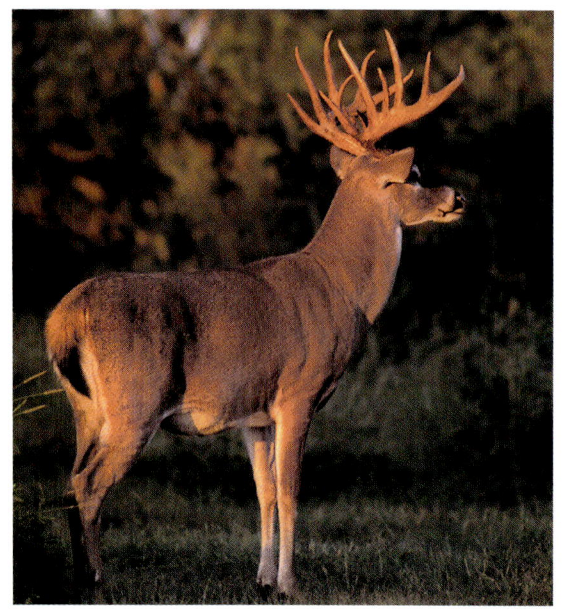

7 1/2-Year-Olds

The bodies of 7 1/2-year-old bucks appear huge. If they appear with younger deer, especially younger bucks, they will almost appear as a larger subspecies. Their bodies will have wrinkles and dimples, and their stomachs and backs will sag. During the rut their necks will be so thick it is difficult to determine where they stop and their briskets begin. If moving, their necks will appear flabby instead of firm like those of 5 1/2-year-olds. Often, the skin under the chin will sag. In the fall, their faces and the hair on the forehead gland will appear gray. However, as the rut approaches, their forehead will usually become darker due to secretions from the forehead gland. Their legs will appear short because their bodies are so large. During the rut, their tarsals will be very large with dark staining extending down the lower inside leg to the hoof. Late in the rut they may have large, grayish-white, scalding under the tarsals that are larger than the tarsal itself. Their testicles will be noticeably large and descended quite low. Many bucks will have their greatest antler mass at this age. Some will grow more total points and nontypical points, although the typical tines may be slightly shorter than at 5 1/2. Many 7 1/2-year-old bucks appear to have a rigid, slow gait when walking, showing the stiffness in their joints that is indicative of older age.

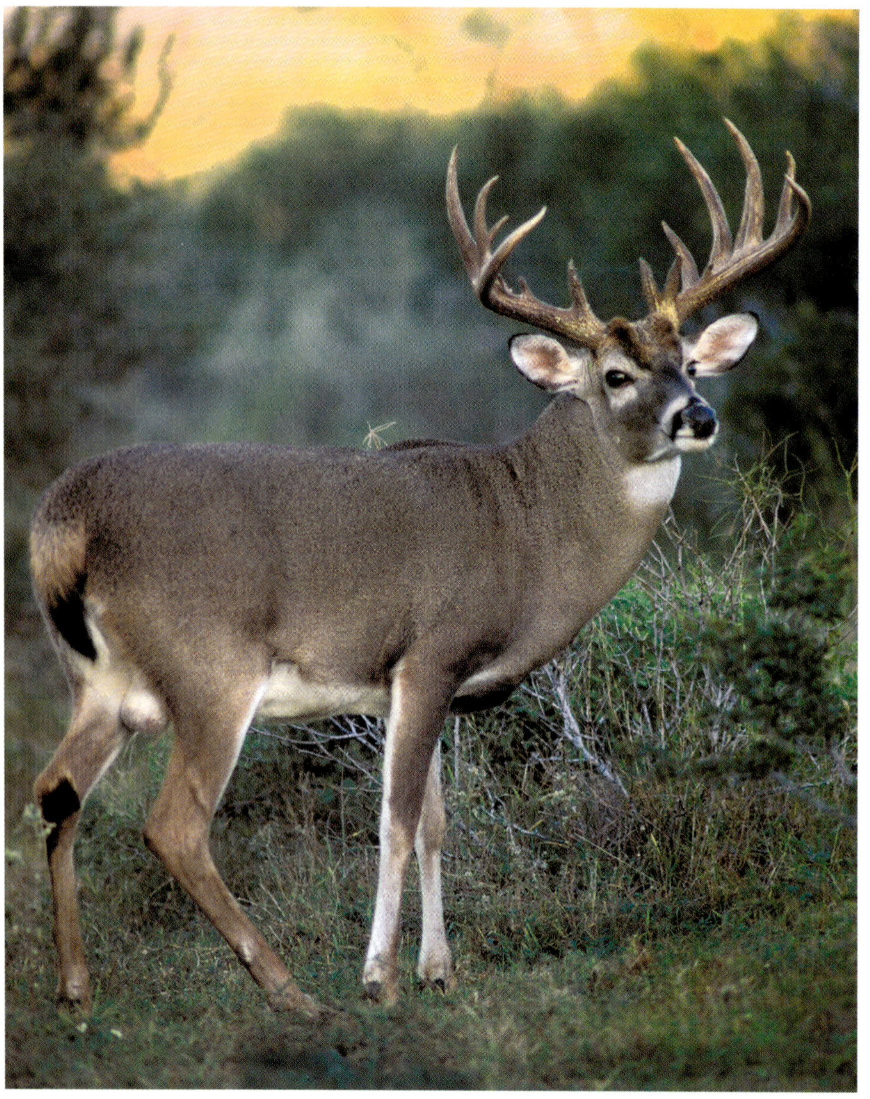

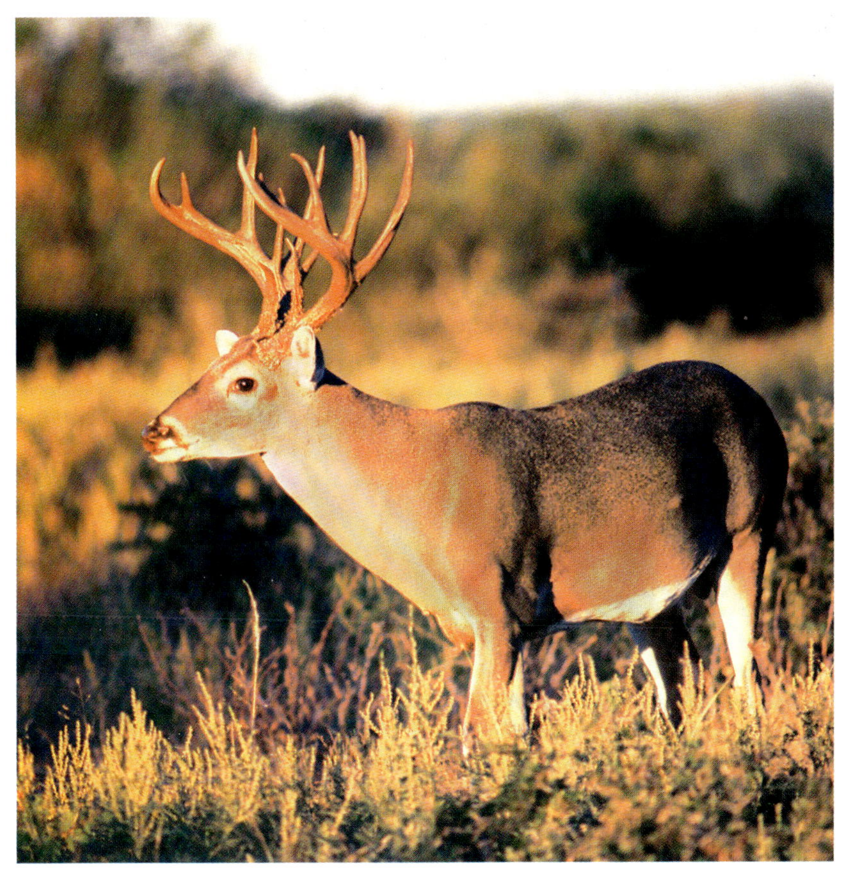
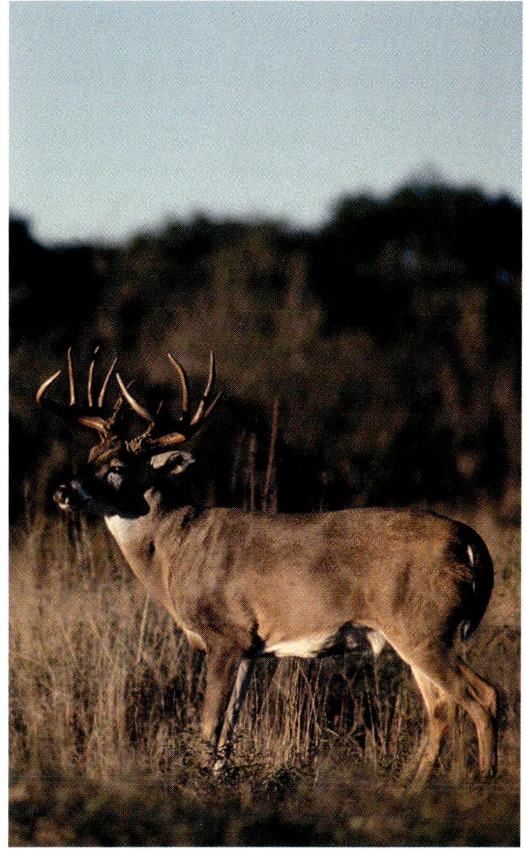
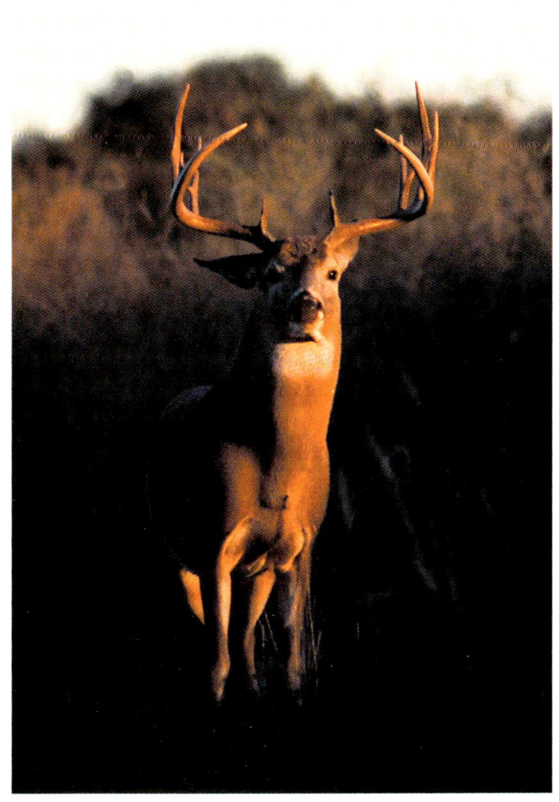
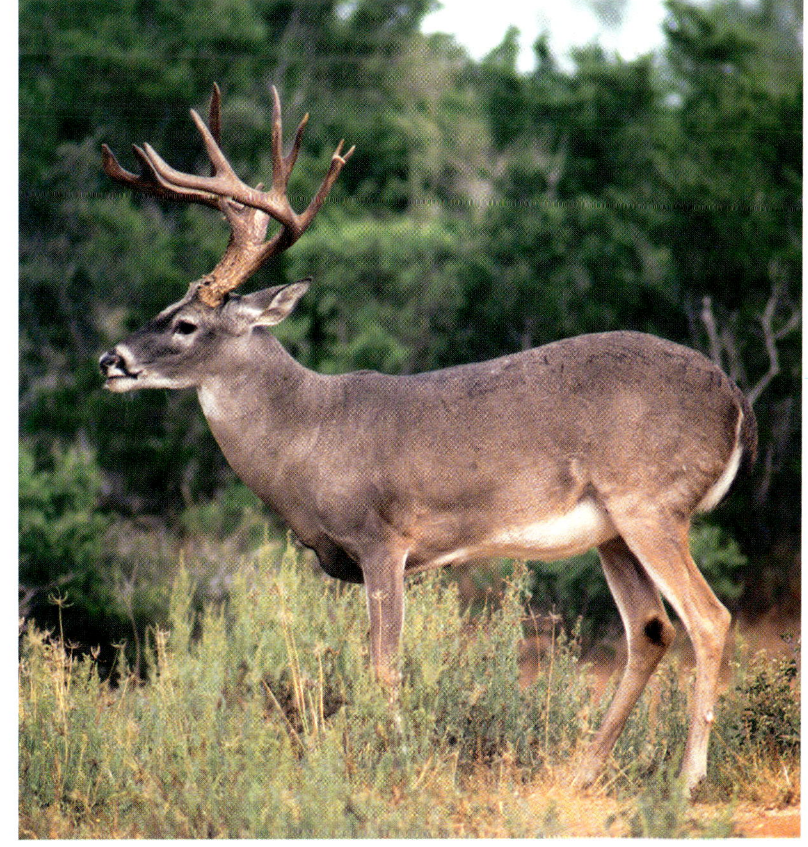

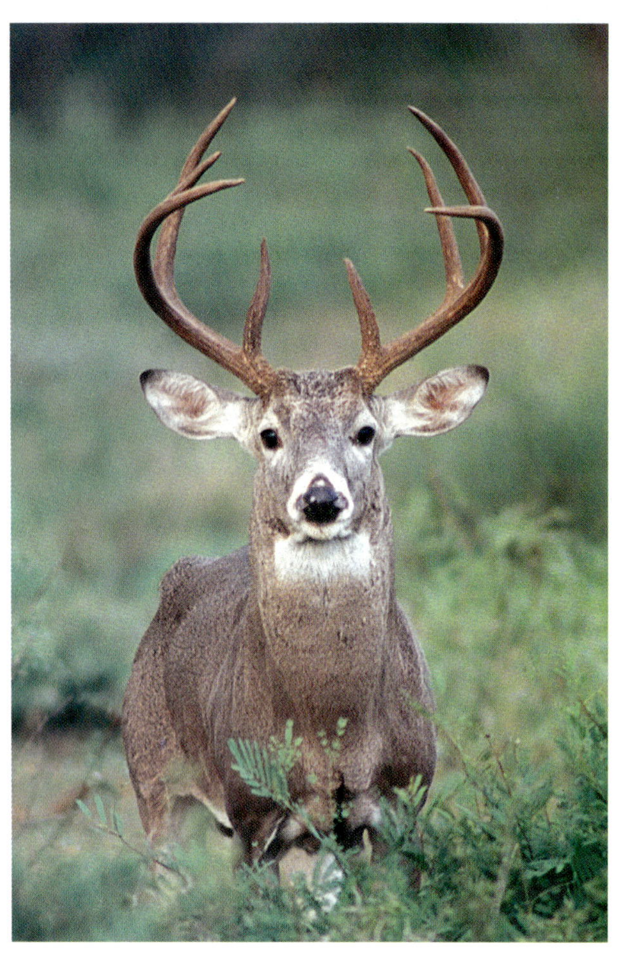

Postmaturity

While some bucks grow sizable antlers at or beyond 8 1/2 years of age, most wildlife managers in south Texas consider 7 1/2 the best age to harvest bucks if antler size is the primary consideration. Beyond 7 1/2 years of age, there also is an increasing chance of loss from natural mortality. Interestingly, as bucks pass 7 1/2 they can become quite a challenge to hunt unless you have patterned and can identify the particular buck. As bucks reach old age their teeth can become badly worn, resulting in reduced nutritional intake and an overall decline in condition. Often, their bodies will resemble those of 3 1/2-year-olds with slimmer bodies and necks. The only clues may be a graying scalp and face and slightly-protruding hip and rib bones. Postmature bucks will often display knocked knees, noticeably-sagging stomachs, and swayed backs with a hump above the shoulders. Also, their rumps appear more pointed than rounded as they

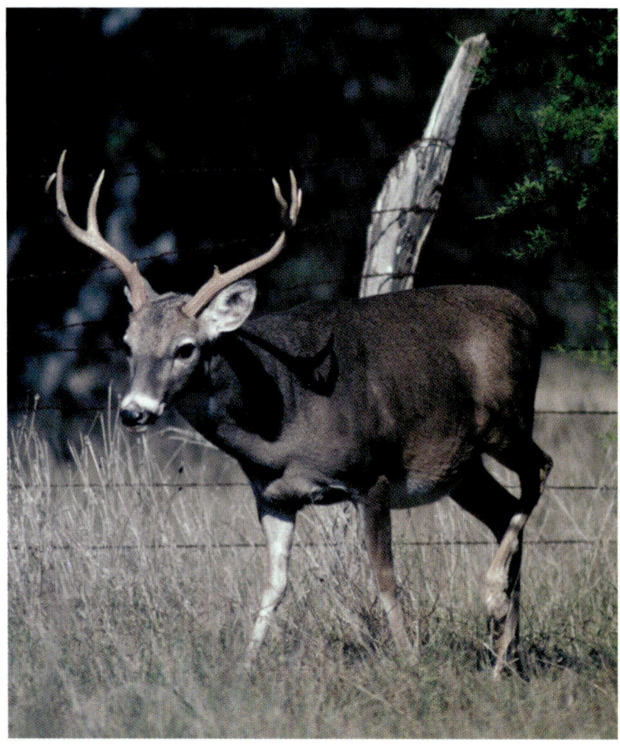

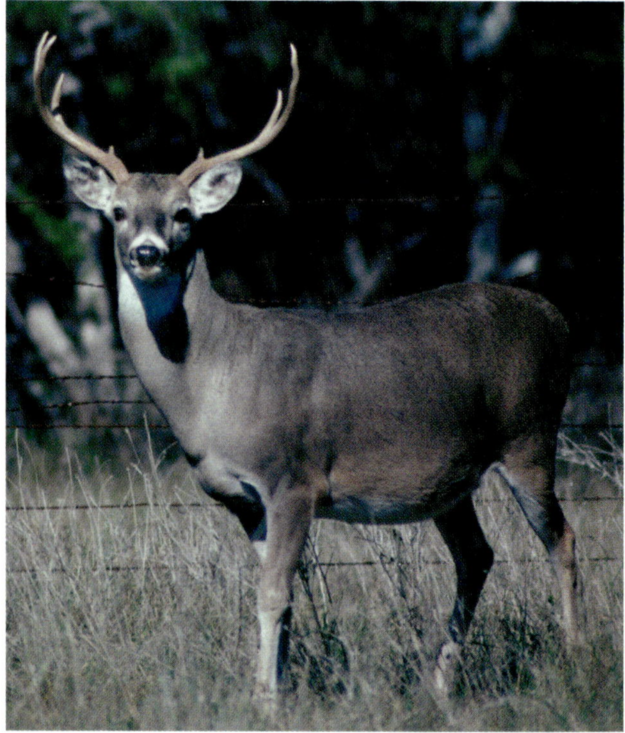

were in prime years. They often are very stiff-legged and slow, showing their old bodies and joints are wearing out. Their antlers will usually decrease in overall size and mass. When the teeth are badly worn, the antlers and body can deteriorate rapidly. Some very old bucks produce antler points that curl or appear crooked as if they were melted in a fire. Often, they will shed their antlers earlier than other bucks. Watching a buck as he relates to other mature bucks will often help determine whether he is postmature. If he acts submissive to younger 4 1/2- to 7 1/2-year-olds, and all the physical characteristics of post maturity are present, his prime years have already passed.

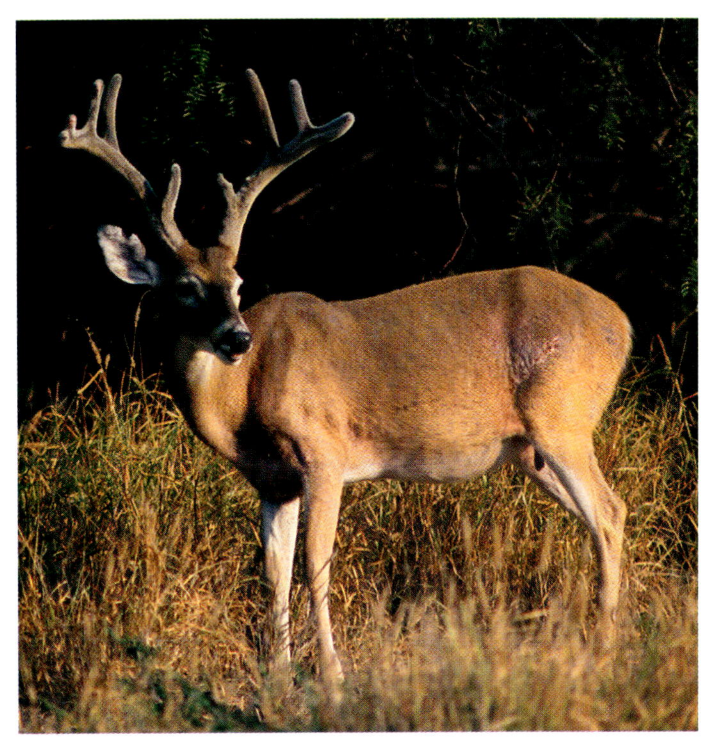

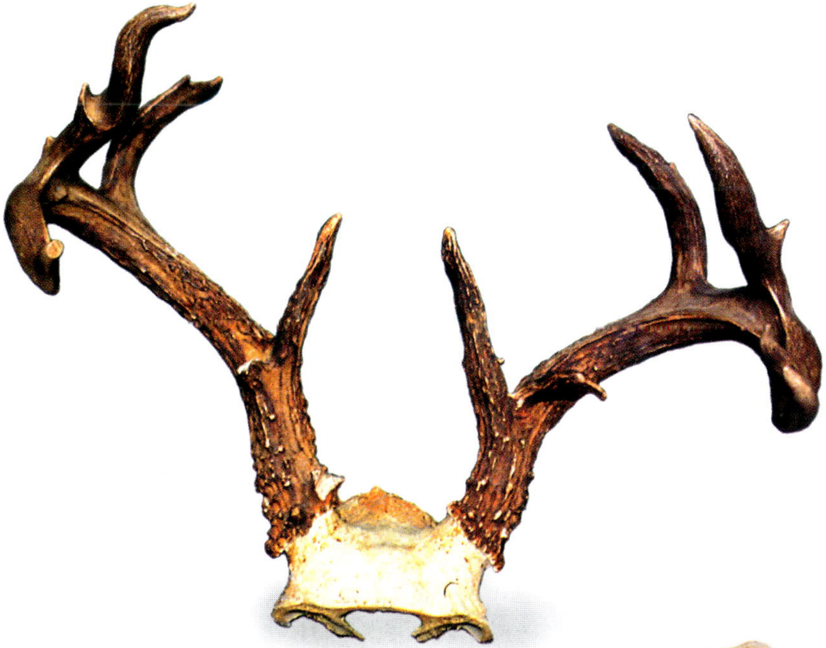

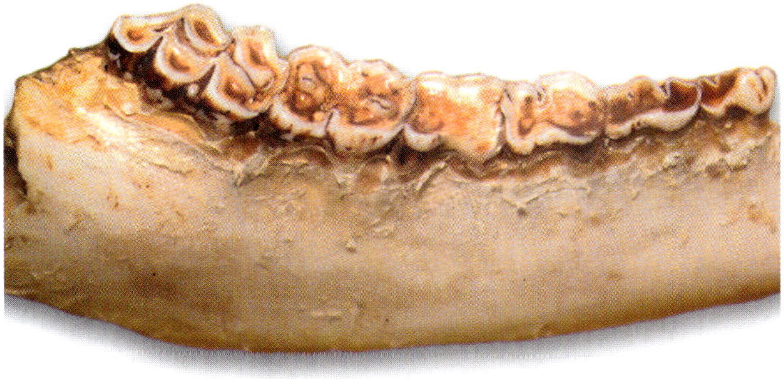

This very old buck's antlers and tooth wear both reveal his age. The antlers of very old bucks are often strangely curved or wavy, as if melted by heat.

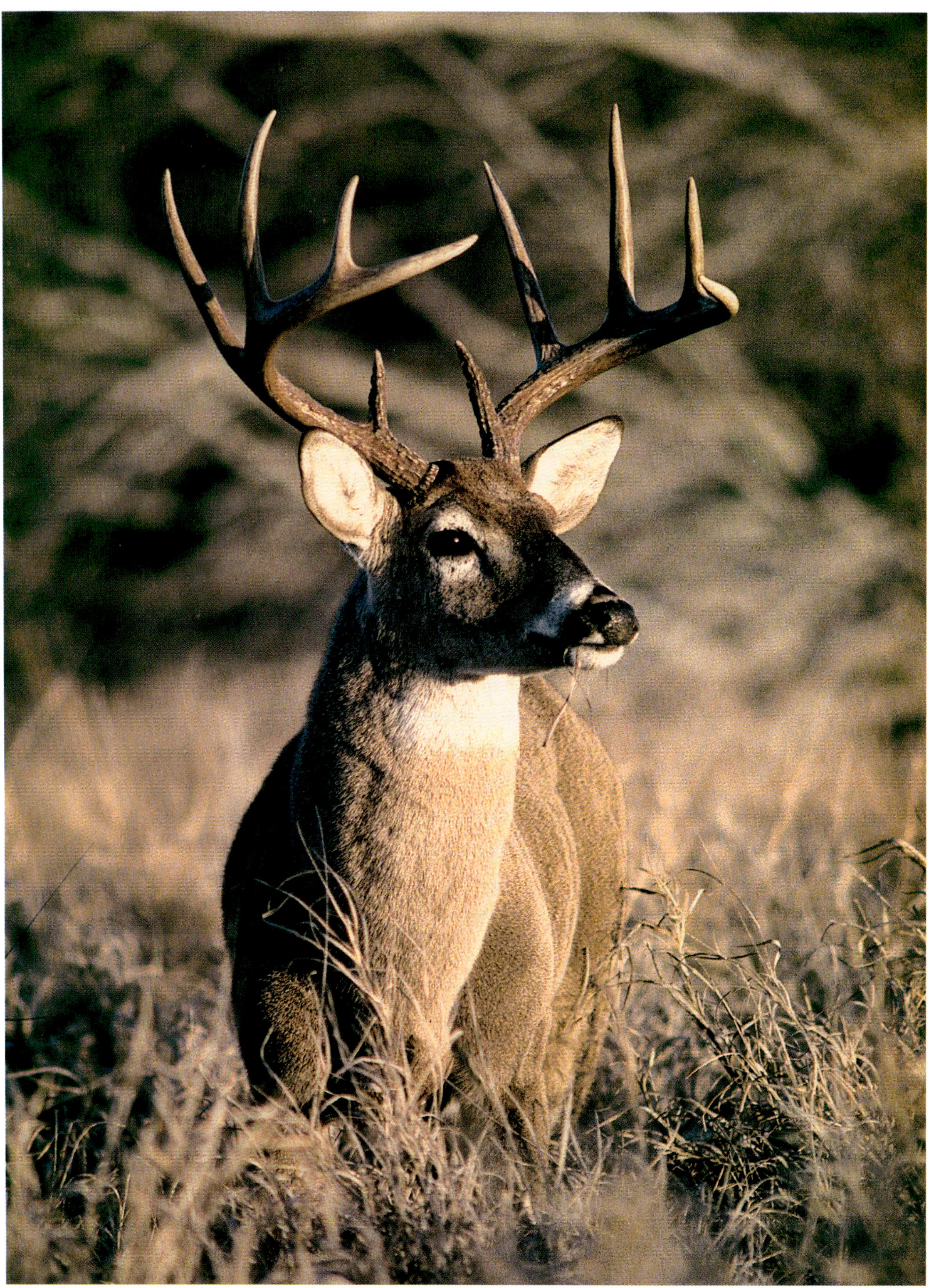

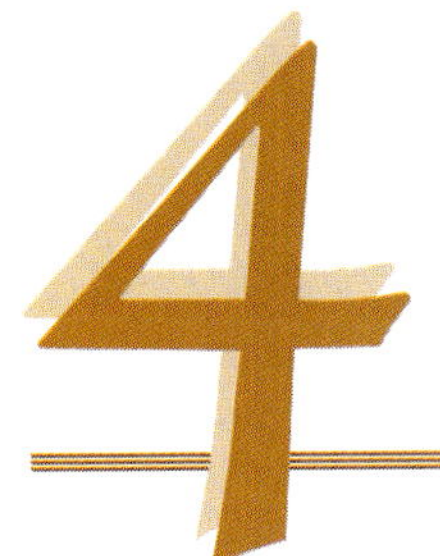

Buck Aging Sequences

Over the years I have been fortunate to follow several bucks throughout their lives. Each buck has been a fascinating learning experience, observing the changes in their body and antler growth each season and the various environmental factors that have affected them.

BUCK # 1

Some bucks catch your eye due to their unique characteristics. This buck, with his double throat patch and beautiful, symmetrical antlers with beams that sweep upward, was always easy to pick out even at a long distance.

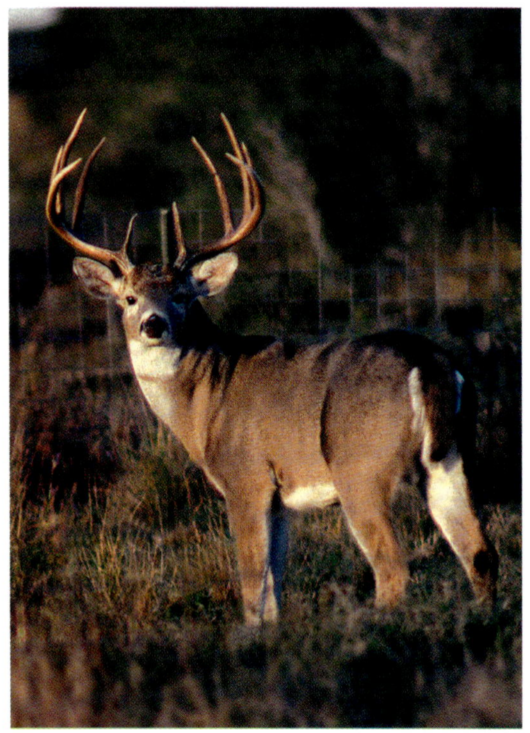
5 1/2

5 1/2

When he was 5 1/2 I only saw him twice and was very fortunate to get a picture of him as he came into a feeder for a few minutes, ate a few bites, and was quickly on his way. He was a very symmetrical 10-point. Notice that his tarsals are dark but not extremely large as they were early in the rut. His stomach area appears full, but does not sag. Also, his neck is swollen making his face appear small in comparison to his neck.

6 1/2

The next year at 6 1/2 his antlers were very similar to those the previous year, though he only had nine points. He did not grow a G-4 on his right antler that year. I will never forget one autumn evening watching five bucks coming out of the brush in single file. Even at 200 yards there was no mistaking that this old boy was bringing up the rear. I noticed that his forehead gland appeared thicker and darker at 6 1/2 and I also noticed that he had dark black spots under each eye, which I had never seen on another buck.

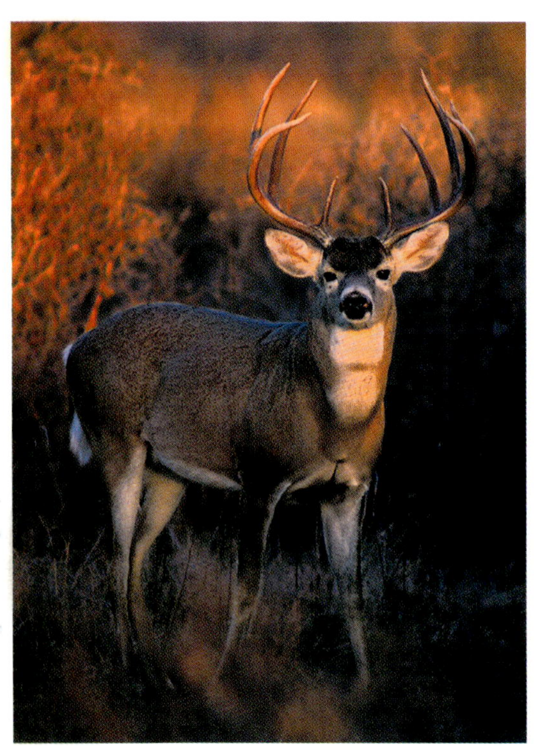
6 1/2

7 1/2

At 7 1/2 he again grew very symmetrical antlers with nine points. Many bucks will grow nontypical points at 7 1/2 but he did not. However, he did grow longer beams and tines than he had in any previous year. The hair on his forehead had grayed considerably. His stomach area was fuller and sagging more than the previous year and his neck and brisket appear as one where they join. This photo was taken in late October and his body appears very full and heavy showing his age. A hunter finally caught up with him that season and he scored 163 6/8 B&C, which is super for a typical 9-point. His body weight was 161 pounds field dressed. I was extremely fortunate that his sheds at both 5 1/2 and 6 1/2 were found, which is quite rare. He is one of the few bucks I have followed over the years that I was able to actually document what each set of antlers scored. He is covered on page 187 in the judging section if you want to see how good your guess is as to how long those tines are.

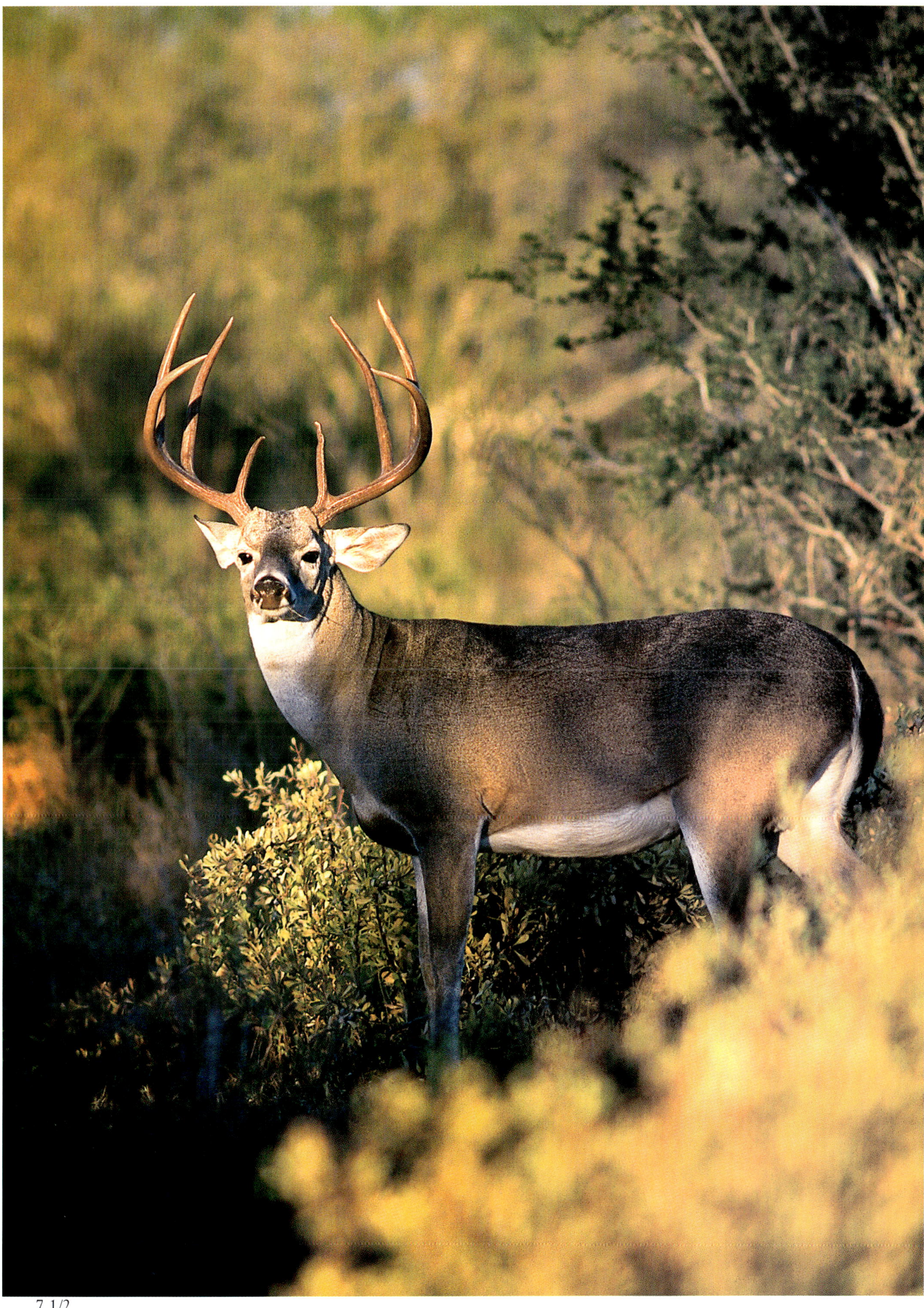

7 1/2

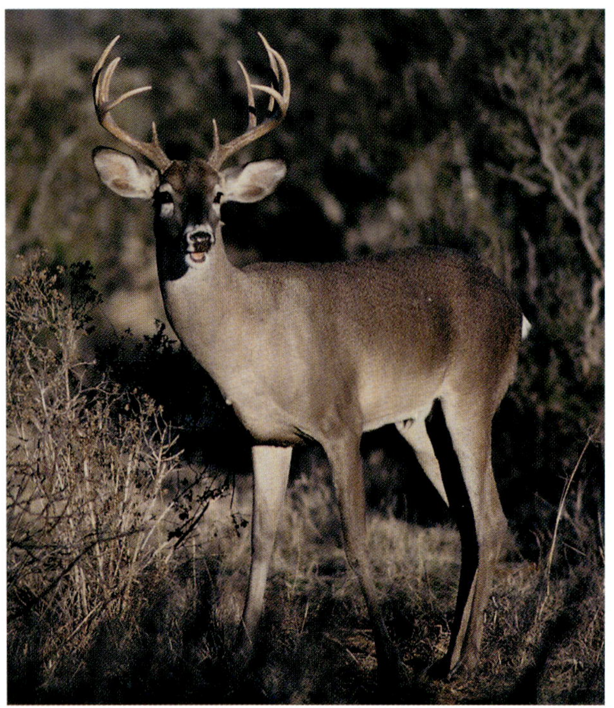

1 1/2 or 2 1/2

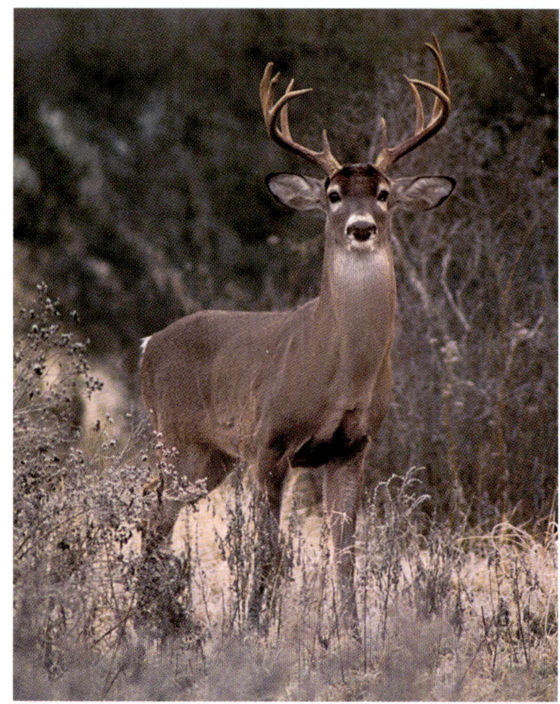

2 1/2 or 3 1/2

BUCK# 2

1 1/2 or 2 1/2

This young buck was very unique and difficult to age, because his antlers were so exceptional. He had beautiful little 10-point antlers, and his spread came to the tips of his ears. He was easy to recognize because he had big, black-tipped ears he always held low, making them appear as if they sagged. He also had amber eyes and a thin, dark strip of hair down the back of his neck. He may represent the rare scenario when a buck's antlers should be given more consideration than his body. His body has many similarities to a 1 1/2-year-old, but his antlers, specifically his beam length, appear too large for a 1 1/2-year-old. So, is he an exceptional 1 1/2-year-old or a small-bodied, average-antlered 2 1/2-year-old? When observing him with another 2 1/2-year-old buck, he reacted more like a 1 1/2-year-old, always acting subordinate. However, that could also be the case for a small-bodied 2 1/2-year-old. This buck is one of those that could go either way and will need to be observed over the years to make the right decision when the time comes. The truth is, in five more years he will be known to be 6 1/2 or 7 1/2, and the decision can be made then whether to harvest him or wait one more season, depending on the circumstances at the time.

2 1/2 or 3 1/2

The next fall he had slightly damaged his right G-2 and G-3 in velvet causing one to be blunt and the other to form an acorn point. He probably injured them in August a few weeks before his antler growth was complete, and it clearly stunted that side of his antlers. However, it was apparent he was in good health, and his antlers had increased in size. This photo was taken in late December near the end of the rut, and his body appears more like a 2 1/2-year-old, but that could be the result of being run-down from the rut.

3 1/2 or 4 1/2

He had 10 points again the following year, and his antlers had increased in mass, beam, and tine length. I was excited knowing that more of the puzzle about his age would be revealed over the next year. It would be interesting to see if his body would take on the characteristics of maturity. I had photos of him for three years and was certain I would be able to follow him throughout his life, because he had so many recognizable features and was quite predictable. However, this photo was the last time I ever saw him. I'm not sure if he moved or died. The rancher thought he saw him once the following season near where I used to photograph him, but he was not certain. It's possible he moved, as there were several bucks in his old stomping grounds. One buck he traveled with in the fall was his same age and quite aggressive toward him. The rancher told me they saw a dead buck with antlers resembling his while flying a helicopter survey that year, but we never were able to locate it on the ground. It would have been interesting to observe his body and antler growth over the next few years and then estimate his age based on tooth wear after harvest. Sadly, his exact age will remain a mystery.

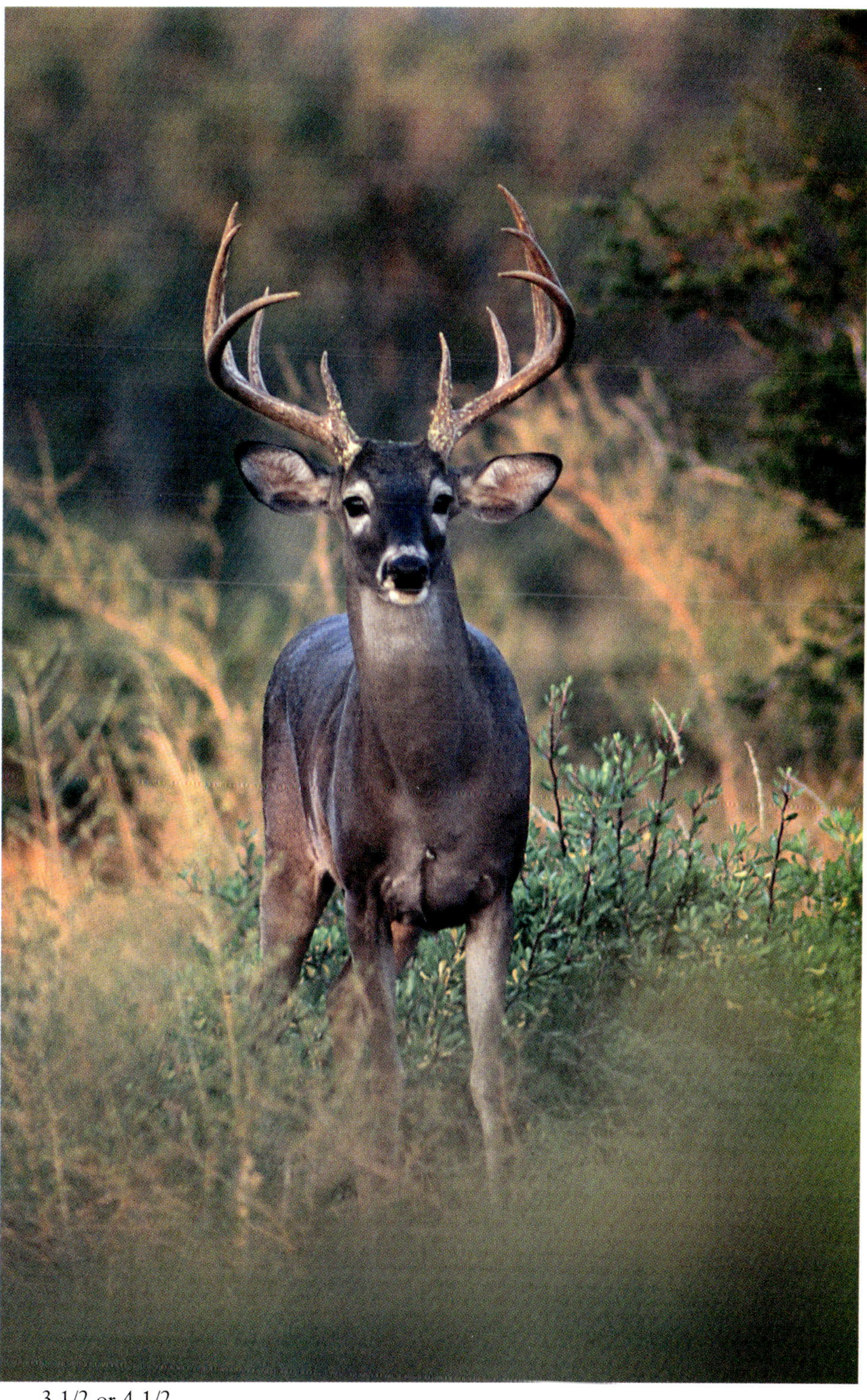

3 1/2 or 4 1/2

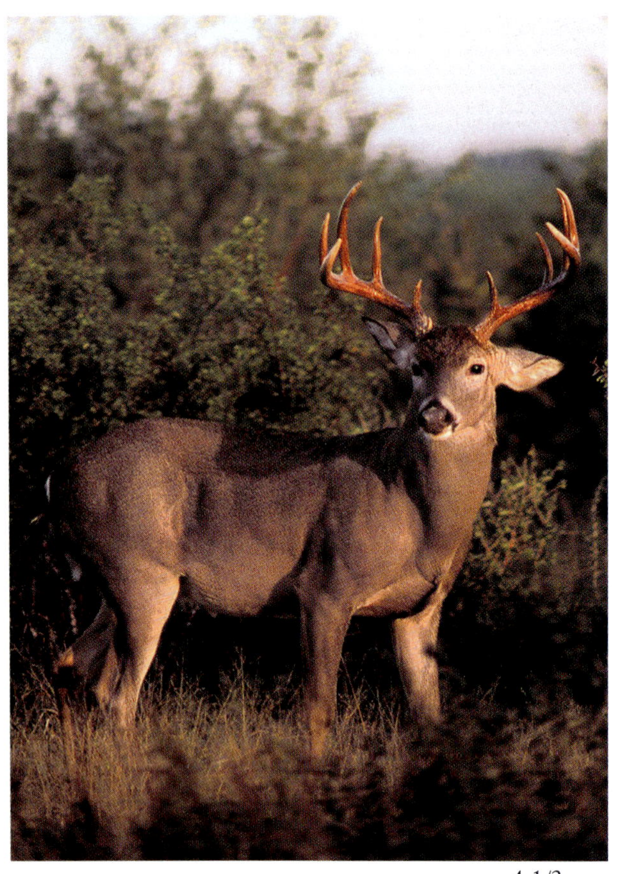

4 1/2

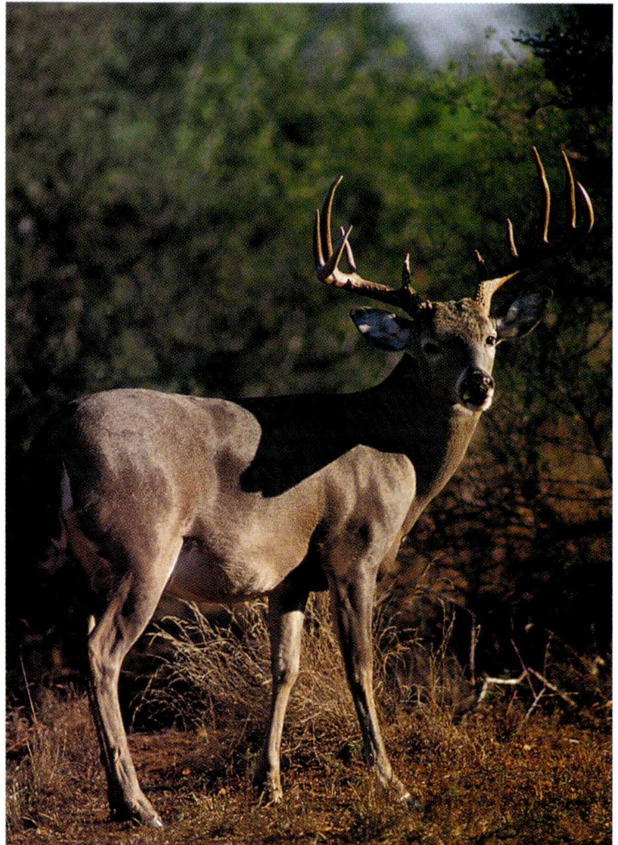

5 1/2

BUCK# 3

4 1/2

The first year I photographed this buck he was 4 1/2 and a basic 10-point. He had very short brow tines and short G-2s, both of which are undesirable traits. I remember the rancher discussing whether to harvest him if the opportunity presented itself. Typical of younger deer, he was fairly predictable, and I believe his mass and spread created just enough hope in the rancher to let him grow another year. Notice that even though his body appears full, his back and stomach are straight.

5 1/2

At 5 1/2 his spread and tines lengths improved, but his brow tines (G-1s) and G-2s were still lacking. His body was continuing to bulk up and appeared fuller than the previous year. Notice that his stomach is starting to sag, but his back is still straight. He moved over a mile and started appearing at a new location that year but was still fairly predictable until the rut started.

6 1/2

At 6 1/2 I did not think I was ever going to see him. He was one of those bucks that became increasingly elusive each year. When I finally did catch up with him, it was January. He was over two miles from where I had seen him the previous year. I imagine he had followed a doe into the new area

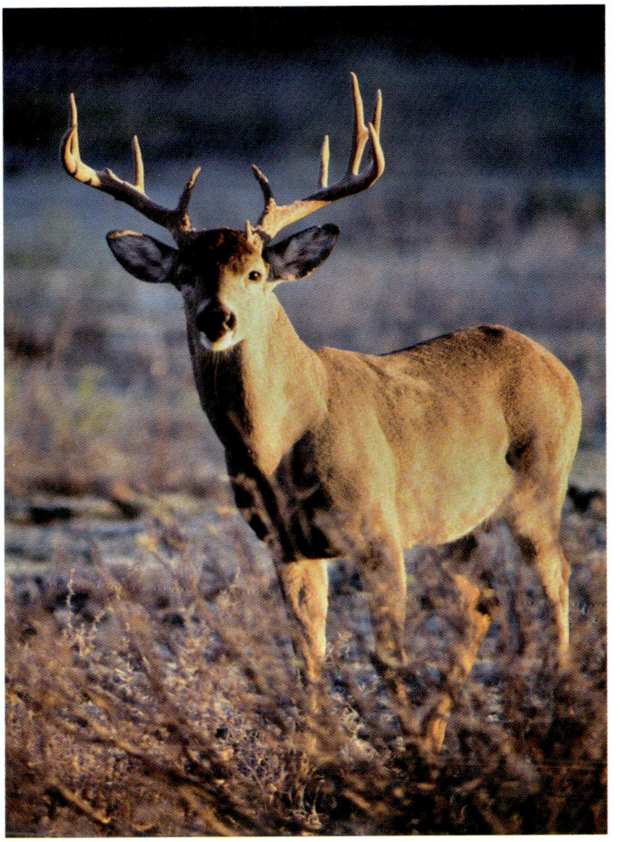
6 1/2

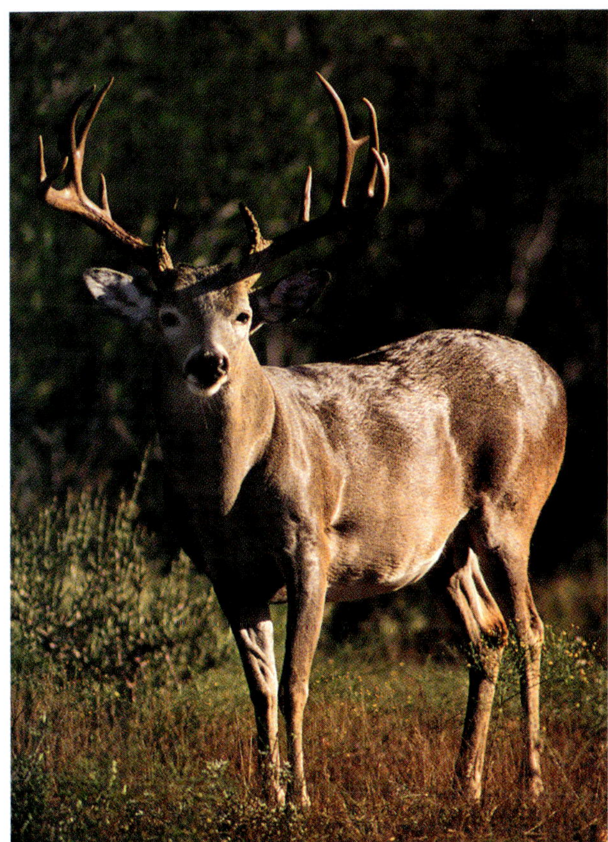
7 1/2

during the rut. His antlers had declined in tine length but appeared to have gained in mass. He had broken his G-3 on his right antler making him appear poorer than he really was. Even in late January during the post-rut, his body appeared in good shape and his neck was still quite swollen. I noticed the hair patch on his forehead appeared very dark and thick. Notice in the photograph that his back is starting to sway.

7 1/2

At 7 1/2 most bucks grow their heaviest and most impressive set of antlers, but this buck still surprised me. His antlers had increased in size from the previous year, and, even with short brow tines and G-2s, he was quite impressive. He had grown a nontypical point on his left G-3 and a deep forked G-3 on the right antler. He had increased in mass and spread and carried 13 points. His body was massive, even well before the rut when this photo was taken. His body was so full it made his legs appear short, which is typical of bucks this age. His stomach and back both have noticeable sags, and his neck and brisket appear as one continuous muscle. I only saw him twice that fall, and then he disappeared. He was finally harvested in the last few days of the season after being hunted hard all season by the same hunter. His gross B&C score will shock you for a buck with very short brow tines and G-2s. How does 165 2/8 B&C sound for a buck that was almost harvested at 4 1/2 for lack of potential? If you want to try and judge him yourself and see how the measurements break down, turn to page 188 in the judging section.

BUCK# 4

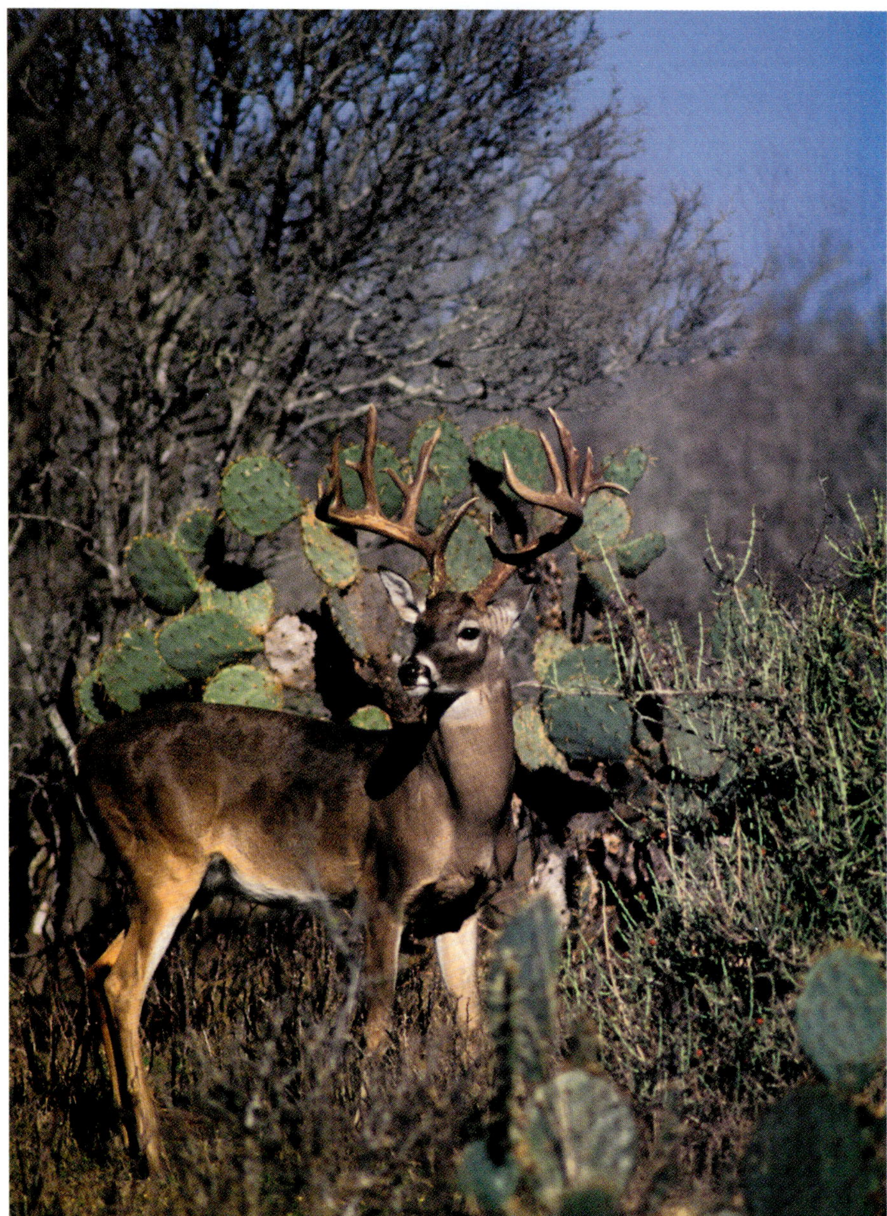
3 1/2

The year this buck was a fawn there was a very gentle doe at a particular feeder with a fawn that was still nursing. The fawn had small 1/2-inch hardened antlers. This was the first year the ranch fed protein. This doe would regularly jump into the pen and feed on the protein pellets. The following year this little buck was a regular with his mother at the feeder. He was 18 months old and had nine points with a nontypical point on each side, and they knew he was special. At 2 1/2 he was a basic 10-point with five nontypical points, and the rancher had to declare him off limits to hunters.

3 1/2

At 3 1/2 he was a 5x6 with five nontypical points. Notice how young he looks in the cactus photo. He has a slender neck, taut stomach, and tight face that still resembles a doe. Most hunters would have never looked at his body because their attention would be fixed on his antlers and he would have been prematurely harvested that year. There are several characteristics in his antlers at 3 1/2 that will be reoccurring year after year. He has high, heavy beams that turn up forming the appearance of crab claws. He has nontypical points on his G-2s and G-3s on both sides and his brow tines turn in toward each other.

4 1/2

At 4 1/2 it is easy to see what a difference a year has made in his body maturing. The whole body and neck are fuller and even the face has matured. The tine lengths and number of nontypical points have decreased. However, it is apparent he has increased significantly in mass and beam length. He also grew a small drop tine on his right main beam for the first time. His personality also changed. He was acting more aggressive toward other bucks and was participating fully in the rut. For the first time, he was not seen throughout much of the season.

5 1/2

At 5 1/2 it was apparent that most of his nutritional intake was going toward antler growth. He had improved in mass, beam length, and tine length. He had a big ridge on the inside of the beams that appeared to have been a very large blood vessel, which could have contributed to the tremendous growth. His stomach sagged, but his back was still straight. He was definitely the dominant buck in the area, and when he was around I did not see any other mature bucks. When the rut hit, he would vanish. Occasionally he would be spotted, but it was apparent he was covering several miles trailing does. Late January that year he showed up back in his home territory with a few abnormal points missing. He was pretty lean, but still in pretty good shape. I often wish I could have seen the buck that knocked off those abnormal points.

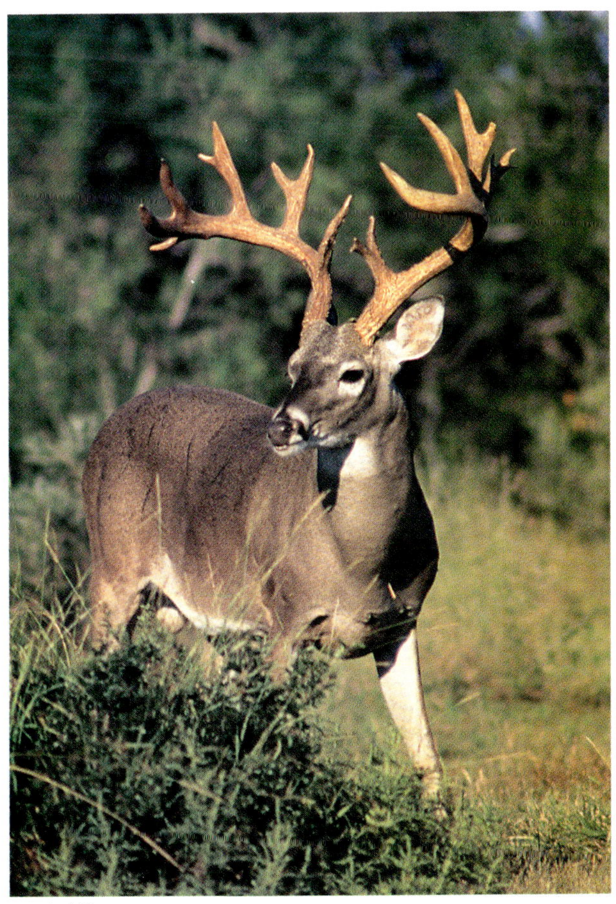

4 1/2

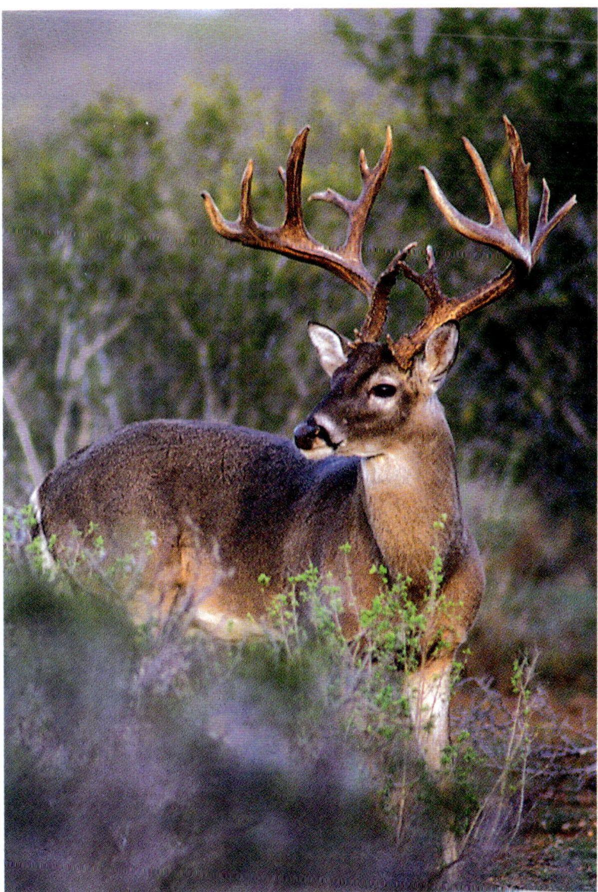

5 1/2

6 1/2

At 6 1/2 he again increased in mass and points and grew the largest set of antlers in his life. Besides being a basic 10-point with nontypical points on his G-2s and G-3s, he had multiple points on his brow tines and grew a nice drop tine out of the ridge on his left beam. The drop tine was on the opposite side of the one he grew at 4 1/2. It was extremely dry the year he was 5 1/2 and most of the antler growth period during his sixth year. This led us to believe he spent a lot of that time eating the high protein supplemental feed, which may explain his enormous antlers. His body was starting to show its age as his stomach and back had noticeable sags. His forehead had gotten quite gray and his jaw line also sagged. He was the dominant buck in the area, and I saw him less than I had any previous year. He again showed up in late January where I had first seen him in October. He had broken a few tines and had a stomach wound. The wound appeared to have been caused by misjudging a fence. He appeared thinner as most bucks do in the post-rut, but not in bad shape.

7 1/2

At 7 1/2 the old buck had declined noticeably. He was still a basic 10-point, but his nontypical points were very small and his antlers had decreased in beam length and mass. He was so big and dominant the year before, his body may have had to recuperate to such a degree that his antlers just never caught up. Also, from October of his sixth year through the antler growth period of his seventh year was a wet period for south Texas. This may have caused him to rely more on native weeds and browse and less on the supplemental feed, causing his antlers to decline. His body appeared in fine shape, and even in October when this photo was taken, the signs of a very mature buck are evident. Whatever the reason for his antler decline, it did not affect his vigor and energy for the rut that year. Typical of the past few years, when the rut started, he was gone. When he showed back up in late January, he had broken his right main beam about halfway between his G-3 and G-4. He was lean but in good shape. However, I saw him again in early February limping badly on an injured back

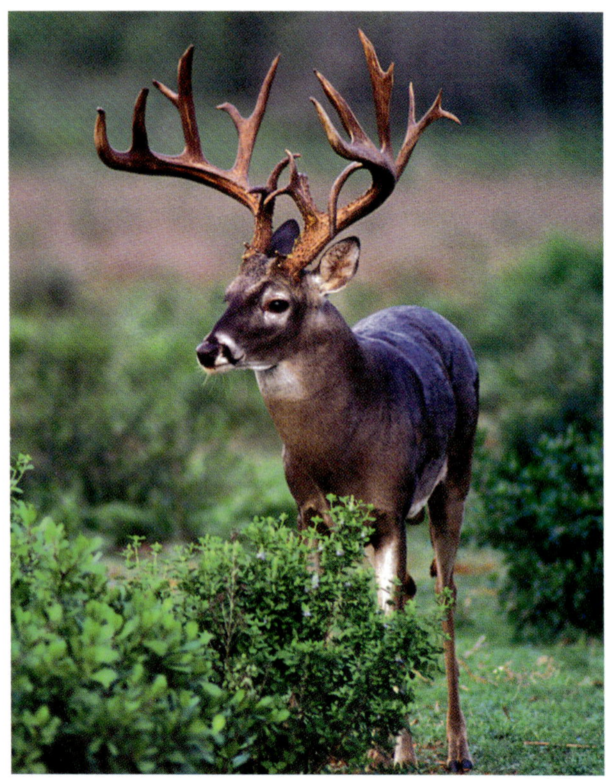

6 1/2

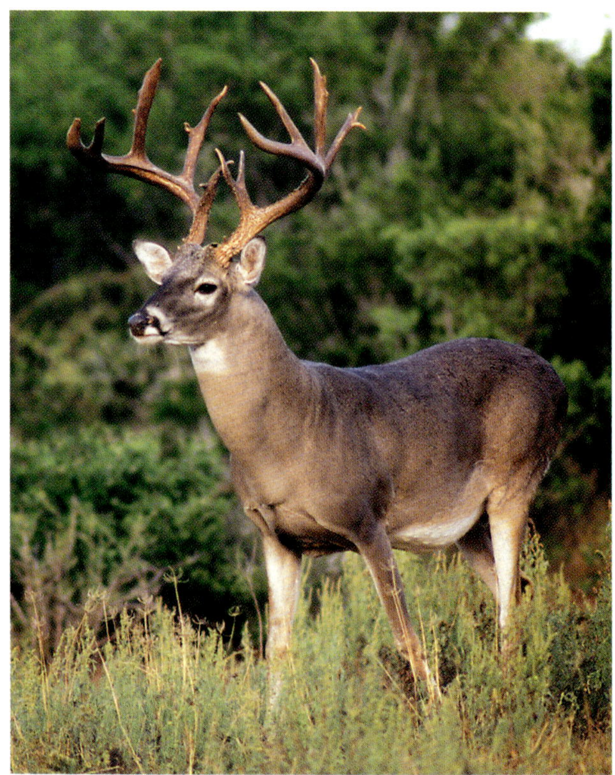

7 1/2

leg. I was certain the leg was not broken but was still sickened to think about how it might affect his antlers the next year.

8 1/2

It was a long spring and summer during which the rancher and I speculated about what this old buck would do at 8 1/2 and if the leg injury would affect his antlers. I could not have dreamed how remarkable a recovery he would make. When he showed up that fall at his old stomping grounds, he was a huge basic 10-point with every accessory you could add to a buck's antlers. He had giant, multipointed brow tines, nontypical points on his G-2 and G-3 on his left side, a deep forked G-2 on the right side, and a big drop tine to help balance him out. Look at the numerous antler characteristics this buck has exhibited year after year. His body is heavy and flabby, which is characteristic of old age. Whichever angle he turned, his stomach and back sagged. In fact, from the side it was apparent he was getting hump-backed over his shoulders, which is very characteristic of old bucks. He also had numerous dimples and wrinkles over his body. This photo was taken in October, so none of the characteristics of the rut would have been present at that time. However, it is easy to see he is a very mature buck. A hunter caught up to him that fall, though I would have been interested to know how active he might have been during the rut. Turn to page 205 and see how well your judging is on what is truly a buck of a lifetime.

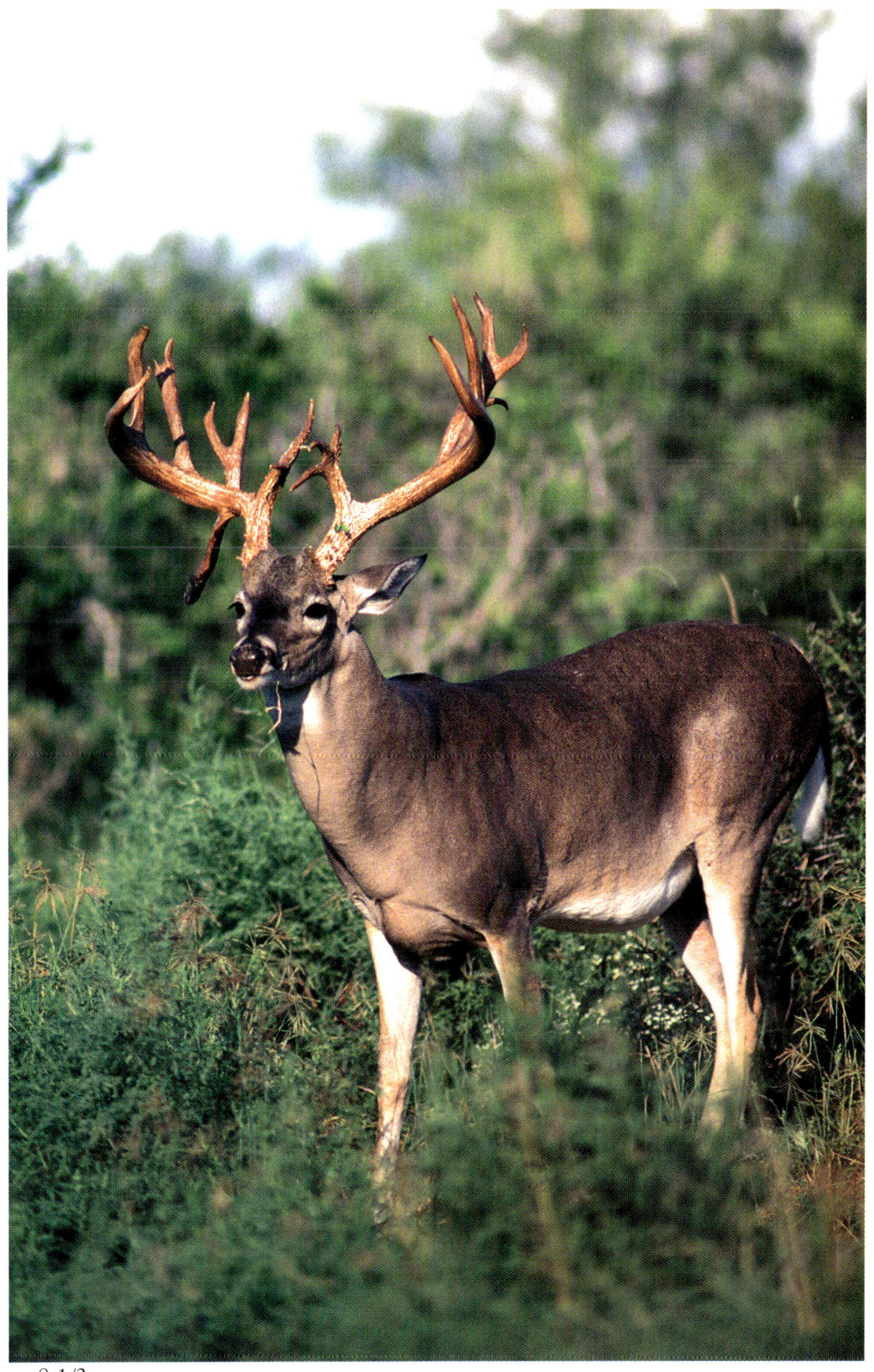

8 1/2

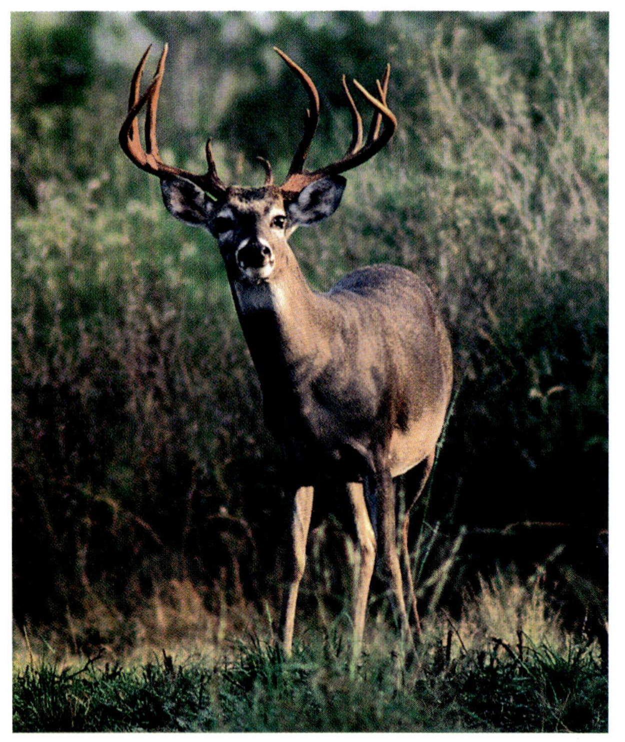

3 1/2

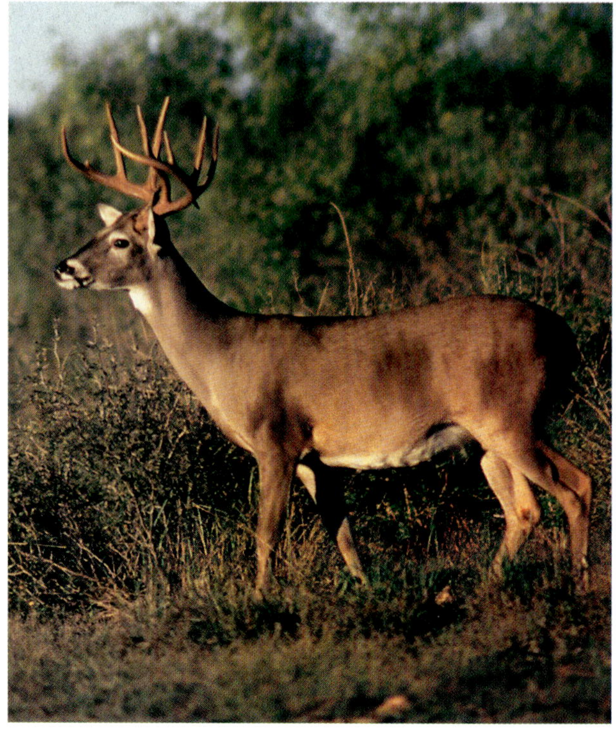

3 1/2

BUCK# 5

3 1/2

This buck was an oddity from the first time I saw him. He had a big, sagging stomach, but his neck was very thin. Notice from the side that he looks like a young buck from the neck up, but his body looks like a much older deer. He also had a very large left brow tine and what appeared to be a small third antler coming out of the back of his skull. At first, it was thought he was post-mature, but no one could identify the buck or was certain they had ever seen him before. The rancher thought the buck could have some type of intestinal problem and was probably younger than he appeared, so he wanted to see what the buck would do in another year.

4 1/2

He was pleasantly surprised the next fall as he was an 8x5 with an estimated spread of 24 inches. His neck never swelled that year, but his stomach area had shrunk back to normal size for his age. The rancher decided he was not over the hill and, after analyzing the shape of his body while taking into consideration the previous year's information, he thought he most closely resembled a 4 1/2- or 5 1/2-year-old.

5 1/2

The next year he was a 7x5, but had broken off most of his left brow tine and the point next to it before I photographed him. I only saw him twice that year, as he had become much more skittish as is typical of older bucks. His left shed was found after the season and his beam was 23 2/8 inches. His other measurements were G-1, (broken) 1 6/8; G-2, 8 7/8; G-3, 10 3/8; G-4, 5 2/8; G-5, 1 5/8; H-1, 5 2/8; H-2, 3 4/8; H-3, 3 5/8; H-4 3 2/8. His spread was estimated to be 26 inches.

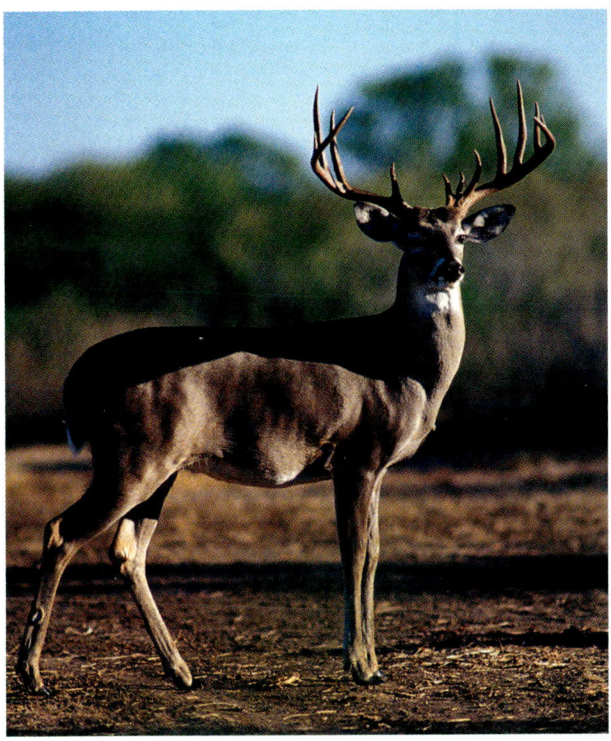

4 1/2

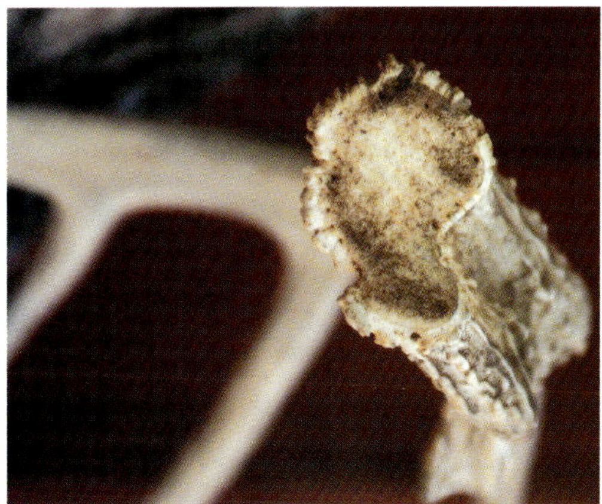

An injury to this buck's left pedicle caused some interesting antler anomalies throughout its life.

The following year the rancher decided it was time to let his hunters go after this buck, because, while there was no way to be certain of his age, he was mature. I am sure another determining factor was that he had become extremely elusive and was rarely seen. I never saw him to get a photograph that year, but a hunter did catch up to him. He was aged at 6 1/2 and scored 166 6/8 B&C, so the rancher had been correct in holding off that first year and waiting to see how the buck would progress. The rancher commented that they never saw this buck with a doe or active in any way during the rut. He noted when the buck was harvested that he had very small testicles that were not descended, which may explain his small neck over the years. Also, after close inspection, the unique brow tines he grew over the years were the result of his base on his left antler being in the shape of a figure eight. This was probably due to a pedicle injury at a young age.

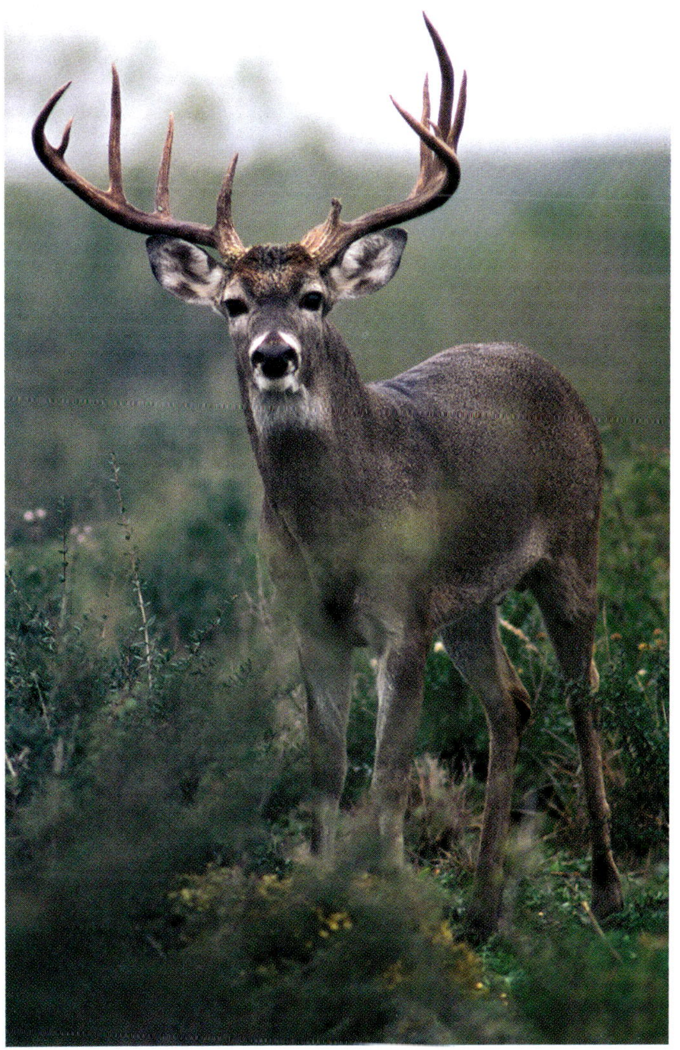

5 1/2

BUCK# 6

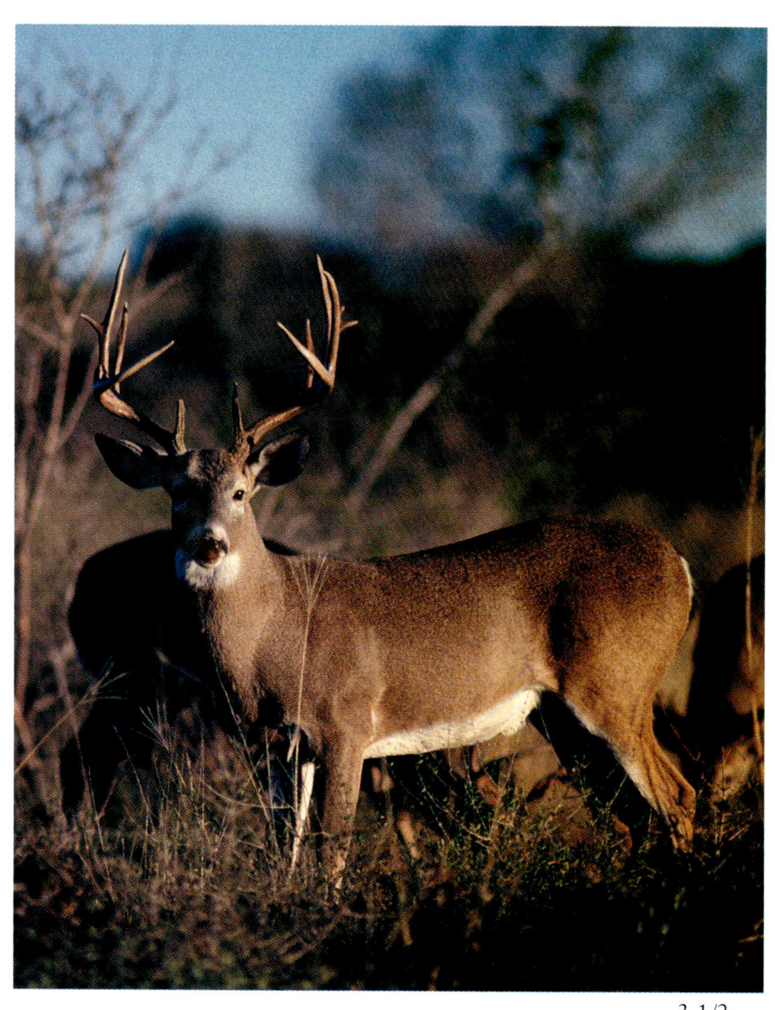
3 1/2

This was one of the most majestic bucks I've ever had the pleasure to photograph. It was not just because of his tall, straight antlers, but the way he carried himself with his head held high. It sounds funny, but he truly had a majestic posture. Many bucks appear as if their bodies are relaxed, but this buck always came in alert like he was surveying his domain.

3 1/2

I first saw him when he was 3 1/2. He was a basic 6x5 with nontypical points off his G-3s on both sides. He repeated that antler trait throughout his life. The photograph was taken in early December, and his neck and body are at their peak. It was during the rut, and his neck is swollen but not very large. His back and stomach are still straight, and it is relatively easy to see he is a young buck — if you don't look at his antlers. He had already broken his G-4 and G-5 on the right side in a fight. His antlers showed great potential, but we had no idea at the time just how magnificent he would become.

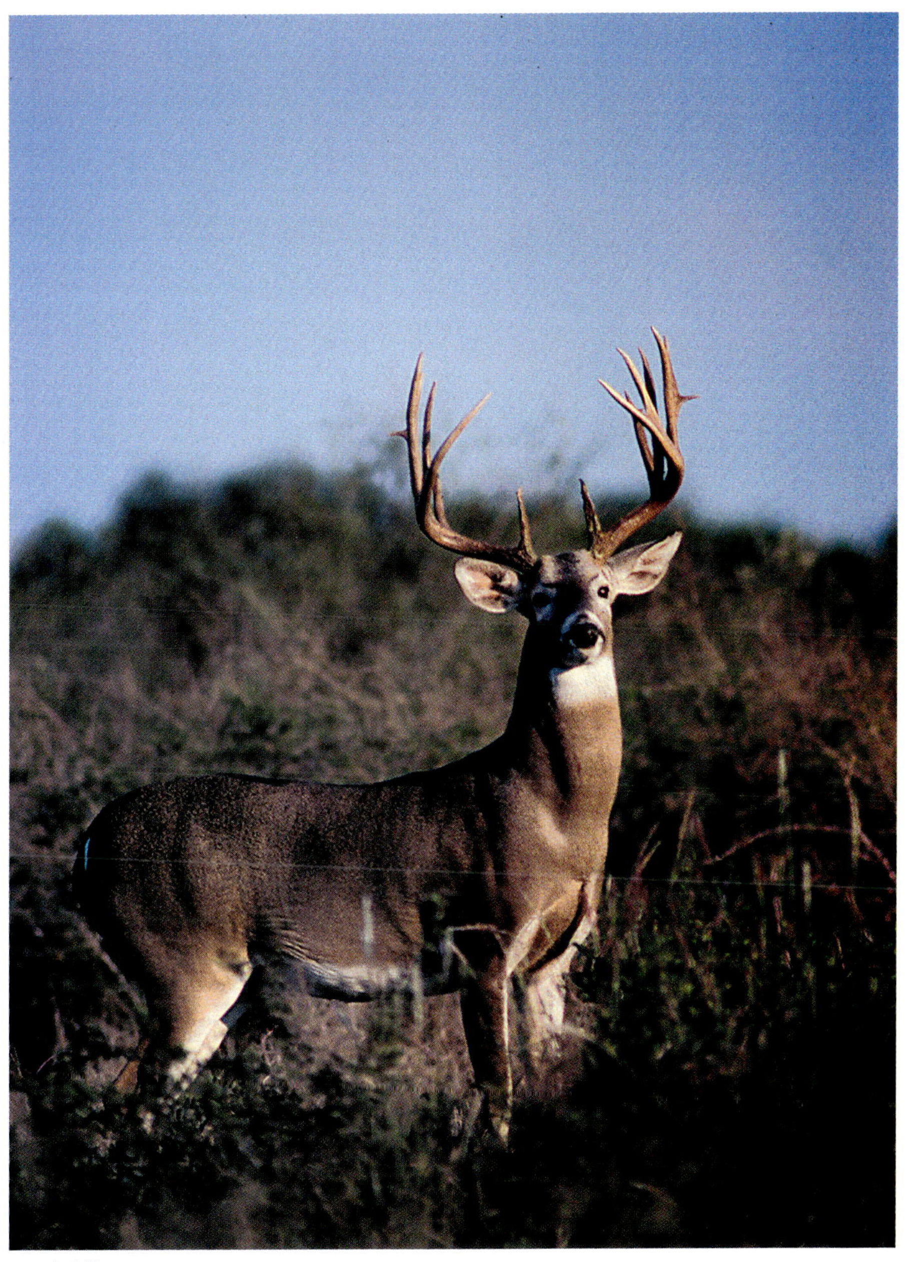

4 1/2

4 1/2

The next fall I could not wait to see him. In late September I was elated when he stepped out one afternoon sporting amazing 6x8 antlers. His G-3 and G-4 on the left side shared a common base and were both over 10 inches long. Years later, the rancher found his right shed. His beam was 25 4/8; G-1, 3 4/8; G-2, 6 7/8; G-3, 11 5/8 +1 2/8; G-4, 10 3/8; G-5, 6 6/8; H-1, 4 2/8; H-2, 3 5/8; H-3, 4; H-4, 3 7/8; totaling 81 6/8 inches. By estimating the measurements on the left antler from photographs, and using the known measurements of the right antler, the buck would have scored in the high 170s B&C. However, he was just getting started.

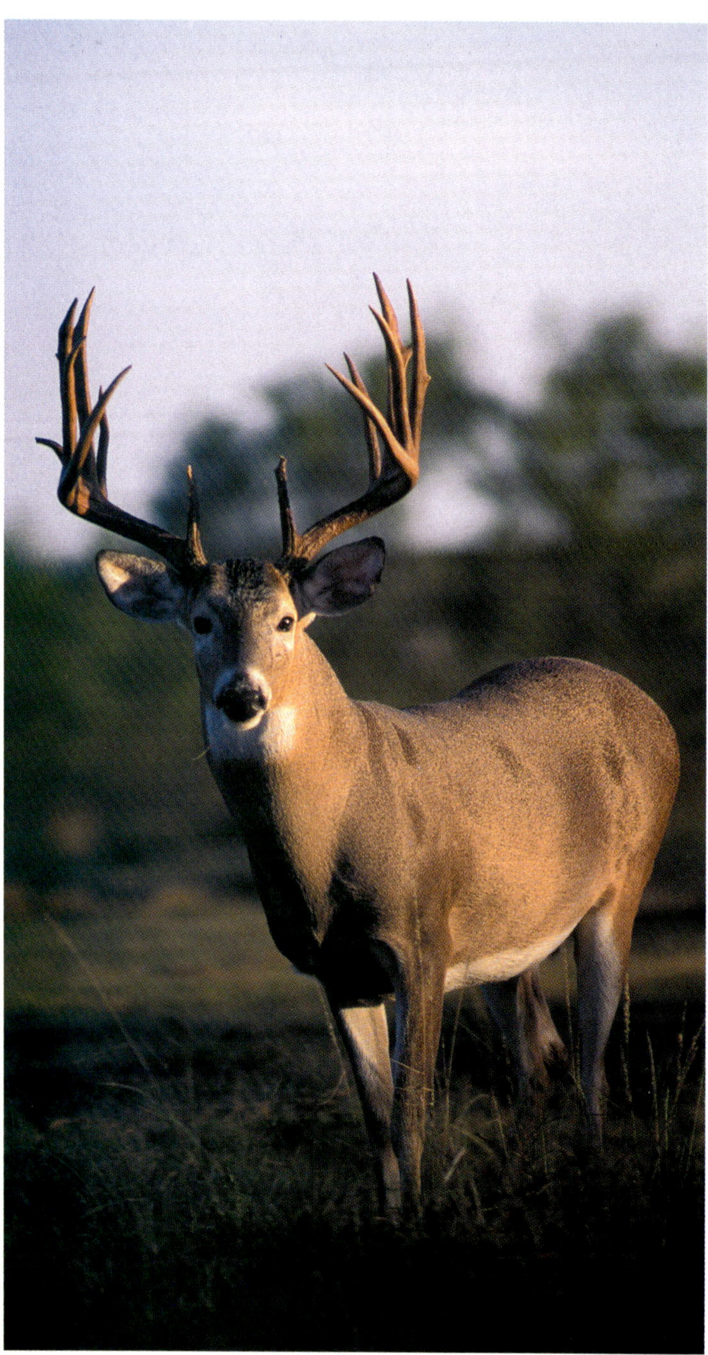

5 1/2

5 1/2

At 5 1/2 he was a 6x7 with nontypical points again off both sides of his G-3s with an abnormal point sharing the base with the G-3 on the right antler. It was apparent his body had bulked up from the previous year, and his neck, chest, and stomach were fuller. He also had gained quite a bit of mass, and it appeared he did so without losing much tine length, which is the case with some bucks. He had moved to another area about two miles from where I had observed him the two previous years. I saw him a number of times that fall but, as the hunting season approached, he became scarce. I did not see him again until late January after the season. It was at last light one evening, and he had busted up his antlers and was pretty lean due to the rut. It was too dark to take a photograph, but I was just happy to see him back in his home range. That was the last time I saw him that year.

6 1/2

The next fall he was more magnificent than ever at 6 1/2. His tine lengths had increased from his brow tines to his G-4s, and he had maintained his mass. His antlers were a 6x6 with his G-4 on the right sporting a deep fork and two small nontypical points. He also had an abnormal point growing out of his right base that curved backward. His body appeared to be in great shape, and his neck was already bulking up in late October (when this photo was taken) making his face appear smaller than his neck. Notice he has quite a bit of excessive skin under his chin, and the hair patch on the forehead has grayed considerably. I only saw him a few times that October and there was no doubt he was the dominant buck in his area. Now turn to page 185, and test your skills at judging this trophy buck.

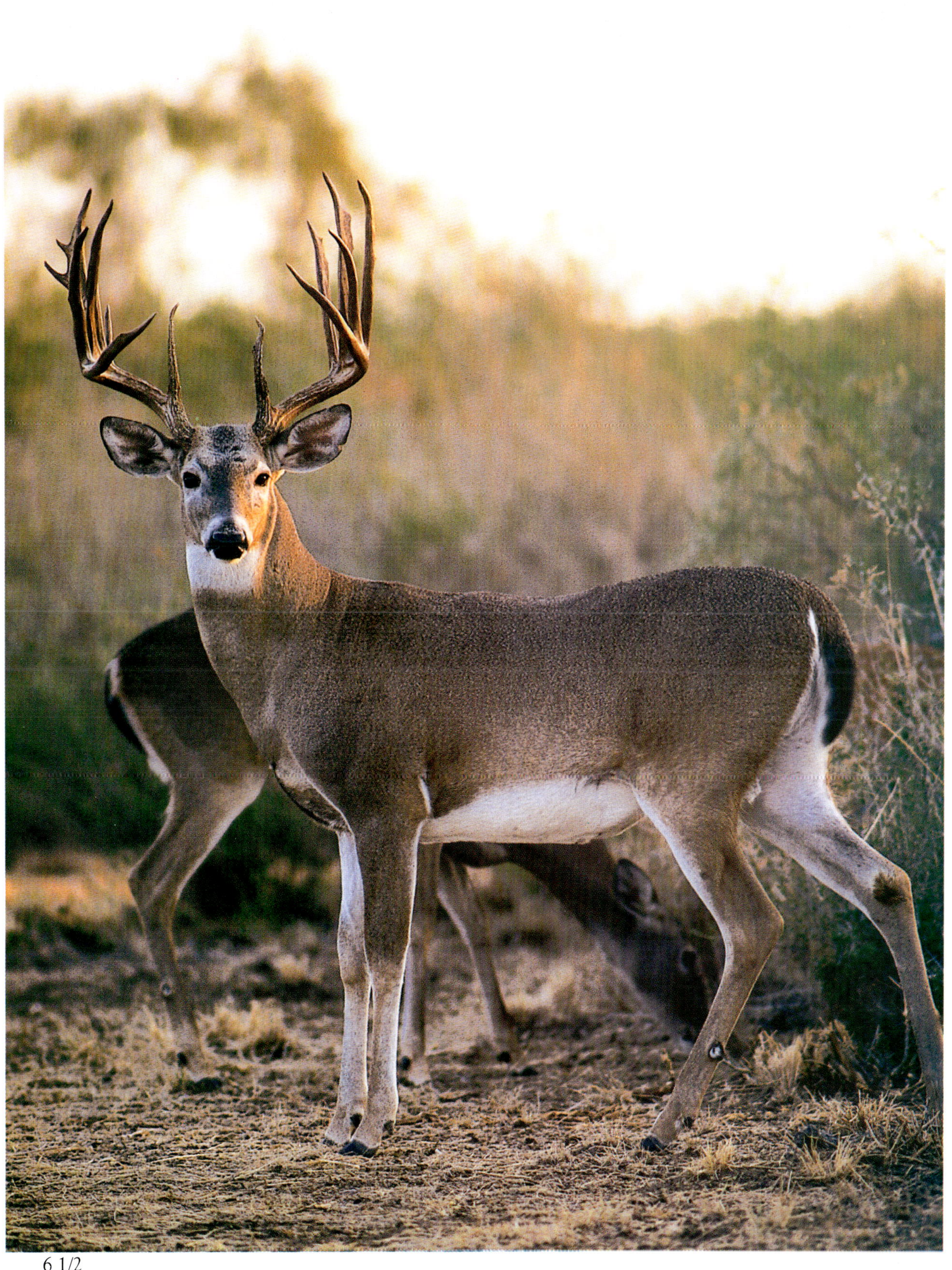

6 1/2

BUCK # 7

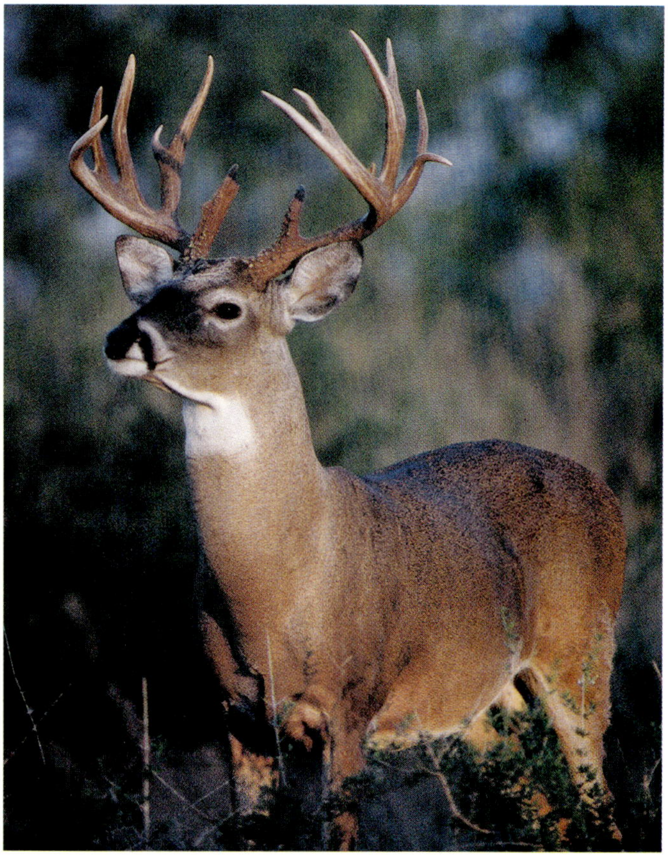

4 1/2

4 1/2

The first year I photographed this buck he was 4 1/2 and a basic 10-point with kickers off both G-2s and a split left G-3. His neck and stomach were muscular and taut, which is characteristic of a 4 1/2-year-old. Whenever he was around, buck #6 would be close by. This was not so unusual when they were young, but these two bucks continued to run with each other as mature bucks. When most bucks were splitting from their summer bachelor groups, these bucks remained together. I watched them feed side by side on numerous occasions, and I never saw either of them display any aggression toward each other. I did see them separately during the rut when one or the other was with a doe, but they would be back together again the next week. They both displayed very distinct, rectangular throat patches, and I wondered if they could have been twins or from the same doe in consecutive years. Whatever the reason, their compatibility allowed for a couple of my most treasured photographs of two south Texas monster bucks together. Pardner, as he became nicknamed because of his compatibility to buck #6, was also unique for another reason. I will never forget sitting in the pitch dark waiting for dawn and hearing something moving in the brush. As the first rays of light dawned, Pardner was standing like a statue in the edge of the brush. He had been there for more than 30 minutes watching and waiting perfectly still to be sure everything was safe. After does and other younger bucks came in, he also would eventually come in with buck #6 a few yards behind. I witnessed this on several occasions over the two years I photographed him and was always impressed by his patience and caution.

5 1/2

This year he was a basic 10-point again without the nontypical points, but his antlers had really gained in mass and tine length. He also showed a lot of palmation on his left antler from his G-2 to his G-4. His body filled out at 5 1/2 and showed his maturity. His neck and brisket showed no distinction where they join, making his neck and brisket appear as one continuous muscle. His stomach and back had noticeable sags, and his face started appearing fuller with excess skin under his chin. His overall body appeared thicker, and his legs appeared short for his body. I saw him several times at 5 1/2 until late January that year, and he appeared to be in great shape after the rut. I was looking forward to seeing what his antlers would do at 6 1/2, but that fall buck #6 showed up by himself. Most bucks become more elusive with age, especially those 6 1/2 and older, which may have been the case with Pardner. As mentioned previously, he was always very cautious and patient, even as a youngster. However, like many mature bucks, he could have experienced any number of mishaps from a rattlesnake, predator, or another buck.

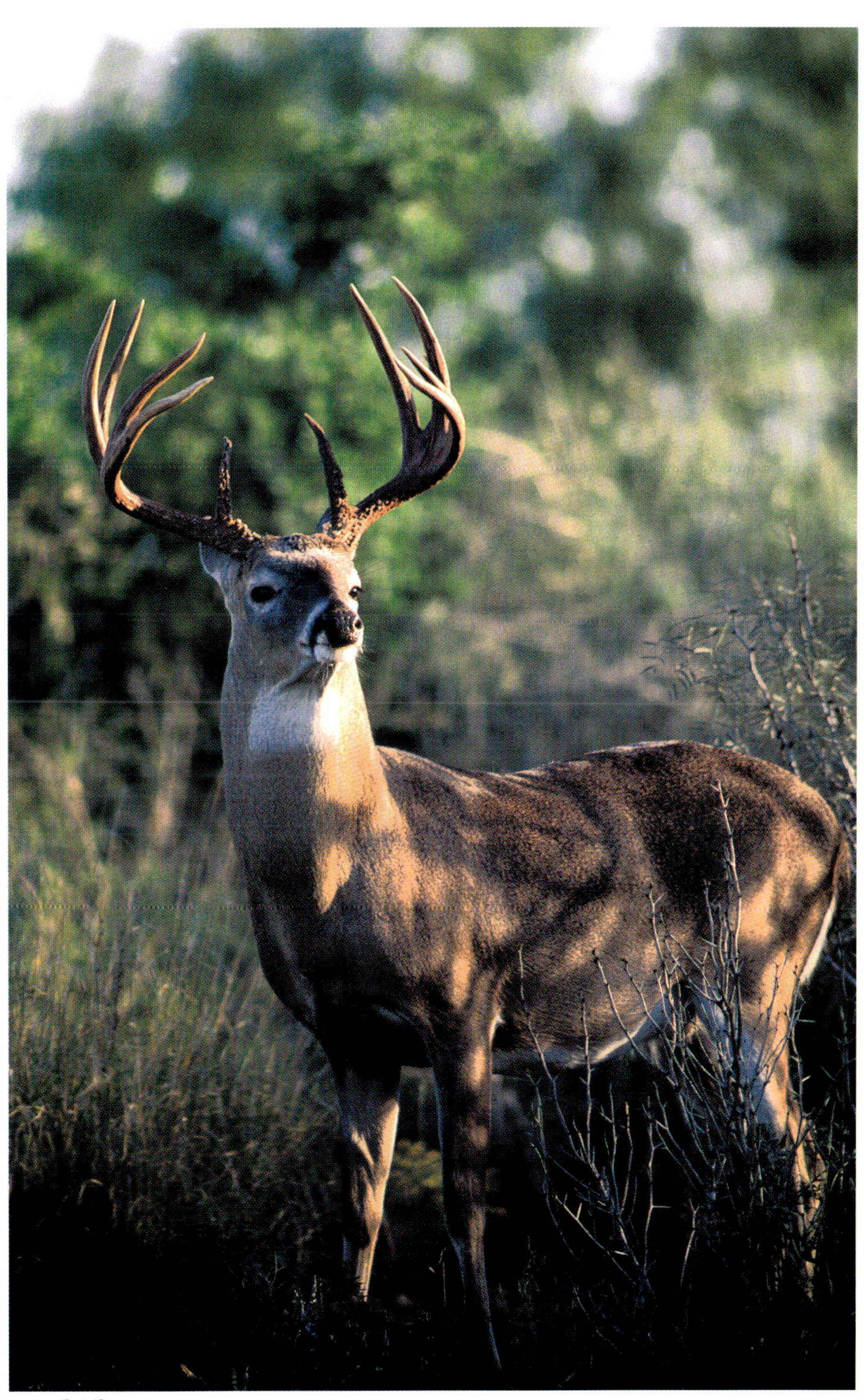

5 1/2

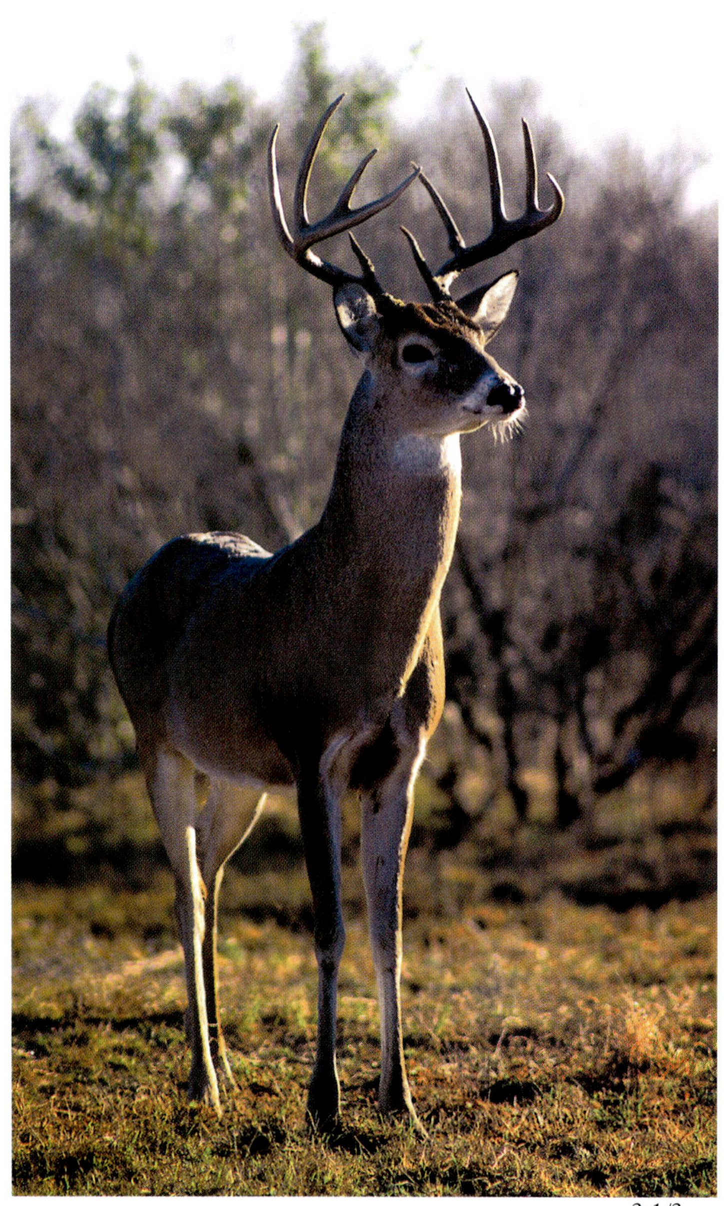

2 1/2

BUCK# 8

2 1/2

The first time I observed this buck he stuck out in the crowd. At 2 1/2 he had beautiful, symmetrical 10-point antlers and very distinct white forelegs that made him appear as if he were wearing white socks. He also had a very white muzzle mark that ran all the way to his throat patch. The photo shown was taken in late January, and he was with eight does at the time. He would run with his head held about a foot off the ground behind the does, and he stopped twice that morning to lip curl for several seconds, then started chasing one of the does again. I remember it impressed me, because I don't see many 2 1/2-year-olds on this ranch running does — there are just too many mature bucks.

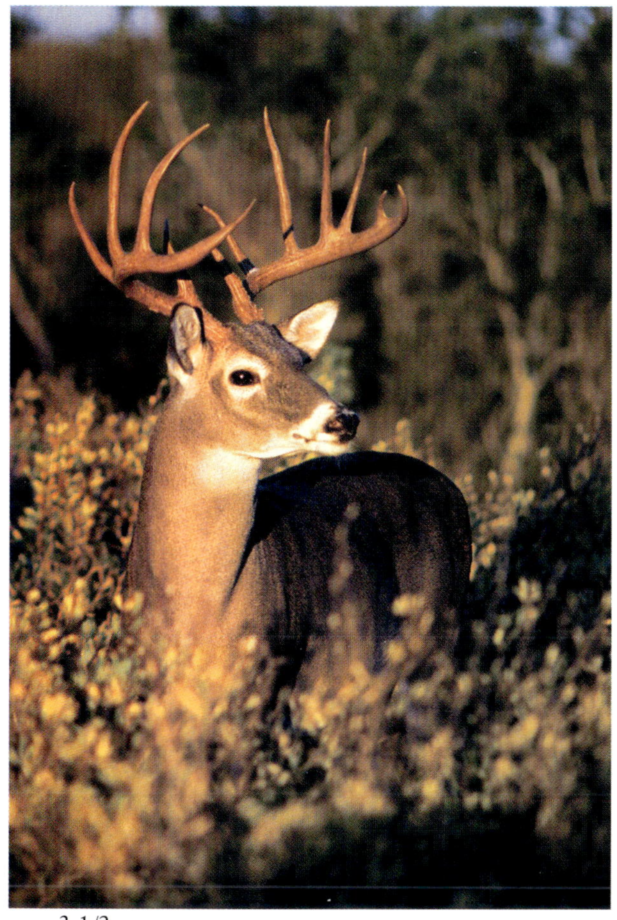

3 1/2

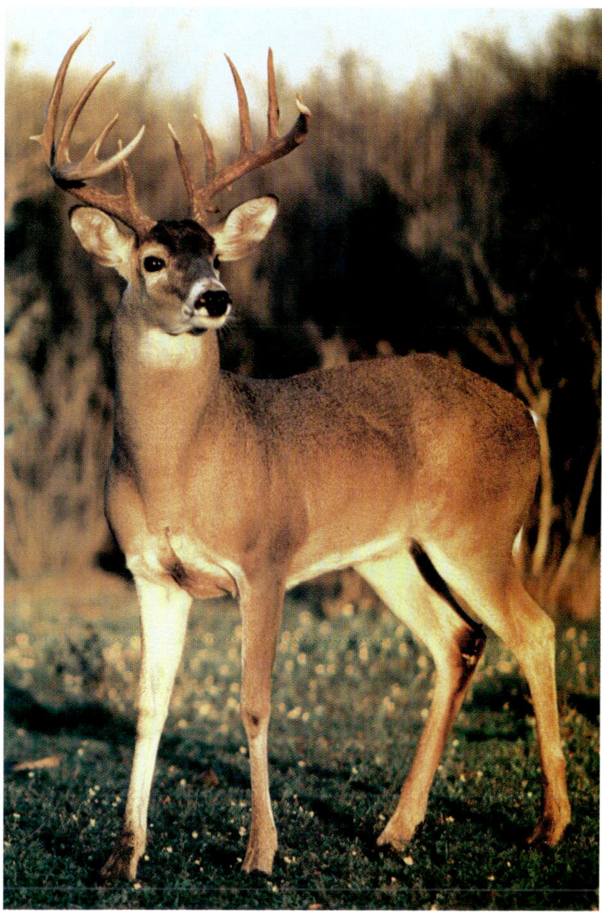

4 1/2

3 1/2

I was very excited when I saw him the next fall because he was a beautiful 5x7. I also noticed that he had become more aggressive toward other bucks. Late that season he got into one heck of a fight and broke his left antler off just above the brow tine. He was limping terribly and his back right leg was injured. It did not appear broken, but I wondered if he was going to survive and, if he did, how it would affect his antlers the next year.

4 1/2

The next fall, he showed up one afternoon at his old haunt, and immediately I noticed his left antler was stunted and smaller. He was a 6x6, but the G-5 on his left antler was only about an inch long. Apparently, the injury to his back right leg the previous season had impacted his antler development on the left side. The good news was he was no longer limping, so I hoped he would bounce back the next year. The photo shown was taken in late January after the rut, and he is much slimmer than when I saw him in the fall. His body appears to have lost 25 or more pounds. Notice that his tarsals are dark and the stain runs down the back of his leg.

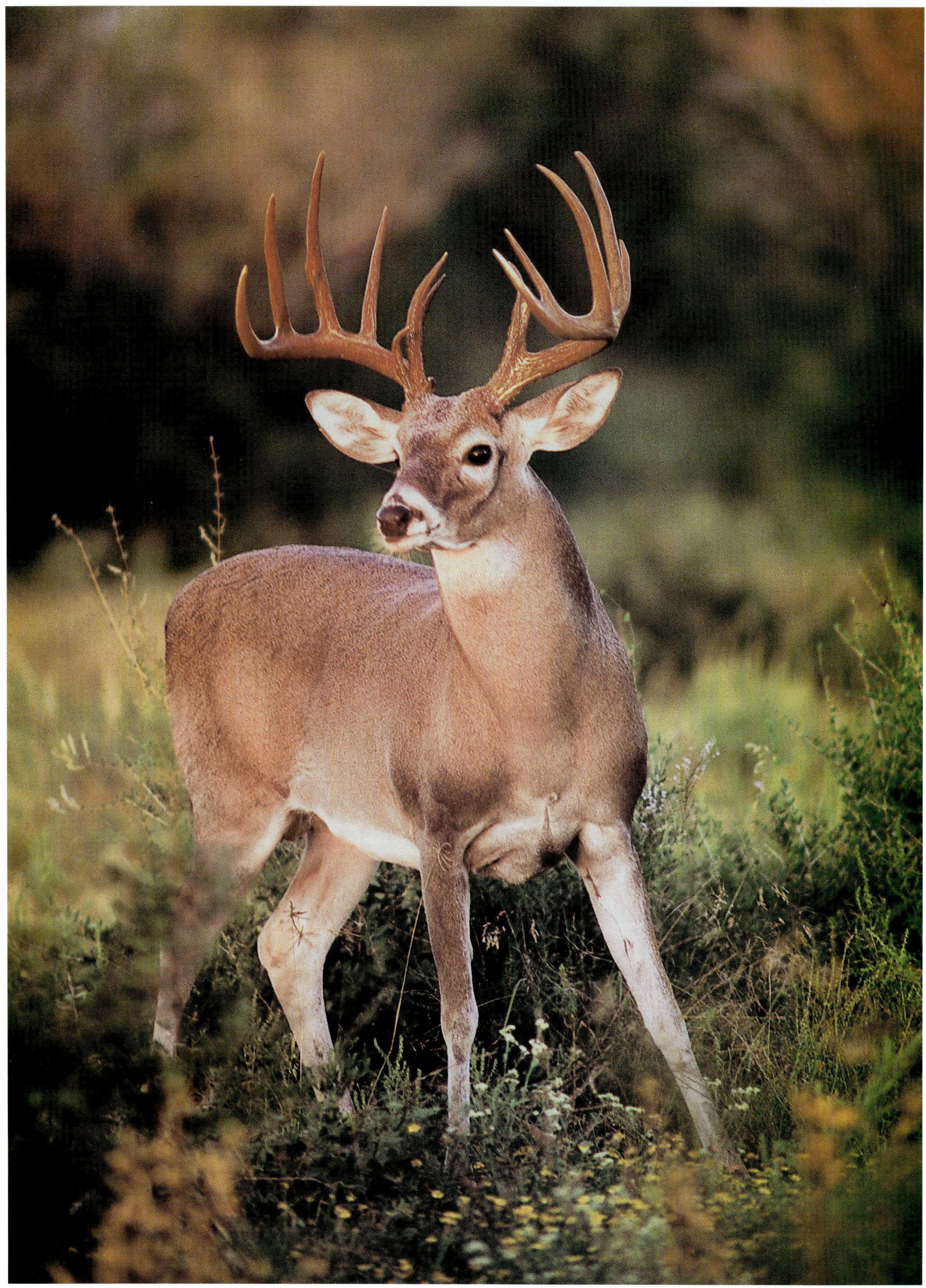

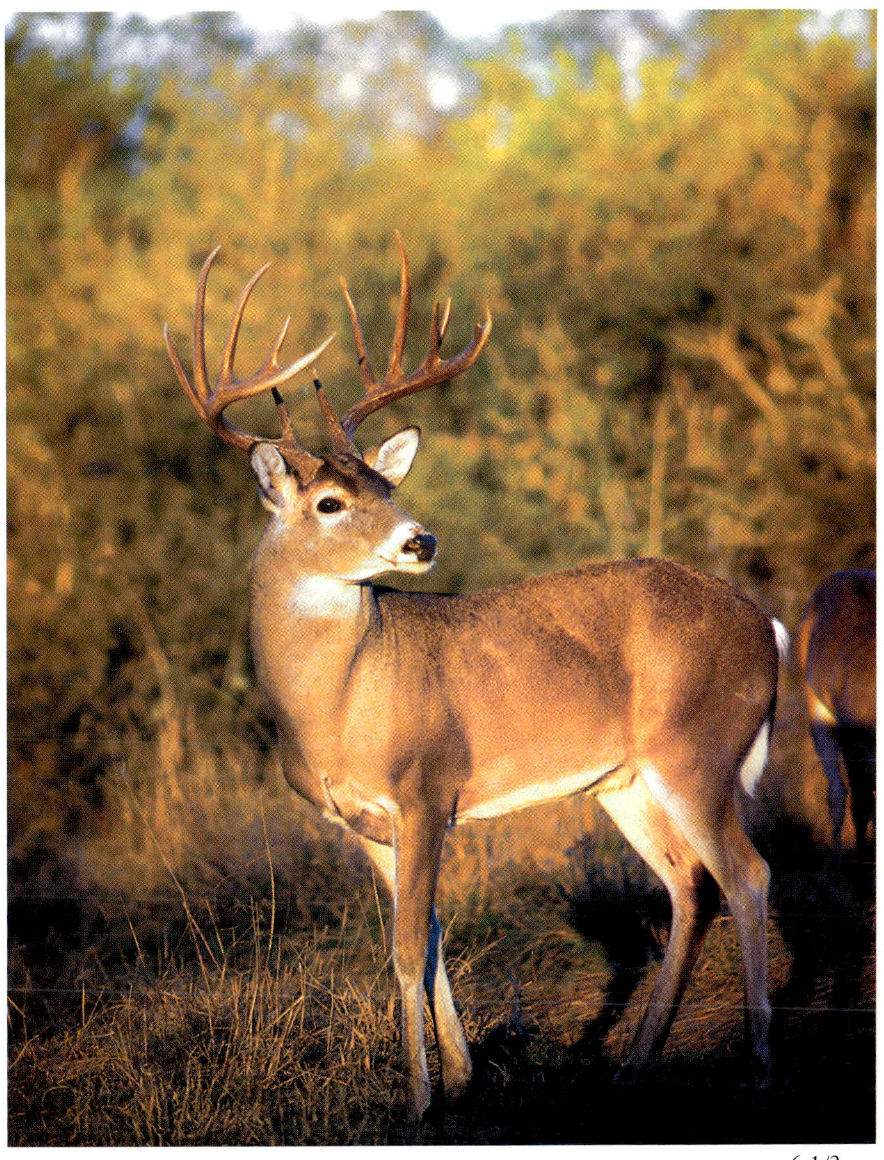

6 1/2

5 1/2

The next year my oldest son James and I were just about to slip out of a blind when motion caught my eye. It was early October and I was elated to see this mature buck coming straight toward us, and his antlers appeared bigger than ever. He was an impressive 8x7 due to multiple brow tines and appeared to be completely healed. I saw him a couple of times during the rut, and he seemed to be in great shape. I hoped he would stick to the does and keep out of a fight, having learned his lesson. However, late in the season after the rut, it was apparent he had gotten into another fight. He was limping badly and his body appeared pretty rundown and poor.

6 1/2

Apparently his injuries had not been as bad as when he was 3 1/2, because when I caught up with him the next year his antlers showed no abnormalities. The multiple brow tines were gone, but he was an impressive 6x7. The photo was taken in late January well after the peak of the rut, so his neck had already begun decreasing in size, and his body was much trimmer than when I saw him earlier in the season. However, his tarsals were still dark to the top of the hoof, indicating he was still ready to participate if a receptive doe should become available.

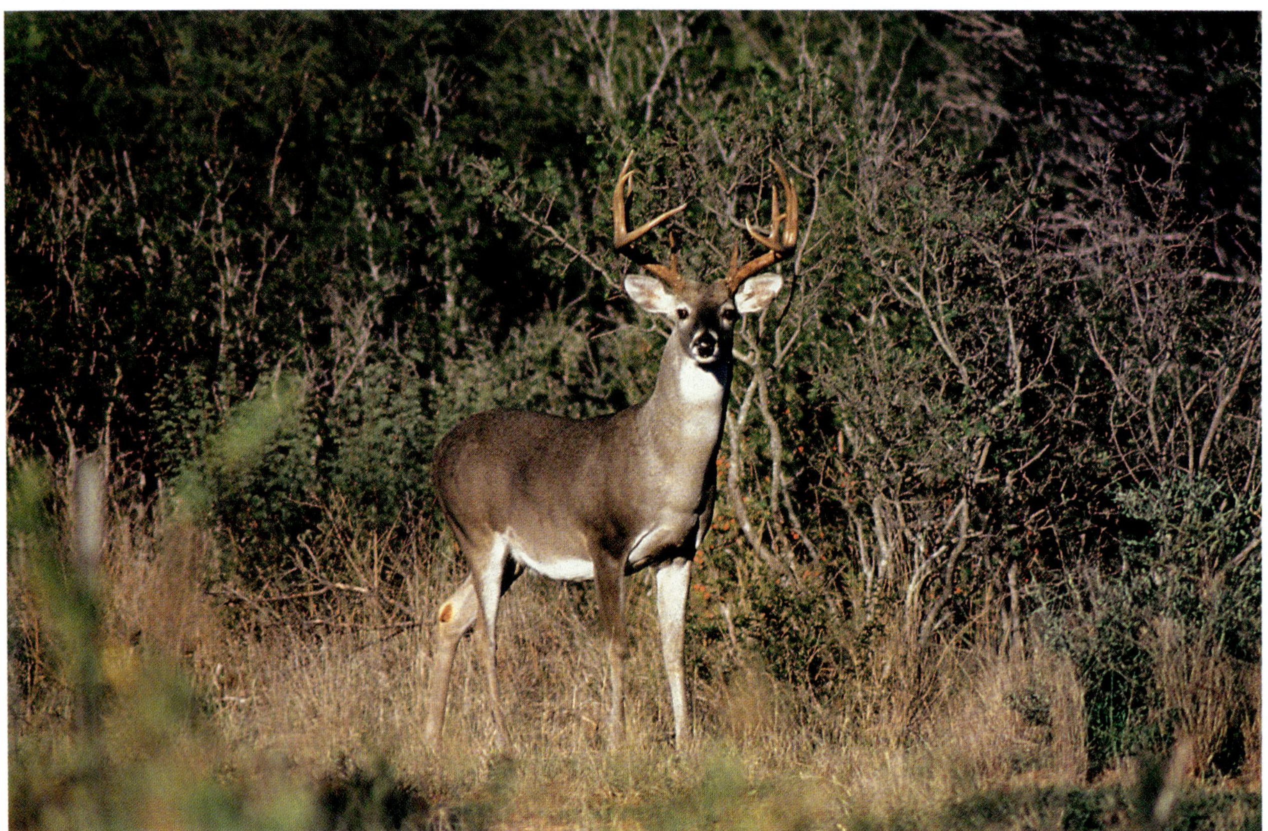

5 1/2

BUCK# 9

5 1/2

This buck was one of the wildest I have ever photographed. This photo of him at 5 1/2 is the only time I saw him that year. At the first picture, he heard the camera and spun around and was gone. Only getting to view him for a few seconds that first encounter, I noticed he had long beams and a picket fence on top of them. Note that his body appears firm, but his stomach is sagging. It was fall and his neck was slightly swollen and his tarsals still lightly colored.

6 1/2

I only saw him twice that year and, as before, after he heard my camera he did not stick around. I managed to snap three pictures in a few seconds, and then he was in the brush. It was apparent he had broken a brow tine and a G-5 on his right antler in a fight. It was late in the season after the rut, and his neck had already shrunk, but his neck and brisket still appeared as one muscle and showed no distinction where they meet. His back had a sag in it, and his tarsals were very dark, but he had run

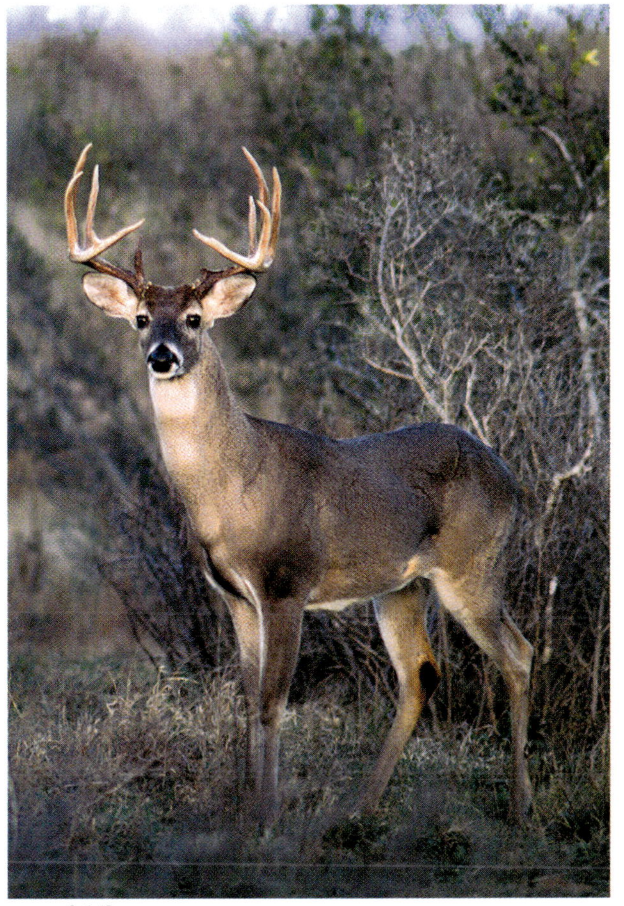

6 1/2

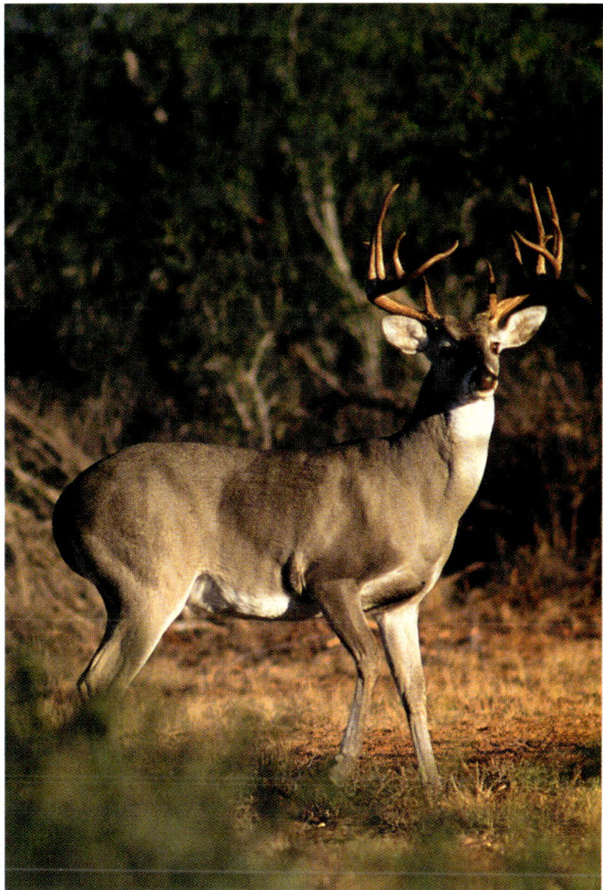

7 1/2

off his stomach during the rut. A couple of months earlier he would have been much fuller in the midsection with a noticeable stomach sag. This is why it is always important to consider the time of year and what their body is going through when aging a buck.

7 1/2

At 7 1/2 I only saw him once and got a few photographs before he turned and ran off as wild-eyed as ever. It was early in the fall before the rut, but his neck was already starting to swell. His body appeared very full and showed numerous ripples in his neck, chest, and stomach. When he walked his body jiggled, appearing flabby instead of firm, which is very characteristic of a 7 1/2-year-old buck. He was a long-beamed 6x6 with small kickers off his G-3s on both sides. A hunter finally caught up to him that season, which surprised me because he was one of those bucks that was only spotted once a season. Of all the bucks in this book, he was probably the least likely to make it into this section because I never thought I would get photos of him in consecutive years. Turn to page 183 and try to judge him in about 30 seconds, and you will have more time than the hunter who finally harvested him.

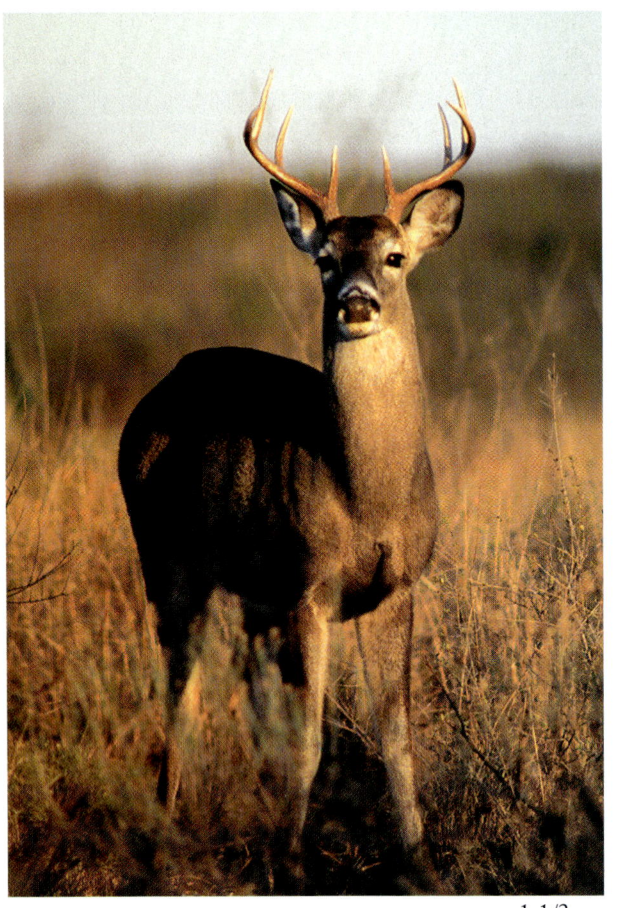

1 1/2

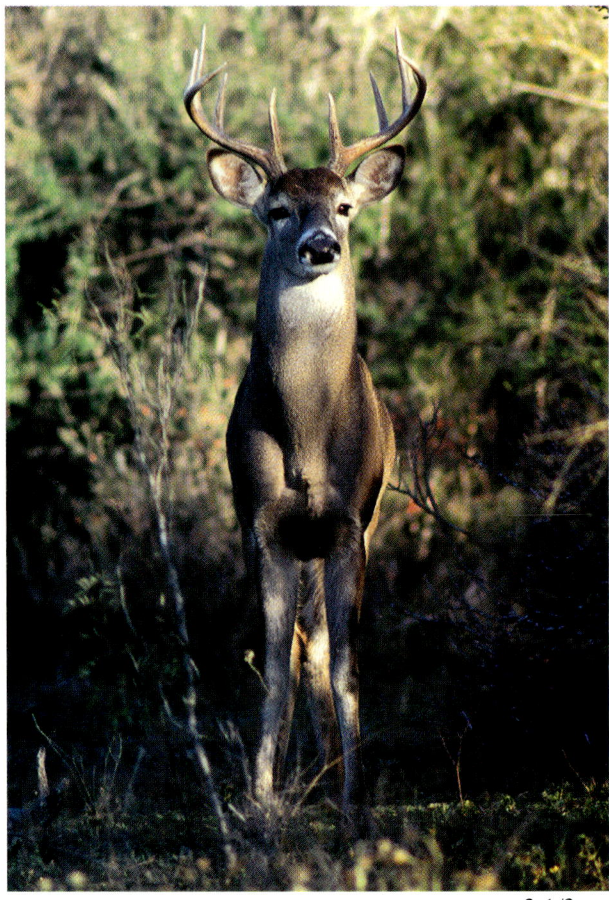

2 1/2

BUCK# 10

1 1/2

Every year I try to photograph as many young bucks as possible. However, it can be extremely tough to point my camera lens at a 1 1/2-year-old buck when a 160-class or better buck is in the vicinity. There are always exceptions, such as a 1 1/2-year-old buck that is spectacular in some way or that has easily-recognizable features like a notch in his ear. This was one of those bucks. At 1 1/2, he had seven points, but what really set him apart were his long, straight brow tines. His ears were black all the way around like they had been highlighted with eyeliner. He also stood with his front legs very close together and his head held high when he approached. It is easy to notice, even during the rut when this photo was taken, that his neck is small and easily distinguishable from his brisket.

2 1/2

The first time I saw him at 2 1/2 he came walking out of the brush and stood with his front legs close together looking straight at me. He was a 10-point, and his antler spread was outside the ears. Again, his long, straight brow tines were what really stood out about him. It was during the rut when I photographed him, and his neck was fuller, but it was still easy to see that his neck was separate from his brisket and both his face and body appeared firm and tight.

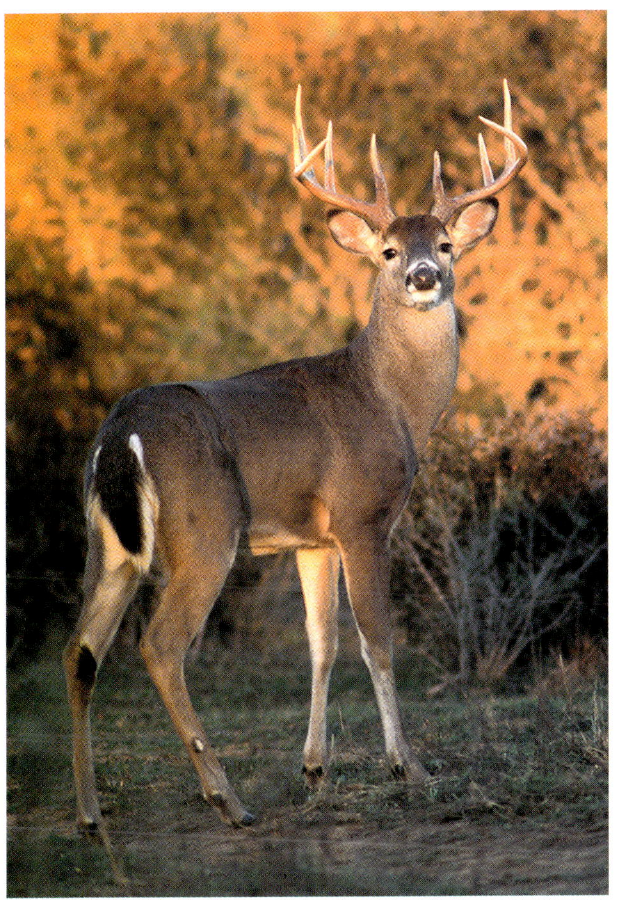
3 1/2

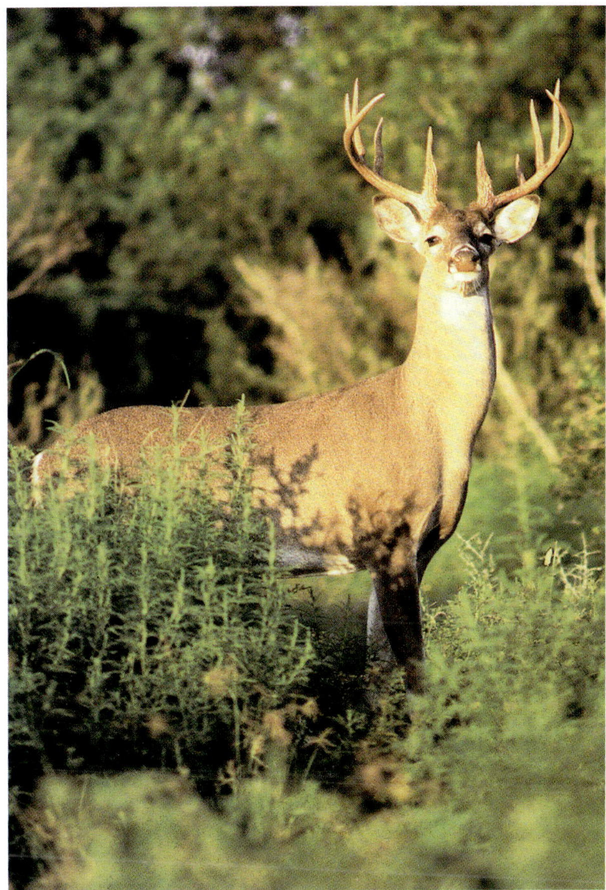
4 1/2

3 1/2

The next year he had grown in every category except number of points. I only saw him once, and he appeared to be a 9-point. He was missing the G-4 on his left antler. If he had knocked it off in a fight, he had knocked it clean off. However, he had grown in mass, spread, and tine length, and his brow tines were so long they appeared longer than his G-2s. The rut was on the wane, and his neck was still somewhat swollen. His stomach was taut, and his back was straight as a board with no signs of sagging. I noticed his tarsals were dark, but not all the way down the back of his leg to the hoof like a mature buck's would have been at that time of year.

4 1/2

In late September the following year, I got to watch this buck for only a couple of minutes. Fortunately, I got a couple of photos before he faded into the brush, because I never saw him again that year. As in the past, his brow tines were his most impressive feature, although he did have 10 points again. His G-2s lay back and were longer than they appear in the photograph. Notice that his neck is small due to the time of year. Even so, it is as thick as it was during the rut when he was 2 1/2 years old. By late November, I'm sure it was quite swollen and had a much different appearance. His back and stomach are still straight and taut, and there is no doubt his body is in its prime.

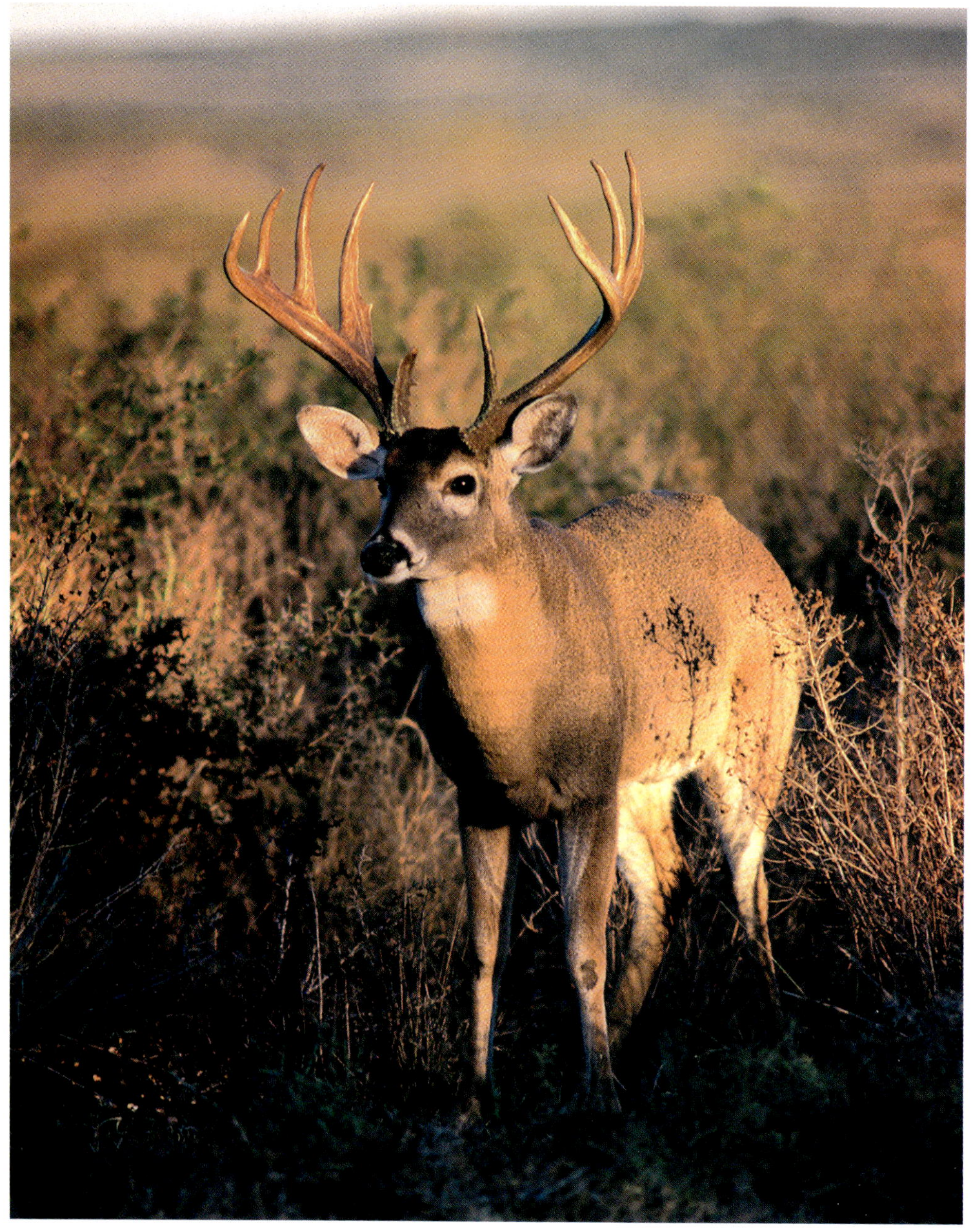

4 1/2

BUCK# 11

If a hunter first saw this buck when he was 4 1/2, they would find it difficult to age him. The younger the buck is when you first see him and learn to recognize him, the more confident you can be in your age estimate. Fortunately, the rancher saw this very recognizable buck when he was 2 1/2 and was able to properly age him. Even at 2 1/2, he was quite a sight with 12 points. At 3 1/2 he was a 6x5, and the rancher told me he was well on his way to becoming a monster buck. He also said that if he had not seen this buck in his early years, it would have been impossible to be sure about his age.

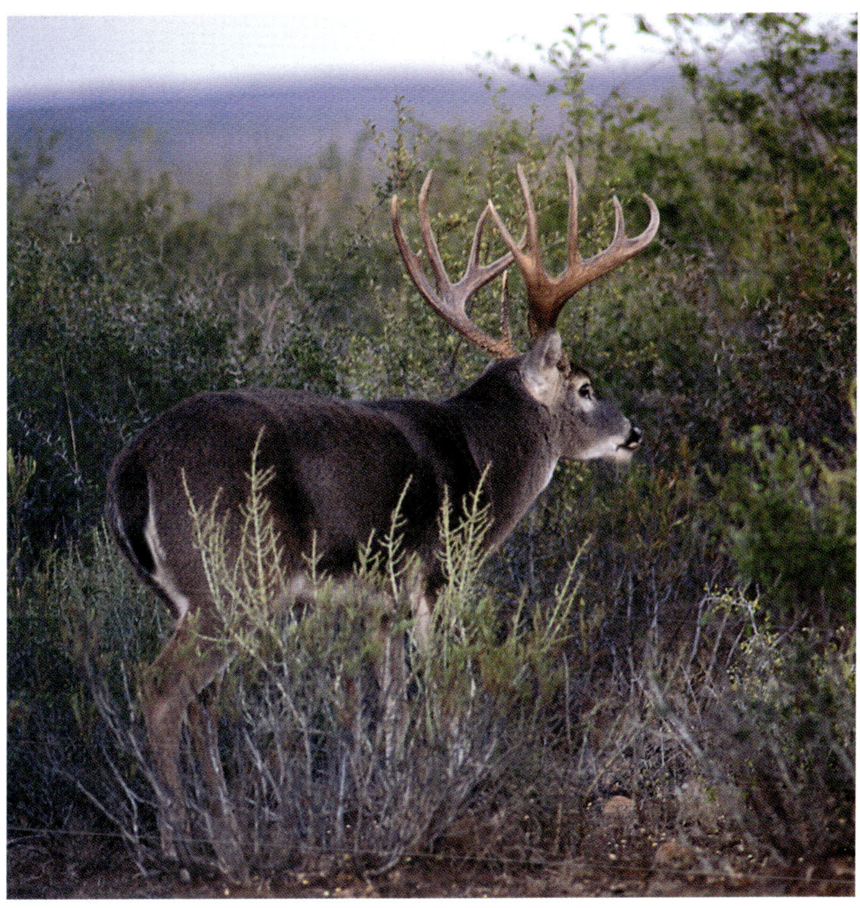

5 1/2

4 1/2

The first time I observed this buck he was 4 1/2, and I was amazed at how big he was in every dimension. Deer are just like livestock, with some animals having larger frames than others. This buck was definitely larger framed, even down to his legs. However, the same characteristics for aging still held true once we were able to look past his enormous size. When he was 4 1/2 he had already become very unpredictable, and I only saw him twice that year. One of those times was in late December. His neck was still swollen but not massive, and his stomach was full but not sagging. His antlers were a high, 6x5 frame, and his beams were extremely heavy.

5 1/2

At 5 1/2 he grew even bigger. He had great mass, especially from his G-2s to G-4s. He grew a forked G-2 on his right antler and a small bump on his left G-2 that we thought might become a point the next year. I sat several times that year to get this photo, and late in the season he came in right before dark. Another buck must have been nearby as his hair is standing erect. Even with some cactus in the way, it is easy to see his body is full, but his stomach is not starting to sag, and his back is still straight.

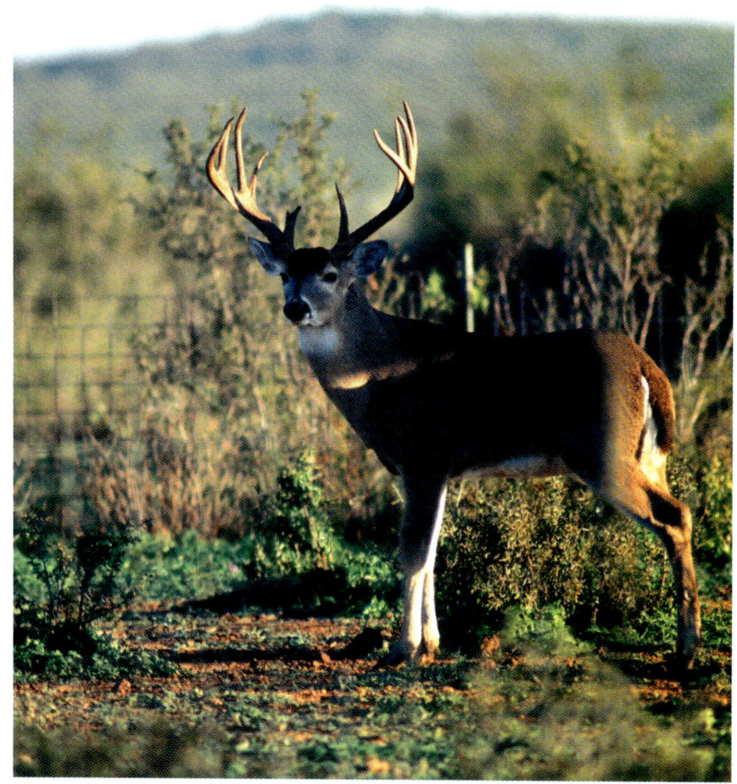

6 1/2

considering he had been shot in the brisket only two months prior. The deer season was over and it appeared he would be around for another year. This photo was taken well after the rut, and it is easy to see at 6 1/2 that his neck and brisket appear as one muscle showing no distinction where they meet. His stomach is not sagging, but I believe that is primarily due to his trauma earlier in the year and the fact that the photo was taken in the post-rut period. The photo also demonstrates how mature bucks, even in the post-rut, appear heavier in their front end due to their massive neck, shoulders, and brisket.

6 1/2

At 6 1/2 the rancher decided to allow his hunters to attempt to harvest this buck because he was so elusive. I knew a hunter was hunting hard for him, so I figured I would not get a photo of him that year. A hunter did get a shot but hit him low in the brisket. There was very little blood, and the buck was not found, so everyone hoped he had a superficial wound that would heal. Late that January, the rancher informed me they thought they had seen him. I set up where I had photographed him before and was rewarded with this photograph. His antlers were a massive 5x6. When I took the photo, he had already broken part of his left brow tine, and it appeared he had knocked off his G-2 clean at the beam. His beams appeared to be even more palmated than the previous year. He had a slight limp, but appeared to be in great shape

7 1/2

The next season the rancher's son spotted this old buck and informed me of his whereabouts. It was late October, and he appeared to be in great physical shape. It was too early in the fall for his neck to have swollen to its full potential. However, his face already appears small in comparison to the thickness of his neck. His stomach was very full and both it and his back had noticeable sags. His antlers were an amazing sight with 10 points on the left and six points on the right. Similar to so many other bucks, he added numerous points in his seventh year. This was the only time I saw him that year, and a hunter harvested him later that season. Turn to page 198 and try your skills at judging a true Muy Grande!

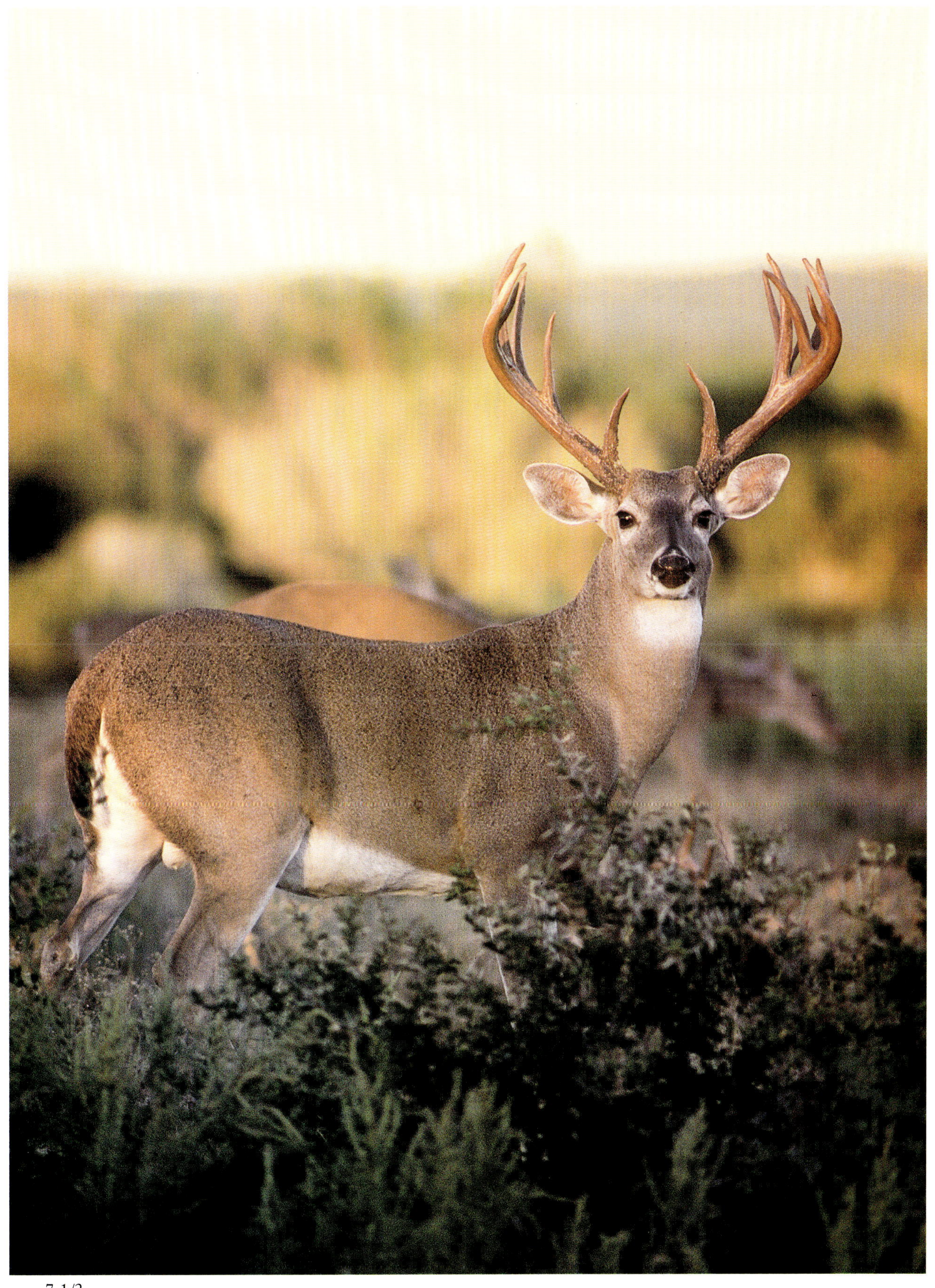

7 1/2

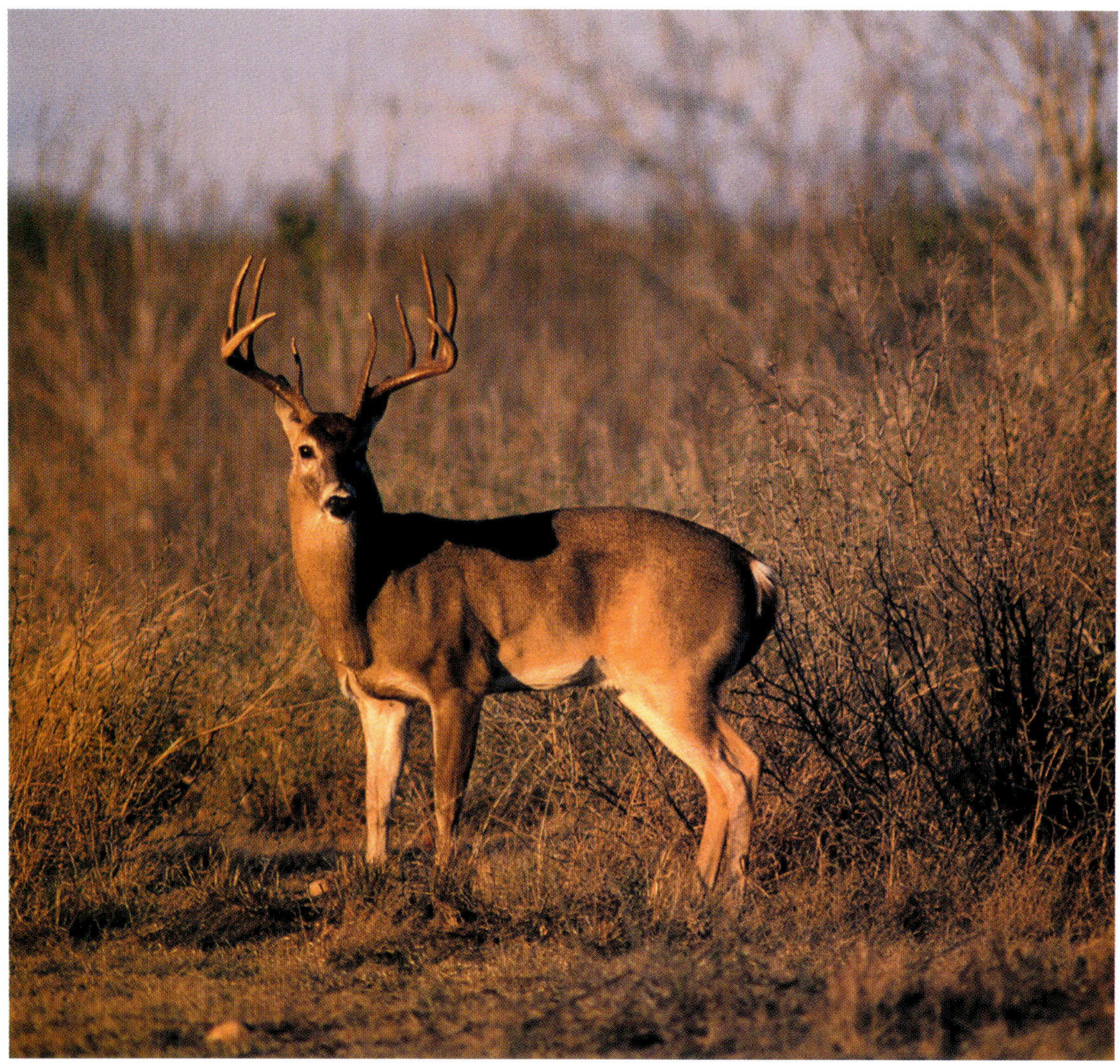
3 1/2

BUCK# 12

3 1/2

The first time I saw this buck he was 3 1/2 and had symmetrical 10-point antlers with long brow tines that flared out. It was during the rut when I took this photo and he had already broken his G-4. His neck was swollen, but his tarsals were fairly light and appeared small. His stomach was full but appeared taut and did not sag, and his back was still straight.

4 1/2

The next year at 4 1/2 he gained in spread and mass, and his antlers still possessed the long, flared brow tines making him easily recognizable. He also had a split fork on his right G-3. I only saw him a couple of times that year, and this photo was taken in early November. His neck was starting to swell, and his tarsals were already starting to darken.

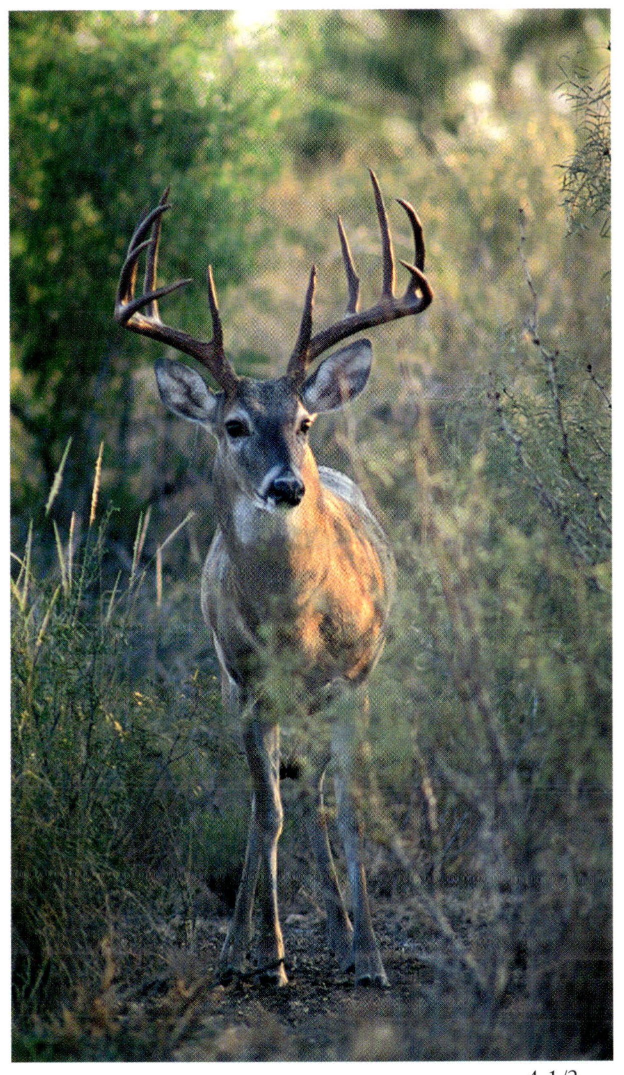

4 1/2

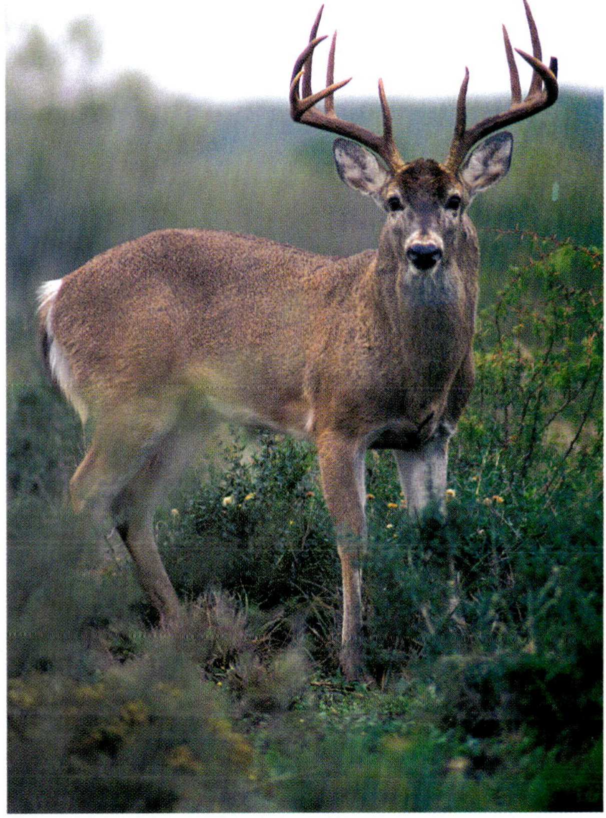

5 1/2

5 1/2

At 5 1/2 I only saw him once, and it was during the rut. When he approached he really put on a show, laying his ears back and erecting his hair while swaggering toward the other bucks. The two other younger bucks present at the time moved off quickly. He was clearly dominant. His neck was extremely swollen, and there was no distinction between it and the brisket where the two muscles join. I noticed that the hair on his forehead appeared longer and darker than it had in previous years. This is because the forehead glands of mature bucks are more active during the rut, which darkens the hair. I also noticed his tarsals were very dark and appeared much larger than the previous year. His stomach did not have a definite sag, but it was well into the rut and, between chasing does and fighting, I am sure he had lost some weight. His antlers appeared to have a wider spread than in previous years, but looked very similar to his earlier sets of antlers except for the addition of a G-5 to his right side making him a 6x5. He had previously broken his G-4 on his left antler in a fight but appeared to be in very good physical shape. A few days after taking this photo, a hunter mistook him for an older buck he had been hunting in the same area. Even at 5 1/2, he was a dandy. If you turn to page 173, you can try your hand at judging him.

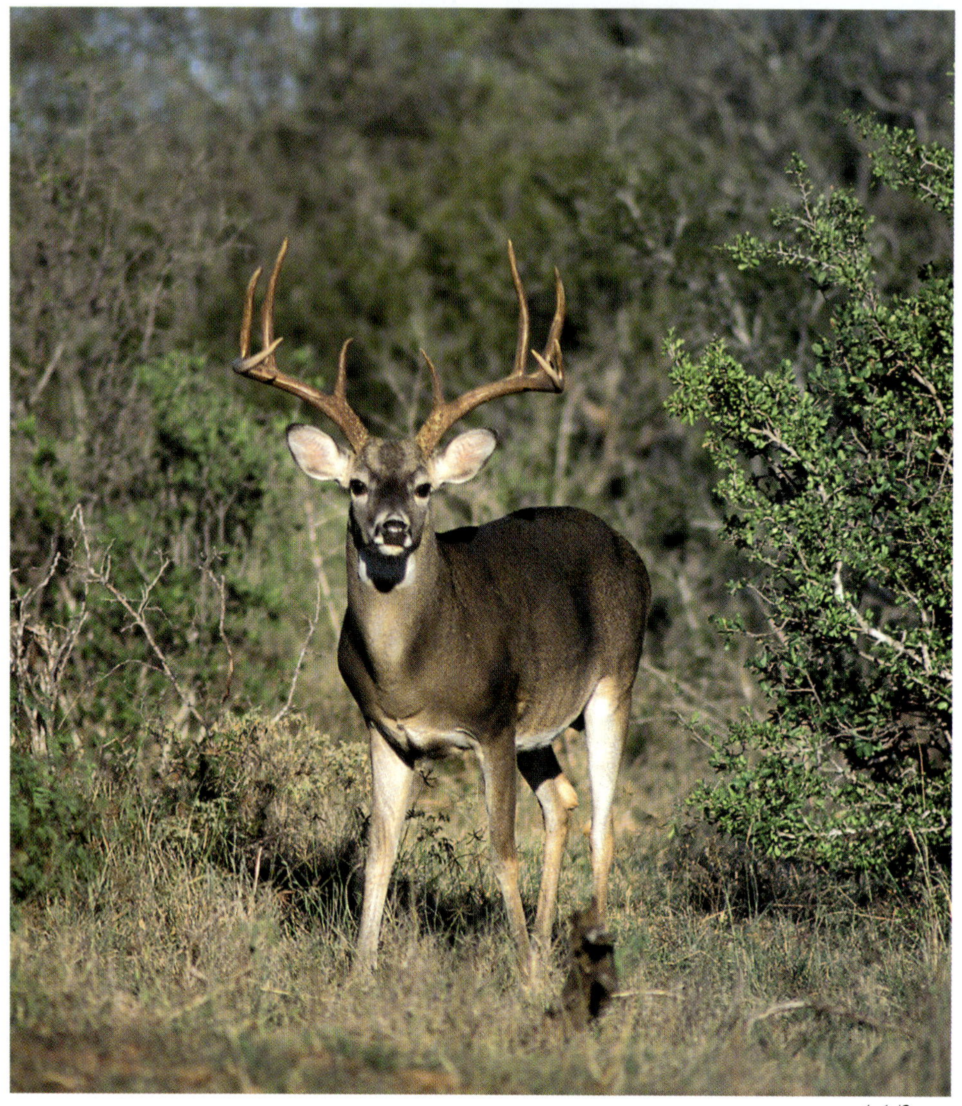
4 1/2

BUCK# 13

4 1/2

Many hunters believe that mature bucks with less than 10 points will never become trophies. At 4 1/2 this buck was well on his way to trophy status. He had an estimated spread of 24 inches and nine typical points. The photograph shown was taken in early October, and it is apparent he had fattened up after rubbing the velvet off his antlers in September. His neck had not started swelling as the rut was still ahead, and his tarsals were very light.

5 1/2

At 5 1/2 I only saw him a couple of times — he was becoming more wary as most bucks do with maturity. I noticed that his brow tines and G-2 on his left antler were almost identical to the previous year, only bigger. However, he was only an 8-point. This photograph was taken late in the rut, and his tarsals were large and dark, though his neck had already shrunk substantially. He had lost much of his stomach during the rut, another example of why you should consider the time of year when estimat-

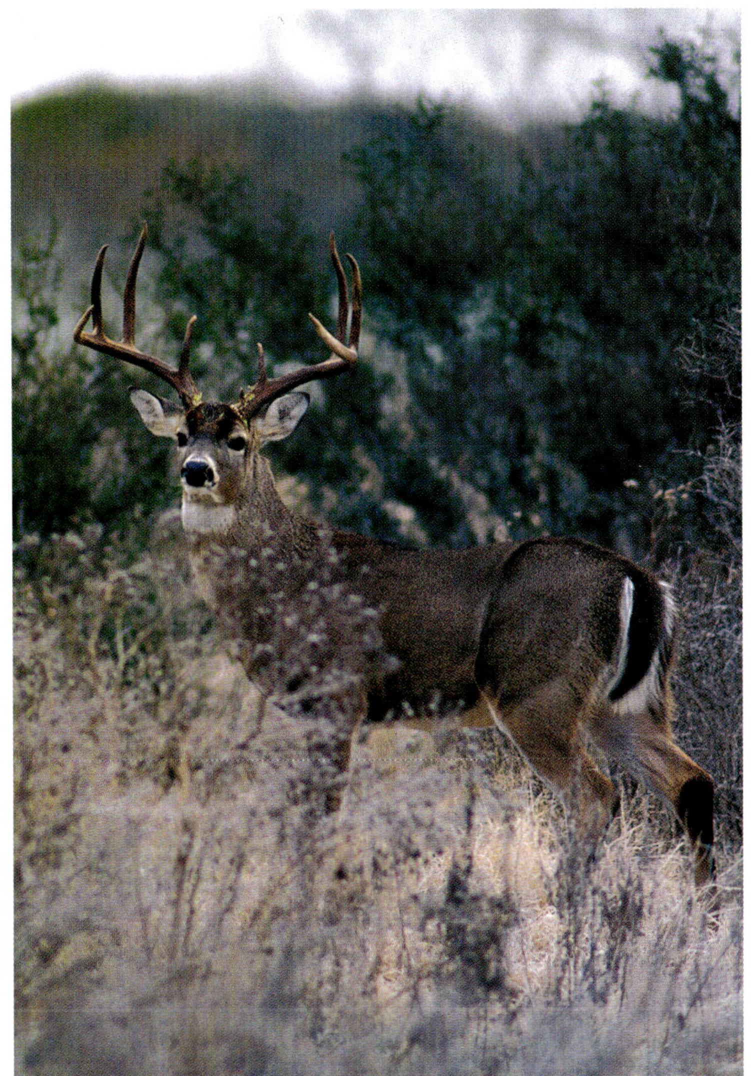

5 1/2

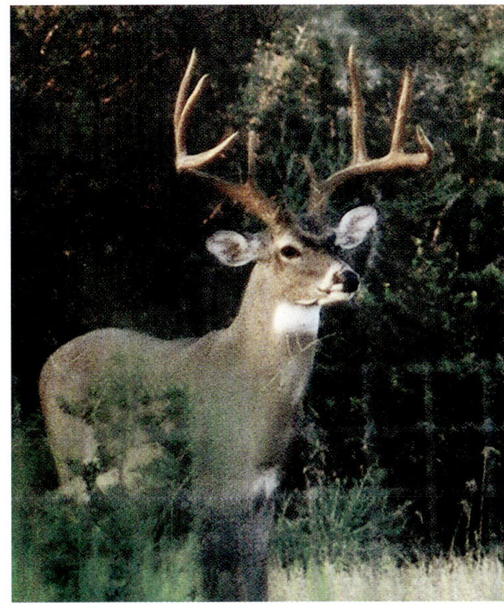

6 1/2

ing a buck's age. The rancher found his left shed antler that spring. The main beam measured 25 2/8 inches, G-1, 3 4/8; G-2, 11 2/8; G-3, 9 1/8; H-1, 4 7/8; H-2, 4 1/8; H-3, 3 5/8; H-4, 2 7/8; and he had a 1 3/8-inch abnormal point off his G-1.

6 1/2

The next year I sat several times waiting for this buck and only saw him once. Late one evening he came out of the brush, stopped, and I took this one photo. He then turned and went back into the brush and did not return. There were other bucks present, so I am not sure if he did not feel comfortable with one of them or sensed my presence. Either way, I was thankful for the opportunity to catch him on film that year. It was apparent that he had gained in mass and had maintained or even increased his spread and tine length. His neck and brisket had no distinction where they joined, and you can see his back and stomach are both starting to sag.

The next year at 7 1/2 the rancher saw him chasing a doe, but I never got to see him. He was a trophy 8-point if there ever was one, and I really wanted to get a photo of him. A hunter who devoted most of his hunting season to chasing this buck finally got him late that year. His inside spread was 26 1/8 with 27 3/8- and 26 4/8-inch beams, and he scored 166 gross B&C. Eight-point bucks of this caliber are more rare than B&C record-book bucks. I was thrilled to have gotten to observe him on the few opportunities I did over the years.

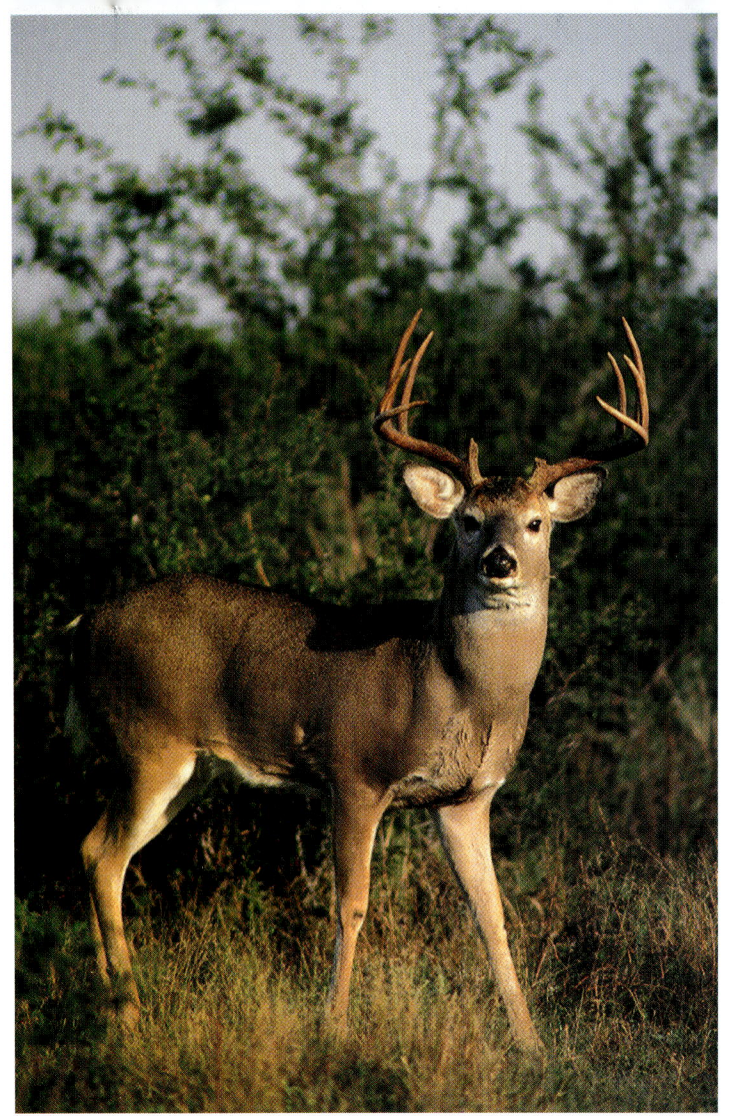

3 1/2

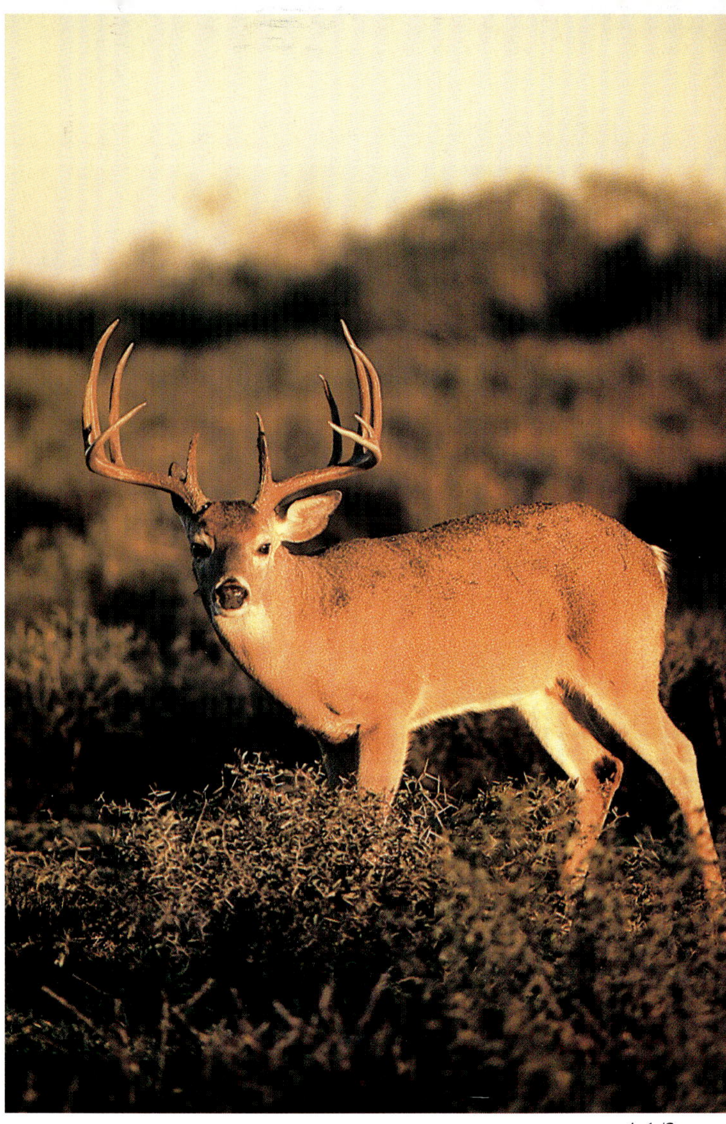

4 1/2

BUCK# 14

3 1/2

The first time I saw this buck his throat was extremely swollen. The rancher felt his swollen neck was the result of a rattlesnake bite. I could also tell he had previously been in a fight because of his broken brow tines. He was 3 1/2 that year, with a taut stomach, long, slender legs, and a young face, except for the swelling in his throat.

4 1/2

The following year his antlers increased in size significantly, which is typical of many bucks at that age. Their bodies have matured, and more of their nutritional intake is directed toward antler growth. He grew a G-5 on his left antler making him a 5x6. His G-2s, G-3s, and G-4s maintained their same shape, but were longer. Also, his neck and brisket began to appear as the same muscle. His stomach is fuller, but still not sagging. His tarsals are dark, but appear quite small.

5 1/2

At 5 1/2 he went back to a 5x5 with an abnormal point on his right G-1. The size of his antlers appeared very close to the size they had been the

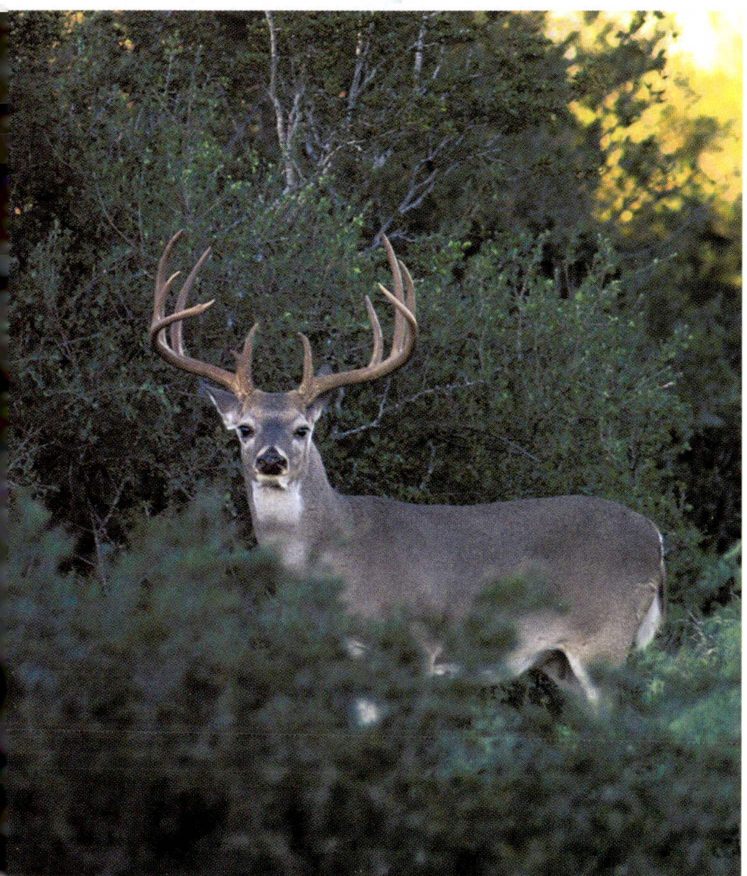

5 1/2

previous year, but his bases and brow tines were obviously heavier. Similar to most 5 1/2-year-old bucks, his body was starting to show its maturity. His stomach was much fuller and had a definite sag, but his back was still pretty straight. His face and chin were showing wrinkles, which is typical of a mature buck. The rancher found his left shed after the season, and it was quite impressive. His beam was 24 2/8; G-1, 5 5/8; G-2, 9 3/8; G-3, 11 5/8; G-4, 7 2/8; H-1, 4 5/8; H-2, 4; H-3, 3 6/8; H-4, 3 3/8; for a gross score of 73 7/8 inches. Considering his right antler is even better than his left, this buck should have scored in the low- to mid-170s B&C that year. At 4 1/2 this buck had a faint second throat patch, and at 5 1/2 it became much more distinct.

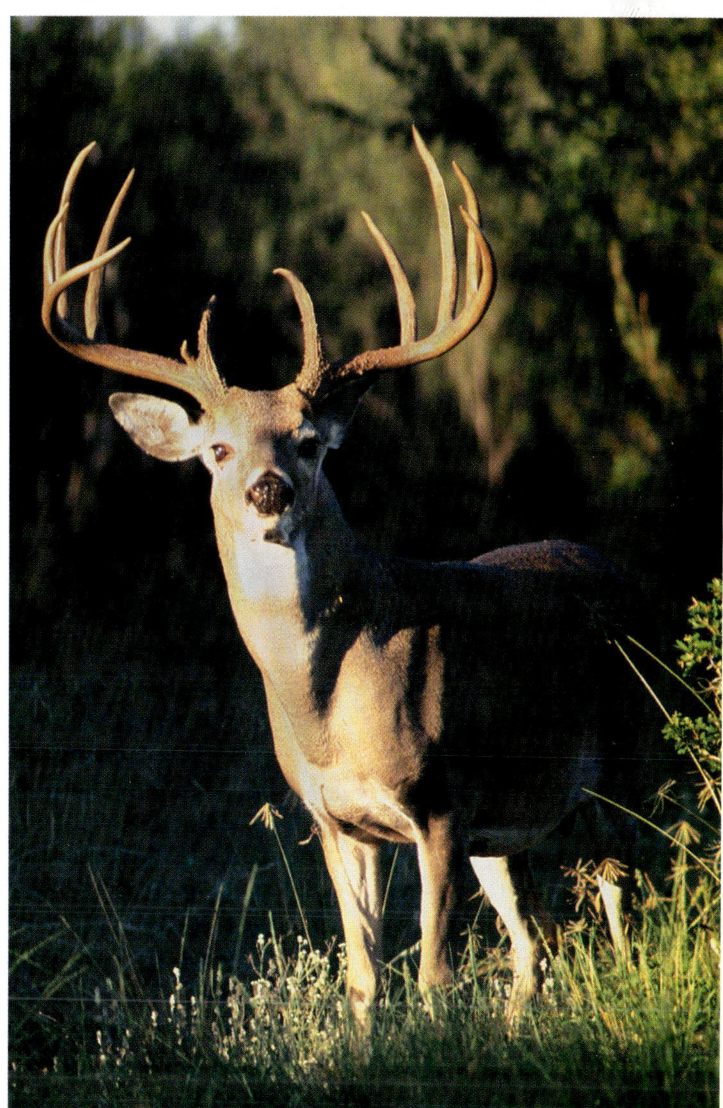

6 1/2

6 1/2

At 6 1/2 this buck's antlers were very similar in shape to the previous year. However, they had grown in mass and tine length. I noticed that he still had a small nontypical point on his right G-1, but it was now closer to where the point met the beam. This photograph was taken in late October, and you can see that his stomach has quite a sag. His neck is already starting to swell, and his legs appear short for his heavy body. I noticed that his right eye had a milky spot in the center, which may have been caused by an antler in a fight or more likely by a branch or thorn. He may have been blind in that eye and, while it did not appear to have affected him physically, he did appear extremely nervous. I only saw him this once and no one else saw him the rest of the season. His bad eye may have caused his demise, or he may simply have become more nervous and elusive, typical behavior for a buck that has lost sight in one eye.

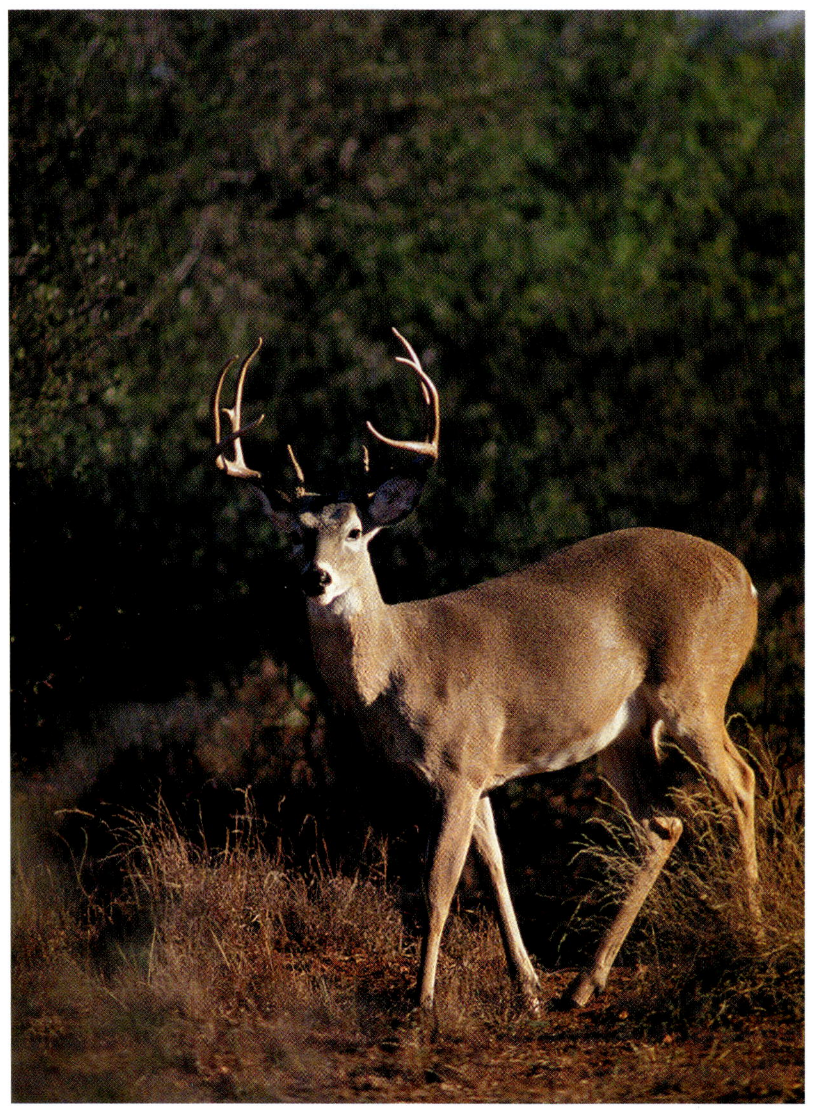

2 1/2

BUCK# 15

2 1/2

I remember the rancher telling me about this buck and convincing me to try to photograph him, as he was one of the best 2 1/2-year-olds he had ever seen. He described him as a basic 8-point with small nontypical points on his G-2s. I was really pleased when he came into my setup. However, at the time I had no idea that the rancher's counsel would prove so valuable. I noticed immediately he had brow tines that pointed backward, and his G-2s and G-3s curved in, particularly on his right antler. I remember thinking he would be pretty recognizable as he grew due to those characteristics. His body was typical of a 2 1/2-year-old with a very thin neck, doe-like face, and straight back and stomach, but his antlers clearly demonstrated this was not going to be an ordinary south Texas buck.

3 1/2

At 3 1/2 his antlers increased in overall size, and he had 10 basic points. His brow tines and G-2s and G-3s were the same shape as the previous year, just bigger. The photo you see is the only time I saw him,

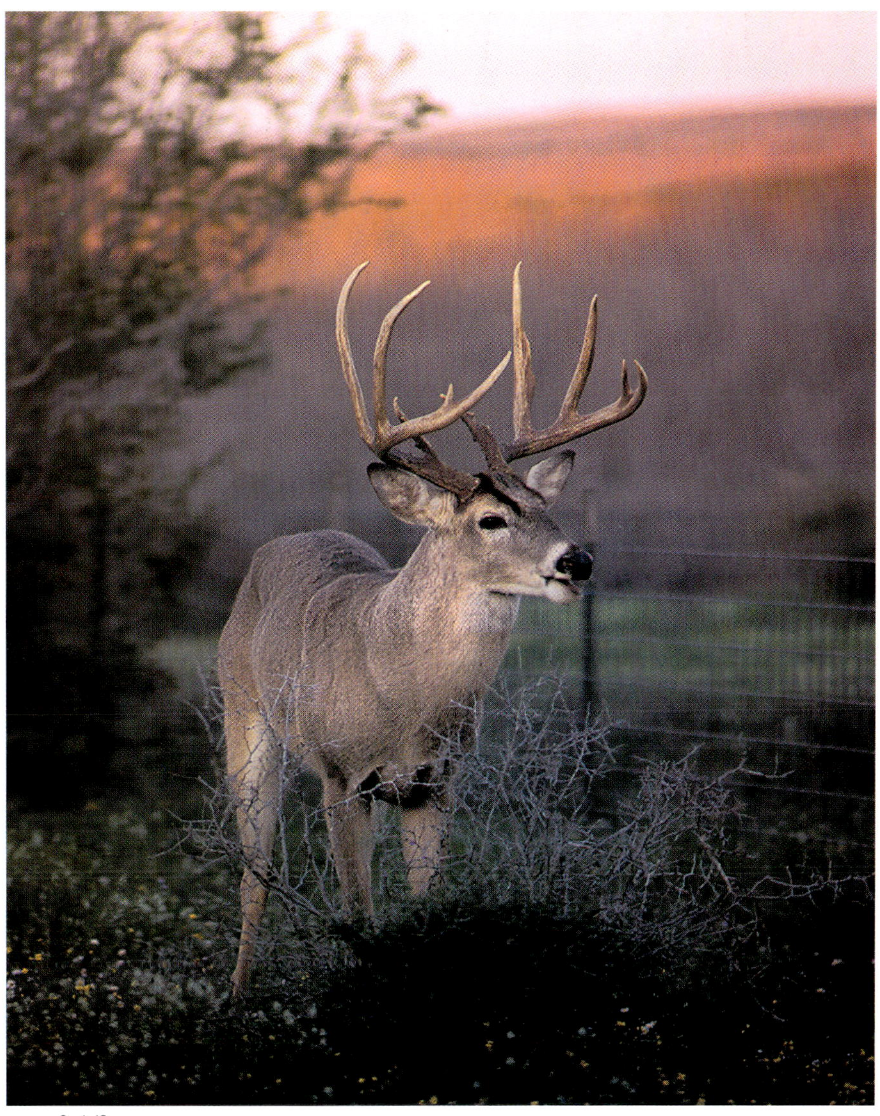

3 1/2

and it was after the rut. His neck is not very swollen, and his stomach is straight and flat.

4 1/2

At 4 1/2 his antlers increased more in one season than any other buck I have ever observed. He was a 6x5 with a nontypical point off his right G-2 and several small points around his heavy bases. His brow tines and G-2s and G-3s had again maintained their same shape as in previous years. Everything about this buck's antlers says he is a mature shooter. However, if you cover those massive antlers and look at his body, there is no doubt he is too young to shoot. He is a perfect example of the need to age a deer by their body and not their headgear. He also demonstrates the importance of recognizing and aging a buck as early in its life as possible. Notice his neck is swollen but not massive. Also, his face appears long and slender when compared to those of 6 1/2- and 7 1/2-year-olds, which are shorter and heavier from this angle. His back and stomach are straight, and even his chin line is straight with no extra flabby skin. Finally, notice that his tarsals are dark, but not stained down the back of his legs to the hoof. Many hours were spent looking for this buck's sheds and, fortunately, the right side was

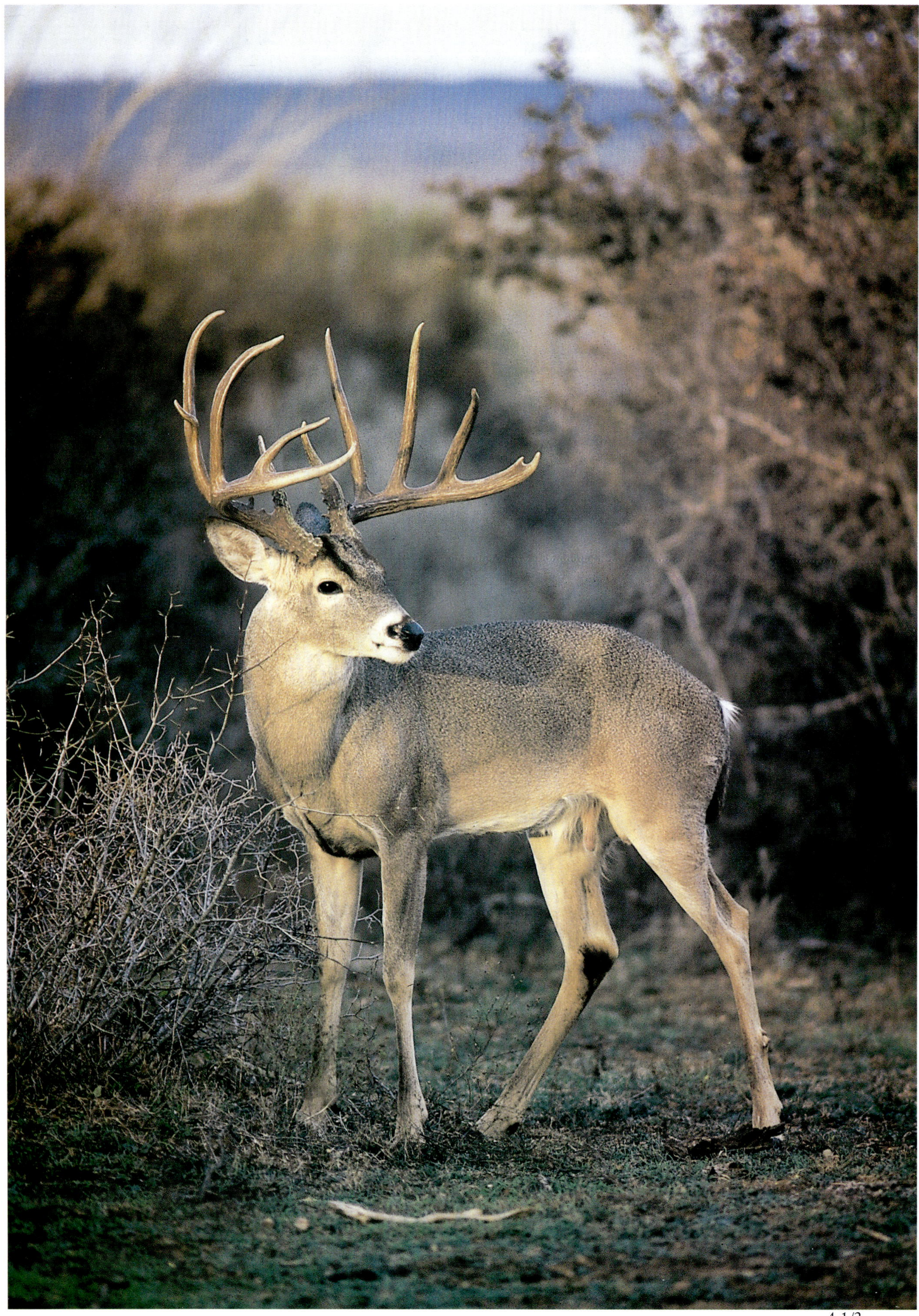

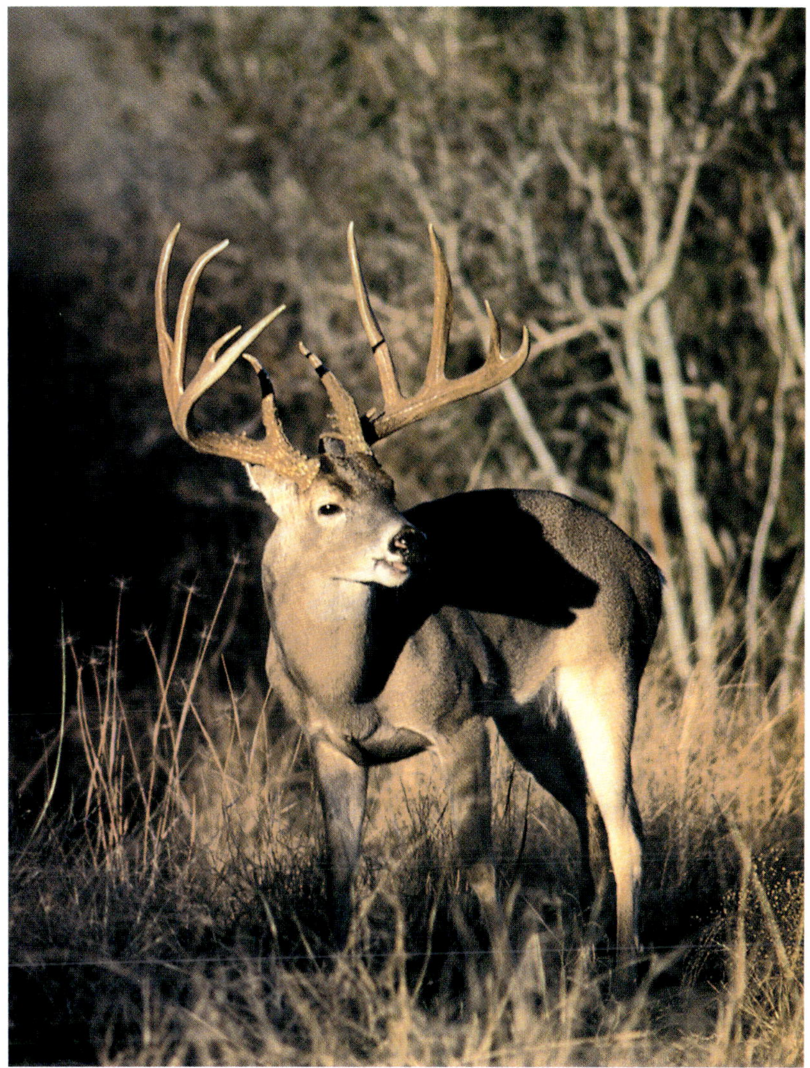

5 1/2

found. The measurements are as follows: main beam, 24 3/8; G-1, 6 4/8 + 1 1/8; G-2, 14 4/8 + 3; G-3, 12 4/8; G-4, 6 4/8; abnormal point off the beam was 1 inch; H-1, 5 2/8; H-2, 4 2/8; H-3, 4 1/8; H-4, 3 4/8; totaling 86 6/8 inches on his right side alone.

5 1/2

At 5 1/2 he continued to amaze me. His antlers were enormous and had noticeably increased in mass. His characteristic long, straight brow tines and thick bases were covered with bumps and small abnormal points. His G-2s and G-3s appeared as long as those from the previous season and possibly even longer. He had grown the nontypical point again on his right G-2 as well. His G-4s were the only area in which he had declined, but they are much longer than they appear when you consider his G-2s and G-3s are at least 14 and 12 inches, respectively. His body had finally taken on many of the characteristics of maturity to accompany his huge antlers. His whole body appeared fuller and thicker from his neck to his stomach. His face had even thickened, giving it the appearance of being short and smaller than his neck when he was looking directly toward me. His tarsals were dark and quite large but were not stained all the way down his legs to the hoof. If this was the first year this buck had been spotted, a hunter would have been hard pressed to determine his age unless it was with tooth wear after harvest.

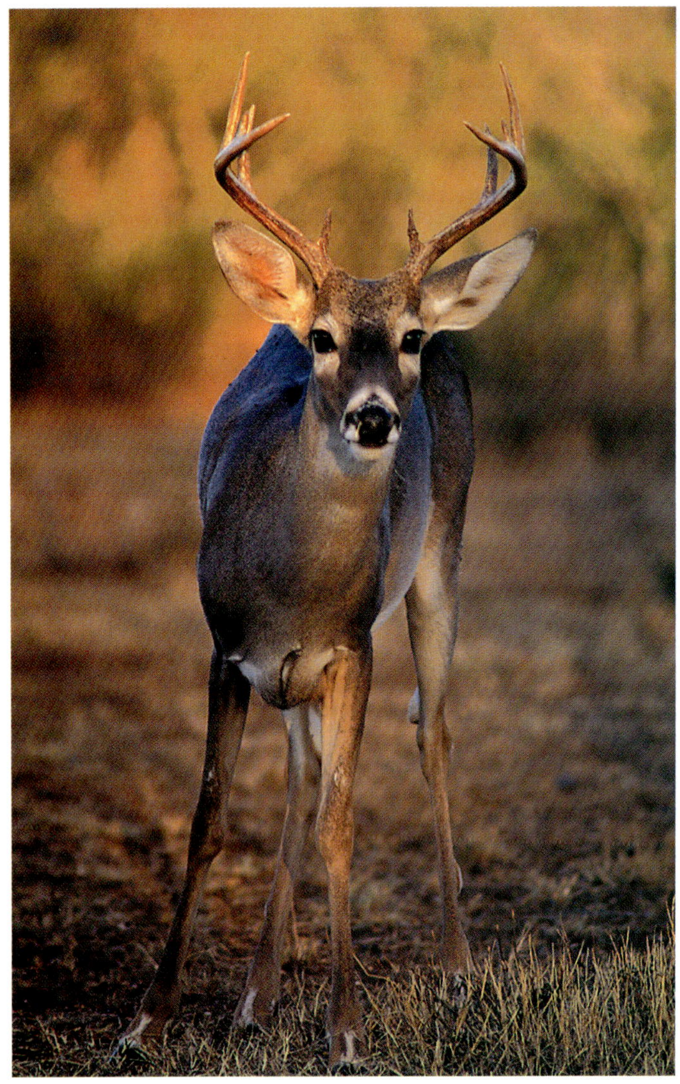

2 1/2

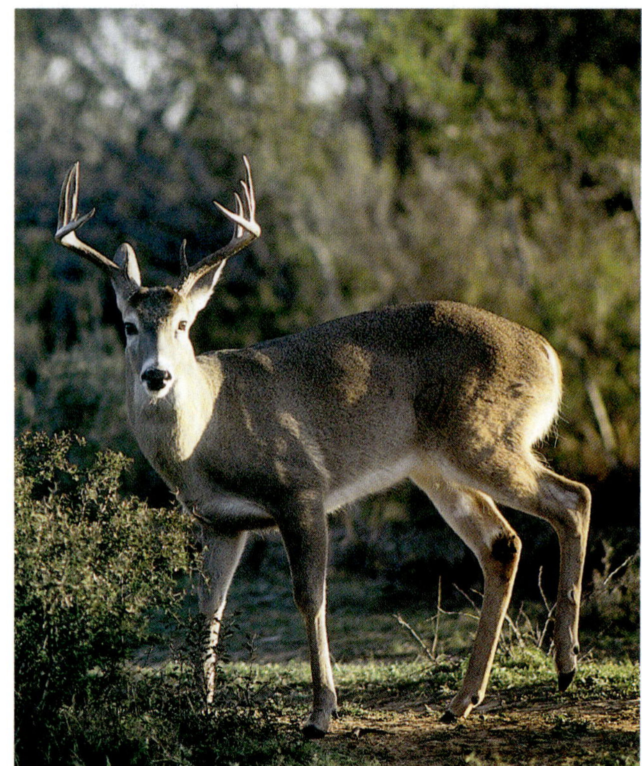

3 1/2

BUCK# 16

As I have mentioned earlier, most bucks do not display recognizable characteristics in their antlers until they are 3 1/2. However, some will display unique features that make them recognizable in the first year or two of life.

2 1/2

Look closely at this buck at 2 1/2 and notice the small white dots a couple inches above his knees. He also had white markings on the inside and outside of his back legs, a small golf ball size spot under his throat patch, and a solid white muzzle, making him appear as if he frequented a milk pail. I only saw him one time late in the evening that year and snapped a couple of quick photographs before an older buck pushed him on his way. He had 10 points, but nothing else about his antlers was extraordinary.

3 1/2

At 3 1/2 I again saw him only once, and he had nine points. He was traveling with a couple of other bucks that appeared to be his age. When I started snapping the shutter on my camera, he stuck around for only a couple of frames. His face appeared long and slender as is typical of a young buck. His body was trim, and his stomach and back were straight.

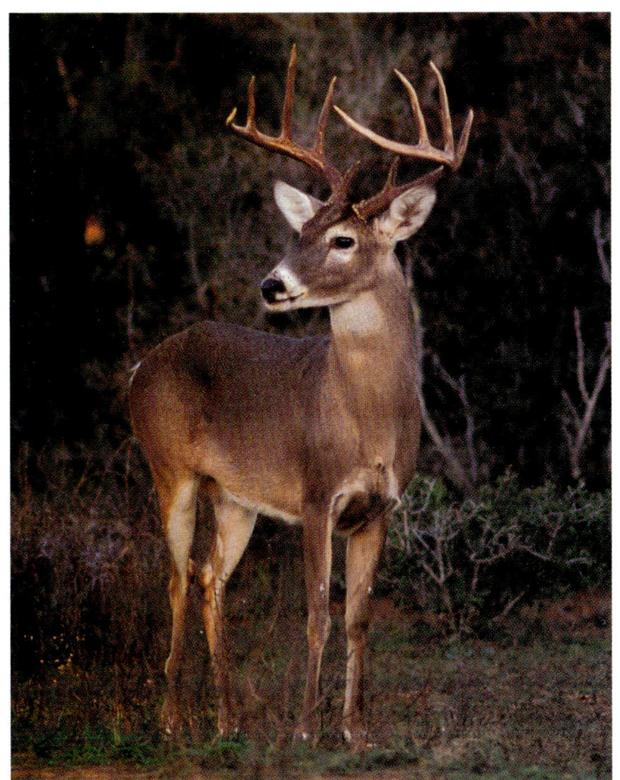
4 1/2

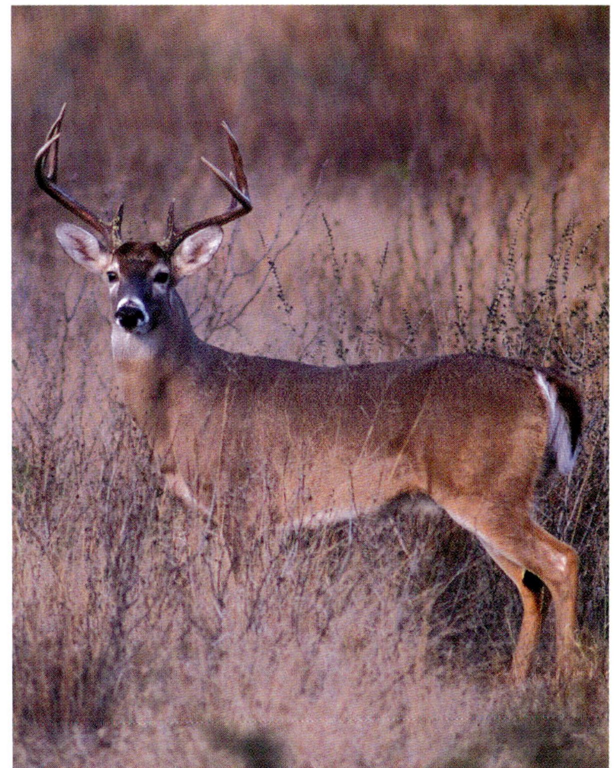
5 1/2

4 1/2

At 4 1/2 his antlers increased noticeably in size and he again had 10 points. His body was filling out but still taut and showed no signs of sagging in his back or stomach area. Notice the white markings on his knees and back legs make what would be just another 10-point buck into a readily identifiable buck. He came in just as the sun was setting and, true to his character, looked the situation over for about two picture frames and headed on his way.

5 1/2

The next year I had all but given up on seeing him when he showed up in January at a feeder. I saw him twice and only got a couple of photos. He came in both days with ears laid back, hair erect, and ran off a much bigger 4 1/2-year-old. This behavior helped confirm he was 5 1/2. Each time, I watched him long enough to see his white knee spots and white markings on his back legs to confirm his identity. I realized for the first time he had noticeably-short brow tines. When I went back and looked at photos from earlier years, I realized he had displayed this characteristic since he was 2 1/2. His spread appeared to have increased from the previous year and was well outside his ears. He had either broken off his G-2 on his right antler or never had one, making him a 9-point. It was well after the rut, but his neck was still quite swollen and there was no distinction where it joined the brisket. His stomach was quite trim, which is typical of 5 1/2-year-old bucks that have been actively participating in the rut. Also typical was how his front end appeared much bigger than his back end.

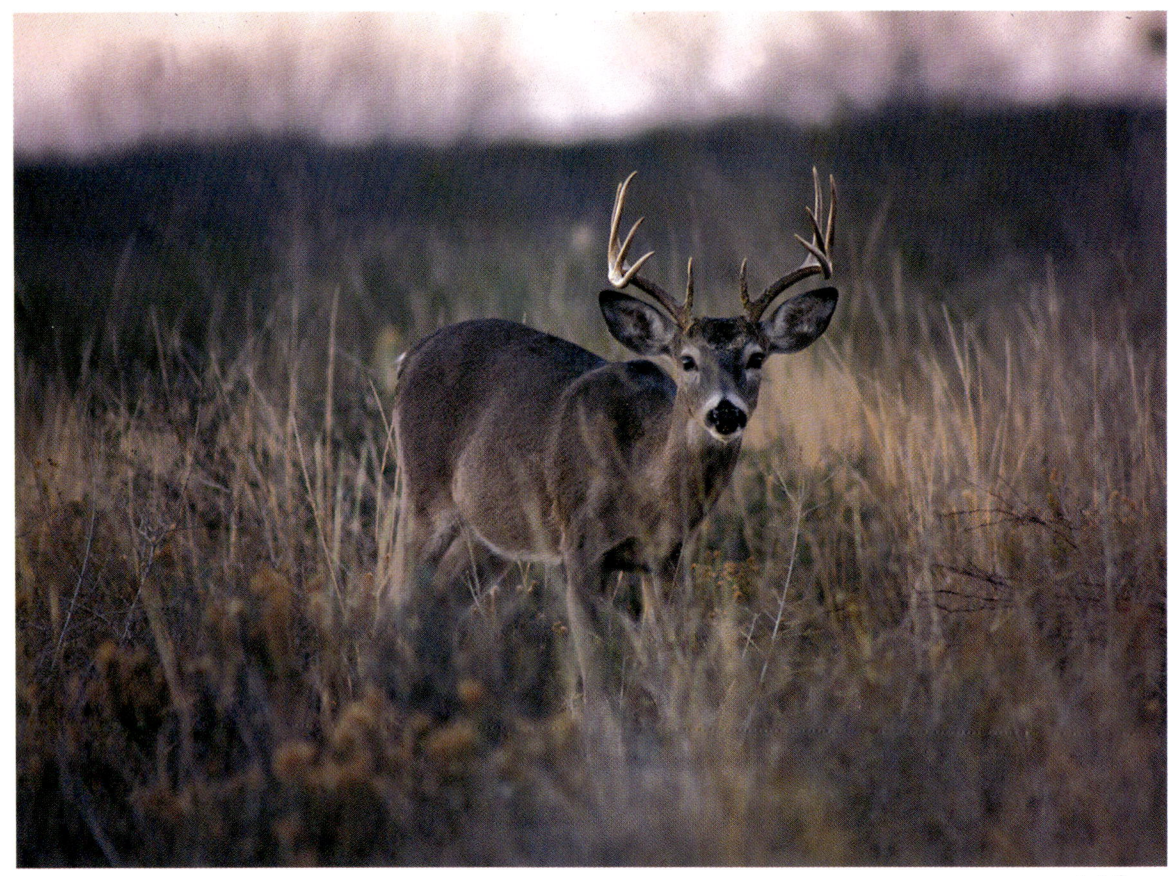

1 1/2

BUCK# 17

1 1/2

I have often been asked if I ever get nervous photographing big bucks, and this one always comes to mind. It was not that he was a monster as a young buck, but he always kept me rattled. I watched him on several occasions over the years, but he would either not come into my setup or would only stay a few seconds. He was always on the move, or at least some part of him was, making it extremely difficult to photograph him. The first year I photographed him he was a 10-point, and I realized he had fairly long brow tines, and that his beams turned up at the ends like crab claws. I also noticed that his ears appeared large for his head. I only saw him two times that year, and he came in with a group of does and other young bucks both times.

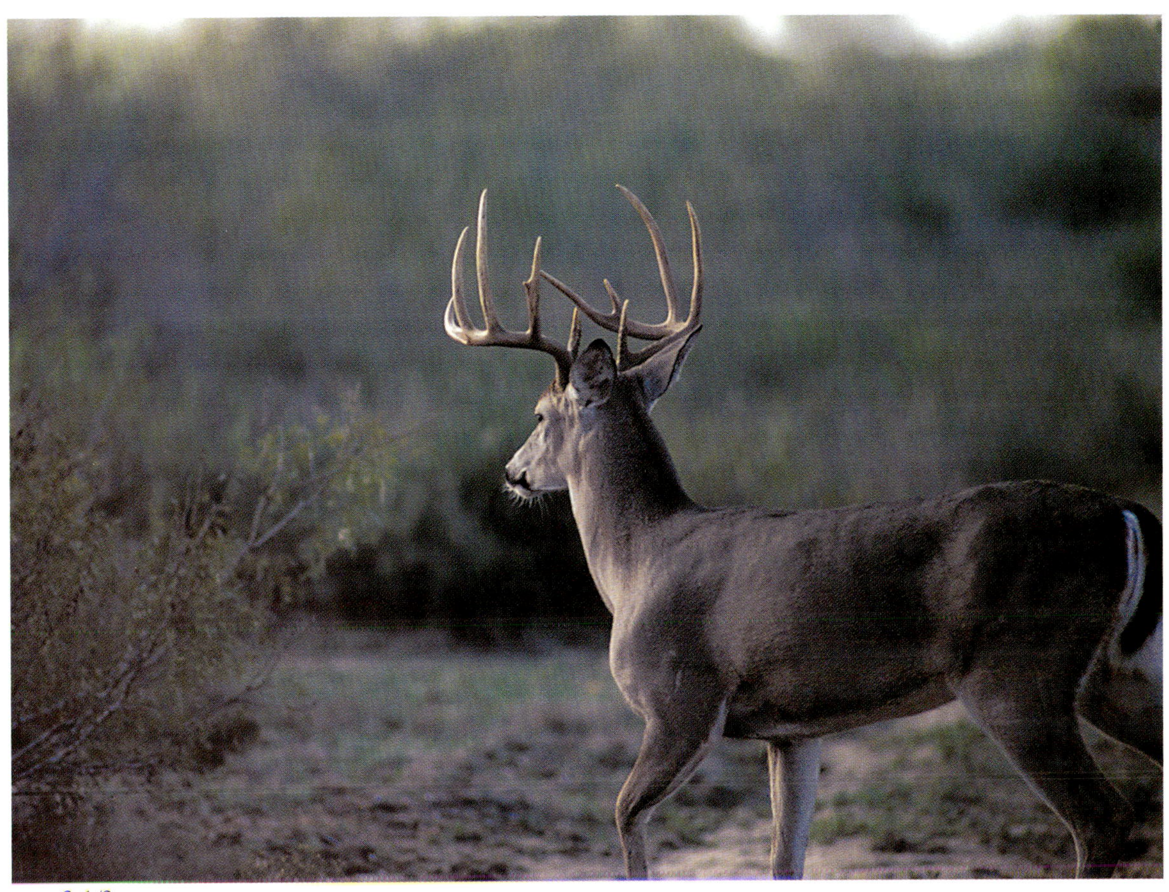
2 1/2

2 1/2

It was late November the next year when I saw him. I immediately recognized him because his antlers were similar in shape to the previous year, and his nervous mannerisms were familiar. Often a buck's mannerisms can help identify him as much as his physical attributes. This buck had 10 points again this year with a small bump on his left G-2. He also still had beams that curved up on the ends and straight brow tines. He came in to my setup that day but never settled down. When he started back toward the brush, I managed to get a couple of quick photos. I'm glad I got them, because it was the only time I saw him that year. Notice that even though it is late November his neck is relatively small, and his body is trim with a taut stomach. This buck is a good example of relatively large antlers on a young buck which can certainly lead to a mistake.

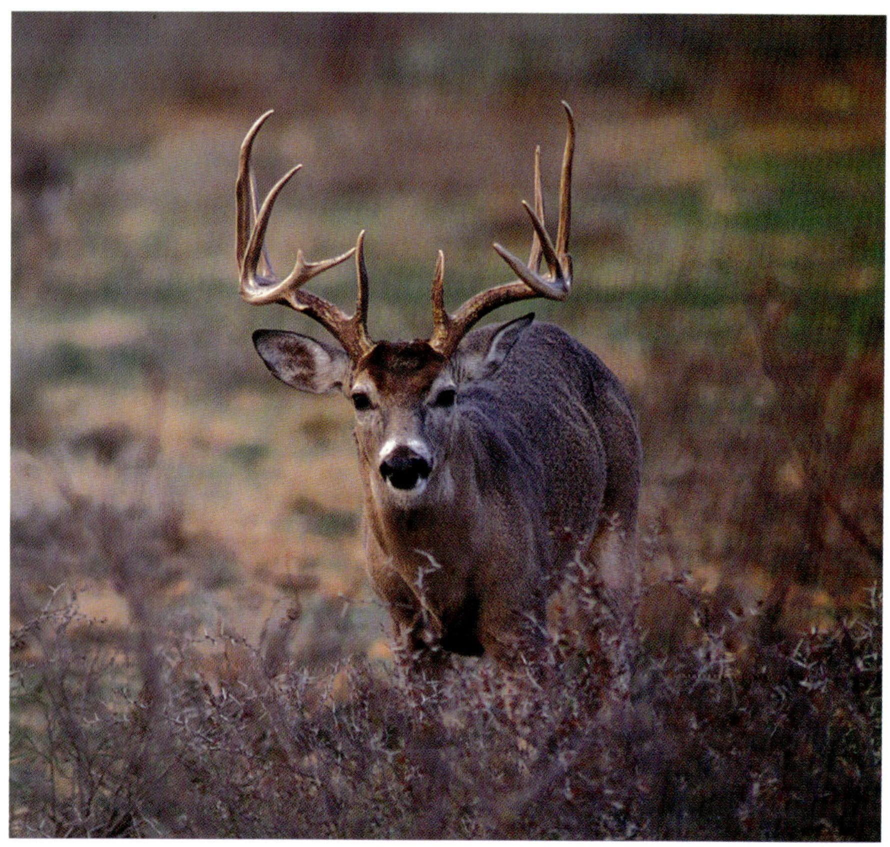

3 1/2

3 1/2

After seeing him a number of times, I finally got a picture of him that year near the end of the rut. His antlers had increased in size significantly, and he was a 6x6 with a small 1 1/2-inch drop tine about four inches from the tip on his right beam. He had broken his G-4 on his left antler but appeared to be in good shape. His body was slender and his back and stomach were straight. His tarsals were dark but small. However, for a 3 1/2-year-old, he was quite an impressive buck.

4 1/2

Each year as this buck got older he was becoming more and more of a surprise. When I observed him from the front, he was merely a nice buck. But when he turned, he would make a hunter's jaw drop. He was a beautiful 12-point with long beams, long tines, and nearly perfect symmetry. His personality had not changed, and he kept me frustrated until late one evening when I got this photo of him. It was early January, and his neck was still a bit swollen. His back and stomach were still straight, and I noticed that he did not appear larger in the chest and shoulders than in his rear quarters as 5 1/2-year-old bucks often do. I also watched a buck that we had determined was 5 1/2 years old run him off on two separate occasions adding to the information we already had to confirm he was 4 1/2. He had a busted nose and slightly torn right nostril but seemed otherwise unaffected.

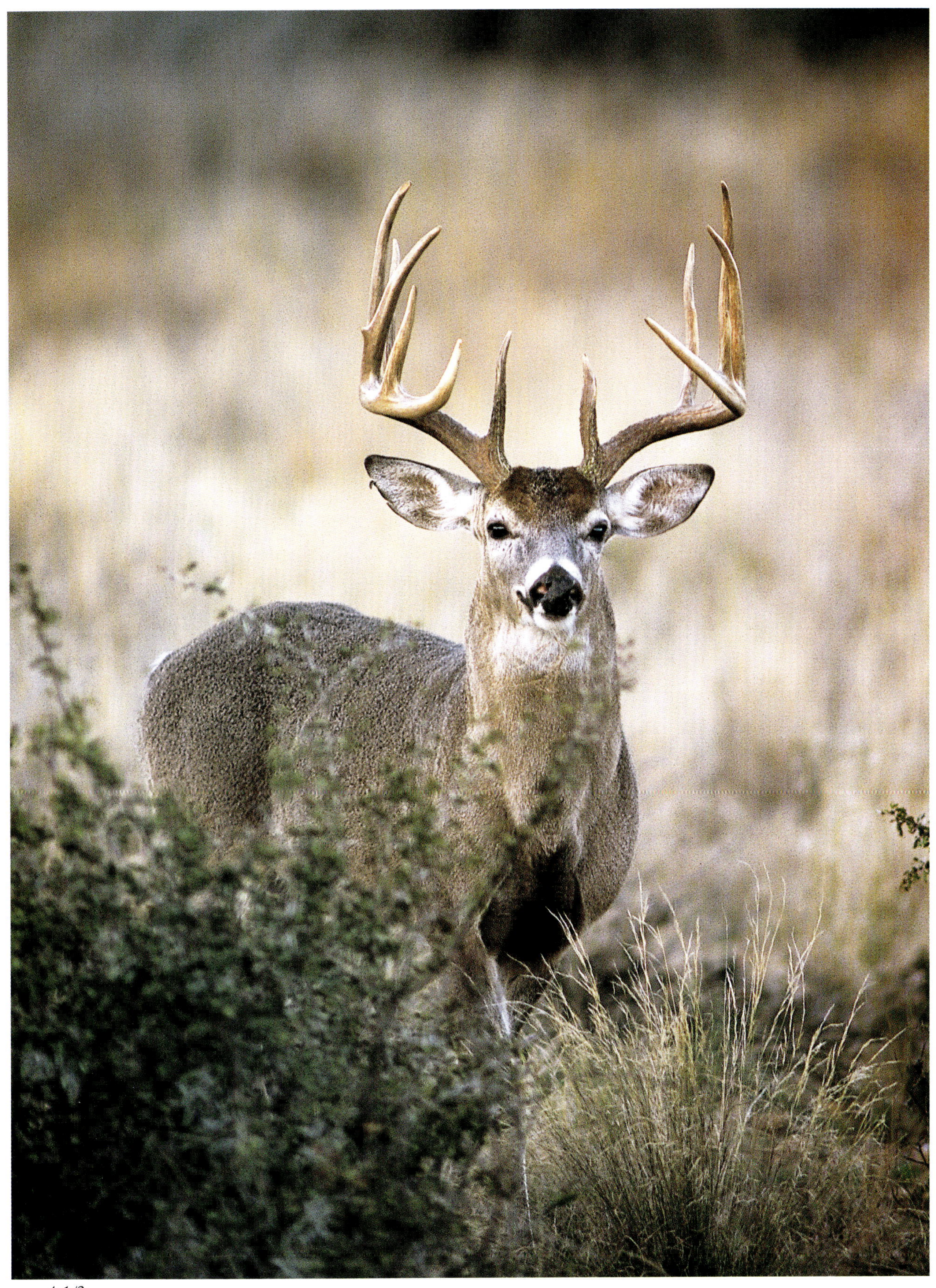

4 1/2

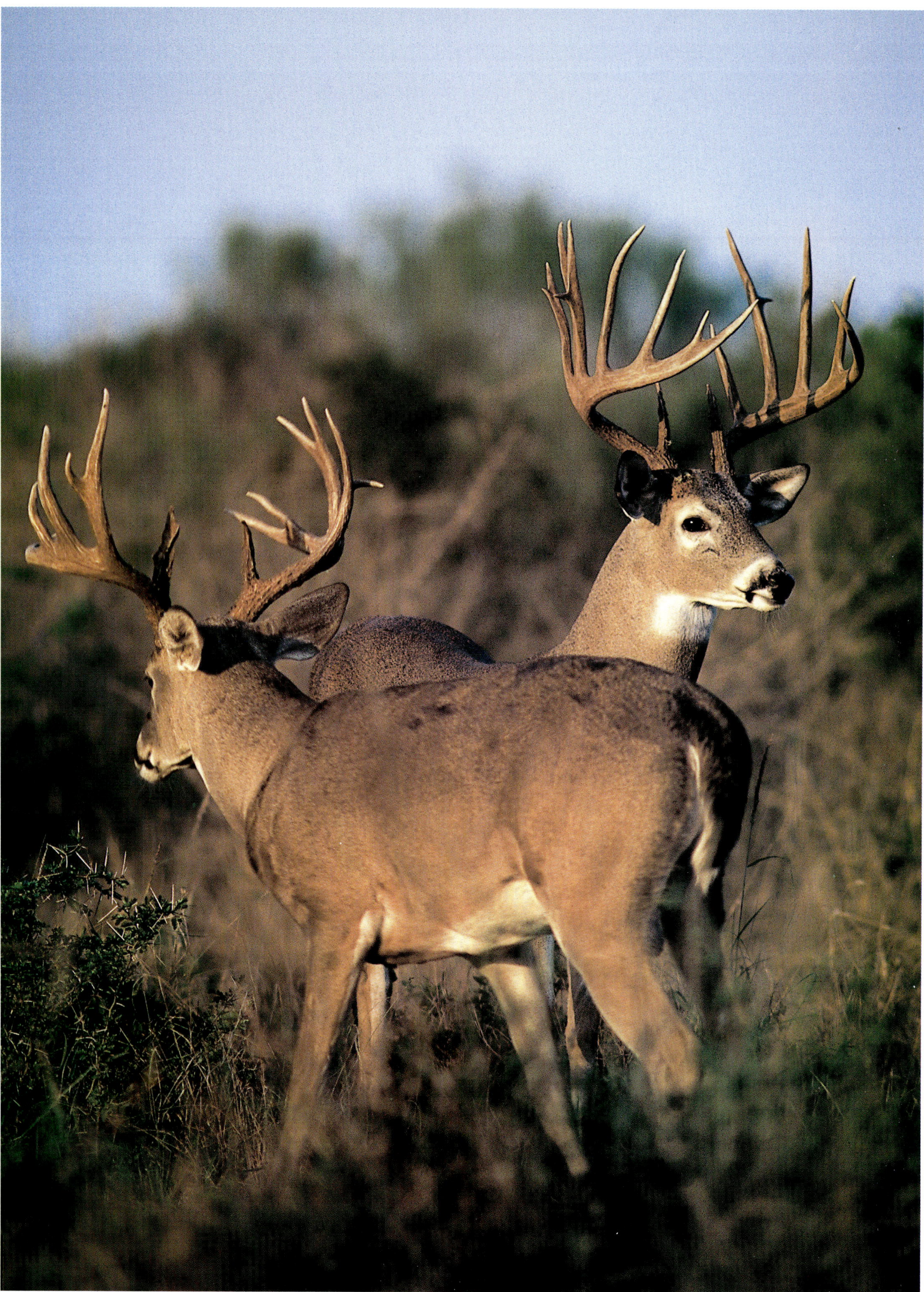

5 Aging Whitetails by Behavior

Often, after all of a buck's physical characteristics have been analyzed, a question still remains as to his exact age. Sometimes physical characteristics alone make it difficult to correctly age bucks in the 3 1/2- to 5 1/2-year-old age group. Observing an individual buck's behavior and especially how he relates and reacts to other bucks can assist you in arriving at a more definitive age.

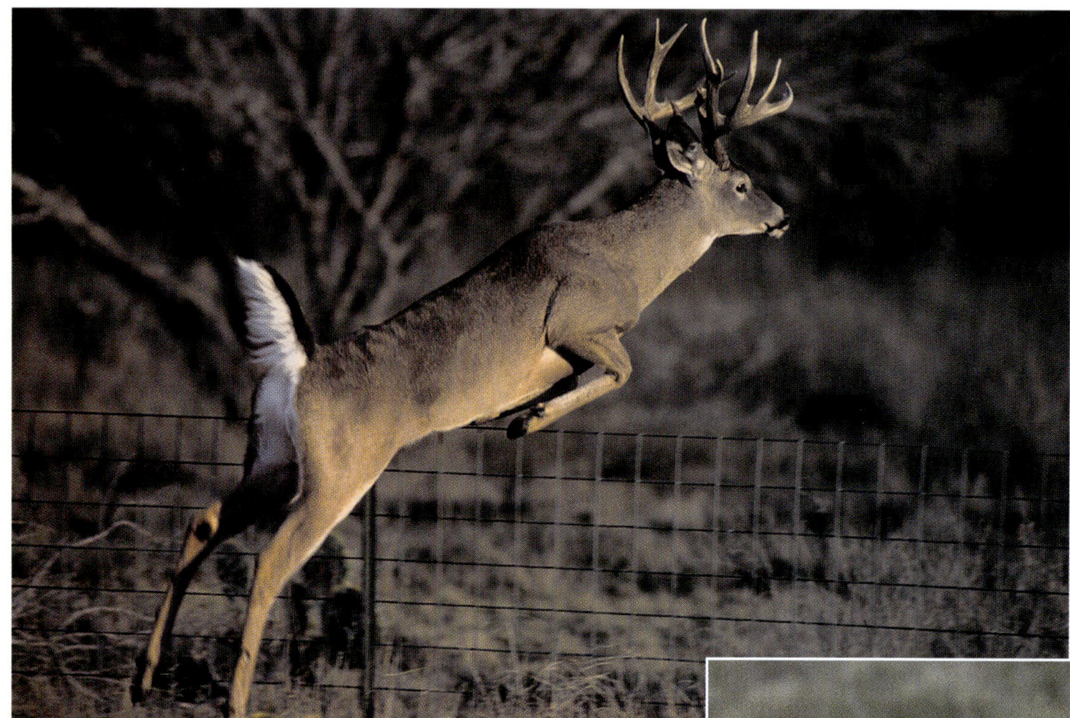

The buck believes that danger is imminent, and it is time to leave with the tail flared and erect, although at times the tail will be tucked as the deer sneaks away. The type of reaction appears to depend on whether the buck is in the open or in heavy cover.

Bucks communicate both vocally and nonvocally. To the occasional observer, it may appear that a buck's use of grunts, snorts, and other vocalizations is limited primarily to the breeding season or when alarmed. However, bucks communicate constantly in many ways. The most familiar nonvocal communication is a deer running away while waving its big white tail for all to see and be alerted to the danger.

Other forms of nonvocal communication include head bobbing and foot stomping. Both occur when a deer senses something suspicious but has not determined if it is truly in danger. A buck will give a stiff-legged stomp with his front leg when he is trying to get a reaction from whatever alerted or aroused his curiosity. He may stomp numerous times over several minutes while simultaneously bobbing his head up and down, all the

This buck, with his tail erect and flared while walking away, indicates he is alert to danger, which could be identified or unidentified at this stage. The buck knows something is not right but has not put all the pieces together. This buck heard my camera and was letting the world know something suspicious was going on.

The two bucks on this page show typical reactions to a predator sighting such as a coyote or bobcat — tail hair flared with the subsequent lifting of the tail to a horizontal position.

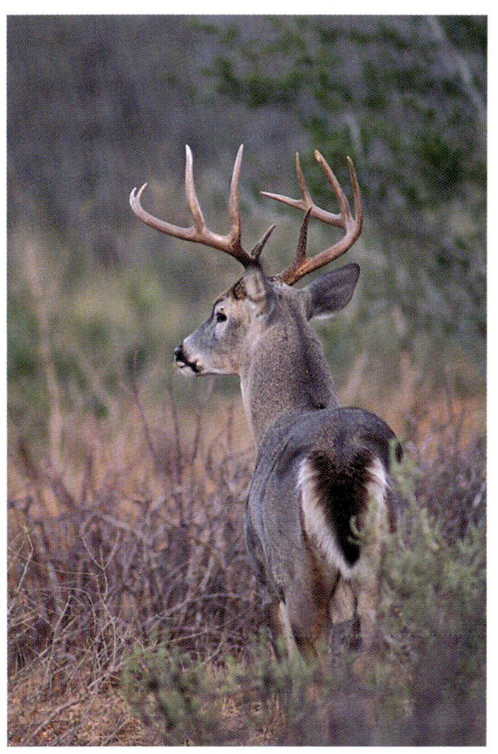

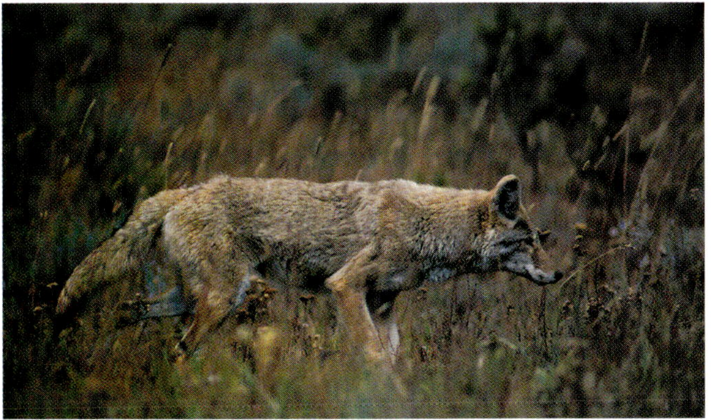

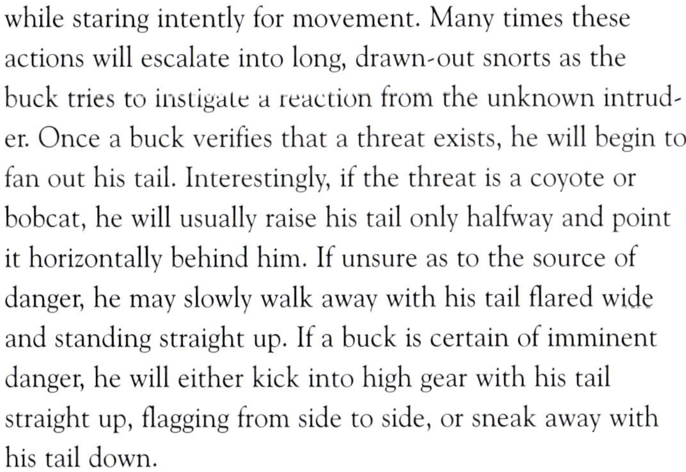

while staring intently for movement. Many times these actions will escalate into long, drawn-out snorts as the buck tries to instigate a reaction from the unknown intruder. Once a buck verifies that a threat exists, he will begin to fan out his tail. Interestingly, if the threat is a coyote or bobcat, he will usually raise his tail only halfway and point it horizontally behind him. If unsure as to the source of danger, he may slowly walk away with his tail flared wide and standing straight up. If a buck is certain of imminent danger, he will either kick into high gear with his tail straight up, flagging from side to side, or sneak away with his tail down.

Recognizing the different types of communication will not necessarily aid in aging bucks, but it will enhance the observer's understanding of what is occurring and, more importantly, what is about to occur. Armed with a basic understanding of behavioral patterns, more subtle clues related to age can be better understood. The "long stare" is an example of such a subtle behavior. Often, when watching a lone buck, the observer can focus primarily on him, because the buck will be the first to notice another deer approaching and greet it with a long stare. The stare can last from a few seconds to a couple of minutes. If it only

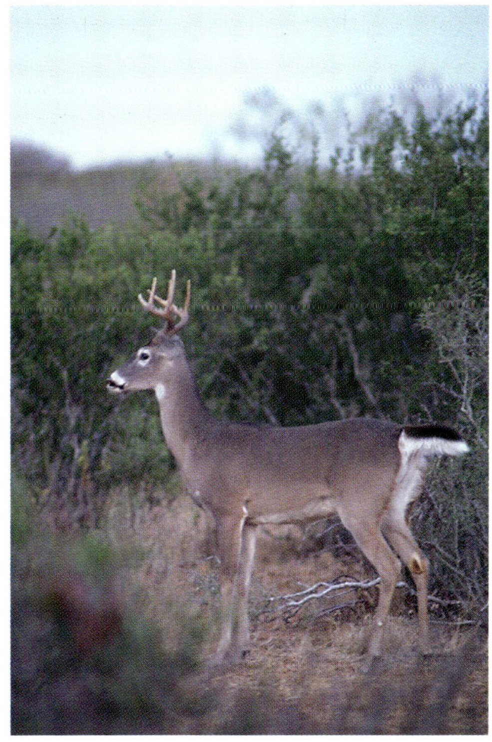

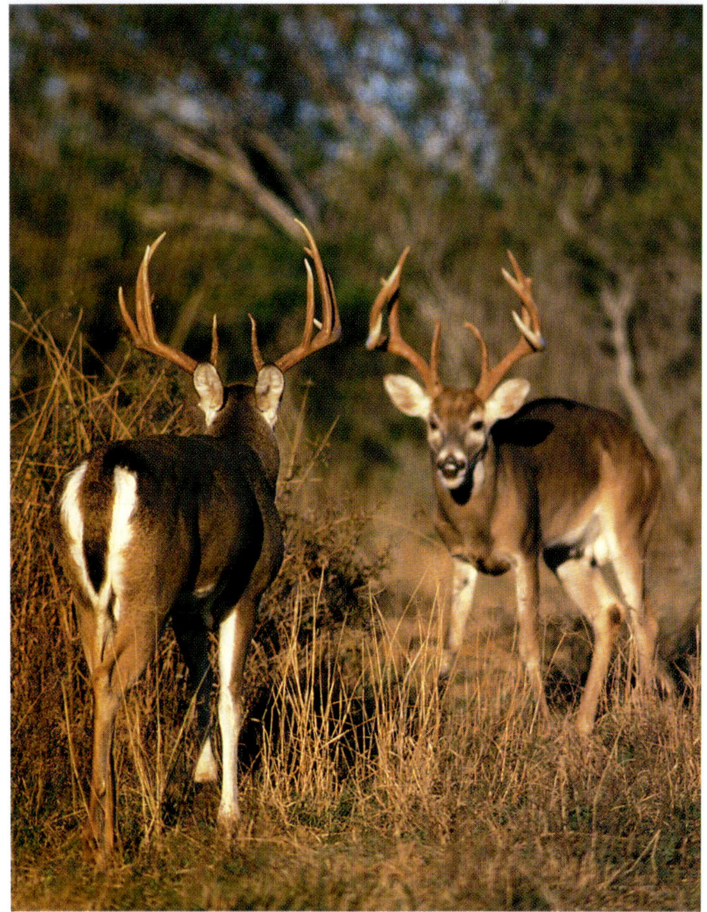

Momentary confrontation — the dominant buck (foreground) with ears laid back and the sub-dominant with ears forward. These head postures often are quite subtle, and the observer must pay close attention to the angles of the head and ears.

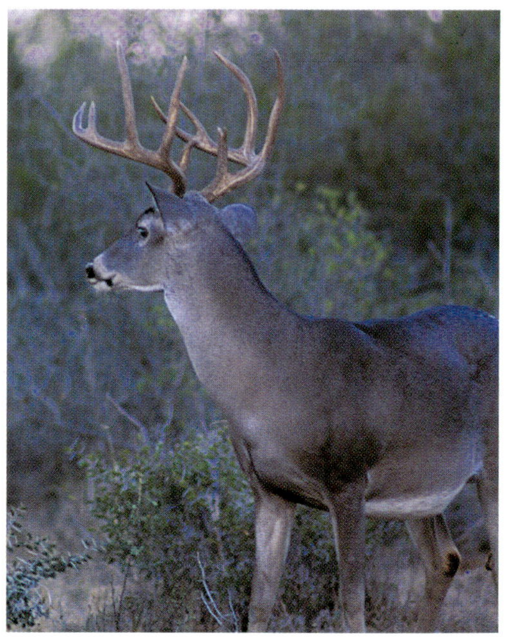

The "long stare" means something of interest is approaching. Keep watching as the buck will give more information through his tail or ears.

lasts a few seconds, it typically means the intruder is of little importance and is generally followed by a sideways twitch of the tail and a resumption of normal activity. However, if the stare is long and intent, pay close attention to the buck's tail and ears. If his tail is starting to flare, he believes a source of potential danger is approaching. It could be anything from someone driving on the property to a coyote making his rounds. However, if he flattens his ears, another buck is likely approaching. If so, he may then flare out his body hair and begin walking with a slow, staggering gait referred to as "sidling." This means another buck perceived to be in the same general age class is nearby, and a staring contest or even a fight might follow.

A buck laying his ears back and erecting his hair are two examples of nonvocal communication that can establish the pecking order and help place bucks into an

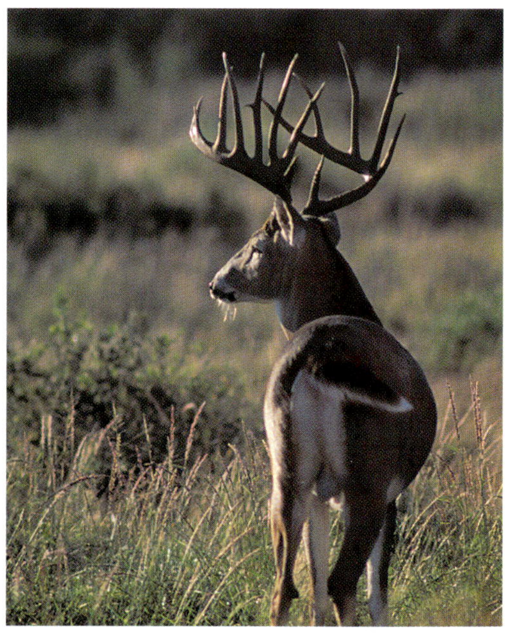

A tail twitch usually indicates the deer is not threatened by what is approaching and is about to resume its previous activity or move on.

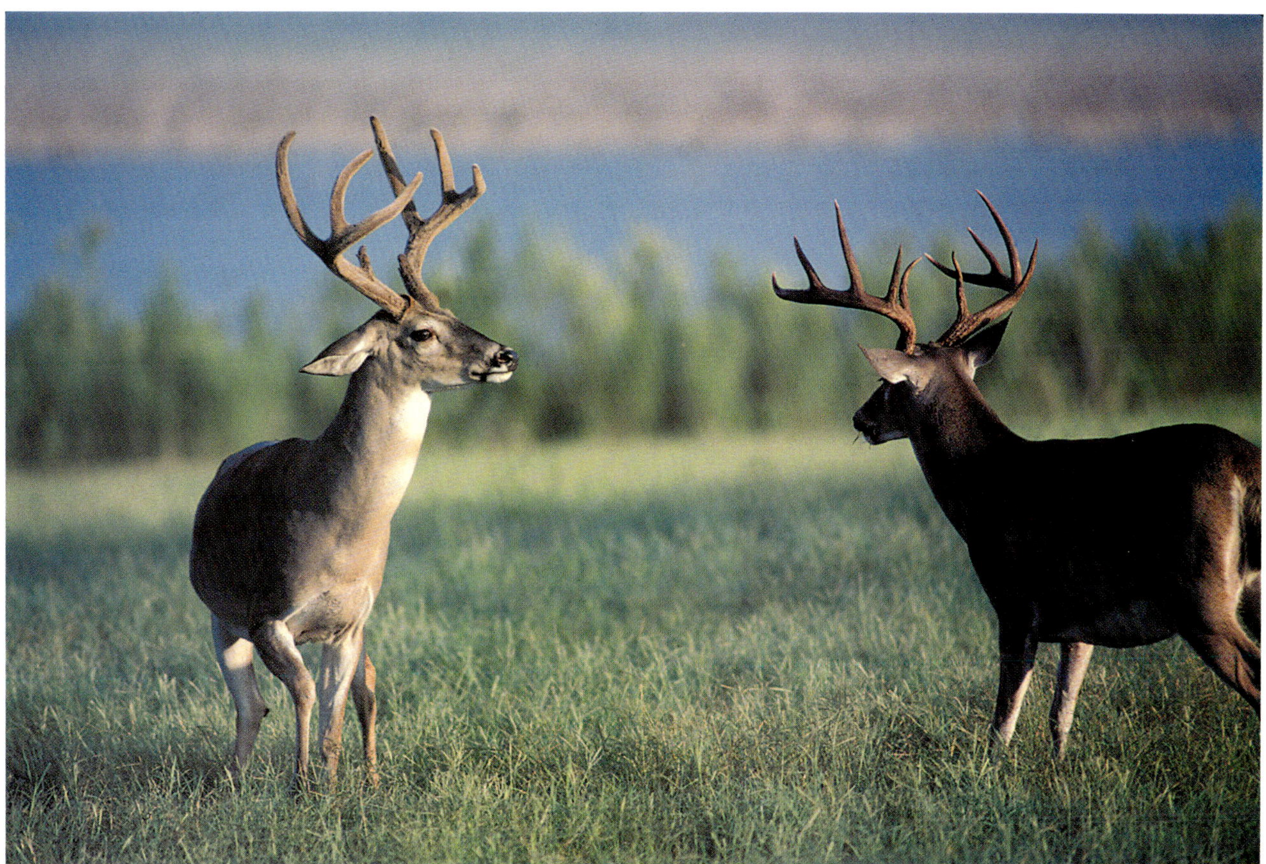

Much can be learned from a buck's interactions with other bucks. In most cases, sub-dominant bucks will be younger than those exhibiting dominance.

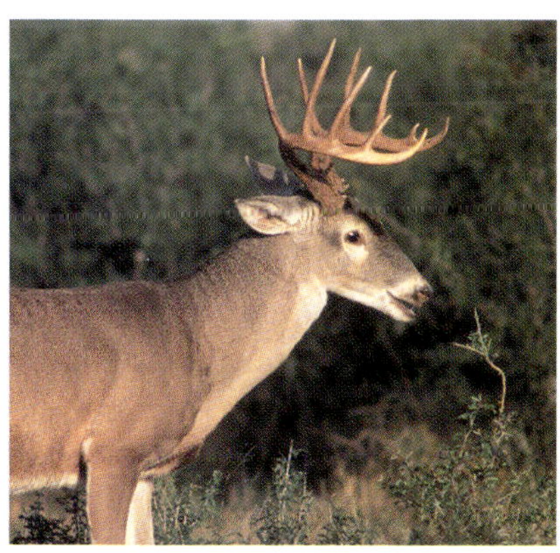

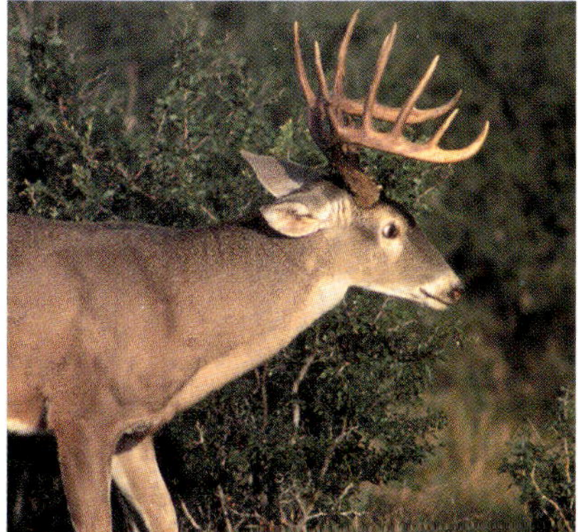

This two-photo sequence shows a buck approaching another with ears laid down and back and neck slightly arched. As the bucks draw closer and the situation intensifies, the buck's eyes are rolled forward showing the whites.

age category. Another important nonvocal communication is head posturing. Simply watching the heads of two bucks will enable the observer to determine which is dominant. The dominant buck will carry his head higher with his ears laid back and will continue doing so until the subordinate buck shows submission with the correct head posture or proceeds on an avoidance course. This typically occurs in just a few seconds and is all that is required to reinforce the pecking order and avoid conflict.

However, if the two bucks are similar in age, a different result may occur. They may begin walking stiffly toward each other with ears laid back, hair flared out, and eyes rolled, until one ceases his dominant posturing or they come face to face. If this happens, there could be a simple clash of the antlers followed by one of the bucks

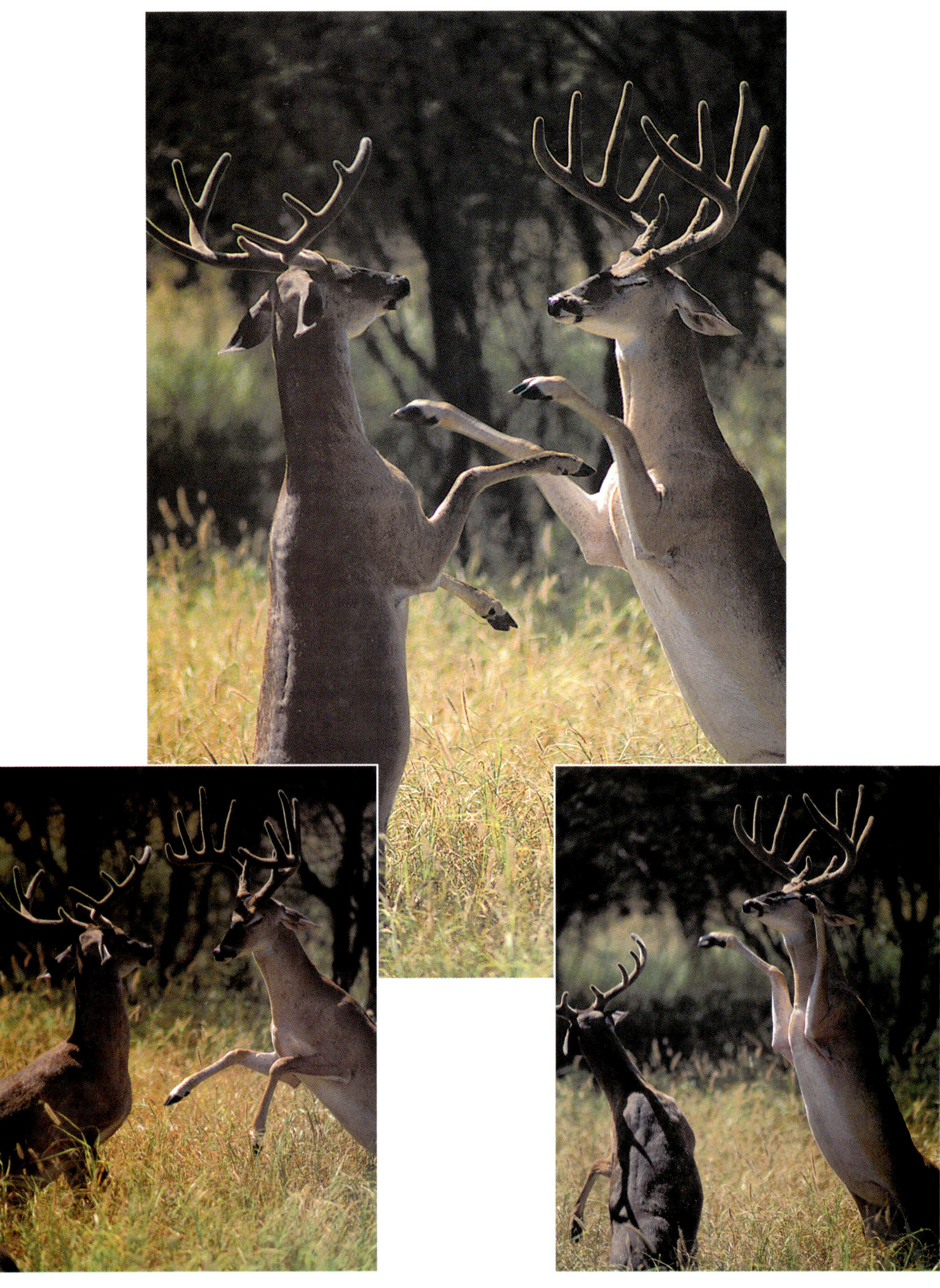

Hoof flailing is used to establish dominance and to drive another deer away while bucks are in velvet. These battles typically only last for a few seconds but can be quite physical.

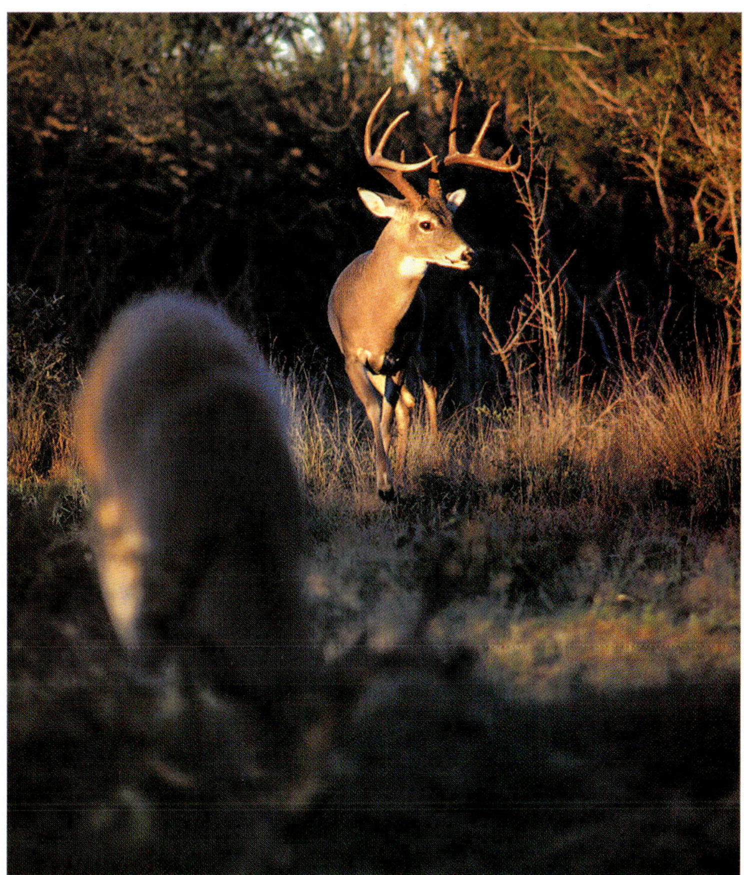

A buck approaching another buck while watching for a reaction.

making a hasty retreat, or it could turn into a serious fight lasting several minutes or, on rare occasions, until death.

In late summer and early fall when bucks are still in velvet, they still go through the same head posturing. However, if the confrontation escalates, a hoof slap or flailing will result. Flailing is when two bucks stand on their hind legs and kick at each other with their front hooves. If it is two young bucks early in the fall with hardened antlers, they may stand toe to toe for several minutes. However, it never escalates into anything more than tickling their antlers together and nudging each other back and forth, similar to two kids on a playground in a playful pushing match.

At times, if one of the bucks is an old, postmature buck, he may walk up and lay his ears back and attempt to bluff other bucks. As he draws closer, he will generally veer away, change his posture, or make a hasty retreat if a younger, more dominant buck continues his aggressive approach. Numerous scenarios similar to these are enacted every day, especially where deer gather to feed. At feeding sites, the immature bucks typically arrive first. Shortly thereafter, the middle age bucks arrive and disperse the immature bucks. Then, just before dark, the mature bucks arrive and disperse any middle-aged bucks present. During the rut, if two or more mature bucks arrive at the same time, it can be extremely exciting. Some sort of confrontation usually takes place. By watching the various forms of behavioral communication, much can be learned that will aid in placing bucks in their respective age classes.

As discussed in Chapter 1, whitetails utter numerous audible sounds from sneezing to grunting,

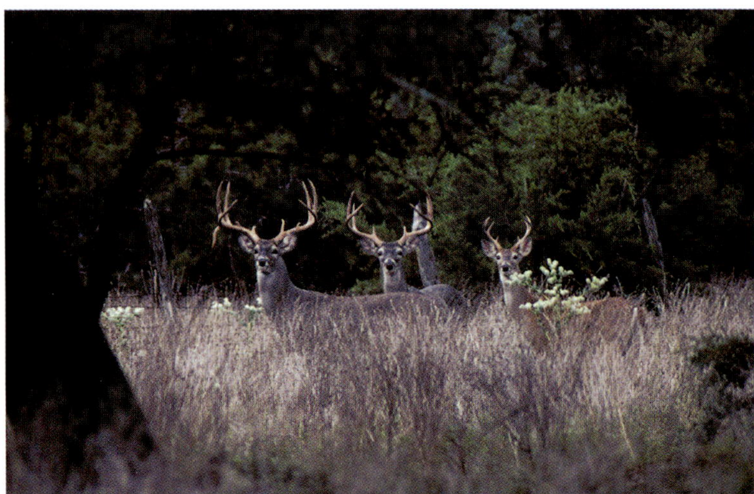

A rare opportunity — capturing a 6 1/2-, 3 1/2-, and 1 1/2-year-old buck standing together.

The most common sound known to hunters is the snort. It is used by both bucks and does of all age classes and is primarily a signal to other deer that danger is present. It can, however, be used out of curiosity or to draw out a perceived predator with the hoof stomp.

The grunt is another form of vocal communication which has been the subject of several studies over the years. Until I started photographing deer, I had never heard a buck grunt. The reason was simple. As a photographer, I was watching several deer undisturbed for longer periods. Watching allowed me to observe many more deer of different age classes interacting with each other than I had while hunting. Another reason is because I had to be much closer.

Until a few years ago, discussing whitetail vocalizations among a group of hunters would have produced many skeptics. However, most hunters today have heard deer grunting in the wild or on videos. I can still remember the first time I heard a buck grunt. It happened in South Texas, and the rut had already begun. While traveling through a ranch to reach a particular spot to photograph a special buck, I caught a glimpse of movement in the brush. I stopped, turned off my truck, and rolled down the window. Within seconds a doe popped out of the brush with a buck hot on her trail. The buck was not a monster by any means — he appeared to be 4 1/2. However, what was fascinating was he would emit a grunt with almost every stride. It was just a short *aaugh* ...*aaugh* ...*aaugh* ...*aaugh*. After both faded into the brush, I hurried to my other spot. Later that day, while passing back through the same area, I was surprised to see the same buck still following the doe and grunting rapidly in succession. This time I was amazed by the presence of three other subordinate bucks following the action. I watched them for 20 or 30 minutes, and when the doe would move, the buck was on her trail with the other bucks slowly following behind. When she stopped, the buck would stop a few feet from her and become silent. As the other bucks closed in on the pair, the dominant buck would either turn on them or, more often, nudge the doe into moving again and resume his grunting routine. This event took place almost 20 years ago and was quite a spectacular introduction to deer grunting. I have been interested in interacting with all sorts of wildlife through game calls since I was a kid. After witnessing that event, I

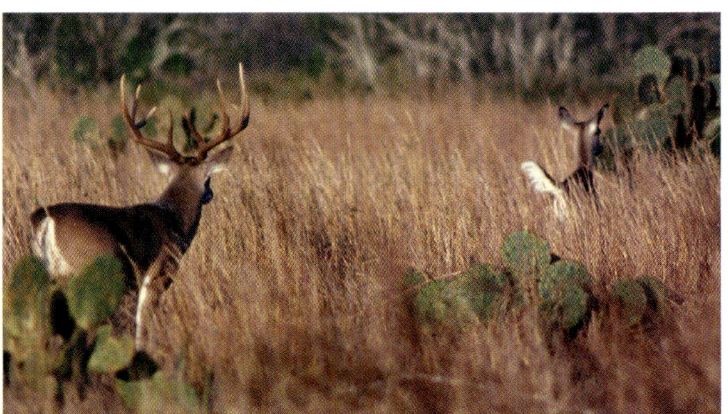

This mature buck is chasing a doe in hopes she is in estrus and ready to mate.

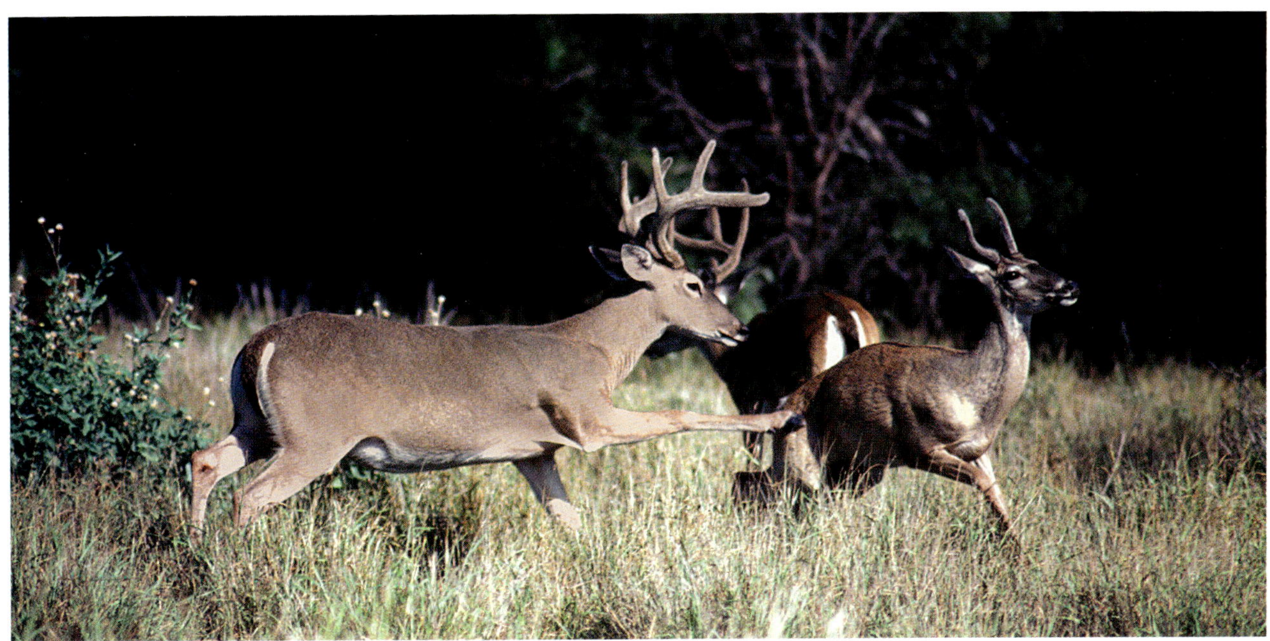

The hoof slap by this dominant buck reminds this spike that he won't be as fortunate once the velvet has been removed.

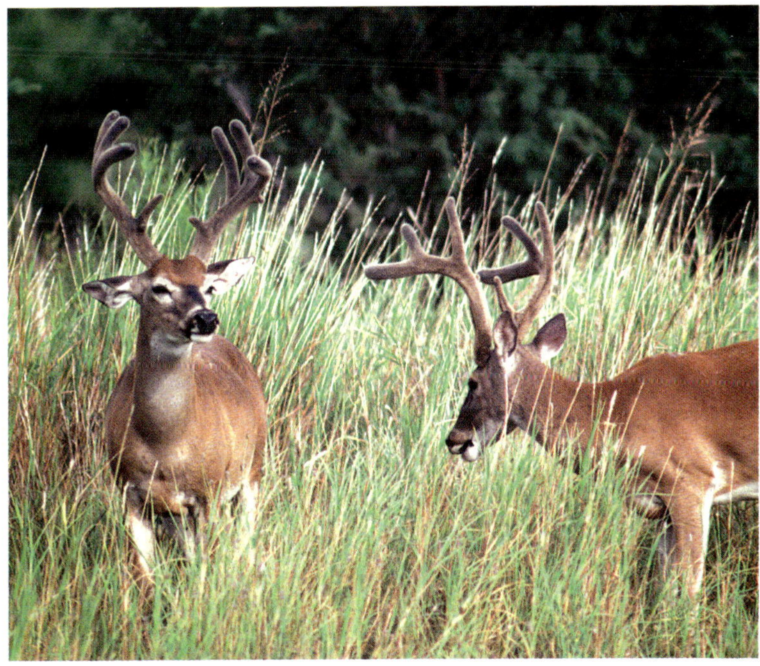

Even when bucks are in velvet, social position is constantly tested and maintained.

gained a new respect for whitetail vocal communication skills, not to mention the possibilities of a deer grunt call.

Another time I heard a buck grunting was in the early fall, and bucks were still in velvet. The buck was a 6 1/2-year-old, and he had two or three younger bucks trying to feed nearby. He grunted at least five times that morning and slapped the younger bucks a time or two with his hooves when they approached too close.

Since those early observations, I have heard bucks grunting many times. When a buck grunts, it usually lasts for a second or two, and his mouth is not noticeably open. If it were not for the sound of the grunt itself, I don't think you would know it had taken place. Numerous times I have heard a buck grunt from behind or beside me before knowing he was present. But, by recognizing the sound, I was ready when he appeared.

Both young and old bucks have the ability to grunt, though I cannot recall ever hearing a young buck grunt. Most bucks I have heard grunting have been at least 4 1/2 years old, with 90 percent or

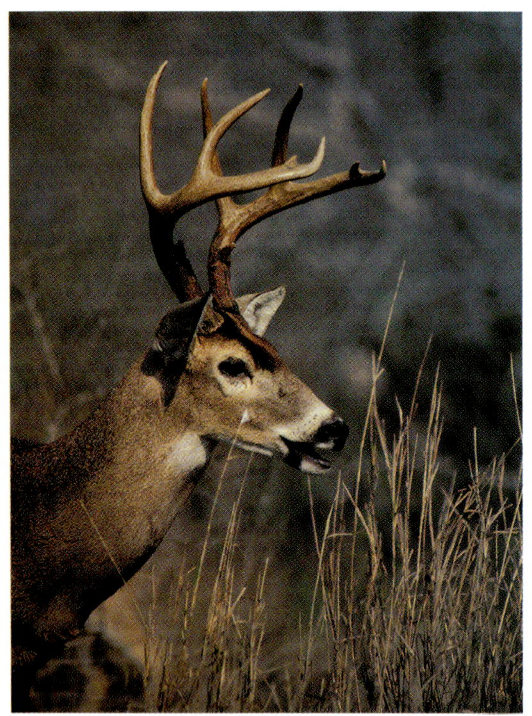

This buck is intently watching an approaching javelina. Most deer will avoid confrontations with javelina, although the authors have observed individual bucks chase javelina away from a feeding area.

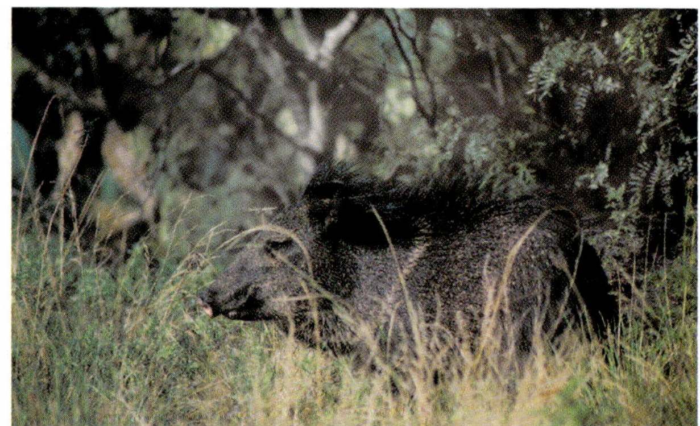

more being 5 1/2 or older. I don't want to imply there is anything scientific about this observation, as young bucks do grunt, particularly if they are dominant in their area. I believe it has to do with the large number of mature bucks on the properties I work and their need to be highly vocal under these circumstances.

Let me explain. The earlier examples I gave were of two distinct periods of the year when I've heard bucks grunting more often — early fall when bucks are still in velvet and during the rut. I believe that when bucks are in velvet, many younger bucks disregard the herd's hierarchy, because the penalties will not be as stiff. This is most noticeable when deer are in close proximity to each other at a food source. The older bucks are more on edge, because they are constantly having to hoof slap and charge younger bucks invading their personal space. Those old bucks appear to be like a time bomb about to explode. They are constantly laying their ears back, grunting a warning, and charging the younger

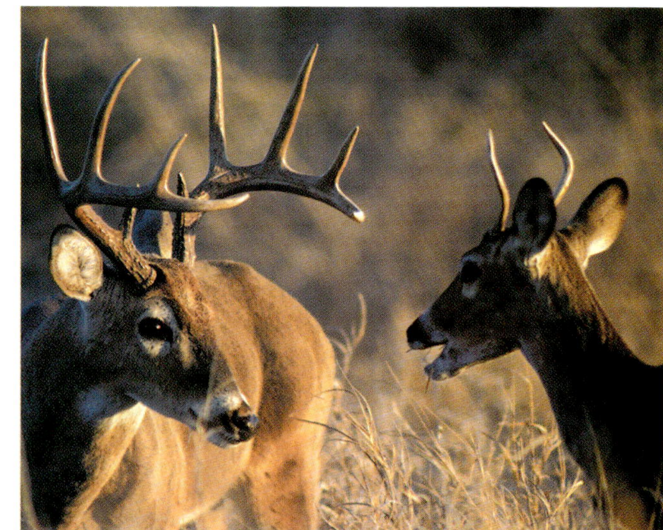

This older buck (left) is showing tolerance of a younger buck in early fall. The older buck's patience will grow shorter as the rut approaches.

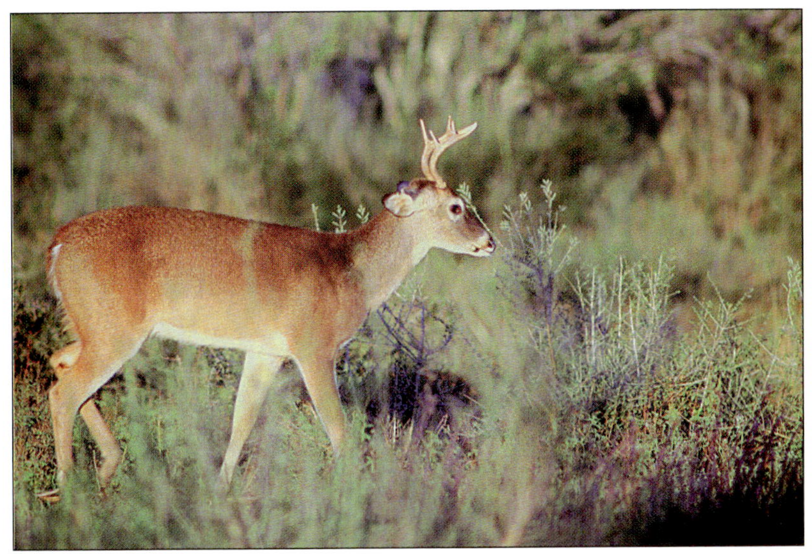

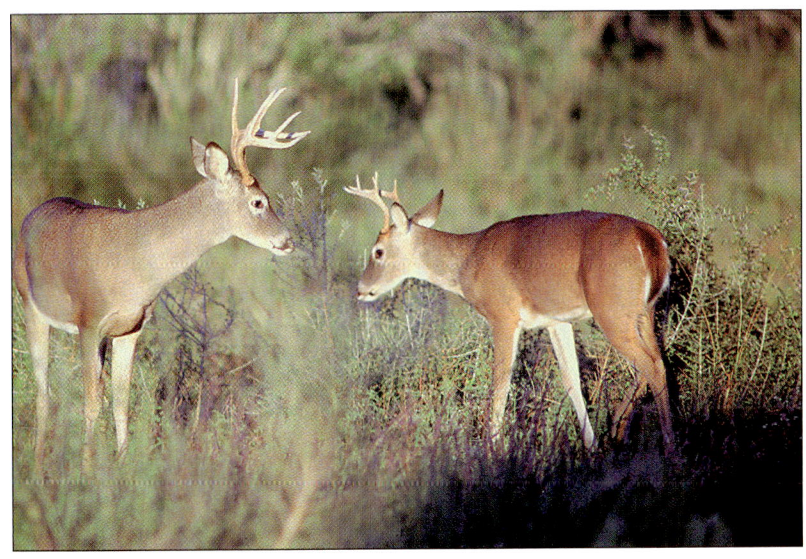

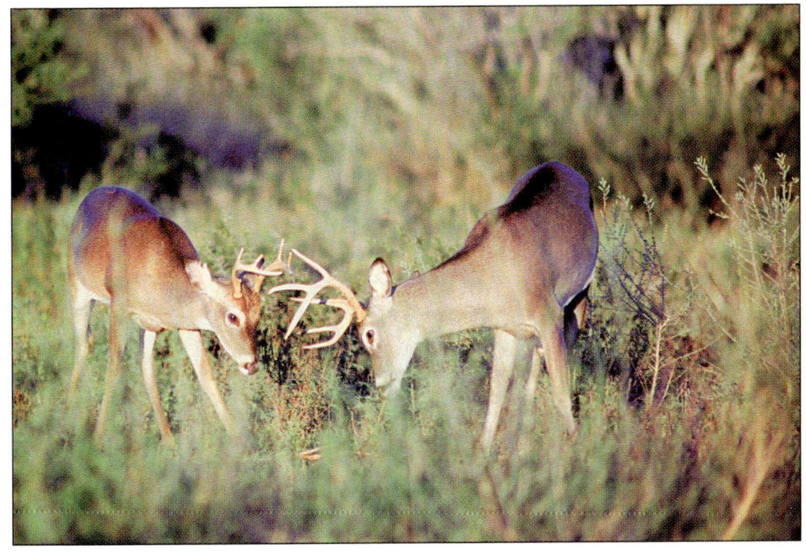

It is common to see a younger buck engage in a friendly sparring match with an older buck. The younger buck usually initiates the sparring, but it rarely becomes aggressive.

A doe and spike buck facing off. In most instances the spike gives way.

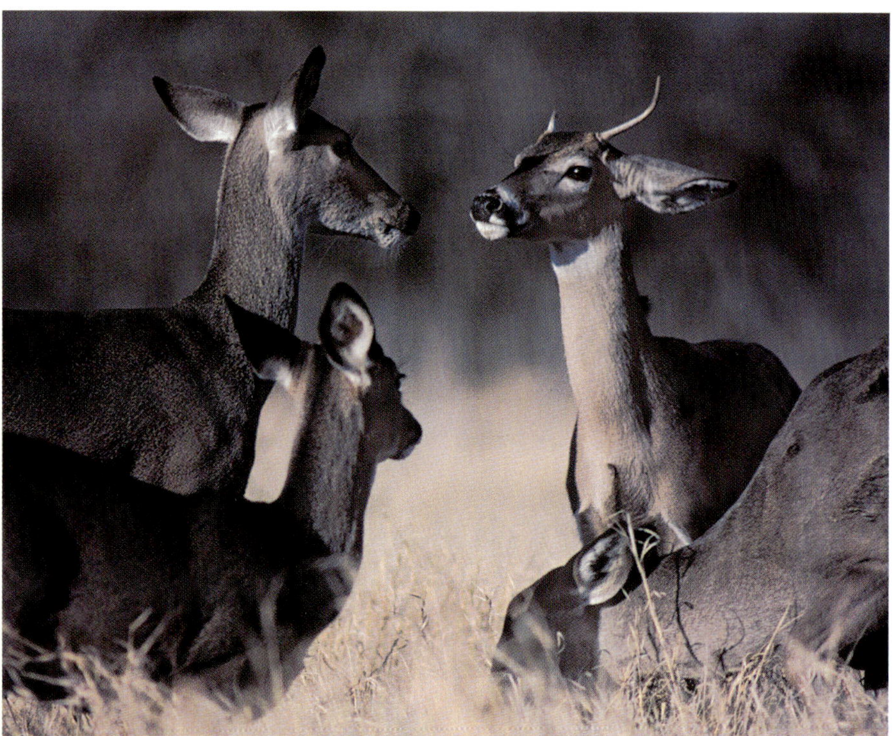

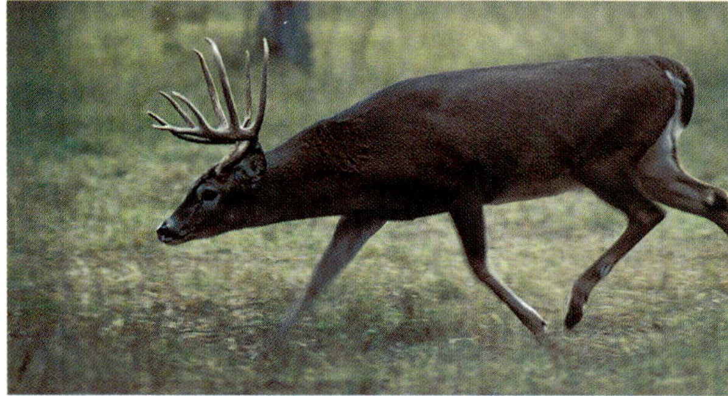

This buck's body language, with head down and neck stretched, indicates he is trailing a doe believed to be in estrus.

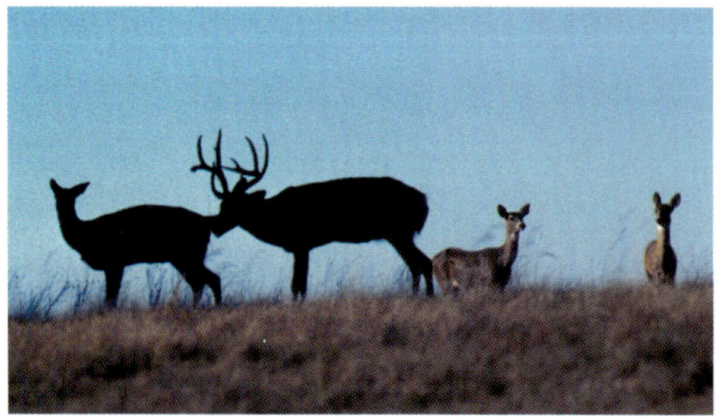

This mature buck is checking this doe for breeding readiness. The fact that she is allowing this to occur is strong evidence that she is ready. Otherwise she would flee from the pursuing buck.

bucks, only to have them back under their feet in a matter of seconds. This scenario plays out over and over again. However, the day that old buck rubs off his velvet he only has to gouge one or two of the younger bucks in the rear or the ribs with his hardened antlers, and they get the picture very quickly. Immediately, the younger bucks fall into line, and the older buck only has to look their direction and lay his ears back. They get out of his way, and his frustration level subsides.

Some years I have observed several bucks rub their velvet off within the same 24-hour period, and the tension level and buck grunting decreased immediately. The following day one would think whitetails are some of the most well-mannered animals on Earth. However, the peaceful period doesn't last for long. Within a few weeks, tension among older bucks begins rising again as the rut approaches.

The rut is the other time of year I have heard

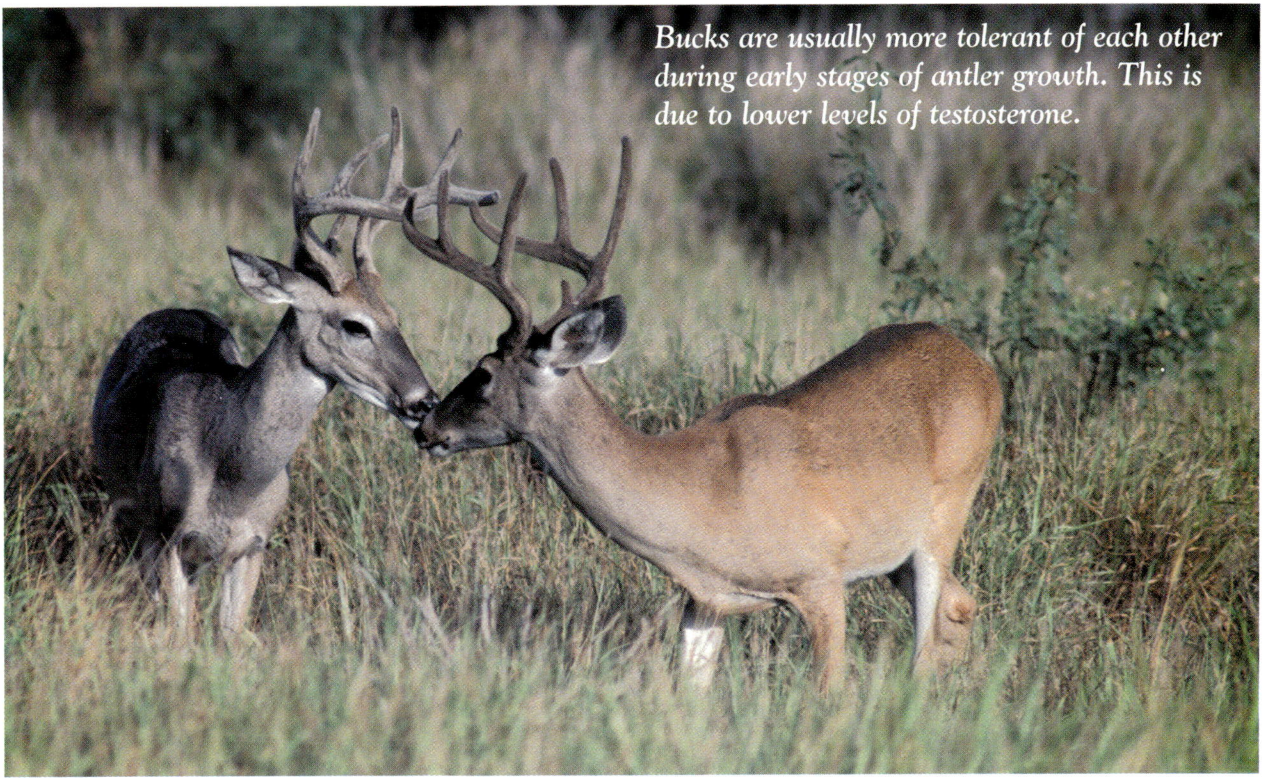
Bucks are usually more tolerant of each other during early stages of antler growth. This is due to lower levels of testosterone.

more bucks grunting. Bucks seem to be on edge due to increased testosterone levels. Older bucks actively rub their antlers on bushes and trees, increasing the size of their neck muscles and becoming increasingly aggressive with each passing week. As more does begin their estrous cycle, it quickly becomes apparent which bucks are dominant and which are not. I have heard bucks grunting at does and other bucks during this period. It often appears they are demonstrating their discontentment with a situation when they grunt, whether it's to get another deer to move on or simply in frustration that a hot doe is not receptive to their advances.

There is little doubt about the reason a buck uses the grunt-snort-wheeze — another important vocal communication. The grunt-snort-wheeze sounds like an agressive grunt followed by a *ff-ff-ff-ff-ffffffffffffff*, and it is the ultimate threat before the confrontation escalates to physical combat. As two mature bucks approach each other with their ears laid back and hair erect, you will sometimes hear

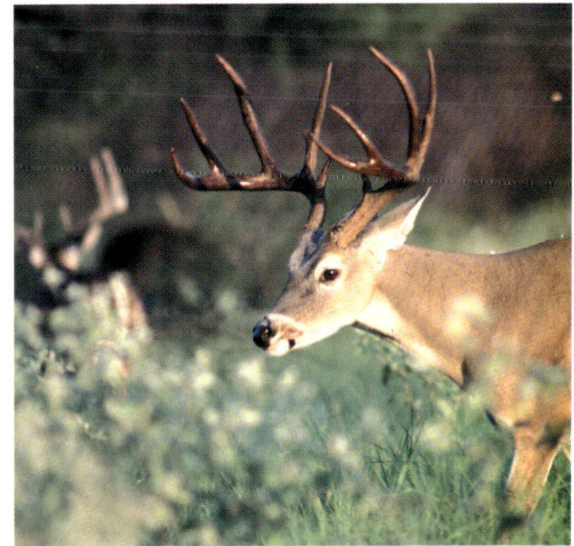
This buck is performing a snort wheeze as he approaches another buck. While I have heard this and other vocalizations numerous times over the years, this is the only time I have knowingly captured any vocalization on film. I could hear the drawn out ffffffff as I snapped the shutter.

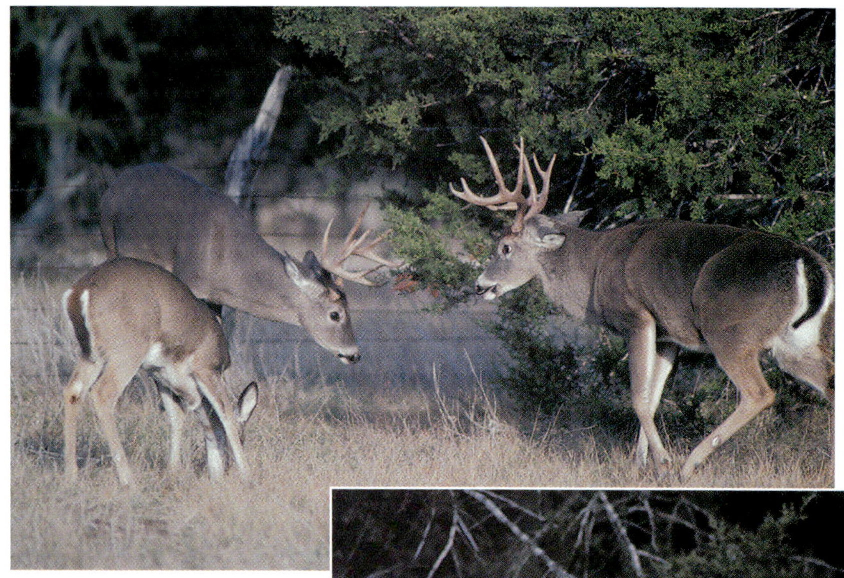

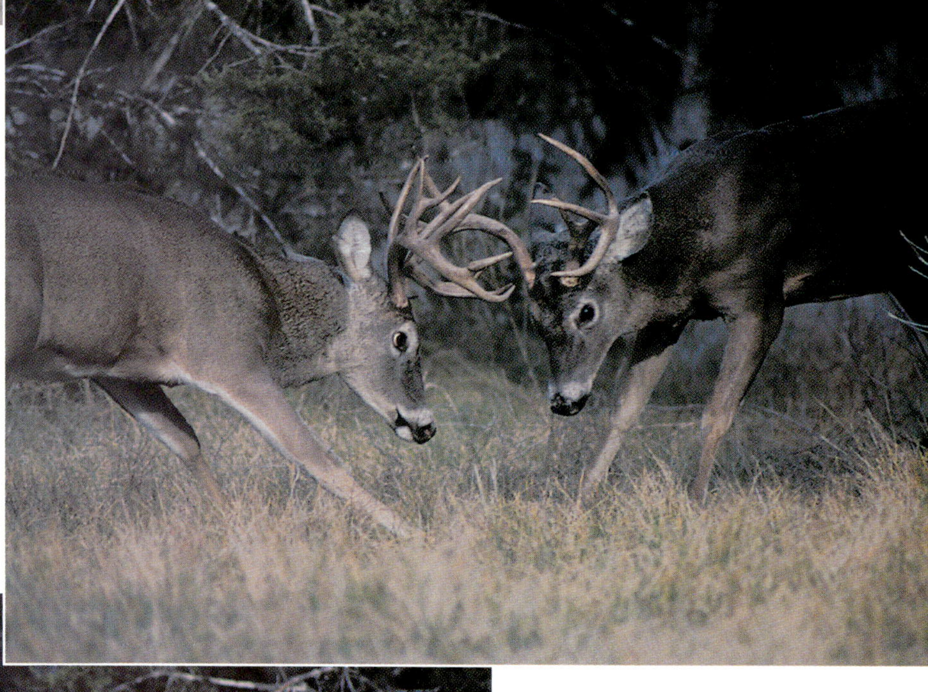

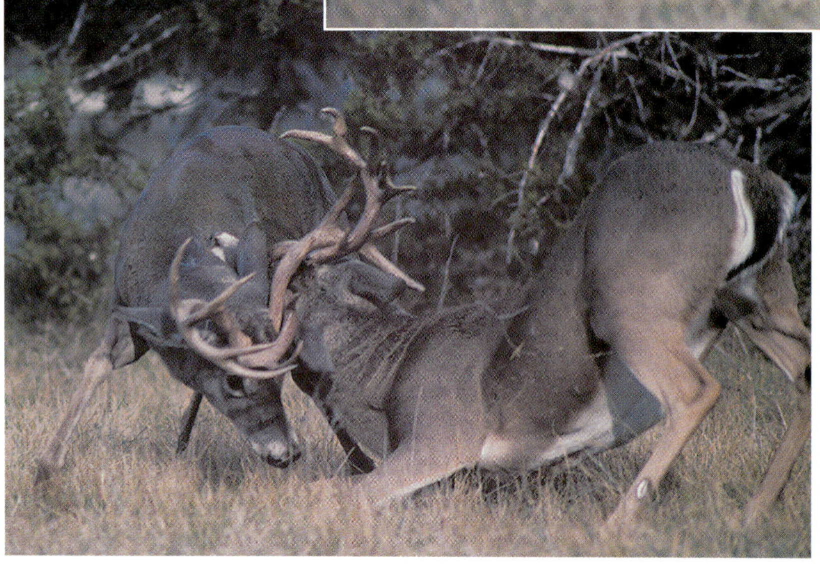

This is the real deal! The buck on the right in the top photo is demonstrating erected hair, antler display, eyes rolled forward, and the sidling step as he approaches. Note how the other buck is starting to lay his ears back as the aggressor approaches. This was a serious battle and the bucks fought for several minutes. They eventually fought into the brush out of sight before separating out of view.

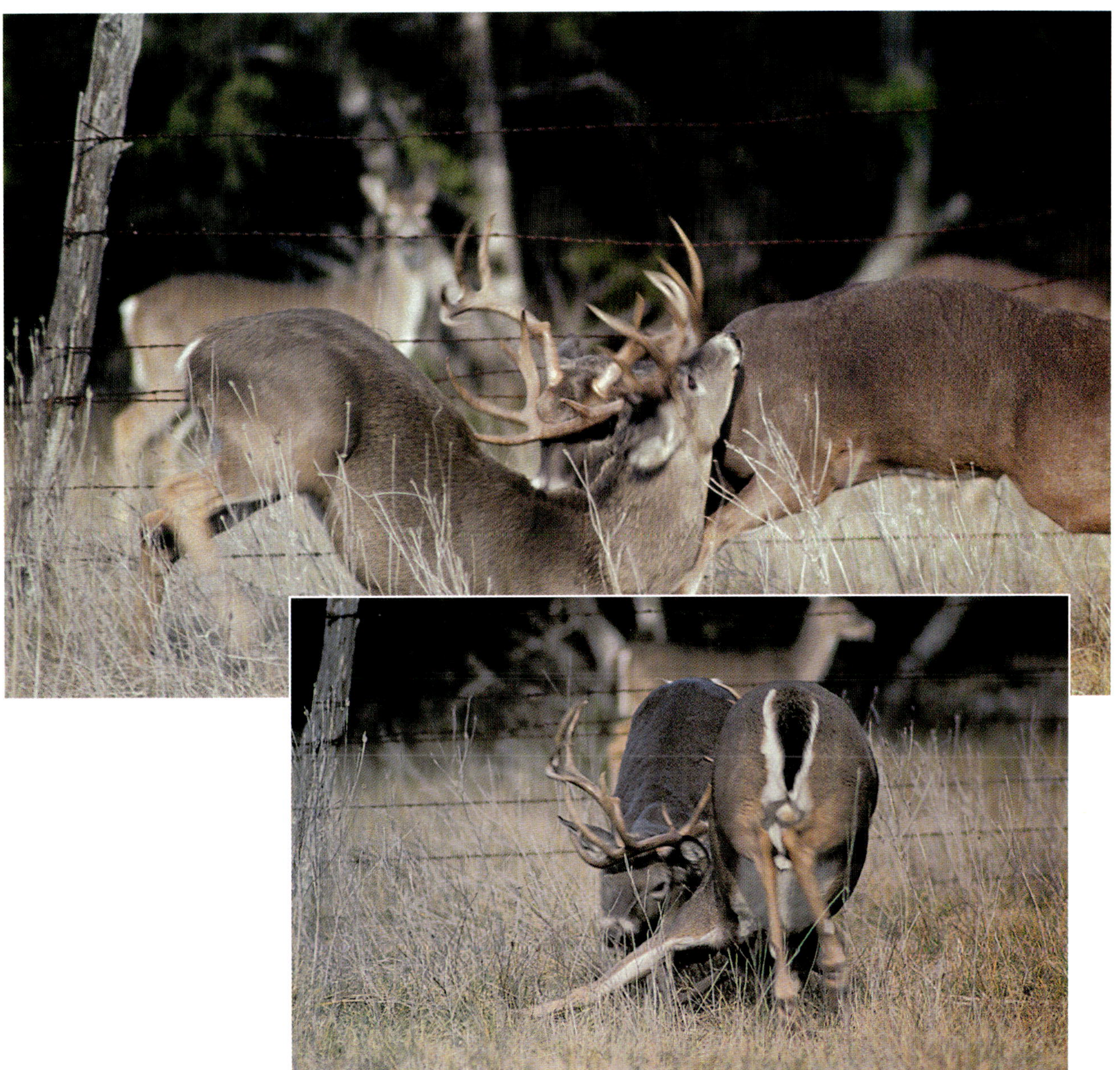

one of them grunt-snort-wheeze. This usually takes place when the bucks are within a few yards of each other. If you hear this, be observant, because you may have the rare chance to witness a fight between two mature bucks. You can be almost certain the buck making the grunt-snort-wheeze is 5 1/2 or older. I have heard this sound several times over the years and cannot remember a single time the buck was younger than 5 1/2. Most of the time it was a dominant 6 1/2- or 7 1/2-year-old buck running off another mature buck. It is quite interesting and even fun to ponder all the different questions about whitetail vocal communication, as there is still much to learn. However, what is noteworthy from an aging perspective is that on well managed properties, the bucks grunting or grunt-snort-wheezing are almost always going to be mature. Of course, there are always exceptions, such as an occasional middle-aged buck that is, or thinks he is, the dominant buck in an area.

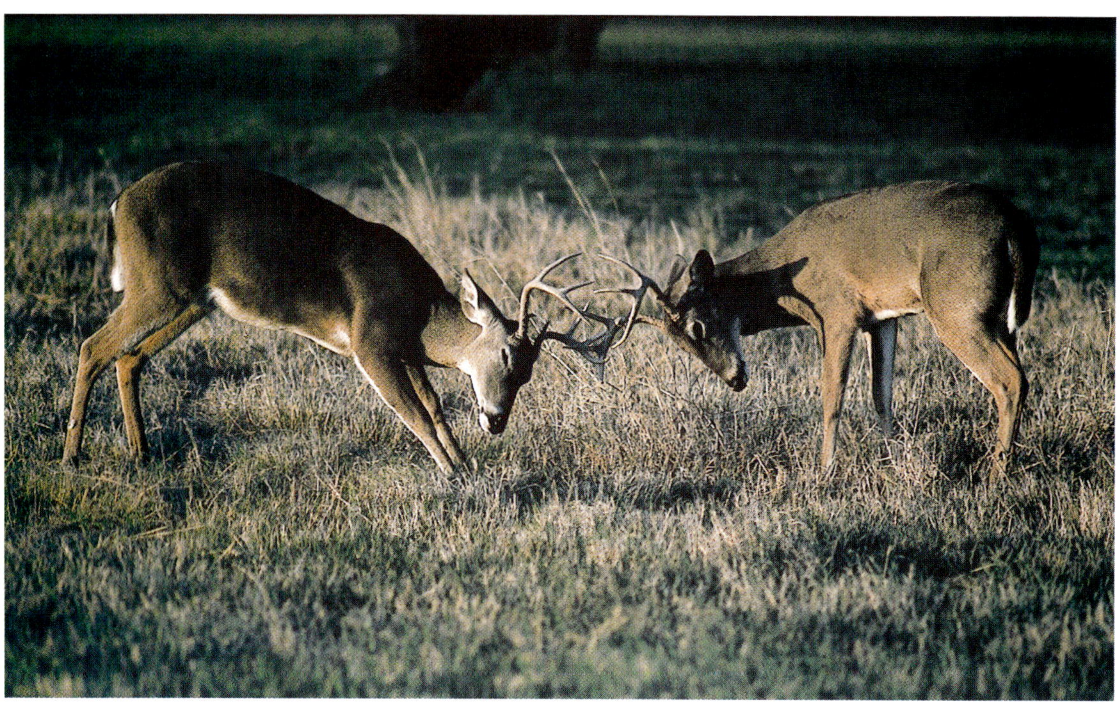

Sparring matches between young bucks help condition them for more serious battles later in life. They also aid in establishing and maintaining their position in the social hierarchy.

Whether two young bucks are playfully sparring in the fall, or an old buck is laying down his ears, grunting, erecting his hair, or grunt-snort-wheezing, they are telling you about the hierarchy in their area. It's also worth noting that the dominant buck is not always the oldest. Some younger bucks are just more aggressive or have antlers that are better suited to fight older bucks, which allows them to be dominant. One evening I watched a 3 1/2-year-old buck whip a 5 1/2-year-old, simply because he was aggressive, and because his antlers were tall, narrow, and heavy. The younger buck's antlers fit inside the older buck's, and he was able to gore him in the head and neck on contact. It only took a few seconds for the older buck to realize the younger buck had an advantage and make a quick retreat in the opposite direction. However, out of hundreds of such conflicts I have seen over the years, this was the exception not the rule. The majority of the time, bucks adhere to their logical pecking order, with age, attitude, and physical condition being the determining factors.

Observing bucks of various ages together will enable you to tell a great deal about the physical differences in their bodies. When you combine this information with how they interact with each other through their vocal and nonvocal communications, you will become more proficient in determining age. Often, when watching an unfamiliar buck and having difficulty determining his age, another buck

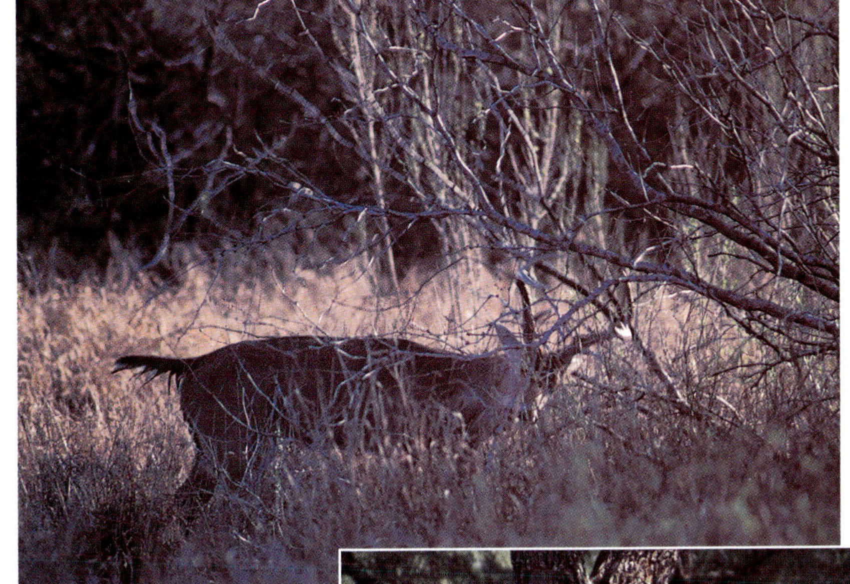

Prior to the peak of the rut, bucks actively rub trees and thrash bushes. This helps strengthen and enlarge neck muscles while depositing important scent information.

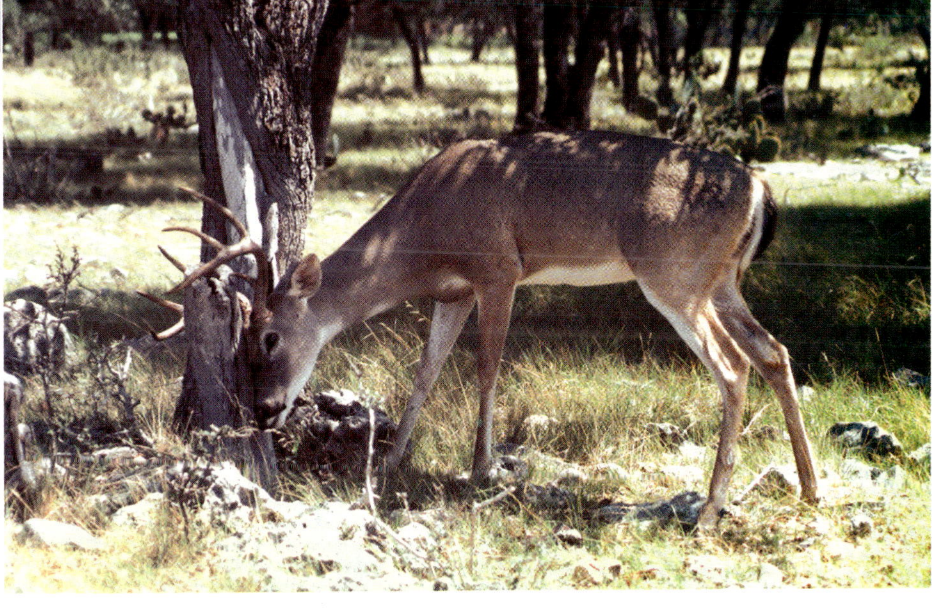

of known age would approach. By watching their reactions to each other, I was able to more confidently determine the age of the unfamiliar buck. Aging is not an exact science, but the more observations you have of a particular buck interacting with other bucks, the closer you will be to correctly estimating his age.

Whitetails also communicate through scents. Whitetails have a number of glands that perform different functions located on several areas of their bodies. The five most recognizable, external glands in the whitetail are the preorbital gland, forehead gland, interdigital gland, tarsal gland, and metatarsal gland. All of these except the metatarsal gland are known to aid deer in recogninzing one another. For instance a buck is leaving scent when he rubs his face on a limb with his preorbital glands or his forehead gland for other deer to know he has been there. Another example is a buck following the scent left by a doe's interdigital glands as she

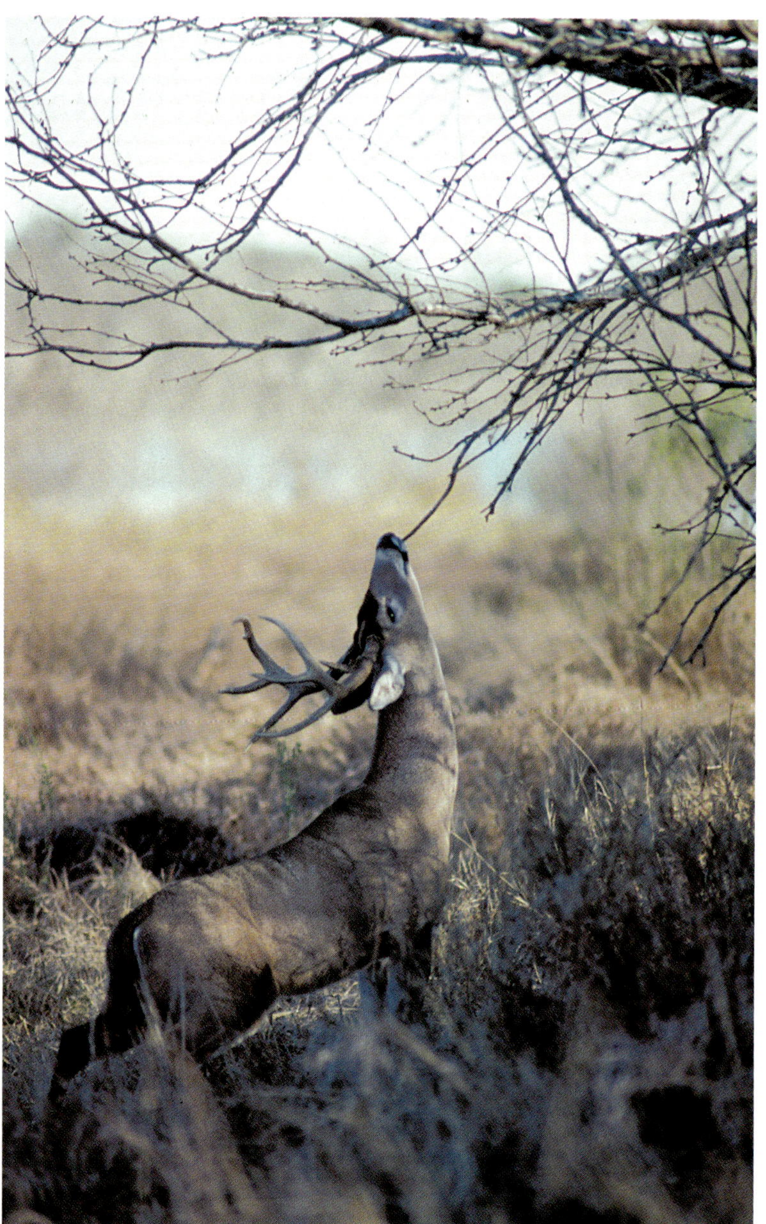

This buck is marking an overhanging limb at a scrape.

walks. Third, during the whitetail breeding season bucks will hold their back legs together and urinate over the inside hock while standing over a scrape thus leaving their scent for receptive does to find. Through my observations and photographs over the years, I have found that the tarsal gland often provides information that helps place a buck into a specific age class or at least narrow the possibilities. Mature bucks are generally more sexually active and urinate more often on their tarsals during the rut, causing them to appear larger and darker than immature or post-mature bucks. For instance, most 1 1/2- and 2 1/2-year-olds have light tarsals during the rut. At 3 1/2, their tarsals will be a little larger and darker during the rut, but are seldom larger than a silver dollar and still round in shape. At 4 1/2, their hocks can appear dark across their entire leg. The hair in and below the hock will also be dark and starting to elongate down the back of the leg. Late in the rut, the hair may even appear grayish-white under the hock as the ammonia in the urine scalds the skin, causing some hair loss. At 5 1/2, their hocks will be very large and darkly stained down the back leg to the hoof. Late in the breeding season, the area under their hocks can appear grayish-white from the scalding and hair loss. At 6 1/2 and 7 1/2, the large, urine-stained areas will be even more exaggerated and are most conspicuous during peak and post-rut. Their hocks will be extremely dark, appearing almost black, and staining will be evident across the entire inside of the leg down the back of the leg to the hoof. Late in the rut, the inside of the back legs can have very large ammonia scalding beneath the hock. As bucks reach post-maturity, their tarsals will appear smaller and lighter during the rut.

Can you identify the body characteristics that differentiate the age classes?

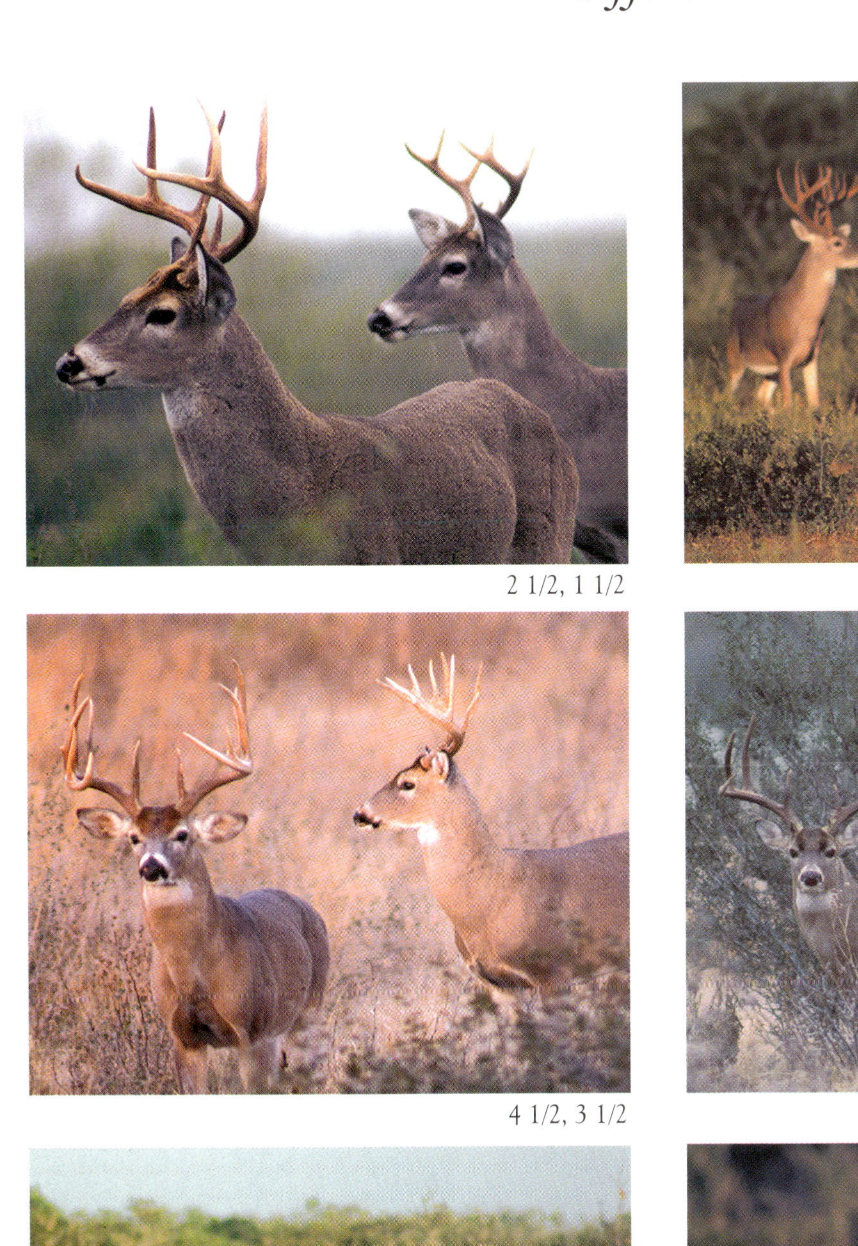

2 1/2, 1 1/2

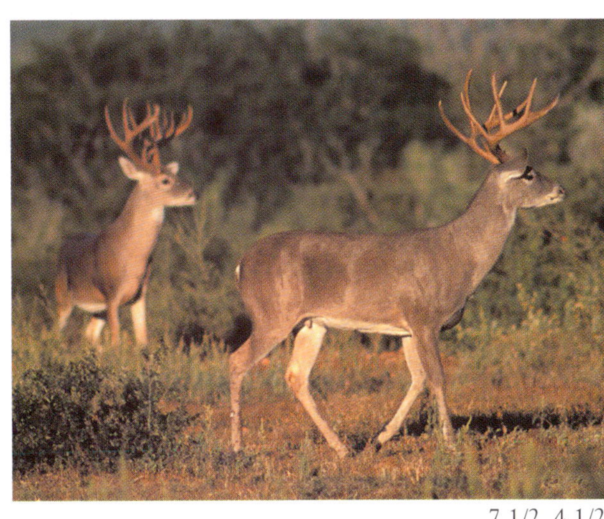

7 1/2, 4 1/2

4 1/2, 3 1/2

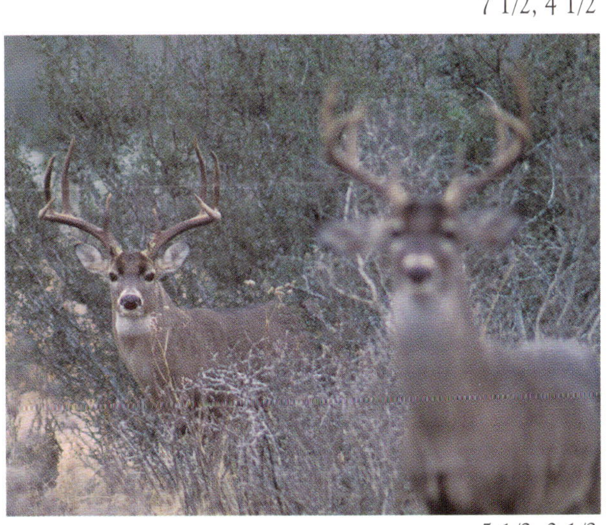

5 1/2, 3 1/2

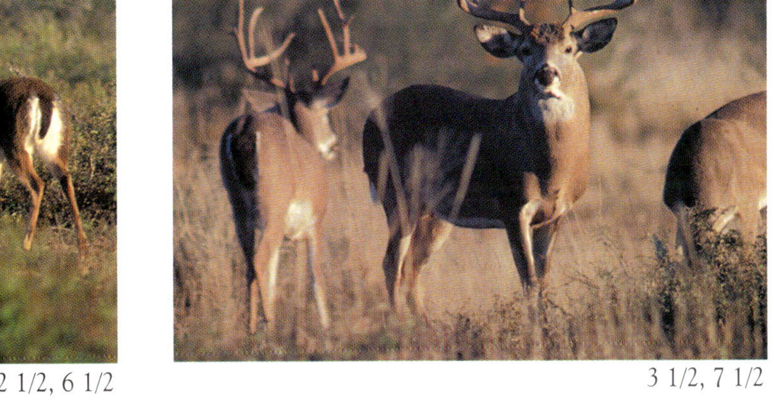

2 1/2, 6 1/2

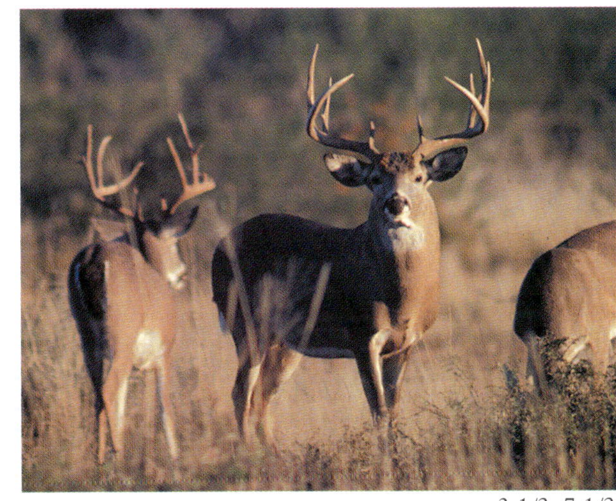

3 1/2, 7 1/2

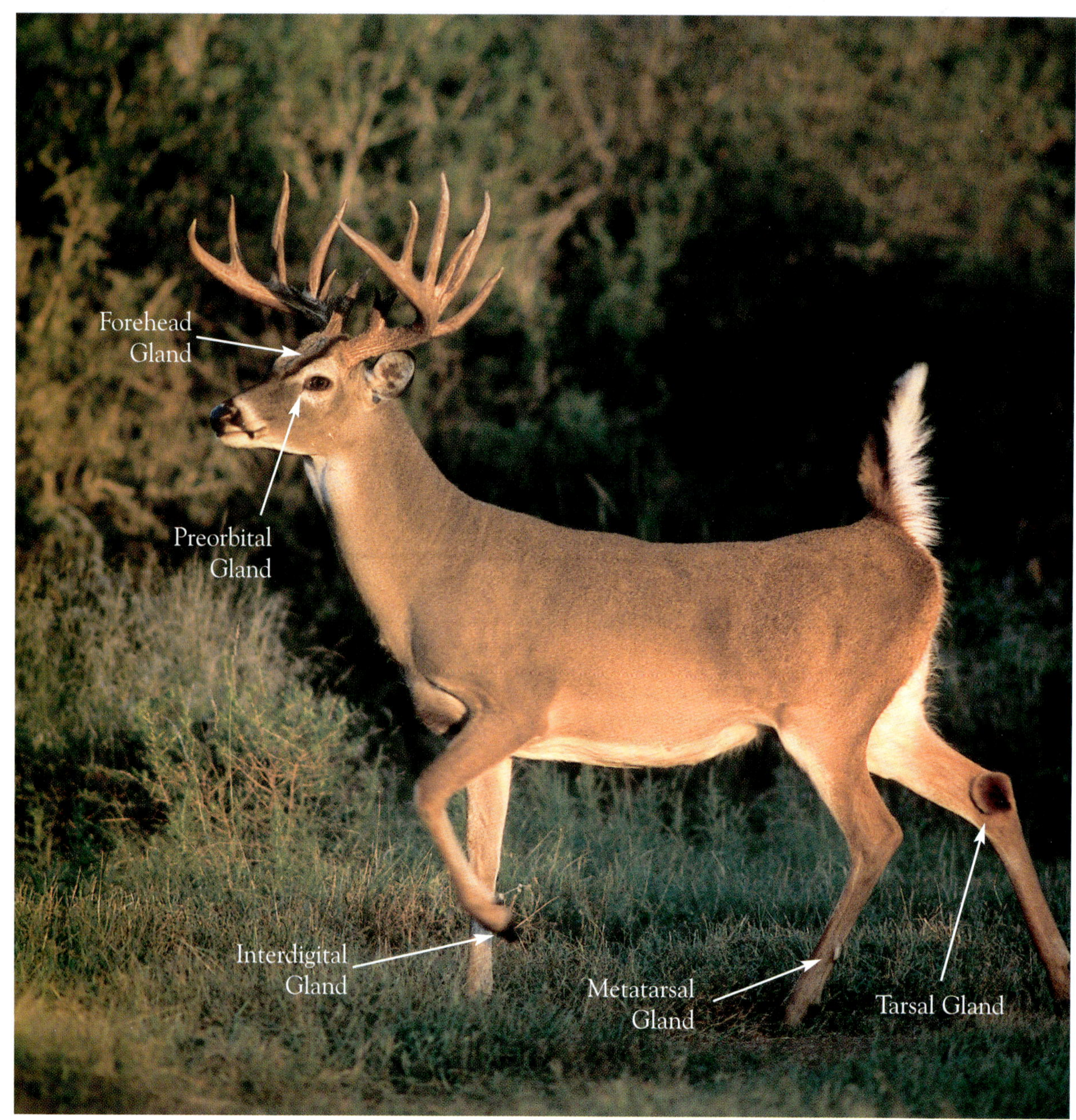

Location of external glands.

A buck's tarsals and hock area are helpful in aging because they are related to his level of involvement in breeding and, therefore, his level of maturity. The forehead gland is another area to pay close attention to. As a buck matures this area of hair between his antlers will appear thicker and darker during the rut from secretions due to increased activity of specialized sweat glands. Studying how these areas appear on different-age bucks will aid in placing them in their respective age classes. For a complete description of deer glands and vocalizations, refer to Chapter 1, written by Dr. R. Larry Marchinton.

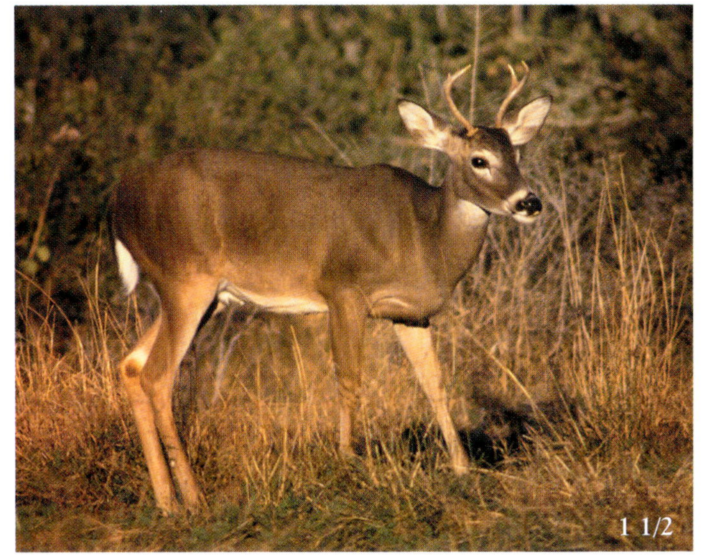

These 1 1/2 through 7 1/2-year-old bucks demonstrate the progressive darkening and chloric scalding of the tarsals and lower legs with increasing age and rutting activity. The tarsal area is a key aging indicator during the rut and post-rut. Close attention should be given to it when observing bucks to determine if they are mature.

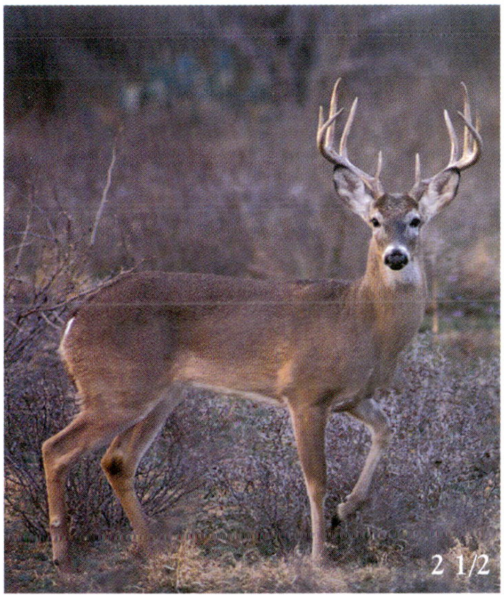

2 1/2

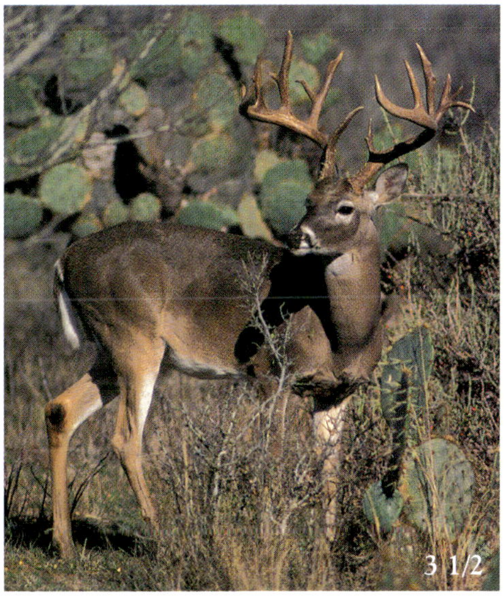

3 1/2

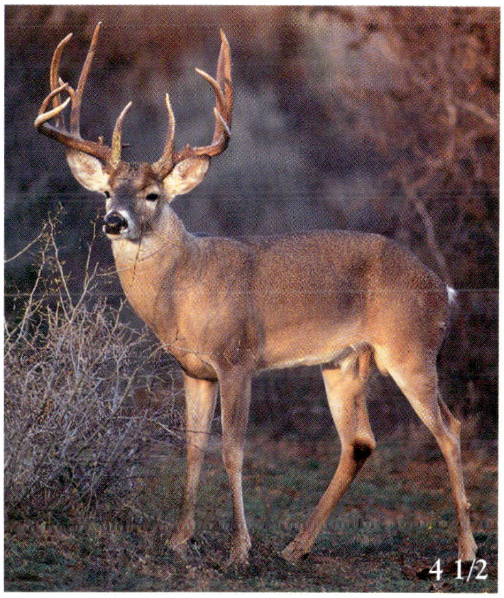

4 1/2

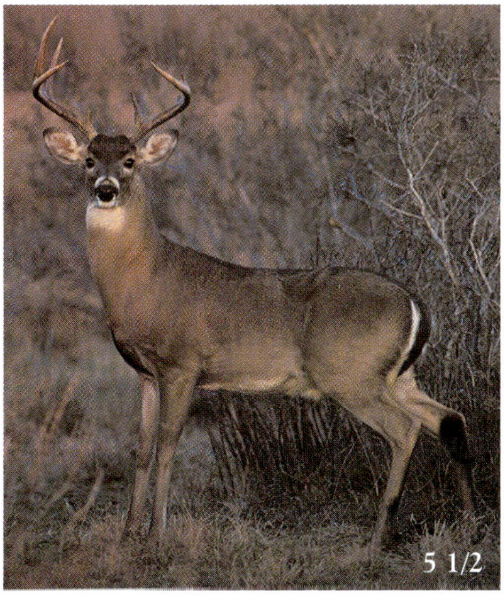

5 1/2

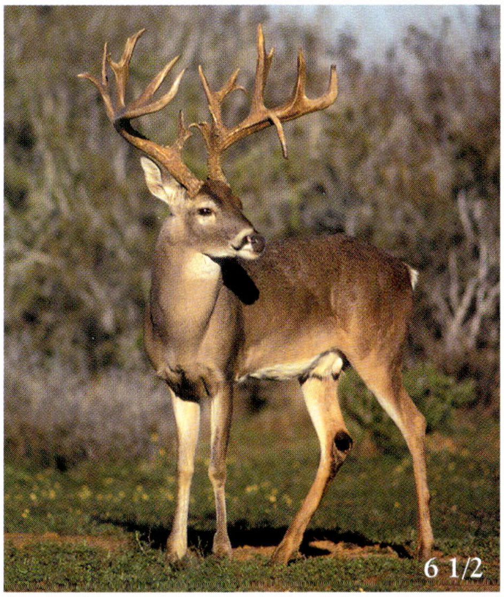

6 1/2

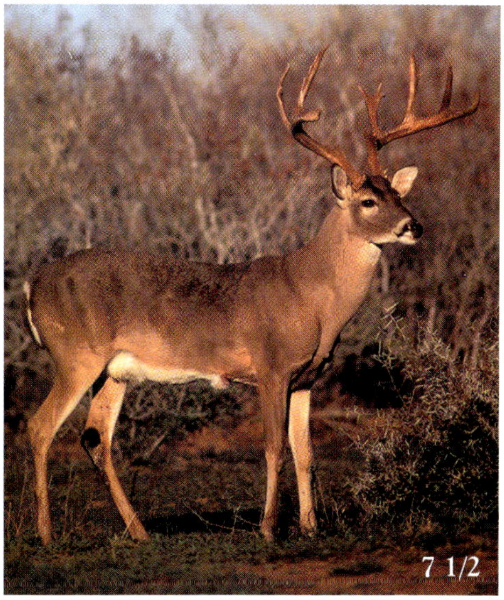

7 1/2

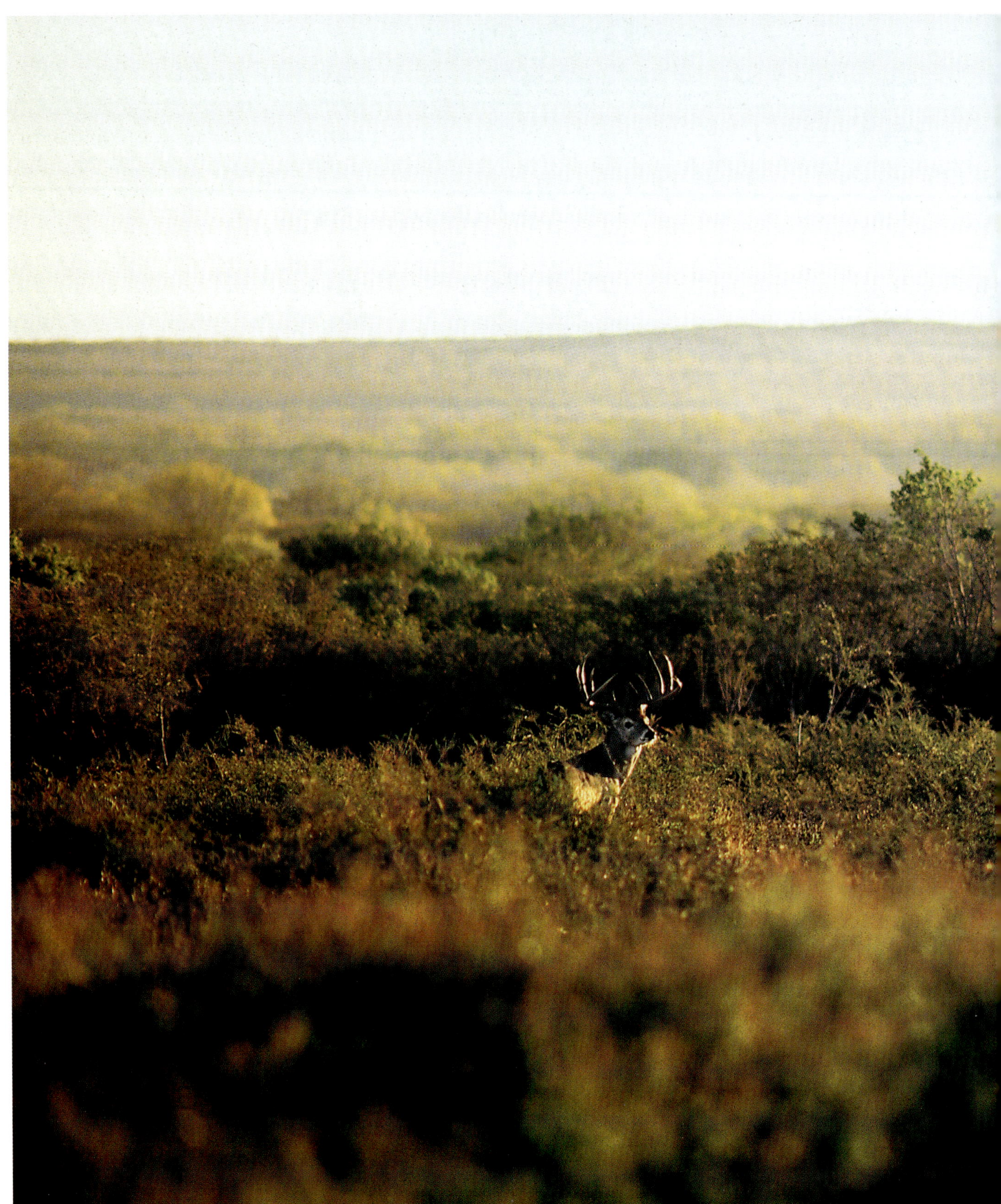

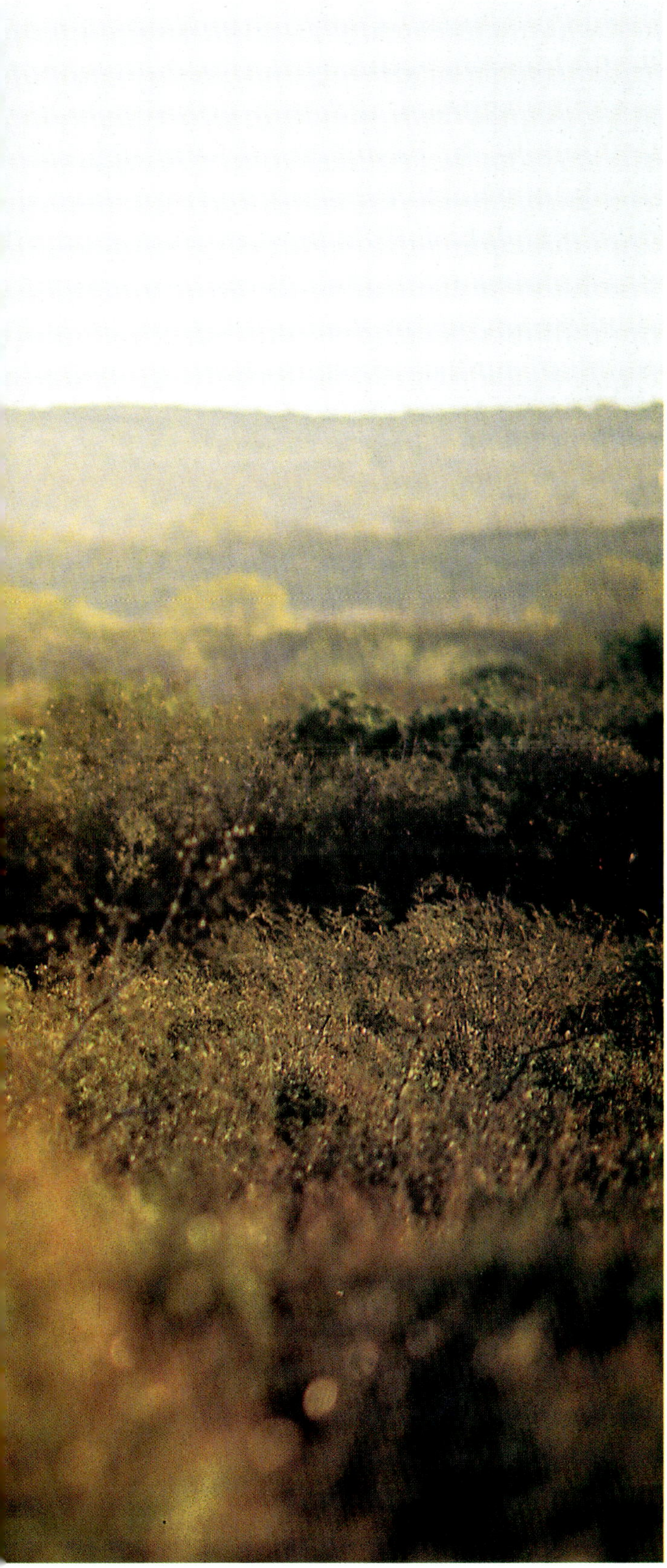

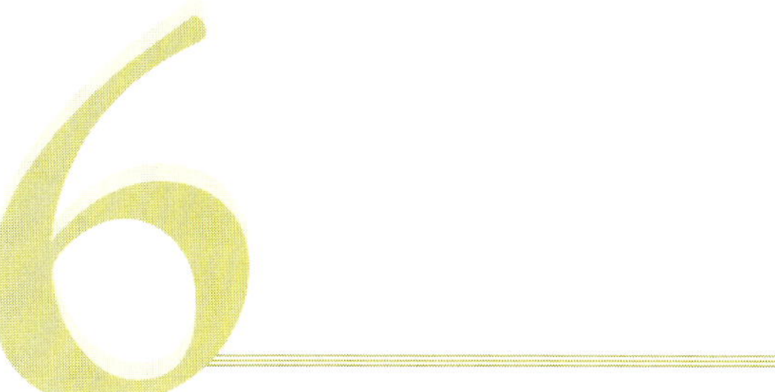

Aging Whitetails after Harvest

By Brian P. Murphy

In any deer management program, aging deer after harvest is the most critical part of the record-keeping process. This is because body weights, antler measurements, and other important data are of little value without corresponding age. Comparing two deer without knowing their age would be like comparing the body weight of a 30-year-old man to that of a 10-year-old boy — it's just not a fair comparison.

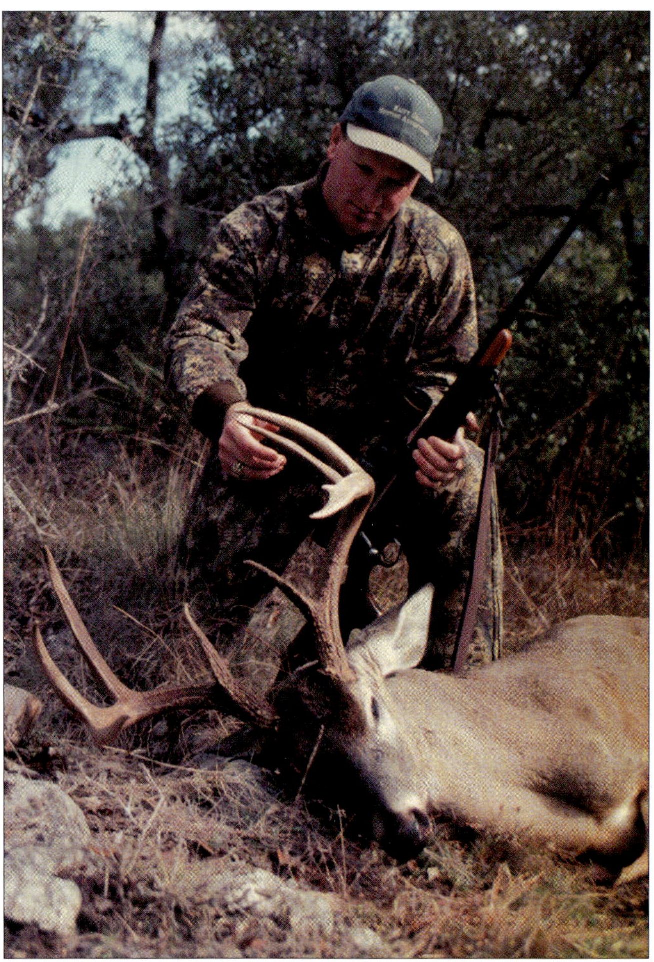

After harvesting a nice buck, don't forget to remove one of its lower jawbones for age estimation. Without the age, other data such as body weight and antler measurements are of little value.

As with aging deer on the hoof, determining the age of deer after harvest is not an exact science. The only sure way to know the exact age of an individual deer is to permanently mark it as a newborn, an impractical or impossible task in most situations. The two most commonly used techniques for aging deer after harvest are the cementum annuli and tooth eruption and wear techniques. Both involve the teeth on a deer's lower jawbone. The cementum technique involves examination of annuli (growth rings) in a stained cross section of a deer's inscisor tooth. This technique requires specialized training and equipment and is performed by one commercial lab in the U.S. (matsonslab.com).

The tooth eruption and wear technique involves comparing the tooth eruption sequences and wear patterns of the lower jaw teeth of deer to established criteria. The vast majority of wildlife biologists, deer managers, and hunters use this technique because it requires no specialized equipment, is relatively easy to learn, costs nothing, and can be performed in the field or at the hunting camp.

Tooth Eruption and Wear Criteria

This technique is based on two processes that occur on a deer's jawbone — tooth eruption and tooth wear. Tooth eruption is used to age deer under 2 1/2 years of age and tooth wear is used to age deer 2 1/2 years of age and older.

Step-by-Step Jawbone Removal

Photos by J. Guthrie

Necessary Equipment:
—Jawbone extractor
—Pruning shears
—Jawbone labels, permanent marker, and storage container

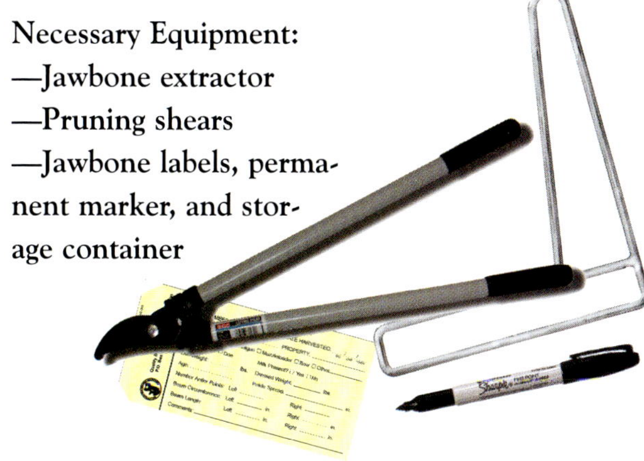

Step 1 - OPEN MOUTH: Place the back of the deer's head on a flat surface and insert the small end of the extractor from the side into the toothless space between the deer's front teeth and the first jaw teeth. Rotate the tool 90 degrees to open the mouth.

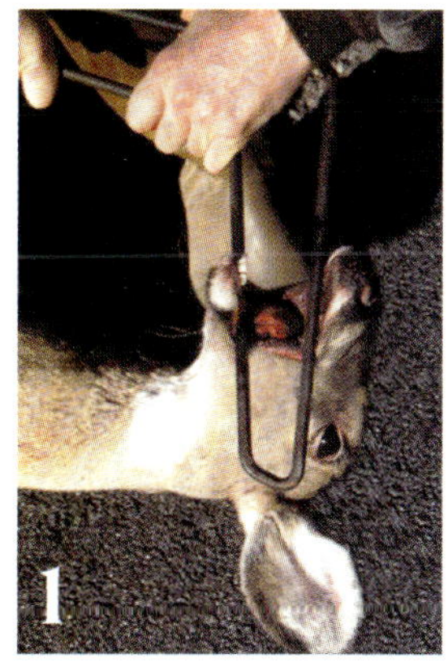

Step 2 - LOOSEN TISSUE: Insert the small end of the extractor between the outside of one lower jaw and the inside of the cheek. Push the extractor downward firmly past the base of the jaw to the base of the ear. Work the extractor back and forth and side-to-side until all attached skin is loose and separated from the jaw.

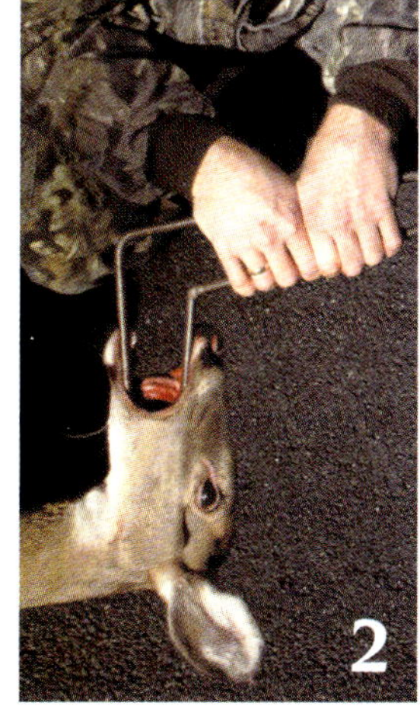

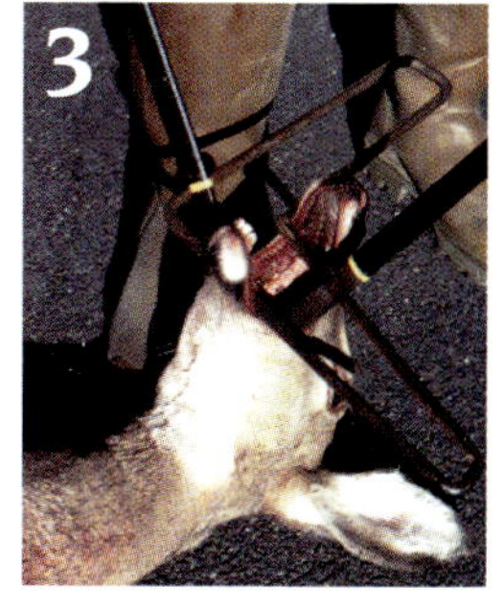

Step 3 - CUT JAWBONE: Insert the pruning shears into the deer's mouth with the unsharpened blade against the deer's cheek. Open the shears and place the center of the blades against the back of the jawbone and above the last jaw teeth (molars). Place the handles of the shears parallel to the roof of the deer's mouth and cut completely through the jawbone. Be careful not to break the back teeth.

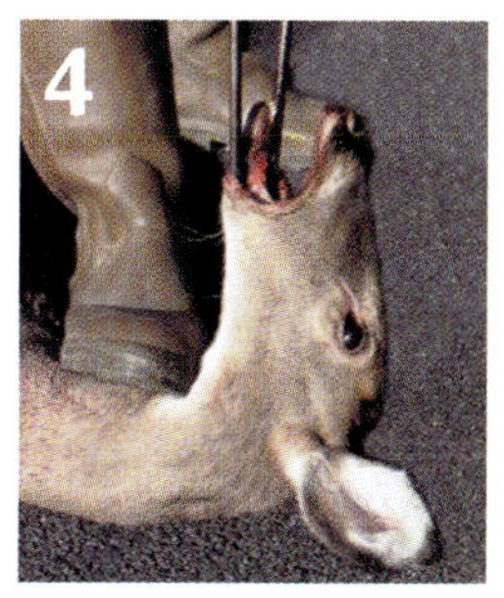

Step 4 - REMOVE JAWBONE: Remove the shears and place the small end of the jaw extractor through the previously made cut. Push the extractor downward until it is positioned below the bottom of the jaw. Place one foot on the deer's neck and pull the tool upward causing it to slide along the underside of the jaw. Once the extractor reaches the front of the mouth where both lower jaws are connected, twist the extractor until the connection breaks. Remove the jaw and check for damage to the teeth. If damaged, age determination may be difficult or impossible resulting in the need to remove the other jawbone.

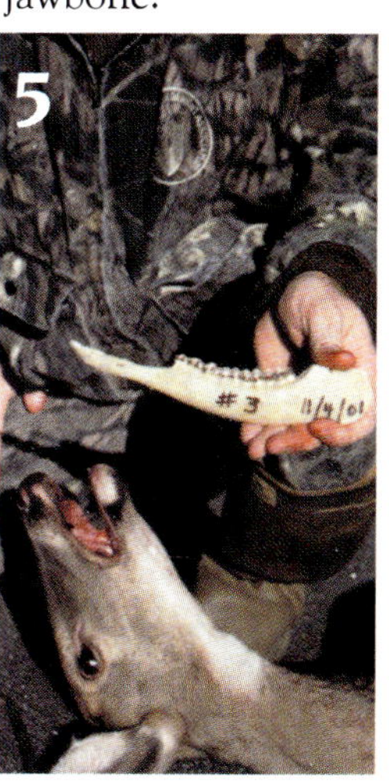

Step 5 - CLEAN & LABEL JAWBONE: Clean and remove remaining tissue. Label the jawbone with the corresponding deer number, date, sex, and other pertinent information. Store in a wire cage or basket to air out. Careful removal of the jawbone does not damage the deer head for mounting.

Tooth Eruption

Tooth eruption criteria are based on the fact that white-tailed deer, like humans, gain additional teeth as they get older and replace some of their temporary teeth with permanent ones. At birth, whitetail fawns have three temporary premolars (called "milk" teeth). All three "milk" teeth are replaced with permanent ones when they are approximately 16-18 months old.

White-tailed deer also gain two additional permanent molars from birth until they are about 18 months old. This knowledge allows us to quickly separate deer into three basic age groups including fawns, yearlings, and adults (Figure 3). This is done by simply examining the number and type of teeth (temporary or permanent) on one side of a deer's lower jawbone. Fawns (1/2 year old) will have three or four teeth, yearlings (1 1/2 years old) will have six teeth, but the first three will be temporary "milk" teeth, and adults (2 1/2 years old and older) will have six teeth and permanent premolars.

Distinguishing between the different teeth may be slightly difficult at first but it can be picked up with minimal practice. The easiest way to determine where the different teeth begin and end is to look at the point where they enter the jawbone. All adult white-tailed deer (2 1/2 + years old) should have six teeth on each side of their lower jaw including three premolars and three molars.

Jawbone Terminology

Before outlining the aging process, it is necessary to review the basic parts of a deer jawbone and learn the terminology that is used (Refer to the diagrams on this page and the following pages of this chapter). It is recommended that you obtain a deer jawbone to use as a reference during the remainder of this chapter.

Premolars: The first three small jaw teeth. These are used for cutting the food. These teeth are labeled P1, P2, and P3 in the diagram.

Molars: The last three large jaw teeth. These are used for grinding the food. These teeth are labeled M1, M2, and M3 in the diagram.

Milk teeth: Temporary premolars that are later replaced by permanent ones.

Enamel: The hard white outer coat of the tooth.

Dentine: The soft inner core of a tooth, much darker in color than the enamel.

Lingual crests: The sharp tooth ridges running from front to back on the tongue side of the jawbone.

Buccal crests: The shorter tooth ridges running from front to back on the cheek side of the jawbone.

Back cusp: The shelf-like surface on the very back of the last molar (M3).

Infundibulum: The dark central depression between the buccal and lingual crests of the teeth.

Tooth Wear

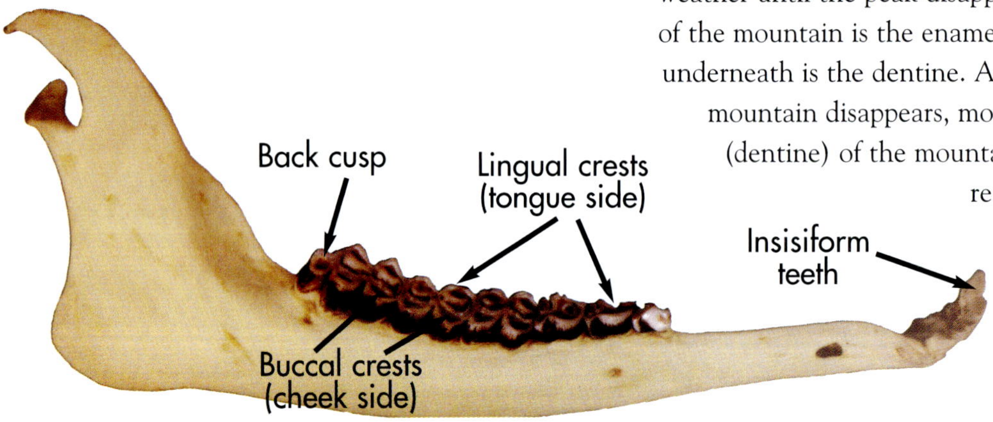

Tooth wear criteria are based on the amount of wear on a deer's teeth. Over time, the width of the dentine increases in relation to that of the surrounding enamel. This process can be described as a sharp mountain peak being slowly eroded by weather until the peak disappears. The outer shell of the mountain is the enamel and the material underneath is the dentine. As the peak of the mountain disappears, more of the inner portion (dentine) of the mountain is exposed. As a result, the dentine appears as if it is getting wider with increasing wear. It is

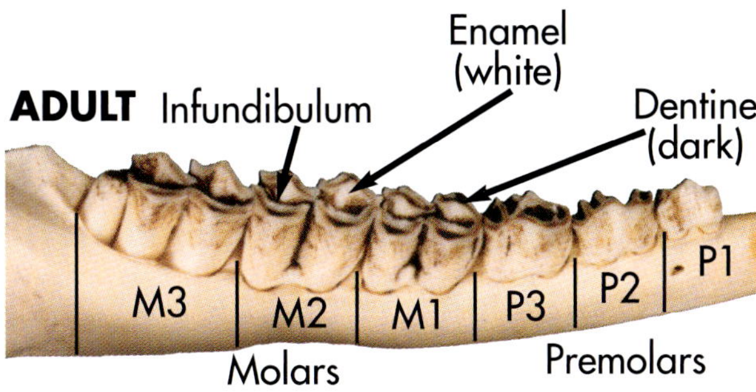

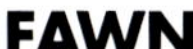

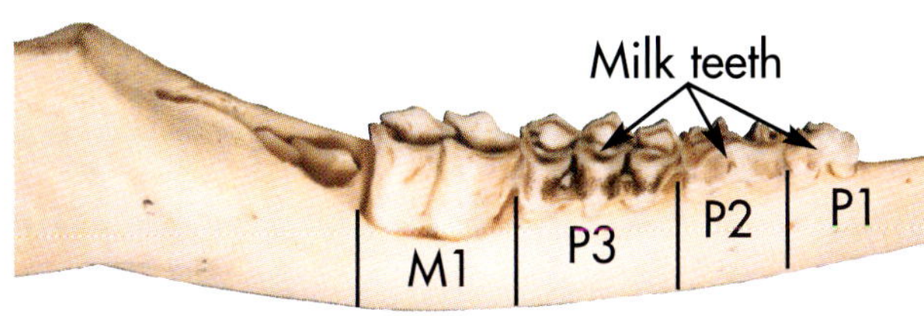

very important to understand this concept because it is the basis of this technique.

Aging Criteria for White-tailed Deer

The following tooth eruption and wear criteria should be used as a general guide only because deer in your area may have slightly different wear patterns. The key to being successful at aging deer is to use all available clues rather than just one or two. The use of multiple characteristics will substantially increase your accuracy and consistency. Other suggestions to maximize the value and success of your aging program include:

1. Collecting a lower jawbone from all deer harvested. In particular, do everything possible to remove the jawbones from trophy bucks before they are taken to the taxidermist because these jawbones often are lost or mixed up with others and are of no value.

2. Establishing a central collection point for all jawbones that is protected from scavengers and well ventilated, allowing jawbones to dry naturally. Wire fish baskets work well as do custom wire mesh boxes.

3. Implementing an identification system that allows the jawbone to be matched with its corresponding harvest data sheet. It is best to mark the necessary details directly on the jawbone with a permanent marker, although tags made of aluminum, plastic, or cardstock may be used.

4. Ensuring that the same person ages all deer every year to ensure consistency. If the person is not a trained biologist, they should have one review their jawbone ages the first few years until they are proficient with the technique. If you practice aging on the hoof and any recognizable deer are harvested, use their jaw age to check your on-the-hoof age.

The ages of the deer illustrated and labeled on the next two pages of this chapter are grouped in half-years because most deer are born during late spring and early summer and harvested in fall and winter. The tooth eruption and wear technique can be used to estimate the age of deer from fawns to at least 6 1/2 years old, though the accuracy decreases with increasing age. Any deer older than 6 1/2 can simply be aged as 7 1/2-plus.

With this information, the charts on the following pages, and a little practice, you will soon become proficient at aging white-tailed deer after harvest. Being able to determine the age of your deer will definitely add to your hunting experience, the value of your trophy, and to your knowledge of deer. So the next time you harvest a deer, remember to save the most important part — the lower jawbone — and give aging a try.

A Guide to Jawbone Aging of White-tailed Deer

The following charts were compiled by the Quality Deer Management Association for their educational poster, "Jawbone Removal and Aging of White-tailed Deer." To purchase a laminated, color poster containing these charts and other information, call the **QDMA** at (800) 209-3337.

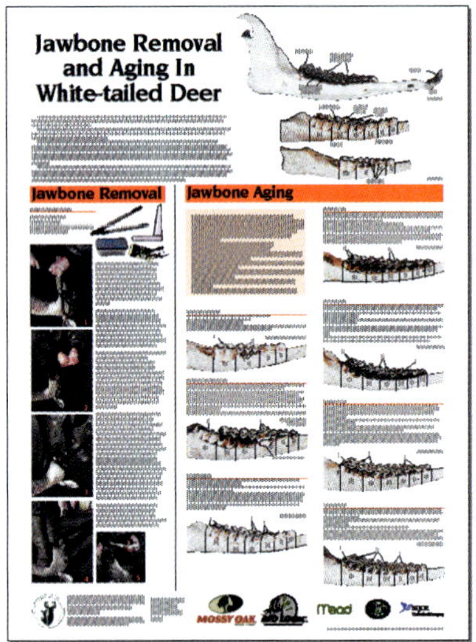

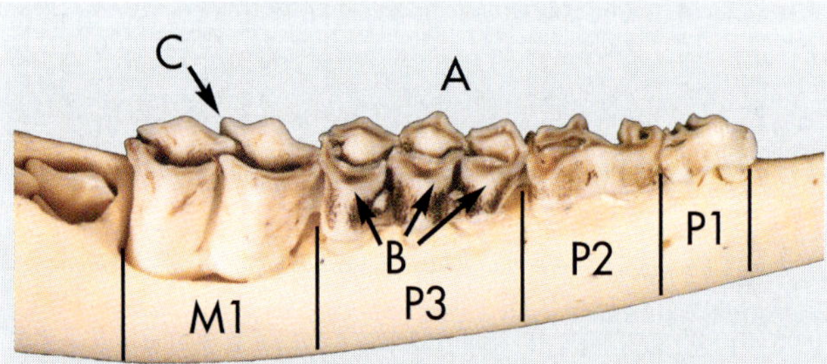

6 Months Old (fawn)

A) 3 or 4 fully erupted teeth on one side of the lower jaw.

B) P3 is a temporary 3-crested "milk" tooth.

C) M1 will be very white and unstained.

Fawns are the easiest group to age. The key to recognizing this group is the number of teeth, the presence of "milk" teeth, and a very short jawbone.

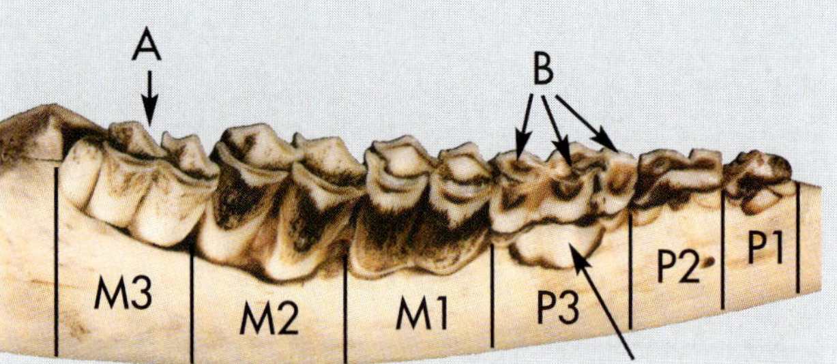

1 1/2 Years Old (yearling)

A) 6 teeth on the lower jaw, although the 6th tooth (M3) may not be fully erupted if the deer was born late or harvested early in the hunting season.

B) In most cases, P3 will be a temporary "milk" tooth with 3 crests. However, if the animal was harvested late in the season or an early-born fawn, it may have already replaced the temporary P3 with a permanent one. This is easily recognizable because the new P3 will have only 2 crests and it will be very white (unstained) and show almost no wear. Note the permanent tooth erupting underneath the temporary one in the photograph.

The key to identifying this group is the presence of 6 jaw teeth, but a three-cusped P3.

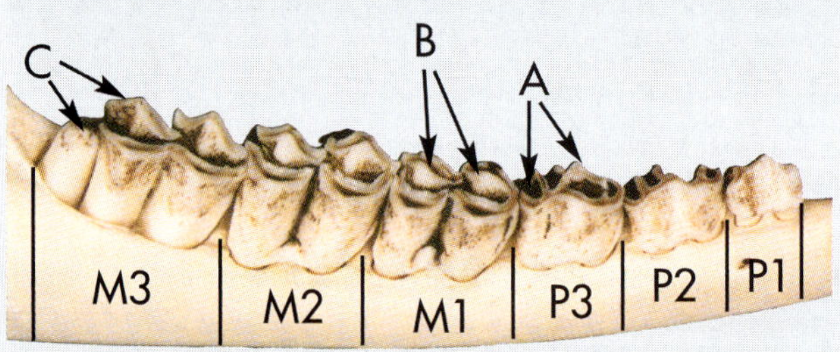

2 1/2 Years Old

A) The presence of all 6 permanent teeth on the lower jaw. P3 is a permanent 2-crested tooth and M3 is fully erupted.

B) The dentine width on the lingual crests of M1 is equal to or narrower than one strip of the surrounding enamel.

C) Little or no dentine is showing on the lingual side of the second crest of M3. The back cusp may be worn level, but not slanting toward the buccal side or cupping.

This age group is identified by the presence of 6 fully-erupted permanent teeth, the narrow dentine width on M1, and by the minimal wear on the last molar (M3), especially on the back cusp.

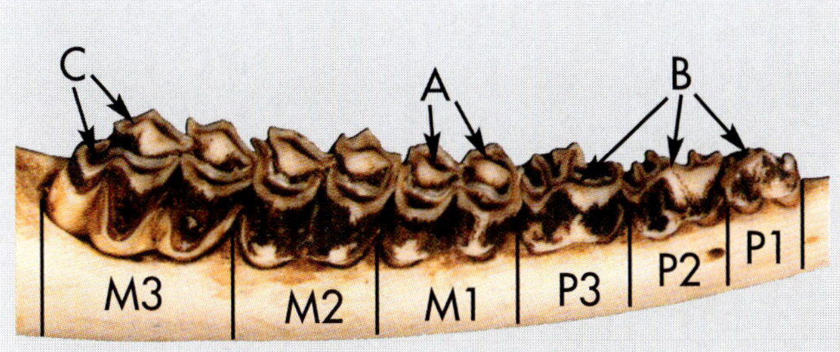

3 1/2 Years Old

A) The dentine width on the lingual crests of M1 is noticeably wider than one strip of the surrounding enamel. The dentine width on M2 and M3 is equal to or narrower than one strip of the surrounding enamel.

B) Light to moderate wear is evident on P1, P2, and P3.

C) Dentine is showing slightly on the lingual side of the second crest of M3. The back cusp of M3 is beginning to show wear and often slanting to the buccal side.

The key to separating this group from the 2 1/2-year-olds is the width of the dentine on the first molar (M1), the presence of dentine on the second lingual crest of M3, and the presence of moderate wear on the back cusp of M3.

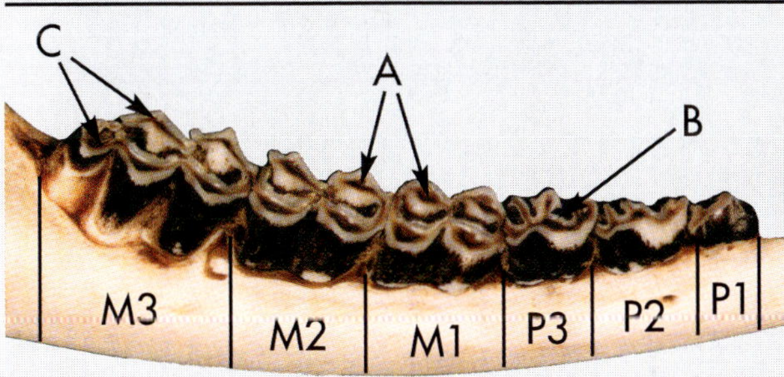

4 1/2 Years Old

A) The dentine width on the lingual crests of both M1 and M2 are noticeably wider than one strip of the surrounding enamel. The dentine width on M3 is equal to or narrower than one strip of the surrounding enamel.

B) Wear is becoming pronounced on P1, P2, and P3. The lingual crests of P3 may be starting to erode away.

C) Dentine is very pronounced on both lingual crests of M3. The back cusp of M3 is showing pronounced wear and slanting sharply to the buccal side or beginning to cup.

The best way to distinguish between a 3 1/2- and 4 1/2-year-old is by the dentine width on the lingual crests of M2 and by the level of wear on the back cusp of M3.

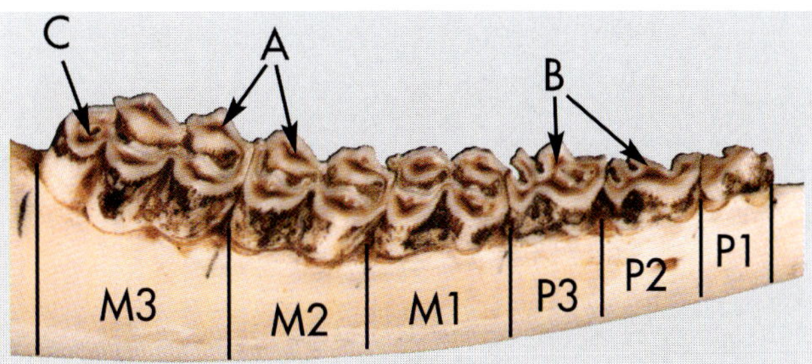

5 1/2 Years Old

A) The dentine width on the lingual crests of M1, M2, and M3 are all noticeably wider than one strip of the surrounding enamel. M1 is showing pronounced wear but the infundibulum remains intact.

B) Wear is becoming heavy on P1, P2, and P3. The lingual crests of P2 and P3 are often worn nearly flat.

C) The back cusp of M3 is slanting heavily to the buccal side. In most cases, a noticeable cup is evident in the center of the back cusp.

Animals 4 1/2 and 5 1/2 years of age are often difficult to separate. The key to making this distinction is by paying close attention to the dentine width on the lingual crests of M3 and the wear on P3 and M1.

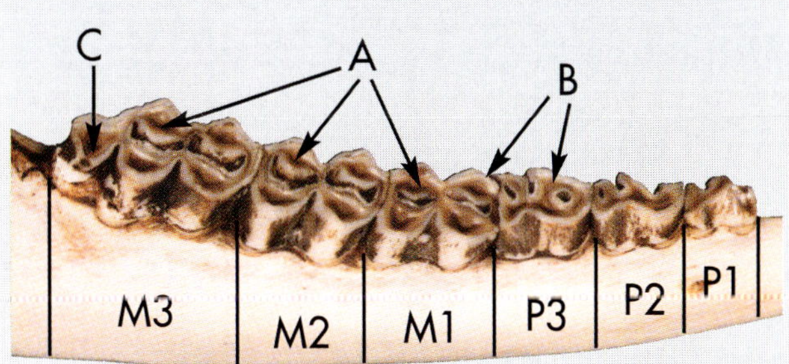

6 1/2 Years Old

A) The dentine width on the lingual crests of M1, M2, and M3 are all noticeably wider than one strip of the surrounding enamel. M1 is heavily worn and the infundibulum is beginning to wear away.

B) Wear is very heavy on P1, P2, and P3. The lingual crests of P2, P3, and M1 are worn nearly flat.

C) The back cusp of M3 is heavily worn and deeply cupped.

The key to separating a 5 1/2-year-old from a 6 1/2-year-old is by the level of wear on M1 and M3 and by the erosion of the lingual crests on P3 and M1. Any deer showing more wear than described here, should be classed as 6 1/2+ years old.

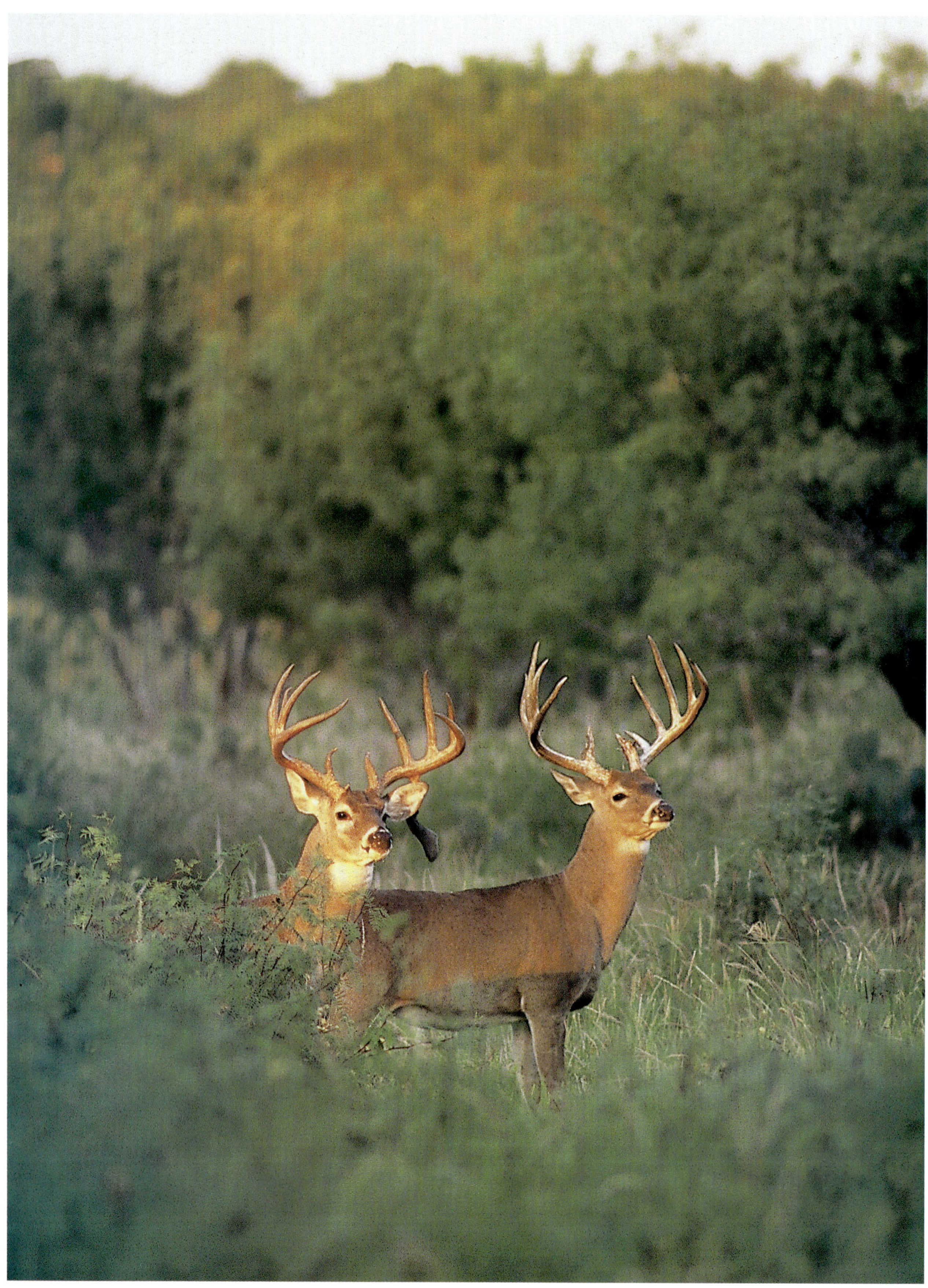

7 Estimating Boone & Crockett Score on the Hoof

Whitetails are unique in that their antlers grow in so many configurations. Mule deer, elk, and moose also have variations, but not to the extent occurring in whitetails. The most recognized scoring system for whitetails, the Boone & Crockett Club (B&C) system, separates all bucks into two categories — typicals and nontypicals. Each category has a gross score that measures the total number of inches of antler grown and a net score that reflects the score after deductions for asymmetry.

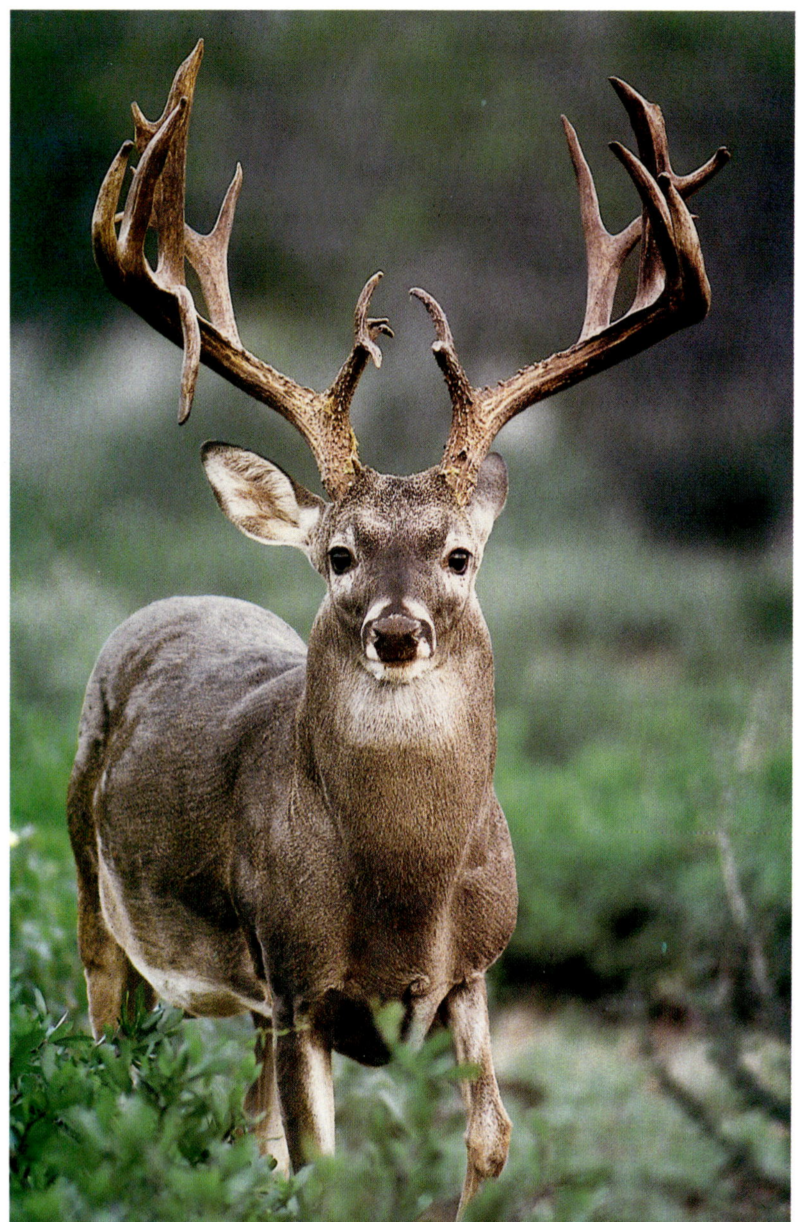

Whitetail antlers can grow in numerous configurations, as this buck's nontypical antlers demonstrate. While some characteristics are genetically influenced, much remains unknown as to why antlers grow in the shapes they do.

The typical category is used for bucks with symmetrical, or nearly symmetrical, antlers. A buck's gross typical score consists of its inside spread, length of each main beam, length of each tine, and four circumference measurements on each main beam. The typical net score includes deductions for anything asymmetrical. It is the gross score minus the differences in corresponding tine, circumference, main beam measurements, and any other nontypical points.

The net nontypical score is similar to the net typical score in that deductions are taken for differences in main-beam length, tine length, and beam circumference between both antlers. The difference is that all nontypical point measurements are included in the net nontypical score. The gross nontypical score does not deduct for differences in beam length, tine length, or beam circumferences and also includes all nontypical points. This explanation of B&C scoring is very simplistic, and by studying the official B&C score sheet on pages 230-233, you will gain a better understanding of how to correctly measure bucks in either category. More detailed information and official score sheets can be obtained from the Boone & Crockett Club (www.boone-crockett.org).

For the purposes of this book we have used gross scores, unless otherwise noted. A gross score provides a more accurate picture of overall antler size, because it gives the animal credit for every inch of antler grown. Judging whitetail antlers involves numerous variables that can deceive and frustrate even the most seasoned observer. However, like any endeavor worth pursuing, practice greatly increases accuracy. What also becomes apparent after judging many sets of antlers is that bucks with drastically different sets of antlers can have B&C scores within a couple inches of each other. One buck may have a wide spread with heavy beams and short tines, while another may have a narrow spread with average beams and long tines. If the two were side by side, most hunters would never guess that both carried nearly identical scores. By practicing and becoming more proficient at judging, hunters can increase their opportunity to harvest mature, high-scoring bucks that previously may have been overlooked. Becoming more proficient at judging antlers will allow you to recognize a buck for what he is, even though he may exhibit a perceived negative quality such as a narrow spread.

To consistently and accurately judge B&C score requires time, practice, and patience. There is simply no shortcut. To estimate score, four groups of measurements have to be estimated — inside spread, beam length of both antlers, four mass measurements on both antlers, and all tine lengths on both antlers. These measurements require a lot of figuring, and most mature bucks are not in the habit of standing around to be sized up. Before actually estimating antler measurements in the field, sit down with a pen and paper and go over some basic scenarios to come up with a 150-class B&C buck, or whatever is realistic for your area. One scenario for a 150-class B&C buck would be as follows:

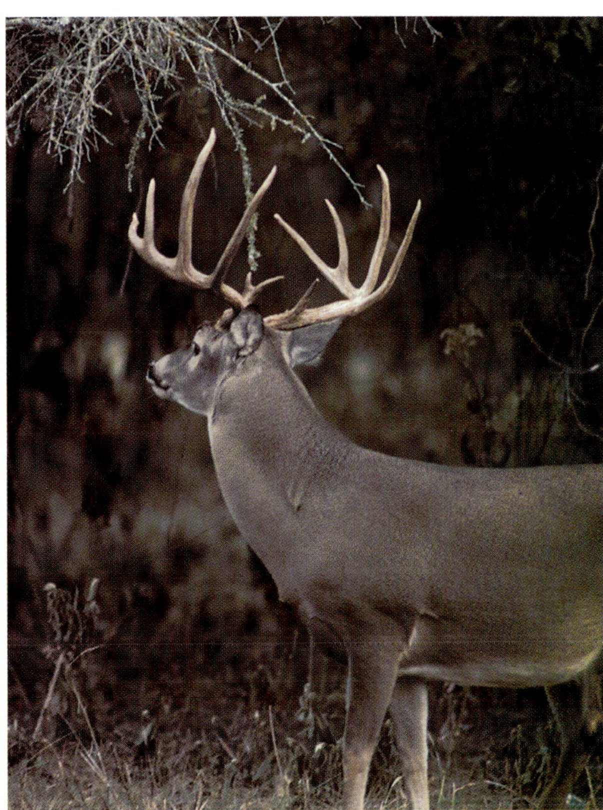

This buck carries an impressive example of a typical 10-point rack with very long tines that curve inward.

TINE LENGTHS (starting with the brow tine):	
Right: 4 + 10 + 10 + 4	28 in.
Left: 4 + 10 + 10 + 4	28 in.
BEAMS: 22 + 22	44 in.
MASS: 4 x 4 per antler (16 x 2)	32 in.
SPREAD:	18 in.
GROSS SCORE:	150 in.

A scenario for a 160-class B&C buck could look as follows:

TINE LENGTHS:	
5 + 10 + 10 + 5	30 in.
5 + 10 + 10 + 5	30 in.
BEAMS: 24 + 24	48 in.
MASS: 4 x 4 per antler (16 x 2)	32 in.
SPREAD:	20 in.
GROSS SCORE:	160 in.

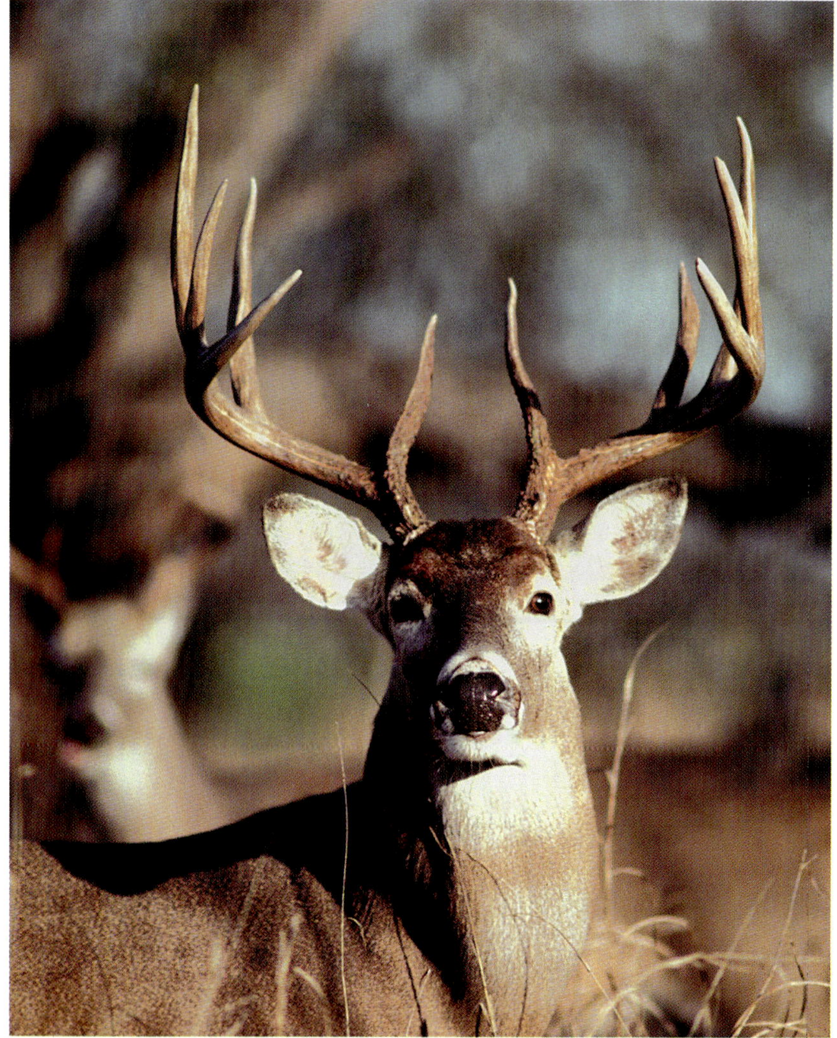

With long brow tines and G-4s, it is quickly recognizable that this buck has well over 30 inches of tine lengths per antler. A quick glance at his spread, beams, and mass and the hunter who has memorized benchmarks quickly recognizes this buck is well over 150 B&C (30-21-16-16) without even adding the measurements.

There are dozens of variables, but practicing a system will provide benchmarks that can be used to recognize where a buck's antlers are deficient in score. For example, a symmetrical 10-point buck with 2-inch G-1s, 8-inch G-2s, 7-inch G-3s, and 3-inch G-4s, would have 20 inches of total tine length on each antler. This buck would need a very heavy mass of 38 inches (both sides combined), main beams of at least 25 inches, and a 22-inch inside spread just to reach 150 B&C. For a buck's antlers to gross 150 B&C or higher, it becomes apparent that his antlers have to reach certain benchmarks in all categories. If antlers are short in any of the four categories, they have to make up the difference in another category.

What also becomes apparent after studying various scenarios is how important tine length is to a buck's score. For example, a buck with 30 or more inches of tine length on each antler has a good chance of scoring above 150 B&C, even with moderate measurements in the other three categories. This buck would only need 21-inch main beams, 16 inches of mass per antler, and a 16-inch spread. Memorizing these benchmarks for bucks of different sizes enables a quicker decision when a mature buck presents itself. It is as simple as 30–21–16–16. Write out several scenarios for 140-, 150-, 160-, 170-, 180-class B&C bucks on 3x5 index cards and study them while sitting in the stand.

There are several whitetail body measurements that can be used to help estimate antler measurements. All are approximations, as bucks of the same age vary in size, even on the same property. While the following measurements are averages in south Texas, the best method is to check these measurements on the bucks harvested in your area and make the necessary adjustments. Since tine length is so critical to a high B&C score, it should be the first estimate made. It is also one of the easiest measurements to determine. The first useful aid in estimating tine length is the length of a buck's ear. The lighter-colored,

Abnormal points can arise from main beams as well as tines. This buck has abnormal points growing out of his beams and tines. Simply add the abnormal points with the typical points for a quick tine length total.

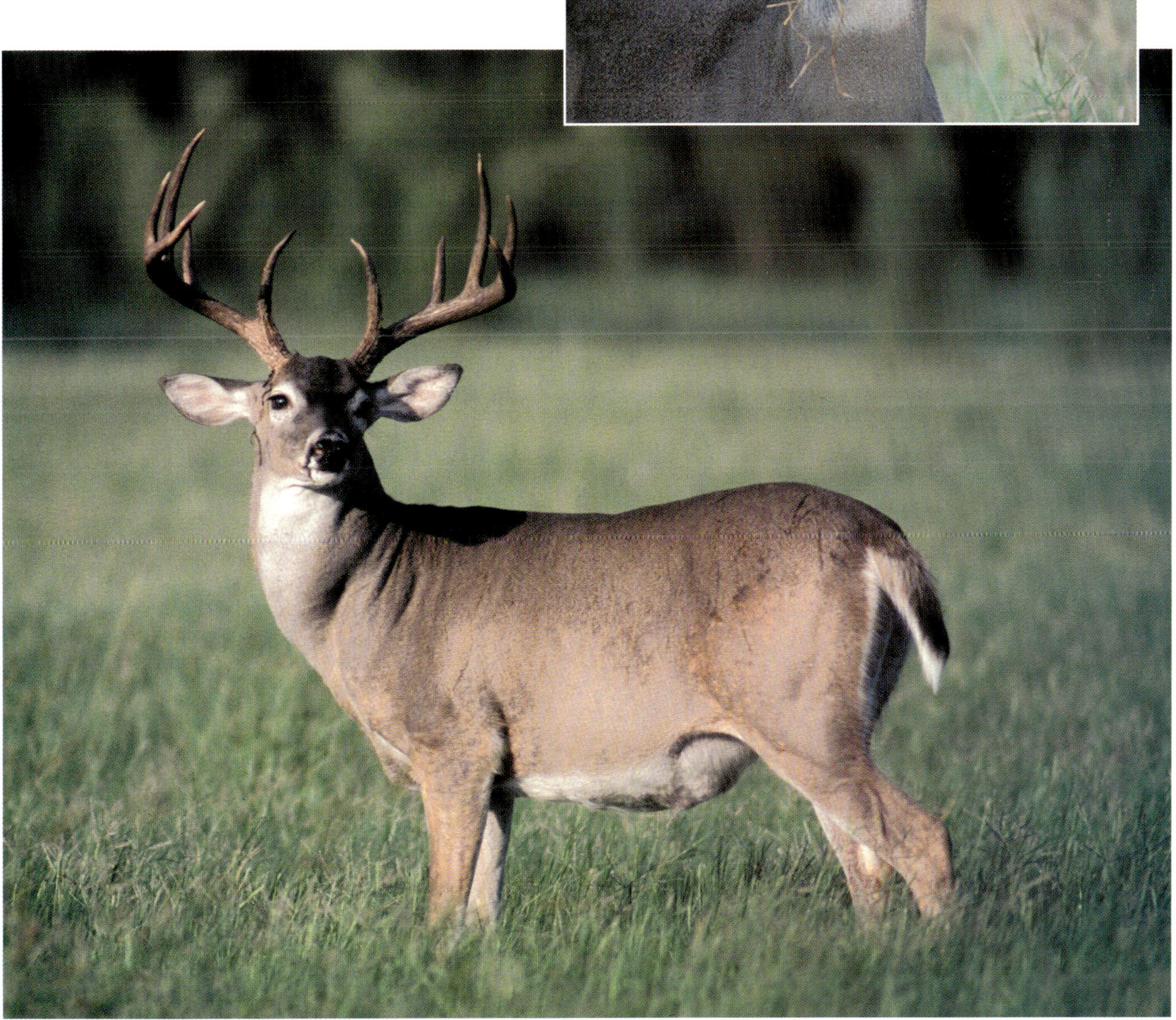

This buck with inward-curving brow tines has G-2s that appear short. Closer examination reveals that they grew backward and are longer than they appear. Viewing antlers from multiple angles is always better for accurate Boone & Crockett estimations.

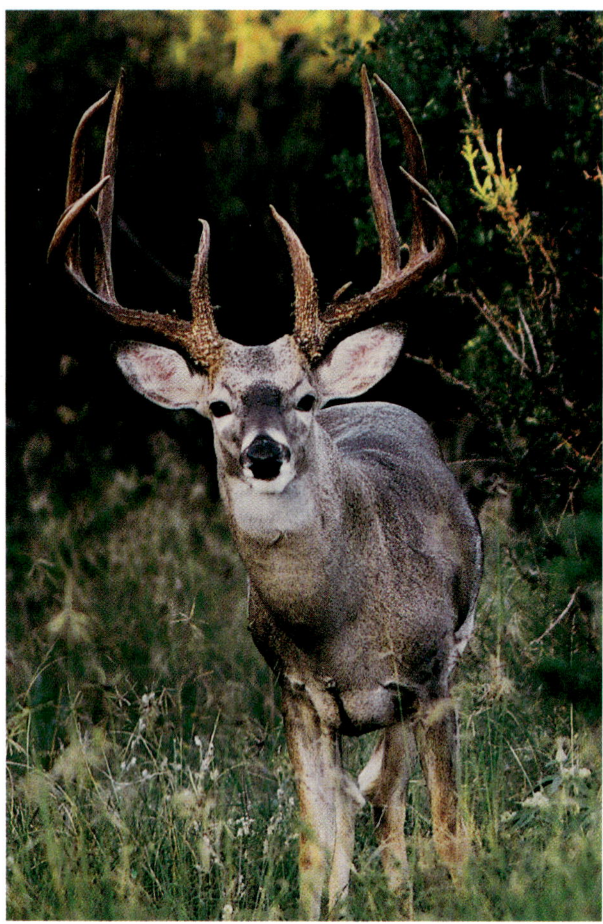

Note the heavy mass, the beading on the bases and G-1s, and the palmated brow tines on this tall-racked buck. Using his eyes for comparison indicates that his bases are well over five inches in circumference.

inside portion of a buck's ear is approximately five inches long. If the buck appears to have very long ears, the measurement could be as long as six inches. If possible, wait until the buck faces you with his ears forward and compare this part of his ear to his brow tines. Once a good estimate of his brow tines (G-1s) is made, the other tines will be easier to estimate. Another measurement that can help estimate tine length is the distance from the outside edge of one eye to the outside edge of the other. This measurement is approximately 5 1/2 inches.

When estimating tines, take notice where the tines grow off the beams. Some bucks' tines grow off the back of the beam with somewhat of a curve, while others grow straight off the top. If they grow off the back and have a distinct curve, they will appear shorter than they are and will score higher than estimated. This was the case of the buck on page 193. He had several inches added to his score, making for a pleasant surprise.

The next measurement to estimate is main beam length. This measurement can be difficult to assess because both front and side views are necessary for an accurate estimate. Even with both views, it is often difficult to estimate the distance in the curve of the antler. From the side view, notice if the beam extends to the buck's nose and if his tines are well spaced or close together. Next, viewing the buck head on, determine if the beams extend past his ears before curving. Finally, do the ends turn in or up for several inches?

One important consideration when judging beam length is how high the main beams climb vertically before they begin leveling off. If a buck's main beams do not climb at all, they are likely quite short. If the buck's beams climb for five or six inches then flatten out, he could have extremely long beams of 25 inches or more. Another situation to watch out for is a buck whose beams curve forward quickly. A buck like this usually has a narrow spread of 15 inches or less. However, from the side his beams may appear to reach his nose. But, unless the beams curve at or beyond the tip of the ear and go almost to his nose, this buck will typically be a disappointment due to very short beams.

Another useful reference measurement is the distance from the tip of a buck's nose to the top of his forehead. This measurement averages nine inches on a mature buck and can be helpful in judging beam length from the side. The final reference measurement is the already estimated tine lengths to use for comparison. The estimated tines can be helpful in judging sections of the beam from the front and side view.

Antler mass, or main beam circumferences, is the next estimate required. This is another measurement that is tough to estimate with consistency. As with judging in general, it is helpful to create

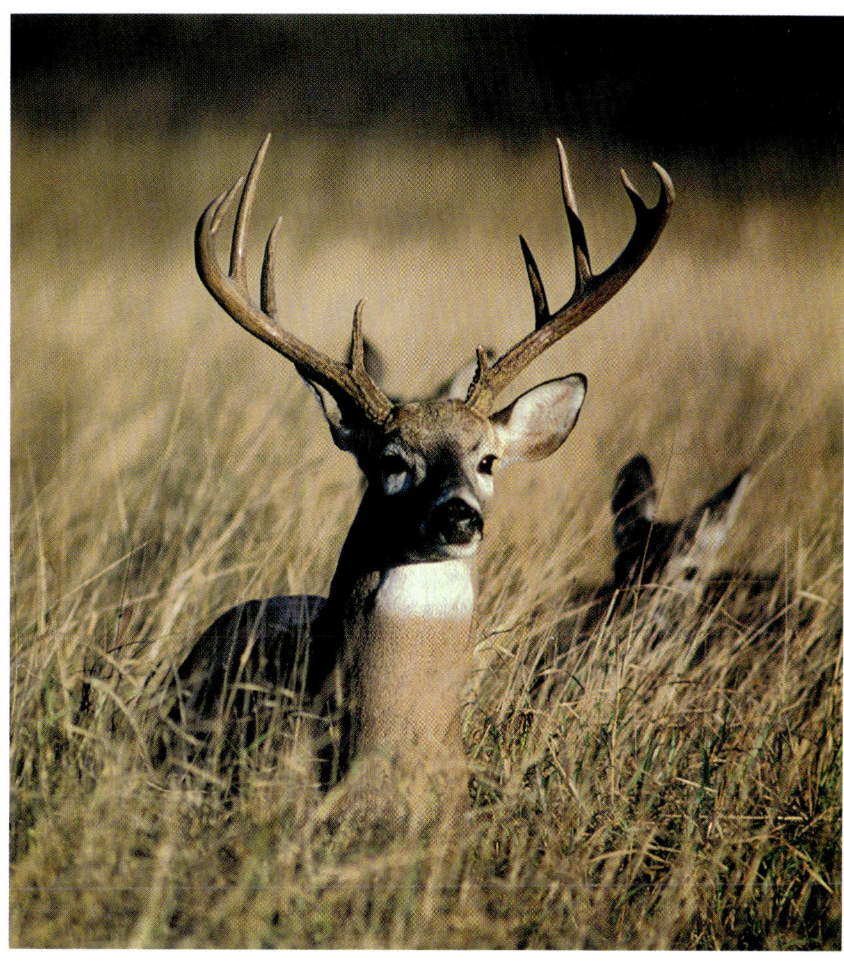

A buck with extremely high, wide antlers with upward curving beams would also need to be viewed from the side to accurately estimate beam length.

likely scenarios of what mature bucks in your area will have in mass measurements. When estimating mass, use whole numbers, and estimate one antler. Unless there is a noticeable difference in the two sides, simply multiply the initial figure by two to achieve a total mass measurement for both antlers.

For simplification, a buck with four-inch circumference measurements at the four locations where this measurement is taken on the main beam will have 16 inches of mass on one antler. Sixteen inches is a good benchmark in most areas, as many mature bucks will exhibit at least 16 inches of mass per antler. However, a more realistic antler with 16 inches of mass might look like this: 4 4/8 inches between the base and the brow tine, followed by 4 inches, 3 7/8 inches, and 3 5/8 inches, as most antlers decrease in circumference as they near the end of the main beam. After other estimates have been taken, if all that remains between a buck and a given B&C category is 12 inches of mass, it's a safe bet he will make the grade.

On the other end of the spectrum, few south Texas bucks have 20 or more inches of mass on each antler. Out of the 27 bucks in the judging section of this book (Chapter 8), only three had total mass measurements of 40 inches or greater. To reach this total, each antler generally must have bases greater than five inches in circumference and maintain almost five-inch circumference measurements to the end. It is rare for a south Texas buck to have six-inch bases. In fact, only one buck in this book had a six-inch base, and it was only on one antler. Thus, if a buck's first circumference measurement is between five and six inches, the antler

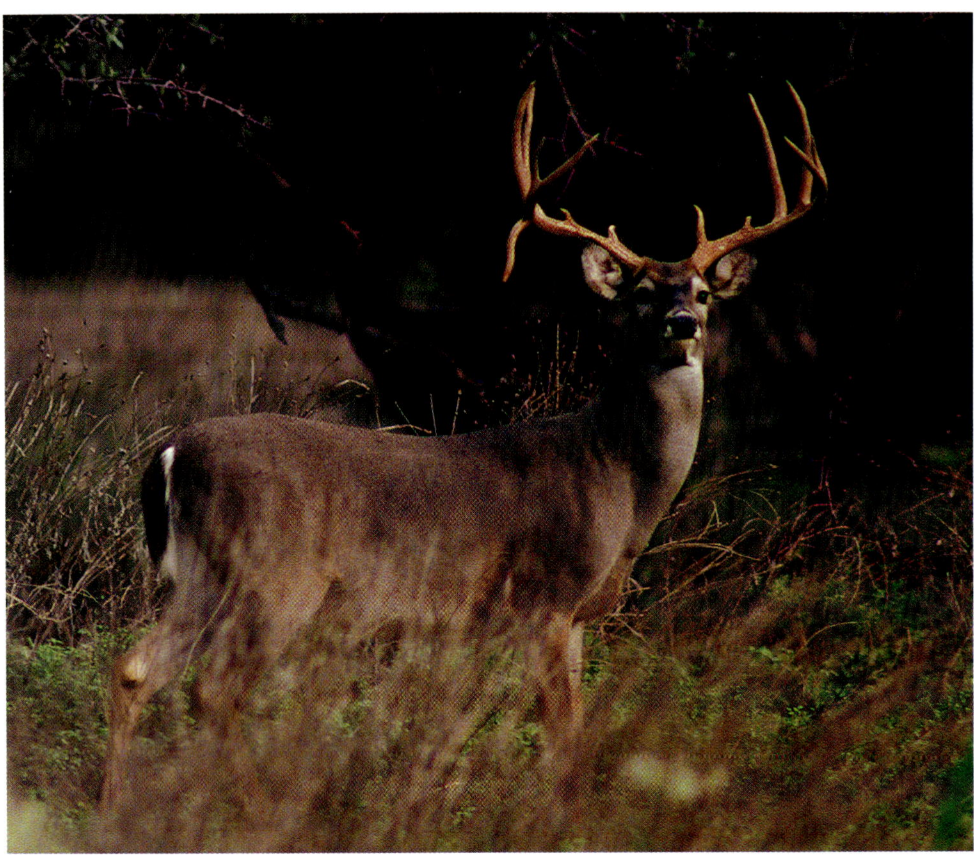

This buck's extremely wide rack can be estimated by adding imaginary inside ear lengths to his 16-inch eartip to eartip measurement. This would put his inside spread at 24 inches.

must maintain its mass in the other three measurements to reach 20 inches. By establishing 16 inches and 20 inches as benchmarks, the estimated mass score for one antler (e.g., 18 inches) can quickly be multiplied by two to arrive at 36 inches, or the total estimated mass estimate. Once this range is established for a given property, it enables rapid and accurate mass estimation.

When estimating the mass of one antler, the size of a buck's eye can be a good reference. Thumb through Chapter 8 of this book and it will become apparent that the circumference of the antler base can be compared to the size of the eye. If the base appears smaller than the eye, it will be under four inches in circumference. If the base appears the same size as the eye, it will be approximately four inches or greater. If the base appears larger than the eye, it will be approximately five inches or greater. These estimates apply to mature bucks only. Once the base has been estimated, notice how large the beam appears at the other three circumference measurements. On some occasions the H-2 measurement can be larger than the base measurement (H-1), so take notice if the beams appear palmated, and adjust the score accordingly.

Judging antlers is a continual learning process. After a buck is harvested, be sure to measure his circumferences, total it separately, and compare your estimation to the buck's actual mass score. The more chances you get to check your field-judging against the actual buck, the faster you will become proficient at judging antler mass.

The final step is to estimate inside spread. I prefer to judge spread last, because it is the easiest to estimate, and, if time is a factor, it can be estimated and added to the total score. To estimate spread, use the buck's ears. The ears of most mature bucks average around 16 inches from tip to

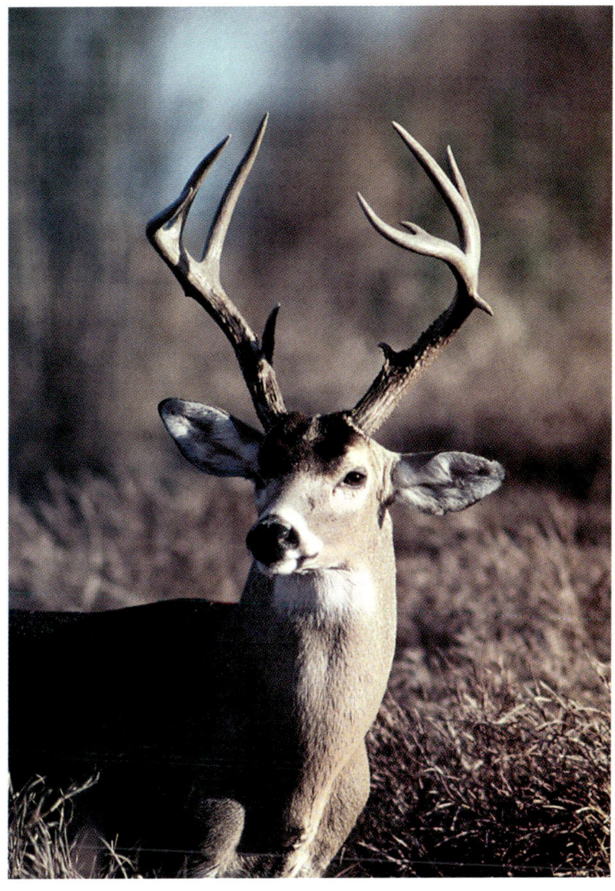

Although this mature buck exhibits short brow tines and short G4s, he still carries a handsome rack worthy of most hunters' serious consideration. This demonstrates that uniqueness sometimes outweighs B&C score.

tip. This can vary one inch either way, as some bucks hold their ears flatter and some more erect. If a buck's spread is wider than its ears, use the inside of his ear (five inches) to estimate the difference. For example, if a buck's spread is approximately half an ear length wider than his ear tips on both sides, he will be approximately 21 inches wide. The equation would be 2.5 plus 16 plus 2.5 equals 21 inches.

There is no substitute for experience when judging antlers. However, some experience can be gained in unique ways. For instance, take advantage of every opportunity to study photographs of bucks for which you know the measurements. Another method is to measure the antlers of mounted bucks and then observe those mounts from typical hunting distances. For many, this is among the most useful exercises, because you have the opportunity to study real antlers with known measurements. Without a doubt, the best experience comes from observing live bucks. The more time spent observing and photographing a particular buck before it is harvested, the better. Once a buck is harvested and antler measurements are known, compare your preharvest estimates with actual measurements, and learn what was judged correctly and incorrectly.

Judging antlers is similar to aging deer on the hoof — occasional mistakes will occur. Mistakes are simply part of the learning process that everyone encounters. However, you should be especially cautious when trying to justify a particular antler measurement to qualify a buck as "shootable." In nearly 100 percent of these cases, the deer should not be harvested, as it is likely too small.

Years ago I harvested a buck that is forever etched in my memory as a personal reminder of this rule. It was late afternoon near the end of my hunt. I was in a tripod stand on a hill that overlooked a draw 200 yards downhill where a big buck had been observed earlier in the afternoon chasing a doe. I observed a buck approaching from a long distance for over five minutes and estimated him to be a 5 1/2-year-old with 10 points. My first estimate of his score was 135 B&C, and I was not even thinking about shooting. I was on a south Texas trophy hunt and looking for a mature deer that scored 150 B&C or higher. As the minutes passed, and the sky grew darker, I began to reevaluate my original score. I started asking myself questions like, "What if his brow tines are five inches instead of three?" That would throw all my other estimates off enough to make him a 150-class deer. I had been observing him for over 20 minutes and there were no other deer with which this buck could be compared. The ranch I was hunting spanned several thousand acres, and the owners asked only that I shoot a mature buck. I continued to watch the buck and, as the light faded, I wondered if I was just being greedy holding out for a bigger buck if this was a mature, shootable buck. As I scored him again in my mind, I was certain he would score over 150 and squeezed the trigger. Needless to say, the buck was not as large as I had convinced myself he was. He was a very symmetrical 10-point that scored 128 B&C. He is mounted in my office as a constant reminder of an enjoyable hunt with good friends and a valuable lesson learned.

I hope this story convinces you not to judge in low light, not to let the lack of time affect your judgment, and to always judge a buck when others are present for comparison. In addition, always try to judge deer as close and clearly as possible with good binoculars or a spotting scope, and beware of reevaluating a buck's measurements in an effort to mentally increase his B&C score. And, when in doubt, pass the deer.

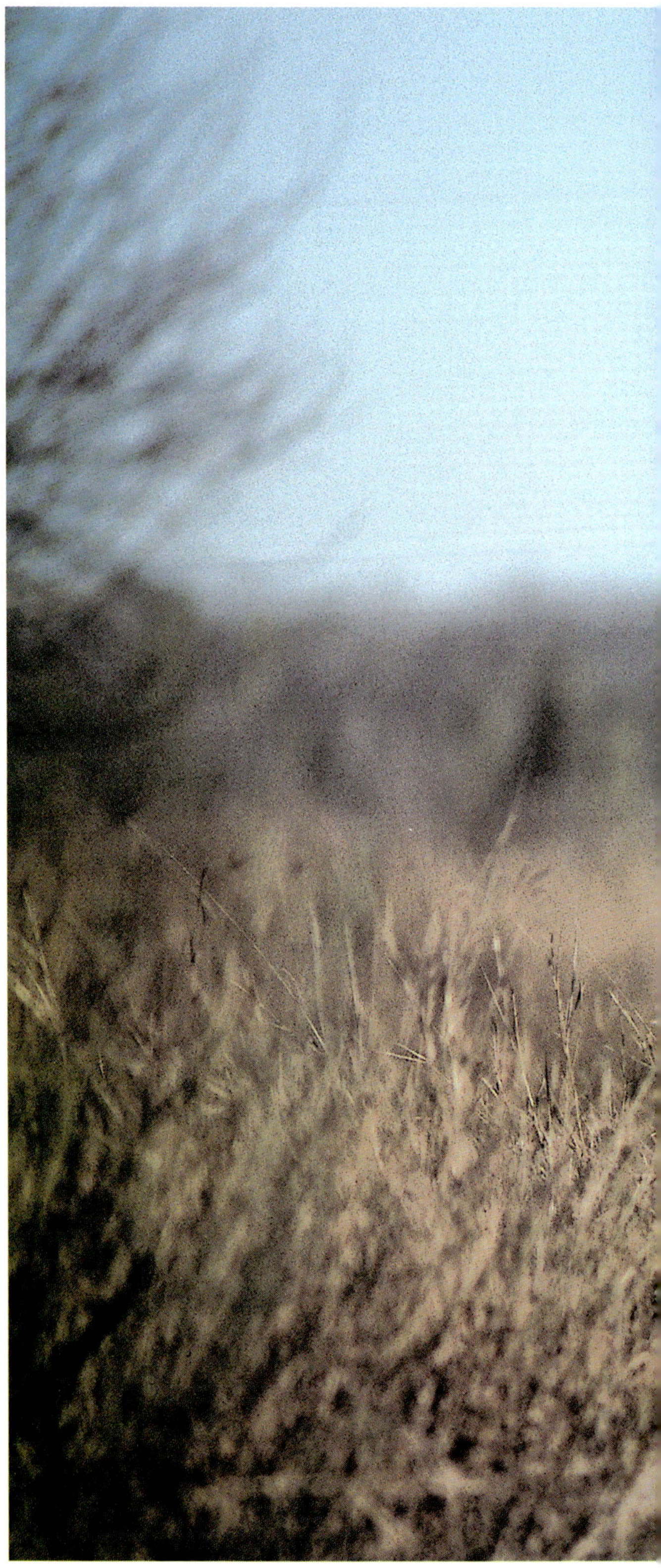

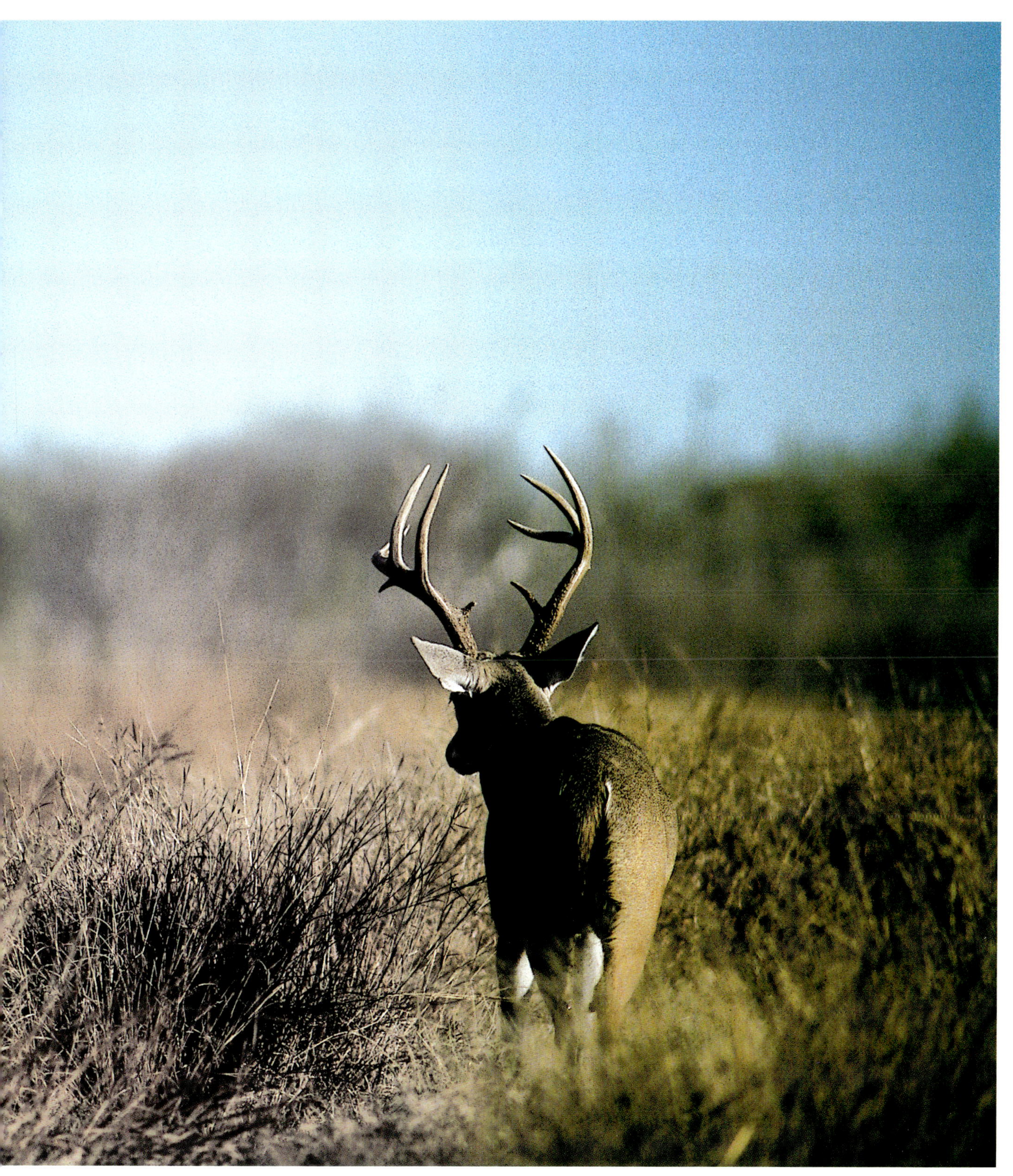

The basket rack on this buck is apparent as he is moving away, but it may have been a surprise if only a side view had been given. Another unique feature of this buck is the distinctive lack of white around the tail.

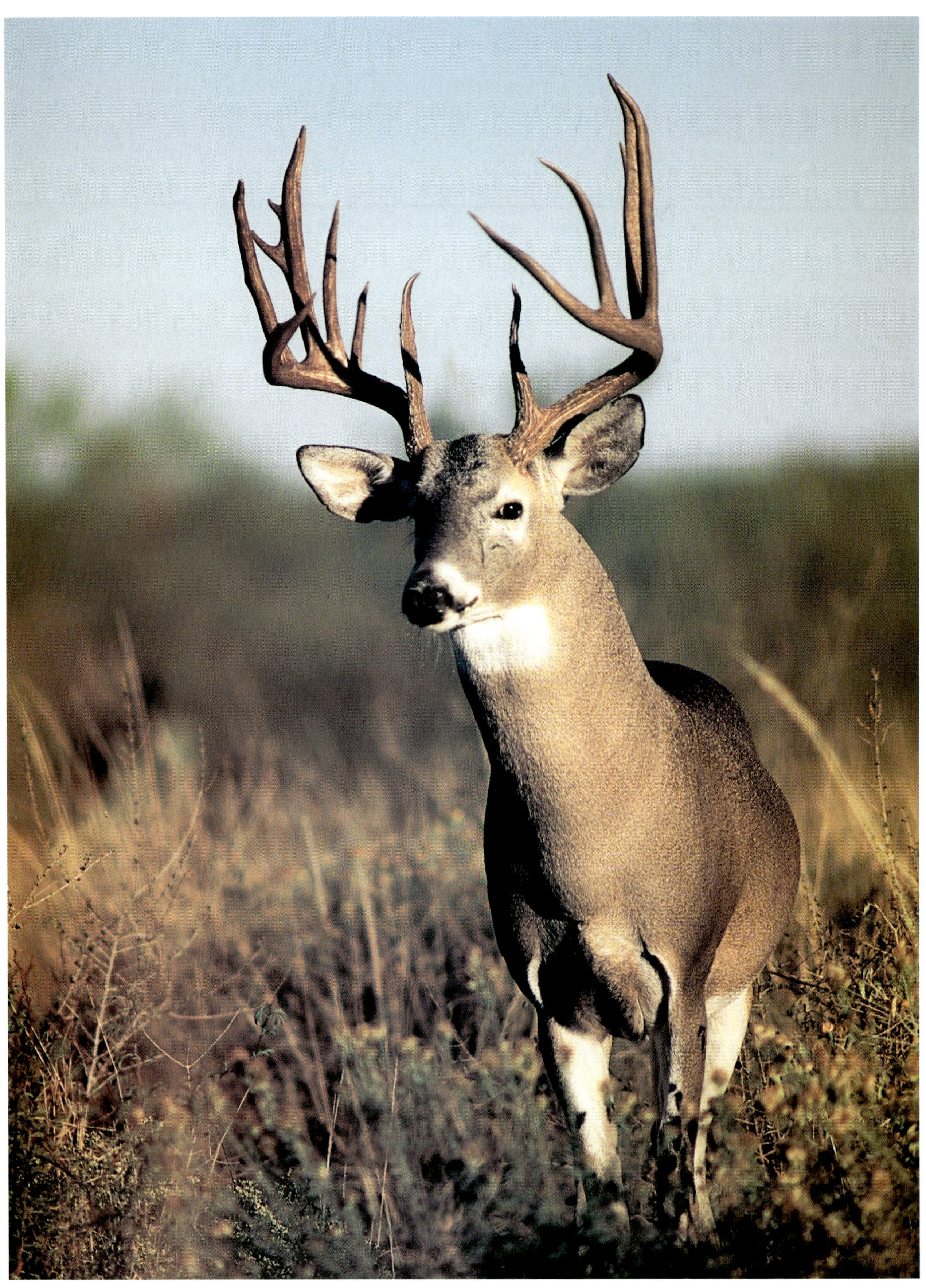

8 Examples of Live Bucks with Known Boone & Crockett Scores

The following bucks were either harvested or both sheds found enabling the actual Boone & Crockett score to be determined. Photos from different angles are provided for each buck to help the observer estimate tine lengths, beam lengths, circumference measurements, and spread. The measurements are categorized in a way to help recognize important benchmarks for each. This will aid in quicker field estimation and help the wildlife manager have antler information in a form that will enable recognition of any deviations from the norm from year to year within their own deer herd.

BUCK# 1

On most properties this buck would have been one of the greatest 3 1/2-year-olds ever harvested. The reason these measurements are known is because both of his sheds were found while he was still alive. He has extremely long beams and demonstrates three key criteria to watch for when judging beams. First, notice that his beams grow upward six or seven inches before turning outward and do not stop climbing until the antlers turn forward. Next, notice from the side view how his antlers grow backward almost the length of his forehead then turn forward and grow twice that far. His spread is well past his ears, so these keys should help the observer realize these are going to be better than average beams.

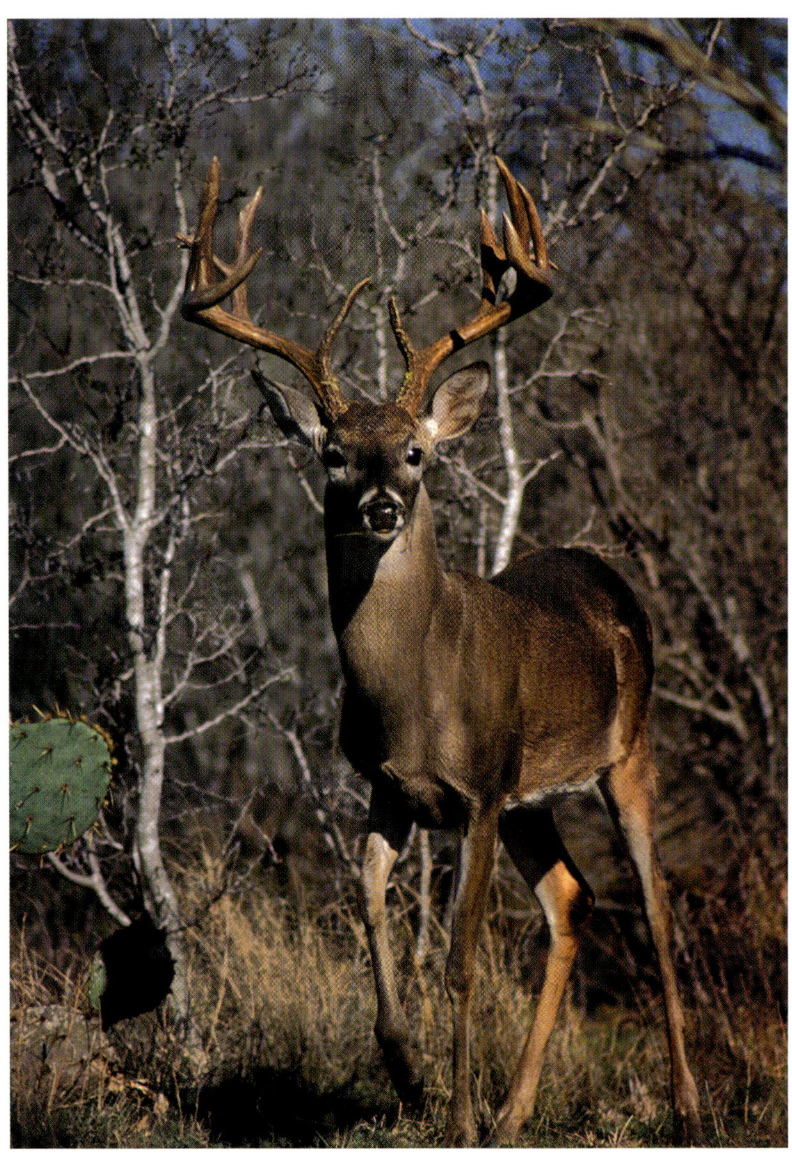

USING THE SCORE CHARTS:

The antler-measurement charts on the following pages will help you practice estimating the various measurements. They are also designed to help you recognize measurement "bench marks" such as the average mass measurements on a given property over time. The four categories of measurement are inside spread, beam length, total inches of tines (typical tines and any abnormal tines combined), and mass. You are estimating a gross B&C score, so these charts do not include deductions for asymmetry (the differences between corresponding left and right measurements, such as the right G-1 and left G-1). The gross B&C score in each chart is the combination of the four categories: spread, beams, tines, and mass (the Antler Total near the bottom of each chart includes all the measurements of actual antler on each side except inside spread. Combining the right and left antler totals and the inside spread also gives you the gross B&C score). Practice estimating the antler measurements on these bucks, then refer to the chart to check your accuracy. **Note**: for measurements taken from sheds, an inside spread was estimated by comparing photographs of the buck then holding his shed antlers in their exact position and measuring the inside spread.

Age: 3 1/2

Inside Spread: 19 0/8

	RIGHT	LEFT
Beams	**27 2/8**	**26 0/8**
G-1	6 6/8	4 2/8
G-2	9 3/8	7 5/8
G-3	8 7/8	8 1/8
G-4	6 6/8	5 5/8
G-5	2 1/8	
	Abn.	**Abn.**
	4 0/8	4 1/8
	1 4/8	2 2/8
Tine Totals	**39 4/8**	**32 0/8**
H-1	4 1/8	4 2/8
H-2	3 6/8	3 6/8
H-3	4 0/8	3 6/8
H-4	3 6/8	3 6/8
Mass Totals	**15 5/8**	**15 4/8**
Antler Total	**82 3/8**	**73 4/8**

Gross B&C: 174 7/8

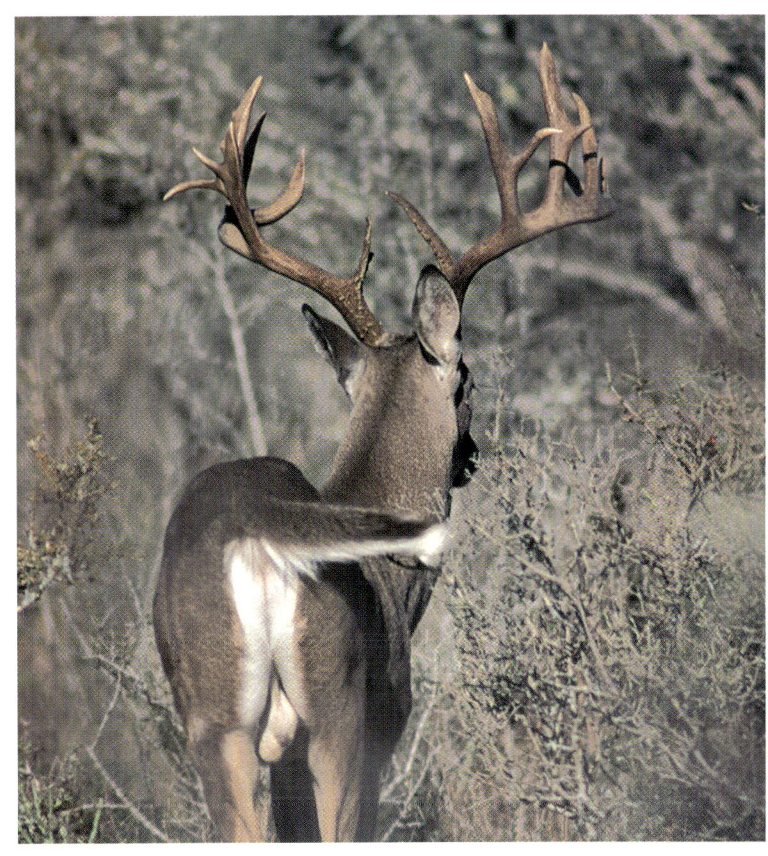

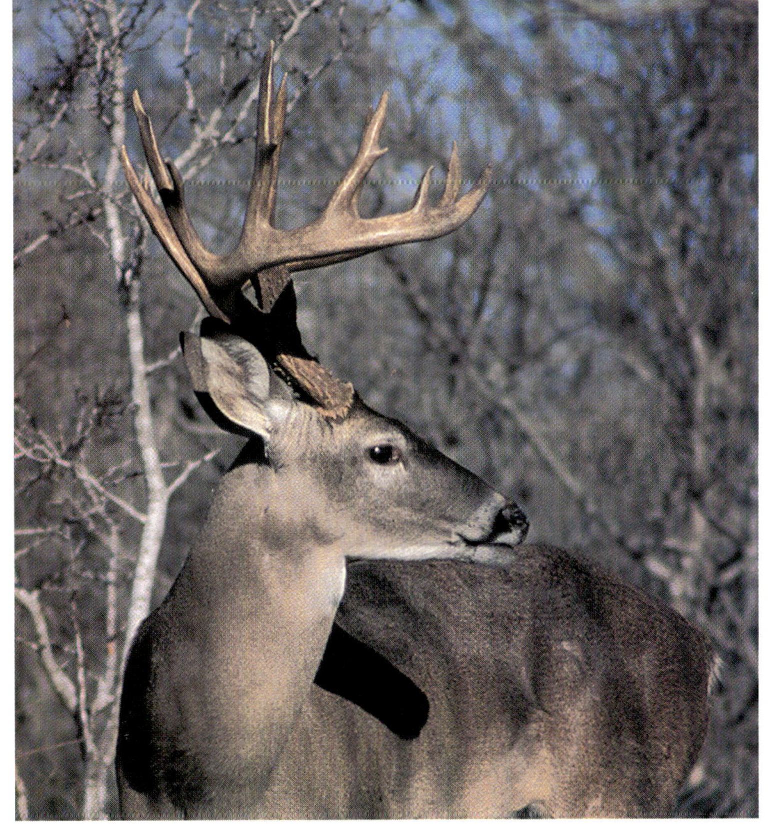

BUCK# 2

Short G-4s are what prevent many bucks from scoring in the 150s. This buck barely misses, and the short G-4 on the left antler kept him from reaching the 30-inch benchmark for total tine length. It is also worth mentioning that this buck's antler bases are about the size of his eyes, indicating they are around four inches in circumference. While the bases are not real heavy, the beams maintain their mass to the end.

Age: 6 1/2

Inside Spread: 17 0/8

	Right	Left
Beams	**22 0/8**	**21 0/8**
G-1	4 5/8	4 0/8
G-2	10 0/8	9 0/8
G-3	10 4/8	10 6/8
G-4	4 4/8	1 7/8
Tine Totals	**29 5/8**	**25 5/8**
H-1	4 3/8	4 3/8
H-2	4 0/8	4 1/8
H-3	3 7/8	4 2/8
H-4	4 0/8	4 2/8
Mass Totals	**16 2/8**	**17 0/8**
Antler Total	**67 7/8**	**63 5/8**

Gross B&C: 148 4/8

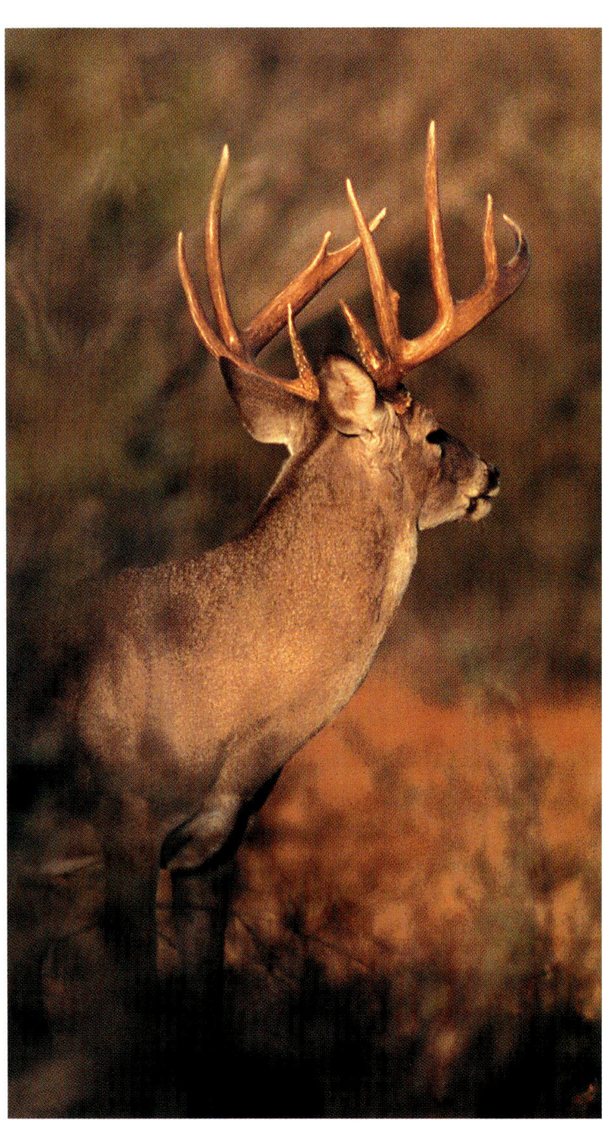

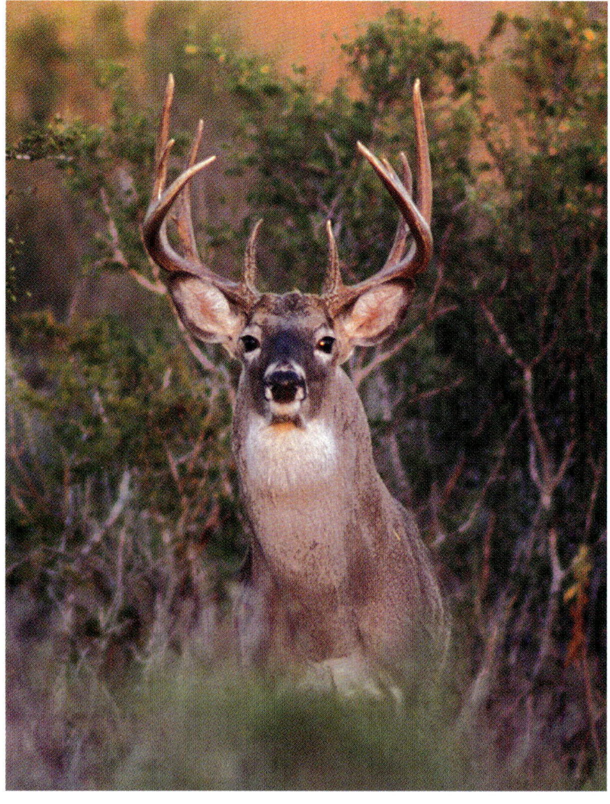

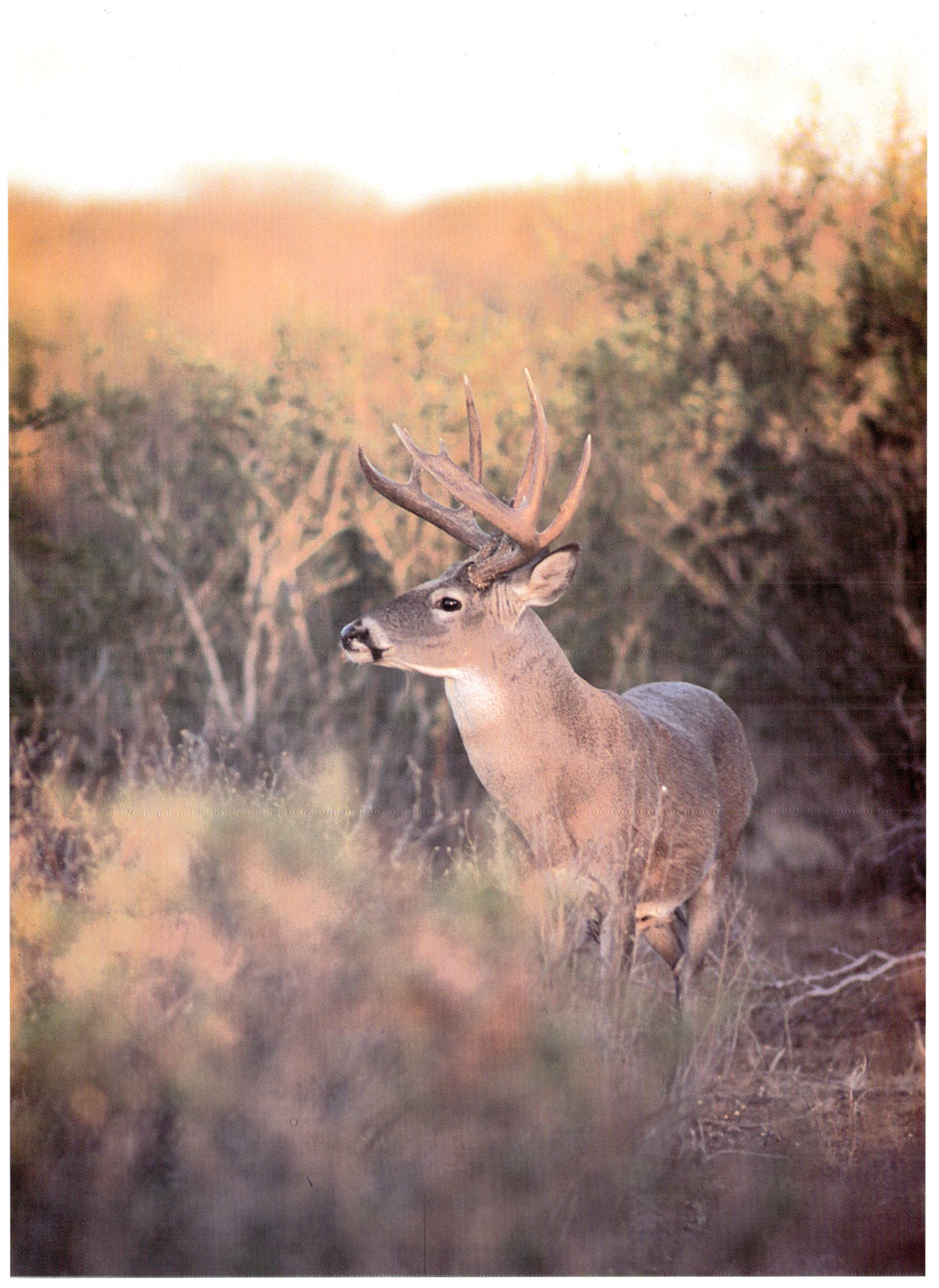

Age: 3 1/2		
Inside Spread: 18 2/8		
	RIGHT	LEFT
Beams	20 4/8	20 6/8
G-1	4 3/8	4 0/8
G-2	7 2/8	8 4/8
G-3	6 2/8	8 0/8
G-4	4 2/8	1 5/8
Tine Totals	22 1/8	22 1/8
H-1	4 0/8	4 1/8
H-2	3 2/8	3 4/8
H-3	3 0/8	3 0/8
H-4	2 4/8	2 3/8
Mass Totals	12 6/8	13 0/8
Antler Total	55 3/8	55 7/8
Gross B&C: 129 4/8		

BUCK# 3

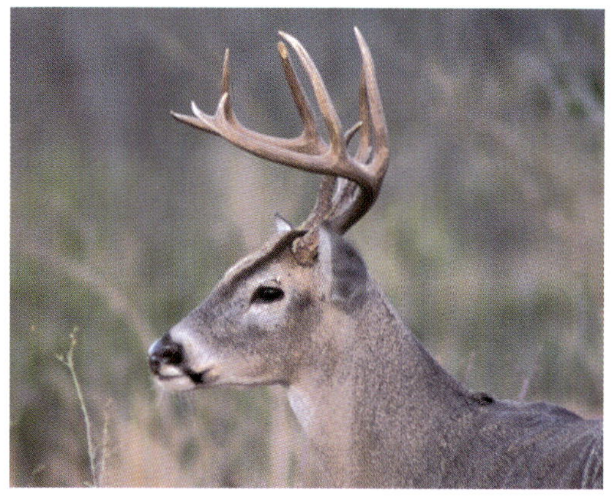

When judging an immature buck, keep in mind that the circumference measurements will rarely reach the standard benchmarks of 16 to 20 inches per antler. This buck's antler base and eye are very close in size, indicating a four-inch base. However, the beam circumferences quickly decrease in size after the G-1s and continue decreasing to the end of the beam, which is typical of immature bucks. By measuring and comparing earlier estimations of harvested bucks, it will become easier to recognize mass measurements in your deer herd.

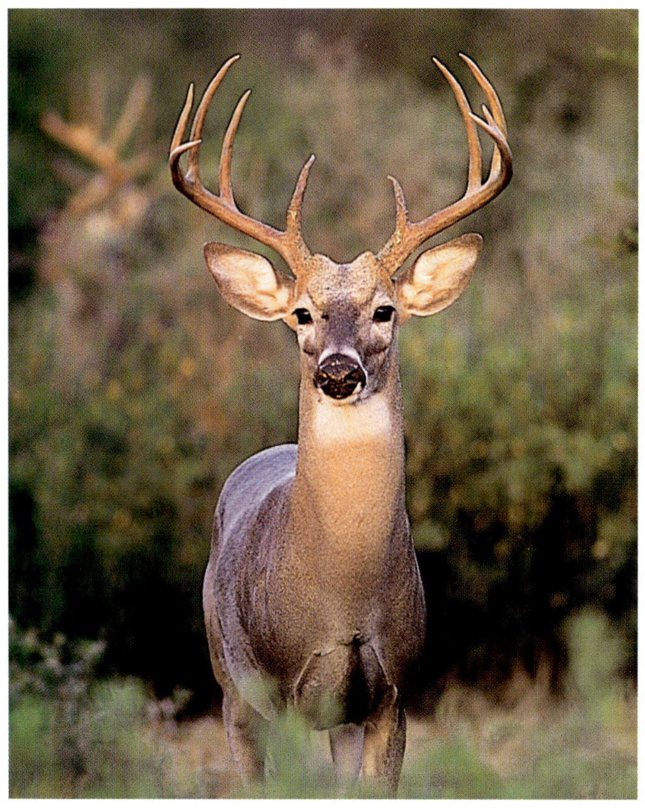

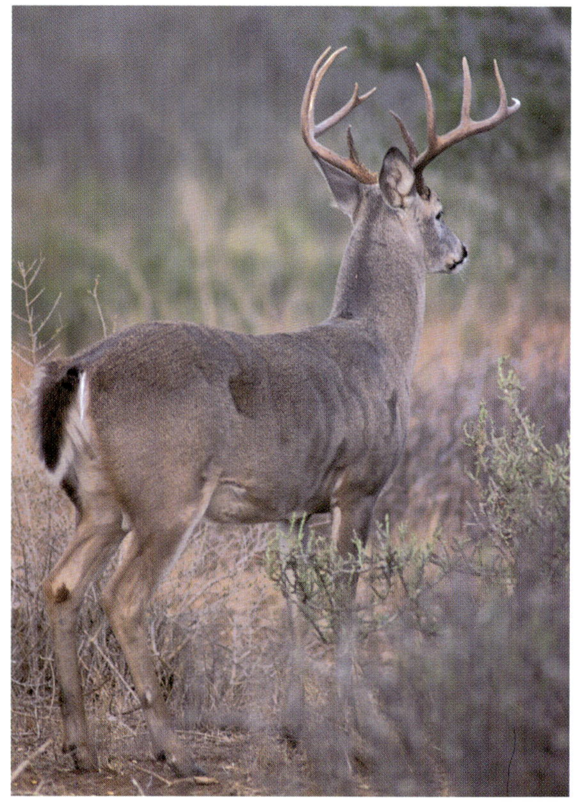

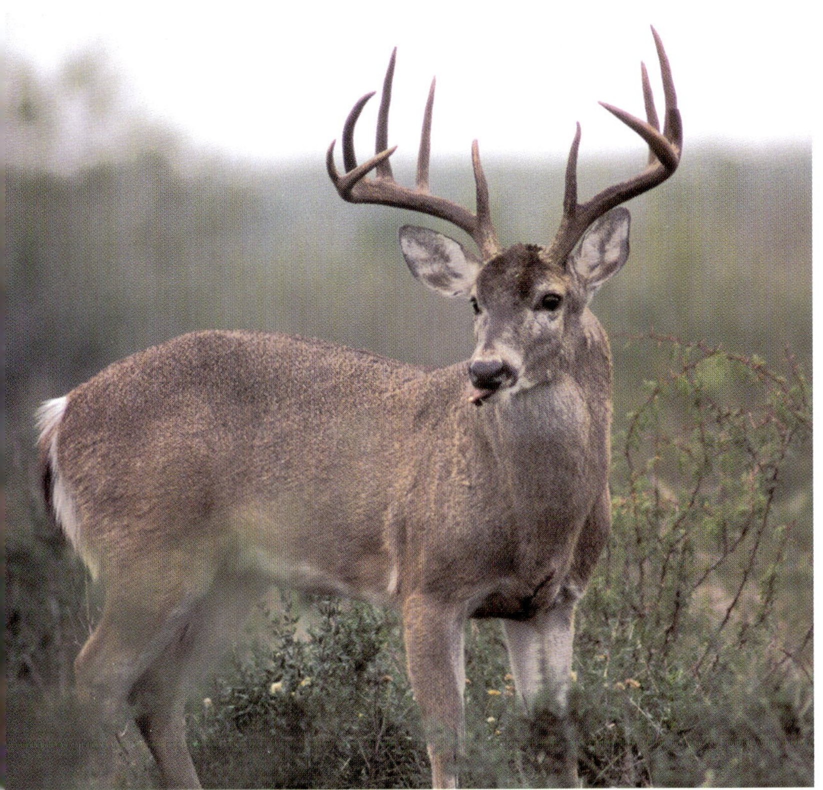

Age: 5 1/2		
Inside Spread: 19 0/8		
	RIGHT	LEFT
Beams	**22 5/8**	**22 0/8**
G-1	5 0/8	5 4/8
G-2	8 0/8	8 0/8
G-3	8 7/8	8 4/8
G-4	8 1/8	3 3/8
G-5	4 0/8	
Tine Totals	**34 0/8**	**25 3/8**
H-1	4 0/8	4 0/8
H-2	4 0/8	4 0/8
H-3	4 0/8	4 0/8
H-4	4 0/8	3 7/8
Mass Totals	**16 0/8**	**15 7/8**
Antler Total	**72 5/8**	**63 2/8**
Gross B&C: 154 7/8		

BUCK# 4

This buck's G-1s are a good example of how the inside of a buck's ear is very close to five inches in length. Lay an index card next to the buck's ear in the photograph and mark the distance from one end of the inside of the ear to the other. Next, lay the measurement next to the right G-1. They should be almost identical, as the buck's right G-1 is five inches. Also, notice the similar size of this buck's antler base compared to his eye, which measures approximately four inches. Finally, this buck holds his ears more erect than many others, so be careful not to overestimate his spread.

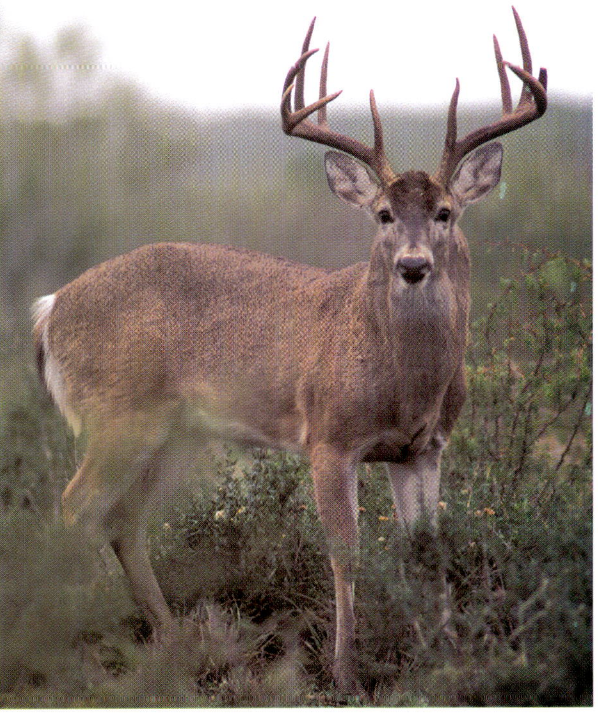

BUCK # 5

Age:	6 1/2	
Inside Spread:	18 6/8	
	RIGHT	LEFT
Beams	**24 6/8**	**26 2/8**
G-1	4 4/8	4 5/8
G-2	9 2/8	8 6/8
G-3	9 4/8	9 2/8
G-4	8 5/8	6 0/8
	Abn.	**Abn.**
	5 6/8	11 4/8
Tine Totals	**37 5/8**	**40 1/8**
H-1	4 4/8	4 4/8
H-2	4 2/8	4 2/8
H-3	4 2/8	4 1/8
H-4	4 1/8	4 0/8
Mass Totals	**17 1/8**	**16 7/8**
Antler Total	**79 4/8**	**83 2/8**

Gross B&C: 181 4/8

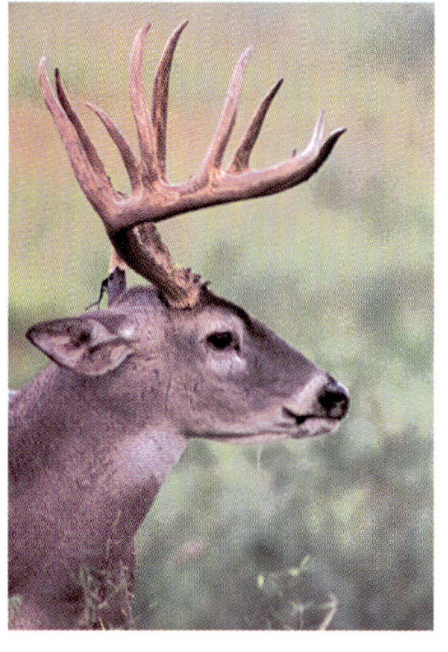

A frontal view of this buck is impressive but deceptive. He does not appear to be a 180-class buck at first glance. His beams do not appear as long as they are, because they are cluttered with so many tines. However, notice how they extend well past the ears and then turn inward several inches toward his head. What helps make him a 180-class buck instead of a 160-class buck, other than his exceptional beams, are his great G-4s. Big G-4s on a mature buck should always alert the observer, especially if his other tines are average or above average. However, the clincher for this buck is the 5 1/2-inch abnormal point on the right antler and the 11 1/2-inch drop tine on the left antler. Those 17 1/4 extra inches are what make a mid 160-class buck into a 180-class deer.

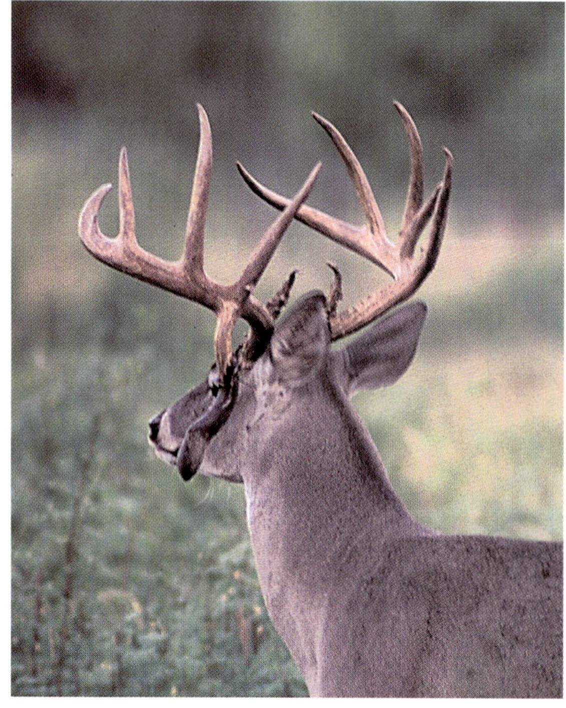

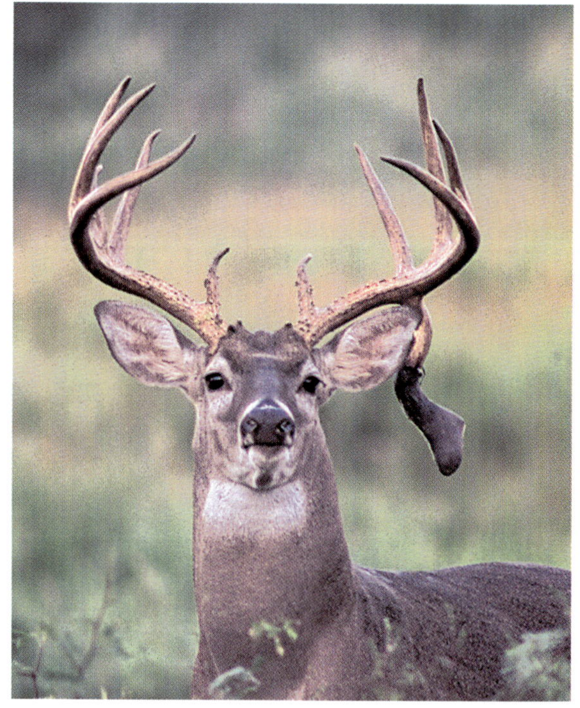

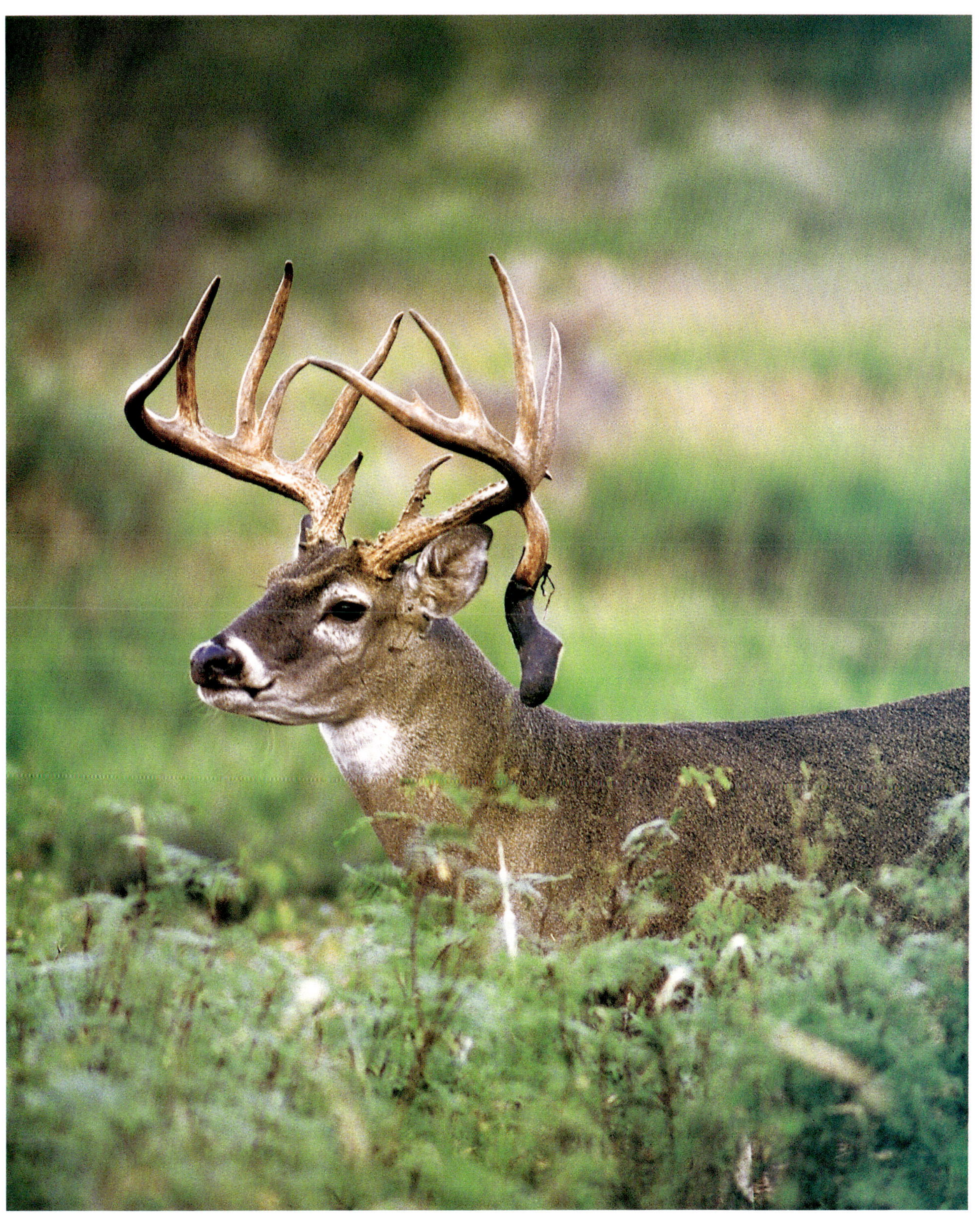

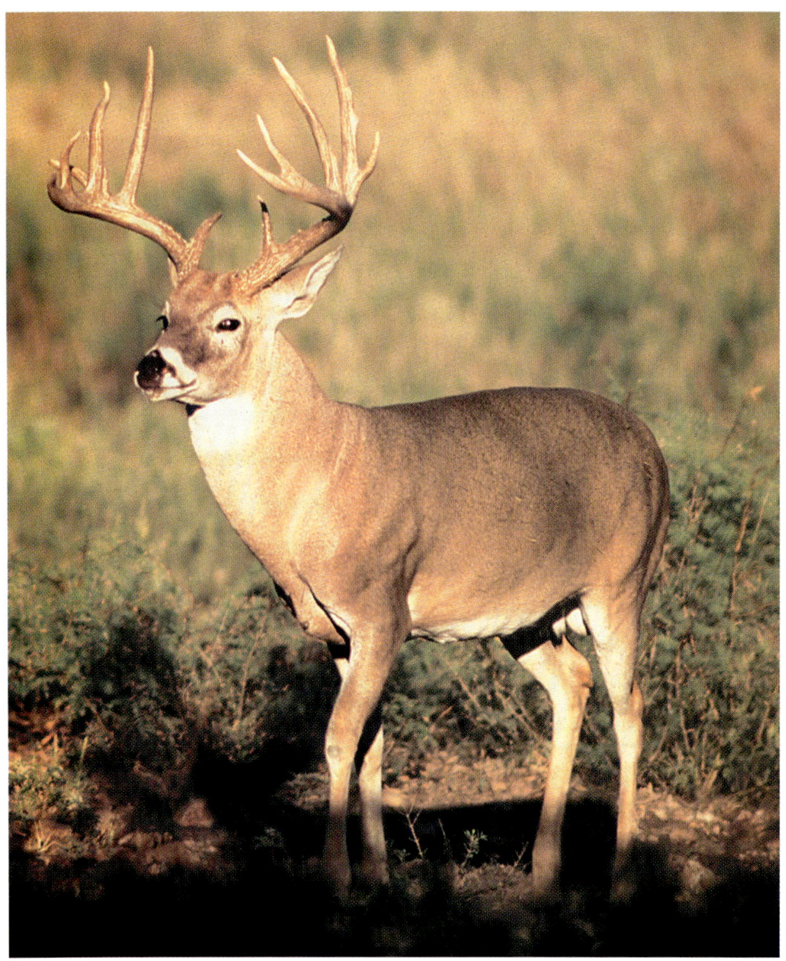

Age: 5 1/2		
Inside Spread: 17 2/8		
	RIGHT	LEFT
Beams	23 4/8	22 0/8
G-1	4 4/8	4 3/8
G-2	10 5/8	11 5/8
G-3	8 4/8	9 4/8
G-4	5 0/8	4 4/8
	Abn.	Abn.
	4 0/8	3 5/8
	4 0/8	
Tine Totals	36 5/8	33 5/8
H-1	4 5/8	4 5/8
H-2	4 2/8	4 2/8
H-3	4 6/8	4 3/8
H-4	3 7/8	3 6/8
Mass Totals	17 4/8	17 0/8
Antler Total	77 5/8	72 5/8
Gross B&C: 167 4/8		

BUCK# 6

This buck had less than an 18-inch inside spread and still scored in the mid 160s because of his strong tine length, beam length, and circumference measurements. The side view shows how his beams grow upward several inches and then forward all the way to his nose to attain 22 and 23 inches on his right and left antlers, respectively.

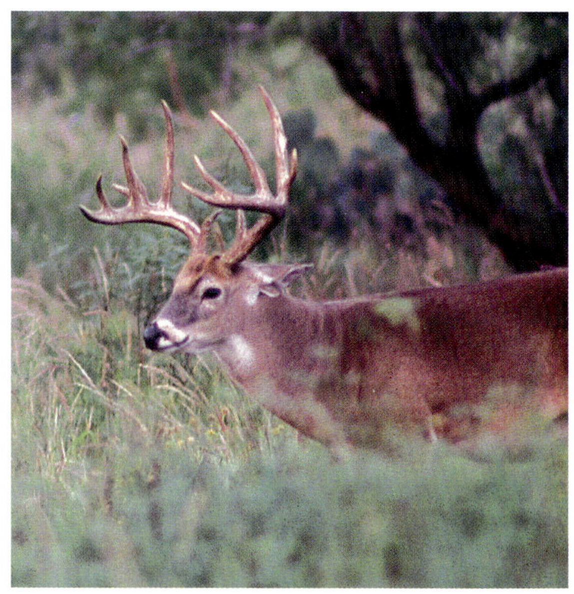

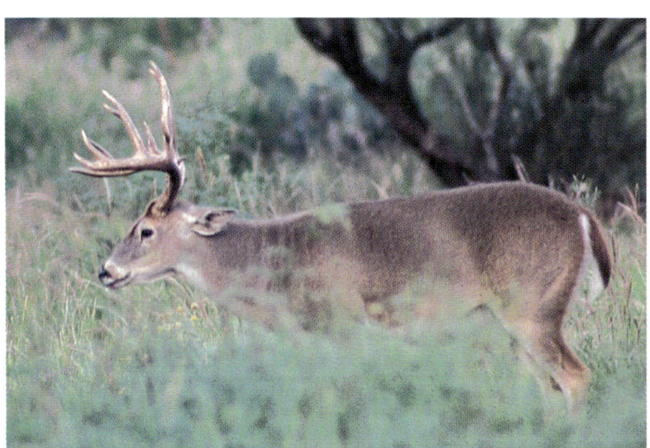

Age: 6 1/2		
Inside Spread: 18 0/8		
	Right	Left
Beams	**23 4/8**	**22 7/8**
G-1	5 2/8	5 1/8
G-2	13 4/8	11 0/8
G-3	11 7/8	11 6/8
G-4		5 3/8
G-5		
Tine Totals	**30 5/8**	**33 2/8**
H-1	4 1/8	4 1/8
H-2	3 6/8	3 5/8
H-3	3 7/8	3 7/8
H-4	3 2/8	3 4/8
Mass Totals	**15 0/8**	**15 1/8**
Antler Total	**69 1/8**	**71 2/8**
Gross B&C: 158 3/8		

BUCK # 7

This buck scores extremely well for a 9-point. Notice how his beams sweep inward and upward, making them longer than they would appear, especially if the side view was the only one given. His right G-2 appears to be the same length as the right G-3, but there is almost two inches difference. The reason for this is the curvature in this type of beam. Do not overlook his double white throat patch for future identification purposes.

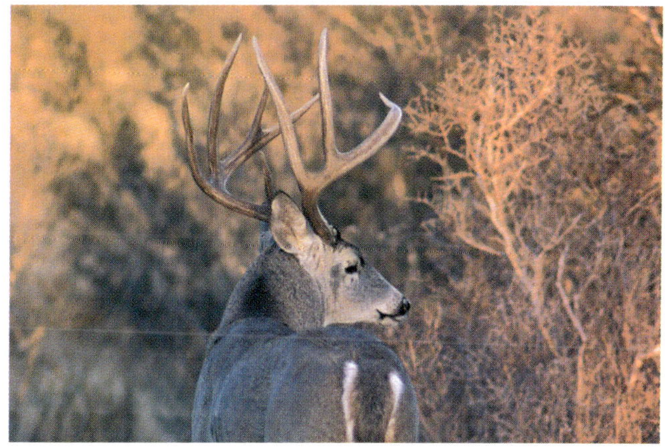

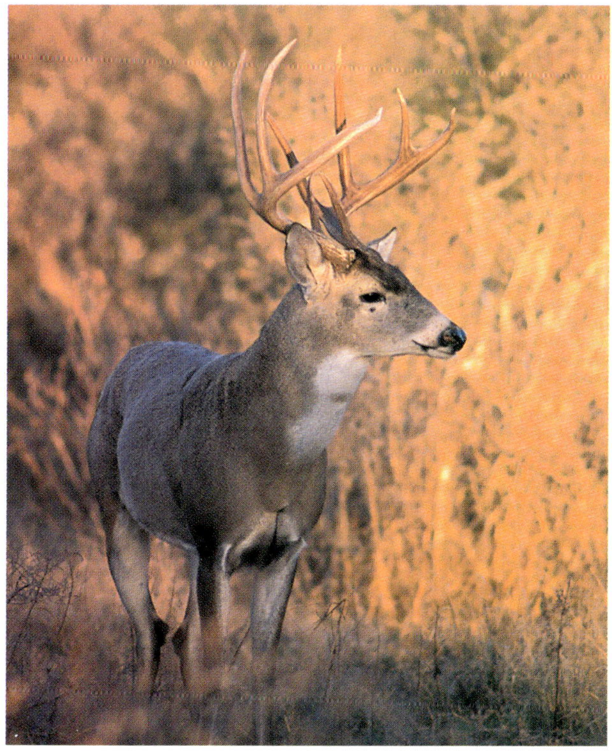

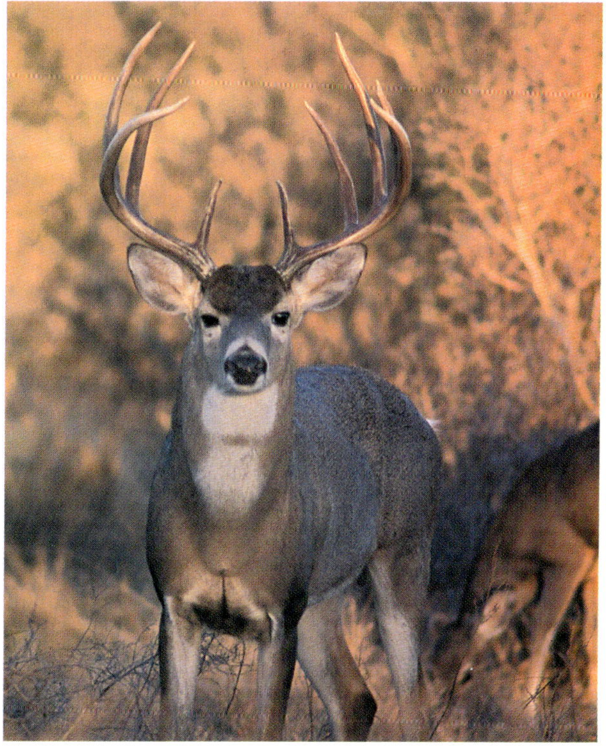

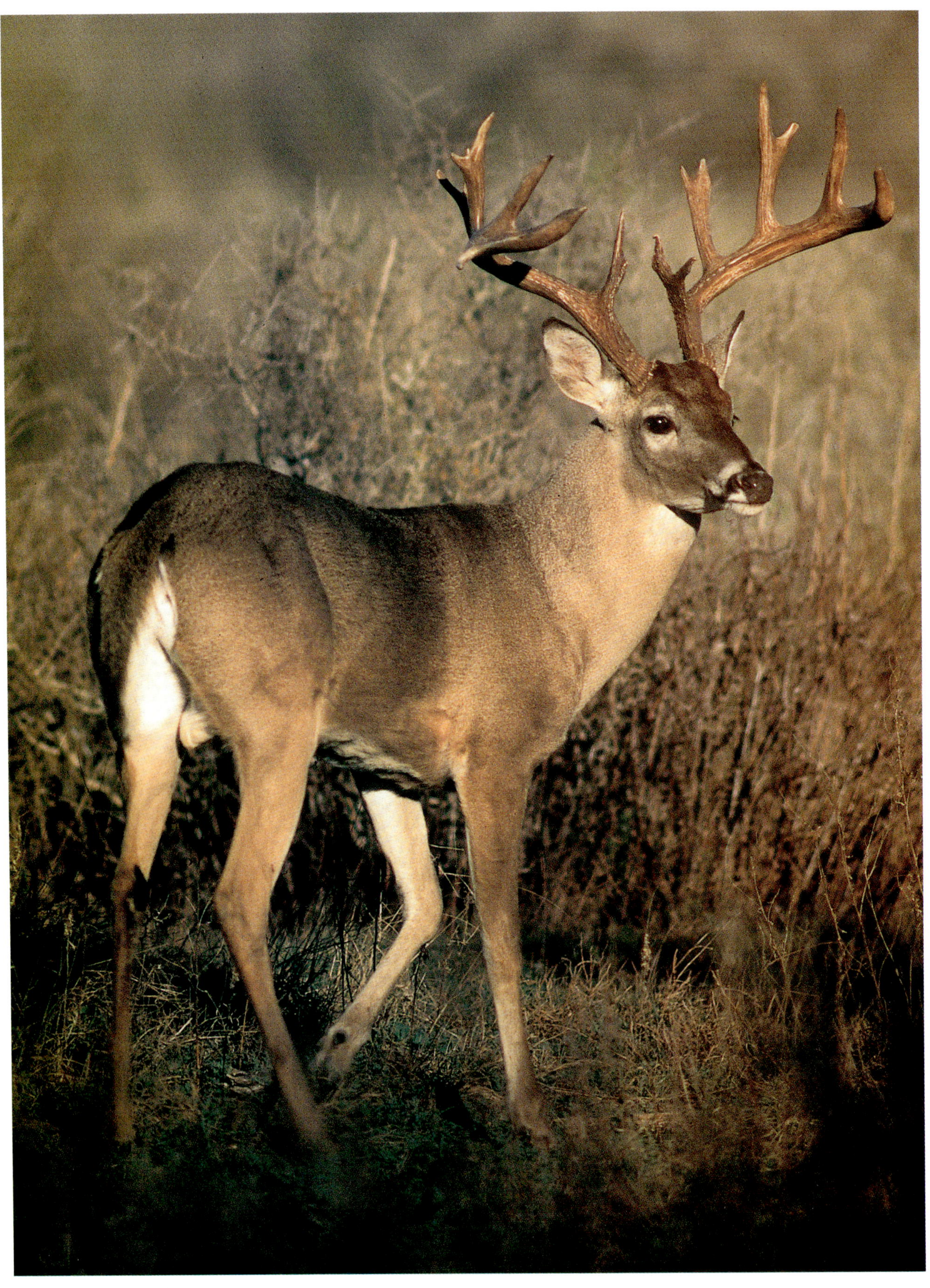

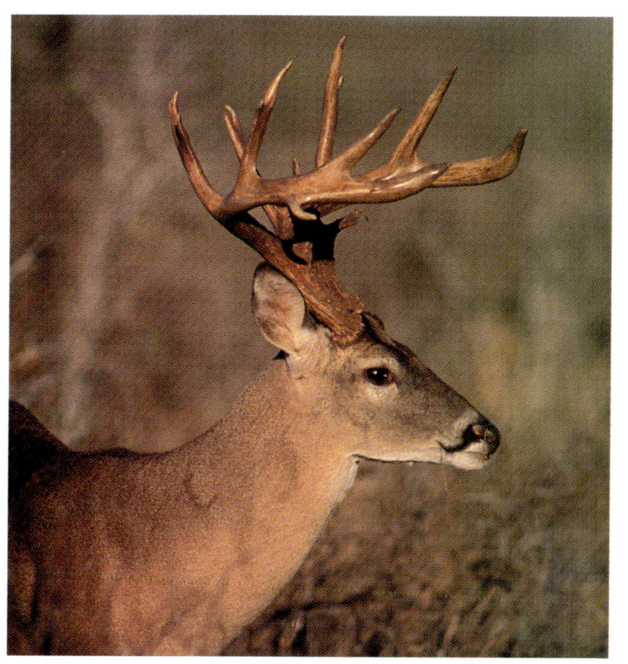

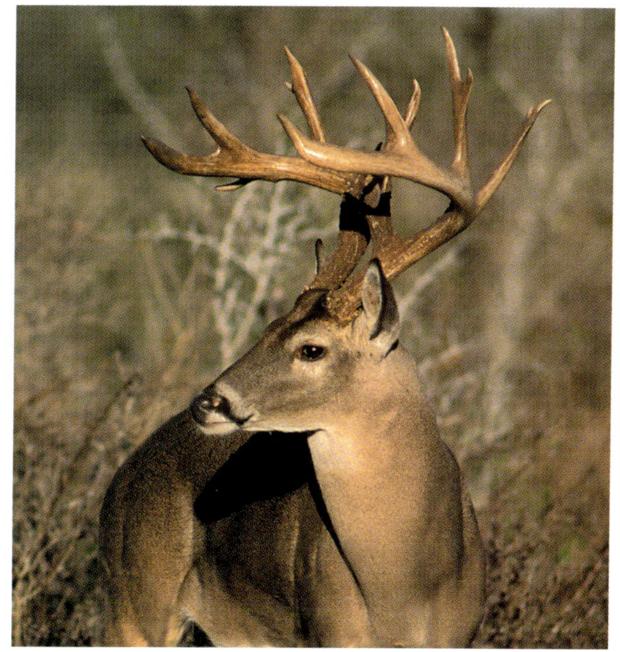

Age: 4 1/2		
Inside Spread: 22 6/8		
	Right	Left
Beams	28 0/8	28 2/8
G-1	6 4/8	5 0/8
G-2	7 6/8	7 4/8
G-3	7 2/8	8 5/8
G-4	5 6/8	7 0/8
	Abn.	Abn.
	2 6/8	2 7/8
	1 5/8	1 5/8
	3 0/8	2 3/8
Tine Totals	34 5/8	35 2/8
H-1	4 6/8	4 6/8
H-2	4 1/8	4 0/8
H-3	4 0/8	4 3/8
H-4	3 7/8	4 3/8
Mass Totals	16 6/8	17 4/8
Antler Total	79 3/8	81 0/8
Gross B&C: 183 1/8		

BUCK # 8

At first glance this buck would not appear to score in the low 180s. His short tines are deceiving, but they total well over 30 inches per side. When his tremendous beam lengths are added, he scores much better than most observers would estimate. Interestingly, the total combined inches on both antlers are very similar.

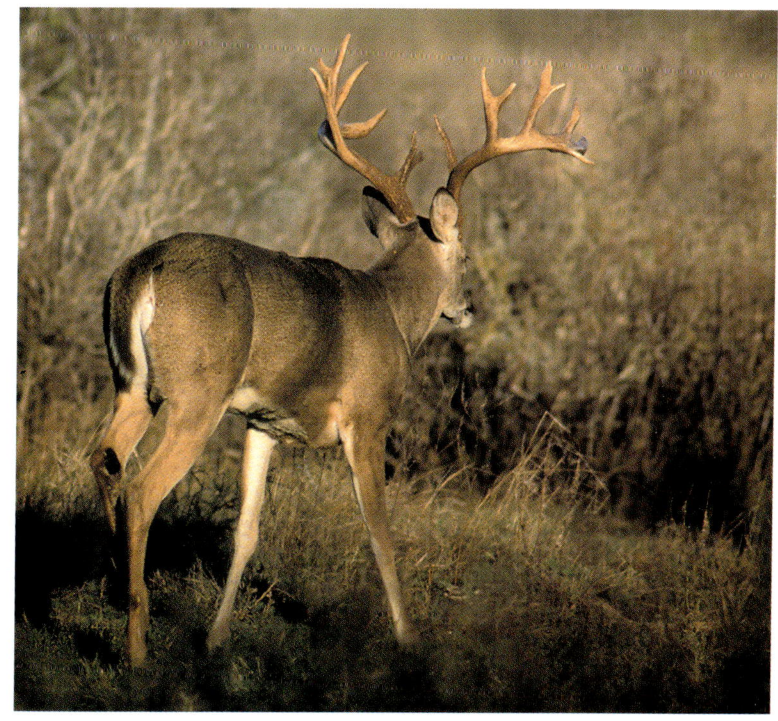

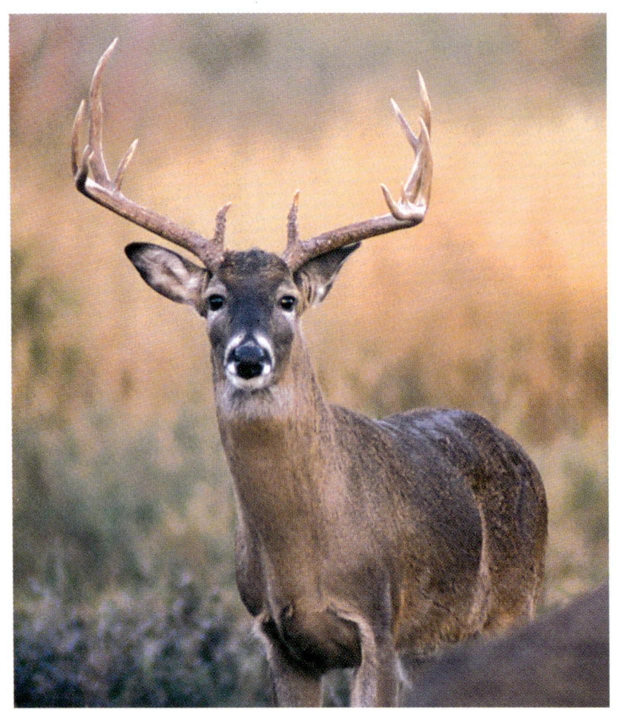

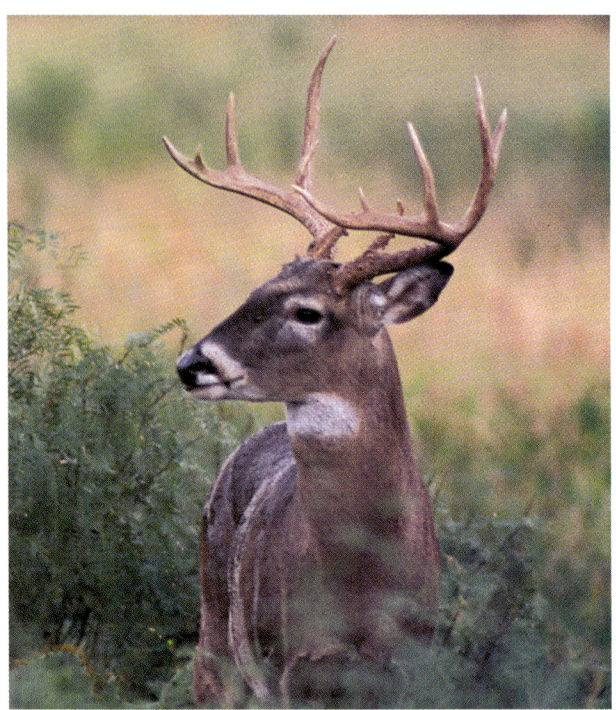

BUCK # 9

Throughout this book we have stated that mistakes will be made. This buck is a good example of one such mistake. When he was harvested, he was aged at 3 1/2 years old. However, based on observations, he was determined to be post-mature due to his thin antlers, relatively thin neck, and a larger spread than was thought possible for a young buck. This is a prime example where body characteristics should have been studied more intensely and weighed more heavily than antler characteristics.

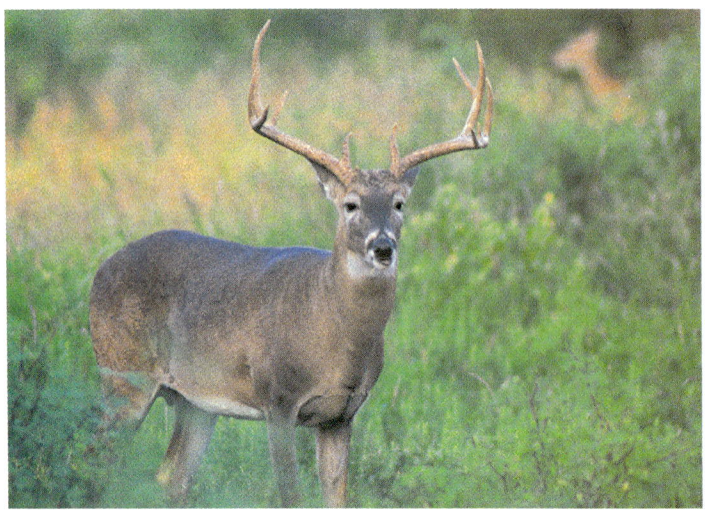

Age: 3 1/2

Inside Spread: 20 1/8

	RIGHT	LEFT
Beams	**20 0/8**	**21 5/8**
G-1	3 0/8	4 0/8
G-2	10 5/8	9 4/8
G-3	4 6/8	6 0/8
G-4	1 2/8	1 4/8
	Abn.	**Abn.**
	3 4/8	3 7/8
Tine Totals	**23 1/8**	**24 7/8**
H-1	4 0/8	4 0/8
H-2	3 6/8	3 4/8
H-3	3 2/8	3 3/8
H-4	2 4/8	2 7/8
Mass Totals	**13 4/8**	**13 6/8**
Antler Total	**56 5/8**	**60 2/8**

Gross B&C: 137 0/8

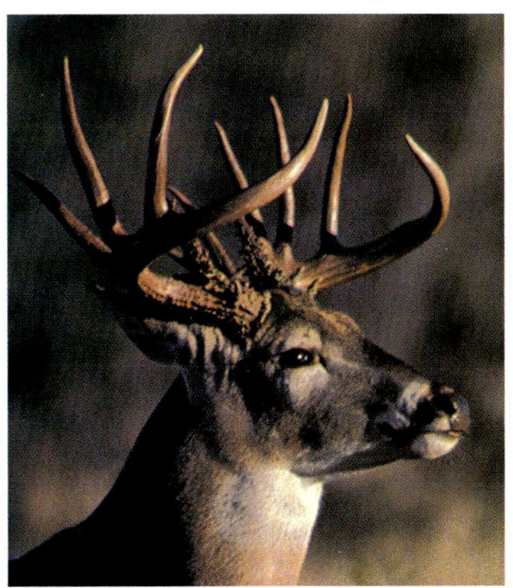

BUCK # 10

This buck's bases clearly appear much larger than his eyes, and they should. Both are well over five inches. In fact, this is the only buck in this book with a six-inch base. Also noteworthy is that this buck scores within one inch of the buck on page 200. They were both harvested from the same area about two years apart. Their antlers were very similar in conformation, possibly suggesting a shared genetic background.

This buck also demonstrates the inward and upward curvature of the beam, which can add significantly to a buck's beam length. When judging this buck's spread, be sure to notice that his ears lay flatter due to his beams spreading just above the base. This is a good example of what is called a "flat-antlered" deer.

Age: 7 1/2

Inside Spread: 20 2/8

	RIGHT	LEFT
Beams	**24 5/8**	**25 2/8**
G-1	5 2/8	5 0/8
G-2	7 1/8	6 6/8
G-3	9 3/8	7 5/8
G-4	8 7/8	7 6/8
	Abn.	**Abn.**
	1 0/8	7 4/8
	2 1/8	1 3/8
	2 4/8	1 0/8
	2 2/8	1 0/8
		1 3/8
		1 4/8
		4 5/8
Tine Totals	**38 4/8**	**45 4/8**
H-1	6 0/8	5 5/8
H-2	4 7/8	4 4/8
H-3	4 5/8	4 4/8
H-4	4 1/8	4 1/8
Mass Totals	**19 5/8**	**18 6/8**
Antler Total	**82 6/8**	**89 4/8**

Gross B&C: 192 4/8

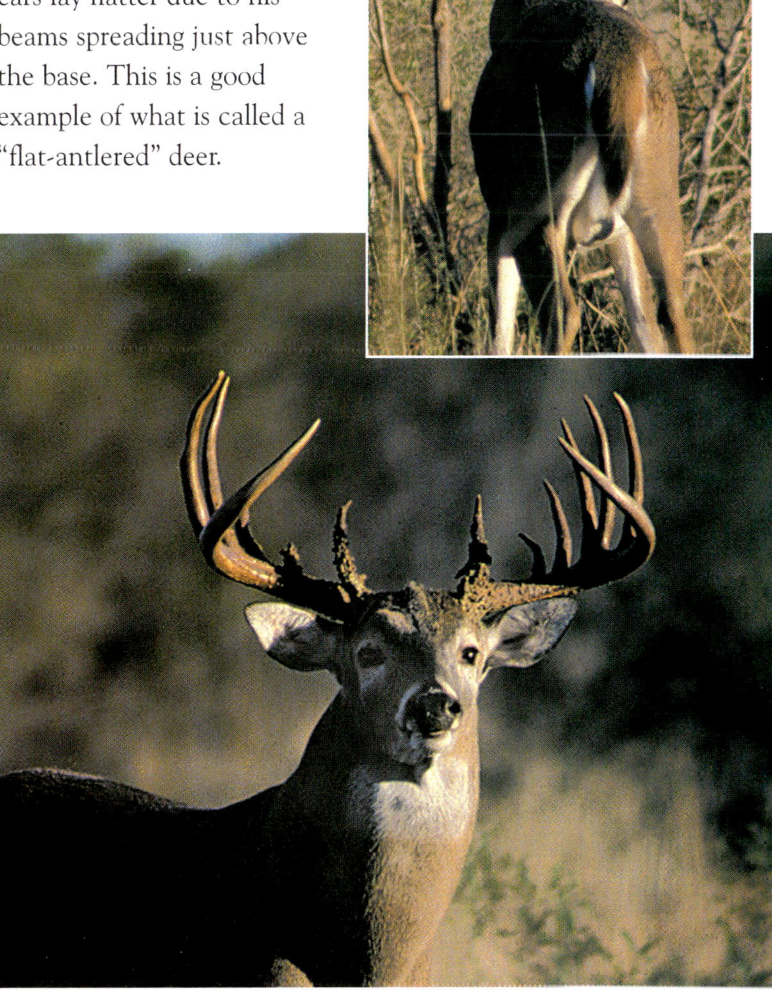

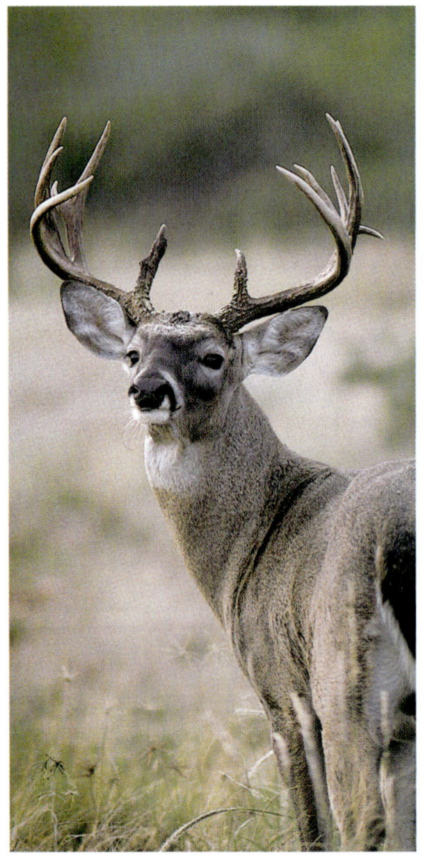

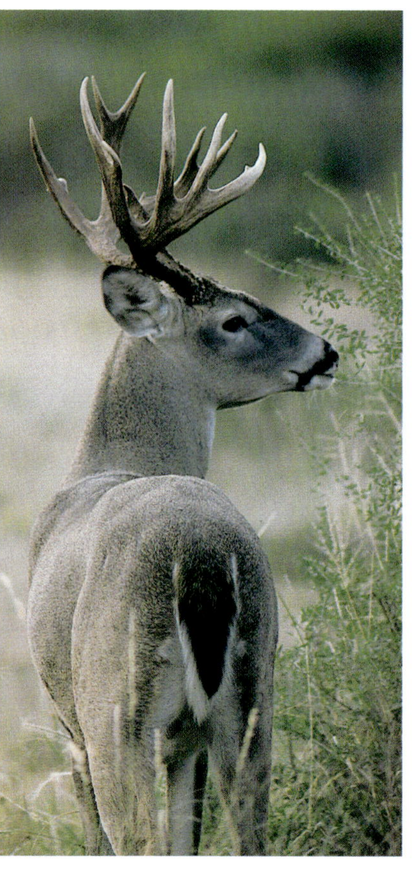

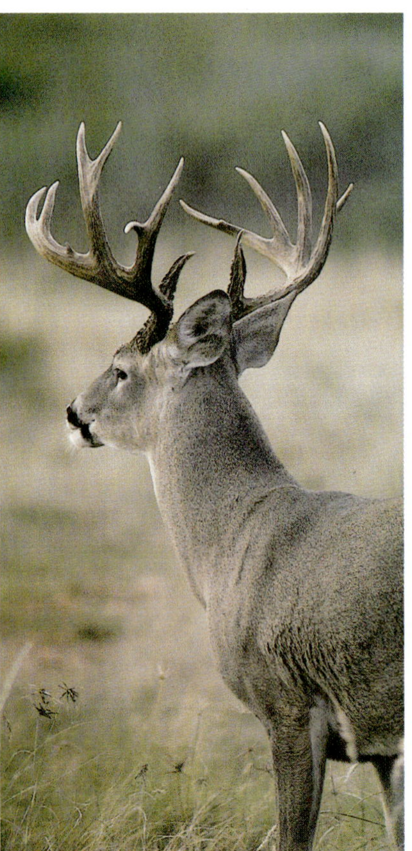

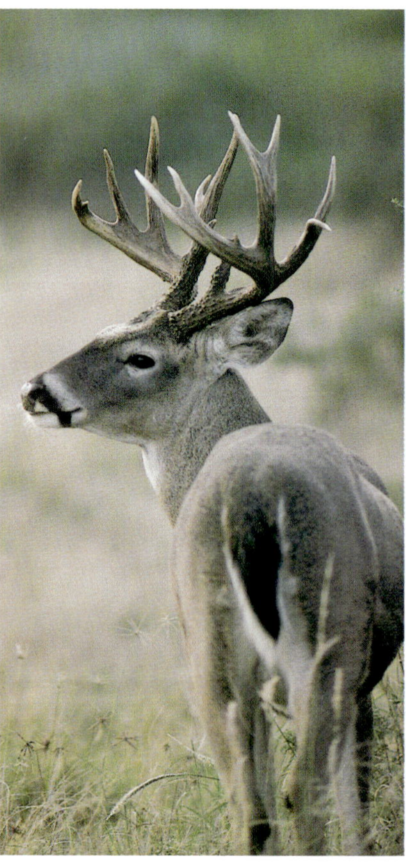

BUCK# 11

This buck is a classic example of a buck with 30 inches of tine length scoring in the 150s, even though his other measurements are quite average. He fits the 30-21-16-16 (tine length, beam length, total circumference, inside spread) benchmark about as close as a buck could, which was discussed in the chapter on judging deer on the hoof. Also, notice the beading on the antler bases that extends through the G-1s and halfway up the G-2s. Beading is considered by many astute whitetail observers to be a genetically inheritable characteristic.

Age: 4 1/2

Inside Spread: 17 0/8

	RIGHT	LEFT
Beams	**19 4/8**	**21 2/8**
G-1	6 1/8	4 3/8
G-2	10 4/8	8 2/8
G-3	7 7/8	8 7/8
G-4	5 4/8	2 4/8
	Abn.	**Abn.**
	2 5/8	2 0/8
		3 2/8
Tine Totals	**32 5/8**	**29 2/8**
H-1	4 4/8	4 3/8
H-2	3 6/8	3 5/8
H-3	4 2/8	4 4/8
H-4	4 0/8	3 1/8
Mass Totals	**16 4/8**	**15 5/8**
Antler Total	68 5/8	66 0/8

Gross B&C:
151 5/8

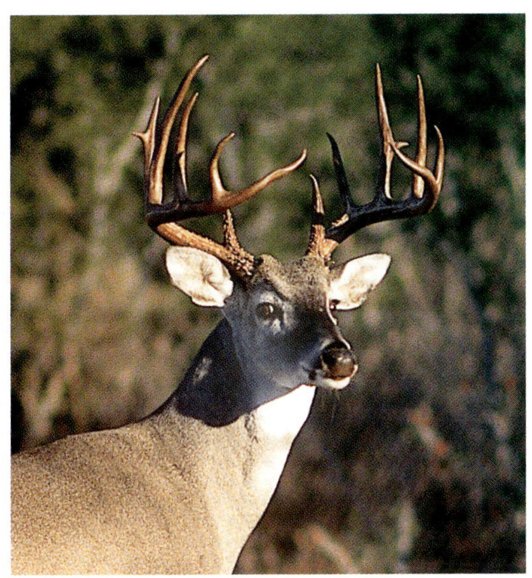

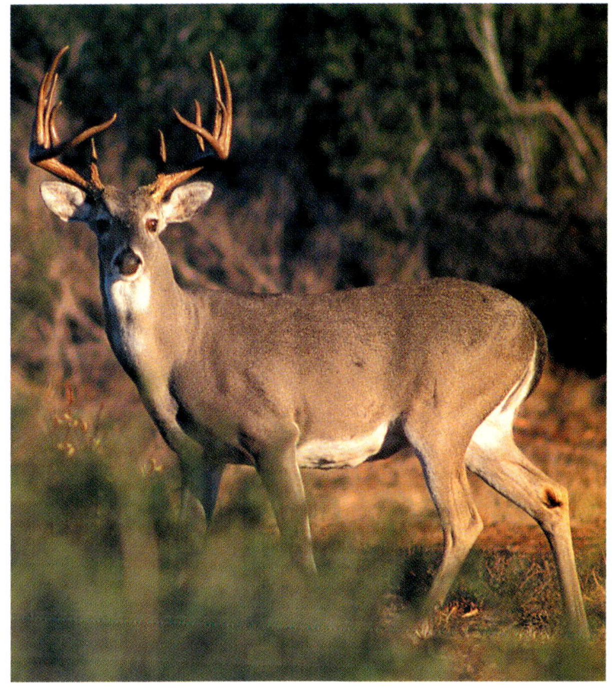

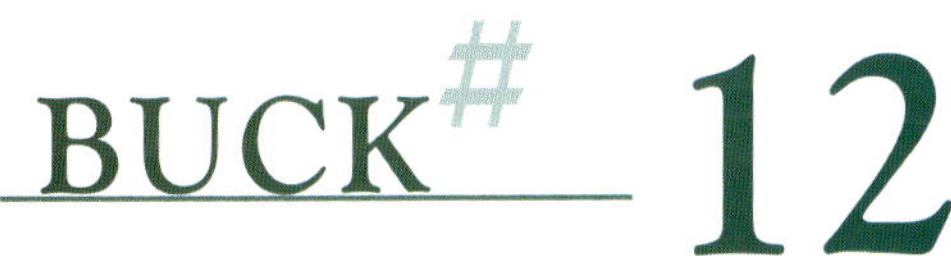

BUCK # 12

This buck has great beams for such a narrow inside spread. Notice from the side view that his beams extend to his nose and from the front view that they turn back within five or six inches of each other. This is a good example of what beams must do to reach 25 or 26 inches on a buck with a narrow inside spread. Also noticeable on this buck is the sag in the stomach area and the length of the antler beams. When combined, these are strong indicators of a buck older than 5 1/2 years.

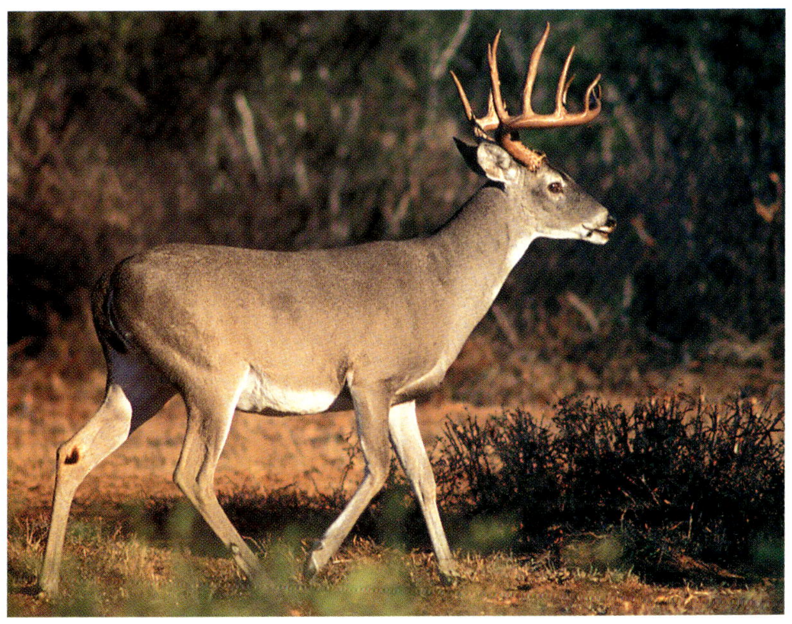

Age: 7 1/2

Inside Spread: 15 7/8

	Right	Left
Beams	**25 0/8**	**26 0/8**
G-1	3 6/8	4 5/8
G-2	7 4/8	5 5/8
G-3	10 2/8	8 4/8
G-4	7 0/8	7 5/8
G-5	4 4/8	4 5/8
	Abn.	**Abn.**
	1 1/8	1 1/8
Tine Totals	**34 1/8**	**32 2/8**
H-1	4 4/8	4 4/8
H-2	4 0/8	4 1/8
H-3	3 7/8	3 7/8
H-4	3 7/8	3 3/8
Mass Totals	**16 2/8**	**15 7/8**
Antler Total	**75 3/8**	**74 1/8**

Gross B&C: 165 3/8

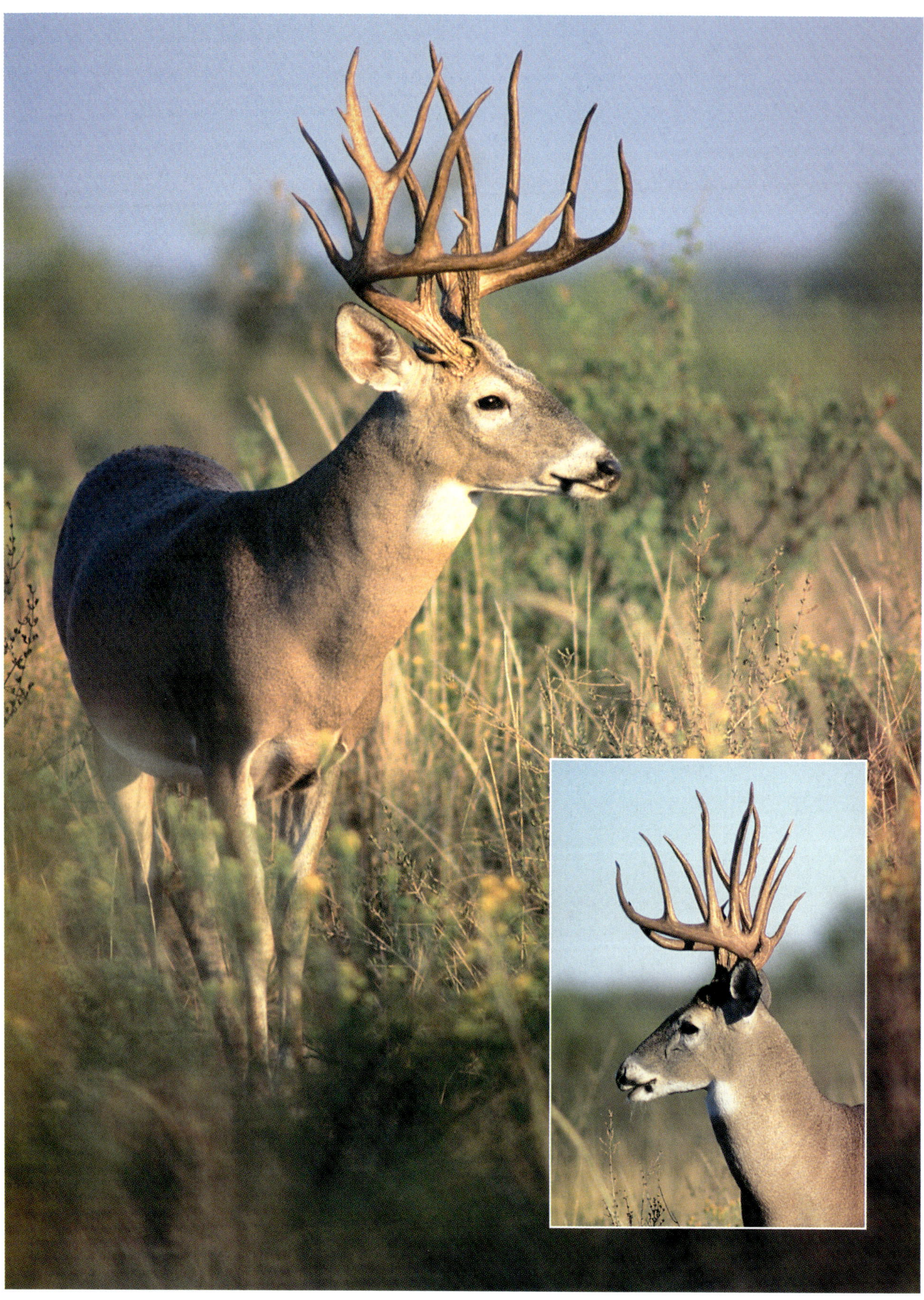

BUCK # 13

This buck has extremely long tines. It is often difficult to convince yourself that the tines are really that long when time is of the essence. Start by comparing his brow tines to the inside measurement of his ear (five inches) for a good starting benchmark. Then, use the brow tine estimations to compare to each of the other antlers. Notice the G-1s are almost seven inches long, and every other tine is longer on both antlers. This is a quick indicator of a high-scoring buck due to total tine length.

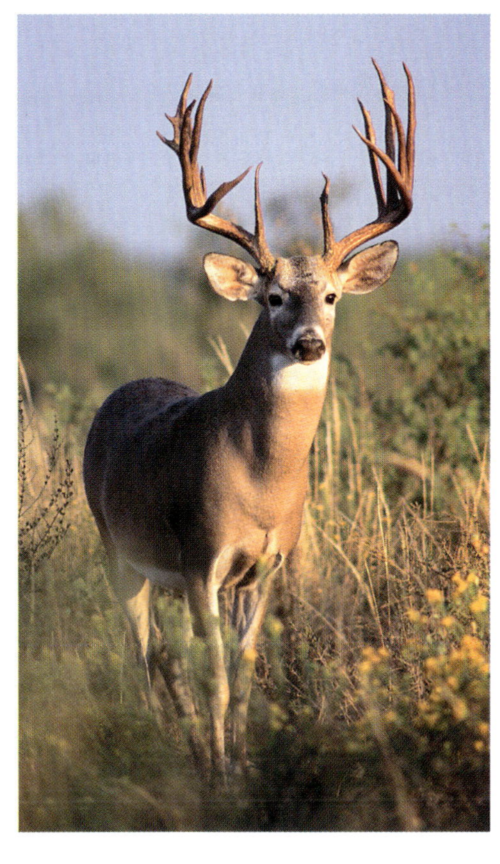

Age: 6 1/2

Inside Spread: 16 3/8

	RIGHT	LEFT
Beams	**24 3/8**	**25 4/8**
G-1	6 6/8	6 6/8
G-2	5 1/8	10 5/8
G-3	7 4/8	12 1/8
G-4	11 0/8	11 1/8
G-5	9 6/8	8 1/8
	Abn.	**Abn.**
	7 5/8	
	2 0/8	
	1 0/8	
	2 7/8	
Tine Totals	**50 6/8**	**48 6/8**
H-1	4 3/8	4 4/8
H-2	3 6/8	4 0/8
H-3	4 5/8	4 5/8
H-4	5 3/8	4 3/8
Mass Totals	**18 1/8**	**17 4/8**
Antler Total	**96 1/8**	**91 6/8**

Gross B&C: 204 2/8

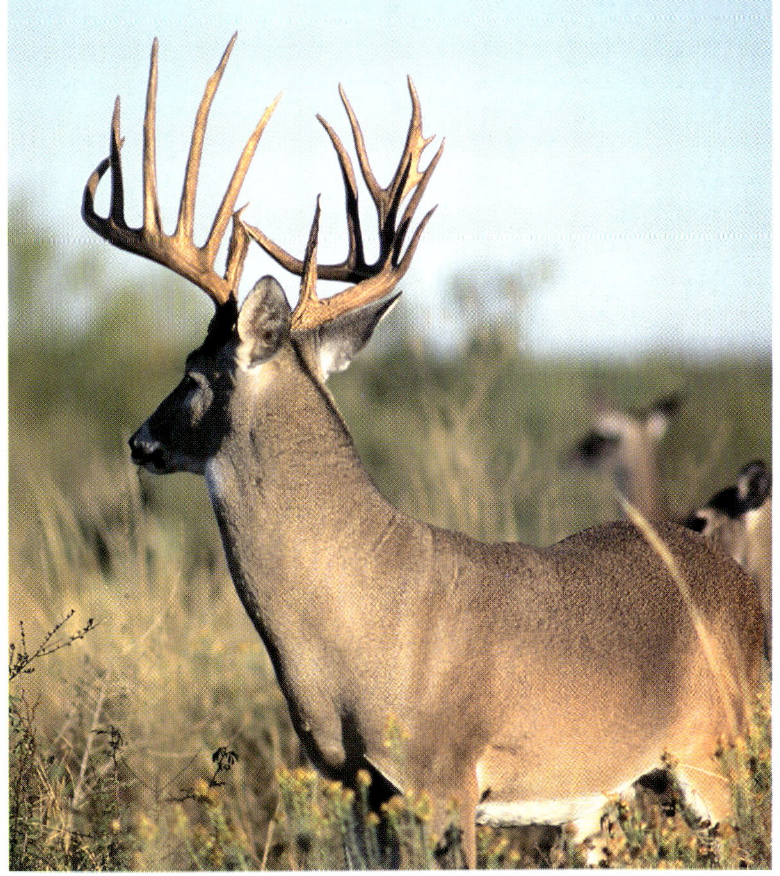

BUCK # 14

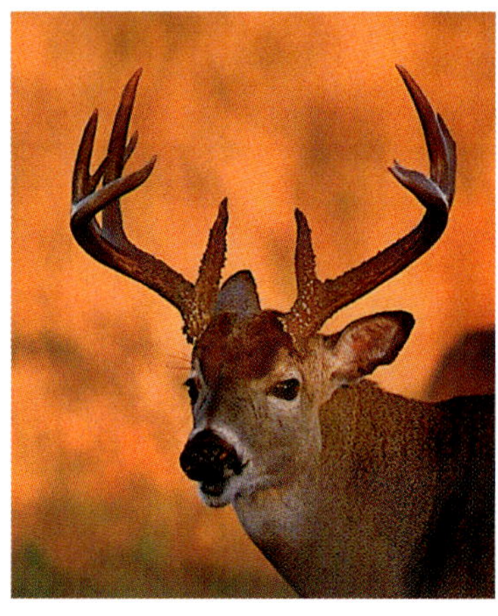

This is a very old buck. His mass is what makes him appear much bigger than he truly is. He has very short beam and tine lengths. Notice his small ears, which make his inside spread appear wider than it actually is. Also, notice the protruding hip bones and sagging skin under the jaw, which are good indicators of old age. Below is a photo of this buck's jawbone, showing the extreme tooth wear indicative of a post-mature buck. See Chapter 6 for more on aging white-tailed deer by tooth wear.

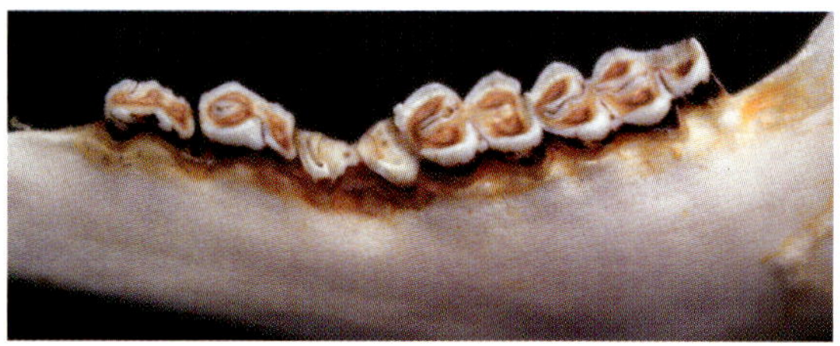

Age: 8 1/2

Inside Spread: 16 0/8

	RIGHT	LEFT
Beams	**17 2/8**	**18 2/8**
G-1	4 4/8	4 3/8
G-2	9 2/8	6 4/8
G-3	4 7/8	6 6/8
	Abn.	**Abn.**
	2 4/8	2 4/8
	1 7/8	
Tine Totals	**23 0/8**	**20 1/8**
H-1	5 1/8	5 1/8
H-2	4 4/8	4 4/8
H-3	4 1/8	4 2/8
H-4	2 7/8	3 3/8
Mass Totals	**16 5/8**	**17 2/8**
Antler Total	56 7/8	55 5/8

Gross B&C: 128 4/8

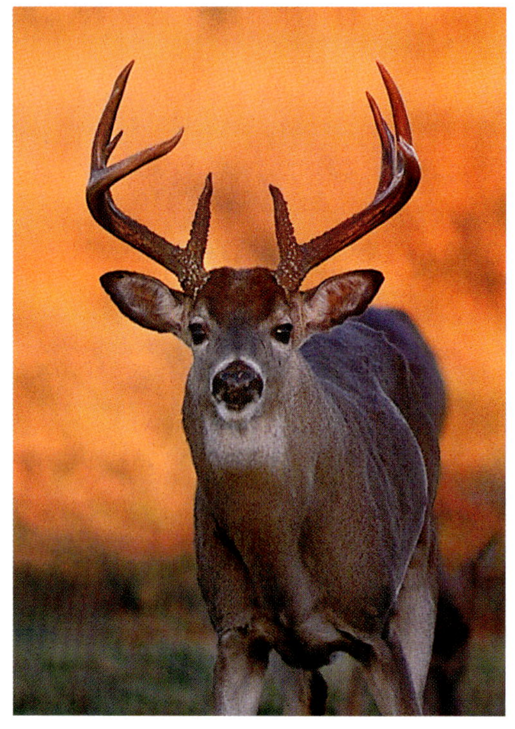

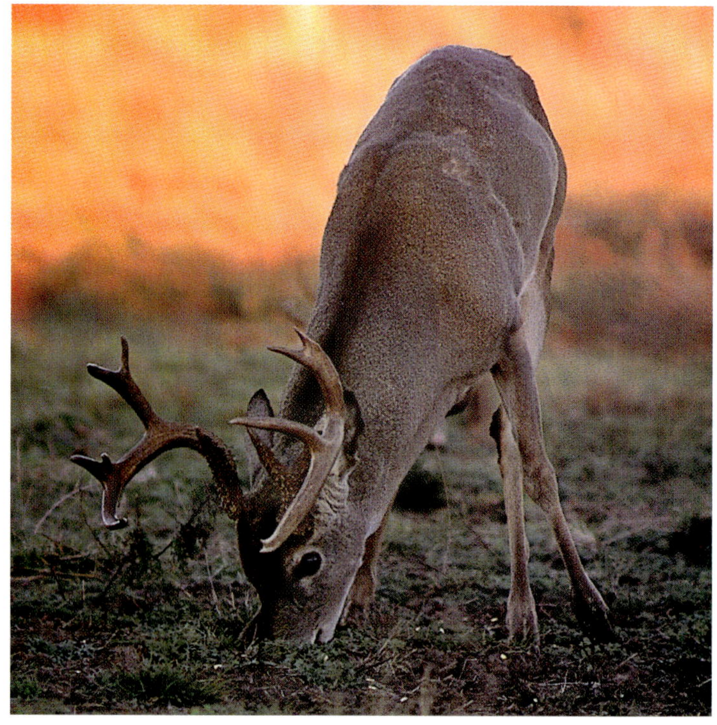

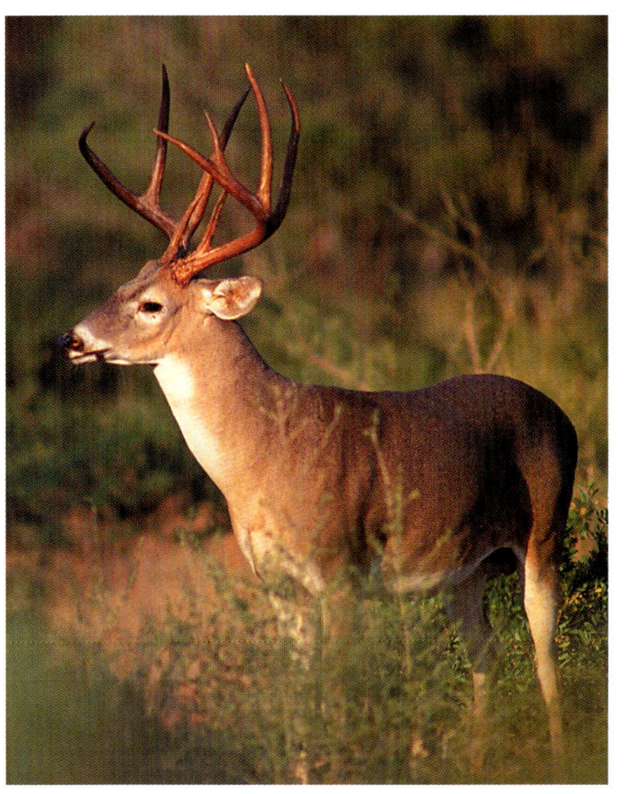

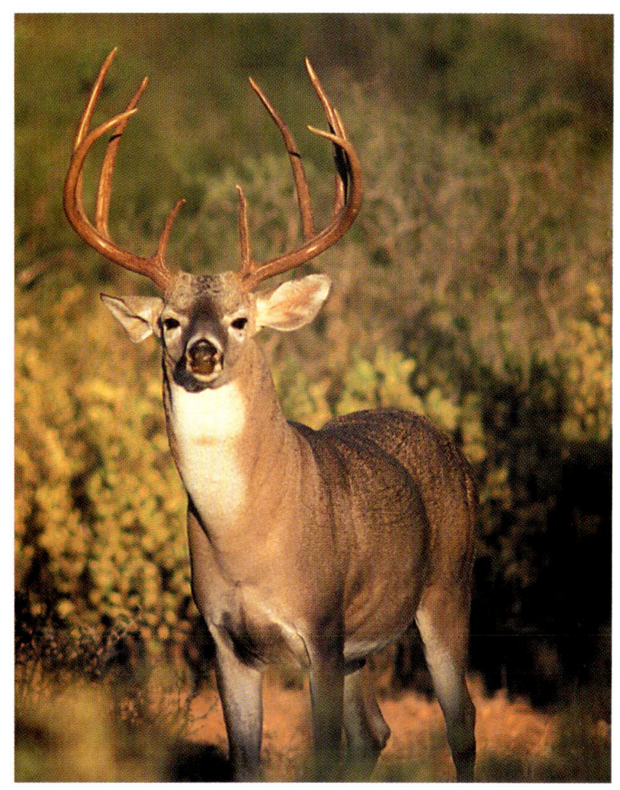

Age: 7 1/2		
Inside Spread: 18 6/8		
	RIGHT	LEFT
Beams	24 2/8	24 1/8
G-1	5 4/8	6 6/8
G-2	13 2/8	13 4/8
G-3	11 4/8	11 2/8
G-4		4 5/8
Tine Totals	30 2/8	36 1/8
H-1	4 1/8	4 4/8
H-2	3 7/8	3 7/8
H-3	3 7/8	3 7/8
H-4	2 7/8	3 2/8
Mass Totals	14 6/8	15 4/8
Antler Total	69 2/8	75 6/8
Gross B&C: 163 6/8		

BUCK # 15

This is another buck with extremely long tines. Always start by comparing a buck's brow tines with the inside measurement of his ear to help confirm his G-2s are 13 inches long. If this buck looks familiar, he is the buck on page 177 the following year. By comparing his scores, you will see he grew another 5 3/8 inches from age 6 1/2 to 7 1/2. Notice that the double white throat patch from the previous year has almost closed up to one, long, white throat patch.

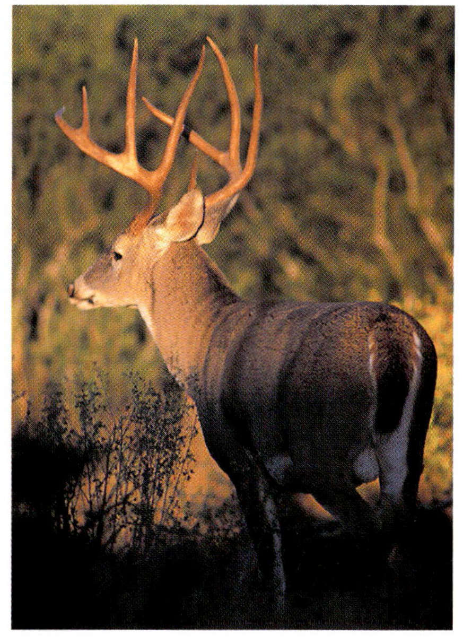

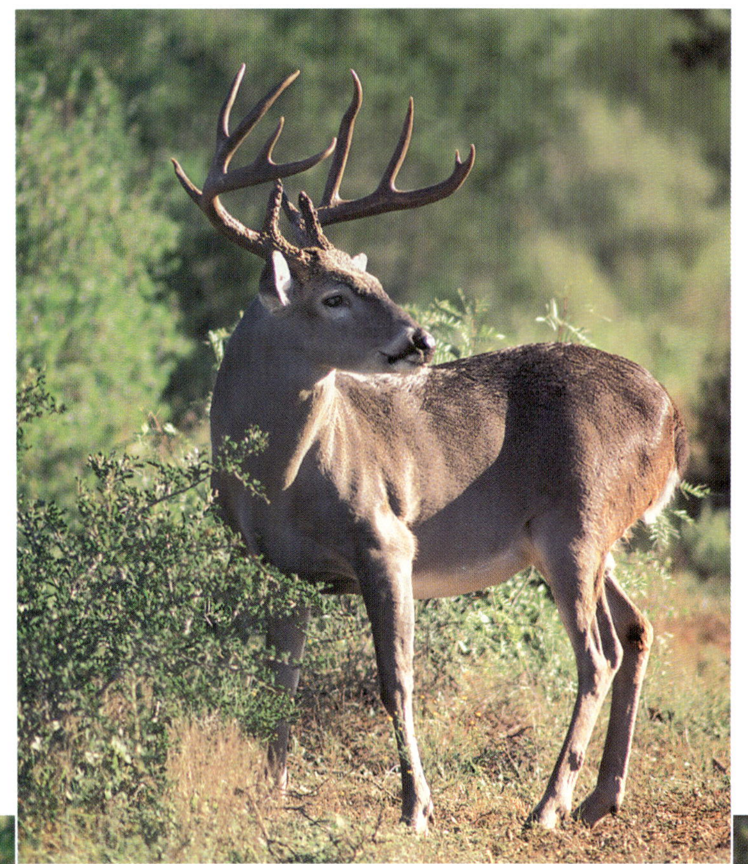

BUCK # 16

At first glance this buck does not appear to score well due to his weak G-1s and G-2s. Yet, when you add in his abnormal points, he has almost 30 inches of tine length. His beams are also difficult to judge, unless they are viewed from both the side and the front showing the backward sweep. His bases appear much larger than his eyes, clearly indicating they are at least five inches. Some hunters would pass this buck due to his short G-1s and G-2s unaware they were passing on what might be the highest-scoring buck of their life.

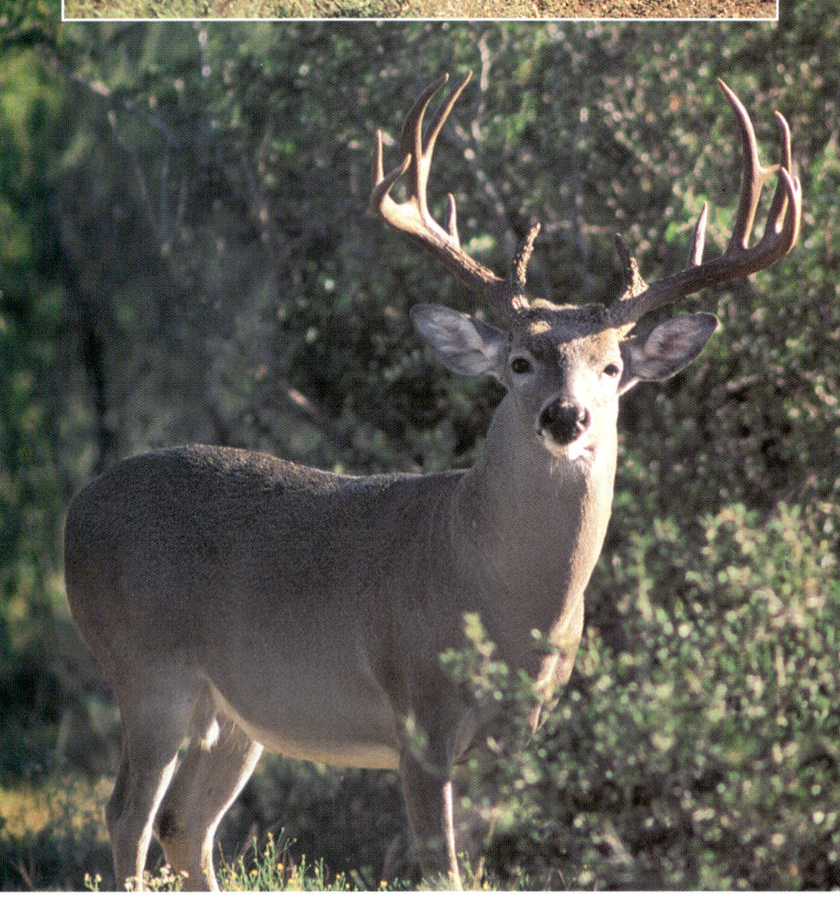

Age: 7 1/2

Inside Spread: 22 2/8

	RIGHT	LEFT
Beams	**25 1/8**	**25 2/8**
G-1	4 2/8	3 4/8
G-2	4 1/8	5 2/8
G-3	10 1/8	10 5/8
G-4	3 5/8	7 1/8
	Abn.	**Abn.**
	7 0/8	1 5/8
Tine Totals	**29 1/8**	**28 1/8**
H-1	5 0/8	5 1/8
H-2	4 4/8	4 4/8
H-3	4 2/8	4 2/8
H-4	3 6/8	4 0/8
Mass Totals	**17 4/8**	**17 7/8**
Antler Total	**71 6/8**	**71 2/8**

Gross B&C: 165 2/8

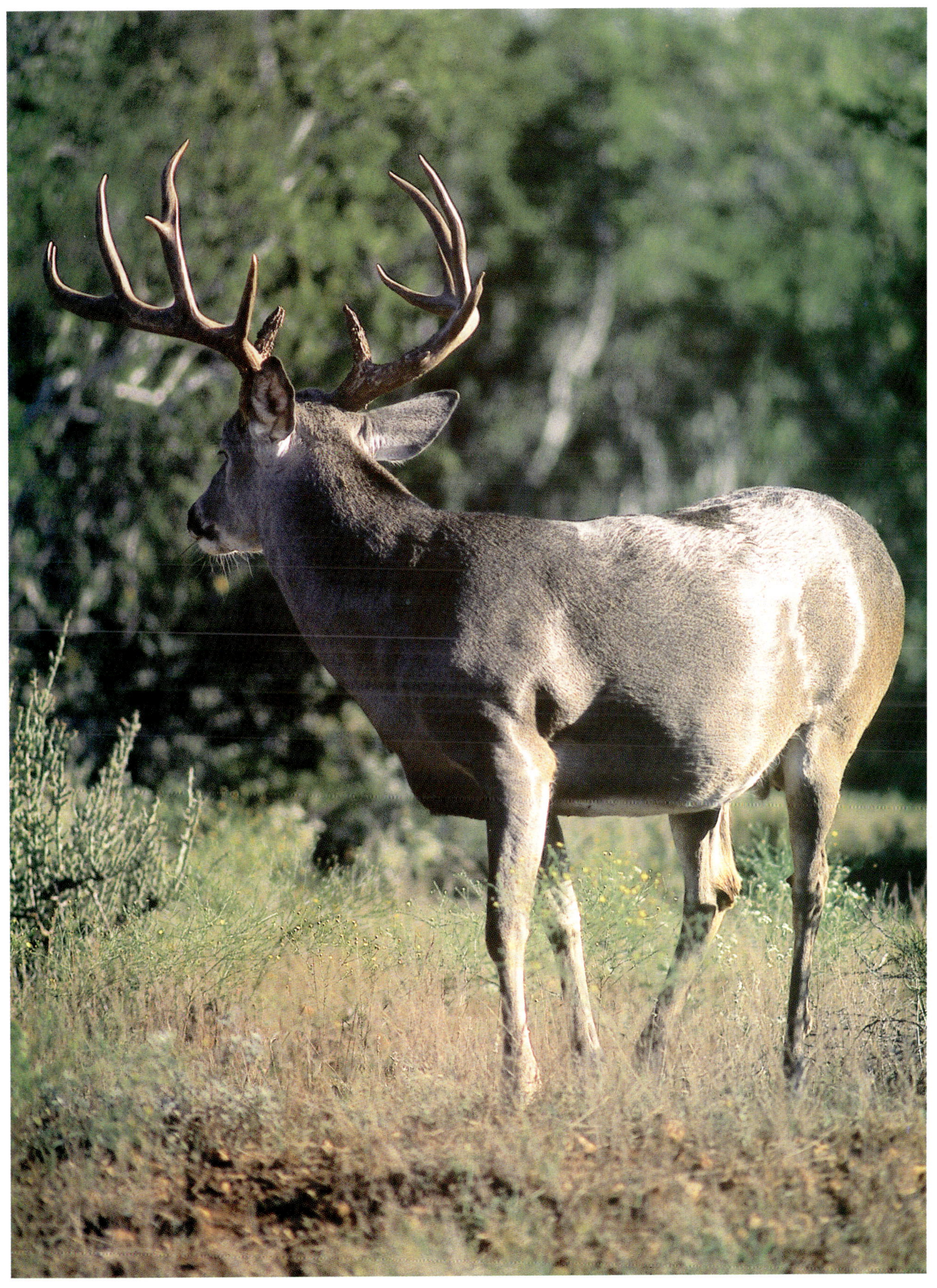

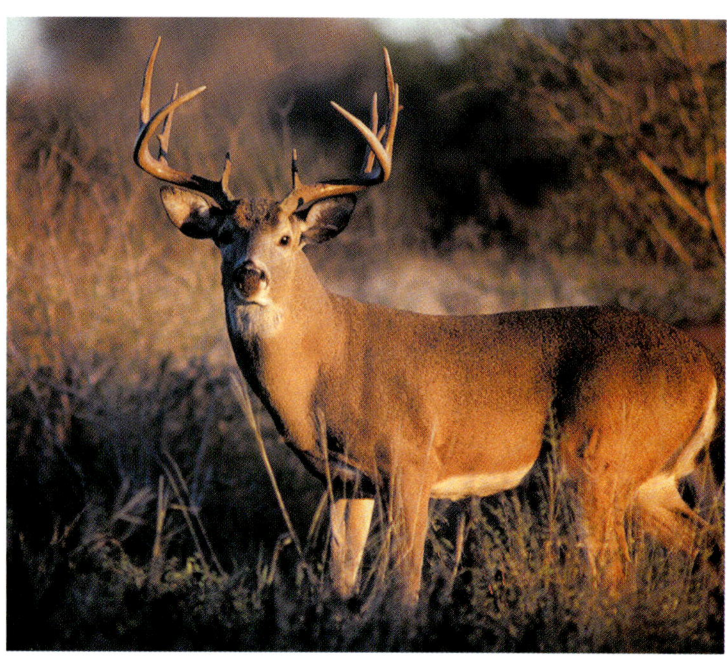

Age: 7 1/2		
Inside Spread: 19 3/8		
	RIGHT	LEFT
Beams	23 0/8	22 7/8
G-1	2 7/8	3 5/8
G-2	7 6/8	8 0/8
G-3	9 2/8	9 5/8
G-4	1 3/8	6 0/8
	Abn.	Abn.
		3 3/8
Tine Totals	21 2/8	30 5/8
H-1	4 0/8	4 0/8
H-2	3 6/8	3 6/8
H-3	3 6/8	3 5/8
H-4	3 2/8	3 2/8
Mass Totals	14 6/8	14 5/8
Antler Total	59 0/8	68 1/8
Gross B&C: 146 4/8		

BUCK # 17

At first glance this buck would appear to easily score in the 150s. However, after close observation it is apparent he has a very short G-4 on his right antler and short brow tines. Always be wary of a buck with short G-4s or brow tines, as these are good indicators of a low-scoring buck. Also, this buck's mass measurements were surprisingly low for a buck his age.

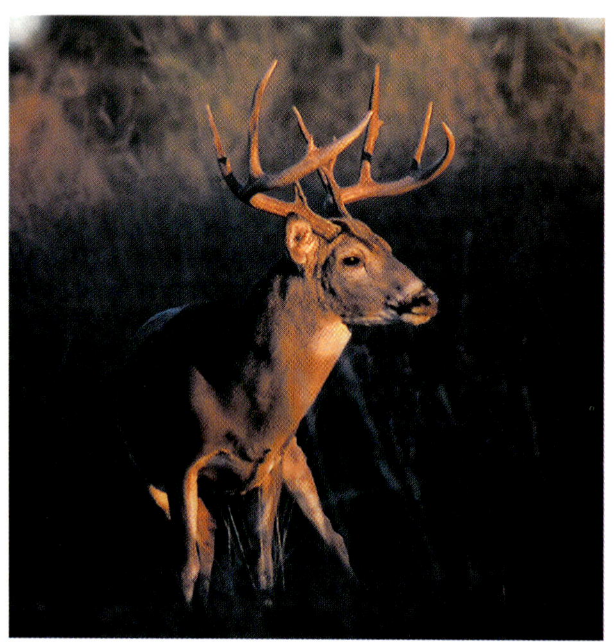

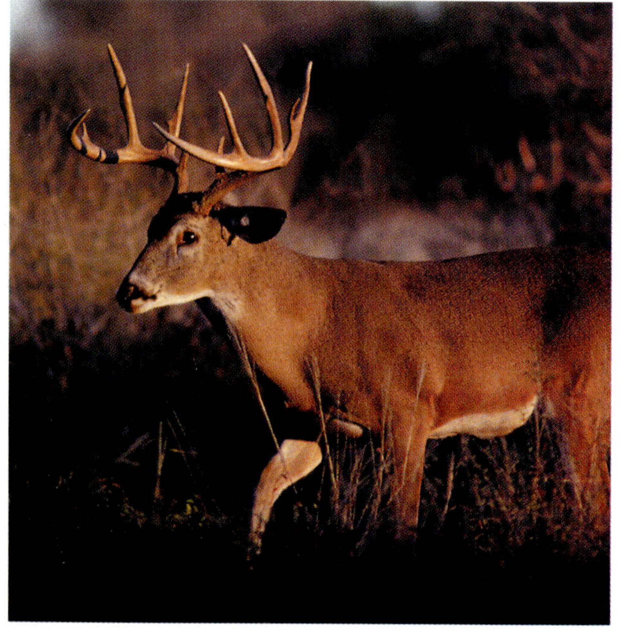

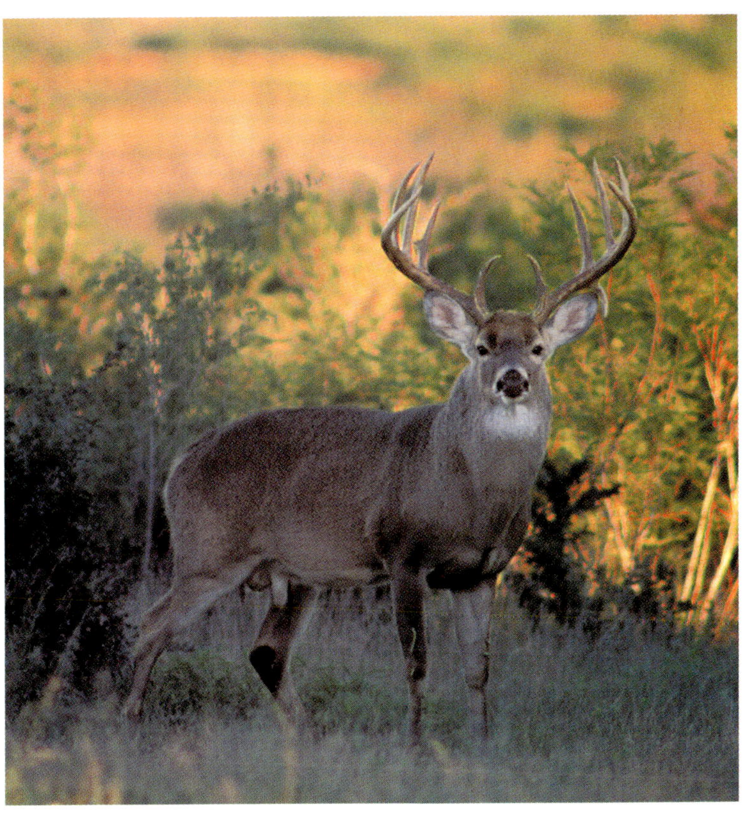

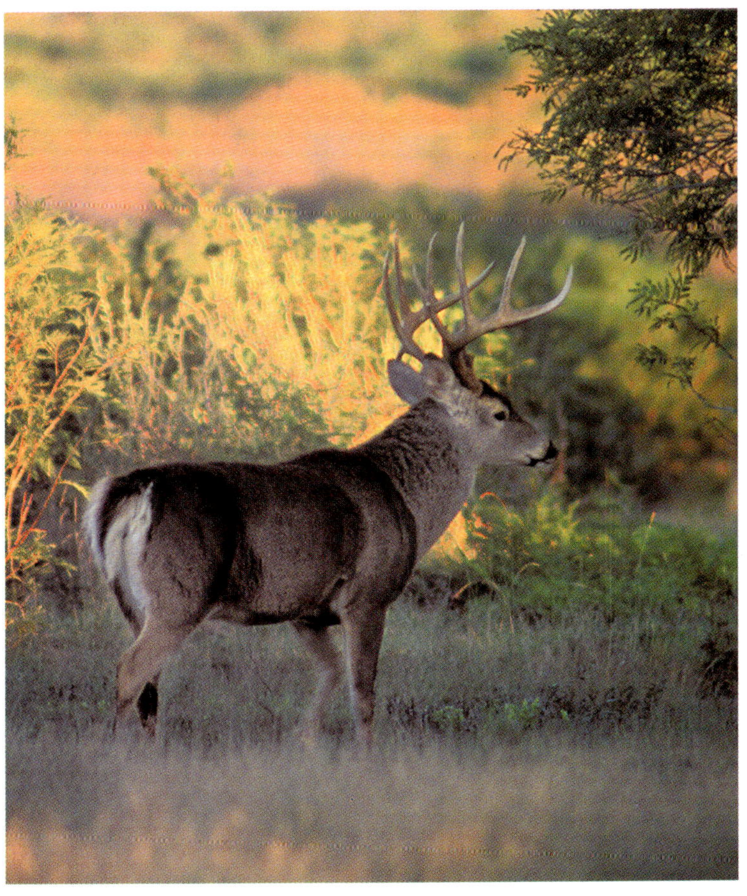

Age: 7 1/2		
Inside Spread: 20 6/8		
	RIGHT	LEFT
Beams	24 3/8	22 4/8
G-1	4 2/8	4 3/8
G-2	7 7/8	8 4/8
G-3	10 0/8	8 5/8
G-4	8 4/8	6 2/8
	Abn.	Abn.
		3 4/8
Tine Totals	30 5/8	31 2/8
H-1	4 5/8	3 7/8
H-2	4 0/8	3 5/8
H-3	4 0/8	3 6/8
H-4	3 7/8	3 4/8
Mass Totals	16 4/8	14 6/8
Antler Total	71 4/8	68 4/8
Gross B&C: 160 6/8		

BUCK # 18

The first things that should catch your eye with this buck are his tall G-4s. This almost always signifies a high-scoring buck unless he is noticeably deficient in another category. A week after I photographed this buck, he was found dead. A buck fight was the apparent cause. Interestingly, after his antlers were measured, it was noticed that his left antler is short in every measurement except for the drop tine, which balances the overall score.

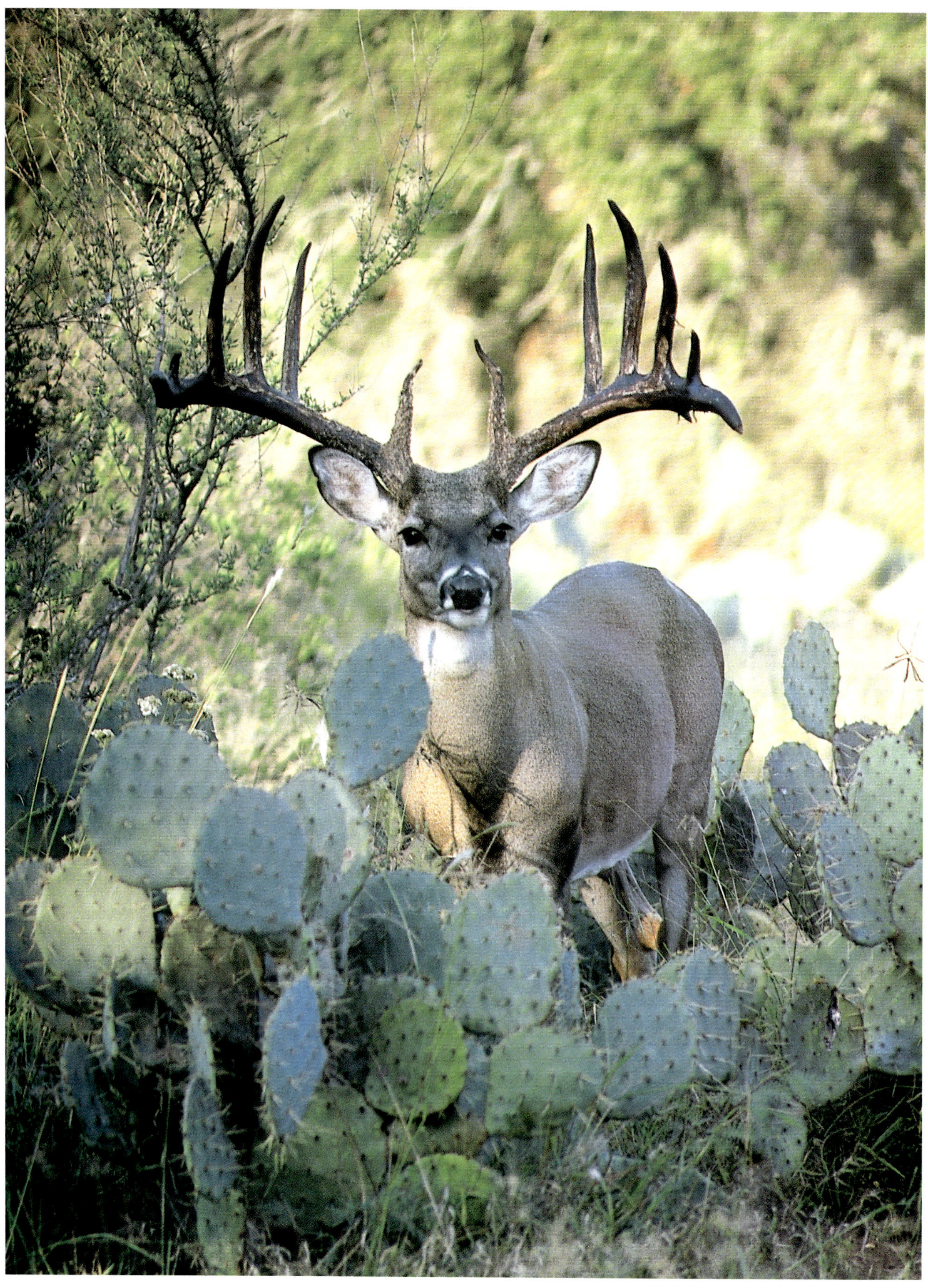

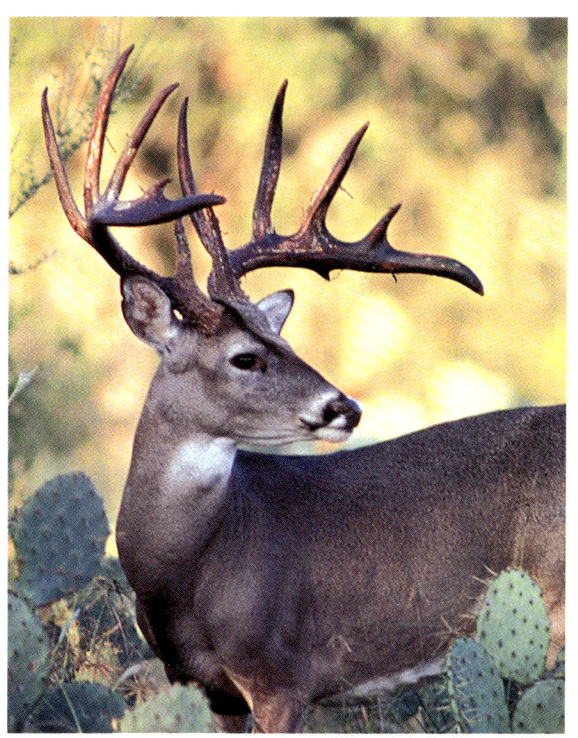

BUCK # 19

This deer's measurements are tremendous in every category. The biggest surprise was his mass. He clearly had antler bases larger than five inches, which you could see by comparing them to his eyes. But, it was hard to realize that he maintained circumferences greater than 4 1/2 inches throughout the beam. To estimate this buck's spread, take the ear tip-to-tip measurement (16 inches) and double it, and it is apparent this only extends about three to four inches outside his actual spread, thus giving an estimation of 28 to 29 inches. Also, notice how this buck's G-2s grow from the back of the beam instead of the top, which added to their length. One final interesting note is that official Boone & Crockett rules do not allow the spread credit to exceed the main beam lengths. In such a case, the difference is deducted from the gross score. We gave the buck full credit for his spread and beams in our score as that is what he actually grew. This buck was the No. 1 Texas Big Game Awards Typical Whitetail harvested in 2002. The body characteristics of sagging skin under the jaw, hipbones showing, and neck size are good indicators of an older-age buck when the stomach line cannot be seen.

Age: 8 1/2

Inside Spread: 28 7/8

	Right	Left
Beams	**26 3/8**	**25 3/8**
G-1	5 5/8	6 4/8
G-2	10 3/8	11 1/8
G-3	10 5/8	10 4/8
G-4	8 1/8	8 4/8
G-5	2 2/8	3 4/8
Tine Totals	**37 0/8**	**40 1/8**
H-1	5 5/8	5 4/8
H-2	4 4/8	4 6/8
H-3	4 5/8	4 5/8
H-4	4 3/8	4 6/8
Mass Totals	**19 1/8**	**19 5/8**
Antler Total	**82 4/8**	**85 1/8**

Gross B&C: 196 4/8

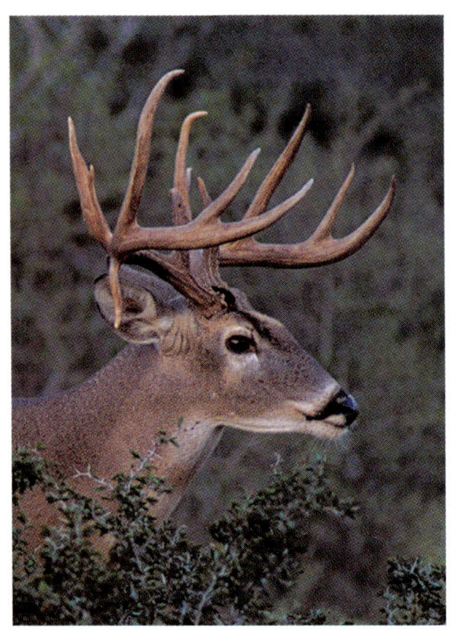

BUCK # 20

This is the type of buck that creates deer legends. He has wide, sweeping beams with tall tines, abnormal points, a drop tine, and a blue-grey eye, which probably was the result of a battle. Typical of deer blind in one eye, this buck became more and more wary, which added to his mystique. Note that his beams did not grow up but back before turning forward. They grew fairly flat but well past his ears before turning and growing several inches forward and upward. Using his large ears as a reference, an observer can quickly estimate his brow tines at over five inches in length. This offers a good rule of thumb for estimating the other tine lengths. Two readily identifiable, physical characteristics of this buck throughout much of its life were the small notch in the top of his left ear and a double white throat patch.

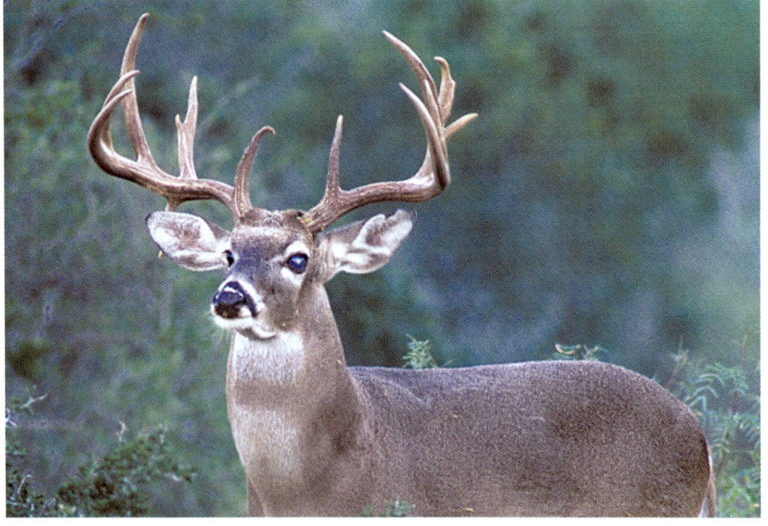

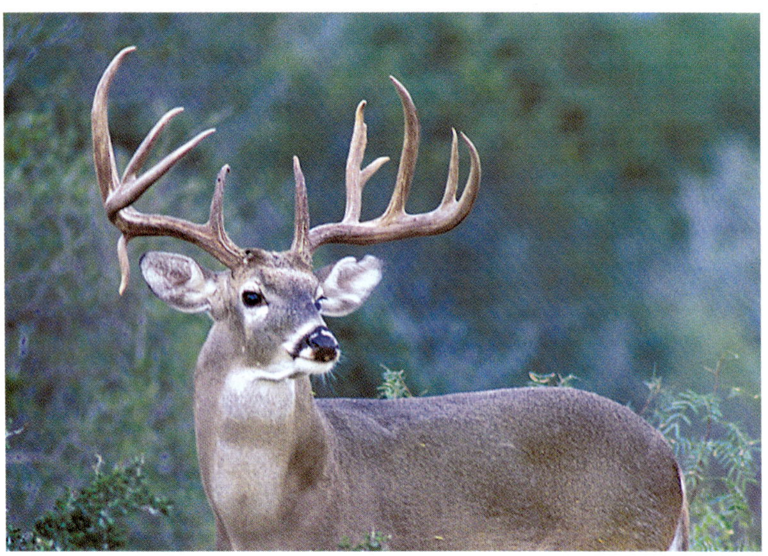

Age: 7 1/2

Inside Spread: 22 4/8

	Right	Left
Beams	**26 3/8**	**25 7/8**
G-1	6 2/8	6 0/8
G-2	8 5/8	10 2/8
G-3	11 5/8	11 0/8
G-4	6 7/8	5 5/8
	Abn.	**Abn.**
	4 2/8	3 0/8
	1 1/8	
Tine Totals	**38 6/8**	**35 7/8**
H-1	4 2/8	4 4/8
H-2	3 7/8	4 0/8
H-3	4 1/8	4 0/8
H-4	3 5/8	3 6/8
Mass Totals	**15 7/8**	**15 2/8**
Antler Total	**81 0/8**	**78 0/8**

Gross B&C: 181 4/8

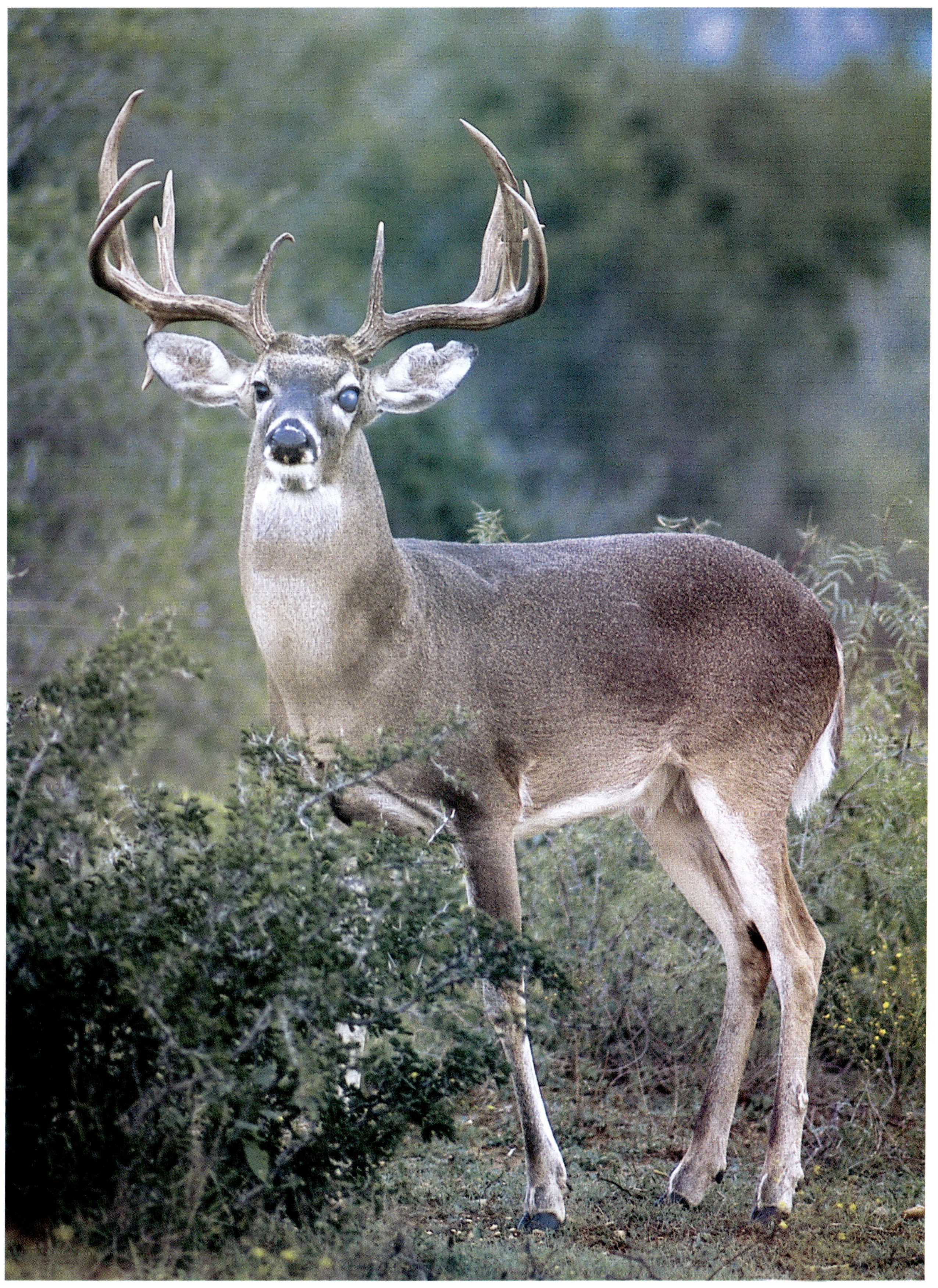

BUCK# 21

This buck demonstrates the 30-inch tine rule again. All of his other measurements are average, yet he easily scores in the 150s. From the side view it is easy to notice that his beams grow backward several inches before turning forward and still almost reach the imaginary line coming up from the tip of his nose. Also, notice the photo with the turned head and ear droop. This indicates another buck is in close proximity.

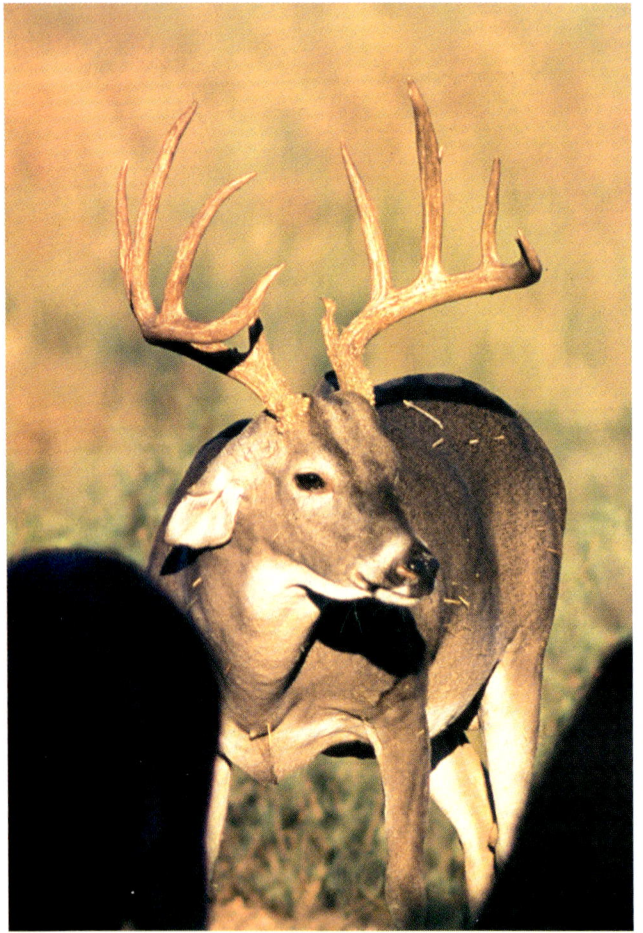

Age: 6 1/2

Inside Spread: 18 2/8

	Right	Left
Beams	**22 6/8**	**23 4/8**
G-1	3 4/8	3 0/8
G-2	7 7/8	8 1/8
G-3	10 5/8	10 7/8
G-4	8 4/8	5 6/8
G-5		1 6/8
Tine Totals	**30 4/8**	**29 4/8**
H-1	4 3/8	4 6/8
H-2	3 7/8	4 0/8
H-3	3 6/8	3 7/8
H-4	3 5/8	3 6/8
Mass Totals	**15 5/8**	**16 3/8**
Antler Total	**68 7/8**	**69 3/8**

Gross B&C: 156 4/8

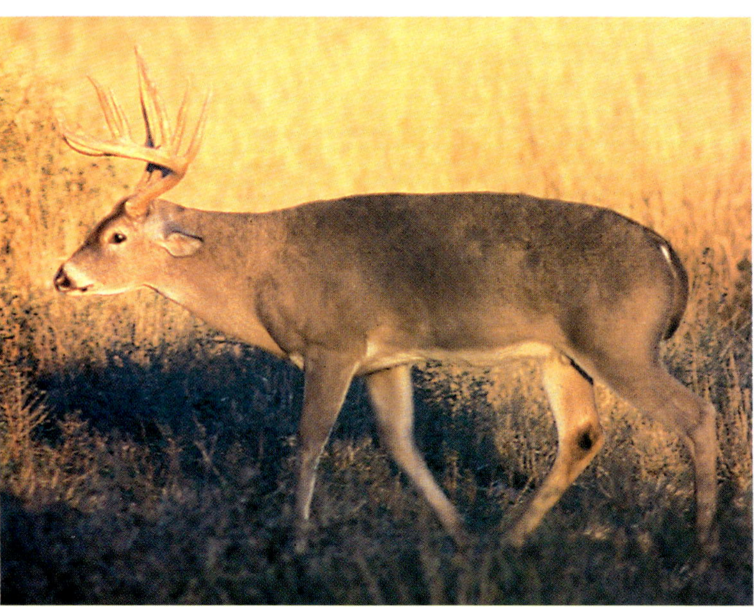

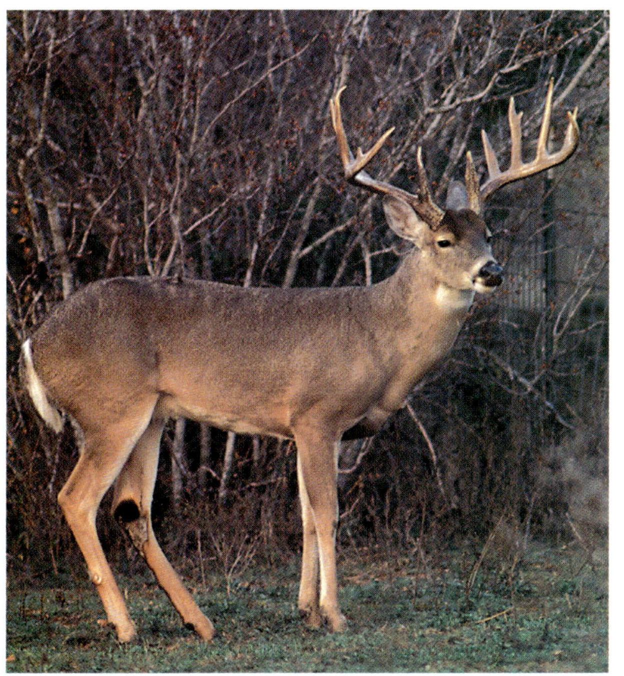

BUCK # 22

This buck showed up in late January after the rut. He is probably 5 1/2, but there is no way to be certain because he had not been recognized earlier. Also, the post-rut made his body appear younger than his actual age. His tarsals and the drooping skin under the jaw are good indicators that he is mature. His antler tines flare out, making his 22 6/8-inch inside spread even wider and more impressive. His antler bases easily appear larger than his eye and were over five inches in circumference. When estimating his spread, notice his right antler is approximately three fourths of an inside ear length (five inches) outside his right ear, and his left antler is a little over half an ear's length outside his left ear. Thus, 3 6/8 plus 16 plus 3 equals 22 6/8 inches of inside spread.

Age: Unknown

Inside Spread: 22 6/8

	Right	Left
Beams	**23 6/8**	**23 0/8**
G-1	5 5/8	4 5/8
G-2	7 2/8	7 2/8
G-3	8 4/8	8 0/8
G-4	8 0/8	8 3/8
G-5	1 0/8	4 1/8
	Abn.	**Abn.**
	1 4/8	1 1/8
Tine Totals	**31 4/8**	**33 4/8**
H-1	5 2/8	5 3/8
H-2	4 4/8	4 5/8
H-3	4 2/8	4 2/8
H-4	3 6/8	3 6/8
Mass Totals	**17 6/8**	**18 0/8**
Antler Total	**73 0/8**	**74 4/8**

Gross B&C: 170 2/8

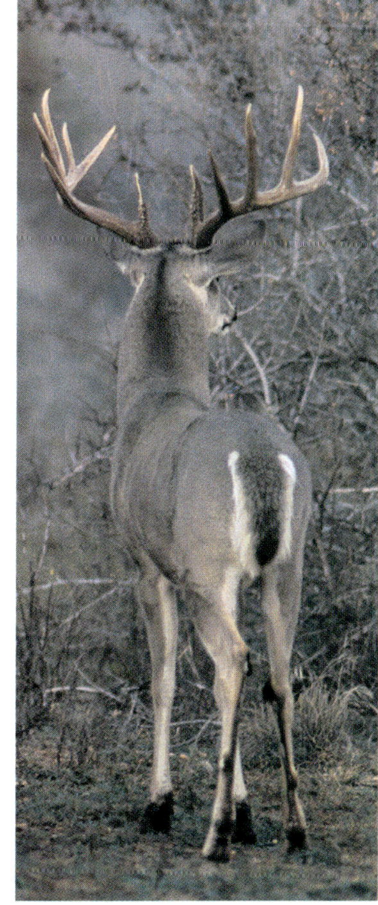

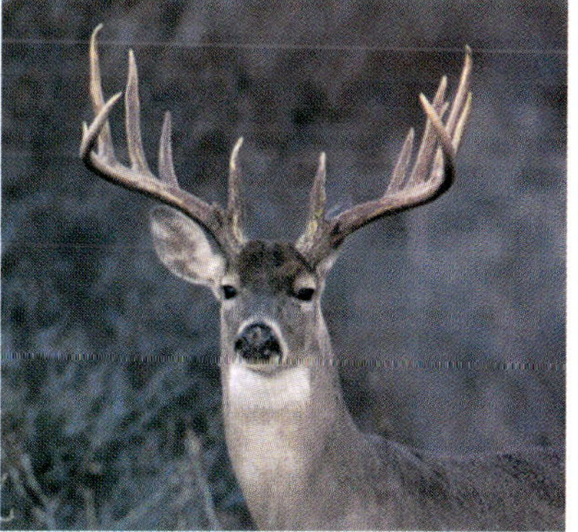

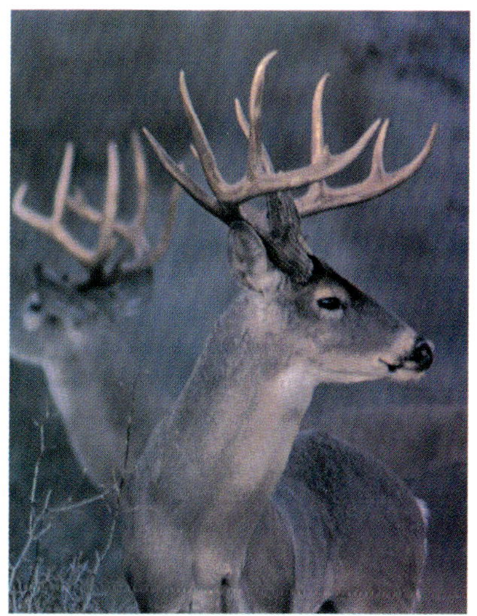

BUCK # 23

Notice how this buck's antler beams appear extremely heavy. With almost 40 inches of mass, he is at the top end of south Texas bucks when it comes to circumference measurements. The beams could easily be misjudged if only a frontal view was available. They are very unique in that they grew at about a 45-degree angle upward from his head. However, the side view clearly shows they grow several inches forward, which enables them to attain 24 inches.

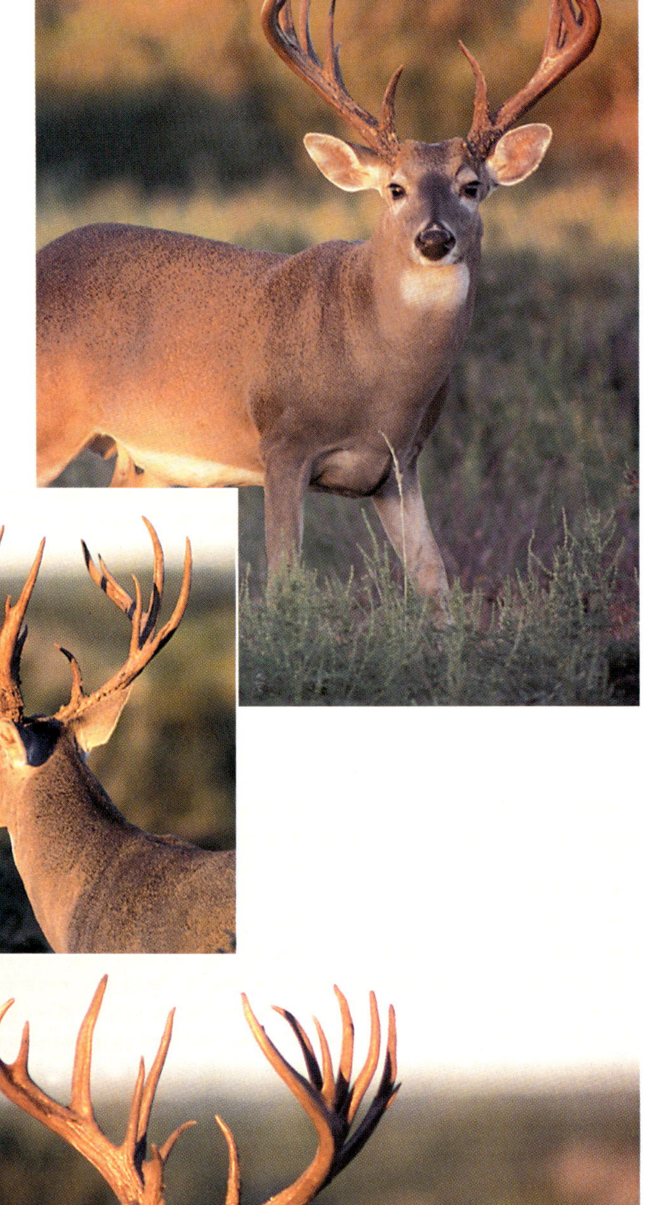

Age: 7 1/2

Inside Spread: 20 5/8

	Right	Left
Beams	**23 5/8**	**24 0/8**
G-1	5 0/8	6 1/8
G-2	10 0/8	10 4/8
G-3	8 5/8	7 5/8
G-4	3 0/8	4 4/8
G-5		3 2/8
	Abn.	**Abn.**
	5 2/8	8 7/8
	5 5/8	1 5/8
		6 6/8
Tine Totals	**38 1/8**	**49 2/8**
H-1	5 3/8	5 4/8
H-2	5 1/8	4 7/8
H-3	4 6/8	5 0/8
H-4	3 7/8	4 7/8
Mass Totals	**19 1/8**	**20 2/8**
Antler Total	**80 7/8**	**93 4/8**

Gross B&C: 195 0/8

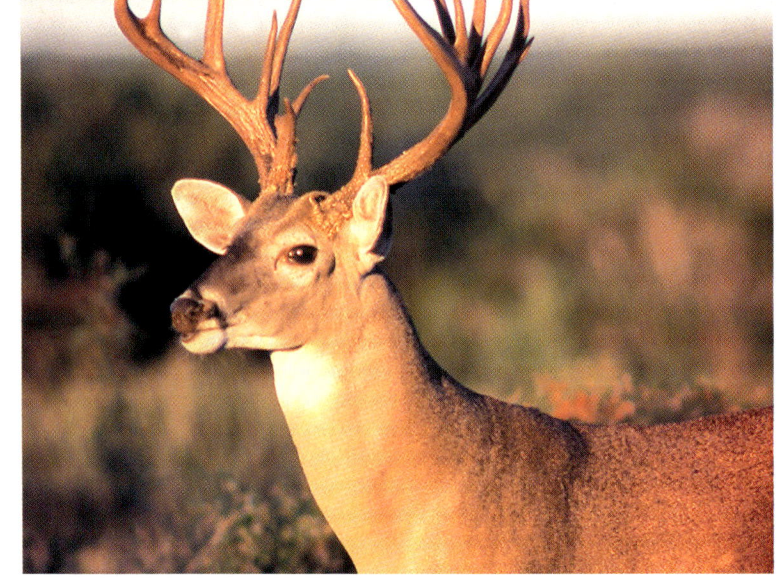

BUCK# 24

The first thing to catch the observer's eye on this buck is his mass. The antler bases are definitely larger than his eyes, putting him in the five-inch basal circumference category. The tines are not long, but they demonstrate that the more tines a buck has the easier it is for them to attain the 30-inch benchmark.

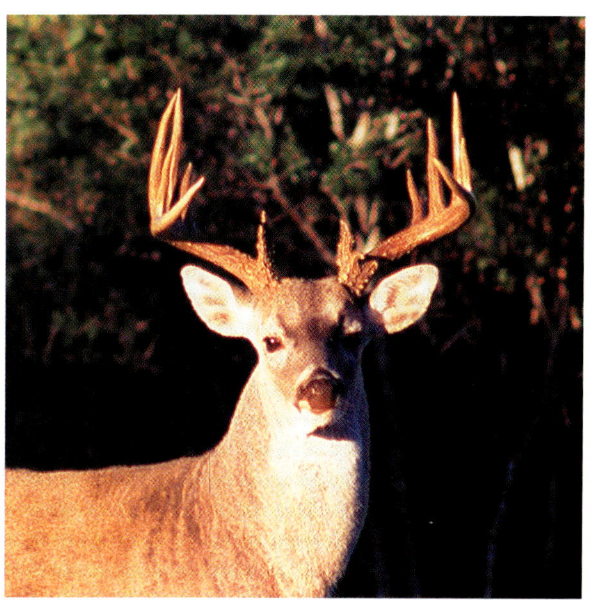

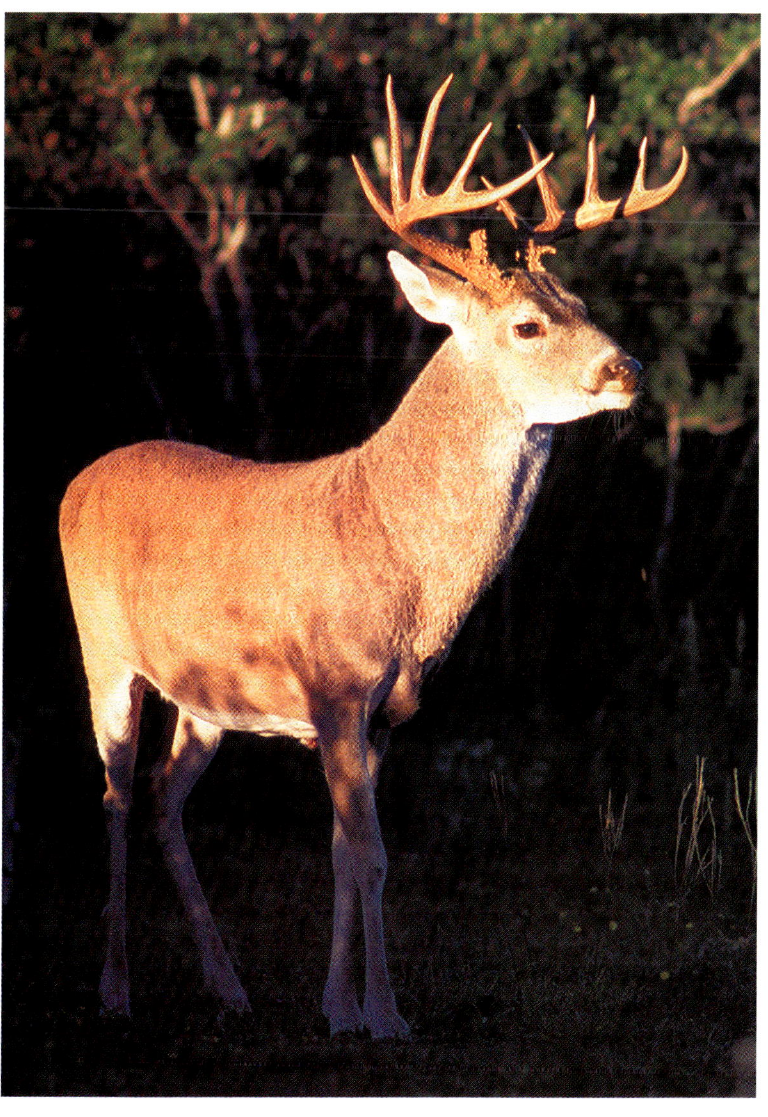

Age: 7 1/2

Inside Spread: 17 7/8

	RIGHT	LEFT
Beams	**23 4/8**	**22 3/8**
G-1	3 4/8	3 4/8
G-2	5 4/8	5 7/8
G-3	6 2/8	8 0/8
G-4	6 4/8	7 7/8
G-5	3 3/8	4 6/8
	Abn.	**Abn.**
	1 3/8	1 1/8
		1 5/8
Tine Totals	**26 4/8**	**32 6/8**
H-1	5 0/8	5 0/8
H-2	4 1/8	4 1/8
H-3	4 1/8	4 2/8
H-4	3 6/8	3 7/8
Mass Totals	**17 0/8**	**17 2/8**
Antler Total	**67 0/8**	**72 3/8**

Gross B&C:
157 2/8

BUCK# 25

When a buck has multiple abnormal tines, add all the tines (typical and abnormal) together on one antler. The reason is that we are only looking for total B&C tine length. Also noteworthy is that this buck's antler bases appear larger than his eyes, which is typical of bases over five inches in circumference. This is another example of a south Texas top-end buck with circumference measurements totaling more than 42 inches. When judging this buck's spread, notice the angle of the ear due to the flatness of the beam. The unique tail coloration pattern is a useful, lifelong, identifying characteristic on this buck.

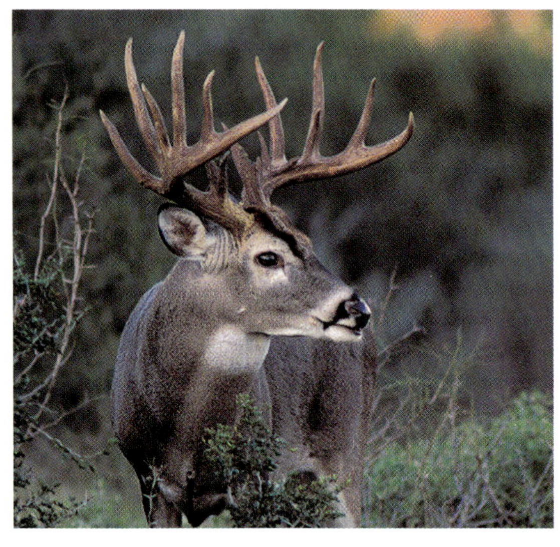

Age: 7 1/2

Inside Spread: 20 0/8

	RIGHT	LEFT
Beams	**22 0/8**	**22 5/8**
G-1	4 0/8	3 7/8
G-2	7 5/8	5 0/8
G-3	10 1/8	8 1/8
G-4	8 7/8	8 4/8
G-5	4 7/8	6 1/8
	Abn.	**Abn.**
	3 3/8	1 4/8
	5 6/8	2 6/8
	1 0/8	1 0/8
		4 1/8
Tine Totals	**45 5/8**	**41 0/8**
H-1	5 1/8	5 3/8
H-2	5 2/8	5 3/8
H-3	5 3/8	5 3/8
H-4	5 3/8	4 7/8
Mass Totals	**21 1/8**	**21 0/8**
Antler Total	**88 6/8**	**84 5/8**

Gross B&C:
193 3/8

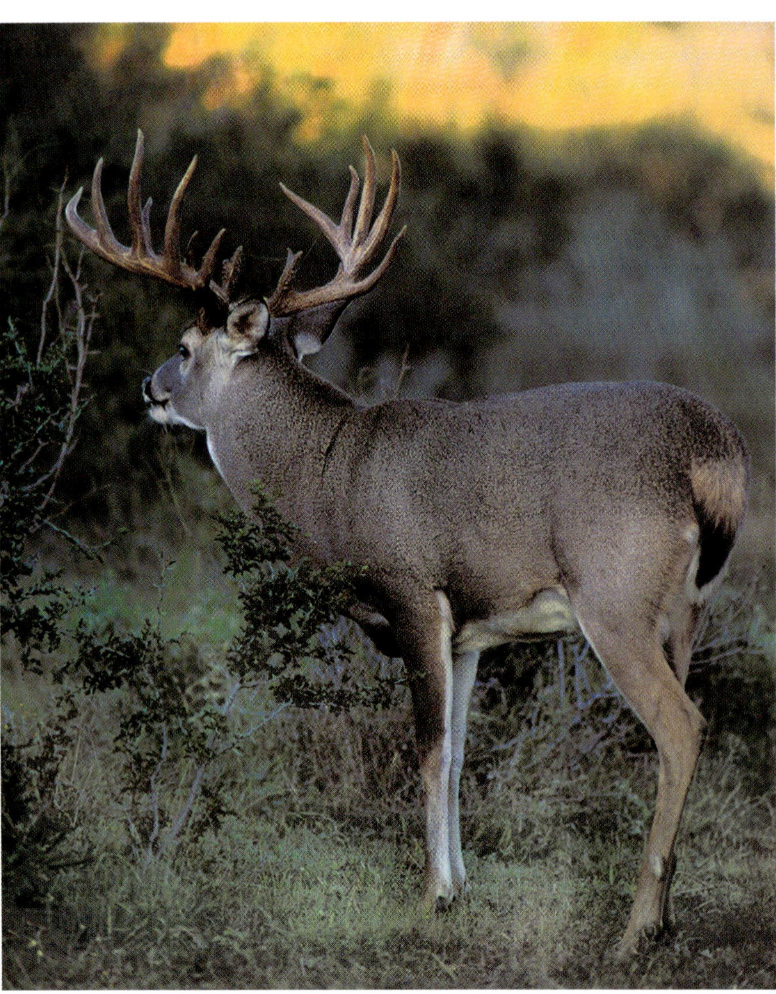

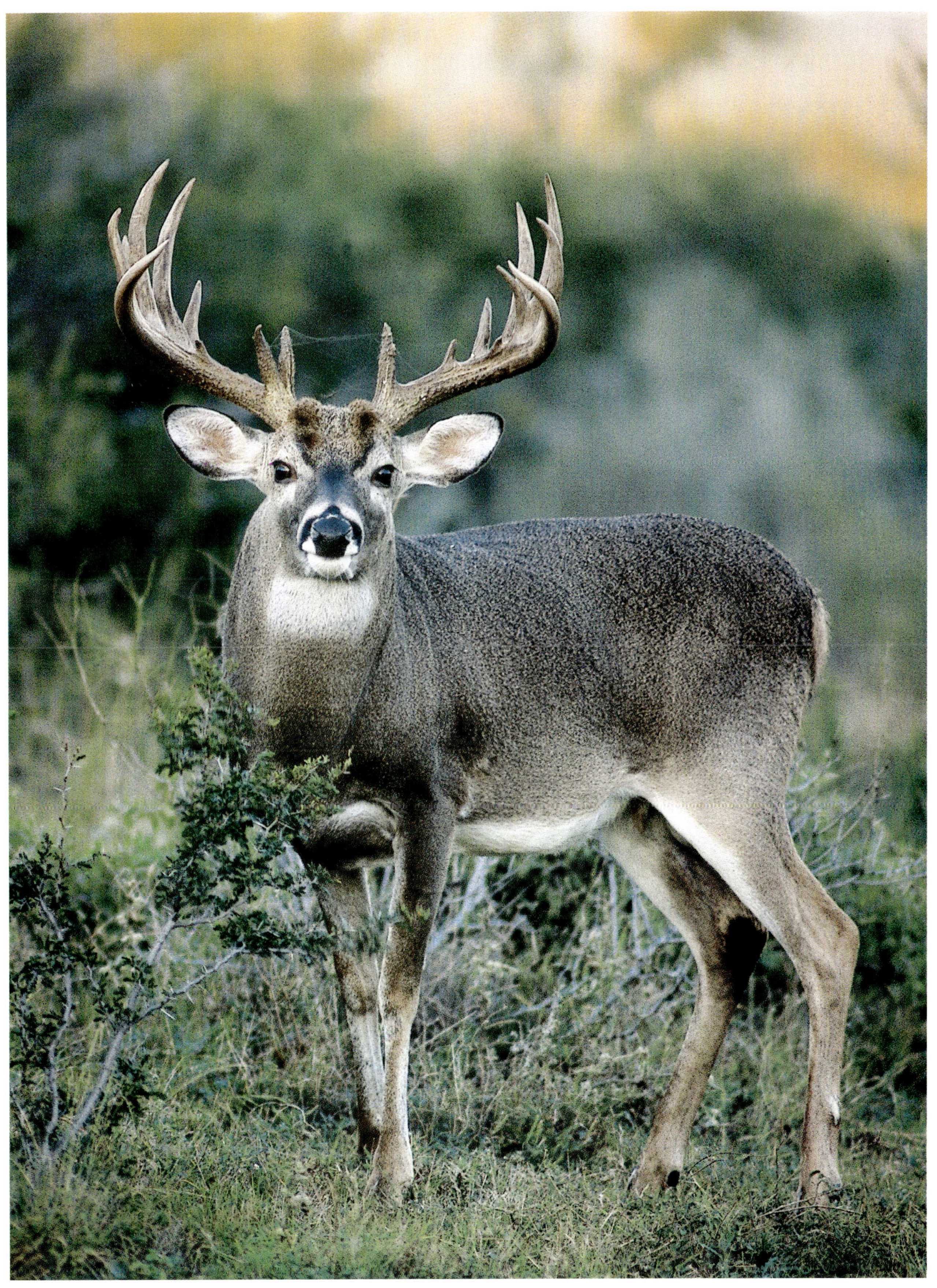

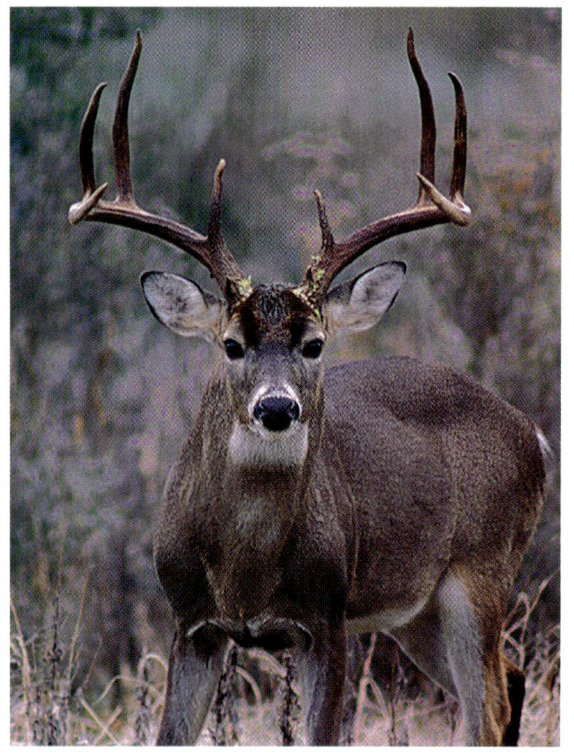

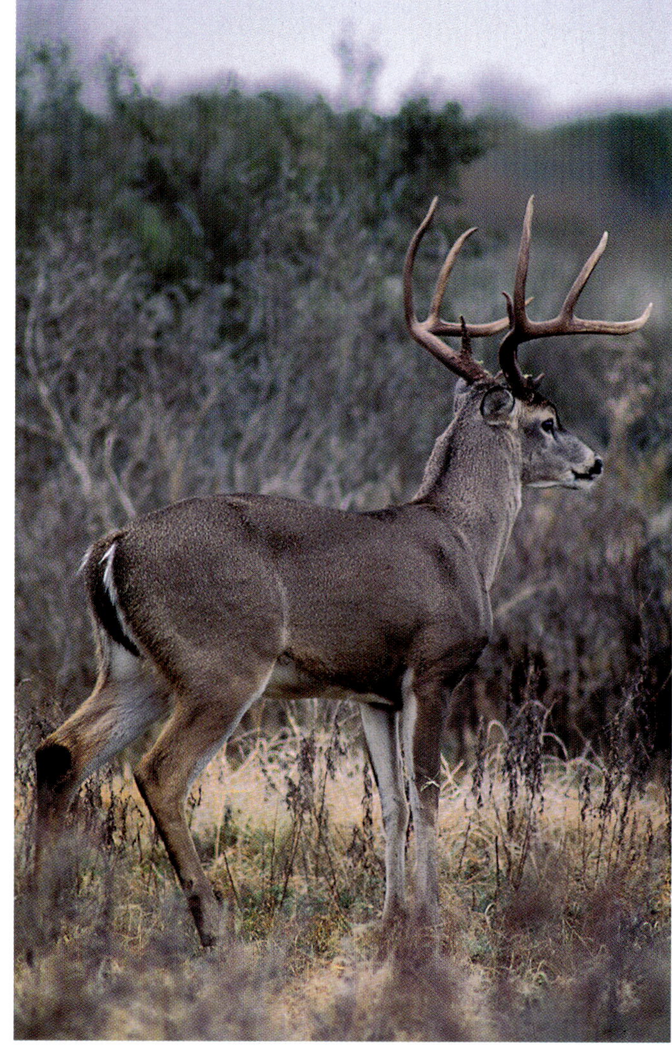

Age:	**5 1/2**	
Inside Spread:	**23 0/8**	
	RIGHT	LEFT
Beams	**24 1/8**	**25 2/8**
G-1	5 4/8	3 4/8
G-2	11 0/8	11 2/8
G-3	8 5/8	9 1/8
	Abn.	**Abn.**
	2 0/8	1 3/8
Tine Totals	**27 1/8**	**25 2/8**
H-1	4 4/8	4 7/8
H-2	4 0/8	4 1/8
H-3	3 4/8	3 5/8
H-4	2 7/8	2 7/8
Mass Totals	**14 7/8**	**15 4/8**
Antler Total	**66 1/8**	**66 0/8**
Gross B&C:	**155 1/8**	

BUCK # 26

If observers had only a head-on view of this buck, they would probably misjudge his beams, as they appear to quickly turn in and stop. However, the side view shows that his beams grow forward almost as far as they are wide. To estimate his spread, use the inside of his ear (five inches) as a guide, and then add the total number inches that extend outside his ears to his ear tip-to-tip measurement (16 inches). The estimate should be about half an ear length outside the ear on the left antler and almost a full ear length on the right antler (16 plus 2 1/2 plus 4 1/2 equals 23).

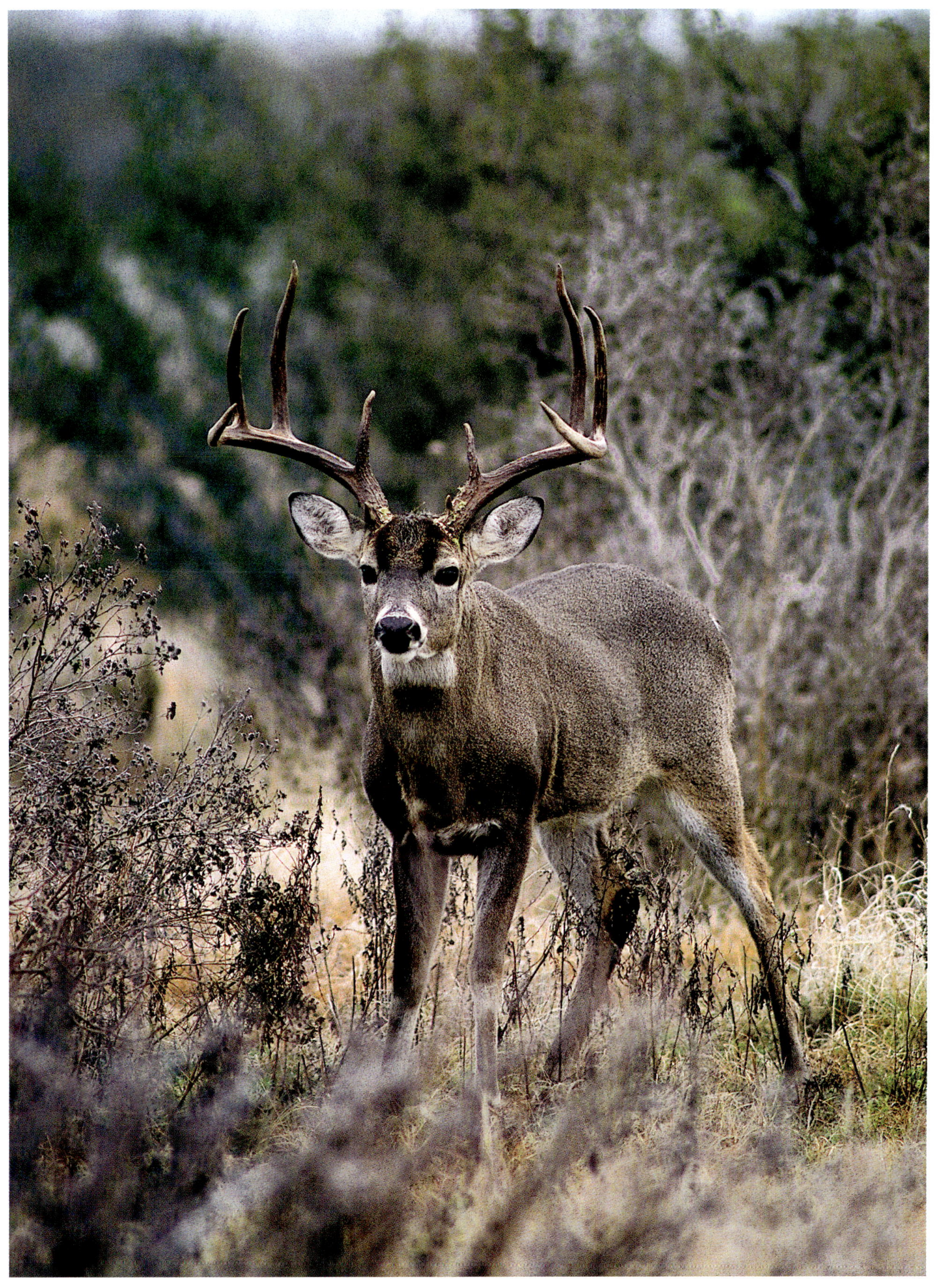

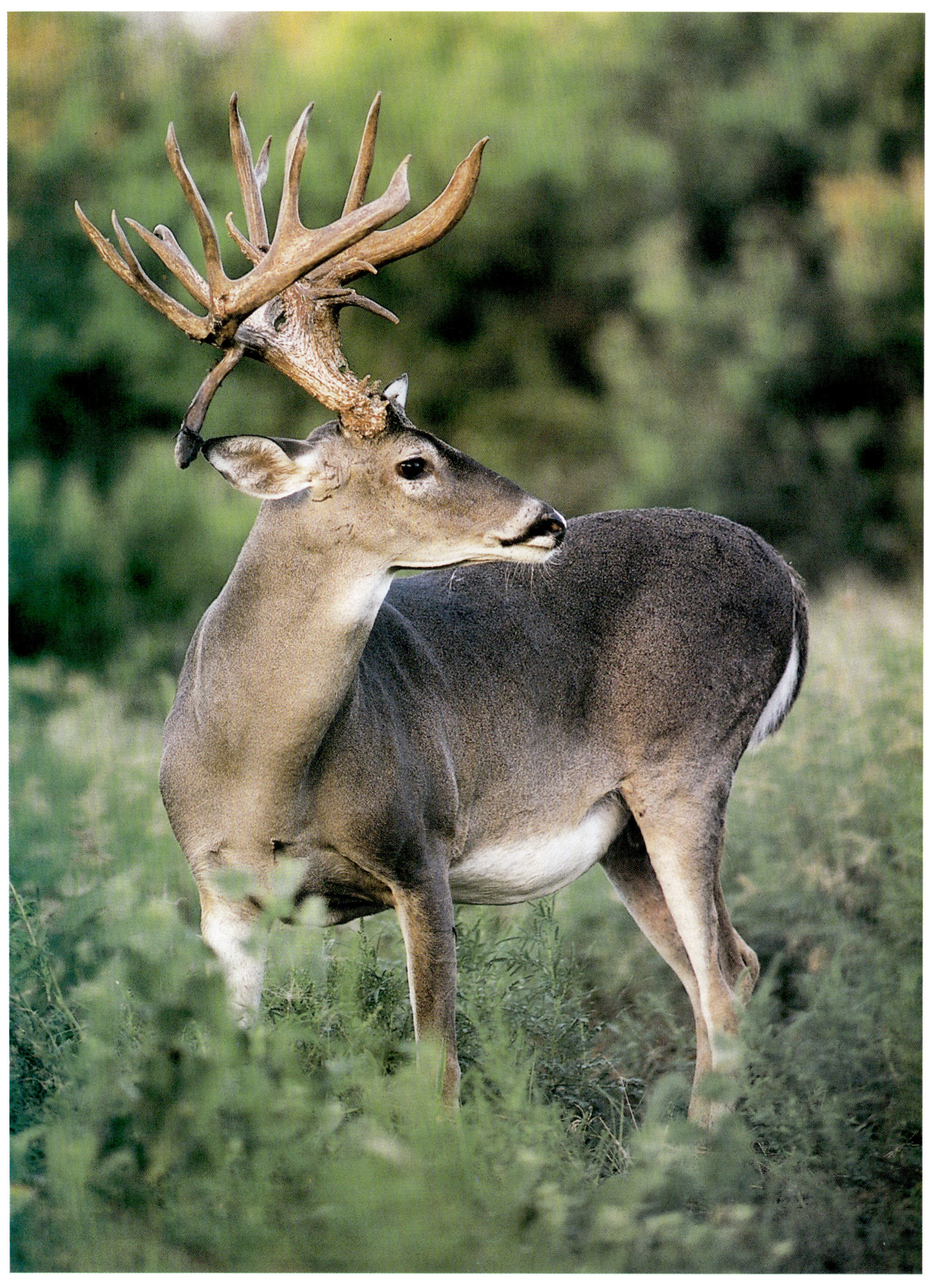

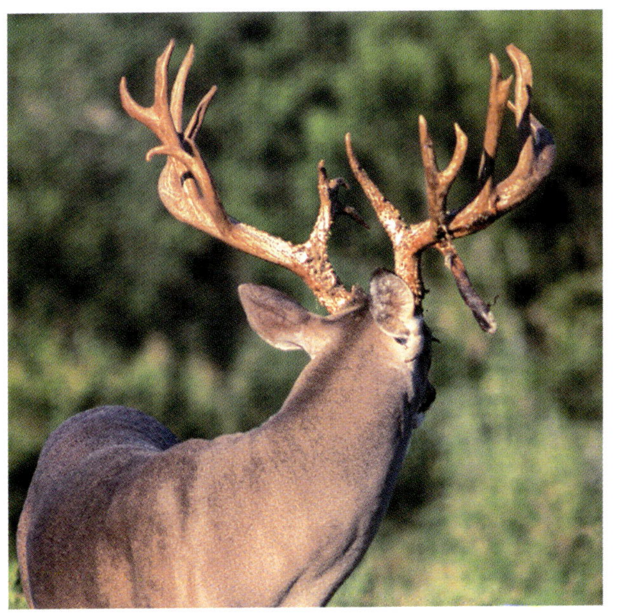

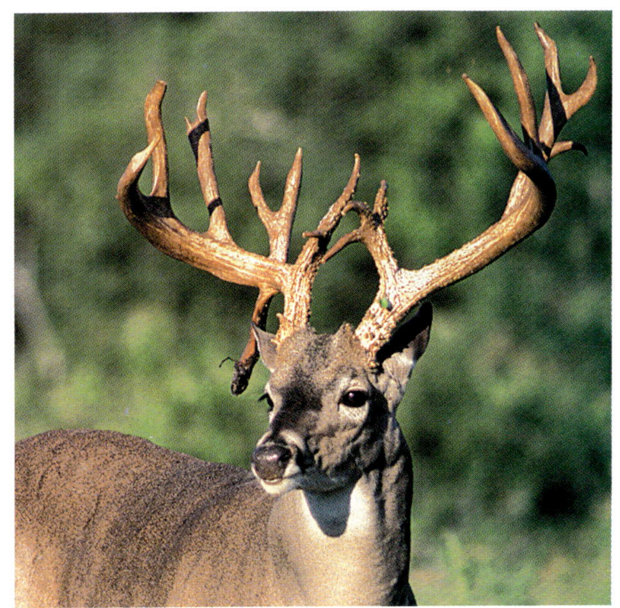

Age: 8 1/2		
Inside Spread: 22 0/8		
	RIGHT	LEFT
Beams	27 3/8	29 3/8
G-1	9 1/8	7 3/8
G-2	9 1/8	8 3/8
G-3	9 7/8	9 5/8
G-4	7 3/8	7 4/8
	Abn.	Abn.
	3 0/8	4 3/8
	4 1/8	3 3/8
	7 1/8	4 0/8
	1 0/8	3 6/8
Tine Totals	50 6/8	48 3/8
H-1	5 0/8	5 0/8
H-2	4 4/8	4 2/8
H-3	4 6/8	4 7/8
H-4	4 4/8	4 6/8
Mass Totals	18 6/8	18 7/8
Antler Total	96 7/8	96 5/8
Gross B&C: 215 4/8		

BUCK # 27

Notice how similar the totals for each category of measurements are with this buck. The antler beam lengths are closer than they appear because he broke off the tip of his right beam. He has extremely long beams that grow upward several inches before they turn outward. The side view also shows how his beams grow backward almost the length of his head before turning forward and growing back almost to the nose. There are many abnormal points that add greatly to the overall score that can only be estimated by viewing from various angles.

This buck is the first buck I discuss in Chapter 7 on estimating Boone & Crockett Score on the hoof. At 3 1/2, he scored 174 7/8, and this is what he grew into at 8 1/2. He is an excellent example of the importance of learning how to age bucks on the hoof to enable them to reach their prime. This buck was the No. 1 Nontypical Texas Big Game Awards buck harvested in 2002.

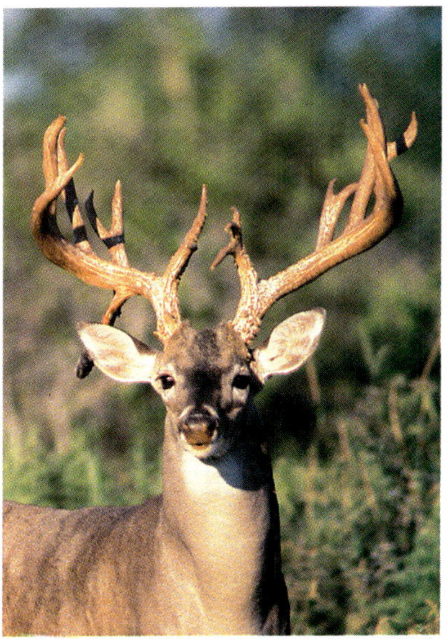

9

Whitetail Antler Anomalies

Misshapen or abnormal antler formations can result from a variety of factors including injuries, genetics, nutrition, and age.

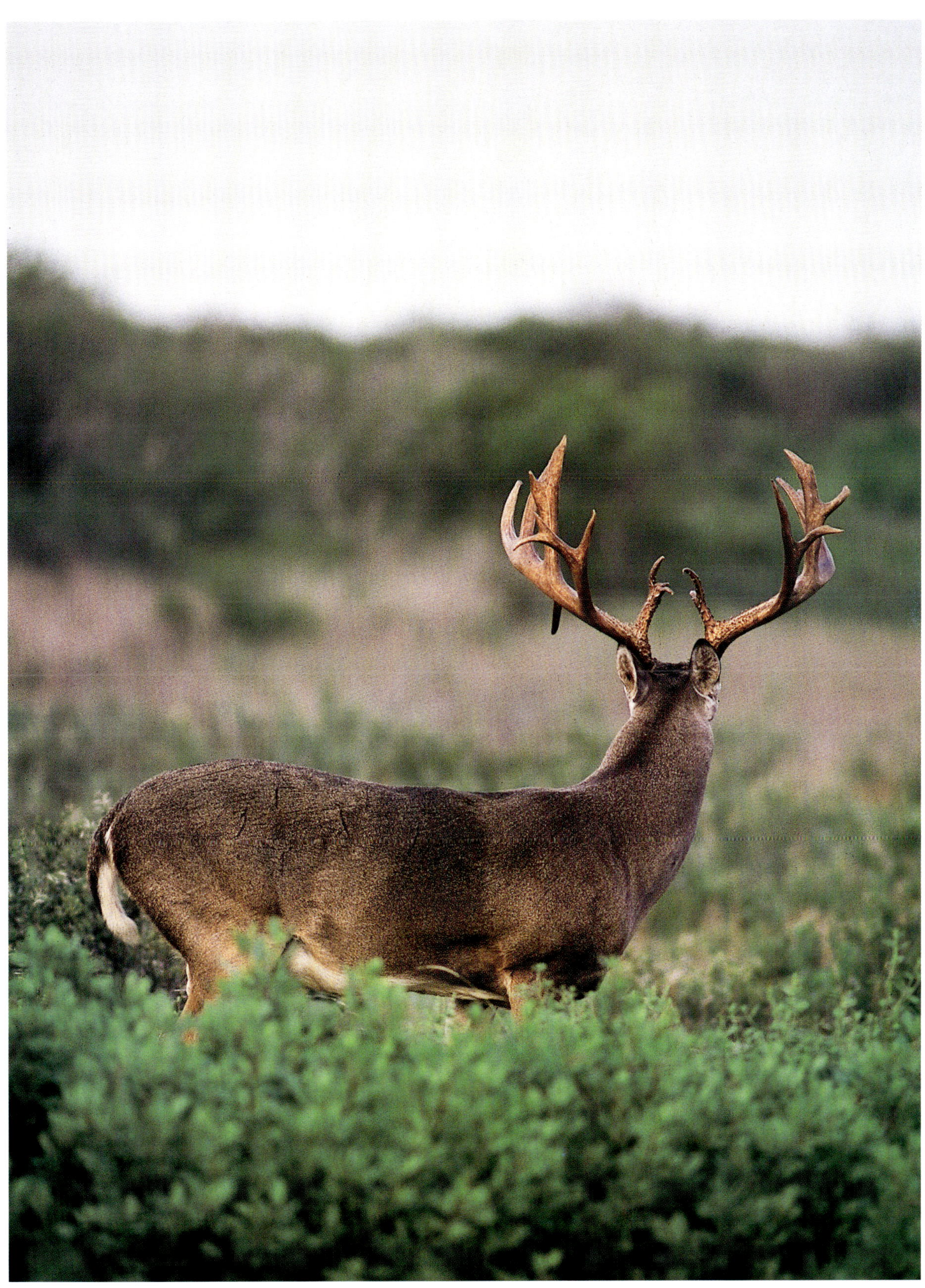

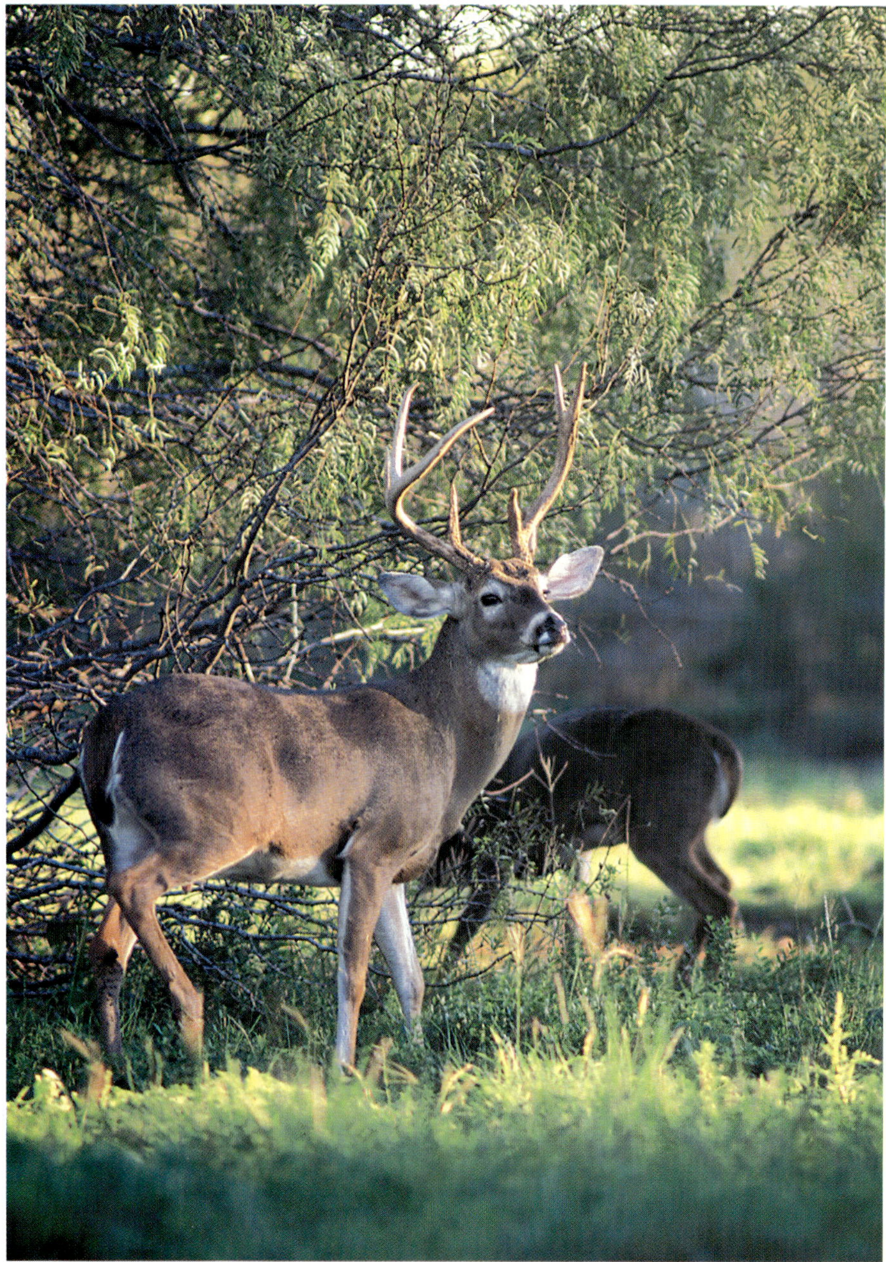

Misshapen or abnormal antler formations can result from a variety of factors including genetics, nutrition, and age. Injuries also play a major role. An injury to a hind leg can result in a deformed antler on the opposite side of the body the following year, as the buck on the left illustrates.

Many factors can affect antler growth including age, nutrition, genetics, diseases, body injuries, pedicle injuries, or injuries to the growing antler. While managers have some control over age, nutrition, and diseases, it is nearly impossible to control genetics and injuries in wild herds. As such, herds managed for older bucks often produce bucks with abnormal antler growth.

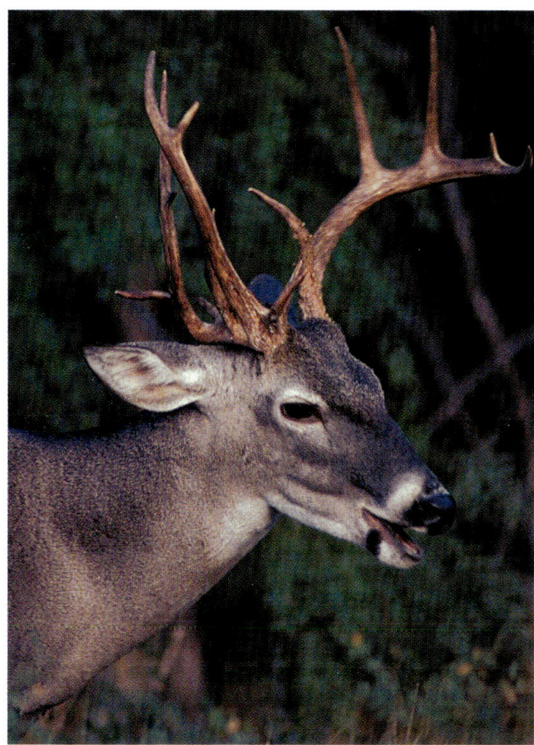

The deformed right antler on the buck to the left was the result of damage to the pedicle or antler while it was still in velvet.

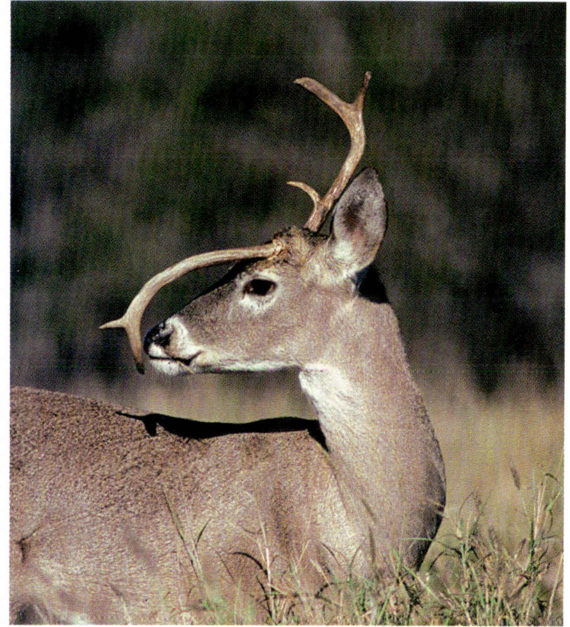

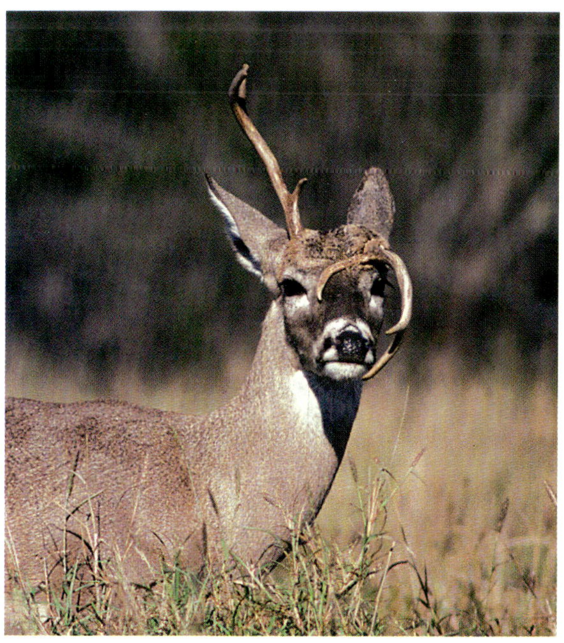

The unusual headgear on this young buck was likely the result of damage to the pedicle before or during antler growth, or a broken skull plate.

The two most common causes of abnormal antler growth in whitetails are antler and body injuries. Antler injuries generally occur to either the growing antler or the pedicle. Depending on the stage of antler growth and severity of the injury, damage to the growing antler can produce a wide range of abnormal growth. Generally, the earlier and more severe the injury, the greater the abnormal growth. In most cases, abnormal growth caused by injury to the growing antler will not be repeated the following year, though some evidence suggests that in severe cases the deformity may be repeated in subsequent years. This is believed to be caused by involvement of parasympathetic nerves. Parasympathetic nerves also appear to be involved in the regulation of antler shape and size.

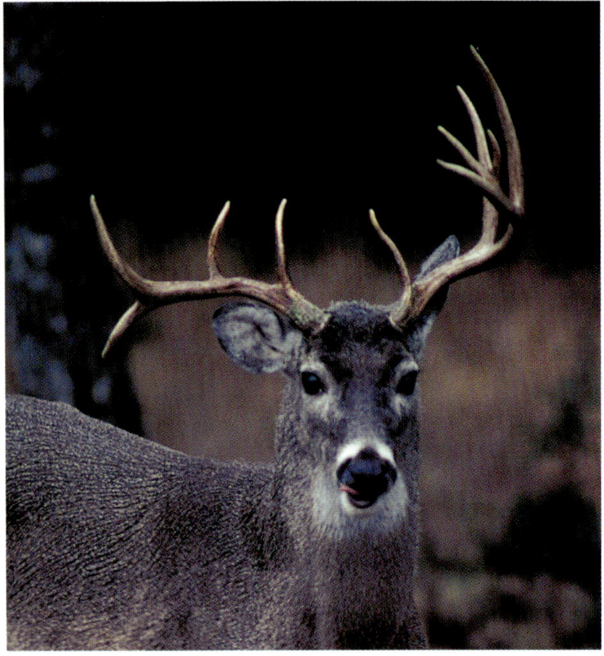

A leg injury prior to antler growth or damage during the velvet stage likely caused this buck's antler deformity.

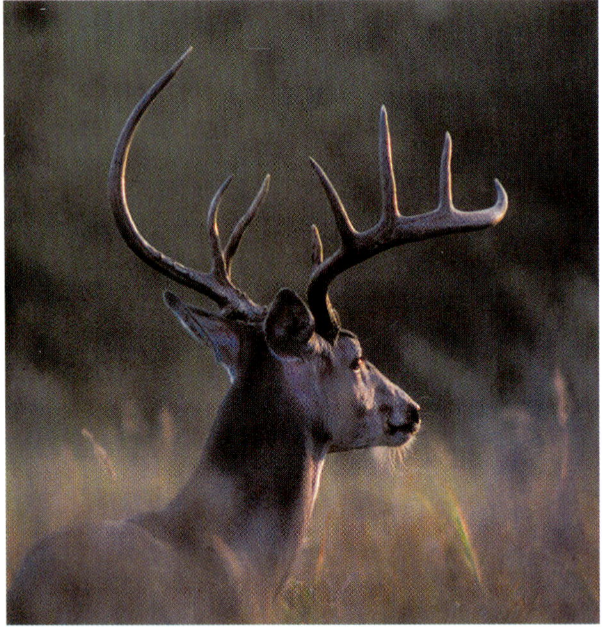

Genetics typically do not result in one normal antler and one deformed antler, as in the case of this buck. A leg injury, damage during early antler growth, or damage to the pedicle is the likely culprit.

Injury to the pedicle often results in the growth of a supplemental main beam and/or prolific "sprouting" of points from the base. These injuries are generally fairly easy to spot because they rarely affect both antlers. In other words, one side of the deer's antlers will appear normal while the other is highly abnormal near the base. Generally, these are permanent injuries.

Antler deformities can also be caused by injury to the skeletal system, particularly the bones in the legs. Generally an injury to the hind leg causes the antler on the opposite side of the body to be deformed. In contrast, an injury to the lower front leg typically causes same-side antler deformities, although both sides can be affected. In most cases, the buck's antlers will be deformed throughout the remainder of his life.

Genetics also play an important role in antler size and configuration. While most antler characteristics are heritable, some are more so than others. In general, nontypical points such as drop tines and "kicker" points are likely caused by genetics rather than injury. This is especially true if the abnormal point is repeated in the same location over multiple years. Many deer researchers believe that half or more of all whitetail bucks possess some genetic traits for abnormal antler growth if allowed to live long enough to express them. This likely explains why drop tines and other abnormal points are common in south Texas — there are simply more mature bucks here than just about anywhere in the whitetail's range.

Many deer researchers believe that half or more of ***all whitetail bucks*** *possess some genetic traits for abnormal antler growth if allowed to* ***live long enough to express them.***

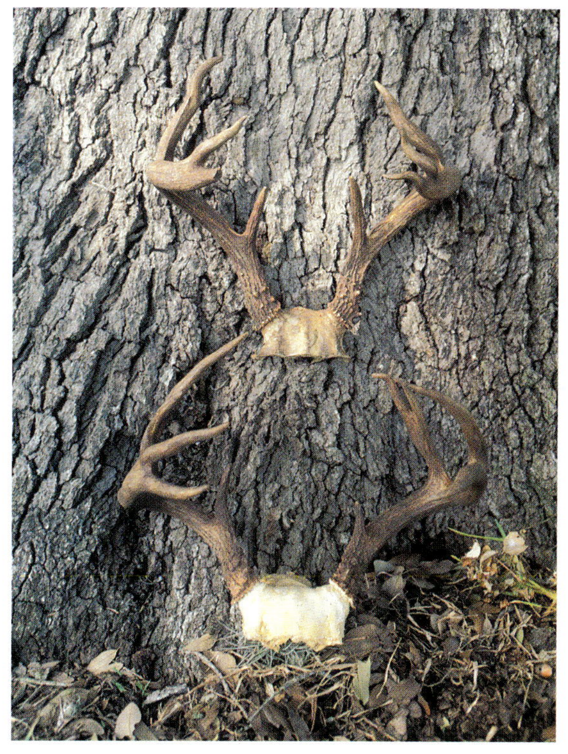

These racks display the waviness characteristic of bucks well past their prime.

One complicating factor in the genetic equation is that does contribute half or more of the genetic code for antler development. This makes it very difficult to manipulate genetics in wild herds. Although the role of genetics in antler development is important, the mechanics of heritability are poorly understood. However, once a buck grows his third set of antlers, they are a profile of the basic antler conformation that will be grown the remainder of his life. Beam length, mass, spread, and points can change with increasing age, but the basic conformation generally remains the same.

By close observation of bucks in this book during sequential years, it becomes evident how the basic shape and conformity remains similar from year to year. Take note of brow-tine lengths, angles or shapes, bifurcation, and palmation. Beam shape can also be helpful. Look for how high the curvature starts above the burr, whether the ends of the beam point straight, curve inward, upward, or downward, and amount and location of mass. Often, antler point configuration can help identify a buck. Look for straightness, curvature, palmation, bifurcation, spacing, and origin on the beam.

A common antler characteristic in bucks well past their prime is curvature or "waviness" of the tines (Also see photos on page 75). Very old deer may also have incomplete ossification of the antler, probably due to dietary deficiencies, especially calcium, that cause the antler to be lighter in weight than a normal antler of equal size. If cross-sectioned, the porosity is plainly evident.

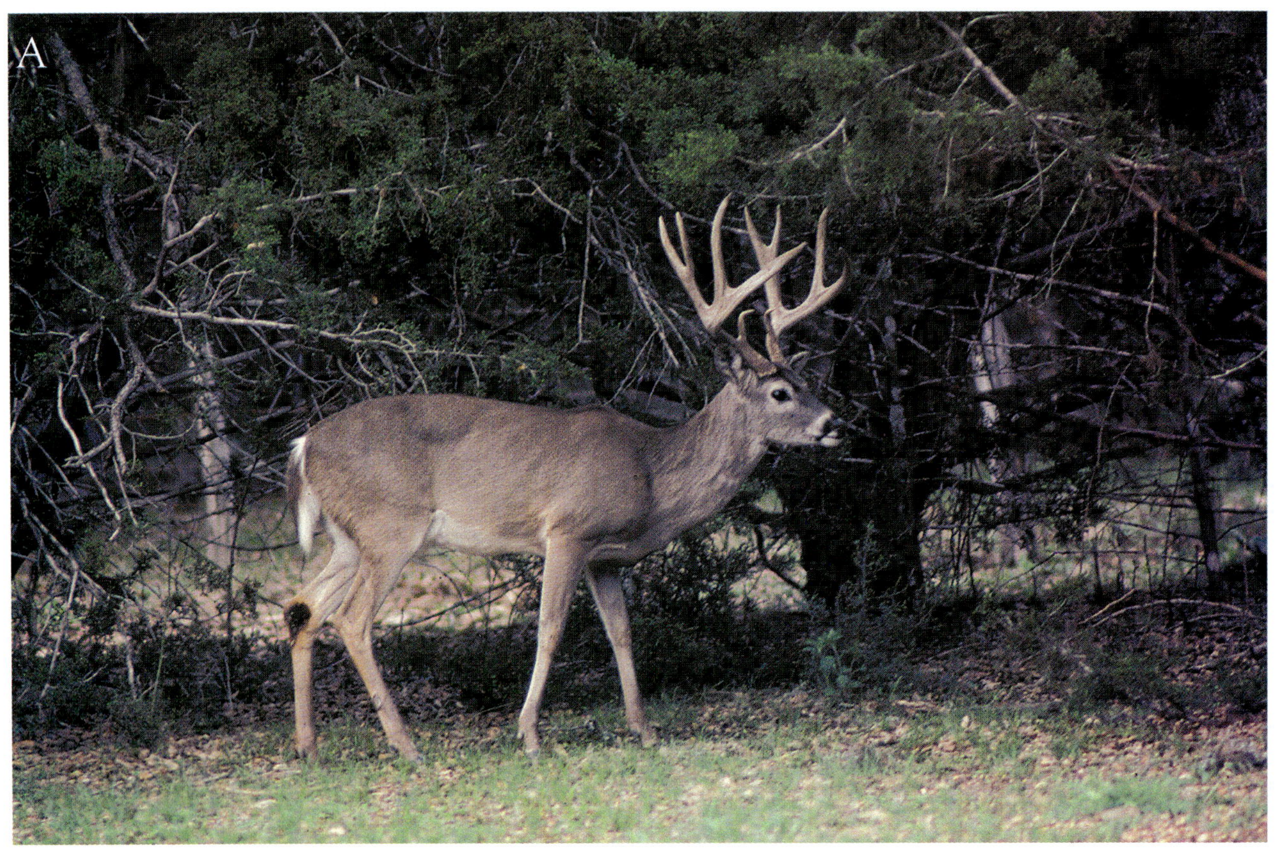

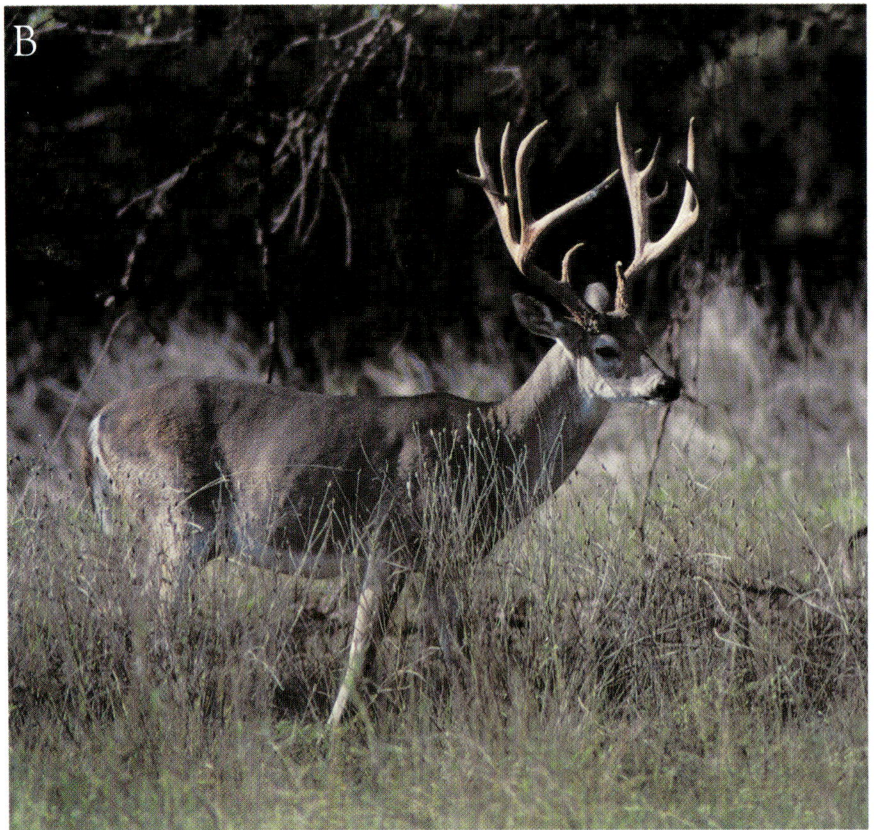

This buck was a 5x5 with split G-2s the first two years I photographed him (A & B). However, the third year(C) he apparently damaged his left antler in the early stages of antler growth, causing it to grow abnormally. The fourth year(D) his antlers again returned to their original conformation of 5x5 with split G-2s.

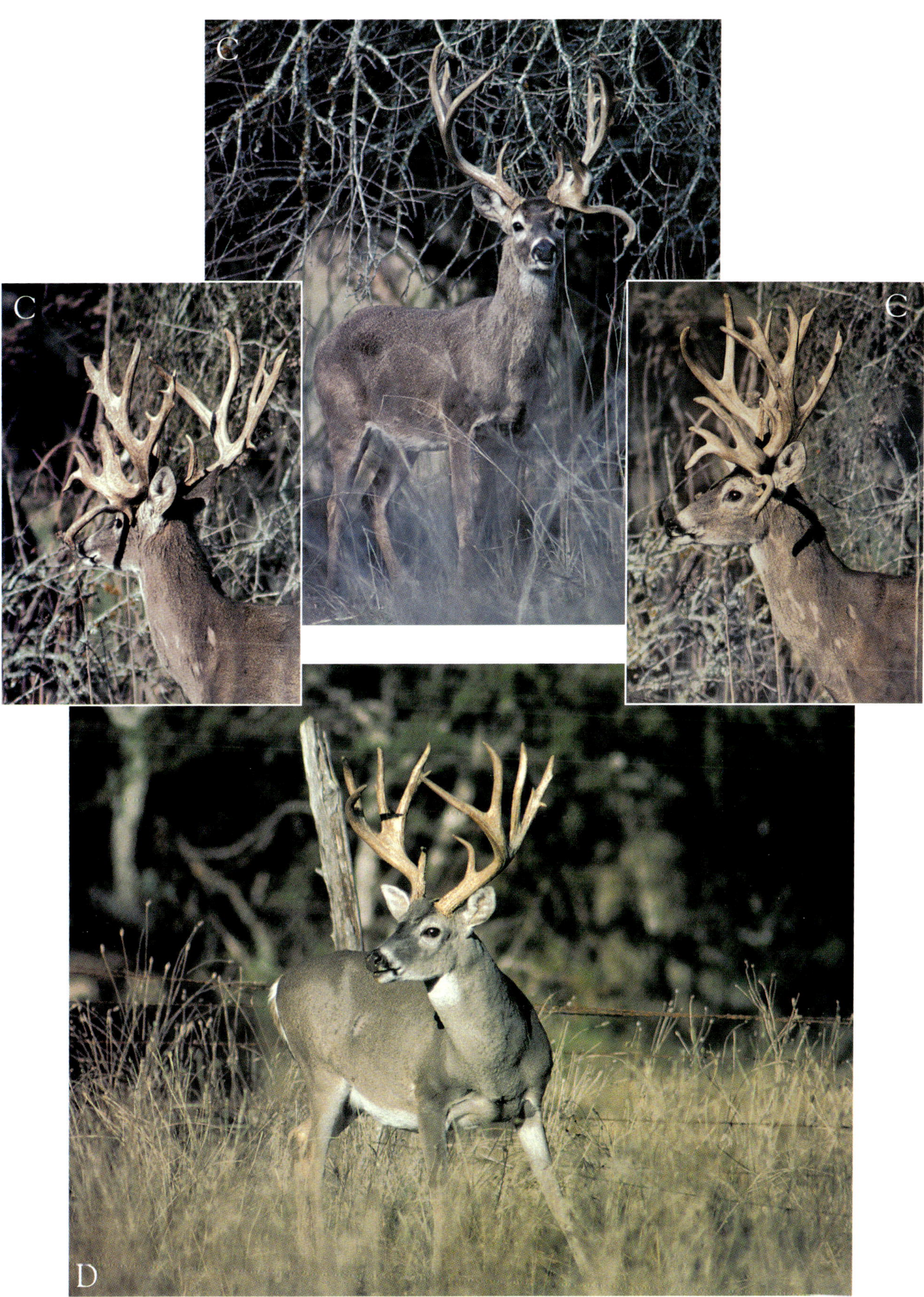
C
C
C
D

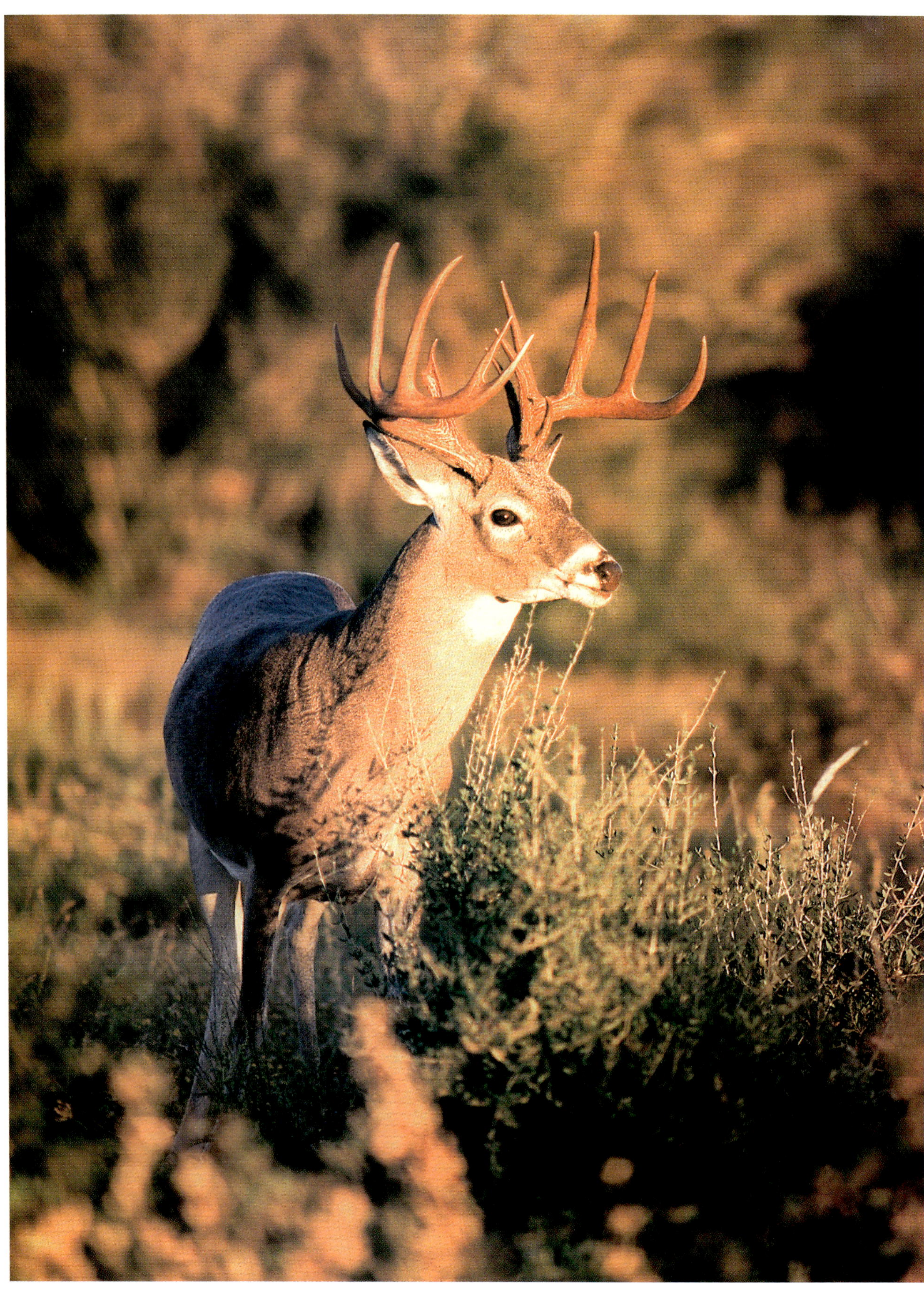

10 Whitetail Diseases, Parasites, and Anomalies

Throughout the whitetail's range, certain diseases, parasites, or anomalies may be encountered. A brief description of some of the most common ones that may be encountered while observing whitetails is provided below. For detailed information on these and other wildlife diseases, obtain a copy of the *Field Manual of Wildlife Diseases in the Southeastern United States*, second edition, by William R. Davidson and Victor F. Nettles. It can be ordered through the College of Veterinary Medicine, The University of Georgia, Athens, Georgia 30602-7393 or through the Quality Deer Management Association at (800) 209-3337.

The information in this chapter was taken from the educational poster "Common Diseases, Parasites, and Anomalies of White-Tailed Deer" produced by the Quality Deer Management Association. Contributing authors include Nikole Castleberry, Brian Murphy, and Dr. Randy Davidson. Copies of the poster can be purchased through the QDMA at (800) 209-3337 or online at www.QDMA.com.

Parasites

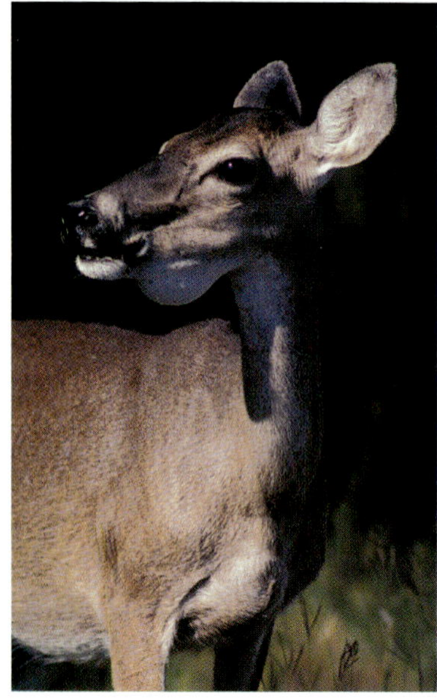

Arterial Worm

Parasite Type: Nematode, *Elaeophora schneideri*

Signs: Food impaction, tooth loss, and occasionally degeneration or fracture of the jawbones. May obstruct blood flow to the head due to blockage of the carotid arteries. Animals with few worms often show no signs.

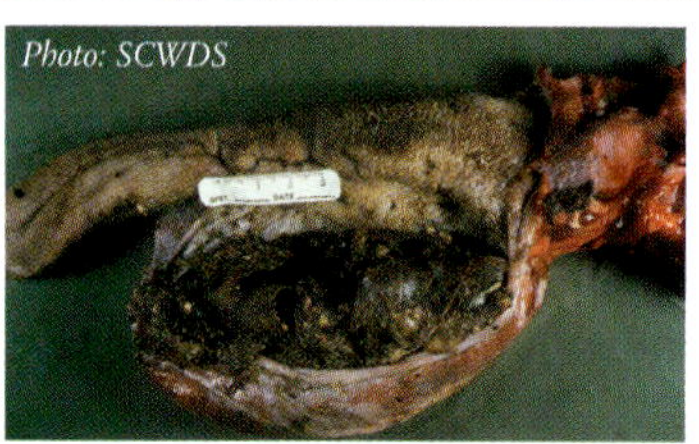
Photo: SCWDS

Cut-away of impacted jaw with tongue

Transmission/Cause: Horseflies, most commonly *Tabanus lineola hinellus* in the Southeast, but other species are important hosts in other regions.

Wildlife Management Significance: In white-tails, arterial worms have been associated with disease and occasional mortality. Food impaction is most commonly found in older deer. Individual animals may die from emaciation, but no significant population impacts have been reported.

Public Health Concerns: None reported, humans are not susceptible to infection.

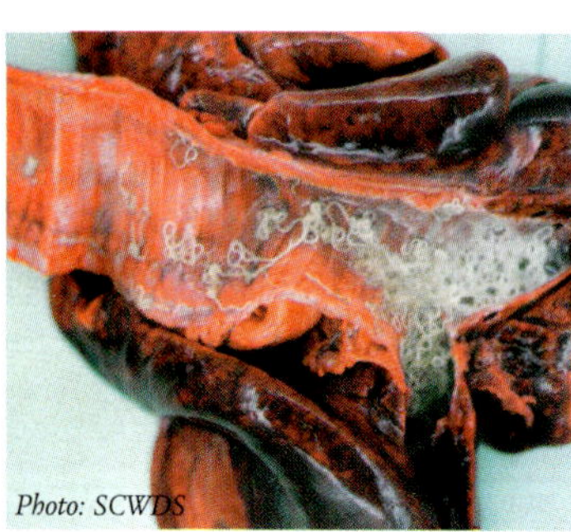
Photo: SCWDS

Large Lungworm

Parasite Type: Nematode, *Dictyocaulus viviparus*

Signs: Most infections are inapparent. Heavily infected animals may be weak, underweight, show respiratory distress, and pneumonia.

Transmission: Larvae are shed in feces and spread to other deer when ingested while feeding on low vegetation.

Wildlife Management Significance: Losses can occur among young animals during winter and early spring. Large lungworms can be an important contributing factor to reduced herd health in areas of overpopulation. Livestock as well as mule deer, elk, and moose can become infected. Maintaining deer within carrying capacity will help reduce losses but not eliminate the parasite.

Public Health Concerns: None reported.

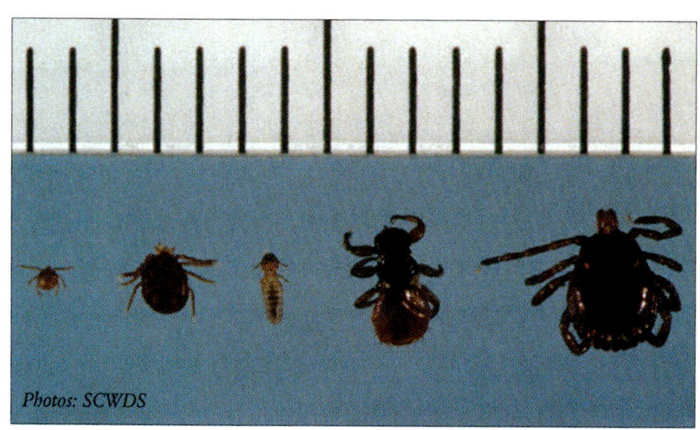
Photos: SCWDS

Ticks

Signs: Ticks embedded in the skin of the animal. Extreme lone star tick infestations can cause weakness, weight loss, abscesses, and in some cases, blindness and death in fawns.

Transmission: Physical attachment.

Wildlife Management Significance: Mortality in fawns and transmission of disease agents. Heavy infestations are frequent complicating factors in overpopulated, malnourished, and heavily parisitized deer populations.

Public Health Concerns: None regarding consumption of infested deer. Ticks spread human diseases such as Lyme disease, babesiosis, and ehrlichiosis.

Parasites

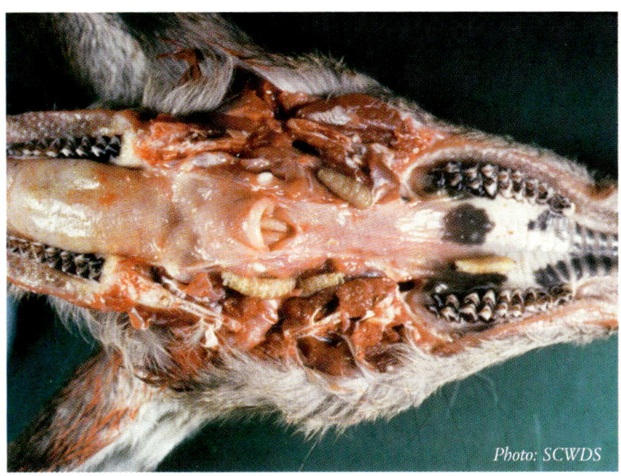
Photo: SCWDS

Nasal Bots

Parasite Type: Larvae of flies in the genus *Cephenemyia*.

Signs: Large fly larvae ("maggots") found in the nose, mouth, and nasal passages.

Transmission: Adult flies deposit a packet of eggs on the skin around the nose or mouth of deer. Larvae are released when the packet is licked by deer. Larvae then migrate to the nasal passages and throat area.

Wildlife Management Significance: Nasal bots are not harmful, even in large numbers, but are often noticed by hunters. Not transmitted to livestock.

Public Health Concerns: None reported.

Liver Fluke

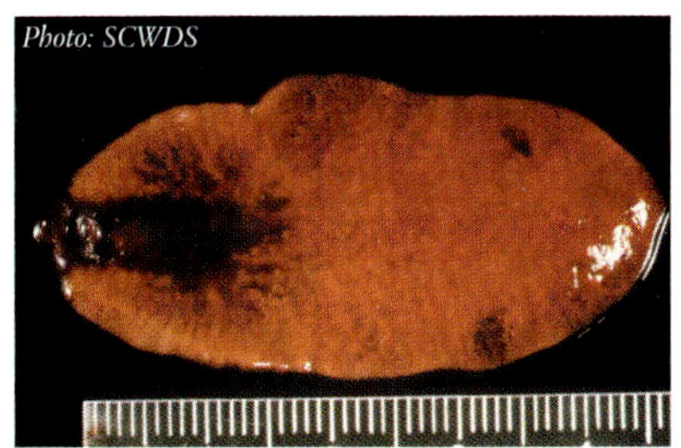
Photo: SCWDS

Parasite Type: Trematode, *Fascioloides magna*

Signs: Found in fibrous, yellowish-white one- to two-inch capsules in the liver. Most deer tolerate liver flukes with no signs of disease. Massive infections (more than 75 per deer) may contribute to poor overall physical condition.

Transmission: Transmission occurs in wetlands or seasonally flooded regions inhabited by certain aquatic snails which are hosts of larval flukes.

Wildlife Management Significance: There is little impact on deer populations. Can be spread to, but not from, livestock. Most infections in cattle are not serious, but infection in sheep can be lethal.

Public Health Concerns: Not transmissible to humans; however, livers of infected deer should be discarded. None reported from consuming venison from infected deer.

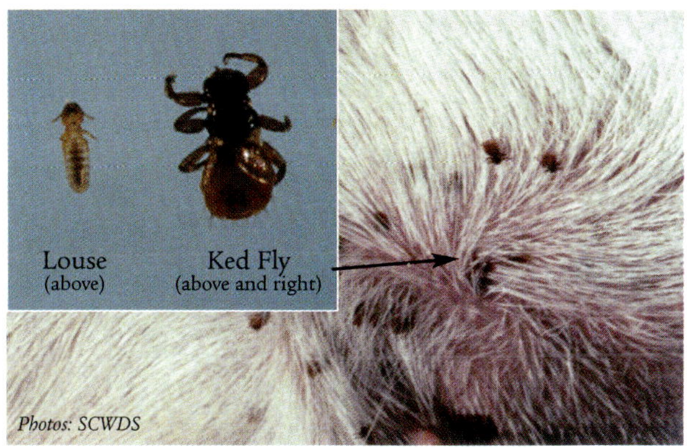

Photos: SCWDS

Louse Flies (Deer Keds) and Lice

Parasite Type: Louse flies - One of four species in the genera *Lipoptena* and *Neolipoptena*; Lice - One of three species in the genera *Solenopotes* and *Tricholipeurus*

Signs: Both are found on the skin.

Louse flies - Similar in size to adult ticks, but have only six legs, a segmented body, and move more quickly.

Lice - Often not noticeable due to small size; however, heavily infested deer may suffer from malnutrition and other parasitic infections.

Transmission: Louse flies - Adults have wings for mobility, which are shed once a suitable host is located. Adults breed on deer. Lice - Contact or frequent use of areas by infected animals.

Wildlife Management Significance: None reported.

Public Health Concerns: None reported.

Diseases

Hemorrhagic Disease (HD)

Disease Agent: Viruses in the genus *Orbivirus* — primarily epizootic hemorrhagic disease virus; less often blue-tongue virus.

Signs: Vary with duration of infection; many do not become ill. **Peracute**: Swollen darkened tongue, heavy fluid-filled lungs. **Acute**: Above signs plus hemorrhages in the heart and rumen, then ulcers on the tongue, and dental pad erosion. **Chronic**: Lameness, sloughing hooves, and emaciation.

Transmission: Biting midges in the genus *Culicoides*. Disease occurs primarily during late summer and early fall as midge numbers increase. Incidence peaks in September and October.

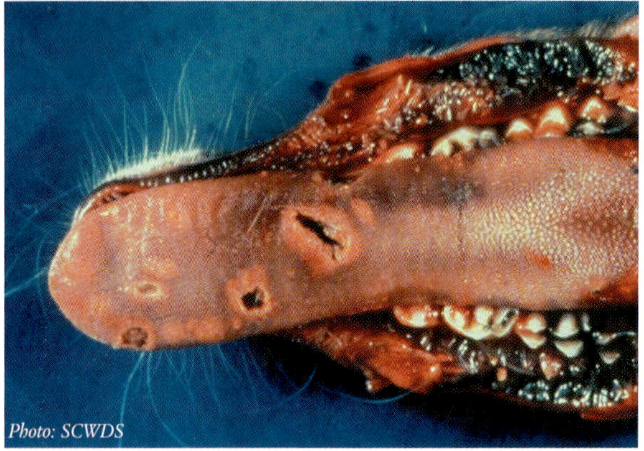

Photo: SCWDS

Acute (10-21 days after infection): Ulcers on the tongue of a deer with acute hemorrhagic disease.

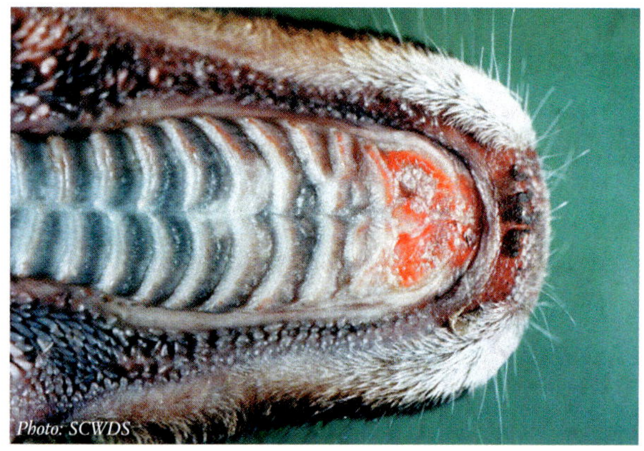

Photo: SCWDS

Acute (10-21 days after infection): Erosion on the dental pad is common in deer with acute hemorrhagic disease.

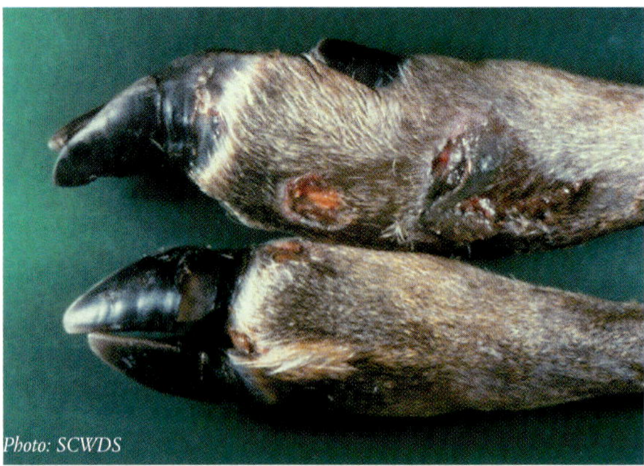

Photo: SCWDS

Chronic (more than 21 days after infection): Growth interruptions and sloughing hooves are typical of deer with chronic hemorrhagic disease.

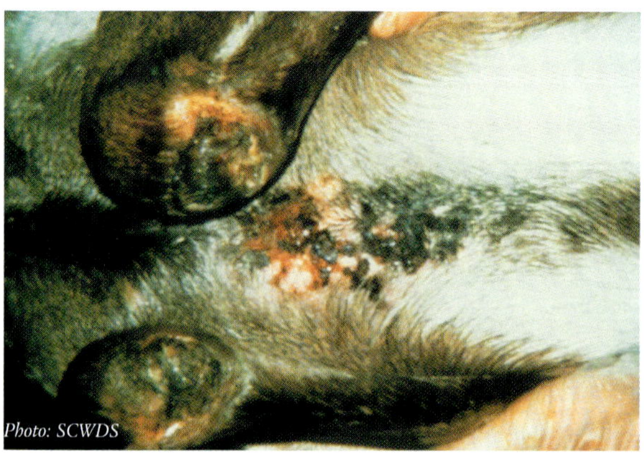

Photo: SCWDS

Chronic (more than 21 days after infection): Sores on the knees and chest due to hoof malformations that become sensitive causing deer to "knee walk."

Diseases

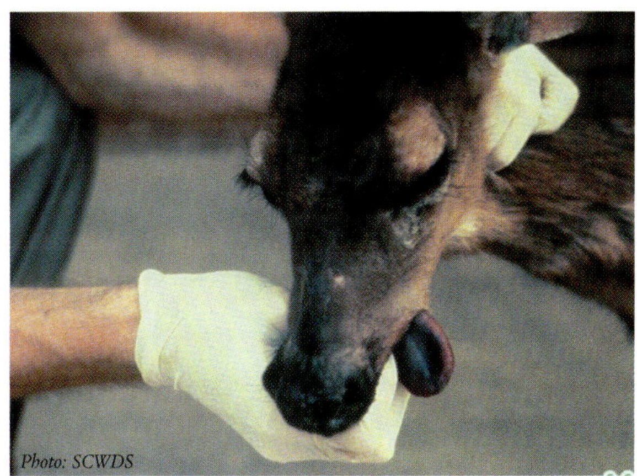

Peracute or Acute (6-21 days after infection): A swollen bluish tongue is often present in deer with peracute or acute hemorrhagic disease.

Wildlife Management Significance: HD is The most frequent infectious disease of white-tailed deer. Herd mortality is usually less than 25 percent, but can be greater than 50 percent. Because disease outbreaks are closely related to herd immunity, midge abundance, distribution, and seasonality, and possibly innate resistance, and not deer density, there is no way to manage for HD. Relocation of susceptible deer is a disease risk.

Public Health Concerns: HD is not infectious to humans, but sick animals are unsuitable to eat. If you suspect an animal has HD, contact your state wildlife agency.

Malnutrition/Parasitism Syndrome

Over 100 parasites, infections, or disease conditions have been identified in white-tailed deer. Of these, only two routinely produce illness or death at levels that impact populations. These are hemorrhagic disease and a syndrome of malnutrition/parasitism. Hemorrhagic disease occurs naturally and is not affected by deer density or management approach. In contrast, the malnutrition/parasitism syndrome is directly related to deer density and can largely be avoided through proper management. As deer populations exceed the carrying capacity of the habitat, forage quantity and quality decrease due to overbrowsing. The resulting nutritional stress causes a decline in deer herd health.

Especially in the Southeast, white-tailed deer with significant nutritional stress usually have high parasite numbers. Similarly, deer with high parasite numbers generally originate from herds with significant nutritional stress whether the result of poor-quality habitat or overbrowsing. The most significant parasites are large stomach worms and large lungworms, although other parasites may be important in specific areas.

Rare Diseases of Concern

Anthrax: Bacterium (*Bacillus anthracis*)

Signs: Sudden death, but may involve weakness, difficulty breathing, blood loss from body openings, and death within hours or days. Often infects many animals at once creating a sudden die-off.

Public Health Concerns: Although outbreaks in the U.S. are infrequent, there is cause for concern due to the potential danger of this disease to humans, wildlife, and livestock. Humans can be infected by breathing spores or coming in contact with blood, meat, bones, or hides from infected animals. Can be fatal to humans if not treated immediately. (Because anthrax is reportable in all states, if an animal is suspected of having anthrax, contact your state animal health authorities immediately and do not handle the animal!)

Diseases

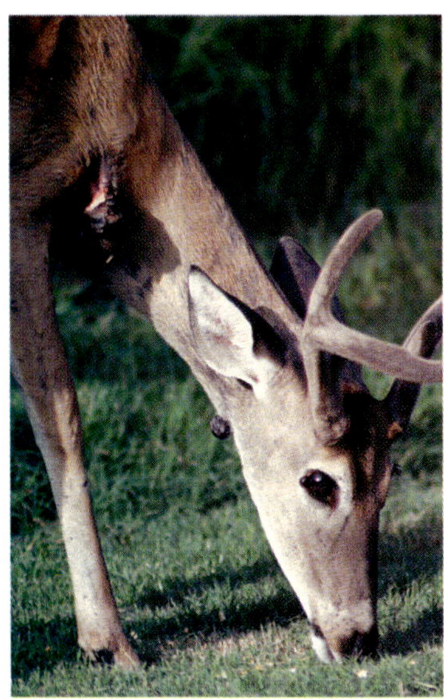

Cutaneous Fibroma

Disease Agent: Virus

Signs: Hairless tumors, usually temporary, found on the skin. Tumors range in size from 1/2-inch to over 8 inches in diameter.

Transmission: Biting insects or direct contact with tumors.

Wildlife Management Significance: Cutaneous fibromas are often merely small blemishes, but can grow large enough to block vision or obstruct eating. They do not affect population size and are not spread to domestic livestock or other wildlife.

Public Health Concerns: None reported. Only tumors with secondary bacterial infections cause venison to be unfit for consumption.

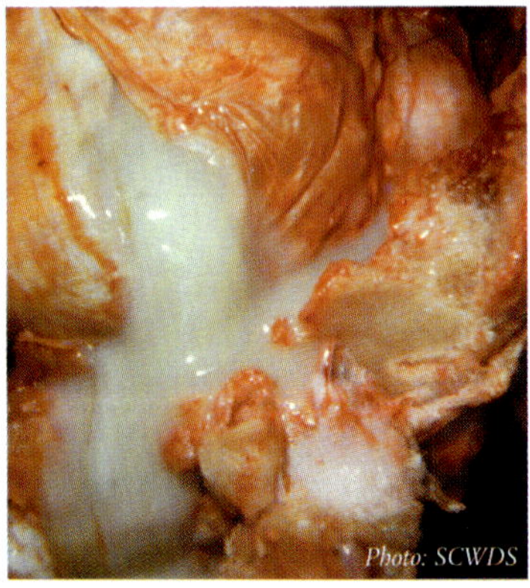

Photo: SCWDS

Brain Abscess

Disease Agents: Various bacteria, primarily Arcanobacterium pyogenes.

Signs: Neurological problems such as circling, incoordination, and abnormal behavior; predominately in males.

Transmission: Infection typically occurs following velvet shedding or antler casting and is associated with antler rubbing and sparring (seasonal, October through April).

Wildlife Management Significance: No significant impact on population size or density. Because it is both gender and age biased—affecting mainly bucks 2 1/2+ years of age—it is a consideration in management programs emphasizing older bucks.

Public Health Concerns: Animals with brain abscesses are not suitable for consumption.

Chronic Wasting Disease (CWD)

Disease Agent: Infectious proteins (prions).

Signs: Poor physical condition, significant weight loss, excessive salivation, thirst, and urination. Behavioral changes include depression, listlessness, grinding of teeth, lowered head, and drooping ears.

Transmission: Appears to be through direct contact or, less importantly, from mother to offspring. There is concern that concentrating animals through such practices as supplemental feeding may facilitate transmission of the disease.

Wildlife Management Significance: Discovered in at least one captive deer or elk herd in Montana, Minnesota, South Dakota, Wyoming, Colorado, Nebraska, Kansas, and Oklahoma in the U.S. and the provinces of Alberta and Saskatchewan in Canada. Many of these populations have been depopulated, although the long-term persistence of the disease in these areas remains uncertain. Also discovered in a small percentage of free-roaming deer and/or elk populations in portions of Colorado, Wyoming, Nebraska, Wisconsin, Illinois, South Dakota, New Mexico, and Utah in the U.S. and the province of Saskatchewan in Canada. Management actions have focused on culling to lower population density, and carcass transportation regulations to reduce the possibility of spreading the disease into new areas. To date, there is no evidence it can be transmitted between wildlife and livestock.

Public Health Concerns: None confirmed. Animals appearing sick should not be consumed and reported to the appropriate wildlife or disease authorities.

Anomalies

Piebald Condition

Anomaly Type: Genetic anomaly or congenital defect.

Signs: Vary from slight deviations in coat color to extreme deviations with large patches of white hair and numerous skeletal deformities. Deformities may include curvature of the spine, short malformed legs, and bowed nasal bones. Severely deformed fawns often die at or shortly after birth.

Transmission: Inherited recessive trait.

Wildlife Management Significance: Piebalds are uncommon, normally less than 1% of births. This condition may be debilitating or lethal to an individual deer, but is not considered important to herd health at the population level. Unfortunately, this detrimental condition sometimes has been encouraged by harvest regulations that protect piebald deer.

Public Health Concerns: None reported.

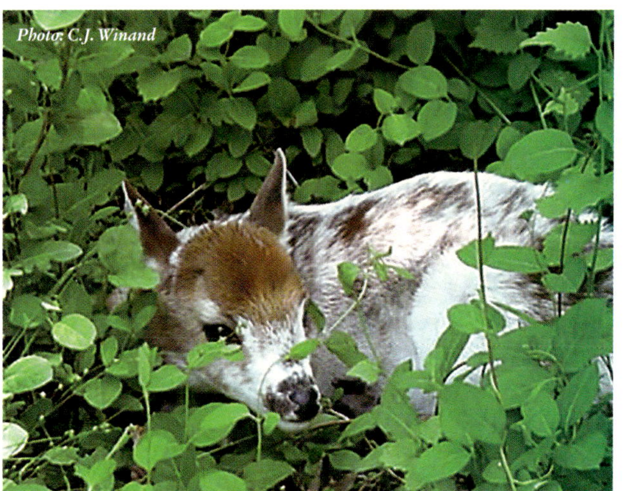
Photo: C.J. Winand

Albino

Anomaly Type: Genetic anomaly.

Signs: A deer that lacks skin pigmentation. They have completely white coats, pink hooves, and red eyes.

Transmission: Inherited recessive trait carried by both parents.

Wildlife Management Significance: Albino deer are even more rare than piebald deer and not considered important management concerns.

Public Health Concerns: None reported.

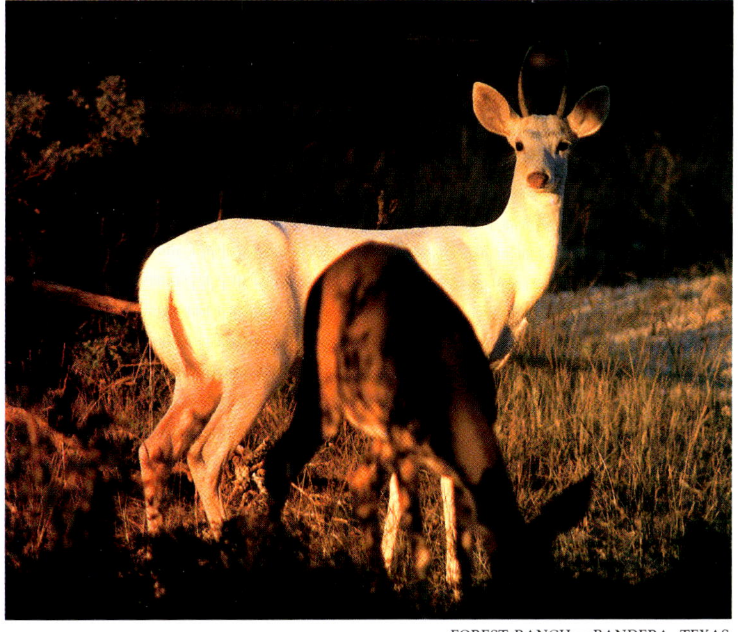
FOREST RANCH – BANDERA, TEXAS

11 Conclusion

Many people see deer, but few really observe them and notice their unique physical characteristics. Also, too few have had the luxury of observing interactions among bucks, especially mature bucks. Usually, it is due to poor buck-to-doe ratios, young buck age structures, and/or low deer densities. When confronted with poor deer herd conditions or low densities, most hunters harvest the first buck encountered. However, during the last few years, deer herd conditions have improved in many areas due to an increasing interest in management, the formation of deer management cooperatives, and improved management practices. In recent years, several states have imposed antler restrictions at the state or county level. These restrictions are designed to increase buck age structure, improve buck-to-doe ratios, and increase the number of does bred during their first estrous cycle. As a result, many hunters are passing younger bucks and observing them for the first time in their hunting careers. Over time, the results of passing these younger bucks will be confirmed through increased observations and harvests of older bucks.

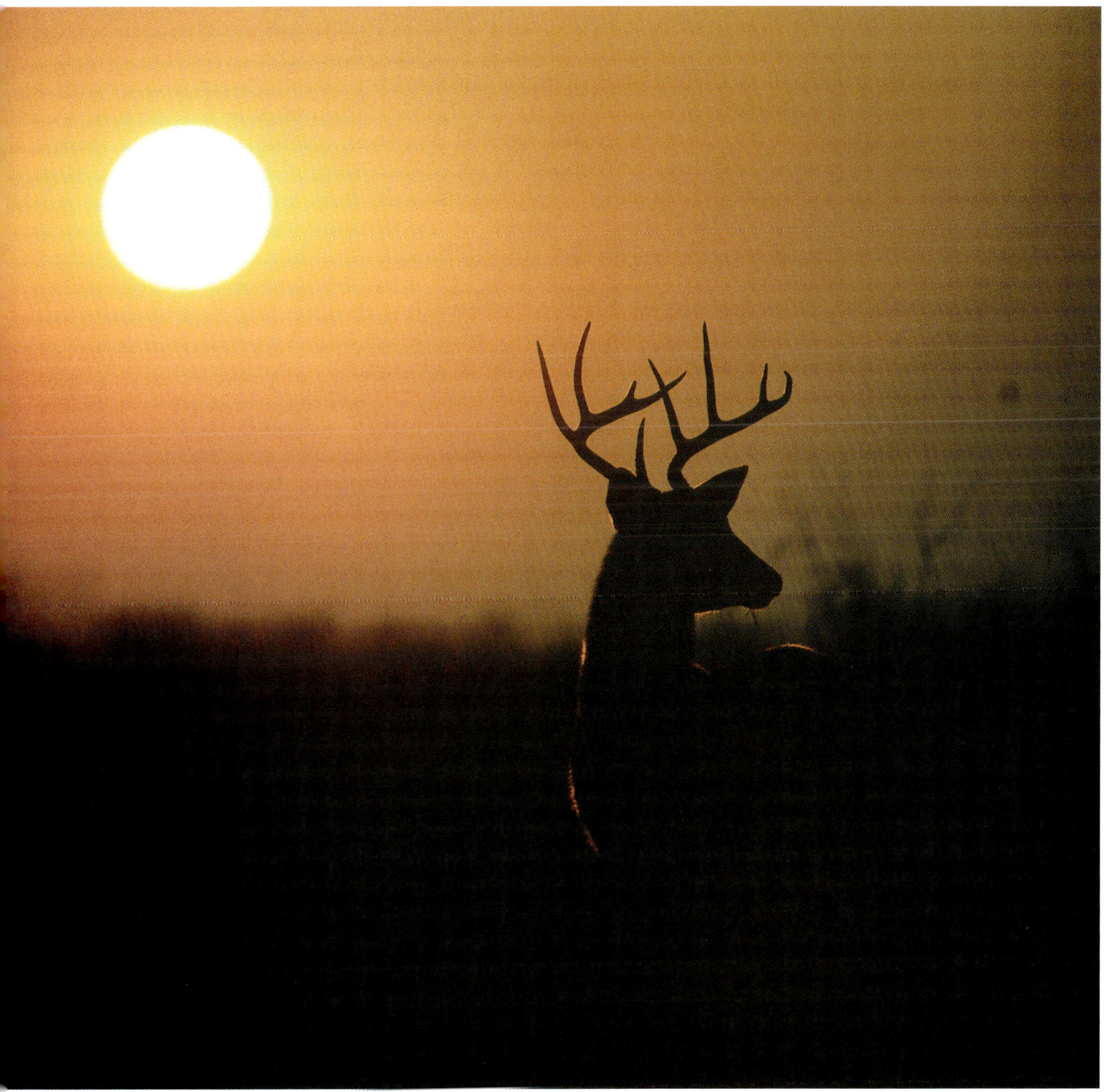

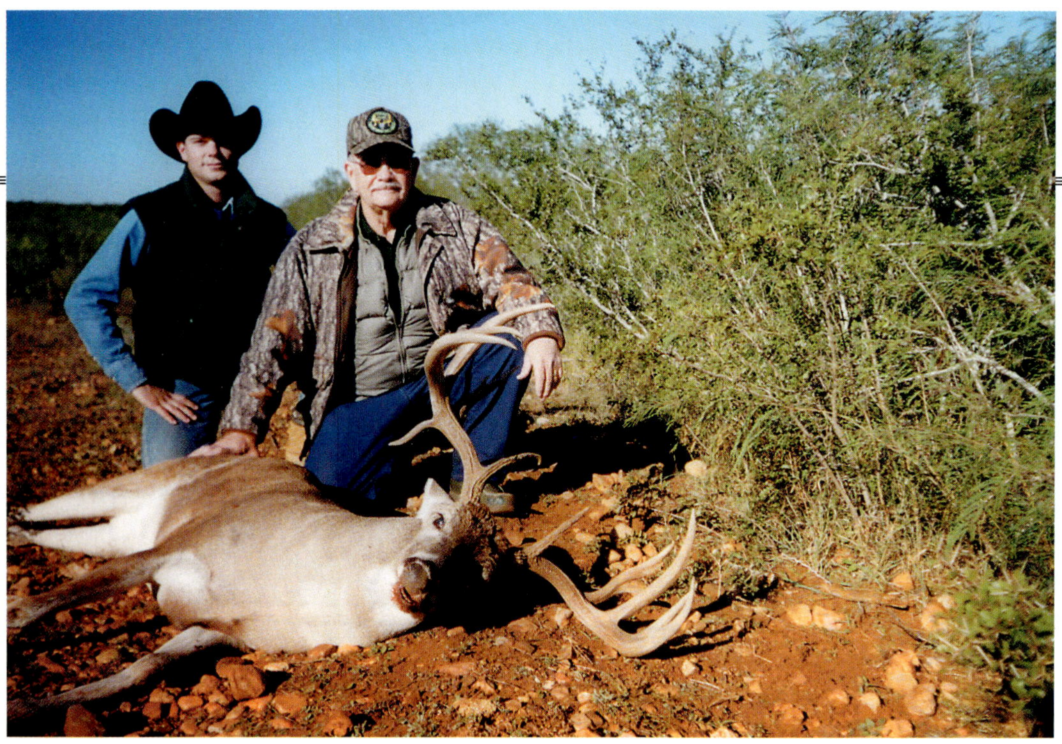

PHOTO COURTESY ROY HINDES III

After several days hunting, Cuatro Hindes rattled up this magnificent buck for long time family friend Billy Patterson. They were able to watch the buck run to the clashing antlers for over 100 yards until stopping at 31 steps where Billy dropped him with one shot. The hard labor and costs of intensive management over several years can produce tremendous payoffs.

From the beginner to the experienced deer observer, we hope new insights will be gained from the material presented between these covers, resulting in improved observational skills and an increased knowledge of white-tailed deer. The bucks in your area may not have the same potential for body and antler growth as those in this book. However, all other physical characteristics and behavioral traits will remain basically the same. It must be remembered that there will always be a few bucks that are exceptions to the rule.

We have pointed out numerous variables that can affect aging criteria on a given property. However, it has been clearly demonstrated that recognizing and aging bucks on the hoof is not only possible, but extremely beneficial for allowing bucks to reach their full potential before harvest. Equally important, it allows management by age, which prevents overharvest within a particular age class or year. Learning how to recognize individual bucks by their identifiable markings at the earliest possible age is critical for effective management. Always record these unique characteristics for future reference. Knowing a buck from previous observations will not always be possible and that is why aging bucks by their physical characteristics and behavior toward other bucks is helpful when attempting to place them in a specific age class.

Experience is the key to becoming proficient at aging bucks and judging antlers. The more time spent in the field watching live deer and then evaluating them once harvested, the better your skills will become. However, much can be learned by studying photographs and videos of bucks as well. The serious observer should study and memorize the various measurements mentioned in this text to be able to compare them to tine, circumference, beam, and spread lengths. They should also know before the hunt the various B&C benchmarks for the size of bucks they are expecting to harvest (e.g., 130-, 140-, 150-, or 160-class buck). The more you study these numbers, the quicker you will be able to judge a buck's antlers in the field. Finally, the more time spent observing deer in your area and the more data collected, evaluated, and studied, the more fine tuned your aging and judging skills will become.

Observational skills can only be as good as the equipment used. The use of the best optical equipment you can afford is critical. Features to look for in high quality optics are resolution (crisp detailed image) at long distances, contrast (optimal light transmission while controlling glare), water and fog proofing, durability, and a lifetime warranty. Even with the best optical equipment, always attempt to observe and evaluate bucks from as close as possible. And, do not make quick decisions and allow as much time as possible for the buck to reveal the information needed for a correct evaluation. A mistake on a buck at today's cost of managing and hunting whitetails is more costly than the finest pair of binoculars or spotting scope. It can be argued that a high quality spotting scope or pair of binoculars is just as important as a good scoped rifle when it comes to managing whitetails.

The ultimate experience when observing deer is the thrill of having that "buck of a lifetime" walk out in front of you. Our hope is that at some point in your life all of you will experience that thrill!

Dave & Al

12

Additional Information

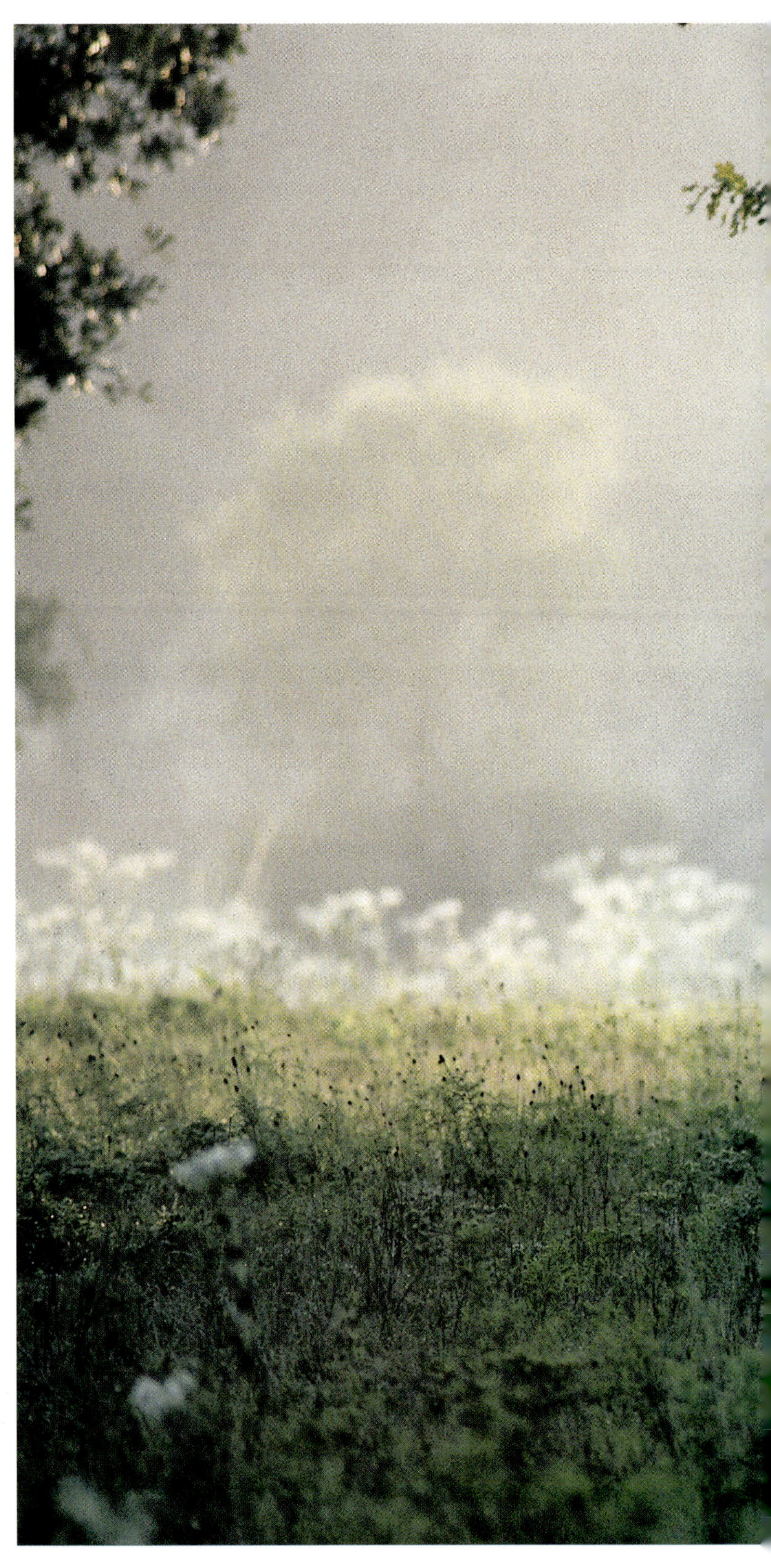

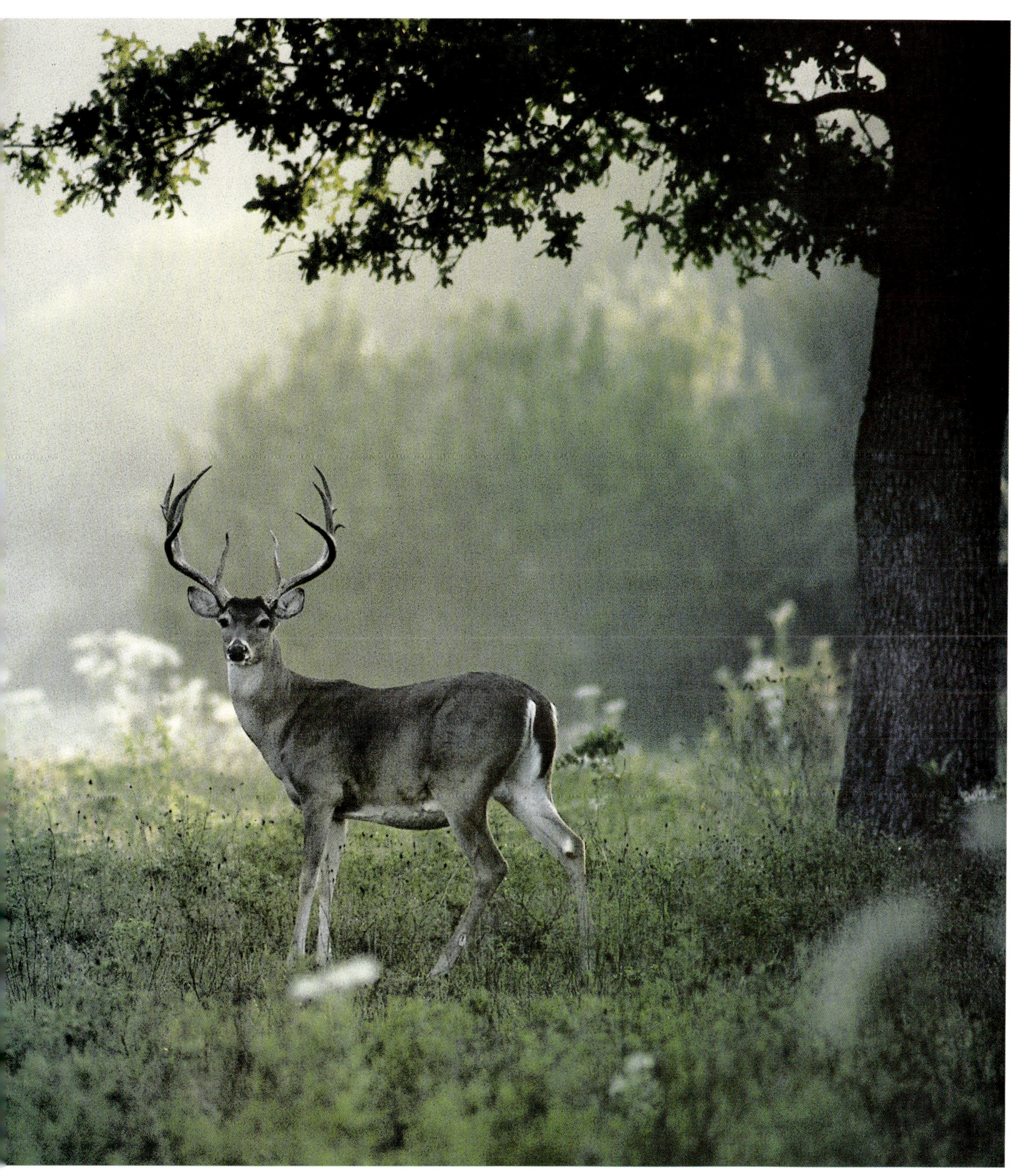

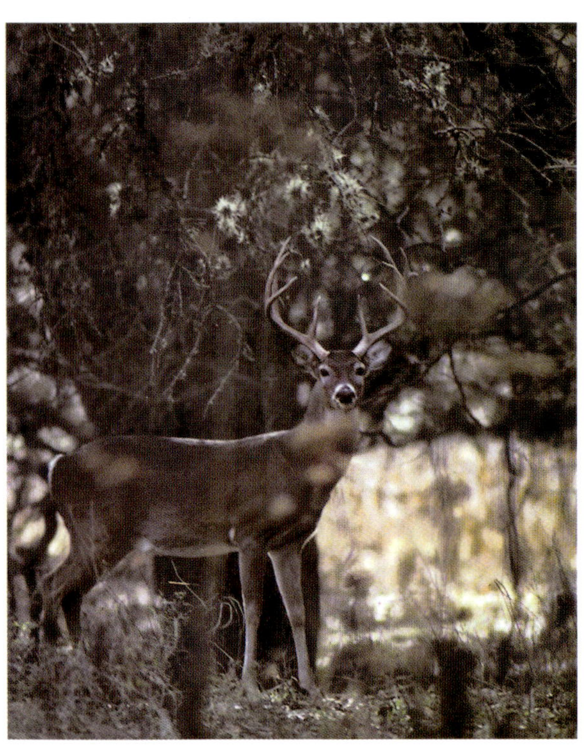

Unlike 25 years ago, today there is an abundance of information on white-tailed deer readily available and in a format designed for the landowner, manager, and hunter. In most areas, the primary source is your state wildlife agency. Universities with wildlife management programs, especially deer research programs, also can be very useful. Wildlife conservation organizations, such as the Quality Deer Management Association, are also great sources of information. While not a complete listing, the following books, magazines, and organizations are recommended to broaden your whitetail knowledge.

Organizations:

Quality Deer Management Association
P.O. Box 160, Bogart, GA 30622

Texas Wildlife Association
401 Isom Rd., Suite 237, San Antonio, TX 78216

Texas Trophy Hunters Association
5413 Bandera Rd., Suite 401, San Antonio, TX 78238

Texas Deer Association
403 E. Ramsey, Suite 204, San Antonio, TX 78216

Boone & Crockett Club
250 Station Dr., Missoula, MT 59801

Ceasar Kleberg Wildlife Research Institute
Kingsville, TX

Institute for Whitetail Deer Management and Research
SFA State Univ., Nacogdoches, TX 75962

Books:

Alsheimer, C., 2002, *Quality Deer Management the Basics and Beyond*. Krause Publications. Iola, WI.

Beyers, R., and Bettas, G., editors, 1999, *Records of North American Big Game* 11th Edition, Boone & Crockett Club Missoula, MO

Biggs, M., 1994, *Amazing Whitetails*, T.P.W., Inc. Fort Worth, TX

Biggs, M., 1996, *Whitetails in Action*, T.P.W., Inc. Fort Worth, TX

Biggs, M., 1998, *The Whitetail Chronicles*, T.P.W., Inc. Fort Worth, TX

Boddington, C. and Robb, B., 1990, *Deer Hunting Coast to Coast*, Safari Press. Long Beach, CA

Brothers, A., and M.E. Ray, JR. 1975, *Producing Quality Whitetails*, Caesar Kleberg Wildlife Inst., Kingsville, TX

Brown, R.D., 1992, *The Biology of Deer*, Springer-Verlag New York Inc.

Caesar Kleberg Wildlife Research Institute, 1983, *Antler Development in Cervidae*, C.K.W.R.I., Kingsville, TX

Fears, J.W., and Weishuhn, L., 2003, *Hunting Whitetails East and West*, Stoeger Publishing, Accokeek, MD.

Halls, L.K., 1984, *Whitetail Deer Ecology and Management by the Wildlife Management Institute*, Stackpole Books, Harrisburg, PA

Kroll, J., 1991, *A Practical Guide to Producing and Harvesting White-tailed Deer*, Center for Applied Studies in Forestry-SFA State Univ., Nacogdoches, TX

Kroll, J., 1996, *Aging and Judging Trophy Whitetails*, Center for Applied Studies in Forestry-SFA State Univ., Nacogdoches, TX

Leopold, A., 1948, *Game Management*, Charles Scribner's and Sons, New York

Miller, K., and Marchinton, L., editors, 1995, *Quality Whitetails — The Why and How of Quality Deer Management*, Stackpole Books, Mechanicsburg, PA

Meinzer, W., and Sasser, R., 1998, *Texas Whitetails*, Collectors Covey, Dallas, TX

Morris, D., 1992, *Hunting Trophy Whitetails*, Safari Press, Huntington, CA

Morris, D., 1998, *Advanced Strategies for Trophy Whitetails*, Safari Press, Huntington, CA

Nesbitt, W. and Wright, P., 2003, *A Boone and Crockett Club Field Guide to Measuring and Judging Big Game*. Boone & Crockett Club, Missoula, MO

Ozoga, J., 1994, *Seasons of the Whitetail* (Books 1-4), Willow Creek Press, Minocqua, WI

Rue III, L., 1978, *The Deer of North America*, Crown Publishers Inc. New York

Sasser, R., 1993, *Texas Whitetails 1992*, Collectors Covey, Dallas, TX

Stein, J., 1993, *Big Antlers IV*, Big rack Publications, San Antonio, TX

Whittington, G., 1998, *World Record Whitetails*, Safari Press, Long Beach, CA

Wooters, J., 1977, *Hunting Trophy Deer*, Lyons & Burford, Publishers. New York

Records of
North American
Big Game

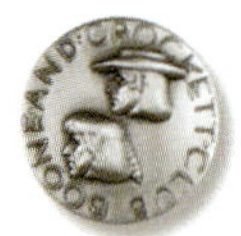

250 Station Drive
Missoula, MT 59801
(406) 542-1888

BOONE AND CROCKETT CLUB®

OFFICIAL SCORING SYSTEM FOR NORTH AMERICAN BIG GAME TROPHIES

MINIMUM SCORES	AWARDS	ALL-TIME
whitetail	160	170
Coues'	100	110

TYPICAL WHITETAIL AND COUES' DEER

KIND OF DEER (check one)
☐ whitetail
☐ Coues'

Abnormal Points	
Right Antler	Left Antler
SUBTOTALS		
TOTAL TO E		

SEE OTHER SIDE FOR INSTRUCTIONS

				COLUMN 1	COLUMN 2	COLUMN 3	COLUMN 4
A. No. Points on Right Antler		No. Points on Left Antler		Spread Credit	Right Antler	Left Antler	Difference
B. Tip to Tip Spread		C. Greatest Spread					
D. Inside Spread of Main Beams		SPREAD CREDIT MAY EQUAL BUT NOT EXCEED LONGER MAIN BEAM					
E. Total of Lengths of Abnormal Points							
F. Length of Main Beam							
G-1. Length of First Point							
G-2. Length of Second Point							
G-3. Length of Third Point							
G-4. Length of Fourth Point, If Present							
G-5. Length of Fifth Point, If Present							
G-6. Length of Sixth Point, If Present							
G-7. Length of Seventh Point, If Present							
H-1. Circumference at Smallest Place Between Burr and First Point							
H-2. Circumference at Smallest Place Between First and Second Points							
H-3. Circumference at Smallest Place Between Second and Third Points							
H-4. Circumference at Smallest Place Between Third and Fourth Points							
TOTALS							

ADD	Column 1		Exact Locality Where Killed:	
	Column 2		Date Killed:	Hunter:
	Column 3		Owner:	Telephone #:
	Subtotal		Owner's Address:	
	SUBTRACT Column 4		Guide's Name and Address:	
	FINAL SCORE		Remarks: (Mention Any Abnormalities or Unique Qualities)	

I, ______________________________________, certify that I have measured this trophy on ____________________
PRINT NAME MM/DD/YYYYY

at ____
STREET ADDRESS CITY STATE/PROVINCE

and that these measurements and data are, to the best of my knowledge and belief, made in accordance with the instructions given.

Witness: ______________________________ Signature: ______________________________ I.D. Number | | | | |
B&C OFFICIAL MEASURER

INSTRUCTIONS FOR MEASURING TYPICAL WHITETAIL AND COUES' DEER

All measurements must be made with a 1/4-inch wide flexible steel tape to the nearest one-eighth of an inch. (Note: A flexible steel cable can be used to measure points and main beams only.) Enter fractional figures in eighths, without reduction. Official measurements cannot be taken until the antlers have air dried for at least 60 days after the animal was killed.

A. Number of Points on Each Antler: To be counted a point, the projection must be at least one inch long, with the length exceeding width at one inch or more of length. All points are measured from tip of point to nearest edge of beam as illustrated. Beam tip is counted as a point but not measured as a point.

B. Tip to Tip Spread is measured between tips of main beams.

C. Greatest Spread is measured between perpendiculars at a right angle to the center line of the skull at widest part, whether across main beams or points.

D. Inside Spread of Main Beams is measured at a right angle to the center line of the skull at widest point between main beams. Enter this measurement again as the Spread Credit **if** it is less than or equal to the length of the longer main beam; if greater, enter longer main beam length for Spread Credit.

E. Total of Lengths of all Abnormal Points: Abnormal Points are those non-typical in location (such as points originating from a point or from bottom or sides of main beam) or extra points beyond the normal pattern of points. Measure in usual manner and enter in appropriate blanks.

F. Length of Main Beam is measured from the center of the lowest outside edge of burr over the outer side to the most distant point of the main beam. The point of beginning is that point on the burr where the center line along the outer side of the beam intersects the burr, then following generally the line of the illustration.

G-1-2-3-4-5-6-7. Length of Normal Points: Normal points project from the top of the main beam. They are measured from nearest edge of main beam over outer curve to tip. Lay the tape along the outer curve of the beam so that the top edge of the tape coincides with the top edge of the beam on both sides of the point to determine the baseline for point measurements. Record point lengths in appropriate blanks.

H-1-2-3-4. Circumferences are taken as detailed in illustration for each measurement. If brow point is missing, take H-1 and H-2 at smallest place between burr and G-2. If G-4 is missing, take H-4 halfway between G-3 and tip of main beam.

ENTRY AFFIDAVIT FOR ALL HUNTER-TAKEN TROPHIES

For the purpose of entry into the Boone and Crockett Club's® records, North American big game harvested by the use of the following methods or under the following conditions are ineligible:

I. Spotting or herding game from the air, followed by landing in its vicinity for the purpose of pursuit and shooting;
II. Herding or chasing with the aid of any motorized equipment;
III. Use of electronic communication devices, artificial lighting, or electronic light intensifying devices;
IV. Confined by artificial barriers, including escape-proof fenced enclosures;
V. Transplanted for the purpose of commercial shooting;
VI. By the use of traps or pharmaceuticals;
VII. While swimming, helpless in deep snow, or helpless in any other natural or artificial medium;
VIII. On another hunter's license;
IX. Not in full compliance with the game laws or regulations of the federal government or of any state, province, territory, or tribal council on reservations or tribal lands;

I certify that the trophy scored on this chart was not taken in violation of the conditions listed above. In signing this statement, I understand that if the information provided on this entry is found to be misrepresented or fraudulent in any respect, it will not be accepted into the Awards Program and 1) all of my prior entries are subject to deletion from future editions of **Records of North American Big Game** 2) future entries may not be accepted.

FAIR CHASE, as defined by the Boone and Crockett Club®, is the ethical, sportsmanlike and lawful pursuit and taking of any free-ranging wild, native North American big game animal in a manner that does not give the hunter an improper advantage over such game animals.

The Boone and Crockett Club® may exclude the entry of any animal that it deems to have been taken in an unethical manner or under conditions deemed inappropriate by the Club.

Date: ____________________ Signature of Hunter: ____
(SIGNATURE MUST BE WITNESSED BY AN OFFICIAL MEASURER OR A NOTARY PUBLIC.)

Date: ____________________ Signature of Notary or Official Measurer: ______________________________

Records of North American Big Game

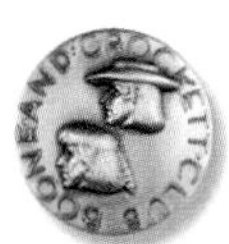

250 Station Drive
Missoula, MT 59801
(406) 542-1888

BOONE AND CROCKETT CLUB®

OFFICIAL SCORING SYSTEM FOR NORTH AMERICAN BIG GAME TROPHIES

NON-TYPICAL WHITETAIL AND COUES' DEER

MINIMUM SCORES	AWARDS	ALL-TIME
whitetail	185	195
Coues'	105	120

KIND OF DEER (check one)
☐ whitetail
☐ Coues'

G2 G3 G4 G5 G6 E E E F H4 H3 G1 H2 H1 Detail of Point Measurement B C D

	Abnormal Points	
	Right Antler	Left Antler
SUBTOTALS		
E. TOTAL		

SEE OTHER SIDE FOR INSTRUCTIONS

				COLUMN 1	COLUMN 2	COLUMN 3	COLUMN 4
A. No. Points on Right Antler		No. Points on Left Antler		Spread Credit	Right Antler	Left Antler	Difference
B. Tip to Tip Spread		C. Greatest Spread					
D. Inside Spread of Main Beams		SPREAD CREDIT MAY EQUAL BUT NOT EXCEED LONGER MAIN BEAM					
F. Length of Main Beam							
G-1. Length of First Point							
G-2. Length of Second Point							
G-3. Length of Third Point							
G-4. Length of Fourth Point, If Present							
G-5. Length of Fifth Point, If Present							
G-6. Length of Sixth Point, If Present							
G-7. Length of Seventh Point, If Present							
H-1. Circumference at Smallest Place Between Burr and First Point							
H-2. Circumference at Smallest Place Between First and Second Points							
H-3. Circumference at Smallest Place Between Second and Third Points							
H-4. Circumference at Smallest Place Between Third and Fourth Points							
TOTALS							

ADD	Column 1		Exact Locality Where Killed:
	Column 2		Date Killed: Hunter:
	Column 3		Owner: Telephone #:
Subtotal			Owner's Address:
SUBTRACT Column 4			Guide's Name and Address:
Subtotal			Remarks: (Mention Any Abnormalities or Unique Qualities)
ADD Line E Total			
FINAL SCORE			

I, ____, certify that I have measured this trophy on ____________________
PRINT NAME MM/DD/YYYYY

at ____
STREET ADDRESS CITY STATE/PROVINCE

and that these measurements and data are, to the best of my knowledge and belief, made in accordance with the instructions given.

Witness: ________________________________ Signature: ________________________________ I.D. Number | | | | |
B&C OFFICIAL MEASURER

INSTRUCTIONS FOR MEASURING NON-TYPICAL WHITETAIL AND COUES' DEER

All measurements must be made with a 1/4-inch wide flexible steel tape to the nearest one-eighth of an inch. (Note: A flexible steel cable can be used to measure points and main beams only.) Enter fractional figures in eighths, without reduction. Official measurements cannot be taken until the antlers have air dried for at least 60 days after the animal was killed.

A. Number of Points on Each Antler: To be counted a point, the projection must be at least one inch long, with the length exceeding width at one inch or more of length. All points are measured from tip of point to nearest edge of beam as illustrated. Beam tip is counted as a point but not measured as a point.

B. Tip to Tip Spread is measured between tips of main beams.

C. Greatest Spread is measured between perpendiculars at a right angle to the center line of the skull at widest part, whether across main beams or points.

D. Inside Spread of Main Beams is measured at a right angle to the center line of the skull at widest point between main beams. Enter this measurement again as the Spread Credit **if** it is less than or equal to the length of the longer main beam; if greater, enter longer main beam length for Spread Credit.

E. Total of Lengths of all Abnormal Points: Abnormal Points are those non-typical in location (such as points originating from a point or from bottom or sides of main beam) or extra points beyond the normal pattern of points. Measure in usual manner and enter in appropriate blanks.

F. Length of Main Beam is measured from the center of the lowest outside edge of burr over the outer side to the most distant point of the main beam. The point of beginning is that point on the burr where the center line along the outer side of the beam intersects the burr, then following generally the line of the illustration.

G-1-2-3-4-5-6-7. Length of Normal Points: Normal points project from the top of the main beam. They are measured from nearest edge of main beam over outer curve to tip. Lay the tape along the outer curve of the beam so that the top edge of the tape coincides with the top edge of the beam on both sides of the point to determine the baseline for point measurement. Record point lengths in appropriate blanks.

H-1-2-3-4. Circumferences are taken as detailed in illustration for each measurement. If brow point is missing, take H-1 and H-2 at smallest place between burr and G-2. If G-4 is missing, take H-4 halfway between G-3 and tip of main beam.

ENTRY AFFIDAVIT FOR ALL HUNTER-TAKEN TROPHIES

For the purpose of entry into the Boone and Crockett Club's® records, North American big game harvested by the use of the following methods or under the following conditions are ineligible:

I. Spotting or herding game from the air, followed by landing in its vicinity for the purpose of pursuit and shooting;
II. Herding or chasing with the aid of any motorized equipment;
III. Use of electronic communication devices, artificial lighting, or electronic light intensifying devices;
IV. Confined by artificial barriers, including escape-proof fenced enclosures;
V. Transplanted for the purpose of commercial shooting;
VI. By the use of traps or pharmaceuticals;
VII. While swimming, helpless in deep snow, or helpless in any other natural or artificial medium;
VIII. On another hunter's license;
IX. Not in full compliance with the game laws or regulations of the federal government or of any state, province, territory, or tribal council on reservations or tribal lands;

I certify that the trophy scored on this chart was not taken in violation of the conditions listed above. In signing this statement, I understand that if the information provided on this entry is found to be misrepresented or fraudulent in any respect, it will not be accepted into the Awards Program and 1) all of my prior entries are subject to deletion from future editions of **Records of North American Big Game** 2) future entries may not be accepted.

FAIR CHASE, as defined by the Boone and Crockett Club®, is the ethical, sportsmanlike and lawful pursuit and taking of any free-ranging wild, native North American big game animal in a manner that does not give the hunter an improper advantage over such game animals.

The Boone and Crockett Club® may exclude the entry of any animal that it deems to have been taken in an unethical manner or under conditions deemed inappropriate by the Club.

Date: ____________________ Signature of Hunter: ____
(SIGNATURE MUST BE WITNESSED BY AN OFFICIAL MEASURER OR A NOTARY PUBLIC.)

Date: ____________________ Signature of Notary or Official Measurer: ________________________________

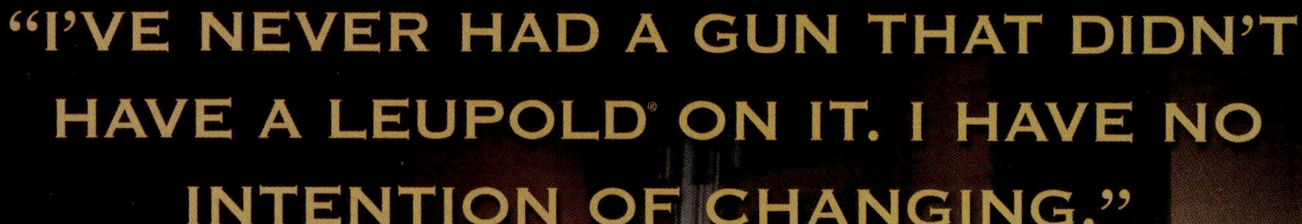

— Jim Shockey, Professional Guide & Outdoor Writer

Jim Shockey hunted the most remote, punishing locales on earth to become the first hunter to complete the Ultimate Slam of North American Big Game with a muzzleloader. Jim faced extreme heat and cold, rain, snow, sand, rough terrain, and none of it could take out his tough, waterproof Leupold® riflescope. At every step, his Leupold's rugged reliability protected its outstanding clarity, low-light capability and accuracy. "I've been fortunate enough to go on some pretty brutal hunts, so I get to see scopes at every extreme," Jim says. "Nothing holds a candle to Leupold for ruggedness."

The world's best competitive shooters, guides, custom gunmakers and outdoor writers choose Leupold over any other scope. If you're looking for an American-made, rugged, waterproof, accurate and reliable hunting optic, it's time you joined them and got a Leupold for yourself. For the Authorized Leupold Golden Ring® Dealer nearest you, call 1-800-929-4949 or visit www.leupold.com.

LEUPOLD®

MADE RIGHT, MADE HERE.

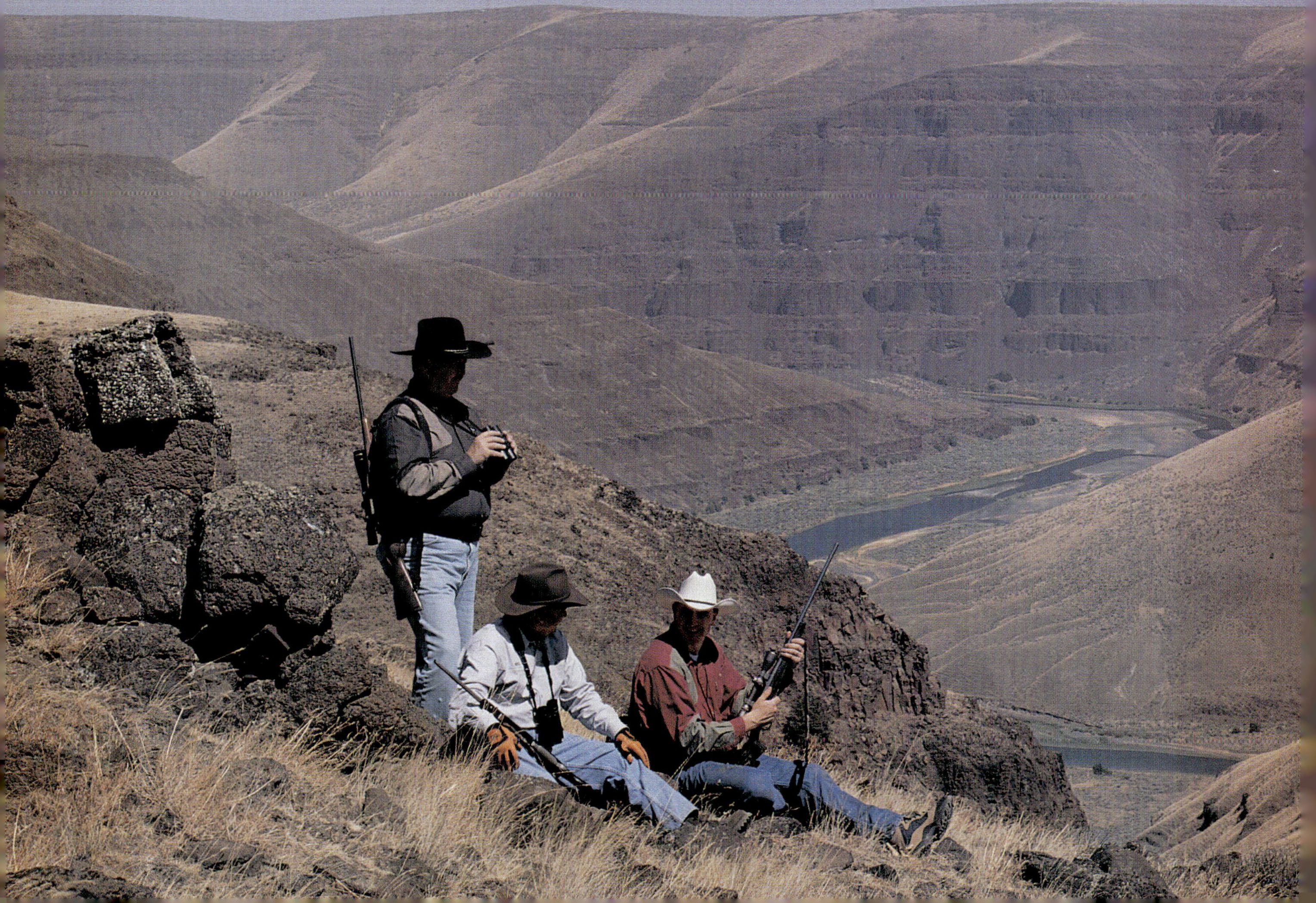

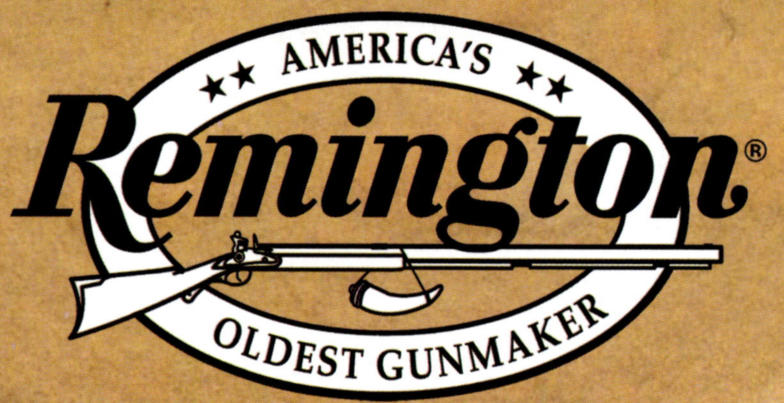

Over the years, hunters worldwide have come to recognize Remington as the leader in manufacturing arms and ammunition. Innovative, safe, and reliable products of the highest quality has been the key to their success for almost two centuries. Remington's goals for the future are the same as in the past. Providing hunters with the best rifles and ammunition for hunting whether its big game on a foreign continent or for America's premier big game animal the white-tailed deer.

We at Bliss-Murski Sales Company want to express our gratitude to Remington Arms Company and its president, Tommy Millner for giving us the opportunity to sell for the number one arms and ammunition company in the world.

It has been the highlight of my thirty-seven year selling career to be associated with the entire Remington organization.

It is also indeed a pleasure to have been selected as a sponsor of Dave Richards new and exciting publication, *"Observing and Evaluating Whitetails."*

Dave has spent years and countless hours photographing some of the most amazing whitetails that have ever lived.

Do yourself a favor and read this outstanding book.

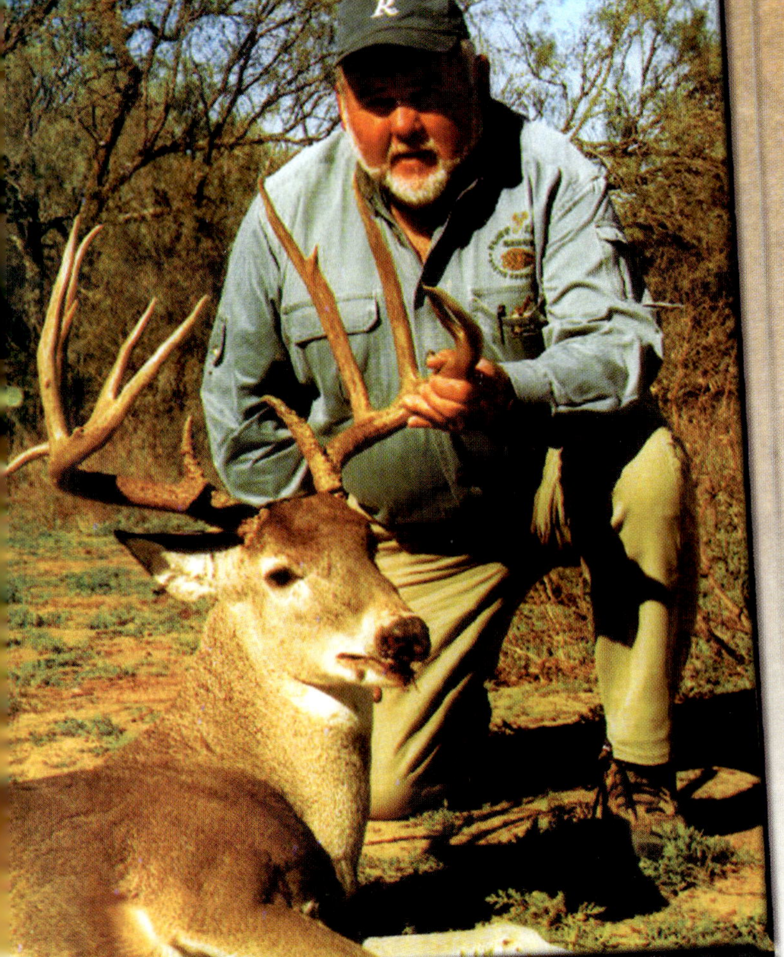

Raymond A. Murski
Owner, Bliss-Murski Sales Company

www.remington.com

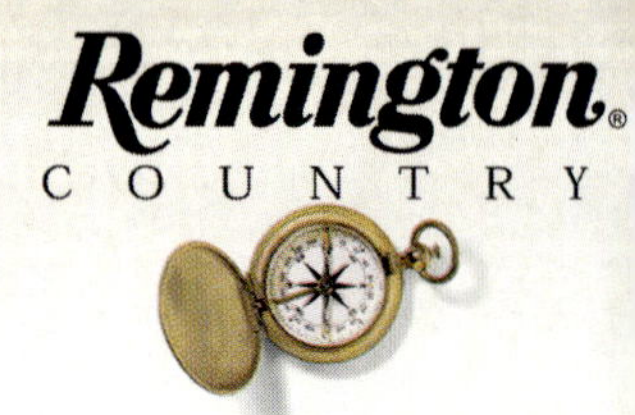

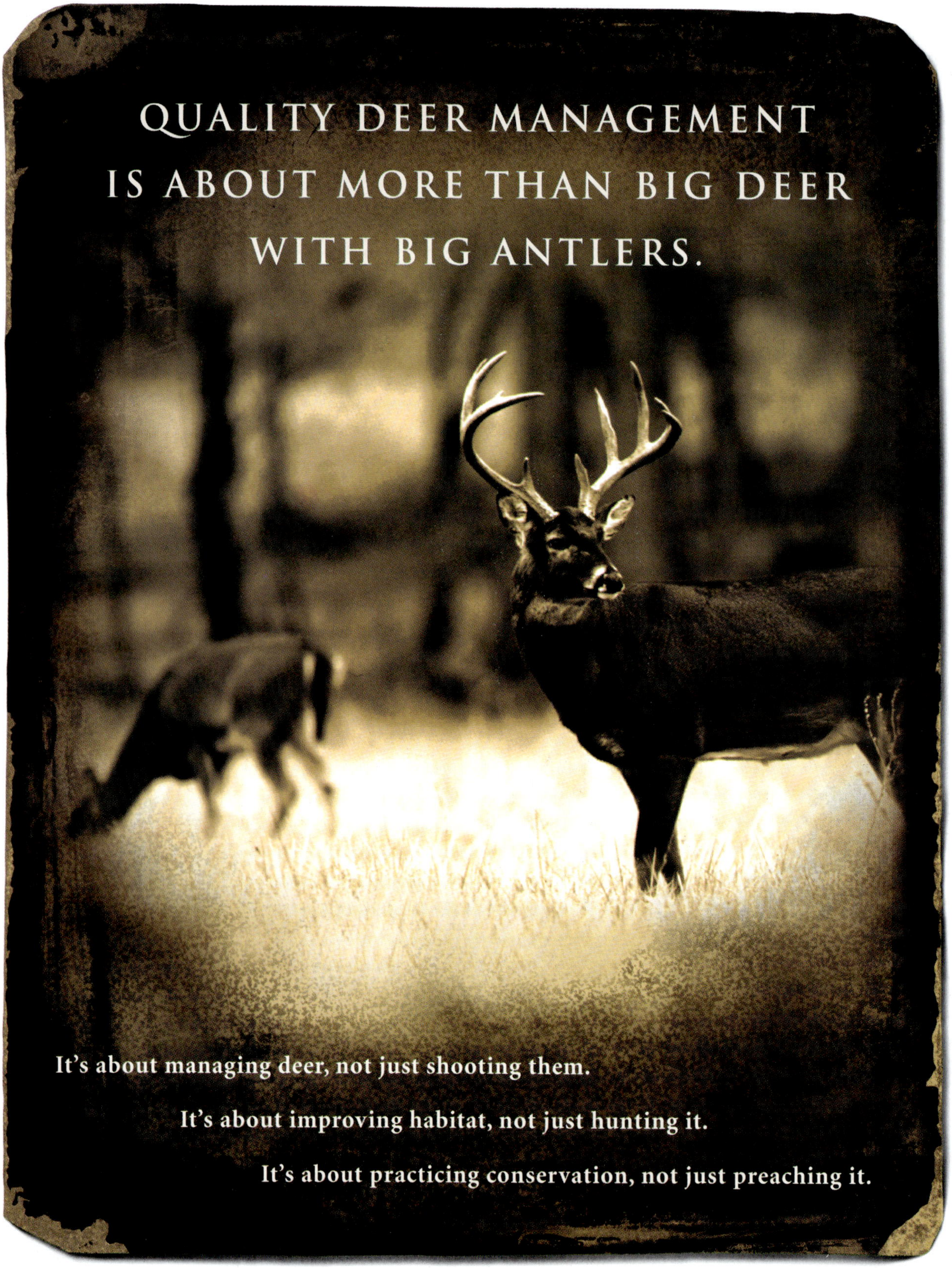

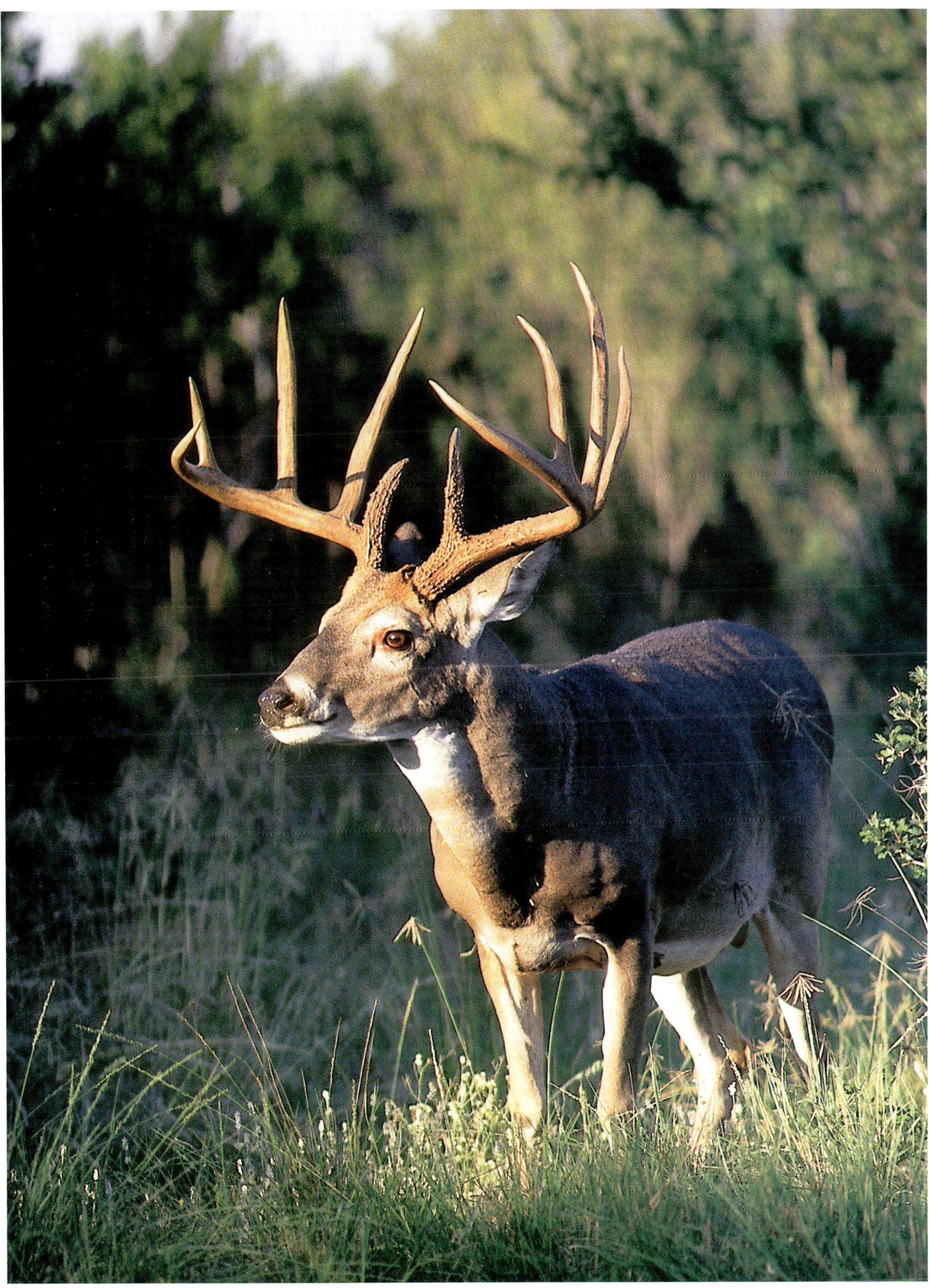

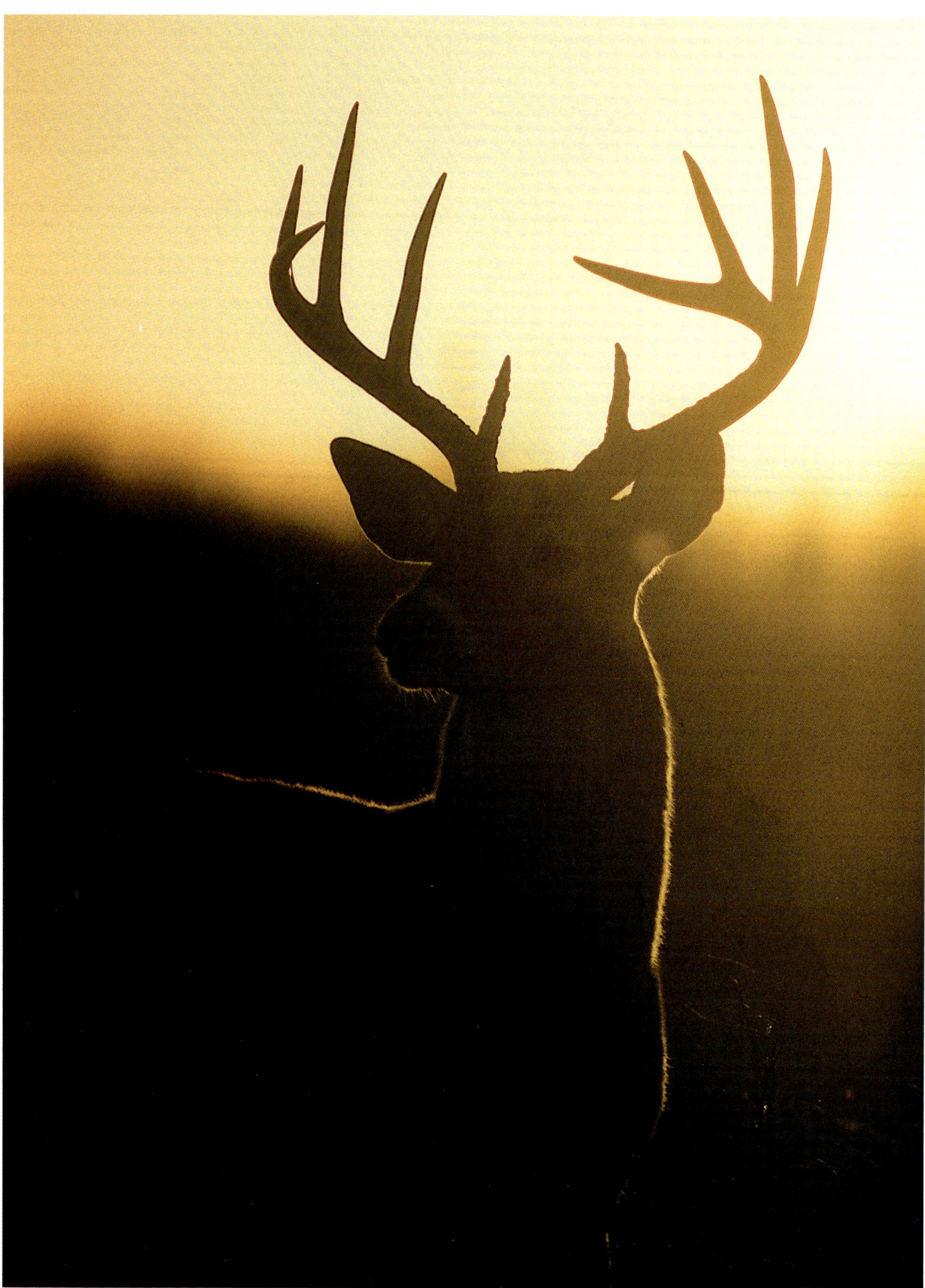